THE NEW TESTAMENT

A New Translation

by

WILLIAM BARCLAY

Fountain Books
Collins + World

First published in 1968 and 1969
by William Collins Sons & Co Ltd, London

First issued in Fontana 1976
© William Barclay 1968, 1969

Made and printed in Great Britain by
William Collins Sons & Co Ltd, Glasgow

Foreword

In making this translation I have had two aims in view. The first was to try to make the New Testament intelligible to the man who is not a technical scholar. The technical New Testament scholar does not need a new translation made for him; he is well able to make his own, and anyone whose business it is to teach the New Testament could have done what I have done—and could very probably have done it better. The second was to try to make a translation which did not need a commentary to explain it. I am well aware that this second aim is an impossibility, for biblical words and manners and customs, the biblical environment, the biblical ideas and categories of thought need explanation. But I have tried in so far as it was possible to make the New Testament speak for itself. In view of these aims I am particularly happy that this translation should be appearing in paperback, because in this form it will reach more people.

The man who attempts to translate the New Testament all by himself cannot but remember Luther's charge against Jerome. Luther's criticism, as W. Schwarz reminds us in his *Principles and Problems of Biblical Translation*, was that Jerome did his rendering alone, without help, and thus lost the promise: 'For where two or three are gathered together in my name, there am I in the midst of them' (Matthew 18.20). But it was my very great privilege to have some small part in the translation of the New English Bible, although not in the New Testament part of it, and to have had over many years a share in the work of the 'Translator's Translation', the Diglot, of the British and Foreign Bible Society. And there I learned far more about translation than ever I contributed So even if the translation and the responsibility for it are mine, there are debts and there was a fellowship.

It was not until my own translation was well-nigh completed that there appeared the Greek New Testament of the United Bible Societies edited by Kurt Aland, Matthew Black Bruce M. Metzger and Allen Wikgren. I had begun by using the second edition of the British and Foreign Bible Society's Greek Testament. But I revised the translation in the light of the newer text, which surely must become the standard New Testament Greek text.

A word of explanation is necessary with regard to the printing layout of the Sermon on the Mount in Matthew chapters 5 to 7, and

3

in the parallel passages such as Luke 6.20-49. The material is arranged in apparently broken lines for three reasons.

i. In the ancient manuscripts the material was sometimes arranged in sense-lines in order to make the public reading of it easier. The lines indicate the phrasing which in reading makes the material easiest to follow and to understand.

ii. The lining is used to show how Jesus, so to speak, built up a saying.

> Yours is this bliss,
>   when men shall heap insults on you,
>   and persecute you,
>   and tell every wicked kind of lie about you
>   for my sake (Matthew 5.11).

The first line is the general principle. Then each of the next three lines lays down a separate instance—insult, persecution, slander—in which the general principle is true. Each indentation of the margin marks a new instance in which the general principle is true.

iii. Hebrew poetry does not rhyme; it is built up on a series of parallels, and often the series is quite elaborate. A good example is in Matthew 7.24-27, where each one of the first ten lines has its exact parallel in each of the second ten lines. A shorter example is in Matthew 5.45.

> If you do that,
>   you will be like your Father in heaven,
>   for he makes his sun to rise,
>   on the bad and on the good alike,
>   and he sends the rain
>   on saint and sinner.

The last four lines have the clear pattern a b a b.

It is to try to reproduce these characteristics of the form of the original Greek that the lay-out I have used has been chosen.

When the translator moves from the Gospels to the Letters, he moves to a new world in translation. It is the difference between translating a narrative and translating an argument. Obviously the argument is far harder to translate. Equally obviously it is an even more obligatory task to try to translate the argument. There are few people who cannot understand the narrative of the Gospels in the

Authorized Version; there are equally few who can understand the arguments of the Letters in the Authorized Version.

In the translation of the Letters there are three things which I have done

Paul particularly tends to write in very long sentences. For instance, in the Greek there is no full stop between Ephesians 1.3 and Ephesians 1.14. I have regularly broken up the long sentences into shorter units. On the other hand, there are times when Paul writes very elliptically, almost as if he was giving us sermon notes rather than the finished article. In these cases I have expanded the translation to try to make the meaning clear. Further, in the New Testament there occur passages in which the point depends on certain Jewish or Greek pictures or customs. I have on occasion incorporated and integrated the explanation into the text for the sake of clarity and for the sake of the person who has to read without a commentary.

No one ever made a translation without the haunting sense of how much better it might have been, and of the imperfections of this translation no one is more conscious than I am. I can but pray that in spite of its inadequacy it may shed for some readers a clearer light on the book which is the word of God to men.

WILLIAM BARCLAY

Contents

CONTENTS

General Introduction to the Gospels

In Revelation 4.7 we read of the four living creatures who were around the throne of God. One was like a lion, another like an ox, another like a man, and another like an eagle. As early as the second century these four living creatures were taken to be the emblems and symbols of the four Gospels, and to this day they are very often thus used in stained-glass windows. Different writers assigned them differently to each of the four Gospels; but the allocation which seems most fitting is that made by Augustine in his book *On the Agreement of the Gospels* (1.6). Augustine takes the man to represent Mark; the lion to represent Matthew; the ox to represent Luke; and the eagle to represent John.

The man represents Mark, because Mark has the simplest and the most human picture of Jesus. The lion represents Matthew, because Matthew is concerned to show us Jesus as the Lion of Judah, the promised Messiah. The ox represents Luke, because the ox is the animal of sacrifice, and Luke shows us Jesus in his all-embracing love as the sacrifice, not for any chosen nation, but for all mankind. The eagle represents John, because of all birds the eagle flies highest, and it is said that of all living creatures the eagle alone can look straight into the blaze of the sun, and not be dazzled. So John's thought climbs highest of all, and John sees furthest of all into the eternities.

So we may think of Mark as the simplest Gospel; of Matthew as the Messianic Gospel; of Luke as the universal Gospel; and of John as the profoundest Gospel.

Introduction to Matthew

Matthew's Gospel was written about twenty years after Mark's Gospel, between A.D. 80 and 90, and it has two great characteristics.

Matthew's Gospel is the most Jewish of the Gospels. It is the Gospel which is most conscious of the unbreakable link between the old and the new. Matthew wished to convince the Jews that Jesus was the Messiah for whom they had so long prayed and hoped. He knew that to a Jew the surest proof of that claim would be to demonstrate that Jesus fulfilled the prophecies of the Old Testament prophets about the Messiah. That is why again and again Matthew says that Jesus did or said something in order that something that some prophet said might come true (1.22; 2.15,17,23; 4.14; 8.17; 12.17; 13.35; 21.4; 26.56; 27.9). Matthew is above all concerned to prove to the Jews that in Jesus the prophecies are fulfilled, and that therefore in Jesus the Messiah has come.

Matthew's Gospel is above all the teaching Gospel. Matthew has a habit of collecting Jesus' teaching in great blocks. He takes certain subjects, and he collects together what Jesus said about them, thus bringing together in an orderly pattern things which are scattered all over the other Gospels. In the Old Testament there are five books of the Law, the Pentateuch as they are called, the first five books of the Old Testament. So Matthew presents us with five great blocks of Jesus' teaching, as if in them he was giving us the new law which supersedes the old law. The five great blocks are:

1. The Sermon on the Mount, or, The Law of the Kingdom (5-7).
2. The Charge to the Twelve, or, The Ambassadors of the Kingdom (10).
3. The Chapter of Parables, or, the Parables of the Kingdom (13).
4. The Discourse about Greatness and Forgiveness, or, the Personal Relationships of the Members of the Kingdom (18).
5. The Discourses about the Future, or, the Coming of the Kingdom (24,25).

Matthew's Gospel could well be called the first handbook of the teaching of Jesus.

Matthew's Gospel has one further characteristic. It is the Gospel of

9

the Church. It is the only Gospel which uses the word Church (16.18; 18.15-17). It has much to say about Church practices. It tells of the right way to fast, to give alms and to pray (6.1-18). It lays down the Christian rule for marriage and divorce (5.27-28; 19.3-9). It gives the authority for baptism (28.19,20). It assures the smallest company of worshipping Christians of the presence of their Lord (18.20). It has indeed been suggested that Matthew's Gospel is deliberately constructed in such a way that it can be read through section by section at the meetings of the Church.

Without Matthew our knowledge of the teaching of Jesus would be very much poorer than it is.

The Story of the Good News
MATTHEW'S VERSION

Chapter 1

THIS is the family tree of Jesus Christ, the Son of David, the son of Abraham.

2Abraham was the father of Isaac, Isaac was the father of Jacob, Jacob was the father of Judah and his brothers, 3Judah was the father of Perez and Zerah, whose mother was Tamar, Perez was the father of Hezron, Hezron was the father of Aram, 4Aram was the father of Aminadab, Aminadab was the father of Naasson, Naasson was the father of Salmon, 5Salmon was the father of Boaz, whose mother was Rahab, Boaz was the father of Obed, whose mother was Ruth, Obed was the father of Jesse, 6Jesse was the father of King David.

David was the father of Solomon, whose mother was Uriah's wife, 7Solomon was the father of Rehoboam, Rehoboam was the father of Abijah, Abijah was the father of Asa, 8Asa was the father of Jehoshaphat, Jehoshaphat was the father of Joram, Joram was the father of Uzziah, 9Uzziah was the father of Jotham, Jotham was the father of Ahaz, Ahaz was the father of Hezekiah, 10Hezekiah was the father of Manasseh, Manasseh was the father of Amos, Amos was the father of Josiah, 11Josiah was the father of Jechoniah and his brothers, in the days of the exile in Babylon.

12After the exile in Babylon, Jechoniah was the father of Shealtiel, Shealtiel was the father of Zerubbabel, 13Zerubbabel was the father of Abiud, Abiud was the father of Eliakim, Eliakim was the father of Azor, 14Azor was the father of Zadok, Zadok was the father of Achim, Achim was the father of Eliud, 15Eliud was the father of Eleazar, Eleazar was the father of Matthan, Matthan was the father of Jacob, 16Jacob was the father of Joseph, the husband of Mary, and Mary was the mother of Jesus, called Messiah.

17From Abraham to David there were in all fourteen generations;

from David to the exile in Babylon there were also fourteen generations; from the exile in Babylon to the coming of the Messiah there
were also fourteen generations.

18This was the way in which the birth of Jesus took place. Mary his
mother was pledged to be married to Joseph, but, before they became
man and wife, it was discovered that she was going to have a child, as
a result of the action of the Holy Spirit. 19Although Joseph, her in
tended husband, was a man who strictly kept the Law, he had no
desire publicly to humiliate her, so he wished to divorce her secretly.
20While he was planning to do this, an angel of the Lord appeared to
him in a dream. 'Joseph, son of David,' the angel said, 'do not hesitate
to marry Mary, for it is as a result of the action of the Holy Spirit that
she is going to have a child. 21She will have a son, and you must call
him by the name Jesus, for it is he who will save his people from their
sins.' 22All this happened that the statement made by the Lord
through the prophet might come true:

> 23'The virgin shall conceive and have a child,
> and they shall give him the name Emmanuel,'

for that name means, 'God is with us.' 24So Joseph woke from sleep
and carried out the instructions of the angel of the Lord. He married
Mary, 25but he did not have any intercourse with her, until she had
had her son. And he called him by the name Jesus.

Chapter 2

WHEN Jesus had been born in Bethlehem in Judaea, in the time of
King Herod, there came to Jerusalem from the East scholars who
were students of the stars. 2'Where,' they asked, 'is the newly born
King of the Jews? We are looking for him, because we have seen his
star rise, and we have come to do homage to him.' 3When King Herod
heard about this he was alarmed, and all Jerusalem shared his alarm.
4So he called a meeting of the chief priests and the experts in the Law,
and tried to find out from them where the Messiah was to be born.
5'In Bethlehem in Judaea,' they told him, 'for scripture through the
prophet says:

6"And you Bethlehem, in land of Judah,
are by no means the least of the leaders of Judah,
for from you there shall emerge
the leader who will be the shepherd of my people Israel." '

7Then Herod secretly sent for the scholars from the East, and carefully questioned them about the date when the star had appeared. 8He sent them to Bethlehem. 'Go,' he said, 'and make every effort to trace the child. And, when you have found him, send word to me, for I too wish to go and do homage to him.' 9When they heard what the king had to say, they set out, and the star, which they had seen when it first rose, led them on, until it came and stopped where the little child was. 10And very great was their rejoicing when they saw the star. 11They went into the house and they saw the little child with Mary his mother, and they knelt down and did him homage. They unpacked their treasures, and offered him gifts, gold, frankincense and myrrh. 12Because a message from God came to them in a dream, warning them not to go back to Herod, they returned to their own country by another way.

13When they had gone, an angel of the Lord appeared in a dream to Joseph. 'Up!' he said. 'Take the little child and his mother and make your escape to Egypt, and stay there until I tell you. Herod is about to institute a search for the little child, for he is out to kill him.' 14So Joseph set out, and took the little child and his mother by night and left for Egypt. 15He remained there till the death of Herod. This happened that the statement made by the Lord through the prophet might come true: 'Out of Egypt I have called my son.'

16Herod was very angry when he saw that he had been tricked by the scholars from the East. So he sent and had all the boy children in Bethlehem and in all the nearby districts killed. He had every child of two years and under killed. This, he reckoned, would be the age of the child about whose birth he had learned in his enquiries from the scholars from the East. 17At the time that statement made through Jeremiah the prophet came true:

18'A voice was heard in Ramah,
weeping and great lamentation,
Rachel weeping for her children,
and refusing to be comforted,
for they were no more.'

19When Herod died, an angel of the Lord appeared in a dream to Joseph in Egypt. 20'Up!' he said. 'Take the little child and his mother, and go into the land of Israel, for those who wanted to kill the child are dead.' 21So he set out and took the child and his mother, and went into the land of Israel.

22When he heard that Archelaus was reigning in Judaea instead of his father Herod, he was afraid to return there. So, after he had received a message from God in a dream, he went away to the district of Galilee, 23and went and settled in a town called Nazareth. This happened so that the statement made through the prophets might come true: 'He shall be called a Nazarene.'

Chapter 3

IT was at that time that John the Baptizer appeared on the scene, preaching in the Judaean desert. 2'Repent,' he preached, 'for the Kingdom of God is almost here. 3It was he who was spoken of by Isaiah the prophet, when he said:

'The voice of one shouting in the wilderness,
'Get ready the road by which the Lord will come,
straighten the paths by which he will travel." '

4John's coat was made of camel's hair, and he wore a leather belt round his waist. His food consisted of locusts and wild honey. 5People from Jerusalem and from all over Judaea and from all over the Jordan valley flocked out to him. 6And a continuous stream of them were baptized in the River Jordan, while they confessed their sins.

7When John saw the Pharisees and Sadducees coming in large numbers to be baptized, he said to them: 'Brood of vipers! Who put it into your heads to flee from the coming wrath? 8Prove the sincerity of your repentance by your life and conduct. 9Don't get the idea that you can say to yourselves: "We have Abraham as our father." For I tell you, God can produce children for Abraham from these stones. 10Even now the axe is poised at the root of the trees. Every tree which does not produce good fruit is going to be cut down and flung into the fire. 11I baptize you with water to make you repent. He who is coming after me is stronger than I am. I am not fit to carry his sandals. He will baptize you with the Holy Spirit and with fire. 12He is going to winnow the chaff from the corn, and he will clear every speck of rubbish from his threshing-floor. His corn he will gather into the store-house; the chaff he will burn with fire that nothing can put out.'

13At that time Jesus came from Galilee to the Jordan to be baptized by John. 14John tried to stop him. 'I need to be baptized by you,' he said, 'and are you coming to me?' 15'For the present,' Jesus answered, 'let it be so, for the right thing for us to do is to do everything a good man ought to do.' Then John let him have his way. 16No sooner had Jesus been baptized and come out of the water, than the heavens were opened, and John saw the Spirit coming down like a dove and settling on him. 17And there came a voice from heaven. 'This is my Son, the Beloved and Only One,' the voice said, 'and on him my favour rests.'

Chapter 4

JESUS was then taken into the desert by the Spirit to undergo the ordeal of temptation by the Devil. 2After he had deliberately gone without food for forty days and forty nights, he was attacked by the pangs of hunger. 3So the tempter came and said to him: 'If you really are the Son of God, tell these stones to become loaves of bread.' 4Jesus answered, 'Scripture says: "It takes more than bread to keep a man alive; man's life depends on every word that God speaks."' 5Then the Devil took him to the holy city, and placed him on the highest spire of the Temple. 6'If you really are the Son of God,' he said to him, 'fling yourself down, for scripture says: "He will give his angels orders to protect you, and they will carry you in their arms to ensure that you will never strike your foot against a stone."' 7Jesus said to him, 'Again, scripture says: "You must not try to see how far you can go with the Lord your God."' 8The Devil took him to a very high mountain, and showed him all the kingdoms of this world and their splendour. 9'I will give you all these,' he said to him, 'if you kneel down and worship me.' 10Then Jesus said to him, 'Begone, Satan! For scripture says: "You must worship the Lord your God, and you must serve him only."' 11Then the Devil left him, and angels came to his help.

12When Jesus heard that John had been committed to prison, he withdrew to Galilee. 13He left Nazareth and went and made his home in Capernaum, a town on the lakeside, in the territory of Zebulun and Naphtali. ₁₄He did this so that the statement made through the prophet Isaiah might come true:

> ₁₅'Land of Zebulun and land of Naphtali!
> Road of the sea beyond Jordan,
> Heathen Galilee!
> ₁₆The people who sat in darkness
>   have seen a great light,
> and a light has arisen for those
>   who sat in the land and the shadow of death.'

₁₇From that time on Jesus began to proclaim his message. 'Repent,' he said, 'for the Kingdom of Heaven is almost here.'

₁₈When Jesus was walking along the shore of the Lake of Galilee, he saw two brothers, Simon, who is called Peter, and his brother Andrew, casting a net into the lake, for they were fishermen. ₁₉'Follow me,' he said to them, 'and I will make you fishermen who catch men!' ₂₀There and then they left their nets and became his followers. ₂₁He went on from there and saw other two brothers, James, Zebedee's son, and his brother John. They were in the boat with Zebedee their father, servicing their nets. He called them. ₂₂There and then they left the boat and their father, and became his followers.

₂₃Jesus made a circular tour of the whole of Galilee, teaching in their synagogues, and proclaiming the Good News of the Kingdom and healing all kinds of illness and all kinds of sickness among the people. ₂₄Reports of what he was doing spread all over Syria. So they brought to him all those who were ill, in the grip of the most varied diseases and pains, those who were possessed by demons, epileptics and paralysed people, and he cured them. ₂₅And huge crowds from Galilee and from the Ten Towns and from Jerusalem and from Judaea and from Transjordan followed him.

Chapter 5

WHEN Jesus saw the crowds, he went up the hill. He sat down to teach, and his disciples came to listen to him. ₂He opened his mind and his heart to them, and this was the substance of his teaching.

3'O the bliss of those who realize
    the destitution of their own lives,
for the blessings of the Kingdom of Heaven
    are theirs here and now.
4O the bliss of those whose sorrow is sore,
    for they shall find courage and comfort.
5O the bliss of those whose strength is in their gentleness,
    for they shall enter into possession of the earth.
6O the bliss of those who hunger and thirst
    for all that sets them right with God,
    for they shall be satisfied to the full.
7O the bliss of those who treat others with mercy,
    for they shall be treated with mercy.
8O the bliss of those who are pure in heart,
    for they shall see God.
9O the bliss of those who make men friends with each other,
    for they shall be ranked as the sons of God.
10O the bliss of those who are persecuted
    for their loyalty to God's way of life,
for the blessings of the Kingdom of Heaven
    are theirs here and now.
11Yours is this bliss,
    when men shall heap their insults on you,
        and persecute you,
            and tell every wicked kind of lie about you
            for my sake.
12When that happens,
    rejoice and exult in it,
for you will receive a rich reward in heaven,
    for it was thus that they persecuted
    the prophets who lived before you.

13'You are the salt of the earth.
    If the salt has lost its taste,
    what can ever give it its saltness back again?
If that happens, you can do nothing with it
    but throw it out for people to tramp on.

14'You are the light of the world.
    A town situated on a hilltop
    cannot be hid.

15A lamp is not lit to be put under a bowl.
   It is lit to be put on a lampstand,
and then it shines for everyone in the house
   to see it.
16Just so, your light must shine
   for everyone to see, so that,
when they see the lovely things you do,
   it may make them want to praise
   your Father who is in heaven.

17'You must never suppose that
   I have come to destroy the Law and the Prophets;
I did not come to destroy them;
   I came to fulfil them.
18This is the truth I tell you,
   so long as heaven and earth shall last,
not the smallest letter,
not the smallest part of a letter of the Law
   will cease to be valid.
It will remain until history comes to an end.

19'So then, anyone who tries to weaken
   the authority of one of these commandments,
   even if it is the least of them,
will have the lowest rank in the Kingdom of Heaven,
   but anyone who obeys them,
   and teaches others to obey them,
will have high rank in the Kingdom of Heaven.
20I tell you, you will certainly not get into
   the Kingdom of Heaven,
unless your loyalty to the Law
   surpasses that of the experts in the Law
   and of the Pharisees.

21'You know very well that
   "You must not kill"
is an ancient law;
   and, if anyone kills,
he is liable to the judgment of the law-courts.

22But I tell you that
anyone who is angry with his fellow man*
will have to stand his trial;
anyone who calls his fellow man a brainless idiot
will have to stand his trial in the supreme court;
anyone who calls his fellow man a wicked fool
is liable to be condemned to hell-fire.
23If, then, you are bringing your gift to the altar,
and, when you are standing there,
you remember that your fellow man has a grievance against you,
24leave your gift there in front of the altar,
and go and make peace with your brother,
and then come and offer your gift.

25'Settle your difference quickly
with the man who is going to prosecute you,
while you are still on the road to the court with him.
If you do not,
the prosecutor may well hand you over to the judge,
and the judge may well hand you over to the court officer,
and you may well be thrown into prison.
26I tell you, if that happens,
you will certainly not be released,
until you have paid the last farthing in full.

27'You know that the Law states,
"You must not commit adultery."
28But I tell you,
if anyone looks at a woman in such a way
as deliberately to awaken within himself
the forbidden desire for her,
he has already committed adultery with her in intention.

29'If your right eye becomes a cause of sin to you,
tear it out, and throw it away,
for it is better that one part of your body
should be destroyed
than that your whole body
should be flung into hell.

*See Notes on pp. 575–6

30If your right hand becomes a cause of sin to you,
   cut it off, and throw it away,
for it is better for you that one part of your body
   should be destroyed
than that your whole body
   should go to hell.

31'The Law states that,
   if a man divorces his wife,
   he must give her an official certificate of divorce.
32But I tell you that
   if a man divorces his wife
   for any reason other than infidelity,
      he makes her commit adultery;
      and if anyone marries a woman who has been divorced,
      he commits adultery.

33'To take another example,
you know very well that it is an ancient law
   that you must not take an oath in God's name
   with no intention of keeping it,
   but you must discharge the obligation of your oaths
      in full to the Lord.
34But I tell you,
   do not take an oath at all,
   neither by heaven,
      for heaven is the throne of God;
   35nor by earth,
      for earth is his footstool;
   nor by Jerusalem,
      for Jerusalem is the city of the Great King;
   36nor by your head,
      for you cannot make one hair white or black.
   37In your speaking,
      when you mean yes, say yes—nothing more;
      when you mean no, say no—nothing more.
   Anything which goes beyond that
      has been prompted by the Evil One.

38'You know that the Law states,
   "An eye in exchange for an eye,
   and a tooth in exchange for a tooth."

39But I tell you
  not to resist evil, but,
    if anyone slaps you on the right cheek,
      let him slap you on the other as well;
      40if anyone wishes to obtain judgment against you
    for possession of your shirt,
      let him have your coat as well.
      41And if a Roman officer commandeers you
    to act as a baggage-porter for one mile,
      go two miles.
42If anyone asks you for anything,
  give it to him,
and do not refuse anyone
  who wishes to borrow from you.

43'You know that the Law states that
  you must love your neighbour
  and hate your enemy.
44But I tell you,
  love your enemies,
  and pray for those who persecute you.
    45If you do that,
    you will be like your Father in heaven,
      for he makes his sun to rise,
        on the bad and on the good alike,
      and he sends the rain
        on saint and sinner.
46What reward can you expect,
  if you love those who love you?
  Do not even the renegade tax-collectors do that?
47Is there anything special about it,
  if you greet only your friends?
  Do not even the heathen do that?
48You must be perfect
as your heavenly Father is perfect.'

Chapter 6

'TAKE care
not to make a public performance
of your goodness,
with the intention of letting everyone see
how good you are.
If you do,
you can expect no reward
from your Father who is in heaven.
₂When you are going to perform an act of charity,
do not announce yourself
with a fanfare of trumpets,
as those whose religion consists
in ostentatious play-acting do
in the synagogues and on the streets,
to win popular applause.
I tell you truly, they have all the reward
they will ever get.
₃But when you perform an act of charity,
your left hand must not know
what your right hand is doing.
₄Your aim must be to keep your charitable giving secret.
And your Father who sees what is done in secret
will give you your reward in full.

₅'When you are saying your prayers
you must not be like those whose religion consists
in ostentatious play-acting.
They love to say their prayers,
standing in the synagogue
and at the street corners.
Their idea is to be seen praying
by as many people as possible.
I tell you truly, they have all the reward
they will ever get.
₆But when you say your prayers,
you must go into your private room,
and shut the door,

and say your prayers to your Father
  who is in secret.
And your Father who sees what is done in secret
  will give you your reward in full.
7When you say your prayers,
  don't pile up meaningless phrases,
    as the heathen do.
Their idea is that God will hear their prayers
  because of their length.
8Don't become like them, you don't need to;
  your Father knows what you need,
    before you ask him.
9So, when you pray, pray like this:
    Our Father in heaven,
    May your name be held in reverence,
      10May your Kingdom come,
    May your will be done,
      as in heaven, so on earth.
      11Give us today our bread for the coming day.
      12Forgive us for our failures in our duty to you,
      as we have forgiven those who have failed
      in their duty to us.
      13Do not submit us to any time of testing,
        but rescue us from the Evil One.★
14For if you forgive your fellow men
  for the wrongs they have done to you,
  your Father will forgive you;
15but if you do not forgive your fellow men,
  then your Father will not forgive you either
  for the wrongs you have done to him.

16'When you are fasting,
  don't put on a gloomy face
  as those whose religion consists
  in ostentatious play-acting do.
They deliberately disfigure their faces,
  so that no one will be able to fail to see
  that they are fasting.

★See Notes on pp. 575-6

I tell you truly, they have all the reward
   they will ever get.
17But when you are engaged in fasting,
   anoint your head and wash your face,
18so that you may look to men
   as if you were not fasting at all,
   although your Father who is in secret will see it.
   And your Father who sees what is done in secret
   will give you your reward in full.

19'Do not amass for yourselves treasures on earth,
   where the moth eats them away,
   and the rust corrodes them,
   and thieves break in and steal.
20Amass for yourselves treasures in heaven,
   where the moth cannot eat them away,
   and the rust does not corrode them,
   and thieves do not break in and steal.
21For your heart is bound to be
where your treasure is.
22The eye is the body's lamp.
So then, if your eye is sound and generous,
   your whole body will be full of light;
23but if your eye is diseased and grudging,
   your whole body will be full of darkness.
If the light that ought to be in you
   has turned to darkness,
   what a terrible darkness that darkness is!

24'No one can be a slave to two owners,
   for he will either hate the one and love the other,
   or he will be devoted to one and despise the other.
You cannot be the servant both of the God of heaven
   and of the god of this world's wealth.

25'That is why I tell you,
Stop worrying about what you are going to eat and drink
   to keep you alive;
stop worrying about the clothes you are going to wear
   to keep your body warm.
Surely there is more to life than food,
   and more to the body than clothes?

26Look at the birds of the sky.
See how they do not sow or reap
or collect things into storehouses.
And yet your heavenly Father gives them their food.
Are you not much more valuable than they?
27Can any of you add half a yard to his height
by worrying about it?
28And why worry about clothes?
Learn a lesson from the way
in which the wild lilies grow.
They do not toil or spin.
29But I tell you,
that not even Solomon in all his splendour
was robed like one of these.
30You have so little faith.
If God clothes like that the wild flowers
which have one brief day,
and which tomorrow are used
to make a fire to heat an oven,
can you not depend on him far more
to clothe you?
31So then, make up your mind to stop worrying,
and to stop saying,
"What are we going to eat?"
or, "What are we going to drink?"
or, "What are we going to wear?"
32These are the kind of things
which the people who don't know God
keep thinking about.
Your heavenly Father knows you need all these things.
33Make the Kingdom of God,
and life in loyalty to him,
the object of all your endeavour,
and you will get all these other things as well.
34So then, make up your mind
to stop worrying about tomorrow.
Tomorrow will worry about itself.
The day's trouble is quite enough for the day.'

Chapter 7

'Don't make a habit of judging others,
  if you do not want to be judged yourselves.
2For the verdict which you pass on others
  will be the verdict that is passed on you.
You will get in exactly the same proportion
  as you give.
3Why do you see the speck of dust
  in your fellow man's eye,
and never notice the plank
  that is in your own eye?
4Or, how can you say to your fellow man:
  "Let me take the speck of dust
  out of your eye,"
while all the time there is a plank
  in your own eye?
5Your trouble is that you completely fail
  to practise what you preach.
Begin by taking the plank
  out of your own eye.
Then you will be able to see clearly
to take the speck of dust
  out of your fellow man's eye.

6'Never give to dogs what is sacred,
  and never offer your pearls to pigs.
If you do, they may well trample on them with their feet,
  and turn on you,
  and tear you in pieces.

7'Keep on asking,
  and you will get;
keep on seeking,
  and you will find;
keep on knocking,
  and the door will be opened for you.

8For everyone who keeps on asking
   gets what he asks for;
he who keeps on seeking,
   finds;
if a man keeps on knocking,
   the door will be opened.
9Is any of you likely to give his son a stone,
   if he asks for a loaf?
10Is he likely to give him a snake,
   if he asks for a fish?
11If then, evil and ungenerous as you are,
   you know how to give your children good gifts,
how much more can you depend on your Father in heaven,
   to give good things to those who ask him for them!

12'In everything you must treat others
   as you would want them to treat you.
This is a summary of the message
   of the Law and the Prophets.

13'Go in by the narrow gate.
There is plenty of room to go through
   the gate that leads to ruin;
   it is no trouble to travel that road;
   and there are crowds who go through it.
14The gate that leads to life is narrow;
   the road is beset with troubles;
   and there are few who find it.

15'Be continually on your guard
   against false prophets,
for they come disguised as sheep
   but they are really rapacious wolves.
16You will recognize them by their conduct.
Obviously, you cannot gather
   grapes from thorn bushes,
   or figs from thistles
17Every good tree
   produces fine fruit,
but every rotten tree
   produces bad fruit;

18It is not possible
for a good tree
  to bear bad fruit,
or for a rotten tree
  to bear fine fruit.
19If a tree does not produce fine fruit,
  it is cut down and thrown into the fire.
20As with trees, so with men—
  you can tell what kind of men they are
  by the conduct they produce.

21'It is not everyone who says to me, "Lord, Lord"
  who will get into the Kingdom of Heaven.
It is the man who does the will
  of my Father who is in heaven.
22On the great day there will be many who will say to me,
  "Lord, Lord, didn't we prophesy in your name?
  Didn't we eject devils in your name?
  Didn't we perform miracles in your name?"
23When that happens, I will tell them straight:
  "You are complete strangers to me!
  Out of my sight!
  Your deeds were sins!"

24'So then, if anyone listens to these words of mine,
  and obeys them,
he will be like a man of sound sense
  who built his house
  with its foundations laid on rock.
25The rains lashed down,
  and the rivers swelled,
  and the winds blew and battered that house,
but it did not collapse,
  for its foundations were laid on rock.
26But if anyone listens to these words of mine,
  and does not obey them,
he will be like a senseless man
  who built his house
  with its foundations laid on sand.
27The rains lashed down,
  and the rivers swelled,

and the winds blew and buffeted that house,
and it collapsed,
and its ruin was complete.'

28When Jesus finished speaking, the crowds were astonished at the way he taught, 29for he taught as one who needed no authority beyond his own, and not like the experts in the Law.

Chapter 8

WHEN Jesus came down from the hill, great crowds of people followed him. 2A leper came and knelt at his feet. 'Sir,' he said, 'if you want to cure me, you can.' 3Jesus reached out his hand and touched him. 'I do,' he said. 'Be cured.' There and then his leprosy was cured. 4'See to it,' Jesus said to him, 'that you do not tell anyone about this, but go and show yourself to the priest, and take to him the gift which Moses prescribed, to prove to them that you really are cured.'

5When Jesus came into Capernaum, a centurion came up to him with an urgent appeal. 6'Sir,' he said, 'my servant is lying at home paralysed and in terrible pain.' 7'I will come and cure him,' Jesus said. 8'Sir,' answered the centurion, 'I am not fit to have you come into my house. All I ask you to do is to say the word, and my servant will be cured. 9For I too know what it is to be under authority, and I have soldiers under my command. I am used to saying to one, "Go" and he goes, and to another, "Come here" and he comes, and to my slave, "Do this" and he does it.' 10Jesus was astonished to hear this. 'I tell you truly,' he said to those who were following him, 'I have not found anyone in Israel with a faith like this. 11I tell you that many will come from the east and the west and will be fellow-guests with Abraham and Isaac and Jacob in the Kingdom of Heaven, 12but those who were born to be members of the Kingdom will be flung out into the outer darkness, where there will be tears and agony. 13Go,' Jesus said to the centurion. 'Because you have a faith like this, your prayer is granted.' And the servant was cured at that very hour.

14When Jesus went into Peter's house, he saw Peter's mother-in-law lying in bed with an attack of fever. 15So he touched her hand and the fever left her, and she got up and began to serve him with his meal.

16When evening came, they brought many demon-possessed people to him, and he ejected the spirits with a word, and cured all those who were ill. 17This happened that the statement made through the prophet Isaiah might come true: 'He took upon himself our weaknesses and carried the burden of our diseases.'

18When Jesus saw the crowds on all sides, he gave orders to his disciples to go away across to the other side of the lake. 19An expert in the Law came up to him. 'Teacher,' he said, 'I will follow you wherever you go.' 20Jesus said to him: 'The foxes have lairs and the birds of the sky have nests, but the Son of Man has nowhere to lay his head.' 21Another man, one of his disciples, said to him: 'Sir, let me go and bury my father first.' 22'Follow me,' said Jesus, 'and let the dead bury their dead.'

23He embarked on the boat, and his disciples accompanied him. 24Such a violent storm blew up on the lake that the boat was engulfed in the waves. Jesus was sleeping. 25They came and wakened him. 'Master,' they said, 'save us! We're drowning!' 26'Why are you such cowards?' he said to them. 'You have so little faith!' Then he got up and reprimanded the winds and the sea, and there was a complete calm. 27The men were astonished. 'What kind of man is this,' they said, 'for even the winds and the waters obey him?'

28When Jesus had crossed to the other side of the lake, to the territory of the Gadarenes, two demon-possessed men met him on their way out of the tombs. They were so fierce that no one was able to pass along that road. 29They shouted at the top of their voices: 'What business have you with us, you Son of God? Have you come here to torture us before the proper time?' 30Some distance away a large herd of pigs was feeding. 31The demons pleaded with Jesus: 'If you eject us from these men, send us into the herd of pigs.' 32'Begone!' he said to them. They came out of the men and went into the pigs, and the whole herd stampeded down the cliff and died in the waters of the lake. 33The herdsmen fled. They went away into the town and related the whole story, and told of what had happened to the demon-possessed men. 34The whole town came out to meet Jesus, and, when they saw him, they begged him to get out of their district.

Chapter 9

JESUS got into a boat, and crossed over to the other side of the lake, and came to his own town. 2They brought to him a paralysed man, lying on a bed. When Jesus saw their faith, he said to the paralysed man: 'Courage, child. Your sins are forgiven.' 3Some of the experts in the Law said to themselves: 'This fellow is insulting God!' 4Jesus knew what was going on in their minds. 'What put such mistaken ideas into your heads?' he said. 5'Which is easier—to say, "Your sins are forgiven," or to say, "Get up and walk"? 6But just to show you that the Son of Man actually has authority on earth to forgive sins'— then he said to the paralysed man—'Up! Lift your bed! And away you go home!' 7He got up and went off home. 8When the crowds saw this, they were moved to awe, and they praised God that he had given power like this to men.

9As Jesus was walking along from there, he saw a man called Matthew, sitting in the office where he collected the customs duties. 'Follow me!' he said. And Matthew rose from his seat and followed him.

10Jesus was sitting at a meal in the house, and many tax-collectors and people with whom no respectable Jew would have had anything to do came to be guests along with Jesus and his disciples. 11When the Pharisees saw this, they said to the disciples: 'Why does your Teacher eat with tax-collectors and with people with whom no respectable Jew would have anything to do?' 12Jesus heard this. 'It is not those who are well who need a doctor,' he said, 'but those who are ill. 13Go and learn the meaning of the saying, "It is mercy I want, not sacrifice." For I did not come to bring an invitation to those who are good but to those who are sinners.'

14John's disciples approached Jesus. 'Why,' they said, 'do we and the Pharisees make a habit of fasting, while your disciples do not?' 15Jesus said to them: 'Obviously, the bridegroom's closest friends cannot be in a state of mourning when the bridegroom is with them. But there will come a time when the bridegroom will be taken away from them, and then they will fast.

16'No one,' Jesus went on, 'sews a patch of unshrunk cloth on an old coat, for, if he does, the patch that was meant to fill the hole tears the coat apart, and the tear becomes worse than ever. 17No more do people pour new fermenting wine into old wineskins that have lost their elasticity. If they do, the skins burst, and the wine is spilled, and the skins are destroyed. New wine is put into new wineskins, and both are preserved.'

18While Jesus was speaking, a man who was president of the local synagogue came and knelt in front of him. 'My daughter has just died,' he said, 'but come and lay your hand on her and she will live.' 19Jesus started out to go with him, and the disciples went too.

20A woman who had had a haemorrhage for twelve years came up behind Jesus and touched the tassel of his cloak. 21She said to herself: 'If I touch only his cloak, I will be cured.' 22Jesus turned and saw her. 'Courage, daughter!' he said. 'Your faith has made you well!' There and then the woman was cured.

23When Jesus reached the president's house, he saw the flute-players, and the crowd in an uproar. 24'Get out of here!' he said. 'The girl is not dead. She is sleeping.' They laughed at him. 25When the crowd had been put out, he went in. He gripped her by the hand, and the girl got up. 26The story of this spread all over the country.

27As Jesus was passing on from there, two blind men followed him shouting. 'Take pity on us, son of David!' they said. 28When he had gone indoors, the blind men approached him. Jesus said to them: 'Do you really believe that I can do this?' 'Yes, sir,' they said. 29He touched their eyes. 'Let your prayer be answered in proportion to your faith,' he said. 30Their sight was restored. Jesus sternly ordered them: 'See that no one gets to know about this.' 31But they went and spread the story all over that district.

32As they were leaving there, a dumb man who was demon-possessed was brought to Jesus. 33When the demon had been ejected from him, the dumb man regained the power of speech. The crowds were amazed. 'Nothing like this,' they said, 'was ever seen in Israel.' 34But the Pharisees said: 'He ejects the demons by the power of the prince of the demons.'

35Jesus made a tour of all the towns and villages, teaching in their synagogues, and proclaiming the Good News of the Kingdom, and healing every disease and every sickness. 36When he saw the crowds he was heart-sorry for them, for they were bewildered and dejected, like sheep who had no shepherd. 37'There is a rich harvest,' he said to the disciples, 'but there are few workers. 38So you must pray to the Lord of the harvest to send out workers to gather in his harvest.'

Chapter 10

JESUS summoned his twelve disciples and gave them such authority over unclean spirits that they were able to eject them, and to cure every disease and every sickness.

2These are the names of the twelve apostles: first, Simon, who is called Peter, and his brother Andrew; James, Zebedee's son, and his brother John; 3Philip and Bartholomew; Thomas and Matthew, the tax-collector; James, Alphaeus' son, and Thaddaeus; 4Simon, the Nationalist, and Judas Iscariot, the man who betrayed him.

5Jesus sent out these twelve, and these were his marching orders to them: 'You must not go off on any road that leads to Gentile territory; you must not go into any Samaritan town; 6it is rather to the sheep of the family of Israel who have gone lost that you must go. 7As you go, make this proclamation: "The Kingdom of Heaven is almost here." 8Cure the sick, raise the dead to life, cleanse the lepers, eject the demons. You paid nothing to get, accept nothing to give.

9'Do not lay in a stock of gold or silver or copper coins in your money-belts. 10Do not take a beggar's knapsack for the road, nor two shirts, nor shoes, nor a staff. The workman deserves his keep.

11'Whenever you enter a town or village, look for someone who deserves the presence of my messengers, and stay there until you leave it. 12When you go into a house, give your greeting to it. 13If the house deserves it, let your prayer for God's blessing rest upon it. If it does not deserve it, let your prayer for God's blessing return to you. 14If anyone refuses you a welcome or a hearing, as you leave that house or town, shake the last speck of its dust from your feet, as if you were leaving a heathen town. 15I tell you truly, it will be easier for the land of Sodom and Gomorrah on the day of judgment than for that town.

16'I am sending you out like sheep among wolves. You must therefore show yourselves to be as wise as serpents and as pure as doves. 17You must be constantly on your guard. They will hand you over to the councils; they will flog you in the synagogues; 18you will be brought before governors and kings for my sake, but you must regard that as an opportunity to demonstrate to them and to the Gentiles your loyalty to me. 19When they hand you over, do not worry about how you are to speak, or about what you are to say. What you are to say will be given you at that time, 20for it is not you who are the speakers; the speaker is the Spirit of your Father, speaking in and through you.

21'Brother will hand over brother to death, and father will hand over child. Children will attack their parents and murder them. 22You will be universally hated because of your connection with me. But the man who sees things through to the end will be saved. 23When they persecute you in one town, make your escape to another. I tell you truly, you will not complete your circuit of the towns of Israel before the Son of Man shall come.

24'A scholar cannot hope to escape what his teacher has to suffer, nor a slave what his owner has to suffer. 25The scholar must be content to undergo the same experience as his teacher, and the slave as his owner. If they called the head of the house a child of the Devil, it is only to be expected that they will do the same to the members of the household.

26'Don't be afraid of them. What is veiled must be unveiled, and what is hidden must be made known. 27What I tell you in the darkness, speak in the full light of day; broadcast from the housetops what is whispered in your ear.

28'Don't be afraid of those who can kill the body but who cannot kill the soul. The one you must fear is the One who is able to destroy both body and soul in hell.

29'Everyone knows that two sparrows can be bought for one farthing, and yet death does not come to one of them without your Father knowing about it. 30Even the hairs of your head have all been counted. 31So, then, don't be afraid. You are more valuable than a whole collection of sparrows.

32'If anyone publicly acknowledges his loyalty to me in front of his fellow men, I will do the same for him in front of my Father who is in heaven. 33If anyone disowns me in front of his fellow men I will disown him in front of my Father who is in heaven.

34'You must not suppose that the result of my coming will be peace for the world. The result of my coming will not be peace but a sword. 35My coming is bound to result in a cleavage between a man and his father, between a daughter and her mother, between a daughter-in-law and her mother-in-law. ₃₆A man's enemies will be his own kith and kin.

₃₇'If a man loves his father and mother more than he loves me, he is not fit to belong to me. If a man loves his son or daughter more than he loves me, he is not fit to belong to me. ₃₈If a man does not take up his cross and follow in my footsteps, he is not fit to belong to me. ₃₉To find your life is to lose it, and to lose it for my sake is to find it.

₄₀'To welcome you is to welcome me; to welcome me is to welcome him who sent me. ₄₁The man who recognizes a prophet and welcomes him as such will receive the same reward as a prophet. The man who recognizes a good man and welcomes him as such will receive the same reward as a good man. ₄₂If anyone recognizes one of these little ones as a disciple of mine, and gives him even a cup of cold water, he can be sure of his reward.'

Chapter 11

WHEN Jesus had completed his instructions to the twelve disciples, he moved on from there to continue teaching and proclaiming his message in their towns.

₂When news of the things that the Messiah was doing reached John in prison, he sent his disciples to ask him: ₃'Are you the One who is to come, or are we to go on waiting and hoping for someone else?' ₄'Go,' answered Jesus, 'and tell John the story of all you are hearing and seeing. ₅Blind men are seeing again; lame men are walking; lepers are being cleansed; deaf men are hearing; dead men are being raised to life; poor men are hearing the Good News. ₆And happy is the man who does not find himself antagonized by me.'

₇As John's disciples were leaving, Jesus spoke to the crowds about John. 'What did you go out to the desert to see?' he said. 'Was it to see what you can see any day there—the long grass swaying in the wind? ₈If it was not that, what was it you went out to see? Was it to see a man dressed in dainty and delicate clothes? The people who wear dainty and delicate clothes live in kings' palaces. ₉If it was not that, what was it you went out to see? Was it to see a prophet? Yes, indeed it was, and, I tell you, more than a prophet. 10This is the man of whom scripture says:

"Look! I am sending my messenger ahead of you,
 And he will go on in advance to prepare your road for you."

11I tell you truly, that among mortal men no greater figure than John the Baptizer has ever emerged in history. All the same, the least in the Kingdom of Heaven is greater than he. 12It was in the days of John the Baptizer that a situation first arose—a situation which still exists—in which the Kingdom of Heaven is stormed, and in which those who are eager to storm their way into it clutch at it. 13For up to John all the prophets and the whole Law told of the things which were destined to happen. 14But, if you are prepared to accept it, John is Elijah who was destined to come. 15If you have ears to hear, then hear.'

16'With what can I compare the people of today? They are like children sitting in the market-place, calling to their companions and saying:

17"When we played you a happy tune,
   you did not dance;
  when we wailed you a sad lament,
   you did not mourn."

18For John came living the life of an ascetic, and they say: "The man is demon-possessed!" 19The Son of Man came enjoying life like a normal person, and they say: "A glutton and a drunkard! The friend of renegade tax-collectors and of people with whom no respectable Jew would have anything to do!" But God's wisdom is vindicated by its results.'

20It was then that Jesus reproached the towns in which very many of his miracles had been performed, because they refused to repent. 21'Tragic will be your fate, Chorazin! Tragic will be your fate, Bethsaida! For, if the miracles which have been done in you had been done in Tyre and Sidon, they would long ago have repented in sackcloth and ashes. 22But I tell you, Tyre and Sidon will get off more lightly in the day of judgment than you. 23And you, Capernaum—do you think you are going to be exalted as high as heaven? You will go down to the depths of hell. For, if the miracles which have been done in you had been done in Sodom, it would still be standing today. 24But I tell you, the land of Sodom will get off more lightly in the day of judgment than you!'

25It was then that Jesus said: 'I thank you, Father, Lord of heaven and earth, that you have hidden these things from the wise and clever and that you have revealed them to those who are as simple as little children. 26Yes, indeed, Father, I thank you, for this is what you chose to do.'

27'All things have been entrusted to me by my Father. No one really knows the Son except the Father, and no one really knows the Father except the Son, and those to whom the Son chooses to make him known.'

28'Come to me, all you who are tired and bent beneath your burdens, and I will give you rest. 29Take my yoke on your shoulders, and let me teach you, for I am gentle and humble in heart, and you will find rest for your souls, 30for my yoke is kindly and my load is light.'

Chapter 12

IT was then that Jesus went for a walk through the cornfields on the Sabbath day. The disciples felt hungry and began to pluck the ears of corn and eat them. 2The Pharisees saw this. 'Look!' they said. 'Your disciples are doing what it is not permitted by the Law to do on the Sabbath day.' 3'Have you not read,' he said to them, 'what David did when he and his friends were hungry? 4Do you not know the story of how he went into the house of God and ate the sacred loaves which are placed in the presence of God, although he and his friends had no right to eat them, because only the priests are permitted to eat them? 5Or, have you not read in the Law how the work of the priests in the Temple compels them to break the Sabbath law, and thus to profane the Sabbath, and yet they remain blameless? 6I tell you that something greater than the Temple is here. 7If you had known the meaning of the saying, "It is mercy I want, not sacrifice," you would not have condemned those who are blameless, 8for the Son of Man's authority extends over the Sabbath.'

9He moved on from there, and went into their synagogue. 10There was a man there with a withered hand. In an attempt to find something which they could use as a charge against him, they asked him: 'Is it permitted to heal on the Sabbath day?' 11'If one of you has a sheep,' he said, 'and the sheep falls into a hole in the ground on the Sabbath day, will he not take a grip of it and lift it out? 12Surely you will admit that a man is more valuable than a sheep? Obviously, there is no law to stop a man doing good on the Sabbath day.' 13Then he said to the man: 'Stretch out your hand!' He stretched it out, and it was restored, healthy as the other. 14The Pharisees went away and concocted a scheme to kill him.

15Jesus was well aware of what they were doing, so he withdrew from there. Large numbers of people followed him, and he healed them all. 16He strictly ordered them not to surround him with publicity. 17All this happened that the statement made through the prophet Isaiah might come true:

> 18'Behold, my servant whom I have chosen!
>   My Beloved and Only One in whom my soul
>   has found delight!
> I will put my Spirit upon him,
>   and he will announce to the nations that the time
>   of judgment has come.
> 19He will not be a loud-mouthed man of strife,
>   nor will anyone hear his voice in the streets.
> 20He will not break a crushed reed,
>   and he will not extinguish a dimly-burning wick,
> until he makes his judgment victorious;
>   21and in his name shall the Gentiles place their hope.'

22It was after that that a demon-possessed man who was blind and dumb was brought to Jesus, and he cured him so effectively that the dumb man was able to speak and see. 23The crowds were all astonished. 'Can this be the Son of David?' they said.

24But when the Pharisees heard of this, they said: 'The only way in which this fellow ejects demons is by the help of Beelzebul, the prince of the demons.' 25Jesus knew what they were thinking. 'Every kingdom,' he said, 'which is split within itself is on the way to being laid waste. No city or household which is split within itself can survive. 26If Satan is ejecting Satan, he is split within himself. How then can his kingdom survive? 27Further, if I eject demons by the help of

Beelzebul, by whose help do your own disciples eject them? Ask them what they think of this argument of yours. 28If I eject demons by the help of the Spirit of God, then the Kingdom of God has reached you here and now. 29To put it in another way, how can anyone enter the house of a strong man and plunder his goods, unless he first ties up the strong man? Then indeed he will be able to plunder his house.

30'If a man is not my ally,' Jesus went on, 'he is my enemy, and if a man is not helping my work he is undoing it. 31That is why I tell you that men will be forgiven for every sin and every insult to God, but they will not be forgiven for insulting the Spirit. 32If any man speaks a word against the Son of Man, he will be forgiven for it, but if anyone speaks a word against the Holy Spirit, he will not be forgiven for it, either in this world or in the world to come. You must make up your minds. 33If the tree is good, the fruit must be good, and if the tree is bad, the fruit must be bad, for you can only tell what kind of tree a tree is by its fruit.

34'You brood of vipers! How can you say anything good when you are evil? A man's words are nothing other than the overflow of what is in his heart. 35A good man brings good things out of his good treasure-house; an evil man brings evil things out of his evil treasure-house. 36I tell you that on the day of judgment men will have to answer for every careless word they shall speak. 37For by your words you will be acquitted, and by your words you will be condemned.'

38Some of the experts in the Law and the Pharisees then said to Jesus: 'Teacher, we would like you to provide us with some visible action of God which will prove your claims.' 39Jesus answered: 'This age which demands some visible action of God is an evil and apostate age, and the only such action that will be given to it is the action of God which was seen in the case of the prophet Jonah. 40For as Jonah was inside the sea-monster for three days and three nights, so the Son of Man will be in the heart of the earth for three days and three nights. 41When the day of judgment comes, the people of Nineveh will rise from the dead at the same time as the people of today and will condemn them, for they repented at the preaching of Jonah, and there is a greater event than Jonah here. 42When the day of judgment comes, the Queen of the South will rise from the dead at the same time as the people of today, and will condemn them, for she came from the ends of the earth to listen to the wisdom of Solomon, and there is a greater event than Solomon here.'

43'When an unclean spirit goes out of a man, it roams through waterless places, looking for rest, and finds none. 44Then it says: "I will go back to the house which used to be mine and which I left." So it comes and finds the house empty, swept and in perfect order. 45Then it goes and brings back along with it seven other spirits worse than itself, and they go in and make their home there. So the last state of that man becomes worse than the first. So it will be with the men of this evil age.'

46While Jesus was speaking to the crowds, his mother and brothers stood outside, wanting to speak to him. 47Someone said to him: 'Look! Your mother and brothers are standing outside, wanting to speak to you.' 48He answered the man who told him: 'Who is my mother? Who are my brothers?' 49He pointed to his disciples. 'See!' he said. 'My mother and my brothers! 50Anyone who does the will of my Father in heaven is my brother and sister and mother.'

Chapter 13

ON that day Jesus went out of the house and sat by the lake-side. 2Such crowds gathered to listen to him that he got into a boat and sat in it, while the crowd all stood on the shore. 3He used parables to tell them many things.

'Look!' he said. 'A sower went out to sow his seed. 4As he sowed, some seeds fell by the side of the road, and the birds came and snapped them up. 5Others fell on ground where there was only a thin skin of earth over the rock, and, because the soil was so shallow, they sprang up immediately, 6but when the sun rose they were scorched, and they withered, because they had no root. 7Some fell among thorn-bushes, and the thorn-bushes shot up and choked the life out of them. 8Others fell on good ground, and produced a crop, some a hundred times, some sixty times, some thirty times as much as had been sown. 9If a man has ears, let him hear.'

10The disciples came to Jesus and asked him: 'What is your reason for speaking to them in parables?' 11'You,' he said, 'have received the privilege of knowing the secrets of the Kingdom of Heaven, secrets which only a disciple can understand, but to them that privilege has not been given. 12For, if anyone already has, he will continue to receive more and more until he has enough and more than enough; but, if anyone has not, even what he has will be taken away from him. 13The reason why I speak to them in parables is that, although they see, they do not see, and, although they hear, they do not hear, nor do they understand. 14In them Isaiah's prophecy has come true:

"You will certainly hear,
    but you will certainly not understand
        the meaning of what you hear;
you will certainly see,
    but you will certainly not perceive
        the meaning of what you see.
15The mind of this people has become lazily shut,
    and their ears have become hard of hearing,
    and they have deliberately obscured their own sight,
lest at any time they should see with their eyes,
    and hear with their ears,
    and understand with their minds,
        and turn and find their cure in me."

16Happy are your eyes, because they are seeing, and your ears, because they are hearing. 17I tell you truly, many a prophet and many a good man longed to see the events which you are seeing, and did not see them, and to hear the words which you are hearing, and did not hear them.'

18'Listen, then, to the meaning of the parable of the sower. 19If anyone hears the message of God's Kingdom, and does not really understand it, the Evil One comes and snatches away what was sown in such a man's heart. This kind of person is represented by the picture of the seed sown on the side of the road. 20The picture of the seed which was sown on the ground which was only a thin skin of earth over the rock represents the man who hears the word and who immediately receives it enthusiastically. 21But he has no inner root, and is at the mercy of the moment, and so, when trouble or persecution comes, he at once stumbles and collapses. 22The picture of the seed which was sown among the thorn-bushes represents the man who hears the word, but the worry of this world and the deceptive seduction of wealth choke the life out of the word, and it never gets a chance to produce a crop. 23The picture of the seed which was sown on the good ground represents the man who hears the word and understands it. He indeed bears a crop which produces sometimes a hundred times, sometimes sixty times, sometimes thirty times as much as he received.'

24Jesus gave them another parable to think about. 'What happens in the Kingdom of Heaven,' he said, 'is like what happened when a man sowed good seed in his field. 25When everyone was asleep, his enemy came and sowed darnel among the corn, and went away. 26When the blade sprouted, and when it began to produce its crop, then the darnel appeared. 27The servants of the master of the house came to him. "Sir," they said, "didn't you sow good seed in your field? How did the darnel get into it?" 28"This is the work of an enemy," he said. "Do you want us to go and gather the darnel?" the servants asked him. 29"No," he said. "If you gather the darnel, the danger is that you may tear up the corn by the roots at the same time. 30Let them both grow together, until the harvest time. At the harvest time I will give instructions to the reapers, first to gather the darnel and tie it up in bundles for burning, and then to gather the corn and to store it in my granary." '

31Jesus gave them another parable to think about. 'The Kingdom of Heaven,' he said, 'is like a grain of mustard seed, which a man took and sowed in his field. 32It is the smallest of all seeds, but when it has reached full growth, it becomes the biggest of all kitchen herbs, and grows into a tree big enough for the birds of the sky to come and nest among its branches.'

33He told them another parable. 'The Kingdom of Heaven works like a piece of leaven,' he said, 'which a woman took and inserted into three pecks of flour, with the result that it was all leavened.'

34Jesus said all this to the crowds in parables, and it was his practice to say nothing to them without a parable. 35He followed this method so that the statement made through the prophet might come true:

'I will speak in parables;
    I will utter things which have been veiled in secrecy
        since the world was created.'

36Jesus left the crowds and went into the house. His disciples came to him. 'Tell us,' they said, 'the meaning of the parable of the darnel in the field.' 37'The sower of the good seed,' Jesus answered, 'stands for the Son of Man. 38The field stands for the world. The good seed stands for the children of the Kingdom. The darnel stands for the children of the Evil One. 39The enemy who sowed them stands for the Devil. The harvest stands for the end of the world as we know it. The reapers stand for the angels. 40The collecting of the darnel and the burning of it in the fire is a picture of what is going to happen at the end of the world. 41The Son of Man will send his angels, to weed out of the Kingdom all those who are a cause of sin to others, and all who act lawlessly, 42and to throw them into the blazing furnace. There will be tears and agony there. 43But the good shall shine like the sun in their Father's Kingdom. If a man has ears, let him hear.'

44Jesus went on: 'The Kingdom of Heaven is like a treasure which lay hidden in a field. A man discovered it and kept his discovery secret. He was so glad that he went off and sold everything he possessed, and bought the field.'

45'To take another illustration, what happens in the Kingdom of Heaven is like what happened to a trader who was searching for lovely pearls. 46When he found one pearl of supreme value, he went and sold everything that he had and bought it.'

47'To take another illustration, what happens in the Kingdom of Heaven is like what happened when a net was cast into the sea. It collected all kinds of things. 48When it was full, they hauled it up on to the shore. Then they sat down and picked out the good things and put them into containers, and flung away the useless things. 49This is what will happen at the end of the world. The angels will come and separate the evil from the good, 50and they will throw them into the blazing furnace. There will be tears and agony there.'

51'Have you understood all that I have been saying to you?' Jesus asked. 'Yes,' they said. 52'That,' he said, 'is why, if an expert in the Law has been instructed in the meaning of the Kingdom, he is like a householder, who brings out of his treasure-store things both new and old.'

53When Jesus had finished these parables, he left there. 54He went to his own native place, and began to teach them in their synagogue. His teaching left them astonished. 'Where did this man get this wisdom?' they said. 'How can he do these miracles? 55Isn't he the carpenter's son? Isn't his mother Mary, and aren't his brothers James and Joses and Simon and Judas? 56Aren't his sisters all here with us? Where did he get all this?' 57They were shocked at him. Jesus said to them: 'The only place in which a prophet has no honour is in his own native town and among his own family.' 58He did not do many miracles there because of their refusal to believe.

Chapter 14

IT was at that time that the reports which were circulating about Jesus reached the ears of Herod the tetrarch. 2'This is John the Baptizer,' he said to his servants. 'He has come back to life. That is why he possesses these miraculous powers.' 3Herod thought this because he had arrested John the Baptizer, and had imprisoned him in chains because of the affair of Herodias, his brother Philip's wife. 4The trouble had arisen because John had told him that he had no right to marry her. 5Herod would have liked to kill John, but he was afraid of the crowd, for they regarded John as a prophet. 6On the occasion of Herod's birthday celebrations Herodias' daughter danced in public and delighted Herod. 7So he pledged himself on oath to give her anything she asked. 8Urged by her mother, she said: 'Give me here and now the head of John the Baptizer on a dish.' 9The king was distressed, but, because he had given his sworn promise in front of his guests, he ordered her request to be granted. 10So he sent and had John beheaded in prison. 11His head was brought in on a dish and given to the girl, and she took it to her mother. 12John's disciples came and took his body away and buried it, and they came and told Jesus what had happened.

13When Jesus heard what had happened, he withdrew from there, and sailed in a boat to a desert place where he could be alone by himself; but when the crowds learned of this, they followed him from the towns on foot. 14When he disembarked, he saw a great crowd, and he was heart-sorry for them, and cured their sick. 15Late on in the day the disciples came to him. 'This place is a desert,' they said, 'and it is now past the time for the evening meal. Send the crowd away into the villages to buy themselves food.' 16'There is no necessity for them to go away,' Jesus said. 'You must give them something to eat.' 17'All that we have here,' they said to him, is five loaves and two fishes.' 18'Bring them to me,' Jesus said. 19So he ordered the crowd to sit down on the grass. He took the five loaves and the two fishes. He looked up to heaven and said the blessing. He broke the loaves into pieces and gave them to the disciples, and the disciples gave them to the crowds. 20They all ate until they could eat no more. They collected twelve basketfuls of pieces of bread that were left over. 21Those who ate numbered about five thousand men, not counting women and children.

22Jesus immediately made his disciples get into the boat and go on ahead to the other side, while he stayed to dismiss the crowds. 23When he had dismissed the crowds, he went up the hill by himself to pray. When evening came he was there alone. 24The boat by this time was a good distance from land. It was being buffeted by the waves, for the wind was dead against them. 25About three o'clock in the morning he came to them, walking on the lake. 26When the disciples saw him walking on the lake, they were terrified. 'It is a ghost,' they said, and they cried out in fear. 27Jesus immediately spoke to them. 'Courage!' he said. 'It is I. Don't be afraid!' 28'Master,' Peter answered, 'if it really is you, give me an order to come to you on the water.' 29Jesus said: 'Come!' Peter got out of the boat and walked on the water, and began to go to Jesus. 30But when he saw the wind, he was afraid. He began to sink below the water. 'Master,' he shouted. 'Save me!' 31Jesus stretched out his hand and gripped him. 'You have so little faith!' he said. 'Why did you begin to doubt?' 32When they got on board the boat, the wind sank to rest. 33The men in the boat knelt in reverence in front of Jesus. 'Beyond a doubt,' they said, 'you are the Son of God.'

34When they had crossed over, they landed at Gennesaret. 35When the people of that place recognized Jesus, they sent all over the countryside, and brought in to him everyone who was ill. 36They begged to be allowed to do no more than touch the tassel of his cloak. All who touched it were completely cured.

Chapter 15

IT was then that a deputation of experts in the Law and Pharisees came from Jerusalem to interview Jesus. ₂'Why,' they said, 'do your disciples break the traditional law of the elders? They do so in that they do not give their hands the prescribed washings when they eat a meal.' ₃Jesus answered: 'Why do you too disobey the commandment of God for the sake of your traditional law? ₄God said: "Honour your father and your mother," and, "The man who curses his father or mother must certainly die." ₅But you say: "If a man says to his father or mother: 'The money I might have contributed to your support is a gift dedicated to God, and usable for no other purpose,' ₆then he must not honour his father." For the sake of your traditional law you have cancelled the word of God. ₇Your fault is that you do not practise what you preach. Isaiah well described you in his prophecy:

₈"This people honour me with their lips,
　　but their heart is far from me.
₉It is a futile worship which they offer me,
　　for they teach as divine commands man-made rules
　　　　　　　　　　　　　　　　　　and regulations." '

₁₀Jesus invited the crowds to listen to him. 'Listen,' he said, 'and understand. ₁₁It is not what goes into a man's mouth that defiles him. On the contrary, it is what comes out of a man's mouth that defiles him.' ₁₂His disciples then came and said to him: 'Do you know that, when the Pharisees heard what you said, they were shocked by it?' ₁₃'Every plant,' he answered, 'which my heavenly Father did not plant will be uprooted. ₁₄Let them alone! They are blind leaders of the blind. If the blind lead the blind, both of them will fall into a hole in the road.' ₁₅'Tell us,' Peter said to him, 'what this difficult saying means.' ₁₆'Are even you still unable to understand?' Jesus said. ₁₇'Do you not realize that everything that goes into a man's mouth goes into his stomach, and is evacuated into the drain by natural processes? ₁₈But what comes out of his mouth comes from his heart, and it is that which defiles a man. ₁₉For from the heart come evil thoughts, murder, adultery, fornication, theft, lies about other people, slander. ₂₀These are the things which really defile a man. To eat with hands which have not been washed as the ritual law prescribes does not defile a man.'

21Jesus left there and withdrew to the districts of Tyre and Sidon. 22A Canaanite woman from these parts came to him. 'Take pity on me, sir, Son of David,' she kept shouting. 'My daughter is possessed by a demon and is very ill.' 23Jesus did not answer her at all. His disciples came and asked him: 'Send her away. She won't stop following us and shouting at us.' 24Jesus said: 'It is only to the lost sheep of the family of Israel that I have been sent.' 25She came and knelt in front of him in entreaty. 'Sir,' she said, 'help me.' 26'It is not proper,' Jesus answered, 'to take the bread which belongs to the children, and to fling it to the pet dogs.' 27'True, sir,' she said, 'but the pet dogs do eat their share of the crumbs which fall from their master's table.' 28At that Jesus answered: 'You have great faith. Let your wish be granted.' From that moment her daughter was cured.

29Jesus left there and went along the coast of the lake of Galilee. He climbed the hill and sat there, 30and the crowds flocked to him, bringing those who were lame and blind, crippled and deaf, and suffering from many other diseases. They laid them at his feet, and he cured them. 31His power to heal left the crowd amazed, when they saw the dumb speaking, the crippled restored to fitness, the lame walking, and the blind seeing, and they praised the God of Israel.

32Jesus called the disciples to him. 'I am heart-sorry for the crowd,' he said, 'for they have stayed with me for three days now, and they have nothing to eat. I don't want to send them away without a meal, because I don't want them to collapse on the road.' 33'Where could we find loaves enough in a desert place to satisfy a crowd like this?' the disciples asked him. 34'How many loaves have you?' Jesus said to them. 'Seven,' they said, 'and a few little fishes.' 35Jesus ordered the crowd to sit down on the ground. 36He took the seven loaves and the fishes. He gave thanks for them, and broke them into pieces, and gave them to the disciples, and the disciples gave them to the crowds. 37They all ate until they could eat no more. They gathered up what was left of the broken pieces of bread, and there was enough to fill seven hampers. 38Those who ate numbered four thousand men, not counting women and children. 39When Jesus had sent the crowds away, he got into the boat, and went to the district of Magadan.

Chapter 16

THE Pharisees and Sadducees came to interview Jesus. They tried to submit him to a test by asking him to show them some visible divine action from heaven. ₂He answered: 'In the evening, you say: "The sky is red. The weather will be good." ₃Early in the morning, you say: "The sky is red and threatening. The weather will be stormy today." You know how to read the weather signs in the sky. Can you not read the signs of the times? ₄It is a wicked and apostate generation which wants to see some visible action of God. The same action as God showed in Jonah is the only divine action which will be given to it.' He went away and left them.

₅When the disciples arrived at the other side, they discovered that they had forgotten to bring any loaves with them. ₆'Watch what you are doing,' Jesus said to them. 'Beware! Be on your guard against the leaven of the Pharisees and Sadducees.' ₇They kept on talking among themselves about bringing no loaves. ₈Jesus knew what they were arguing about. 'You have so little faith,' he said. 'Why do you keep on talking about having no loaves? ₉Do you not even yet understand? Don't you remember the five loaves and the five thousand, and how many basketfuls you collected? ₁₀Don't you remember the seven loaves and the four thousand, and how many hamperfuls you collected? ₁₁Why can't you understand that it was not about loaves that I spoke to you? Be on your guard against the leaven of the Pharisees and Sadducees.' ₁₂Then they understood that he was not telling them to beware of leaven in the sense of leaven that is in loaves, but in the sense of the evil influence of the teaching of the Pharisees and Sadducees.

₁₃When Jesus had come to the districts of Caesarea Philippi, he put a question to his disciples. 'Who are people saying that the Son of Man is?' he asked. ₁₄They said: 'Some are saying, John the Baptizer; others, Elijah; others, Jeremiah, or one of the prophets.' ₁₅'And you,' he said to them, 'who do you say that I am?' ₁₆Simon Peter answered: 'You are the Messiah, the Son of the living God!' ₁₇'You are indeed blessed, Simon Barjona,' Jesus said, 'for it was no human being who revealed this to you; it was my Father who is in heaven. ₁₈I tell you, you are Peter—the man whose name means a rock—and on this rock

I will erect my Church, and the powers of death will be helpless to harm it. 19I will give you the keys of the Kingdom of Heaven, and whatever you forbid on earth will be forbidden in heaven, and whatever you allow on earth will be allowed in heaven.' 20Jesus gave strict orders to his disciples not to tell anyone that he was the Messiah.

21From then on Jesus began to show his disciples that he must go to Jerusalem, and that he must undergo many sufferings at the hands of the elders and the chief priests and the experts in the Law, and that he must be killed, and that he must be raised to life again on the third day. 22Peter caught hold of him, and sternly forbade him to talk like that. 'God forbid, Master!' he said. 'This must never happen to you!' 23Jesus swung round. 'Get out of my sight, Satan!' he said to Peter. 'You're doing your best to trip me up! Your ideas are not God's, but man's!'

24Jesus went on to say to his disciples: 'If anyone wishes to walk in my steps, he must once and for all say No to himself; he must decide to take up his cross, and he must keep on following me. 25Anyone who wishes to keep his life safe will lose it, but anyone who is prepared to lose his life for my sake will find it. 26What good will it do to a man to gain the whole world, if in so doing he forfeits his own life? What could a man give that would be an equal exchange for his life? 27For the Son of Man will come with his angels in his Father's glory, and he will settle accounts with each man on the basis of how each man has lived. 28I tell you truly, there are some of those who are standing here who will not experience death until they see the Son of Man coming in his Kingdom.'

Chapter 17

ABOUT a week later Jesus took with him Peter and James and John, James's brother, and brought them up into a high mountain alone. 2He was transformed before their very eyes. His face shone like the sun, and his clothes became as white as the light. 3Moses and Elijah appeared to them, talking to Jesus. 4'Master,' Peter said to Jesus, 'it is a wonderful thing for us to be here. Would you like me to make three shelters here, one for you, one for Moses, and one for Elijah?' 5While he was still speaking, a shining cloud enveloped them, and out of the cloud a voice said: 'This is my Son, the Beloved and Only One, on whom my favour rests. Listen to him!' 6When the disciples heard this, they flung themselves face down on the ground, for they were terrified. 7Jesus came and touched them. 'Up!' he said. 'Don't be afraid!' 8And when they looked up, the only person they could see was Jesus, all by himself.

9On the way down from the mountain Jesus gave them strict orders not to tell anyone what they had seen, until the Son of Man had been raised from the dead.

10The disciples put a question to him. 'Why,' they asked, 'do the experts in the Law say that Elijah must come first?' 11'It is quite true,' Jesus answered, 'that Elijah is to come and is to set everything in order. 12But the fact is, Elijah has already come, and, so far from recognizing him, they did what they liked to him. In exactly the same way the Son of Man is going to suffer at their hands.' 13Then the disciples understood that it was about John the Baptizer that Jesus had been speaking to them.

14When they reached the crowd, a man came to Jesus and knelt at his feet. 15'Sir,' he said, 'take pity on my son. He is an epileptic, and he is very ill. He often falls into the fire and into the water. 16And I brought him to your disciples, and they were quite unable to cure him.' 17'This modern generation has no faith,' Jesus answered. 'There is a fatal perversity about it. How long have I to be with you? How long must I endure you? Bring him here to me!' 18Then Jesus spoke to him with a stern authority, and the demon came out of him, and there and then the boy was cured. 19Afterwards when they were alone, the disciples came to Jesus. 'Why were we unable to eject the demon?' they asked him. 20'Because,' he said, 'you have so little faith. I tell you truly, if you have faith as big as a mustard seed, you will say to this mountain: "Move from here to there," and it will remove itself. There will be nothing that you cannot do.'*

22When they were moving about in Galilee together, Jesus said to them: 'The Son of Man is going to be handed over into the power of men, 23and they will kill him, and on the third day he will be raised to life again.' And they were very distressed.

24When they arrived in Capernaum, the collectors of the Temple tax approached Peter. 'Does your teacher not pay the twenty-five
*See Notes on pp. 575-6

pence Temple tax?' they asked. ₂₅'Yes, he does,' said Peter. When Peter came into the house, before he could even mention the matter, Jesus said to him: 'Tell me your opinion, Simon—who do earthly kings collect tolls and taxes from? Is it from their own family or from strangers?' ₂₆'From strangers,' Peter said. 'So then,' Jesus said, 'their own family are exempt. ₂₇All the same, we do not want to give offence to anyone. So go to the lake. Throw in a hook. Take the first fish that comes up. Open its mouth and you will find a fifty-pence piece. Take it and give it to the collectors for me and for you.'

Chapter 18

THE disciples came to Jesus at that time. 'Who,' they said, 'is the greatest in the Kingdom of Heaven?' ₂Jesus called a little child, and made him stand where they could all see him. ₃'I tell you truly,' he said, 'unless you change the whole direction of your lives, and become like little children, you will certainly not get into the Kingdom of Heaven at all. ₄It is the man who thinks as little of his importance as this little child, who is the greatest in the Kingdom of Heaven.

₅'To welcome a little child like this in my name is to welcome me. ₆It would be better for a man to have a huge millstone hung round his neck and to be drowned in the deepest part of the sea than to do anything to cause one of these little ones who believe in me to sin.

₇'The tragedy of the world is the existence of the things which make men sin! True, things which make men sin must come, but tragic is the fate of the man who is responsible for the coming of such a thing!

₈'If your hand or your foot becomes a cause of sin to you, cut it off and throw it away. It is better for you to enter into life maimed or crippled than to be thrown into eternal fire with two hands or two feet. ₉If your eye becomes a cause of sin to you, tear it out and throw it away. It is better for you to enter into life with one eye than to be thrown into hell-fire with two eyes.

₁₀'Be very careful never to think of one of these little ones as of no importance. I tell you that in heaven their guardian angels always have the right of access to the presence of my Father who is in heaven.'*

*See Notes on pp. 575–6

12'What do you think? If a man has a hundred sheep, and if one of them has wandered away, will he not leave the ninety-nine on the hillside, and go and search for the wandering one? 13And, if he finds it, I tell you truly, he rejoices more over it than over the ninety-nine which never wandered away. 14Just so, your Father in heaven doesn't want one of these little ones to be lost.'

15'If your fellow man wrongs you, go, and with no one but him and you there, try to persuade him to admit his fault. If he listens to you, you have gained a friend. 16If he refuses to listen to you, take one or two other people with you, and go and see him, so that everything that is said may be confirmed by the evidence of two or three witnesses. 17If he refuses to listen to them, report the whole trouble to the church. And, if he refuses to listen even to the church, then he must be regarded as no better than a heathen and a renegade tax-collector.'

18'I tell you truly, all that you forbid on earth will be forbidden in heaven, and all that you allow on earth will be allowed in heaven.'

19'Still further, I tell you truly, if two of you on earth agree about anything for which you are praying, they will receive it from my Father who is in heaven. 20For, where two or three have met in my name, I too am there with them.'

21Peter came to Jesus. 'Master,' he said to him, 'how often ought I to forgive my fellow man, if he goes on wronging me? As many as seven times?' 22'I tell you,' Jesus said to him, 'not as many as seven times, but as many as seventy times seven. 23That is why what happens in the Kingdom of Heaven can be compared with the situation which arose when a king wished to settle accounts with his servants. 24When he began to settle up, one debtor was brought in who owed him two and a half million pounds. 25He was quite unable to pay. So his master gave orders for him to be sold, along with his wife and children and everything he had, and the money to be paid over. 26The servant threw himself on his knees at his master's feet. "Give me time," he said, "and I will pay you everything in full." 27The servant's master was heart-sorry for the man, and let him go free, and remitted the debt. 28That same servant went out and met one of his fellow-servants who owed him five pounds. He seized him by the throat. "Pay your debt!" he said. 29His fellow-servant threw himself at his feet. "Give me time," he begged, "and I will pay you in full." 30He refused, and went and had him thrown into prison, until he should pay the debt in full. ₃₁When his fellow-servants saw what had happened, they were very distressed. So they went to their master and informed him of all that had happened. ₃₂The master sent for the servant. "You utter scoundrel!" he said. "I remitted that whole debt of yours, because you pleaded with me to do so. ₃₃Surely you should have had the same pity for your fellow-servant as I had for you." ₃₄The master was furious, and handed him over to the torturers until he should repay the whole debt in full. ₃₅My heavenly Father will do the same to you, if you do not, each one of you, genuinely forgive your fellow man.'

Chapter 19

WHEN Jesus had finished what he had to say on this occasion, he left Galilee, and went to that part of Judaea which lies on the far side of the Jordan. ₂Great crowds followed him, and he healed them there.

₃The Pharisees came to him with what they intended to be a test question. 'Is a man permitted,' they asked, 'to divorce his wife for any reason he likes?' ₄'Have you not read,' he answered, 'that in the beginning the Creator made mankind male and female? ₅And that he said: "For this reason a man will leave his father and mother, and will be joined inseparably to his wife; ₆and they two shall become so completely one that they shall be no longer two persons but one"? What God has united man must not separate.' ₇They said to him: 'Why did Moses prescribe a regulation allowing a man to give his wife a deed of divorce, and so to send her away?' ₈'Moses would never have allowed you to divorce your wives,' Jesus said, 'if it had not been that your hearts are quite impervious to the real commandment of God. That was not the original intention. ₉I tell you, anyone who divorces his wife for any reason other than infidelity and marries another woman commits adultery.'* ₁₀His disciples said to him: 'If that is the only ground on which a man may divorce his wife, then it is better not to marry at all!' ₁₁'This principle,' he said to them, 'is not practicable for everyone. It is only practicable for those whom God has

*See Notes on pp. 575-6

53

enabled to accept it. 12There are some who have been born incapable of marriage. There are some who by the action of men have been made incapable of marriage. There are some who have voluntarily made marriage impossible for themselves for the sake of the Kingdom of Heaven. Let the man who is able to accept this principle accept it.'

13Little children were brought to Jesus for him to lay his hands on them and to say a prayer over them, but the disciples warned them off. 14Jesus said: 'Let the little children come to me, and don't try to stop them. It is to such as they are that the Kingdom of Heaven belongs.' 15So he laid his hands on them, and then he moved on from there.

16A man came to Jesus. 'Teacher,' he said, 'what must I do to make myself good enough to possess eternal life?' 17'Why do you ask me about what is good?' Jesus said to him. 'One and One alone is good. If you want to get into life, obey the commandments.' 18'What commandments?' he said. Jesus said: 'The commandments which say: You must not kill, You must not commit adultery, You must not steal, You must not tell lies about anyone, 19Honour your father and your mother, and, You must love your neighbour as yourself.' 20'I have obeyed all these,' the young man said to him. 'What is still missing in me?' 21'If you really want to be perfect,' Jesus said to him, 'go and sell everything you have and give the proceeds to the poor, and you will have treasure in heaven. Then come! Follow me!' 22When the young man heard Jesus say this, he went sadly away, for he was very wealthy.

23'I tell you truly,' Jesus said to his disciples, 'it is very difficult for a rich man to get into the Kingdom of Heaven. 24I repeat, it is easier for a camel to go through the eye of a needle than it is for a rich man to get into the Kingdom of God.' 25The disciples were astonished to hear this. 'Who then can be saved?' they said. 26Jesus looked at them. 'With men this may be impossible,' he said, 'but everything is possible with God.'

27Peter said to him: 'We have left everything to become your followers. What will we get for this?' 28'I tell you truly,' Jesus said to them, 'at the rebirth of the world, when the Son of Man takes his seat upon his glorious throne, you who chose to follow me will sit on twelve thrones, as the judges of the twelve tribes of Israel. 29Anyone who has left houses or brothers or sisters or father or mother or children or estates for my sake will get them back a hundred times over, and will receive the promised gift of eternal life. ₃₀But many who are first will be last, and the last will be first.'

Chapter 20

'THE situation in the Kingdom of Heaven is like the situation in the following story. There was a householder who went out first thing in the morning to engage workmen to work in his vineyard. ₂He came to an agreement with the workmen to work for a normal day's wage, and sent them to his vineyard. ₃He went out again about nine o'clock in the morning, and saw other men standing in the market-place unemployed. ₄"Go to my vineyard along with the other men," he said to them, "and I will pay you whatever is a fair wage." ₅So they went off to the vineyard. He went out again about twelve o'clock midday and about three o'clock in the afternoon, and did the same. ₆He went out about five o'clock in the evening and found others standing there. "Why have you stood here all day unemployed?" he said to them. ₇"Because no one engaged us," they said. "Go to my vineyard as well as the other men," he said. ₈When evening came, the owner of the vineyard said to his foreman: "Call the workers and give them their pay. Start with the last ones and go on to the first." ₉When those who had started work at five o'clock in the evening came, they each received a normal full day's wage. ₁₀When those who had been engaged first came, they expected to get more. But they too received a normal day's wage. ₁₁When they got their pay, they began to grumble at the way in which the householder had treated them. ₁₂"The men who came last," they said, "worked for one hour, and you have treated them the same as us, and we have done a whole day's work, and in a wind like a furnace too." ₁₃"Friend," he said to one of them, "I am not doing you any wrong. Did you not agree with me to work for the usual day's wage? ₁₄Take what is due to you, and go. It is my wish to give the last man the same as I gave you. ₁₅Have I not a perfect right to do what I like with my own money? Are you going to be mean, because I am generous?" ₁₆Just so, the last will be first, and the first will be last.'

₁₇When Jesus was on his way up to Jerusalem, he took the Twelve aside by themselves, and spoke to them as they walked along the road. 18'We are on our way up to Jerusalem,' he said, 'and the Son of Man will be handed over to the chief priests and to the experts in the Law; they will condemn him to death; 19they will hand him over to the Gentiles to mock and to flog and to crucify; and on the third day he will be raised to life again.'

20It was then the mother of Zebedee's sons came to him with her sons. She knelt before him and asked him to give her a special favour. 21'What is it you want?' he said to her. 'I want my two sons,' she said, 'to sit one on your right hand and one on your left in your Kingdom.' 22'You do not know what you are asking for,' Jesus said. 'Can you pass through the bitter experience through which I must pass?' 'We can,' they said. 23He said to them: 'You will pass through the same experience as I must go through, but to sit on my right hand and on my left is not in my power to give you. That is reserved for those for whom it has been prepared by my Father.'

24When the ten heard about this, they were annoyed with the two brothers. 25Jesus called them to him. 'You know,' he said, 'that the leaders of the Gentiles lord it over them, and that in their society the mark of greatness is the exercise of authority. 26But in your society the situation is very different. With you, if anyone wishes to be great, he must be your servant; 27and with you, if anyone wishes to hold the first place, he must be everyone's slave, 28just as the Son of Man did not come to be served but to serve, and to give his life as a ransom for many.'

29They were leaving Jericho followed by a large crowd. 30There were two blind men sitting at the roadside. When they heard that Jesus was passing, they shouted: 'Master! Take pity on us! Son of David!' 31The crowd sharply told them to be quiet, but they shouted all the louder: 'Master! Take pity on us! Son of David!' 32Jesus stopped and called them. 'What do you want me to do for you?' he said. 33'Sir,' they said to him, 'the only thing we want is to be able to see.' 34Jesus was heart-sorry for them. He touched their eyes, and there and then their sight returned, and they followed him.

Chapter 21

WHEN they were near Jerusalem, and when they had reached Bethphage, at the Hill of Olives, Jesus sent on two of his disciples. ₂'Go into the village opposite you,' he said, 'and you will at once find a tethered donkey, and a foal with her. Untie them and bring them to me. ₃If anyone says anything to you, you will say: "The Master needs them," and he will send them at once.' ₄This happened so that the statement made through the prophet might come true:

> ₅'Say to the daughter of Sion:
> "Look! Your king is coming to you,
> gentle, and riding on an ass,
> and on a colt, the foal of a beast of burden." '

₆The disciples went off and carried out Jesus' instructions. ₇They brought the donkey and the foal. They put their cloaks on them, and Jesus mounted them. ₈The huge crowd spread their cloaks on the road, while others cut down branches from the trees, and spread them on the road. ₉The crowds who were going on ahead and the crowds who were following behind kept shouting:

> 'God save David's Son!
> God bless him who comes in the name of the Lord!
> O send your salvation from the heights of heaven!'

₁₀When Jesus entered Jerusalem, the whole city seethed with excitement. 'Who is this?' they said. ₁₁The crowds said: 'This is the prophet Jesus from Nazareth in Galilee.'

₁₂Jesus went into the Temple precincts, and drove out all who were selling and buying there, and upset the tables of the money-changers, and the seats of the pigeon-sellers. ₁₃'Scripture says,' he said to them, ' "My house must be regarded as a house of prayer," but you are making it a brigands' den.'

₁₄The blind and the lame came to him in the Temple precincts and he cured them. ₁₅When the chief priests and the experts in the Law saw the astonishing things that Jesus did, and when they heard the children shouting in the Temple precincts: 'God save David's Son!'

they were enraged. 16'Do you hear what the children are saying?' they said to him. 'I do,' Jesus said to them. 'Have you never read: "Out of the mouths of babes and sucklings you have brought perfect praise"?' 17So he left there, and went out of the city to Bethany, and spent the night there.

18When Jesus was on his way back to the city early in the morning, he felt hungry. 19He saw a fig tree at the roadside. He went up to it, and found nothing but leaves on it. 'May no fruit ever grow again on you,' he said. And there and then the fig tree withered. 20The disciples were astonished to see what had happened. 'How did the fig tree wither on the spot?' they said. 21'I tell you truly,' Jesus answered, 'if you have unquestioning faith, you will be able to do not only what was done to the fig tree, but even if you were to say to this hill: "Be picked up and flung into the sea," it will happen. 22You will receive everything you ask in prayer, if you ask in faith.'

23Jesus went into the Temple precincts. As he was teaching there, the chief priests and the elders of the people approached him. 'What right have you to act as you are doing,' they said, 'and who gave you the right to do so?' 24'I will ask you one question,' Jesus answered, 'and, if you tell me the answer to it, I will tell you what right I have to act like this. 25What was the source of the baptism that John administered? Was it divine or human?' They began to argue with each other. 'If,' they said, 'we say, "Divine," he will say: "Why then did you not believe in him?" 26On the other hand, we are afraid to say, "Human," because of the crowd, because they all regard John as a prophet.' 27So they answered Jesus: 'We do not know.' So Jesus said to them: 'No more am I going to tell you what right I have to act as I do.'

28'What do you think?' Jesus went on. 'There was a man who had two sons. He went to the first son and said: "Son, go and work in my vineyard today." 29He answered: "I will not." But he afterwards changed his mind and went. 30So the father went to the second and said the same to him. He said: "Certainly, sir." But he didn't go. 31Which of these two really obeyed his father?' 'The first,' they said. 'I tell you truly,' Jesus said to them, 'the tax-collectors and the prostitutes are going to go into the Kingdom of Heaven before you. 32For John came to you, and showed you how to live as God wants you to live, and you refused to believe him. But the tax-collectors and the prostitutes did believe him. And, even when you saw the effect of his preaching on them, you still did not change your mind and believe him.'

33'Listen to another parable. There was a householder who planted a vineyard. He surrounded it with a hedge, and dug out a pit in which the juice could be extracted from the grapes, and built a watch-tower. He then let it out to tenants and went abroad. 34When the fruit season arrived, he sent his servants to the tenants to receive his due share of the crop. 35The tenants took the servants, and beat one up, and killed another, and stoned another. 36Again he sent other servants, more than the first lot he had sent, and they treated them in the same way. 37He then sent his son to them. "They will treat my son with respect," he said. 38But, when the tenants saw the son, they said to themselves: "This is the heir. Come on! Let's kill him! And let us seize his estate!" 39So they took him, and threw him out of the vineyard and killed him. 40When the owner of the vineyard comes, what will he do to these tenants?' 41They said, 'He will see to it that these bad men come to a bad end, and he will let out the vineyard to other tenants, who will pay him his full share of the crops when it is due.' 42Jesus said to them: 'Have you never read in the scriptures:

"The stone which the builders rejected,
    this has become the headstone of the corner.
This is the action of God,
    and it is marvellous in our eyes"?

43I tell you, that is why the Kingdom of God will be taken from you, and given to a nation whose conduct befits it. 44Anyone who falls against this stone will be shattered, and it will crush anyone it falls upon.'

45When the chief priests and Pharisees heard Jesus' parables, they were well aware that he was speaking about them. 46They tried to find a way to arrest him, but they were afraid of the crowds, for they re-garded him as a prophet.

Chapter 22

ONCE again Jesus spoke to them in parables. 2'The situation in the Kingdom of Heaven,' he said, 'is like the situation which arose when a king gave a wedding banquet for his son. 3He sent out his servants to tell the guests, who had already received their invitations to the banquet, to come, and they refused to come. 4He sent out a second lot of servants. "Tell those who have been invited," he said, "that I have completed the preparations for the dinner I am giving. My oxen and specially fattened calves have been killed. Everything is ready. Come to the wedding banquet." 5They completely disregarded the invitation, and went off, one to his farm and another to his business. 6The others seized the servants, and wantonly ill-treated them, and killed them. 7The king was furious and sent his troops and wiped out those murderers, and burned their town. 8Then he said to the servants: "The wedding banquet is all ready, but those who received invitations to it did not deserve them. 9Go out to the open roads and invite everyone you meet to the banquet." 10So the servants went out to the roads and collected everyone they met, good and bad alike, and so the room where the wedding banquet was to be held was filled with guests.

11'When the king came in to look at the guests, he saw a man there who was not dressed in wedding clothes. 12"Friend," he said to him, "why have you come like this, without wedding clothes?" The man had nothing to say. 13Then the king said to the attendants: "Tie him up, hand and foot, and fling him out into the outer darkness." There will be tears and agony there. 14For many are invited but few are chosen.'

15The Pharisees went and concocted a scheme to lay a verbal trap for Jesus. 16They sent their disciples to him along with Herod's supporters. 'Teacher,' they said to him, 'we know that you speak the truth, and that you really do teach the life that God wishes us to live. We know that it makes no difference to you who or what anyone is, and that man-made prestige means nothing to you. 17Well, then, tell us, what is your opinion—is it right for us to pay the poll-tax to Caesar, or is it not?' 18Jesus was well aware of their malicious motives. 'You are not out for information,' he said to them, 'you are out to make trouble in your two-faced maliciousness. 19Show me the coin with which the poll-tax is paid.' They brought him a silver piece. 20'Whose portrait and whose inscription is this?' he asked. 21'Caesar's,' they said. 'Well, then,' he said to them, 'pay to Caesar what belongs to Caesar, and to God what belongs to God.' 22When they heard that answer, they were astonished, and went away and left him.

23On the same day a group of Sadducees approached Jesus. It is their contention that there is no such thing as a resurrection from the dead. So they put a question to Jesus. 24'Teacher,' they said, 'Moses said that, if a man dies childless, his brother must marry his wife, and raise a family for his brother. 25There were amongst us seven brothers. The first married and died, and, since he died childless, he left his wife to his brother. 26The same happened with the second, and with the third, and with the whole seven. 27After them all, the woman died. 28Well then, at the resurrection, of which of the seven will she be the wife, for they all had her as a wife?' 29Jesus said to them: 'You are on the wrong track altogether, because you do not know either the meaning of the scriptures or the power of God. 30At the resurrection men and women neither marry nor are married, but are like angels in heaven. 31As for the resurrection of the dead, have you never read what God said to you, when he said: 32"I am the God of Abraham and the God of Isaac and the God of Jacob"? He is not the God of the dead, but of the living.' 33When the crowds heard this answer, they were astonished at his teaching.

34When the Pharisees heard that Jesus had silenced the Sadducees, they came in a body. 35One of them, a legal expert, put a question to Jesus as a test. 36'Teacher,' he said, 'which is the greatest commandment in the Law?' 37Jesus said to him: 'You must love the Lord your God with your whole heart and your whole soul and your whole mind. 38This is the first and greatest commandment. 39And there is a second one like it: You must love your neighbour as yourself. 40On these two commandments the whole message of the Law and of the Prophets depends.'

41When a group of the Pharisees had come to him, Jesus put a question to them. 42'What is your opinion about the Messiah?' he said. 'Whose son is he?' 'David's,' they answered. 43'How, then,' he said to them, 'does David, moved by the Spirit, call him Lord? For he says:

₄₄"The Lord said to my Lord,
Sit at my right hand,
until I give you the victory over your enemies."

₄₅If then David calls him Lord, how can he be his son?' ₄₆No one was able to give Jesus any answer; and from then on no one dared to ask him any more questions.

Chapter 23

JESUS spoke to the crowds and to his disciples. ₂'The experts in the Law and the Pharisees,' he said, 'have inherited the authority of Moses. ₃Their instructions you must carry out, but you must not copy their actions, for their practice is very different from their profession. ₄They take heavy burdens, and strap them on to men's shoulders, but they themselves will not lift a finger to help to move them.

₅Their every action is designed for self-display. They wear outsize prayer-boxes, and exaggerate the size of the tassels on their robes. ₆They like the top places at banquets and the front seats in the synagogues. ₇They like to be deferentially greeted as they move through the market-places, and to be called Rabbi by ordinary people. ₈You must not let anyone call you Rabbi. There is One who is your teacher, and you are all brothers. ₉You must not call any man on earth father. There is One who is your Father, and he is in heaven. ₁₀You must not let anyone call you leaders. There is One who is your leader, I mean the Messiah. ₁₁Your top-ranking man must be your servant. ₁₂If a man exalts himself, he will be humbled; and, if he humbles himself, he will be exalted.'

₁₃'Tragic will be the fate of you experts in the Law and you Pharisees with your façade of ostentatious piety! You shut the door of the Kingdom of Heaven in men's faces. You will not go in yourselves, and you will not allow those who are trying to get in to go in.*

₁₅'Tragic will be the fate of you experts in the Law and you Pharisees

*See Notes on pp. 575–6

with your façade of ostentatious piety! You roam sea and land to make one convert, and, when he has become a convert, you make him twice as much hell-begotten as yourselves.

16"Tragic will be your fate, for you are blind guides! You say:"If a man swears by the Temple, there is no necessity to keep the oath, but, if a man swears by the gold of the Temple, he is bound to keep it." 17You are senseless and blind! Which is greater—the gold, or the Temple which makes the gold sacred? 18You say: "If a man swears by the altar, there is no necessity to keep the oath, but, if a man swears by the gift that is on it, he is bound to keep it." 19You are blind! Which is greater—the gift, or the altar which makes the gift sacred? 20If a man swears by the altar, he swears by it and by all that is on it. 21If a man swears by the Temple, he swears by it, and by him whose home it is. 22If a man swears by heaven, he swears by the throne of God, and by him who sits on it.

23"Tragic will be the fate of you experts in the Law and you Pharisees with your façade of ostentatious piety! For you meticulously pay the tenth part of your crop of mint and dill and cummin to the Temple, and you completely neglect the more important demands of the Law—justice, mercy and loyalty. You ought to have kept the second without neglecting the first. 24You are blind guides, you who carefully filter a midge out of your drink and then swallow a camel!

25"Tragic will be the fate of you experts in the Law and you Pharisees with your façade of ostentatious piety! For you carefully clean the outside of the cup and the plate while you leave the inside full to overflowing with greed and unbridled self-indulgence. 26You blind Pharisee! First clean the inside of the cup, and then outside and inside will both be clean.

27"Tragic will be the fate of you experts in the Law and you Pharisees with your façade of ostentatious piety! For you are like white-washed tombs, which look beautiful from the outside, but which are full of dead men's bones and all kinds of filth. 28So you too, as far as external appearances go, seem to people to be carefully obeying the Law, but you are really putting on an act, for inside you are full of disobedience to the Law.

29"Tragic will be the fate of you experts in the Law and you Pharisees with your façade of ostentatious piety! You build tombs for the prophets and erect lovely memorials to good men, 30and you say: "If we had lived in the days of our ancestors, we would not have been partners with them in the murder of the prophets." 31By your very statement you provide evidence that you yourselves are the descendants of those who killed the prophets. ₃₂Carry on! Equal your fathers in their sins! ₃₃You serpents! You brood of vipers! How can you escape being condemned to hell?

₃₄'Let me tell you why I send you prophets and sages and experts in the Law. Some of them you will kill and crucify. Some of them you will flog in your synagogues, and hunt from town to town. ₃₅The reason is that there may rest on you the responsibility for the murder of every good man from the murder of the good Abel to the murder of Zachariah, Barachiah's son, between the Temple and the altar. ₃₆I tell you, retribution for all this will descend upon the people of today.'

₃₇'O Jerusalem, Jerusalem! Killer of the prophets! Stoner of those who were sent to you by God! How often I have wanted to gather your children together as a bird gathers her nestlings under the shelter of her wings—and you refused! ₃₈God no longer has his home among you, ₃₉for, I tell you, you will not see me again until you say: "God bless him who comes as the representative of the Lord." '

Chapter 24

WHEN Jesus had come out of the Temple precincts, and when he was walking away, his disciples came to tell him to look at the Temple buildings. ₂'You see all these?' he said. 'I tell you truly that not one stone of them will be left standing on another here. There is not a building here which will not be utterly demolished.'

₃When he was sitting on the Hill of Olives, his disciples came to him privately. 'Tell us,' they said, 'when these events will take place, and what will be the sign of your coming and of the end of this world.'

₄'You must be careful that no one misleads you,' Jesus answered. ₅'For many will come claiming that they are my representatives. They will claim to be the Messiah, and they will mislead many. ₆You will hear of wars and reports of wars. See that you don't get into a panic, for these things must happen, but it is not yet the end. ₇Nation will attack nation, and kingdom will attack kingdom. There will be outbreaks of famine and earthquakes here and there. ₈All these events are the beginning of the birth-pangs of the new age.

₉'You will have much to suffer at the hands of men at that time.

They will kill you, and because of your connection with me you will be hated in every country. 10At that time the faith of many will collapse; they will betray each other and they will hate each other. 11Many false prophets will emerge, and they will mislead many. 12Lawlessness will flourish increasingly, and it will be characteristic of that time that men's love for each other will grow cold. 13But the man who sees things through to the end will be saved.

14'This Good News of the Kingdom will be proclaimed all over the inhabited world, so that all nations may be confronted with the truth, and after that the end will come.

15'When you see the desolating abomination, of which the prophet Daniel spoke, standing in the Holy Place' (let the reader mark this well) 16'then those who are in Judaea must flee to the hills. 17Anyone who happens to be on the housetop must not go down to take his possessions out of his house. 18Anyone who is at work in the field must not turn back to pick up his coat. 19It will be a tragic day for women who are carrying children in the womb or feeding them at the breast. 20Pray that you may not have to flee in winter or on the Sabbath, 21for at that time there will be suffering so great that nothing like it has happened from the beginning of the world to this present day, or will ever happen again. 22Unless this period had been cut short, no human being could survive. But this period will be cut short for the sake of God's chosen ones.

23'If at that time anyone says to you: "Look! Here is the Messiah!" or "There he is!" do not believe him. 24False Messiahs and false prophets will emerge, and will perform such miracles and wonders, that, if possible, they will mislead even God's chosen ones. 25I have forewarned you about these things before they happen. 26If they say to you: "See! Here he is out in the wilderness!" do not go out. If they say: "See! Here he is in the secret rooms!" do not believe it. 27For, as the lightning flashes across the whole sky from east to west, so will be the coming of the Son of Man. 28Where the carrion is, there the vultures will gather.

29'Immediately after the period of suffering of that time,

> "The sun will be darkened,
>   and the moon will not give its light;
>   the stars will fall from the sky,
>   and the powers in the heavens will be shaken."

30Then the sign of the Son of Man will appear in the sky, and then every nation will lament, when they see the Son of Man coming in the clouds of the sky with great power and glory. 31With a blast on the trumpet he will send out his angels, and they will gather in his chosen ones from the four points of the compass, from the limits of heaven to the furthest bounds of the universe.'

32'Learn the lesson which the fig tree offers you. When the sap rises in its branches, and when it produces its leaves, you know that summer is near. 33So, when you see all these events happening, you must realize that he is near, standing at the very door. 34I tell you truly, all these events will happen within the lifetime of this generation. 35Heaven and earth will cease to be, but my words will never cease to be. 36No one knows about that day or hour, not even the angels in heaven, not even the Son, no one except the Father.'

37'What happened in the time of Noah will happen again at the coming of the Son of Man. 38As in the days before the flood they spent their time eating and drinking, marrying and being married, right up to the day when Noah went into the ark, 39and just as they did not realize what was happening until the flood came and swept them all away, so it will be at the coming of the Son of Man. 40At that time two men will be working in the field; one will be taken and the other will be left. 41Two women will be grinding corn at the mill; one will be taken and the other will be left.'

42'Be sleeplessly on the watch, for you do not know the day when your Lord is coming. 43It is obvious that, if the householder had known at what hour of the night the thief was going to come, he would have been awake, and would not have allowed his house to be broken into. 44The reason why you too must be ready is that the Son of Man is coming at an hour when you do not expect him.

45'Suppose there is a dependable and sensible servant whose master put him in charge of the household staff, with instructions to issue them with their food at the right time. 46That servant is a happy man, if his master, when he comes, finds him engaged on that very task. 47I tell you truly, his master will put him in charge of all his property. 48But, if a bad servant says to himself: "I need not expect my master for a long time yet," 49and if he begins to beat his fellow-servants, and to eat and drink with drunkards, 50the master of that servant will come on a day when he is not expecting him—he doesn't know at what hour to expect him—51and he will cut him in pieces, and will assign to him the same fate as the fate of those whose religion is only a pretence. There will be tears and agony there.'

Chapter 25

'WHAT will happen in the Kingdom of Heaven is like what happened to ten bridesmaids, who took their lamps and went out to meet the bridegroom. 2Five of them were foolish and five were sensible. 3The foolish ones brought their lamps, but they did not bring any oil with them. 4The sensible ones took oil in jars along with their lamps. 5When the bridegroom was a long time in coming, they grew drowsy. They were all asleep, 6when in the middle of the night there was a shout: "Here comes the bridegroom! Out you go and meet him!" 7At this all the girls woke up and trimmed their lamps. 8The foolish ones said to the sensible ones: "Our lamps have gone out. Give us some of your oil." 9"We can't do that," the sensible ones answered, "because then there might not be enough oil for us and for you. You had better go to those who sell oil, and buy some for yourselves." 10While they were away buying it, the bridegroom arrived. The bridesmaids who were ready went in to the banquet with him, and the door was shut. 11Later on the other girls arrived. "Sir!" they said, "Sir! Open the door for us!" 12"I tell you truly," he said, "I don't know who you are!" 13So, then, be sleeplessly on the watch, because you do not know the day or the hour.'

14'What will happen in the Kingdom of Heaven is like what happened when a man went on a journey abroad. He called his servants and handed over his property to them. 15He gave twelve hundred and fifty pounds to one, five hundred to another, and two hundred and fifty to a third. He gave each man a sum proportionate to his ability, and went abroad. 16The man who had been given the twelve hundred and fifty pounds lost no time in going and trading with the money, and made a profit of another twelve hundred and fifty pounds. 17In the same way the man who had been given the five hundred pounds made a profit of another five hundred pounds. 18But the man who had been given the two hundred and fifty pounds went away and dug a hole in the ground, and hid his master's money in it.

19'After a long time the master of these servants returned and settled accounts with them. 20The man who had been given the twelve hundred and fifty pounds came up with another twelve hundred and fifty pounds. "Master," he said, "You handed over twelve hundred and fifty pounds to me. I have made a profit of another twelve hundred and fifty pounds." 21"Well done!" his master said to him. "You have shown yourself a good and trustworthy servant. Because you have shown that I could depend on you to do a small job well, I will give you a big job to do. Come and share your master's joy." 22The man who had been given the five hundred pounds came up. "Sir," he said, "you handed over five hundred pounds to me. I have made a profit of another five hundred pounds." 23"Well done!" his master said to him. "You have shown yourself to be a good and trustworthy servant. Because you have shown that I could depend on you to do a small job well, I will give you a big job to do. Come and share your master's joy."

24The man who had been given the two hundred and fifty pounds came up. "Sir," he said, "I am well aware that you are a shrewd and ruthless business man. I know that you have a habit of letting someone else do the work and of then taking the profits. I know you often step in and appropriate the results of some enterprise which you did not initiate. 25So I went and hid your two hundred and fifty pounds in a hole in the ground, because I was afraid to take the risk of doing anything with it. Here you are! Your money is safe!" 26"You lazy good-for-nothing!" his master answered. "You knew very well that I have a habit of letting other people do the work and of then taking the profits. You knew very well that I often step in and appropriate the results of some enterprise which I did not initiate. 27That is all the more reason why you ought to have lodged my money with the bankers, and then, when I came home, I would have got my money back with interest. 28Take the two hundred and fifty pounds from him, and give it to the man who has two thousand five hundred pounds. 29For, if any man has much, he will be given still more, but, if any man has nothing, he will lose even what he has. 30Fling the useless servant out into the outer darkness. There will be tears and agony there." '

31'When the Son of Man comes in his glory, accompanied by all the angels, he will take his seat on his glorious throne. 32The people of every nation will be assembled before him, and he will separate them into two groups, in the same way as a shepherd separates the sheep from the goats. 33He will place the sheep on the right hand and the goats on the left. 34Then the king will say to those on the right: "You have earned my Father's blessing. Come and take possession of the kingdom, which has been prepared for you since the creation of the world. 35For, when I was hungry, you gave me food to eat; when I was thirsty, you gave me water to drink; when I was a stranger, you took me into your home circle; 36when I was naked, you clothed me; when I was ill, you came to visit me; when I was in prison, you came to see me." 37Then the good people will answer: "Sir, when did we see you hungry and feed you, or thirsty and give you water to drink? 38When did we see you a stranger and take you into our home circle, or naked and clothe you? 39When did we see you ill or in prison and come to visit you?" 40The king will answer: "The truth is that every time you did these things for one of my brothers, even for the least of them, you did them for me." 41Then he will say to those on the left: "God's curse is on you! Begone to the eternal fire which has been prepared for the devil and his angels! 42For, when I was hungry, you did not give me food to eat; when I was thirsty, you did not give me water to drink; 43when I was a stranger, you did not take me into your home circle; when I was naked, you did not clothe me; when I was ill and in prison, you did not come to visit me." 44At that they will answer: "Sir, when did we see you hungry or thirsty or a stranger or naked or ill or in prison, and fail to give you help?" 45Then he will answer: "The truth is that every time you failed to do these things for one of these, even for the least of them, you failed to do them for me." 46These will go away to eternal punishment, but the good will go to eternal life.'

Chapter 26

WHEN Jesus had finished all he had to say on this occasion, he said to his disciples: 2'You know that in two days' time it will be the Passover, and the Son of Man is going to be handed over to be crucified.' 3It was then that the chief priests and the elders of the people met in the palace of the High Priest, whose name was Caiaphas, 4and discussed how to arrest Jesus by some stratagem, and so to kill him. ₅Their problem was that they could not arrest him during the festival, because they could not take the risk of a popular riot breaking out among the people.

₆When Jesus was in Bethany as the guest of Simon the leper, ₇a woman came up to him with an alabaster phial of very expensive perfume, which she poured over his head as he sat at table. ₈The sight of her action annoyed the disciples. 'What is the point of this waste?' they said. ₉'This could have been sold for a large sum of money, and the proceeds could have been used to help the poor.' ₁₀Jesus knew what they were saying. 'Why are you distressing the woman?' he said. 'She has done a lovely thing to me. ₁₁You have the poor with you always, but you do not have me always. ₁₂By pouring this perfume over my body, she has by her action prepared me for my burial. ₁₃I tell you truly, wherever this Good News is proclaimed all over the world, what she has done will be told too, so that she will always be remembered.'

₁₄It was at this time that one of the Twelve, called Judas Iscariot, went to the chief priests. ₁₅'What are you prepared to give me,' he said, 'if I deliver him into your hands?' They settled with him for five pounds. ₁₆From then on Judas was always looking for a good opportunity to deliver Jesus into their hands.

₁₇On the first day of the Festival of Unleavened Bread Jesus' disciples came and said to him: 'Where do you wish us to make the necessary preparations for you to eat the Passover meal?' ₁₈Jesus said to them: 'Go into the city to so-and-so, and tell him: "The teacher says: 'My hour of crisis will not be long now. I am going to celebrate the Passover festival at your house with my disciples.' " ' ₁₉The disciples carried out Jesus' instructions, and made all the necessary preparations for the Passover.

₂₀When evening came, Jesus took his place at the table with his twelve disciples. ₂₁During the meal he said to them: 'I tell you truly, one of you will betray me.' ₂₂They were very distressed, and each of them said to him: 'Master, surely it can't be me?' ₂₃Jesus answered: 'It is one who has dipped his bread with me in the dish who is going to betray me. ₂₄The Son of Man goes out on the road the scripture says he must go. But tragic is the fate of the man by whom the Son of Man is betrayed! It would have been better for that man, if he had never been born!' ₂₅Judas, who was busy trying to betray him, said: 'Master, surely it can't be me?' Jesus said to him: 'You have said it yourself!'

₂₆During the meal Jesus took a loaf. He said the blessing over it, and broke it into pieces, and gave it to his disciples. 'Take! Eat!' he said. 'This means my body.' ₂₇He took a cup, and gave thanks to God. He gave it to them and said: 'All of you drink it. ₂₈This means my life-blood, through which the new relationship between man and God is made possible, the blood which is being shed for many, that their sins may be forgiven. ₂₉I tell you, I shall not drink of this fruit of the vine, until the time comes when I drink it new with you in my Father's kingdom.'

₃₀When they had sung the psalm of praise, they went out to the Hill of Olives. ₃₁Then Jesus said to them: 'There is not one of you whose courage will stand the test of what is going to happen to me tonight, for scripture says: "I will smite the shepherd, and the sheep of the flock will be scattered." ₃₂But, after I have risen, I will go on ahead of you into Galilee.' ₃₃Peter answered: 'Even if everyone else's courage fails because of what is going to happen to you, mine never will.' ₃₄'I tell you truly,' Jesus said to him, 'that this very night, before the cock crows, you will disown me three times.' ₃₅'Even if I have to die with you,' Peter said to him, 'I will never disown you.' And all the disciples said the same.

₃₆Then Jesus went with them to a place called Gethsemane. 'Sit here while I go over there and pray,' he said to his disciples. ₃₇He took with him Peter and Zebedee's two sons, and he began to be distressed and distraught in mind. ₃₈'My soul is grief-stricken with a grief like death,' he said to them. 'Wait here and share my vigil.' ₃₉He went a little farther, and flung himself face down on the ground in prayer. 'My Father,' he said, 'if it is possible, don't let this bitter ordeal come to me. But not what I will, but what you will.' ₄₀He came to his disciples and found them sleeping. He said to Peter: 'So the three of you could not keep vigil with me for one hour? ₄₁Sleeplessly watch and pray, for you may well all have to face your ordeal of temptation. I know that you mean well and that you want to do the right thing, but human nature is frail.' ₄₂He went away a second time and prayed again. 'My Father,' he said, 'if there is no escape from this situation, unless I go through it to the bitter end, your will be done.' ₄₃He came back again, and again he found them sleeping, for they could not keep their eyes open. 44Again he went away and left them, and again a third time he prayed the same prayer. 45Then he came to his disciples and said to them: 'Are you still lying there sleeping? The hour has come for the Son of Man to be delivered into the hands of sinful men. 46Up! On your way! The traitor is coming!'

47Just as he was saying this, Judas, one of the Twelve, arrived, accompanied by a mob armed with swords and cudgels, sent by the chief priests and elders of the people. 48The traitor had given them a signal. 'The man I shall kiss is the man you want,' he said. 'Hold him!' 49He went straight up to Jesus and said: 'Greetings, Rabbi!' and kissed him lovingly. 50'Comrade,' Jesus said, 'get on with what you came to do!' Then they came up to Jesus and seized and held him. 51One of Jesus' friends reached out and drew his sword, and struck the High Priest's servant, and cut off his ear. 52'Put your sword back in its place,' Jesus said. 'All who draw the sword will die by the sword. 53Do you think that I cannot appeal to my Father and he will here and now provide me with twelve regiments of angels? 54But, if I were to do this, how could the scriptures, which say things must be so, come true?' 55At the same time Jesus said to the mob: 'Have you come out with swords and cudgels to arrest me, as if you were out to arrest a brigand? I sat teaching in the Temple precincts every day, and you made no attempt to arrest me. 56All this has happened that the writings of the prophets should come true.' It was then that all the disciples abandoned him and ran away.

57Those who had arrested Jesus took him to the house of Caiaphas the High Priest, where the experts in the Law and the elders had assembled. 58Peter followed him at a distance, right into the courtyard of the High Priest's house. He went in and sat down with the attendants to see the end.

59The chief priests and the whole Sanhedrin made repeated attempts to find fabricated evidence against Jesus, which could be used to justify them in putting him to death. 60Many witnesses who were prepared to perjure themselves came forward, but the court was unable to find any evidence upon which it could legitimately proceed. At last two witnesses came forward 61and said: 'This man said: "I can demolish God's Temple, and in three days I can rebuild it."' 62The High Priest stood up and said to Jesus: 'Have you no answer to these allegations which these witnesses are making against you?' 63Jesus remained silent. The High Priest said to him: 'I call on you to tell us on oath, in the name of the living God—are you the Messiah, the Son of God?' 64'If you like to say so,' Jesus said. 'But I tell you, from now on you will see the Son of Man sitting at the right hand of Almighty God, and coming on the clouds of heaven.' 65At that the High Priest ripped his clothes in horror. 'This statement is blasphemy,' he said. 'What further witnesses do we need? You have actually here and now heard his blasphemous claim. 66What is your verdict?' They answered: 'He is guilty of a crime for which the penalty is death.' 67Then they spat in his face, and punched him with their clenched fists. Some of them slapped him across the face. 68'Prophesy to us, Messiah,' they said. 'Who struck you?'

69Peter was sitting outside in the courtyard. One of the maid-servants came up to him. 'You too were with Jesus the Galilaean,' she said. 70He denied it in front of them all. 'I have no idea what you're talking about,' he said. 71He went out to the gateway. Another maid-servant saw him. She said to the people there: 'This man was with Jesus the Nazarene.' 72Again he denied it. 'I swear I do not know the man,' he said. 73Shortly afterwards the bystanders came up to Peter and said to him: 'You certainly are one of them. Indeed you are. Your Galilaean accent makes it obvious.' 74Peter swore he was telling the truth, and called down curses on himself if he was not. 'I do not know the man,' he said. 75Just then the cock crew, and Peter remembered how Jesus had said: 'Before the cock crows, you will disown me three times.' And he went out and wept bitterly.

Chapter 27

WHEN morning came, all the chief priests and elders of the people laid their plans to make sure that Jesus would be put to death. 2So they put him in chains and took him away and handed him over to Pilate, the Roman governor.

3When Judas, who had betrayed him, saw that Jesus had been condemned, he realized the horror of what he had done. He took the five pounds back to the chief priests and elders. 4'I sinned,' he said, 'when I betrayed to death a man who is completely innocent.' 'That has nothing to do with us,' they said. 'That's your look-out!' 5He flung the money into the Temple and went out and went away and hanged himself. 6The chief priests took the money. 'It is not right,' they said, 'to put this into the treasury, for it is the price of a man's life.' 7So, after conferring about the matter, they bought the Potter's Field with it, to serve as a burying-ground for strangers. 8That is why to this day that field is called the Bloody Field. 9Then the statement made through the prophet Jeremiah came true: 'They took the five pounds, the price of him on whom a price had been set by the sons of Israel, 10and they paid for the Potter's Field with them, as the Lord had instructed me.'

11Jesus was brought before the governor, and, as he stood there, the governor put the question to him. 'Are you the King of the Jews?' he asked. Jesus said: 'If you like to put it so.' 12Jesus made no reply to the accusations of the chief priests and elders. 13Pilate said to him: 'Do you not hear all the evidence they are alleging against you?' 14But to Pilate's surprise Jesus did not answer even one single word.

15At the festival it was the governor's custom to release any one prisoner whom the crowd chose. 16At that time a notorious prisoner called Jesus Barabbas was under arrest. 17When they had assembled, Pilate said to them: 'Whom do you wish me to release for you, Jesus Barabbas, or Jesus called the Messiah?' 18He was well aware that it was malicious ill-will which had prompted them to hand Jesus over to him.

19When he was presiding over his court, his wife sent a message to him. 'Have nothing to do with this innocent man,' she said, 'for today I have had the most disturbing dream about him.' 20But the chief priests and the elders persuaded the crowds to ask for the release of Barabbas and the death of Jesus. 21'Which of the two do you wish me to release for you?' the governor asked. 'Barabbas,' they said. 22'What am I to do with Jesus called the Messiah?' said Pilate. 'To the cross with him!' they all said. 23'Why? What crime has he committed?' Pilate asked. They kept on shrieking the more insistently: 'To the cross with him!' 24When Pilate saw that nothing was any use, and that there was every prospect of a riot, he took water and publicly washed his hands. 'I am not responsible for this man's death,' he said. 'The responsibility is yours.' 25The whole people answered: 'Let the responsibility for his death be on us and on our children.' 26Then

Pilate released Barabbas for them, and he had Jesus flogged, and handed him over to be crucified.

27Then the governor's soldiers took Jesus to their headquarters. They collected the whole company. 28They stripped him of his clothes, and dressed him in a scarlet cloak. 29They plaited a crown of thorns and placed it on his head. They put a cane in his right hand and knelt mockingly before him. 'Hail, King of the Jews!' they said. 30They spat on him. They took the cane and hit him across the head with it. 31When they had finished their horseplay, they took the cloak off, and dressed him in his own clothes, and took him away to crucify him.

32On the way out they came on a man from Cyrene called Simon, and they forcibly commandeered him to carry Jesus' cross.

33When they came to a place called Golgotha, which means the Place of a Skull, 34they offered Jesus drugged wine mixed with gall to drink. He tasted it and refused to drink it. 35When they had crucified him, they shared out his clothes between them by drawing lots for them; 36and they sat there and kept watch on him. 37Above his head they placed a written copy of the charge against him: 'This is Jesus, the King of the Jews.' 38Two brigands were crucified at the same time as he was, one on his right and one on his left.

39The passers-by tossed their heads at him and hurled their insults at him. 40'You are the man who was going to demolish the Temple and rebuild it in three days,' they said. 'If you really are God's Son, save yourself, and come down from the cross.' 41The chief priests too joined in the mockery with the experts in the Law and the elders. 42'He saved others,' they said. 'He cannot save himself! He is the King of Israel! Let him come down from the cross here and now, and we will believe his claims! 43He trusted in God! He claimed to be God's Son! Let God rescue him now—if he wants him!' 44The brigands who were crucified with him flung the same taunts at him.

45From twelve o'clock midday until three o'clock in the afternoon there was darkness over the whole land. 46About three o'clock in the afternoon Jesus gave a great shout: 'Eli, Eli, lama sabachthani?' which means: 'My God, my God, why have you abandoned me?' 47When some of the bystanders heard this, they said: 'He is calling Elijah!' 48One of them at once ran and took a sponge and soaked it in vinegar and put it on a cane, and offered it to him to drink. ₄₉The others said: 'Wait! Let us see if Elijah is coming to save him.'* ₅₀Jesus again shouted at the top of his voice, and died.

₅₁The curtain of the Temple which veiled the Holy of Holies was ripped from top to bottom, and the ground was shaken and the rocks were split. ₅₂The tombs were burst open, and the bodies of many of the people of God who slept in death were raised to life. ₅₃They came out of their tombs, and after his resurrection they went into the holy city, and appeared to many. ₅₄When the company commander and his men who were watching Jesus saw the earthquake and the things which were happening, they were awe-stricken. 'Beyond a doubt,' they said, 'this man was indeed a son of God.'

₅₅There were many women looking on from a distance. They had followed Jesus from Galilee, attending to his needs. ₅₆Among them were Mary from Magdala, and Mary the mother of James and Joseph, and the mother of Zebedee's sons.

₅₇When evening came, a wealthy man from Arimathaea called Joseph, who had himself been a disciple of Jesus, ₅₈went to Pilate and asked for Jesus' body. Pilate gave orders for it to be given to him. ₅₉Joseph took Jesus' body away, and wrapped it in clean linen, ₆₀and placed it in his new tomb, which had been hewn out of the rock. He rolled a huge stone up to the doorway of the tomb, and went away. ₆₁Mary of Magdala was there with the other Mary, sitting opposite the tomb.

₆₂On the next day, the day after the Day of Preparation, the Pharisees went in a body to Pilate. ₆₃'Sir,' they said, 'we remember that, while he was alive, that impostor claimed that after three days he would rise from the dead. ₆₄In view of this, please issue orders for special security measures to be taken in regard to the tomb for the next three days, to prevent his disciples coming and stealing his body and telling the people that he has risen from the dead. If that happens the deception will go from bad to worse.' ₆₅Pilate said to them: 'You can have a military guard. Go and take all possible security measures.' ₆₆They went and secured the tomb by affixing a seal to the stone as well as posting a military guard.

*See Notes on pp. 575–6

Chapter 28

LATE on the Sabbath, just as the day was breaking on the Sunday, Mary from Magdala and the other Mary came to look at the tomb. ₂There was a great earthquake, for the angel of the Lord came down from heaven, and came and rolled away the stone, and sat on it. ₃His face shone like lightning, and his clothes were as white as snow. ₄The guards were shaken with fear, and lay like dead men. ₅The angel said to the women: 'Do not be afraid. I know that you are looking for Jesus who was crucified. ₆He is not here, for he has risen, as he said he would. Come! See for yourselves the place where his body lay. ₇Hurry and tell his disciples that he has risen from the dead, and that he is going on ahead of you into Galilee. You will meet him there. That is the message I have for you.' ₈They hurried away from the tomb in mingled awe and great joy, and ran to tell the news to the disciples. ₉Suddenly Jesus was standing in their path. 'Joy be with you,' he said. They went up to him, and clasped his feet, and knelt before him. ₁₀Then Jesus said to them: 'Don't be afraid. Go and tell my brothers to leave for Galilee. They will see me there.'

₁₁While the women were on their way, some of the military guard went into the city, and told the chief priests the news of what had happened. ₁₂When they had met and conferred with the elders, they gave the soldiers a considerable sum of money. ₁₃'You must say,' they said, 'that his disciples came at night and stole his body, while you were sleeping, ₁₄and, if the governor gets to know about this, we will make it all right with him, and we will see to it that you have nothing to worry about.' ₁₅They took the money, and carried out their instructions, and this story is still current in Jewish circles.

₁₆The eleven disciples made their way to Galilee, to the mountain to which Jesus had instructed them to go. ₁₇When they saw him, they worshipped him, but some were not sure. ₁₈Jesus came to them and said: 'All authority in heaven and on earth has been given to me. ₁₉You must therefore go and make the people of all nations my disciples. You must baptize them in the name of the Father and of the Son and of the Holy Spirit, ₂₀and you must teach them to obey all the commands I have given you. And there is not a day when I will not be with you to the end of time.'

Introduction to Mark

IT is generally agreed that Mark is the earliest Gospel, and that it was written in Rome about A.D. 65. There is a very old tradition that Mark contains the preaching material which Peter was in the habit of using. Peter, the Galilean fisherman, was unable to write it down for himself, and Mark, acting as his interpreter, wrote it down for him.

There is in Mark what has been called 'an incomparable touch of reality'. Mark has many little incidental touches which read as if they went back to an eye-witness of the scene which is being described. When Mark is telling the stories of Jesus and the children, only he tells us that Jesus took the children *in the crook of his arm* (Mark 9.36; Matthew 18.2; Luke 9.47; Mark 10.16; Matthew 19.15; Luke 18.16). In the story of the Gerasene demoniac only Mark tells us that the man was always crying out and bruising himself with stones (Mark 5.5). In the story of the storm at sea only Mark tells us that Jesus was in the stern of the boat sleeping on a rower's cushion (Mark 4.38).

Far oftener than any other Gospel Mark has the habit of giving Jesus' words in the original Aramaic (3.17; 5.41; 7.11; 7.34; 14.36; 15.22). It looks as if Peter, when he told these stories, could not help hearing again the voice of Jesus speaking these words, not in Greek, but in his native tongue.

Mark was written before the days when theology had thrown a curtain of too much reverence around the events of the Gospels. When Mark tells the story of the ambitious request of James and John for the chief places in Jesus' kingdom, he does not hesitate to say that it was James and John themselves who made the request (10.35-45), but when Matthew tells the story, he does not wish to record anything that might bring discredit on an apostle, so he says that their mother made the request for them (Matthew 20.20-28). When Mark tells the story of Jesus' rejection by the people of Nazareth, he ends it by saying that Jesus could do no mighty works there (6.5); but when Matthew tells the story he says that Jesus did not do many mighty works there because of their unbelief (Matthew 13.58), because he does not like to say that Jesus was unable to do anything.

This is not to say that in Mark there is not deep reverence and great thought; but it is to say that in this the first of the Gospels we come nearest of all to a simple account of the man Jesus in the days of his flesh, the man who was also the Son of God.

The Story of the Good News
MARK'S VERSION

Chapter 1

THIS is the beginning of the story of how Jesus Christ, the Son of God, brought the Good News to men. ₂It all began as the passage in Isaiah the prophet said it would:

> 'See! I am sending my messenger ahead of you,
> and he will prepare your road.
> He will be like a voice shouting in the wilderness:
> ₃Get ready the road by which the Lord will come,
> straighten the paths by which he will travel.'

₄This came true when John the Baptizer emerged in the wilderness, announcing a baptism, which was a sign of the repentance which leads to the forgiveness of sins. ₅People from all over Judaea flocked out to him, and so did all the people of Jerusalem, and a continuous stream of them were baptized by him in the River Jordan, while they confessed their sins.

₆John was dressed in clothes made of camel's hair; he wore a leather belt round his waist; and his food consisted of locusts and wild honey. ₇This was his message: 'The One who is stronger than I is coming after me. I am not fit to stoop down and to untie the strap of his sandals. ₈I have baptized you with water; he will baptize you with the Holy Spirit.'

₉It was then that Jesus came from Nazareth in Galilee, and was baptized by John in the Jordan. ₁₀At the very moment when he was coming up out of the water, Jesus saw the heavens opening, and the Spirit coming down like a dove upon himself. ₁₁A voice came from heaven. 'You are my Son,' it said, 'the Beloved and Only One, and on you my favour rests.'

₁₂No sooner had Jesus had this experience than the Spirit compelled him to go out into the desert. 13He was in the desert for forty days, and all the time he was undergoing the ordeal of temptation by Satan. His companions were the wild animals, and the angels were helping him.

14After John had been committed to prison, Jesus came into Galilee proclaiming God's Good News. 15'The appointed time has come,' he said. 'The Kingdom of God is almost here. Repent, and believe that the Good News is true.'

16When Jesus was walking along the shore of the Lake of Galilee, he saw Simon and Andrew, Simon's brother, casting their nets into the sea, for they were fishermen. 17'Follow me!' he said to them. 'I will make you into fishermen who catch men!' 18There and then they left their nets and became his followers. 19He went on a little farther, and saw James, Zebedee's son, and his brother, John. They were in the boat servicing their nets. 20There and then he called them, and they left their father Zebedee in the boat with the hired servants, and took the decision to leave home and to become his followers.

21Jesus and his disciples went into Capernaum, and, as soon as the Sabbath came round, he went into the synagogue, and began to teach. 22They were astonished at the way he taught, for he taught them like a teacher who needed no authority other than his own, and not like the experts in the Law. 23No sooner had Jesus entered the synagogue than a man there with an unclean spirit shouted: 24'What business have you with us, Jesus of Nazareth? Have you come to destroy us? I know who you are! You are God's Holy One!' 25Jesus reprimanded the spirit. 'Silence!' he said. 'Come out of him!'. 26The unclean spirit threw the man into a convulsion, and shrieked, and came out of him. 27They were all astonished. 'What is this?' they kept on asking. 'A new kind of teaching! A teaching with the accent of authority! When he gives his orders to the unclean spirits, even they obey him!' 28And in no time the story of what Jesus had done spread everywhere, all over the surrounding district of Galilee.

29They went straight out of the synagogue, with James and John, into the home of Simon and Andrew. 30Simon's mother-in-law was confined to bed with an attack of fever. They lost no time in telling Jesus about her. 31He went in to her, gripped her hand, and lifted her up. The fever left her, and she began to serve them with their meal.

32When evening came, and when the sun had set, they kept on

bringing to Jesus all who were ill and demon-possessed. 33Everyone in the town gathered at the door. 34He healed many who were ill with many different kinds of diseases, and ejected many demons. He would not allow the demons to speak, for they knew who he was.

35Very early in the morning, long before the night had gone, Jesus left the town and went away to a lonely place. He was praying there. 36Simon and his friends tracked him down. 37'They are all looking for you,' they said, when they had found him. 38He said to them: 'Let us move on somewhere else to the nearby villages. I want to proclaim my message there too, for that is what I came to do.' 39So he went all over Galilee, proclaiming his message in their synagogues, and ejecting demons.

40A leper came to him, urgently appealing for help. 'If you want to cure me,' he said, kneeling before Jesus, 'you can.' 41Jesus was heart-sorry for him. He reached out his hand and touched him. 'I do,' he said. 'Be cured!' 42Then and there the leprosy left him, and he was cured. 43Jesus at once sent him away with a stern warning. 44'See to it,' he said, 'that you don't tell anyone anything about this. But go and show yourself to the priest, and take to him the offering for your cleansing which Moses prescribed, to prove to them that you really are cured.' 45But he went off and told everyone, and spread the story everywhere. The result was that Jesus could no longer appear in any town, but had to stay outside in the lonely places, and even then people kept coming to him from all over.

Chapter 2

WHEN Jesus returned to Capernaum some days later, the news went round that he was at home there. 2Such crowds gathered that there was no room, not even round the door. 3While he was speaking to them, a party of people came to him, bringing a paralysed man carried by four men. 4When they could not carry the man in to him, because the crowd was so dense, they removed part of the roof of the house in which Jesus was; and, when they had dug their way through, they let down the stretcher on which the paralysed man was lying. 5When Jesus saw their faith, he said to the paralysed man: 'Child, your sins are forgiven.' 6There was a group of experts in the Law sitting there. Their minds immediately began to ask: 'How can this fellow speak like this? 7This is an insult to God! Can anyone but God forgive sins?' 8Jesus was at once inwardly aware of what was going on in their minds. 'What put questions like that into your heads?' he said. 9'Which is easier—to say to this paralysed man, "Your sins are forgiven", or to say, "Get up! Lift your stretcher and walk?" 10Just to show you that the Son of Man actually has authority on earth to forgive sins'—with this he said to the paralysed man—11'I tell you, Get up! Lift your stretcher, and away you go home!' 12On the spot, in front of them all, the man got up, lifted his stretcher, and went off. This left them in such a state of astonishment that they kept on praising God. 'Never,' they kept on saying, 'have we seen anything like this.'

13Jesus went out again and walked along the seashore. The people all crowded to him, and he continued to teach them. 14As he was walking along, he saw Levi, Alphaeus' son, sitting in the office in which he collected the customs duties. 'Follow me!' Jesus said to him. He rose from his seat and followed him.

15Jesus was sitting at a meal in Levi's house. Many tax-collectors and people with whom no respectable Jew would have had anything to do were guests along with him and his disciples, for there were many people like that who were eager for Jesus' company. 16When the experts in the Law, who belong to the school of the Pharisees, saw that he was eating with disreputable characters and tax-collectors, they said to his disciples: 'Why does he eat with tax-collectors and with people with whom no respectable Jew would have anything to do?' 17Jesus heard what they were saying. 'It is not those who are well who need a doctor,' he said, 'but those who are ill. I did not come to bring an invitation to those who are good but to sinners.'

18John's disciples were in the habit of fasting, and so were the Pharisees. Some people came to Jesus and said: 'Why do John's disciples and the disciples of the Pharisees fast, while your disciples do not fast?' 19'Obviously,' Jesus said to them, 'the bridegroom's closest friends cannot fast so long as he is with them. So long as they have the bridegroom they cannot fast. 20But the time will come when the bridegroom will be taken from them, and then, when that time comes, they will fast.

21'No one,' Jesus went on, 'sews a patch of unshrunk cloth on an old coat. If he does, the patch that was meant to fill the hole tears the cloth apart—the new from the old—and the tear becomes worse.

22No one puts new fermenting wine into old wineskins that have lost their elasticity. If he does, the wine will burst the wineskins, and the wine and the wineskins will both be lost. No! New wineskins for new wine!'

23Jesus was walking through the cornfields on a Sabbath day. His disciples, as they walked along, began to pluck the ears of corn. 24The Pharisees said to him: 'Why are they doing what may not legally be done on the Sabbath?' 25'Have you never read,' he said to them, 'what David did, when he and his friends were hungry and needed food? 26Don't you know the story of how he went into the house of God, when Abiathar was High Priest, and ate the sacred loaves, which are placed in the presence of God, and which legally only the priests may eat, and gave them to his companions as well? 27The Sabbath,' he said to them, 'was made for the sake of man, and not man for the sake of the Sabbath. 28So the Son of Man's authority extends over the Sabbath too.'

Chapter 3

JESUS went into the synagogue again, and there was a man there whose hand was withered. 2They were watching Jesus closely to see if he would heal on the Sabbath, for they wanted to find something which they could use as a charge against him. 3Jesus said to the man with the withered hand: 'Get up, and stand where everyone can see you! 4Whether is it permitted,' he said to them, 'to help or to hurt on the Sabbath, to save life or to kill?' They remained silent. 5His gaze swept round them, and there was anger in his eyes, for he was saddened by the imperviousness of their hearts. 'Stretch out your hand!' he said to the man. He stretched it out, and his hand was restored to health.

6Thereupon the Pharisees went out and began to concoct a scheme with Herod's supporters to kill Jesus.

7Jesus withdrew to the lakeside with his disciples, and crowds of people from Galilee followed him. The crowds flocked to him also from Judaea 8and from Jerusalem and from Idumaea and from Transjordan and from the neighbourhood of Tyre and Sidon. They came because the story of his deeds was common knowledge. 9The crowd was so dense that he told his disciples to keep a boat ready to avoid being crushed by the crowd, 10for he performed many cures, and the result was that all who were suffering from the scourges of disease rushed forward to touch him. 11Whenever the unclean spirits saw him, they flung themselves down at his feet. 'You are the Son of God,' they kept shouting. 12But he strictly ordered them not to surround him with publicity.

13Jesus went up to the hill country, and there he called to his service the men of his choice. They left their homes and their jobs and came to him. 14He appointed twelve, because he wanted them to be with him, and he planned to send them out to proclaim his message, 15and to have power to eject the demons. 16He chose Simon to whom he gave the new name Peter; 17and James Zebedee's son, and his brother John, to whom he gave the new name Boanerges, which means Sons of Thunder; 18and Andrew and Philip and Bartholomew and Matthew and Thomas, and James Alphaeus' son, and Thaddaeus, and Simon the Nationalist, 19and Judas Iscariot, who was the man who betrayed him.

20Jesus went into a house, and once again such a crowd gathered that it was impossible for them even to eat a meal. 21When his own family heard what was going on, they left home to come and forcibly restrain him. 'He has taken leave of his senses,' they said.

22The experts in the Law, who had come down from Jerusalem, said: 'He has Beelzebul as his ally. It is by the help of the prince of demons that he ejects the demons.' 23Jesus called them to him, and used these illustrations to answer them. 'How,' he said, 'can Satan eject Satan? 24If a kingdom is split against itself, it cannot survive. 25If a household is split against itself, it will not be able to survive. 26So, if Satan is attacking himself, and if he is split against himself, he cannot survive—he is finished. 27The fact is that no one can go into a strong man's house and plunder his goods, unless he first ties up the strong man. Then indeed, he will be able to plunder his house. 28This is the truth I tell you,' Jesus went on. 'Men will be forgiven for everything, for all their sins and their insults to God. 29But if anyone insults the Holy Spirit, he will never be forgiven for ever. He is guilty of a sin that not even eternity can wipe out.' 30Jesus said this because they were saying that he had an unclean spirit.

31Jesus' mother and brothers came and stood outside. They sent in a message to him to ask him to come out and see them. 32A crowd of people were sitting round him. 'Look!' they said to him. 'Your mother and your brothers and your sisters are outside asking for you.' 33'Who is my mother?' Jesus answered. 'Who are my brothers?' 34His gaze swept round the circle of people sitting round him. 'See!' he said. 'My mother and my brothers! 35Anyone who obeys God's will is my brother and sister and mother!'

Chapter 4

JESUS was again teaching by the lakeside, and a very large crowd gathered round him. There was such a crowd that he got into a boat and sat in it on the lake, while the whole crowd stood on the land facing the lake. 2Much of his teaching was in the form of parables, and this is what he said to them as he taught.

3'Listen! Look! A sower went out to sow his seed. 4As he sowed, some seed fell by the side of the road, and the birds came and snapped it up. 5Some seed fell on ground where there was only a thin skin of earth over the rock. It sprang up immediately, because the soil was so shallow. 6But, when the sun rose, it was scorched, and it withered, because it had no root. 7Other seed fell among thorn-bushes, and the thorn-bushes shot up and choked the life out of the seed, and it produced no crop. 8Other seeds fell on good ground, and, as they sprang up and grew, they produced a good crop, yielding up to thirty and sixty and a hundred times as much as had been sown. 9If a man has ears,' said Jesus, 'let him use them!'

10When Jesus was alone, the Twelve and his other friends asked him about the meaning of the parables. 11'You,' he said, 'have received the privilege of knowing the meaning of the Kingdom of God, a secret which only a disciple can understand, but to those who are not disciples everything has to be expounded by means of parables, 12so that

"They may certainly see,
 and yet not perceive the meaning of what they see;
 and so that they may certainly hear,
 and yet not understand the meaning of what they hear,
 in case at any time they should turn to me,
 and have their sins forgiven."

13You do not know the meaning of this parable?' Jesus said to them. 'Then how will you understand the meaning of all the parables? 14It is the word that the sower sows. 15The picture of the seed that was sown by the side of the road represents the people who hear the word, but no sooner have they heard it, than Satan snatches away the word that was sown into them like seed. 16In the same way the picture of the seed that was sown on the ground which was only a thin skin of earth over the rock represents the people who immediately and enthusiastically welcome the word, whenever they hear it; 17they have no inner root, and they are at the mercy of the moment. And so, when trouble or persecution comes because of the word, they at once stumble and collapse. 18Then there are those who are represented by the picture of the seed that fell among the thorn-bushes. These are the people who hear the word, 19but the worry of this present world, and the deceptive seduction of wealth, and the desire for other things, get into them at the same time, and choke the life out of the word, and it never gets a chance to produce a crop. 20The picture of the seed that was sown on the good ground represents the people who hear the word, and who really make it part of their lives, and produce a crop, some thirty, some sixty, some a hundred times as much as they received.'

21'Surely,' Jesus said to them, 'a lamp is not brought into the room to be put under a bowl or under the bed? Surely a lamp is brought into the room to be placed on its stand? 22If anything is hidden, it is only in order that it should be revealed; and if anything is secret, it is only that it should be brought out into the open. 23If a man has ears, let him use them!'

24'Pay attention to what you are hearing,' Jesus said to them. 'What you get depends on what you give—only more so. 25For, if a man already has, more will be given to him, and if a man has not, even what he has will be taken from him.'

26'This,' said Jesus, 'is what the situation in the Kingdom of God is like. It is like what happens when a man sows seed on the ground. 27He wakens in the morning and he goes to sleep at night. The seed sprouts and grows—he does not know how. 28With no help from anyone the ground produces its crop, first the shoot, then the ear, then the ripe grain in the ear. 29And, as soon as the crop is ready for it, he sends out the sickle, for the time to reap the harvest has come.'

30'How,' said Jesus, 'will we find something with which to compare the Kingdom of God, or what picture can we use to represent it? It is like a grain of mustard seed. 31When mustard seed is sown on the ground, it is the smallest of all seeds which are sown on the ground. 32But when it is sown, it keeps on growing, until it becomes the biggest of all kitchen herbs, and produces branches so big that the birds nest in its shade.'

33Jesus talked to them in many parables like these, in so far as they were capable of receiving his message. 34He never spoke to them without using parables, but in private he explained the meaning of everything to his disciples.

35Late on that day Jesus said to them: 'Let us cross over to the other side of the lake.' 36So they left the crowd, and took him with them without disembarking. Other boats accompanied them. 37A violent squall of wind swept down on them, and the waves broke over the boat with such force that it was on the point of being completely swamped. 38Jesus was sleeping on a cushion in the stern of the boat. They woke him up. 'Master,' they said, 'we're drowning. Can't you do something about it?' 39He woke up and reprimanded the wind, and said to the waters: 'Silence! Quiet!' The wind dropped, and there was a complete calm. 40'Why are you such cowards?' he said to them. 'Can you not trust me even yet?' 41They were awe-struck. 'Who can this be?' they said. 'Even the wind and the waters obey him!'

Chapter 5

JESUS and his disciples crossed over to the other side of the lake to the district of the Gerasenes. 2No sooner had he disembarked from the boat than there met him out of the tombs a man with an unclean spirit. 3This man had his home among the tombs. He had reached such a pitch of madness that it was no longer possible to bind him with a chain, 4for he had often been bound with fetters and chains, but he had wrenched the chains apart and had smashed the fetters in pieces. No one was able to tame him. 5Night and day amongst the tombs and on the hills he never stopped shrieking and gashing himself with stones. 6When he saw Jesus in the distance, he ran and knelt in front of him. 7'What business have you got with me, Son of the Most High God?' he shouted at the top of his voice. 'For God's sake don't torture me!' 8He said this because Jesus had been ordering the unclean spirit to come out of him. 9'What is your name?' Jesus asked him. 'My name is Regiment,' he said, 'for we are many.' 10Repeatedly he pleaded with Jesus not to send them out of the country.

11A large herd of pigs was grazing on the hillside. 12'Send us into the pigs,' they pleaded with him. 'Let us go into them.' 13Jesus allowed them to do as they asked. So the unclean spirits left the man and went into the pigs, and the herd—there were about two thousand of them—stampeded down the cliff into the lake, and were drowned in the sea. 14The herdsmen fled, and told the story both in the town and all over the countryside. So the people came to see what had actually happened. 15They came to Jesus and found the demon-possessed man sitting fully clothed and in his senses—that very man who had had the regiment of devils—and they were terrified. 16Those who had seen what had taken place told them what had happened to the demon-possessed man and the whole story of the pigs; 17and they begged Jesus to get out of their neighbourhood. 18When Jesus was getting on board the boat, the man who had been demon-possessed pleaded to be allowed to stay with him, 19but Jesus would not allow him. 'Go back,' he said, 'to your own home and your own friends, and tell them the story of all that the Lord has done for you, and how he took pity on you.' 20So he went back and told all over the Ten Towns the story of all that Jesus had done for him, and everyone was astonished at the tale.

21When Jesus had made the return voyage in the boat to the other side, crowds of people gathered to meet him. 22Before he had got any farther than the shore, one of the presidents of the local synagogue, Jairus by name, came to him. As soon as he saw Jesus, he threw himself at his feet 23with an urgent appeal. 'My little daughter,' he said, 'is at death's door. Please come and lay your hands on her. Please come and cure her and save her life.' 24Jesus went with him. Crowds of people were following him, and they were jostling in on him on all sides.

25There was a woman who for twelve years had suffered from a haemorrhage. 26She had undergone many different kinds of treatment at the hands of many doctors. She had spent her last penny trying to find a cure. It had done her no good at all. Indeed her trouble grew worse and worse. 27She had heard the stories about

Jesus. She came up behind him in the crowd and touched his cloak, 28for she said to herself: 'If I touch even his clothes, I will be cured.' 29There and then her flow of blood was staunched, and she felt in her body that she was cured of the trouble which had been her scourge for so long. 30Jesus was aware that his power had gone out of him. Immediately he swung round in the crowd. 'Who touched my clothes?' he said. 31The disciples said to him: 'Don't you see the crowd jostling you on every side? What's the sense in asking who touched you?' 32But Jesus continued to search the crowd with his eyes to discover who had done it. 33The woman was so scared that she was still shaking. She knew what had happened to her. So she came and threw herself at Jesus' feet, and told him the whole truth. 34'Daughter,' he said, 'your faith has cured you. Go and God bless you! Go and enjoy your new health, free from the trouble that was your scourge.'

35While Jesus was still speaking, messengers came from the president's house. 'Your daughter has died,' they said. 'Why trouble the Teacher any further?' 36Jesus heard the message, but he disregarded it. 'Don't be afraid,' he said to the president. 'Keep on trusting!' 37He allowed no one to come with him except Peter, James and John, James's brother. 38They arrived at the president's house. Jesus saw the uproar. He saw them weeping and wailing unrestrainedly. 39He went in. 'Why all this uproar? Why these tears?' he said. 'The child is not dead—she's sleeping.' 40They laughed at him. He put them all out. He took with him the child's father and mother and his own men and went into the room where the child was. 41He gripped the child's hand. 'Talitha kum,' he said to her, which means, 'Little girl! I tell you, Get up!' 42There and then the little girl got up and began to walk about. She was about twelve years old. They were suddenly and completely amazed. 43He gave them very definite instructions that no one should be told about this, and he told them to give the child something to eat.

Chapter 6

JESUS left there and went to his own native place, and his disciples accompanied him. 2When the Sabbath came round he taught in the synagogue. The general reaction of his hearers was complete astonishment. 'Where did he get these things he is teaching?' they said.

'What wisdom is this that has been given to him? How can he perform such miracles? 3Isn't this the carpenter, Mary's son, the brother of James and Joses and Judas and Simon? Aren't his sisters here with us?' They were shocked and resentful that someone they knew so well should speak and act like that. 4Jesus said to them: 'The only place in which a prophet has no honour is his own native place, and among his own relations and in his own family.' 5He could not do any miracles there. All he could do was to lay his hands on a few sick people and cure them. 6He was amazed at their unwillingness to believe.

Jesus made a teaching tour of the villages. 7He summoned the Twelve and sent them out in twos. He gave them authority to deal with unclean spirits. 8He gave them orders to take nothing for the road except a staff. They were not to take any bread, or a beggar's knapsack, or any money in their money-belts. 9They were to wear sandals. 'And,' he said to them, 'you must not wear two shirts. 10Wherever you enter a house,' he went on, 'stay there until you leave that place. 11And if any place refuses you a welcome or a hearing, shake the last speck of its dust from your feet, as you would do if you were leaving a heathen town, to make them see the seriousness of what they have done.' 12So they went out with a summons to repent, and, 13everywhere they went, they ejected many demons, and anointed many sick people with oil, and cured them.

14King Herod heard of what was going on, for the name of Jesus was widely known. Some people were saying: 'John the Baptizer has come back to life. That is why he possesses these miraculous powers.' 15Others said: 'He is Elijah.' Others said: 'He is a prophet, like one of the great prophets.' 16When Herod heard what was going on, he said: 'This is John whom I beheaded come back to life.' 17Herod himself had sent and arrested John, and had imprisoned him in chains, because of the affair of Herodias, his brother's wife. The trouble had arisen because Herod had married her, 18for John had told Herod that he had no right to marry his brother's wife. 19Herodias nourished a grudge against John, and would have liked to kill him, but she was unable to succeed in her purpose, 20because Herod was afraid of John, for he well knew that John was a good and holy man, and he did his best to protect him. When Herod listened to John, he did not know what to do, and yet he found a certain pleasure in listening to him. 21But a day came when Herodias got her chance, when Herod on his birthday gave a banquet for his courtiers and commanders and for the leading men of Galilee. 22On that occasion Herodias' daughter came in and danced for them. Herod and his guests were delighted with her performance. The king said to the girl: 'Ask me for anything, and I will give you it.' 23He pledged his oath to her: 'I will give you whatever you ask for, up to half of my kingdom.' 24She went out and said to her mother: 'What will I ask for?' 'John the Baptizer's head,' her mother said. 25She at once went in and hurried to the king, and made her request. 'I want you,' she said, 'to give me John the Baptizer's head on a dish.' 26The king was very distressed, but because he had given her his sworn promise in front of his guests, he would not break his word to her. 27So there and then he despatched a soldier of the guard with orders to bring John's head. The soldier went and beheaded John in prison, 28and brought his head on a dish, and gave it to the girl, and the girl gave it to her mother. 29When John's disciples heard what had happened, they came and took away his body, and laid it in a tomb.

30The apostles returned to Jesus and told him all about what they had done and taught. 31'Come away by yourselves into a lonely place,' he said, 'and rest for a little while.' For so many people were continually coming and going that they did not even get time to eat an uninterrupted meal. 32So they went away in the boat to a lonely place where they hoped they could be by themselves. 33But many saw them go and recognized them, and hurried there on foot from all the towns, and went on ahead of them. 34So when Jesus disembarked he saw a great crowd, and he was heart-sorry for them, because they were sheep who had no shepherd, and he taught them many things.

35By this time it was late in the day. So the disciples came to Jesus. 'This place is a desert,' they said, 'and it is late in the day. 36Send them away to the farms and the villages round about to buy themselves something to eat.' 37'You,' Jesus answered, 'must give them something to eat.' 'Are we,' they said to him, 'going to spend a year's wages buying bread to give them a meal?' 38'How many loaves have you?' Jesus said. 'Go and find out.' 'Five,' they said when they had checked up, 'and two fishes.' 39He ordered them all to sit down in groups on the green grass. 40So they sat down in sections of hundreds and fifties. 41Jesus took the five loaves and the two fishes. He looked up to heaven and said the blessing. Then he broke the loaves into pieces, and gave them to the disciples to serve to the people, and he shared out the two fishes among them all as well. ₄₂They ate until they could eat no more, and ₄₃they collected enough broken pieces of bread and scraps of fish to fill twelve baskets. ₄₄Those who ate the loaves numbered five thousand men.

₄₅Jesus immediately made his disciples get into the boat and go on ahead to the other side to Bethsaida, while he himself dismissed the crowd. ₄₆When he had taken leave of them, he went away up to the hill country to pray. ₄₇When evening came, the boat was half way across the lake, and Jesus was alone on the land. ₄₈He saw that they were being buffeted by the storm as they rowed, for the wind was dead against them. About three o'clock in the morning he came to them, walking on the water, and it looked as though he meant to walk past them. ₄₉When they saw him walking on the water, they thought he was a ghost, and they cried out in terror, ₅₀for they all saw him, and they were distracted with fear. At once he spoke to them. 'Courage!' he said. 'It is I! Don't be afraid.' ₅₁Then he got into the boat with them, and the wind sank to rest. They were astonished, ₅₂for they did not understand about the loaves, because their minds were dully uncomprehending.

₅₃When they had crossed over, they landed at Gennesaret, and moored the boat there. ₅₄When they had disembarked from the boat, the people at once recognized Jesus. ₅₅They hurried all over the countryside, and from all over they carried the sick on stretchers to where they heard that he was. ₅₆And wherever he came into villages or towns or country places, they laid the sick in the market-places, and kept pleading with him to be allowed to touch even the tassel of his cloak; and everyone who touched it was cured.

Chapter 7

A GROUP of Pharisees and experts in the Law came down from Jerusalem to meet Jesus. ₂They saw that some of his disciples ate food with hands which were ceremonially unclean, that is, with hands which had not been washed in the way which the ceremonial law prescribes, ₃for the Pharisees and indeed all the orthodox Jews do not eat unless they first wash their hands as meticulously as the Law prescribes, for they strictly observe the tradition of the elders. ₄When they come in from business, they do not eat until they have carried out the ritual washing of themselves with water. There are many other traditions which they observe, traditions connected with the ritual washing of cups and pots and utensils of bronze. ₅So the Pharisees and experts in the Law asked Jesus: 'Why do your disciples not behave as the traditional law of the elders prescribes? Why do they eat food with hands which are ceremonially unclean?' ₆Jesus said to them: 'Isaiah well described the insincerity of your religion in his prophecies in the passage which says:·

> "This people honours me with their lips,
>   but their heart is far from me.
> ₇It is a futile worship which they offer me,
>   for they teach as divine commandments
>   man-made rules and regulations."

₈You abandon the commandment of God, while you carefully observe man-made traditions. ₉You are experts,' he went on to say to them, 'in finding a way to cancel the commandment of God in order to preserve your man-made traditions. ₁₀Moses said: "Honour your father and your mother," and, "The man who curses his father or mother must certainly be put to death," ₁₁but you say that if a man says to his father or mother: "This money that I might have contributed to your support is Korban" (that is, a gift dedicated to the service of God and usable for no other purpose), ₁₂he can, so far as you are concerned, no longer be allowed to give any help to his father or mother. ₁₃You thereby use your humanly transmitted tradition to render null and void the word of God. And this is only one of many such things that you do.'

₁₄Again he invited the crowd to listen to him. 'Listen to me, all of you,' he said, 'and try to understand. ₁₅Nothing which enters a man from outside can defile him. On the contrary, it is what comes out of a man that defiles him.'*

₁₇When he had left the crowd and had gone indoors, the disciples asked him what this difficult saying meant. ₁₈'Are even you not able to understand?' he said to them. 'Do you not realize that anything which goes into a man from outside cannot defile him, ₁₉because it goes, not into his heart, but into his stomach, and is then evacuated into the drain by natural processes?' (By this statement he in effect

*See Notes on pp. 575-6

declared all foods to be clean.) 20It is what comes out of a man that defiles him, 21for it is from within, from the heart, that there emerge evil thoughts, fornication, theft, murder, 22adultery, the desire to possess what a man has no right even to desire, wickedness, deceitful trickery, shameless immorality, jealousy, slander, arrogance, folly. 23All these wicked things come from inside, and it is they which defile a man.'

24Jesus left there and went away into the districts of Tyre. He went into a house because he did not want anyone to know that he was there, but his presence could not remain concealed. 25As soon as she had heard that he was there, a woman whose daughter had an unclean spirit came and threw herself at his feet. 26This woman was a Greek by birth, a Syro-Phoenician. Persistently she asked him to eject the demon from her daughter. 27'You must first allow the children to eat their fill,' he said, 'for it is not proper to take the food which belongs to the children and to fling it to the pet dogs.' 28'True, sir,' she said, 'but the pet dogs below the table eat their share of the crumbs that the children drop!' 29'Because of this answer,' Jesus said to her, 'go! The demon has gone out of your daughter!' 30So she went home, and found the child lying in bed, and the demon gone.

31Jesus left the district of Tyre, and went by way of Sidon to the Lake of Galilee. On the way he went through the district of the Ten Towns. 32They brought to him a deaf man who had also a bad impediment in his speech, and begged him to lay his hand on him. 33Jesus took the man away from the crowd because he wanted to be alone with him. He put his fingers into his ears, and spat and touched his tongue with the spittle. 34He looked up to heaven, and took a deep breath. 'Ephphatha!' he said to him, which means: 'Be opened!' 35The man's hearing returned, and then and there the impediment in his speech was removed, and he spoke clearly. 36Jesus instructed them not to tell anyone; but the more he so instructed them, the more eagerly they broadcast the story to everyone. 37They were completely astonished. 'He has done everything well!' they said. 'The deaf get back their hearing, and the dumb their speech!'

Chapter 8

There was at that time another occasion when there was a great crowd with Jesus, and when they had nothing to eat. He summoned his disciples. 2'I am heart-sorry for the crowd,' he said, 'for they have stayed with me for three days now, and they have nothing to eat. 3If I send them away home without a meal, they will collapse on the road, and some of them have come a long way.' 4'Where could anyone find food here in a desert to satisfy them?' his disciples answered. 5'How many loaves have you?' he asked them. 'Seven,' they said. 6He ordered the crowd to sit down on the ground. He took the seven loaves and gave thanks for them. Then he broke them into pieces and gave them to the disciples to serve to the crowd. They served them to them. 7They had a few little fishes as well. Jesus said the blessing for them and told them to serve them to the crowd too. 8They ate until they could eat no more. They gathered up the broken pieces that were left over, and there were seven hamperfuls of them. 9There were about four thousand people there. He sent them away 10and immediately got into the boat with his disciples and went to the district of Dalmanutha.

11The Pharisees came and tried to involve Jesus in an argument. They were trying to subject him to a test by demanding that he should produce some visible divine action from heaven. 12Jesus sighed deeply. 'Why,' he said, 'are the people of today always looking for some visible action of God? This is the truth I tell you, no such action will be given to them.' 13So he left them, and got into the boat, and went away to the other side.

14It so happened that the disciples had forgotten to bring any loaves with them, and they had only one loaf with them in the boat. 15Jesus proceeded to give them a warning. 'Watch what you are doing,' he said. 'Be on your guard against the evil influence of the Pharisees and against the evil influence of Herod.' 16They kept talking to each other about having no loaves. 17Jesus knew what they were arguing about. 'Why do you keep on talking about having no loaves?' he said to them. 'Do you not even yet understand, and do you not even yet see the meaning of things? Are your minds so completely impervious to the truth? 18You have eyes—can you not see? You have ears—can you not hear? Don't you remember the time 19when I broke the five loaves into pieces and shared them out among the five thousand people? Don't you remember how many basketfuls of fragments you collected?' 'Twelve,' they said. 20'Don't you remember,' he said, 'the time when I divided the seven loaves among the four thousand people? Don't you remember how many hamperfuls of fragments you collected?' 'Seven,' they said. 21'Do you still not understand?' he said to them.

22They went to Bethsaida. A blind man was brought to Jesus with the earnest request that Jesus should touch him. 23Jesus took the blind man by the hand and led him out of the village. He spat into his eyes and laid his hands on him. 'Do you see anything?' he asked him. 24The man's sight began to come back. 'I see men,' he said. 'I see them walking about, and they look like trees.' 25Jesus laid his hands on his eyes again. The man saw clearly; his sight was completely restored; and he was able to see everything plainly. 26Jesus sent him away home. 'Don't even go into the village,' he told him.

27Jesus and his disciples went away to the villages of Caesarea Philippi, and on the way Jesus put a question to his disciples. 'Who are people saying that I am?' he asked them. 28'Some,' they said, 'are saying John the Baptizer. Others, Elijah. Others, one of the prophets.' 29'And you,' he asked them, 'who do you say I am?' 'You are the Messiah,' said Peter. 30Jesus sternly insisted that they must not tell anyone about him.

31He now began to teach them that the Son of Man must undergo many sufferings, and that he must be rejected by the chief priests and the experts in the Law, and that he must be killed, and that after three days he must rise again. 32He kept telling them this very plainly and very definitely. Peter caught hold of him and sternly forbade him to talk like that. 33Jesus swung round and looked at his disciples. 'Get out of my sight, Satan!' he said sternly to Peter. 'Your ideas are not God's but man's.'

34Jesus called both the crowd and his disciples to him. 'If anyone,' he said, 'wishes to walk in my steps, he must once and for all say No to himself; he must decide to take up his cross; and he must keep on following me. 35Anyone who wishes to keep his life safe will lose it, but anyone who is prepared to lose his life for my sake and for the sake of the Good News will save it. 36What good will it do a man to gain the whole world, if in so doing he forfeits his own life? ₃₇For what could a man give that would be an equal exchange for his life? ₃₈If anyone is ashamed of me and my words in this apostate and sinful age in which we live, the Son of Man will be ashamed of him, when he comes with the glory of his Father and with the holy angels.'

Chapter 9

'I TELL you truly,' Jesus said to them, 'that there are some of those who are standing here who will not experience death until they see the arrival in power of the Kingdom of God.'

₂About a week later Jesus took with him Peter and James and John, and brought them up into a high mountain alone, all by themselves. He was transformed before their very eyes. ₃His clothes became glistening, intensely white, with a whiteness with which no earthly laundering could whiten them. ₄Elijah appeared to them, along with Moses. These two were talking with Jesus. ₅'Rabbi,' Peter said to Jesus, 'it's a wonderful thing for us that we are here. Let us make three shelters, one for you, one for Moses and one for Elijah.' ₆He did not know what to say, for they were terrified. ₇There came a cloud, enveloping them, and out of the cloud there came a voice: 'This is my Son, the beloved and only One. Listen to him!' ₈And suddenly, when they looked round, they no longer saw anyone with them, except Jesus.

₉On the way down from the mountain Jesus gave them strict injunctions not to tell to anyone the story of what they had seen, until the Son of Man had risen from the dead. ₁₀They could not stop thinking of this saying of his, and they discussed with each other what to rise from the dead could mean. ₁₁They put a question to Jesus. 'Why,' they said, 'do the experts in the Law say that Elijah must first come?' ₁₂'It is quite true,' he said to them, 'that Elijah is to come first, and is to set everything in order. But what does scripture say about the Son of Man? It says that he must go through many sufferings, and that he must be treated with utter contempt. ₁₃But, to return to your question, I tell you that the fact is that Elijah has come, and they did what they liked to him, as scripture said they would.'

₁₄When they came to the other disciples, they saw a large crowd round them, and the experts in the Law engaged in an argument with them. 15The crowd were all astonished to see Jesus, and, as soon as he came in sight, they ran up to him, and welcomed him. 16'What are you arguing about with my disciples?' he asked. 17'Teacher,' a man in the crowd answered, 'I brought my son to you, because he has a spirit that makes him dumb. 18And, whenever he has a seizure, the spirit tears him, and he foams at the mouth and grinds his teeth, and the boy is wasting away. And I asked your disciples to eject the spirit, and they could not.' 19'This modern generation has no faith,' Jesus said. 'How long have I to be with you? How long must I endure you? Bring him to me.' 20So they brought the boy to Jesus. When the spirit saw Jesus, it immediately threw the boy into a convulsion, and he collapsed on the ground, and rolled about, foaming at the mouth. 21'How long has he been like this?' Jesus asked the father. 'Since he was a child,' the father said, 22'and it often throws him into the fire and into the water, for it is out to kill him. If you can do anything, take pity on us and help us.' 23Jesus said: ' "If you can do anything," you say—everything is possible for the man who has faith.' 24Immediately the father cried out: 'I do have faith. Help me, if I haven't enough!' 25When Jesus saw a crowd running up, he spoke to the unclean spirit with stern authority. 'Deaf and dumb spirit,' he said, 'it is I who order you—come out of him and never enter him again!' 26The spirit shrieked and violently convulsed the boy, and came out of him. The boy was left so like a corpse that most of them said: 'He's dead.' 27Jesus gripped the boy by the hand and lifted him up, and the boy stood up. 28When Jesus had gone indoors and when they were by themselves, the disciples asked him: 'Why were we not able to eject it?' 29'This kind,' he said to them, 'can only be driven out through prayer.'

30They left there and were travelling through Galilee, but Jesus did not wish his presence to be known, 31for he was trying to teach his disciples about what was going to happen. 'The Son of Man,' he said to them repeatedly, 'is to be handed over into the power of men, and they will kill him, and three days after he has been killed, he will rise again.' 32But they did not understand what he was saying, and they were afraid to ask him what he meant.

33They came to Capernaum, and, when Jesus was in the house, he asked his disciples: 'What were you arguing about on the road?' 34They remained silent, because on the road they had been arguing with each other about which of them was greatest. 33Jesus sat down and called the Twelve to him. 'The man who wishes to be first,' he said, 'must be the last of all and the servant of all.' 36He took a little child and made him stand where they could all see him. Then he took him up in the crook of his arm and said to them: 37'To welcome a little child like this in my name is to welcome me; and to welcome me is to welcome not me but him who sent me.'

38'Teacher,' John said to Jesus, 'we saw a man ejecting demons by the use of your name, and we tried to stop him because he is not a follower of yours like us.' 39'Don't try to stop him,' Jesus said. 'A man cannot do a miracle in my name and then immediately go on to slander me. 40For the man who is not our opponent is our supporter.'

41'If anyone gives you a cup of water to drink for my sake because you belong to the Messiah, I tell you truly, he will not be unrewarded.'

42'If anyone does anything to cause one of these little ones who believe in me to sin, it would be better for him to have a huge millstone hung round his neck and to be thrown into the sea.'

43Jesus went on to say: 'If your hand becomes a cause of sin to you, cut it off. It is better that you should enter into life maimed than that you should go to hell with two hands to the fire that can never be quenched.* 45If your foot becomes a cause of sin to you, cut it off. It is better that you should enter into life a cripple than that you should be flung into hell with two feet.* 47If your eye becomes a cause of sin to you, throw it away. It is better that you should enter into the Kingdom of God with one eye than that you should be thrown into hell with two eyes, 48where the destructive worm never dies and the fire is never put out.

49'Every man's life must be a sacrifice to God, and the salt of the sacrifice is the purifying fire of affliction.

50'Salt is good, but if the salt has lost its saltness, with what can you give it back its flavour?

'Have a heart seasoned with the salt of purity, and then you will be able to live at peace with one another.'

*See Notes on pp. 575–6

Chapter 10

JESUS moved on from there, and went into the districts of Judaea and of the country on the far side of the Jordan. Once again crowds of people flocked to him and again, as his custom was, he continued to teach them.

2A group of Pharisees came to him with what they intended to be a test question. 'Is a man permitted to divorce his wife?' they asked. 3'What was the regulation which Moses prescribed for you?' Jesus said. 4'Moses,' they said, 'allowed a man to draw up a deed of divorce and to send his wife away.' 5Jesus said to them: 'Moses would never have prescribed any such regulation, if it had not been for the fact that your hearts are quite impervious to the real commandment of God. 6From the beginning of creation God made mankind male and female. 7For this reason a man will leave his father and mother and will be joined inseparably to his wife, 8and the two will become so completely one that they will no longer be two persons but one. 9What God has united man must not separate.' 10In the house the disciples again questioned him about this. 11'If,' he said to them, 'a man divorces his wife and marries another woman, he is guilty of adultery against her; 12and if she divorces her husband and marries another man, she commits adultery.'

13Little children were brought to Jesus for him to touch them, but the disciples warned off those who were trying to bring them. 14When Jesus saw what the disciples were doing, he was vexed. 'Let the little children come to me,' he said, 'and don't try to stop them, for it is to such as they are that the Kingdom of God belongs. 15I tell you truly, if a man does not receive the Kingdom of God like a little child, he will certainly not get into it.' 16And he took them up in the crook of his arm, and laid his hands on them, and blessed them.

17As Jesus was going out of the house on to the road, a man came running to him, and knelt in front of him. 'Good teacher,' the man said, 'what am I to do to get this eternal life that God has promised?' 18'Why call me good?' Jesus said to him. 'No one is good except God. 19You know the commandments, Do not kill. Do not commit adultery, Do not steal, Do not tell lies about anyone, Do not cheat anyone, Honour your father and mother.' 20'Teacher,' the man said to Jesus, 'I have obeyed all these since I was a child.' 21Jesus looked at him and loved him. 'One thing is missing in your life,' he said. 'Go, sell everything you have, give the proceeds to the poor, and you will have treasure in heaven. Then come! Follow me!' 22When he heard Jesus saying this, a look of the deepest gloom came over the man's face, and he went sadly away, for he was very wealthy.

23Jesus' eyes swept over the company. 'With what difficulty,' he said to his disciples, 'will the wealthy get into the Kingdom of God!' 24His disciples were very surprised to hear this. 'Children,' said Jesus again, 'how difficult it is to get into the Kingdom of God! 25It is easier for a camel to go through the eye of a needle than for a rich man to get into the Kingdom of God.' 26They were utterly astonished. 'Who, then,' they said to each other, 'can be saved?' 27Jesus looked at them. 'With men,' he said, 'it may be impossible, but not with God, for everything is possible with God.'

28Peter said to Jesus: 'We have left everything to become your followers.' 29'I tell you truly,' Jesus said to him, 'there is no man who has left a house or brothers or sisters or mother or father or children or estates for my sake and for the sake of the Good News 30who will not now in this present world get them back a hundred times over—houses and brothers and sisters and mothers and children and estates, yes, and persecution too—and in the world to come eternal life. 31But many who are first will be last, and the last will be first.'

32They were on their way up to Jerusalem, and Jesus was walking ahead of them. They were in a state of bewildered astonishment. They went with him, but they were frightened. Once again he took the Twelve aside, and talked to them about what was going to happen to him. 33'We are going up to Jerusalem,' he said, 'and the Son of Man will be handed over to the chief priests and to the experts in the Law. They will condemn him to death, and they will hand him over to the Romans. 34They will mock him and spit on him and flog him and kill him, and after three days he will rise again.'

35James and John, Zebedee's two sons, came to Jesus. 'Teacher,' they said, 'we want you to do for us whatever we ask you.' 36'What do you want me to do for you?' Jesus said. 37They said to him: 'Give us the right to sit one on your right hand and one on your left in your glory.' 38'You do not know what you are asking,' Jesus said. 'Can you pass through the bitter experience through which I must pass? Can you be submerged in the sea of troubles in which I must be submerged?' ₃₉'We can,' they said. Jesus said to them: 'You will pass through the bitter experience through which I must pass. You will be submerged in the sea of troubles in which I must be submerged. ₄₀But the right to sit on my right and left hand is not mine to give you. That is reserved for those for whom it has been prepared.'

₄₁When the ten heard this, they were annoyed with James and John. ₄₂Jesus called them to him. 'You know,' he said, 'that those who have the prestige of ruling the Gentiles lord it over them, and that in their society the mark of greatness is the exercise of authority; ₄₃but in your society the situation is very different. With you, if anyone wishes to be great, he must be your servant; ₄₄and with you, if anyone wishes to hold the first place, he must be everyone's slave. ₄₅Yes, indeed! For the Son of Man did not come to be served but to serve, and to give his life a ransom for many.'

₄₆They came to Jericho, and, as Jesus was leaving Jericho accompanied by his disciples and a large crowd of people, Bartimaeus, the son of Timaeus, a blind beggar, was sitting at the roadside. ₄₇When he heard that it was Jesus of Nazareth who was passing, he shouted: 'Son of David! Jesus! Take pity on me!' ₄₈Many sharply told him to be quiet, but he kept shouting all the more: 'Son of David! Take pity on me!' ₄₉Jesus stopped. 'Call him!' he said. They called the blind man. 'Keep your heart up!' they said. 'Get up! He's calling you!' ₅₀Bartimaeus threw off his cloak, leapt to his feet and went to Jesus. ₅₁'What do you want me to do for you?' Jesus said. 'Master,' the blind man said, 'the one thing I want is to see again!' ₅₂'Go!' said Jesus. 'Your faith has cured you.' There and then his sight returned, and he followed Jesus along the road.

Chapter 11

WHEN they were nearing Jerusalem, at Bethphage and Bethany, near the Hill of Olives, Jesus sent on two of his disciples. ₂'Go into the village opposite you,' he said, 'and, as soon as you enter it, you will find a tethered colt which no one has ever ridden. Untie it and bring it to me. ₃And, if anyone says to you: "Why are you doing this?" say: "The Master needs it; and he will return it very soon." ' ₄So they went off, and they found a colt tethered at a door, outside on the open street, and they untied it. ₅Some of the bystanders said to them: 'What are you doing untying this colt?' ₆They told them what Jesus had told them to say, and the bystanders made no effort to stop them.

₇They brought the colt to Jesus; they put their cloaks on it; and he mounted it. ₈Many of the people spread their cloaks on the road; others cut down leafy branches from the fields and spread them on it. ₉Those who were going on ahead and those who were following behind kept shouting:

'God save the people!
God bless him who comes in the name of the Lord!
₁₀God bless the kingdom of our father David, which is
   now on the way!
O send your salvation from the heights of heaven!'

₁₁So Jesus entered Jerusalem. He went into the Temple precincts and surveyed the scene, and then, since it was late in the day, he went out to Bethany with his disciples.

₁₂On the next day, when they had left Bethany, Jesus felt hungry. ₁₃In the distance he saw a fig tree in full leaf. He went up to it to see if he could find any fruit on it; but, when he reached it, he found nothing but leaves, for it was not yet the season for figs. ₁₄'May no one ever again eat figs from you!' he said. His disciples were listening.

₁₅So they came to Jerusalem. Jesus went into the Temple precincts, and proceeded to drive out those who were selling and buying there, and to upset the tables of the money-changers and the seats of the pigeon-sellers. ₁₆And he would not allow anyone to use the Temple court as a short-cut between the shops and their houses. ₁₇He began to teach them. 'Does not scripture say,' he said, ' "My house must be regarded as a house of prayer for all nations"? But you have made it a brigands' den.' ₁₈The chief priests and the experts in the Law heard about this, and they tried to find a way to kill Jesus, for they were afraid of him, because the crowd were all astonished at his teaching.

₁₉When evening came, they left the city. ₂₀In the morning on their way into the city they passed the fig tree, and they noticed that it was withered root and branch. ₂₁Peter remembered the incident of the previous day. 'Look, Rabbi!' he said. 'The fig tree you cursed is withered!' ₂₂'Have faith in God,' Jesus answered. ₂₃'I tell you truly, if anyone were to say to this hill: "Be picked up and flung into the sea," if there are no doubts in his mind, but if he really believes that what he is saying will happen, what he asks will be done. ₂₄That is why I tell you that you must believe that you have as good as received everything for which you pray and ask, and then you will receive it. ₂₅And, whenever you stand praying, if you have anything against anyone, forgive it, for it is then that your Father in heaven will forgive your sins.'*

₂₇Once again they came to Jerusalem. When Jesus was walking in the Temple precincts, the chief priests and the experts in the Law and the elders came to him. ₂₈'What right have you to act as you are doing?' they asked him. 'Or, who gave you this right to do so?' ₂₉'I will put one question to you,' Jesus said. 'Answer it, and I will tell you what right I have to act like this. ₃₀Was the source of the baptism which John administered divine or human? Answer me!' ₃₁They began to argue with each other. 'If,' they said, 'we say, "Divine," he will say: "Why then did you not believe in him?" ₃₂On the other hand, suppose we say, "Human" '—they were afraid of the people, for everyone was quite sure that John was genuinely a prophet. ₃₃So they answered Jesus: 'We do not know.' Jesus said to them: 'No more am I going to tell you what right I have to act as I do.'

Chapter 12

JESUS went on to speak to them in parables. 'A man,' he said, 'planted a vineyard, and surrounded it with a hedge, and had a pit dug in which the juice could be extracted from the grapes, and built a watch-tower. He then let it out to tenants and went abroad. ₂At the proper time he sent a servant to the tenants to collect from the tenants his due share of the crop of the vineyard. ₃They took the servant and beat him up and sent him away empty-handed. ₄Again he sent another servant to them. They knocked him on the head and shamefully maltreated him. ₅He sent still another. They killed him. He sent many others. They beat up some of them and killed others. ₆He had still one person to send, a beloved and only son. Last of all he sent him. "They will treat my son with respect," he said. ₇But these

*See Notes on pp. 575-6

tenants said to each other: "This is the heir. Come on! Let's kill him! Then the estate will be ours!" 8So they seized him and killed him, and threw his body out of the vineyard. 9What will the owner of the vineyard do? He will come and wipe out these tenants, and give the vineyard to others. 10Have you never read this passage of scripture?

> "The stone which the builders rejected,
>> this has become the headstone of the corner.
> 11This is the action of the Lord,
>> and it is marvellous in our eyes." '

12They tried to find a way to arrest Jesus, but they were afraid of the crowd, for they were well aware that Jesus had directed this parable against them. So they left him and went away.

13A group of the Pharisees and of Herod's supporters were sent to set a verbal trap for Jesus. 14'Teacher,' they came and said to him, 'we know that you speak the truth, and that it makes no difference to you who or what anyone is. Man-made prestige means nothing to you, and you really do teach the life that God wishes us to live. Is it right for us to pay the poll-tax to Caesar, or not? Are we to pay it, or are we not to pay it?' 15Jesus was well aware that they were not asking for information but that they were out to make trouble for him. 'Why are you trying to catch me out?' he said. 'Bring me a shilling and let me see it.' 16They brought him one. 'Whose portrait and whose inscription is this?' he said. 'Caesar's,' they answered. 17Jesus said to them: 'Pay to Caesar what belongs to Caesar, and to God what belongs to God.' They were astonished at the way in which he had parried their question.

18A group of Sadducees came and put a question to him. They belong to the school of thought which denies that there is any resurrection from the dead. They put a question to him. 19'Teacher,' they said, 'Moses prescribed a regulation in the Law for us that, if a man's brother dies, and leaves a wife behind him, but leaves no child, his brother should marry the wife, and raise a family for his brother. 20There were seven brothers. The first married a wife, and, when he died, he left no family. 21The second married her and died, leaving no family. The third did the same. 22The whole seven left no family. Last of all the woman died. 23When they rise from the dead at the resurrection, whose wife will she be, for she was married in succession to the whole seven?' 24'Surely you are on the wrong track altogether,'

Jesus said to them, 'and it is because you do not know either the meaning of the scriptures or the power of God. 25When men and women rise from the dead, they neither marry nor are married, but are like the angels in heaven. 26As for the fact that the dead are raised, have you not read in the Book of Moses in the passage about the bush how God said to him: "I am the God of Abraham and the God of Isaac and the God of Jacob"? 27He is not the God of the dead but of the living. You are on the wrong track altogether.'

28One of the experts in the Law came to Jesus. He had listened to the course of the discussion between Jesus and the Sadducees, and he had seen how well Jesus had met their arguments. So he put a question to Jesus: 'Which is the commandment which takes priority of all the others?' 29Jesus answered: 'The commandment which takes priority over all the others is, "Hear, O Israel, the Lord our God is the only Lord 30and you must love the Lord your God with your whole heart and your whole soul, and your whole mind and with all your strength." 31The second commandment is this: "You must love your neighbour as yourself." These are the two commandments which take priority over all the others.' 32'Well said, Teacher!' answered the expert in the Law. 'You spoke the truth when you said that God is one, and there is no other but him; 33and that for a man to love him with his whole heart and his whole intelligence and with all his strength, and to love his neighbour as himself, far outweighs all burnt-offerings and sacrifices.' 34Jesus saw that he had answered wisely. 'You are not far from the Kingdom of God,' he said to him. And no one dared to ask him any more questions.

35Jesus was teaching in the Temple precincts. 'How,' he said, 'can the experts in the Law say that the Messiah is David's son? 36David himself, moved by the Holy Spirit, said:

> "The Lord said to my Lord,
> Sit at my right hand
> until I give you the victory over your enemies."

37David calls him Lord—how can he be David's son?'
The thronging crowd listened to Jesus gladly.
38In his teaching Jesus said: 'Be on your guard against the experts in the Law, for they like to walk about in long flowing robes; they like to be deferentially greeted as they move through the market-places; 39they like the front seats in the synagogue and the top places at ban-

quets. 40They greedily extract the last penny from credulous widows, and then with their long prayers they try to give an impression of exceptional piety. They will receive all the heavier a sentence.'

41Jesus sat down opposite the Temple treasury. He was watching how the crowds of people put their money into the treasury. Many wealthy people put in large contributions. 42A poor widow came and dropped in two little copper coins, which were together worth half a farthing. 43Jesus summoned his disciples and said to them: 'I tell you truly, this poor widow has put in more than all the others who put money into the treasury put together. 44They all have more than they need, and it was out of their surplus that they made their contributions. She has far less than she needs, and it was out of her want that she put in every farthing she possessed, all that she had to live on.'

Chapter 13

As Jesus was leaving the Temple, one of his disciples said to him: 'Teacher! Look! What a size these stones and buildings are!' 2'You see these huge buildings?' Jesus said. 'Not one stone of them will be left standing on another. There is not a building here which will not be utterly demolished.'

3When Jesus was sitting on the Hill of Olives, opposite the Temple buildings, Peter and James and John and Andrew privately asked him: 4'Tell us, when will these events take place? What will be the sign that the time has come when all these events are actually going to happen?' 5Jesus said to them: 'You must be careful that no one misleads you. 6Many will come claiming to be my representatives. They will say: "I am he," and they will mislead many. 7Don't get into a panic when you hear of wars and reports of wars. These things must happen, but it is not yet the end. 8For nation will attack nation, and kingdom will attack kingdom. There will be earthquakes here and there. There will be outbreaks of famine. These events are the beginning of the birth-pangs of the new age.

9'You must be continually on your guard. They will hand you over to the councils; you will be flogged in synagogues; you will have to stand your trial before governors and kings for my sake. This will be an opportunity for you to show them what you believe. 10And first the Good News must be proclaimed to all nations. 11When they bring you to trial and hand you over to the authorities, do not worry beforehand about what you are to say, but say whatever is given you to say at the moment, for it is not you who are the speakers; it is the Holy Spirit. 12Brother will hand over brother to death; father will hand over child; children will attack their parents and murder them. 13You will be universally hated because of your connection with me. But the man who sees things through to the end will be saved.

14'When you see the desolating abomination standing where it has no right to be' (let the reader mark this well), 'then those who are in Judaea must flee to the hills. 15Anyone who happens to be on the housetop must not even come down and go into his house to take something out of it. 16Anyone who is at work in the field must not turn back to pick up his coat. 17It will be a tragic day for women who are carrying children in the womb or feeding them at the breast. 18Pray that it may not be winter time when all this happens. 19For these days will mean suffering such as has never happened since the beginning, when God created the world, to this present day, and such as will never happen again. 20And if the Lord had not cut short the period during which the suffering lasted, no human being could survive. But for the sake of the elect whom he had chosen, he has cut it short.

21'If at that time anyone says to you: "Look! Here is the Messiah! Look! There he is!" do not believe him. 22False Messiahs and false prophets will emerge, and, by performing miracles and wonders, will try everything possible to mislead God's chosen ones. 23But you must be on your guard. I have forewarned you about these things before they happen.

24'At that time, after the period of suffering,

> "The sun will be darkened,
>   and the moon will not give its light,
>   25the stars will fall from the sky,
>   and the powers in the heavens will be shaken."

26Then they will see the Son of Man coming on the clouds with great power and glory. 27Then he will send out his angels, and they will gather in God's chosen ones from the four points of the compass, from the limits of the earth to the limits of the sky.

28'Learn the lesson which the fig tree offers you. When the sap rises in its branches, and when it produces its leaves, you know that summer is near. 29So when you see these events happening, you too must realize that he is near, standing at the very door. 30I tell you truly, all these things will happen within the life-time of this generation. 31Heaven and earth will cease to be, but my words will never cease to be.

32'No one knows about that day or hour, not even the angels in heaven, not even the Son—no one except the Father.

33'Be on your guard. Be sleeplessly on the watch! For you do not know when the crucial moment will come. 34You are in a situation like that which arises when a man leaves home and goes abroad, after putting his servants in full charge of his affairs, and assigning to each his task, and after issuing orders to the doorkeeper to be always on the watch. 35So then you must be always on the watch, for you do not know when the master of the house is coming, late in the evening, at midnight, at dawn, or early in the morning. 36You must watch all the time in case he comes all unexpectedly and finds you asleep. 37What I say to you, I say to everyone—Be always on the watch!'

Chapter 14

IT was now two days before the Passover and the Festival of Unleavened Bread. The chief priests and the experts in the Law were trying to work out some stratagem which would enable them to arrest and to kill Jesus. 2Their problem was that they could not arrest him during the festival without serious danger of a popular riot.

3When Jesus was in Bethany as the guest of Simon the leper, as he sat at table, a woman came in with an alabaster phial of very expensive pure spikenard perfumed oil. She broke the alabaster phial, and poured the perfume over his head. 4Some of the guests were annoyed at what she had done. They said angrily to her: 'What is the point of wasting the perfume like this? 5This perfume could have been sold for more than fifteen pounds—a year's wages—and the money could have been used to help the poor.' And they snarled their reproaches at her. 6But Jesus said: 'Let her alone! Why distress her? It is a lovely thing that she has done to me. 7You have the poor with you always, and you can do something for them any time you like, but you do not have me always. 8She has done all that she had it in her power to do.

She has anointed my body in advance for burial. 9I tell you truly, wherever the Good News is proclaimed all over the world, what she has done will be told too, and she will always be remembered.'

10Judas Iscariot, one of the Twelve, went to the chief priests with an offer to deliver Jesus into their hands. 11They were delighted when they heard his proposal, and promised to pay him well; and Judas began to look for a good opportunity to deliver Jesus into their hands.

12On the first day of the Festival of Unleavened Bread, the day on which it was the custom to kill and to sacrifice the Passover lamb, Jesus' disciples said to him: 'Where do you wish us to go and make the necessary preparations for you to eat the Passover meal?' 13So he despatched two of his disciples. 'Go into the city,' he said, 'and a man carrying an earthenware water-jar will meet you. Follow him, 14and say to the owner of whatever house he goes into: "The teacher says: 'Where is my guest-room where I am to eat the Passover meal with my disciples?' " 15He will show you a big upstairs room, with everything ready, and with the couches spread with rugs. There make all the necessary preparations for us.' 16So the disciples went off into the city, and found everything exactly as Jesus had told them. And they made all the necessary preparations for the Passover.

17In the evening Jesus went to the room with the Twelve. 18When they had taken their places at the table, during the meal, Jesus said: 'I tell you truly, one of you will betray me, one who is eating with me.' 19They were all distressed, and one by one they said to him: 'Surely it can't be me?' 20'It is one of the Twelve,' Jesus said, 'one who is dipping his bread in the dish with me. 21For the Son of Man goes out on the road that scripture says he must go, but tragic is the fate of that man through whom the Son of Man is betrayed! Better for that man if he had never been born!'

22During the meal Jesus took a loaf and said a blessing over it. He broke it into pieces and gave it to them. 'Take it,' he said, 'this means my body.' 23Then he took a cup, and gave thanks to God, and gave it to them, and they all drank from it. 24'This means my life-blood,' he said, 'through which the new relationship between man and God is made possible, the blood which is being shed for the sake of many. 25I tell you truly, I shall not drink again of the fruit of the vine until the time comes when I drink it new in the Kingdom of God.' 26When they had sung the psalm of praise, they went out to the Hill of Olives.

27Jesus said to them: 'There is not one of you whose courage will stand the test, for scripture says: "I will smite the shepherd and the sheep will be scattered." 28But after I have risen, I will go on ahead of you into Galilee.' 29Peter said to him: 'Even if everyone else's courage fails, mine will not.' 30'I tell you truly,' Jesus said to him, 'today, this very night, before the cock crows twice, you will disown me three times.' 31Peter strenuously insisted: 'If I have to die with you, I will never disown you.' And they all said the same.

32They went to a place called Gethsemane. Jesus said to his disciples: 'Sit here, while I pray.' 33He took with him Peter and James and John. The increasing realization of what lay ahead came to him with such a sense of overwhelming shock that he was distraught in mind. 34'My soul is grief-stricken with a grief like death,' he said to them. 'Wait here, and stay awake.' 35He went a little farther on, and threw himself on the ground, and prayed again and again that, if it was possible, he might not have to face this terrible crisis. 36'Dear Father,' he said, 'everything is possible to you. Save me from having to go through this bitter ordeal. But not what I will, but what you will.' 37He came and found them sleeping. 'Simon,' he said to Peter, 'are you asleep? Were you not able to stay awake for one hour? 38Stay awake and pray, for you may well have to face an ordeal of temptation. I know that you mean well and that you want to do the right thing, but human nature is frail.' 39He went away again and prayed in the same words. 40Again he came back and found them sleeping, for they could not keep their eyes open, and they did not know what to say for themselves. 41He came a third time. 'Sleep on now,' he said to them, 'and take your rest. He has had his pay! The crisis is here! The Son of Man is betrayed into the hands of sinful men! 42Up! On your way! The traitor is coming!'

43Just as he was saying this, Judas, one of the Twelve, arrived, accompanied by a mob armed with swords and cudgels, sent from the chief priests and the experts in the Law and the elders. 44The traitor had given them a prearranged signal. 'The man I shall kiss is the man you want,' he said. 'Hold him and make sure of his arrest!' 45As soon as Judas arrived, he went up to Jesus and said to him: 'Rabbi!' and kissed him lovingly. 46They seized Jesus and held him. 47One of those who were standing beside Jesus drew his sword, and struck the High Priest's servant, and cut off his ear. 48Jesus said to them: 'Have you come out with swords and cudgels to arrest me as if you were out to arrest a brigand? 49I was with you daily, teaching in the Temple precincts, and you made no attempt to arrest me. But this has happened this way that what the scriptures say should come true.' 50And they all abandoned him and ran away.

51A young man was following Jesus, wearing nothing but a linen sheet over his naked body. They tried to catch him, 52but he left the sheet in their hands and fled naked.

53They took Jesus away to the High Priest, and all the chief priests and the elders and the experts in the Law assembled. 54Peter followed him at a distance, right into the courtyard of the High Priest's house. He was sitting there with the High Priest's attendants. He was warming himself at the fire.

55The chief priests and the whole council made repeated attempts to find evidence against Jesus, which would justify them in putting him to death, but they could find none. 56There were many who were quite prepared to perjure themselves, but their evidence did not agree. 57Some men came forward and falsely alleged in evidence against him: 58'We heard him say: "I will demolish this Temple made with hands, and in three days I will build another not made with hands."' 59But not even so did their evidence agree. 60Then the High Priest rose in the middle of the council. 'Have you nothing to say in answer?' he asked Jesus. 'What are these allegations that these witnesses are making against you?' 61But Jesus remained silent and made no reply. Once again the High Priest questioned him. 'Are you the Messiah, the Son of the Blessed One?' he asked. 62Jesus said: 'I am, and you will see the Son of Man seated at the right hand of Almighty God, and coming with the clouds of heaven.' 63The High Priest ripped his clothes in horror. 'What further witnesses do we need?' he said. 64'You have heard his blasphemous claim. What is your verdict?' They all condemned Jesus as guilty of a crime for which the penalty was death. 65Some of them spat on him, and blindfolded him, and punched him with their clenched fists. 'Prophesy!' they said to him. And the guards slapped him across the face, as they took him into custody.

66While Peter was below in the courtyard, one of the High Priest's maidservants came up to him. 67She saw him warming himself and looked at him closely. 'You too were with the Nazarene, Jesus,' she said. 68He denied it. 'I don't know him,' he said, 'and I don't under-stand what you're talking about.' He went outside into the forecourt. 69The maidservant saw him, and again she said to the bystanders: 'This man is one of them.' 70Again he repeatedly denied it. Shortly afterwards the bystanders again said to Peter: 'You certainly are one of them, for you are a Galilean.' 71Peter swore that he was telling the truth, and called down curses on himself if he was not. 'I do not know this man you are talking about,' he said. 72Just then the cock crew the second time, and Peter remembered how Jesus had said to him: 'Before the cock crows twice you will disown me three times.' He flung himself out and wept.

Chapter 15

FIRST thing in the morning the chief priests and the elders and the experts in the Law and the whole Sanhedrin prepared a plan of action. They put Jesus in chains and took him away and handed him over to Pilate. 2Pilate put the question to him: 'Are you the King of the Jews?' Jesus answered: 'If you like to put it so.' 3The chief priests brought many charges against him. 4Once again Pilate questioned him. 'Have you nothing to say in answer?' he said. 'Look how many charges they are making against you.' 5But to Pilate's astonishment Jesus made no answer.

6It was Pilate's custom at the festival to release for them any one prisoner for whom they asked. 7There was a man named Barabbas in detention, along with the rebels who had committed murder in the recent revolt. 8The crowd came and asked Pilate to observe his usual custom. 9Pilate answered: 'Do you wish me to release the King of the Jews for you?' 10For he was well aware that it was malicious ill will which had prompted the chief priests to hand Jesus over to him. 11But the chief priests incited the mob to demand that he should release Barabbas to them rather than Jesus. 12Once again Pilate asked them: 'What am I to do with the man you call King of the Jews?' 13'Crucify him!' they shouted back. 14'Why?' Pilate said. 'What crime has he committed?' But they shouted all the more insistently: 'Crucify him!' 15It was Pilate's desire to satisfy the mob, so he released Barabbas for them. He had Jesus flogged, and handed him over to be crucified.

16The soldiers led Jesus away, and took him inside the courtyard, that is, into the governor's headquarters. They summoned the whole company to come. 17They dressed him in a purple robe, and they plaited a crown of thorns and put it on him. 18Then they began to salute him: 'Hail, King of the Jews!' 19Repeatedly they struck him on the head with a cane, and spat on him, and knelt down and offered him a mocking homage. 20When they had finished their horseplay, they took off the purple robe, and dressed him in his own clothes, and led him out to crucify him.

21A man called Simon of Cyrene was passing, on his way into the city from the country. He was the father of Alexander and Rufus. They forcibly commandeered him to carry Jesus' cross. 22So they brought Jesus to the place called Golgotha, which means the Place of a Skull. 23They tried to give him wine drugged with myrrh, but he refused to take it. 24So they crucified him. They shared out his clothes between them by drawing lots for them, to see who should take what. 25It was nine o'clock in the morning when they crucified him. 26On the placard stating the charge against him was written: 'The King of the Jews.' 27They crucified two brigands along with him, one on his right and one on his left.*

29The passers-by tossed their heads at him and hurled their insults at him. 'Aha!' they said. 'You are the man who was going to demolish the Temple and build it in three days! 30Come down from the cross and save yourself!' 31So the chief priests and the experts in the Law jested with each other. 'He saved others,' they said. 'He cannot save himself. 32Let us see the Messiah, the King of Israel, coming down from the cross here and now, if he wants to make us believe in him!' And those who were hanging on their crosses with him flung their taunts at him.

33When it was twelve o'clock midday, darkness came over the whole country, and it lasted until three o'clock in the afternoon. 34At three o'clock in the afternoon Jesus shouted at the top of his voice: 'Eloi, Eloi, lama sabachthani?' which means: 'My God, my God, why have you abandoned me?' 35When some of the bystanders heard this, they said: 'Look! He is calling for Elijah!' 36One of them ran and soaked a sponge in vinegar, and offered it to him to drink. 'Wait!' he said. 'Let's see if Elijah is coming to take him down.' 37Jesus gave a great shout and died. 38And the curtain of the Temple which veiled the

*See Notes on pp. 575-6

Holy of Holies was ripped from top to bottom. ₃₉When the company commander, who was standing facing him, saw how Jesus had died, he said: 'This man was indeed a son of God!'

₄₀Some women were looking on from a distance. Among them were Mary from Magdala, and Mary the mother of James the Little and of Joses, and Salome. ₄₁They had attached themselves to Jesus when he was in Galilee, and had attended to his needs there; and there were many other women who had come up with him to Jerusalem.

₄₂It was already late in the day, and, since it was the Day of Preparation, that is, the day before the Sabbath, ₄₃Joseph of Arimathaea, who was a well-respected member of the Sanhedrin, and who was himself waiting for the Kingdom of God, greatly daring, went to Pilate and asked for Jesus' body. ₄₄Pilate wondered if it could be the case that Jesus had died so soon. So he sent for the company commander and asked if Jesus had been dead for long. ₄₅When he had ascertained from the commander that he was dead, he allowed Joseph to have the body. ₄₆Joseph brought linen, and took Jesus' body down from the cross, and wrapped it in the linen, and laid it in a tomb which had been hewn out of the rock. And he rolled a stone against the door of the tomb. ₄₇Mary of Magdala and Mary the mother of Joses were watching where the body of Jesus was laid.

There is more than one ending to Mark's Gospel in the ancient manuscripts. All the manuscripts agree down to 16.8. It is after that that the variation comes. i. In the best and most ancient manuscripts the Gospel ends at 16.8. ii. In the great majority of the later manuscripts there is the longer ending which finishes at 16.20, and which is the ending in the Authorised Version. iii. In certain manuscripts there is an alternative shorter ending. iv. In one important manuscript there is additional material following 16.14. In this translation all the various endings are given.

Chapter 16

WHEN the Sabbath had ended, Mary of Magdala, and Mary the mother of James, and Salome bought perfumed oils to go and anoint Jesus' body. ₂Very early on the Sunday morning they came to the tomb, just after sunrise. ₃They were saying to each other: 'Who will roll the stone away from the door of the tomb for us?' ₄They looked up and saw that the stone, for all its immense size, had been rolled away. ₅They went into the tomb, and they were very surprised to see a young man sitting there, on the right-hand side, dressed in a white robe. 6'There is no need to be so surprised,' he said to them. 'You are looking for Jesus of Nazareth who was crucified. He has risen! He is not here! Look! There is the place where they laid him. 7Go, and tell his disciples and Peter that he is going on ahead of you to Galilee. You will see him there as he told you you would.' 8They came out of the tomb and fled, for they were reduced to a state of trembling bewilderment; and they did not tell anyone about their experience, for they were afraid.

THE LONGER ENDING

9When Jesus had risen from the dead early on Sunday morning, he appeared first of all to Mary of Magdala, out of whom he had ejected seven demons. 10She went and told the story to those who had been with Jesus, and who were in mourning and tears. 11When they were told that Jesus was alive, and had been seen by her, they refused to believe it. 12After that, he appeared in another form to two of them, when they were walking on their way to the country. 13They went back and told the news to the others, but they did not believe them either. 14Later he appeared to the eleven themselves, as they were sitting at a meal, and he reprimanded them for their refusal to believe and for the stubbornness of their hearts, because they had refused to believe those who had seen him after he had risen.

15'Go all over the world,' he said to them, 'and proclaim the Good News to the whole of creation. 16He who believes and is baptized will be saved but he who refuses to believe will be condemned.

17'These are the visible demonstrations of the action of God which will accompany the life of those who believe. By using my name they will eject demons. They will speak in strange languages. 18They will lift snakes in their bare hands. Even if they drink any deadly poison, it will not hurt them. They will place their hands on the sick and they will be cured.'

19After he had spoken to them, the Lord Jesus was taken up into heaven, and took his seat at the right hand of God. 20They went and preached everywhere, and all the time the Lord worked with them, and confirmed their message by visible demonstrations of his power.

THE SHORTER ENDING FOLLOWING 16.8

They gave to Peter and his friends a brief account of all the instructions they had received. After that, Jesus through them sent out from east to west the holy and imperishable proclamation of eternal salvation.

THE ADDITIONAL MATERIAL FOLLOWING 16.14

They defended themselves by saying: 'This lawless and faithless generation is under the domination of Satan, who does not allow those who are subject to the unclean spirits to understand the truth and power of God. Therefore, reveal your righteousness now.' So they said to Christ, and Christ said to them: 'The limit set for the years of the power of Satan has been finally reached, but other terrible things are near. And I was delivered to death for the sake of those who had sinned, that they might turn to the truth, and no longer go on sinning, so that they might enter into the promised possession of the spiritual and incorruptible glory of righteousness, which is in heaven.'

Introduction to Luke

LUKE's Gospel was written between A.D. 80 and 90. There must always be for us a very special interest about Luke's Gospel, because Luke is the only writer in the New Testament who was a Gentile and not a Jew. This can even be seen in Luke's Greek. The preface to his gospel (1.1-4) is written on the model of the Greek classical writers and is in the best Greek in the New Testament.

One characteristic of Luke's Gospel stands out very clearly. Luke is the universal gospel. Matthew traces the genealogy of Jesus back to Abraham, the father and founder of the Jewish nation (Matthew 1.2), but Luke traces it right back to Adam, the father of the human race (3.38). All the Gospel writers quote Isaiah 40.3 in connection with John the Baptist, the forerunner of Jesus. Matthew (3.3), Mark (1.2,3) and John (1.23) all have:

> The voice of one crying in the wilderness:
> Prepare the way of the Lord,
> make his paths straight.

Only Luke (3.4-6) continues the quotation:

> Every valley shall be filled,
> and every mountain and hill shall be brought low,
> and the crooked shall be made straight,
> and the rough ways shall be made smooth,
> and all flesh shall see the salvation of God.

Right from the beginning Luke sees Jesus in terms of the world.

In this universal sweep the Samaritans are included. The one grateful leper is a Samaritan (17.11-19), and the hero of the parable is a Samaritan (10.30-37). The Gentiles are included. The aged Symeon sees in the child Jesus a light for revelation to the Gentiles (2.32). The faith of the Gentile centurion surpasses any faith in Israel (7.1-10). The poor are included. It is to the poor that the Gospel is preached (4.18; 7.22), and it is the poor who are blessed (6.20-25). In the parable of the rich man and Lazarus it is godly poverty which is in heaven and selfish wealth which is in hell (16.19-31). Even the disreputable, the outcast and the sinner are included. It is precisely the lost things that

God loves to find (15). Luke is concerned to show the universal embrace of the love of God.

Women have a very special place in Luke's Gospel. It is there that we meet Anna the prophetess (2.36-38); the widow of Nain (7.11-17); the woman who was a sinner but whose love was great (7.35-50); Martha and Mary (10.38-41); the weeping daughters of Jerusalem (23.27-31). In those days the place of women in society was very low, and we see in Luke the beginning of Christian chivalry to women.

Prayer has a very special place in Luke's Gospel. There are seven occasions when only Luke shows us Jesus at prayer (3.21; 5.16; 6.12; 9.18; 9.29; 11.1; 23.46); and it is in Luke that we find the two prayer parables of the friend at midnight and the unjust judge (11.5-8; 18.1-8).

Luke's Gospel is the Gospel of praise. The phrase *praising God* occurs oftener in the writings of Luke, the Gospel and Acts, than in all the rest of the New Testament put together.

Renan, the famous French scholar, called Luke's Gospel the most beautiful book in the world, and certainly no book gives such a picture of the universal love of God in Jesus Christ.

The Story of the Good News
LUKE'S VERSION

Chapter 1

THERE have been many who attempted the task of drawing up an account of the events on which our faith is based. ₂They have transmitted the story in the form in which it was handed down to us by those who were the original eye-witnesses of the events, and who were given the task of spreading the Christian message. ₃I, too, therefore, have made up my mind to carry out a careful investigation of the history of all these events, and to write to you, Theophilus, your Excellency, an orderly account of them, ₄because I want you to have in your mind a full and reliable knowledge of the things about which you may well have been misinformed.

₅In the time of Herod, the King of Judaea, there was a priest called Zacharias, who belonged to the Abia section of the priests. He had a wife called Elisabeth who like himself was a direct descendant of Aaron. ₆They were both good people in God's sight, for they lived in blameless obedience to all the commandments and ordinances of the Lord. ₇They were childless, because Elisabeth had been unable to have a child, and by this time they were both far advanced in years. ₈When Zacharias was performing his priestly offices before God, during the week when his section was on duty, ₉it fell to him by lot, in the normal priestly arrangements, to enter the Lord's Temple to burn incense. ₁₀The assembled people were praying outside at the hour when the incense was being offered. ₁₁The angel of the Lord appeared to him, standing on the right of the altar of incense. ₁₂When Zacharias saw him, he was alarmed and afraid. ₁₃'Don't be afraid, Zacharias,' the angel said to him, 'for your prayer has been heard. Your wife Elisabeth will bear you a son, and you must give him the name John. ₁₄His birth will bring a thrill of joy to you and happiness to many. ₁₅God will give him a great task to do. He must never drink wine or strong drink, and from the day of his birth he will be filled with the Holy Spirit. 16He will be the means whereby many of the sons of Israel turn to the Lord their God. 17God means him to be the forerunner, and the spirit and the power of Elijah will be his. It will be his task to reconcile fathers and children, to persuade the disobedient to accept the wisdom of the good, and to make ready a people prepared for the Lord.' 18Zacharias said to the angel: 'How shall I know that this is really going to happen, for I am an old man and my wife is far advanced in years?' 19'I am Gabriel,' the angel answered. 'I stand in God's presence awaiting his command, and I have been sent to speak to you and to bring you this good news. 20You will be silent, and you will not be able to speak, until this happens, because you did not believe my words, and my words are such that in their own due time they will come true.'

21The people were waiting for Zacharias, and they were surprised that he was lingering so long in the Temple. 22When he came out, he was unable to speak to them, and they realized that he had seen a vision in the Temple. He made signs to them, but he remained speechless. 23When his period of Temple duty was completed, he returned home. 24After this time his wife Elisabeth conceived a child, and for five months she did not see anyone. 25'The Lord has done this for me,' she said, 'and now in his kindness to me he has taken away the thing that was always a public humiliation to me.'

26In Elisabeth's sixth month the angel Gabriel was sent by God to a town in Galilee called Nazareth, 27to a girl who was pledged to marry a man called Joseph, who was a direct descendant of David. The girl's name was Mary. 28He went in to her and said: 'Joy be with you! You are specially dear to God! The Lord is with you!' 29She was deeply moved at what he said, and wondered what a greeting like this could mean. 30'Don't be afraid, Mary,' the angel said to her. 'God has chosen you for a very precious privilege. 31You will conceive, and you will have a son, and you must give him the name Jesus. 32He will be great; his title will be the Son of the Most High. The Lord will give him the throne of David his ancestor. 33He will reign over the house of Jacob for ever, and his reign will never come to an end.' 34Mary said to the angel: 'How can this happen when I have no husband?' 35The angel answered: 'The Holy Spirit will come upon you, and the power of the Most High will overshadow you. That is why the holy child who will be born will be called Son of God. 36Elisabeth, your kinswoman, has also conceived a son in her old age. They said that she could never have a child. But now she is in her sixth month, 37for there is nothing impossible to God.' 38Mary said: 'I am the Lord's servant. Whatever you say, I accept.' And the angel went away and left her.

39At that time Mary set out and went as fast as she could to a town of Judah in the hill country. 40She went into Zacharias' house and greeted Elisabeth. 41When Elisabeth heard Mary's greeting, the baby stirred in her womb. Elisabeth was filled with the Holy Spirit, 42and burst into speech. 'You are the most blessed of women,' she said, 'and blessed is the child you will bear. 43Why have I received this privilege that the mother of my Lord should come to me? 44For, when I heard your greeting, the baby in my womb leaped for joy. 45Blessed is she who has believed that the message she received from the Lord will come true.'

46Mary said:
'My soul tells of the greatness of God,
    47and my spirit thrills in God my Saviour,
48because he has looked kindly on his servant,
    even though my place in life is humble.
From now on those of all time to come will call me blessed,
    49for the Mighty One has done great things for me,
    and holy is his name.
50His mercy is from age to age
    to those who reverence him.
51He has done mighty deeds with his right arm.
    He has scattered the proud with their arrogant plans.
52He has thrown down the mighty from their seats of power.
    He has exalted the humble,
53He has filled those who are hungry with good things,
    and those who are rich he has sent empty away.
54He has come to the aid of Israel his servant.
    55He has kept the promise that he made to our fathers,
the promise never to forget his mercy to Abraham,
    and to his descendants for ever.'

56Mary stayed with Elisabeth for about three months, and then returned to her own home.

57When the time for her baby to be born came, Elisabeth gave birth to a son. 58When her neighbours and relations heard of God's great kindness to her, they shared in her joy. 59On the eighth day they went to have the child circumcised, and it was their intention to call him Zacharias after his father. 60But his mother said: 'No! He is to be called John.' 61They said to her: 'There is no one in your family circle who is called by that name.' 62They asked his father by signs what he wished him to be called. 63He asked for a writing-tablet and wrote: 'John is his name.' They were all very surprised. 64There and then he recovered his powers of speech, and he was able to talk again, and he began to praise God. 65The neighbours regarded these events with awe, and the story was the talk of the whole hill country of Judaea. 66No one who heard it could forget it. 'What will this child turn out to be?' they said. 'For indeed it is to the action of God that he owes his existence.'

67His father Zacharias was filled with the Holy Spirit. With prophetic inspiration he said:

68'Blessed be the Lord, the God of Israel,
for he has kindly cared for his people,
and has rescued them from their bondage.
69From the family of David his servant,
he has raised up a champion to save us,
70as long ago through the words of the holy prophets
he said he would, when he promised
71to deliver us from our enemies
and from the power of those who hate us,
72to fulfil the promise of mercy which he made to our fathers,
and to remember his holy covenant.
73It was his sworn promise to Abraham our father
74that he would rescue us from the power of our enemies,
and enable us to serve him with nothing to fear,
75in holiness and goodness all our lives.
76And you, child, shall be called the prophet of the Most High,
for you will be the Lord's forerunner,
to prepare the roads by which he will travel,
77for it will be your task to tell his people
how they may be saved and have their sins forgiven,
78through the deep compassion of our God
which has graciously sent heaven's dawn to break upon us,

79to shine on those who sit in darkness and in the shadow of death, and to direct our steps in the road that leads to peace.'

80So the child grew physically and developed spiritually; and he lived in the desert places until he publicly emerged upon the scene of Israel's history.

Chapter 2

AT that time a decree was issued by Caesar Augustus that a census should be taken of the whole inhabited world. 2This was the first census, and it took place when Quirinius was governor of Syria. 3Everyone went to his own native town to be registered. 4So Joseph went up from Galilee, from the town of Nazareth, to Judaea, to David's town, which is called Bethlehem, 5to register himself, along with Mary, who was pledged to marry him, and who was expecting a child. 6When they were there, the time for her to have her baby came, 7and she gave birth to a son, her first child, and wrapped him in swaddling clothes, and laid him in a manger, because there was no room for them inside the village guest-house.

8In that district there were shepherds out in the fields, guarding their flock by night. 9An angel of the Lord appeared to them, and the glory of the Lord shone round them, and they were terrified. 10'Don't be afraid,' the angel said to them, 'for I am bringing you good news of great joy, a joy in which all peoples will share. 11For today there has been born to you in David's town a saviour who is the Messiah, the Lord. 12This is how you will recognize him. You will find a baby, wrapped in swaddling clothes, lying in a manger.' 13Suddenly there was with the angel a crowd of heaven's army, singing God's praise. 14'Glory to God in the heights of heaven,' they sang, 'and on earth peace to mankind, on whom God's favour rests.'*

15When the angels had left them and gone back to heaven, the shepherds said to each other: 'Come! We must go over to Bethlehem and see what has happened, and what the Lord has told us about.' 16So they went as fast as they could, and they found Mary and Joseph, and the baby lying in the manger. 17When they saw him, they told everyone what they had been told about this child. 18And everyone

*See Notes on pp. 575-6

who heard it was astonished at the shepherds' story. 19Mary treasured all this in her memory, and wondered in her mind what it all meant. 20So the shepherds went back glorifying and praising God for all that they had heard and seen, for everything was exactly as they had been told.

21When the eight days which must precede circumcision had elapsed, he was named Jesus, the name given him by the angel, before his mother had conceived him.

22When the days which, according to the law of Moses, must precede the ceremony of their purification had elapsed, his parents brought him to Jerusalem to present him to the Lord, 23in accordance with the regulation in the Lord's law, which states that every first-born male creature must be regarded as consecrated to the Lord, 24and to make the sacrifice prescribed in the Lord's law, that is, a pair of doves or two young pigeons.

25There was a man in Jerusalem called Simeon. He meticulously observed the Law and devoutly reverenced God. He was waiting for the comforting of Israel, and the Holy Spirit was upon him. 26He had received a special message through the Holy Spirit that death would not come to him until he had seen the Lord's Messiah. 27Guided by the Spirit, he went into the Temple precincts. When his parents brought in the baby Jesus, to carry out the customary ceremonies of the Law, 28he took him in his arms. He blessed God and said:

29'Now, O Lord, as you promised,
   you are giving your servant his release in peace,
30because my eyes have seen the saving power
   31which you have prepared for all peoples to see,
   32to be a light to bring your revelation to the Gentiles,
   and glory to your people Israel.'

33His father and mother were astonished to hear this said about him. 34Symeon blessed them, and said to Mary his mother: 'As for this child, he is destined to be the cause whereby many in Israel will fall, and many will rise, and to be a message from God which men will reject. 35As for you, a sword will pierce your soul. It will be his work to lay bare the secret thoughts of many a heart.'

36There was a prophetess called Anna, the daughter of Phanuel, a member of the tribe of Asher. She was far advanced in years. For seven years after she grew to womanhood she had lived with her husband,

37and now she was a widow of eighty-four years of age. She was never away from the Temple precincts, and day and night she worshipped continually with fasting and prayers. 38Just at that moment she came up. She began to thank God, and to speak about him to all who were waiting expectantly for the deliverance of Jerusalem.

39When they had discharged all the duties which the Lord's law prescribes, they returned to Galilee, to their own town of Nazareth. 40The child grew bigger and stronger; he was full of wisdom, and the grace of God was on him.

41Every year Jesus' parents used to go to Jerusalem for the Festival of the Passover. 42When he was twelve years old, they went up to the festival as they usually did. 43They stayed to the very end of the festival, and, when they were on their way back home, the boy Jesus stayed on in Jerusalem. His parents were not aware that he had done so. 44They thought that he was in the caravan, and, at the end of the first day's journey, they began to search for him among their relations and friends. 45When they did not find him, they turned back to Jerusalem, searching for him as they went. 46It was three days before they discovered him in the Temple precincts, sitting in the middle of the teachers, listening to them, and asking them questions. 47All the listeners were amazed at his intelligence and at his answers. 48They were very surprised to see him there. 'Child,' his mother said to him, 'why have you behaved like this to us? Your father and I have been searching for you, and we have been worried to distraction.' 49'Why had you to look for me?' he said. 'Didn't you know that I was bound to be in my Father's house?'

50They did not understand the meaning of what he said. 51So he went down with them, and came to Nazareth, and he was obedient to them. His mother stored all these things in her memory and kept thinking about them. 52And Jesus grew wiser in mind and bigger in body, and more and more he won the approval of God and of his fellow men.

Chapter 3

In the fifteenth year of the reign of Tiberius Caesar, when Pontius Pilate was governor of Judaea, when Herod was tetrarch of Galilee, his brother Philip tetrarch of Ituraea and of the district of Trachonitis, and Lysanias tetrarch of Abilene, ₂in the high priesthood of Annas and Caiaphas, the word of God came to John, Zacharias' son, when he was in the desert. ₃So he went all over the Jordan valley, proclaiming a baptism which was a sign of the repentance which leads to the forgiveness of sins. ₄It was all as scripture said it would be in the book of the words of the prophet Isaiah:

> 'The voice of one shouting in the wilderness,
>   Get ready the road by which the Lord will come,
>   straighten the paths by which he will travel.
>   ₅Every ravine will be filled in,
>   every mountain and hill will be levelled;
>   the twisted paths will be made into straight ways,
>   and the rough tracks into smooth roads,
>   ₆and all men shall see the saving power of God.'

₇John's message to the crowds who came out to be baptized by him was: 'Brood of vipers! Who put it into your heads to flee from the coming wrath? ₈Prove the sincerity of your repentance by your life and conduct. Don't begin to say to yourselves: "We have Abraham as our father." For I tell you that God can produce children for Abraham from these stones. ₉Even now the axe is poised at the root of the trees. Every tree which does not produce good fruit is going to be cut down and flung into the fire.'

₁₀The crowds kept asking: 'What does this mean that we must do?' ₁₁'If a man has two shirts,' he answered, 'he must share with the man who has none, and the man who has food must do the same.' ₁₂The tax-collectors came to be baptized. 'Teacher,' they said to him, 'what ought we to do?' ₁₃'Exact no more than the rate fixed,' he said to them. ₁₄The soldiers too asked him: 'What ought we to do?' 'Treat no man with violence,' he said to them. 'Never be a blackmailer. Be content with your pay.'

₁₅When the people were in a state of expectancy, and when they were all debating in their minds whether John could be the Messiah, 16John said to them all: 'I baptize you with water, but the One who is stronger than I is coming. I am not fit to untie the strap of his sandals. He will baptize you with the Holy Spirit and with fire. 17He is going to winnow the chaff from the corn. He will cleanse every speck of rubbish from his threshing-floor, and gather the corn into his granary, but he will burn the chaff with fire that nothing can put out.'

18So, then, appealing to the people with these and many another plea, John announced the Good News to them. 19But, when Herod the tetrarch was reproved by him for his conduct in the matter of Herodias, his brother's wife, and for all the other wicked things he had done, 20in addition to all his other crimes, he shut up John in prison.

21When all the people had been baptized, Jesus too was baptized, and, while he was praying, heaven was opened, 22and the Holy Spirit in bodily form came down like a dove on him, and there came a voice from heaven: 'You are my Son, the Beloved and Only One, on whom my favour rests.'*

23When Jesus entered upon his ministry, he was about thirty years of age. He was the son, so it was believed, of Joseph, the son of Heli, 24the son of Matthat, the son of Levi, the son of Melchi, the son of Jannai, the son of Joseph, 25the son of Mattathias, the son of Amos, the son of Nahum, the son of Esli, the son of Naggai, 26the son of Maath, the son of Mattathias, the son of Semein, the son of Josech, the son of Joda, 27the son of Joanan, the son of Rhesa, the son of Zerubbabel, the son of Salathiel, the son of Neri. 28the son of Melchi, the son of Addi, the son of Cosam, the son of Elmadam, the son of Er, 29the son of Joshua, the son of Eliezer, the son of Jorim, the son of Matthat, the son of Levi, 30the son of Symeon, the son of Judah, the son of Joseph, the son of Jonam, the son of Eliakim, 31the son of Melea, the son of Menna, the son of Mattatha, the son of Nathan, the son of David, 32the son of Jesse, the son of Obed, the son of Boaz, the son of Sala, the son of Naasson, 33the son of Aminadab, the son of Admin, the son of Arni, the son of Esrom, the son of Phares, the son of Judah, 34the son of Jacob, the son of Isaac, the son of Abraham, the son of Terah, the son of Nahor, 35the son of Serouch, the son of

*See Notes on pp. 575-6

Ragau, the son of Phalek, the son of Eber, the son of Sala, 36the son of Cainam, the son of Arphaxad, the son of Shem, the son of Noah, the son of Lamech, 37the son of Methuselah, the son of Enoch, the son of Jared, the son of Maleleel, the son of Cainam, 38the son of Enos, the son of Seth, the son of Adam, the son of God.

Chapter 4

JESUS came back from the Jordan full of the Holy Spirit. 2For forty days he was under the direction of the Spirit in the desert, 2and during all that time he was undergoing the ordeal of temptation by the Devil. During that time he ate nothing, and at the end of the period he was attacked by the pangs of hunger. 3The Devil said to him: 'If you really are the Son of God, tell this stone to become a loaf of bread.' 4Jesus answered: 'Scripture says, "It takes more than bread to keep a man alive." ' 5The Devil took him up and showed him in a flash all the kingdoms of the inhabited world. 6The Devil said to him: 'I will give you control over all these, and I will give you their splendour, for it has all been handed over to me, and it is mine to give to anyone I wish. 7If you worship me, all of it will be yours.' 8Jesus answered: 'Scripture says, "You must worship the Lord your God, and you must serve only him." 9The Devil took him to Jerusalem, and placed him on the highest spire of the Temple. 'If you really are the Son of God,' he said to him, 'fling yourself down from here, 10for scripture says, "He will give his angels orders to guard you through all dangers," and, 11"They will carry you in their arms to ensure that you never strike your foot against a stone." ' 12Jesus answered: 'It has been said, "You must not try to see how far you can go with the Lord your God." ' 13So when the Devil had exercised his every tempting wile, he left him until another opportunity of putting him to the test should come.

14So Jesus returned to Galilee equipped with the power of the Spirit. The whole countryside was talking about him. 15He went on teaching in their synagogues, and he was held in high reputation by all.

16He went to Nazareth, where he had been brought up, and, as his habit was, he went into the synagogue on the Sabbath. He rose to read the scripture lesson. 17The roll containing the prophecies of Isaiah was handed to him. He unrolled the roll and found the passage where it is written:

18'The Spirit of the Lord is upon me,
    because he has anointed me,
    to bring good news to the poor.
He has sent me to announce to the prisoners
    that they will be liberated,
    and to the blind that they will see again,
to send away in freedom
    those who have been broken by life,
19to announce that the year
    when the favour of God will be shown has come.'

20He rolled up the roll, and handed it back to the officer. He took the preacher's seat, and the eyes of everyone in the synagogue were fixed intently on him. 21'Today,' he said to them, 'this passage of scripture has come true, as you listened to it.'

22They all agreed that the reports that they had heard of him were true, and they were astonished at the gracious words he spoke. 'Isn't this Joseph's son?' they said. 23He said: 'You are bound to quote the proverb to me, "Doctor, cure yourself." Do here in your home country all that we have heard about you doing in Capernaum.' 24He went on: 'This is the truth I tell you, no prophet is accepted in his own native place. 25You know quite well that it is the fact that there was many a widow in Israel in Elijah's time, when the sky was closed for three and a half years, and there was a severe famine all over the country; 26but to none of them was Elijah sent; he was sent to a widow in Sarepta in Sidon. 27There was many a leper in Israel in the time of Elisha; and none of them was cured; but Naaman the Syrian was.' 28The people in the synagogue were all enraged, when they heard him speak like this. 29They rose from their seats and hustled him out of the town. They took him to the brow of the hill on which their town is built, to hurl him down. 30But he walked straight through the middle of them, and went on his way.

31So he went down to Capernaum, a town in Galilee. On the Sabbath he was teaching there, 32and they were astonished at the way in which he taught, because he spoke like a man who needed no other authority than his own.

33In the synagogue there was a man who had a spirit of an unclean demon. This man shrieked at the top of his voice: 34'Let us alone! What business have you with us, Jesus of Nazareth. Have you come to destroy us? I know who you are. You are God's Holy One.' 35Jesus reprimanded the spirit. 'Silence!' he said. 'Come out of him!' The demon threw the man into a convulsion right in front of them all, and then came out of him without doing him any harm. 36Astonishment gripped them. They kept saying to one another: 'What kind of way is this to speak? He gives his orders to unclean spirits with authority and power, and they come out.' 37The report of what Jesus had done spread all over the surrounding district.

38Jesus went out of the synagogue, and went into Simon's house. Simon's mother-in-law was in the grip of a major fever. They asked him to do something for her. 39He stood over her and reprimanded the fever, and it left her. There and then she got up, and began to serve them with their meal.

40When the sun was setting, everyone who had friends who were ill with all kinds of troubles brought them to Jesus, and he laid his hands on each of them, and cured them. 41Demons too went out of many people, shouting: 'You are the Son of God.' He reprimanded them, and would not allow them to speak, because they knew that he was the Messiah.

42At daybreak he left the house and went out to a lonely place. The crowds kept searching for him, and, when they found him, they tried to keep him from leaving them. 43'I must tell the good news of the Kingdom of God to the other towns too,' he said to them, 'because that is what I was sent to do.' 44So he continued to proclaim his message in the synagogues of Judaea.

Chapter 5

JESUS was standing on the shore of the Lake of Gennesaret, and the crowd were pressing in upon him in their eagerness to hear the word of God. 2He saw two boats drawn up on the lake-side. The fishermen had disembarked and were washing their nets. 3He got into one of the boats, which belonged to Simon, and asked him to push out a little from the land. He sat down and went on teaching the crowds from the boat.

4When he had finished speaking, he said to Simon: 'Push out into the deep water, and let down your nets for a catch.' 5'Master,' Simon answered, 'we have worked our hardest all night and we have caught nothing. All the same, if you say so, I will let down the nets.' 6When they had done so, they caught so many fish in the nets that they were on the point of breaking. 7They signalled to their partners in the other boat to come to their help. They came and filled both boats so full that they were in danger of sinking. 8When Simon Peter saw what had happened, he threw himself at Jesus' feet. 'Lord,' he said, 'leave me, for I am a sinful man.' 9The size of the catch of fish they had taken left Peter and his crew in wondering amazement, 10and James and John, Zebedee's sons, Peter's partners, were equally astonished. 'Don't be afraid,' Jesus said to Simon. 'From now on it will be men that you catch.' 11Then they hauled the boats up on to the land, and left everything, and became his followers.

12When Jesus was in one of the towns, a man who was a mass of leprosy came and threw himself prostrate in front of him. 'Sir,' he appealed to Jesus, 'if you want to cure me, you can.' 13Jesus reached out his hand and touched him. 'I do,' he said. 'Be cured!' There and then the leprosy left him. 14Jesus gave him orders not to tell anyone. 'But go,' he said, 'and show yourself to the priest, and take him the offering for your cleansing which Moses prescribed, to prove to them that you really are cured.' 15But the news about Jesus spread all the more, and huge crowds gathered to listen to him and to have their illnesses cured. 16But Jesus withdrew into the lonely places and remained there in prayer.

17One day, as Jesus was teaching, a group of Pharisees and legal experts were sitting listening. They had come from every village in Galilee and from Judaea and from Jerusalem. The Lord's power made Jesus able to make sick people well. 18A party of men came carrying on a bed a man who was paralysed. They tried to carry him in to lay him in front of Jesus. 19They were unable to find any way to carry him in because of the crowd. So they went up on to the roof, and they let him down, bed and all, through the tiles, right into the middle of the crowd, in front of Jesus. 20When Jesus saw their faith, he said: 'Man, your sins are forgiven you.' 21Then questions began to arise in the minds of the experts in the Law and of the Pharisees. 'Who is this fellow who is insulting God?' they said. 'Can anyone but God forgive sins?' 22Jesus was well aware of what was going on in their minds. 'What are your minds going on about?' he said. ₂₃'Which is easier, to say, "Your sins are forgiven you," or to say, "Get up and walk"? ₂₄Just to show you that the Son of Man actually has power to forgive sins on earth'—he said to the paralysed man—'Get up, I tell you! Lift your bedding and go home!' ₂₅On the spot the man got up in front of them all, lifted the mattress on which he had been lying, and went away home, praising God. ₂₆They were absolutely astonished. They kept on praising God; they were filled with awe. 'We have seen things beyond belief today,' they said.

₂₇After that, Jesus went out and saw a tax-collector called Levi sitting in the office where he collected the customs duties. 'Follow me!' he said to him. ₂₈Levi rose from his seat, left everything, and began to be his follower. ₂₉Levi gave a big reception for Jesus in his house, and there was a large crowd of tax-collectors and other guests. ₃₀The Pharisees and the experts in the Law complained to the disciples: 'Why do you eat and drink with tax-collectors and with people with whom no respectable Jew would have anything to do?' ₃₁Jesus answered: 'It is not those who are well who need a doctor, but those who are ill. ₃₂I did not come to bring an invitation to repent to those who are good, but to those who are sinners.'

₃₃They said to him: 'John's disciples fast frequently and carefully observe the prescribed prayers, and so do the disciples of the Pharisees. But your disciples eat and drink when and what they like.' ₃₄'Obviously,' Jesus said to them, 'you cannot expect the bridegroom's closest friends to fast while the bridegroom is with them. ₃₅The time will come when the bridegroom will be taken away from them. When that time comes, they will fast.'

₃₆He used an illustration to speak to them. 'No one,' he said, 'tears a piece from a new coat and uses it to patch an old coat. If he does, he will tear the new coat, and, at the same time, the patch from the new coat will not match the old coat. ₃₇No one puts new fermenting wine into old wineskins which have lost their elasticity. If he does, the new wine will burst the wineskins, and the wine itself will be spilled, and the wineskins will be ruined too. ₃₈Newly made wine must be put into new wineskins. ₃₉No one wants to drink new wine when he has old wine, for he says: "The old is mellow."'

Chapter 6

JESUS was walking through the cornfields on a Sabbath day. His disciples began to pluck the ears of corn, and to rub them in their hands and eat them. 2Some of the Pharisees said: 'Why are you doing what it is not permitted by the Law to do on the Sabbath?' 3'Have you never read,' Jesus answered, 'what David did when he and his friends were hungry? 4Don't you know the story of how he went into the house of God, and took and ate the sacred loaves which are placed in the presence of God, and which only the priests are permitted to eat, and how he gave them to his friends as well? 5The Son of Man's authority,' he said to them, 'extends over the Sabbath.'

6On another Sabbath he went into the synagogue and was teaching there. There was a man there whose right hand was withered. 7The experts in the Law and the Pharisees were watching him closely, to see if he would heal the man on the Sabbath, for they wanted to find something to use as a charge against him. 8Jesus was well aware of what was going on in their minds. He said to the man with the withered hand: 'Get up, and stand where everyone can see you!' The man stood up. 9'I will put a question to you,' Jesus said to them. 'Is it permitted on the Sabbath day to help or to hurt, to save life or to destroy life?' 10His gaze swept round them all. 'Stretch out your hand,' he said to the man. The man did so, and his hand was restored to health. 11They were furious, and they began to discuss with each other what they could do to Jesus.

12At that time Jesus went away to the hillside to pray. He spent the whole night in prayer to God. 13When day came, he summoned his disciples, and from them he chose twelve, whom he called apostles; 14Simon, to whom he gave the name Peter, and his brother Andrew, and James and John, and Philip and Bartholomew, 15and Matthew and Thomas and James, Alphaeus' son, and Simon who was called the Nationalist, 16and Judas, James's son, and Judas Iscariot, who became a traitor.

17He came down with them, and took his stand on a level place. There were with him a huge crowd of his disciples, and a great mob of people from all over Judaea, and from Jerusalem, and from the sea coast of Tyre and Sidon. They had come to listen to him and to have their illnesses cured. 18Those who were troubled by unclean spirits were cured. 19The crowd were all trying to touch him, for power issued from him, and he healed them all.

20Jesus looked up at his disciples and said:

O the bliss of you who are destitute,
for the Kingdom of God belongs to you!
21O the bliss of you who are hungry in this world,
for you will be satisfied to the full!
O the bliss of you who weep in this world,
for you will laugh!
22Yours is this bliss,
when men will hate you,
and when they will shut the door in your face,
when they will heap insults on you,
when they will banish your very name
as an evil thing,
for the sake of the Son of Man.
23Rejoice when that happens,
and thrill with joy.
You will receive a rich reward in heaven,
for their fathers treated the prophets
in exactly the same way.

24But tragic is the fate of you who are rich,
for you have received all the comfort you will ever get.
25Tragic is the fate of you who have eaten your fill in this world,
for you will be hungry.
Tragic is the fate of you who laugh in this world,
for you will mourn and weep.
26Tragic is your fate, when everyone sings your praises,
for their fathers treated the false prophets
in exactly the same way.

27'I say to those of you who are listening to me:
Love your enemies.
Be kind to the people who hate you.
28Bless those who curse you.
Pray for those who abuse you.

29 If anyone strikes you on one cheek,
  offer him the other to strike as well.
If anyone tries to take your shirt from you,
  make no attempt to stop him taking your coat too.
30 If anyone asks you for anything,
  give it to him,
  and don't demand your possessions back
    from anyone who takes them from you.

31 'Treat others as you would wish them to treat you.
32 What credit is it to you,
  if you love the people who love you?
  Even sinners love the people who love them.
33 What credit is it to you,
  if you are kind to the people who are kind to you?
  Even sinners are that.
34 What credit is it to you,
  if you lend to those
  from whom you have every hope of getting your money back?
  Even sinners lend to sinners,
  when they are sure they will get it back.
35 You must love your enemies;
  you must be kind to them;
  you must lend without hope of getting anything back.
If you do that,
  you will receive a rich reward,
  and you will be like the Most High,
    for he is kind to the ungrateful and to the mean.
36 You must show yourself merciful,
  as your Father is merciful.

37 'Do not make a habit of judging other people,
  and you will not be judged yourselves.
Do not make a habit of condemning other people,
  and you will not be condemned yourselves.
Forgive, and you will be forgiven.
38 Be generous, and you will find others generous to you.
Good measure, close-packed, and shaken down,
  brimming over, will be poured into your lap.
You will get in exactly the same proportion
                    as you give.'

³⁹Jesus went on to use an illustration. 'Surely,' he said, 'one blind man cannot lead another blind man. If he tries to, both of them are sure to fall into a hole in the road.'

⁴⁰'A scholar is not superior to his teacher;
every well-equipped scholar will be like his teacher.

⁴¹'Why do you see the speck of dust
   in your brother's eye,
and never notice the plank
   that is in your own eye?
⁴²How can you say to your fellow man,
   "Brother, let me remove the speck of dust that is in your eye,"
when you don't see the plank in your own eye?
   Your trouble is that you completely fail
   to practise what you preach.
Begin by removing the plank
   out of your own eye,
and then you will be able to see clearly
   to remove the speck of dust
   in your brother's eye.

⁴³'A fine tree does not produce rotten fruit,
   nor, on the other hand, does a rotten tree produce fine fruit.
⁴⁴You can tell
   what kind of tree any tree is
by its fruit.
You can't gather figs from thorn-bushes,
   and you can't pluck grapes from a bramble-bush.
⁴⁵A good man produces good
   from his heart's good treasure-house.
An evil man produces evil
   from his evil.
A man's words are the overflow
   of the thoughts that are in his heart.

⁴⁶'Why do you call me Lord, Lord
   and not do what I tell you?
⁴⁷I will tell you
what every man who comes to me,
   and who listens to my words,
   and obeys them, is like.

48He is like a man,
who, in building his house,
dug and excavated,
until he laid the foundations on the rock.
Then when a flood arose,
the river swept down on the house,
but it was powerless to shake it,
because it was well and truly built.
49But a man who has listened to me,
and who has not obeyed my words,
is like a man
who built a house on earth,
without any foundations.
The river swept down upon it,
and it collapsed at once,
and the ruin of that house was complete.'

Chapter 7

WHEN Jesus had finished telling the people what he wanted them to hear, he went to Capernaum. 2There was a centurion there whose slave was so ill that there was no hope of his recovery. This slave meant a great deal to him. 3He heard about Jesus, and sent a party of Jewish elders to him, with a request that Jesus should come and save his slave's life. 4They came to Jesus with an urgent appeal. 'He deserves to have you do this for him,' they said, 5'for he loves our nation, and it was he who built our synagogue for us.' 6Jesus started out with them, but, when he was not far from the house, the centurion sent some friends with a message to him. 'Don't trouble yourself, sir,' he said. 'I am not fit to have you come into my house. 7That is why I did not even think myself fit to approach you personally. All I ask you to do is to say the word, and so to answer my prayer that my servant should be cured. 8I know what it is to be under authority, and I have soldiers under my command. I am used to saying to one, "Go!" and he goes, and to another, "Come here!" and he comes, and to my slave, "Do this!" and he does it.' 9Jesus was astonished to hear this. He turned to the crowd which was following him. 'I tell you,' he said, 'not even in Israel have I met a faith like this.'

10When those who had been sent returned to the house, they found the slave in perfect health.

11Soon afterwards Jesus went into a town called Nain. He was accompanied by his disciples and a large crowd of people. 12When he was near the town gate, a dead man was being carried out for burial. He had been his mother's only son, and she was a widow. A great crowd of the townspeople were with her. 13The Lord was heart-sorry for her when he saw her. 'Stop crying,' he said to her. 14Then he stepped forward, and put his hand on the coffin, and the bearers halted. 'Young man,' he said, 'I tell you, Rise up!' 15The dead man sat up and began to talk, and Jesus gave him to his mother. 16They were all awestruck and praised God. 'A great prophet has emerged among us,' they said. 'God has come in kindness to his people!' 17The story of what Jesus had done spread all over Judaea and all over the surrounding countryside.

18John's disciples brought him news about all that was going on. 19John summoned two of his disciples and sent them to the Lord. 'Are you the One who is to come,' he said, 'or are we to go on waiting and hoping for someone else?' 20When the men reached Jesus, they said: 'John the Baptizer has sent us to ask, "Are you the One who is to come, or are we to go on waiting and hoping for someone else?"' 21At that time Jesus cured many who were ill and suffering and possessed by evil spirits, and he gave the gift of sight to many who were blind. 22'Go!' he said, 'and tell John the story of all that you have seen and heard. Blind men are seeing again; lame men are walking; lepers are being cleansed; deaf men are hearing; dead men are being raised to life; poor men are hearing the good news. 23And happy is the man who does not find himself antagonized by me!'

24When John's messengers had gone away, Jesus spoke to the crowds about John. 'What did you go out to the desert to see?' he said. 'Was it to see what you can see any day there—the long grass swaying in the wind? 25If it was not that, what did you go out to see? Was it to see a man clothed in dainty and delicate clothes? Those who are magnificently dressed, and who live in luxury, are in royal palaces. 26If it was not that, what did you go out to see? Was it a prophet? Yes, indeed it was, I tell you, and more than a prophet. 27This is the man of whom scripture says:

"Look! I am sending my messenger ahead of you,
    and he will go on in advance to prepare your road for you."

28I tell you that among mortal men no greater figure than John has ever emerged in history. All the same, the least in the Kingdom of God is greater than he.' 29All the people who heard this, and especially the tax-collectors, praised God for his goodness, for they had been baptized by John; 30but the Pharisees and legal experts had frustrated God's purposes for themselves, because they refused to be baptized by John.

31Then Jesus went on: 'In view of all this, with what can I compare the people of today? What are they like? 32They are like children sitting in the market-place, calling to each other:

> "When we played you a happy tune,
>   you did not dance;
> when we wailed you a sad lament,
>   you did not weep."

33For John the Baptizer came living the life of an ascetic, and you say: "He is demon-possessed." 34The Son of Man came enjoying life like a normal person, and you say: "A glutton and a drunkard! The friend of renegade tax-collectors and people with whom no respectable Jew would have anything to do." 35And yet wisdom is vindicated by all her children.'

36One of the Pharisees asked Jesus to have a meal with him. Jesus went into the Pharisee's house and took his place at table. 37There was a woman in the town who was a notoriously bad character. When she heard that Jesus was a guest at a meal in the Pharisee's house, she took an alabaster phial of perfumed oil, 38and, as Jesus reclined on his couch, she stood behind him at his feet. She began to let her tears pour down on his feet, and she wiped them with her hair, and she kissed his feet, and she poured the perfumed oil over them. 39The Pharisee who had invited Jesus to the meal saw this. 'If this fellow was really a prophet,' he said to himself, 'he would have known who and what this woman who is touching him is, for she is a notoriously bad character.' 40'Simon,' Jesus said, 'I would like to say something to you.' 'Go ahead and say it, Teacher,' Simon answered. Jesus said: 41'There was a creditor who had two people in debt to him. One owed him twenty-five pounds, the other owed him two pounds ten shillings. 42When they were unable to settle the debt, he let both of them off without paying anything. Which of them will love him more?' 43'I suppose,' Simon answered, 'the one he let off the greater debt.' 'Your conclusion is correct,' Jesus said. 44Then Jesus turned to the woman. 'You see this woman?' he said to Simon. 'When I came into your house, you did not give me any water to wash the dust off my feet. This woman has drenched my feet with her tears, and has wiped them with her hair. 45You did not give me any kiss of welcome. Since I came in, she has not stopped kissing my feet. 46You did not anoint my head with oil. She has anointed my feet with perfume. 47This is why I tell you that, although she has sinned greatly, her sins are forgiven, because she loved greatly. He who is forgiven little loves little.' 48He said to her: 'Your sins are forgiven.' 49'Who is this who forgives even sins?' his fellow-guests said to themselves. 50Jesus said to the woman: 'Your faith has saved you. Go, and God bless you!'

Chapter 8

AFTER this Jesus went through one town and village after another, preaching, and spreading the Good News of the Kingdom of God. The Twelve accompanied him, 2and so did a group of women, who had been cured of evil spirits and of illnesses. There was Mary, known as Mary from Magdala. Seven demons had come out of her. 3There was Joanna, the wife of Chuza, one of Herod's financial secretaries. There was Susanna, and there were many others, who used their private means to provide for the needs of Jesus and his comrades.

4A great crowd was gathering, and from one town after another people were coming to him. He used a parable to speak to them.

5'A sower,' he said, 'went out to sow his seed. As he sowed, some seed fell by the side of the road, and it was trampled on, and the birds of the sky snapped it up. 6Some seed fell on the rock in pockets of soil, and it withered as soon as it grew, for it had no moisture. 7Some seed fell in the middle of thorn-bushes, and the bushes, as they grew along with it, choked the life out of it. 8Some seed fell on good ground, and grew, and produced a crop a hundred times more than was sown. If a man has ears to hear,' Jesus went on to say, 'let him hear.'

9Jesus' disciples asked him what the parable meant. 10'You,' he said, 'have received the privilege of knowing the secrets of the Kingdom of God, secrets which only a disciple can understand. But to other people the truth is spoken in parables, so that, although they see, they may not see, and, although they hear, they may not understand.

11'This is the meaning of the parable. The seed is the word of God. 12The picture of the seed which fell on the side of the road represents those who hear, and then the devil comes and snatches the word out of their hearts to stop them from believing and being saved. 13The picture of the seed which fell on the rock represents those who enthusiastically welcome the word as soon as they hear it; but these have no root. Their faith is at the mercy of the moment; and, when they are involved in any situation which puts their faith to the test, they quit. 14The picture of the seed which fell among the thorn-bushes represents those who have heard the word, but who go away and allow their lives to be all choked up with worries and wealth and the pleasures of life. The seed never gets a chance to mature. 15The picture of the seed which fell into the good ground represents those who hear the word with a fine and good heart, and who keep fast hold of it, and bear fruit through thick and thin.'

16'No one lights a lamp, and then hides it under a bowl or puts it below the bed. He puts it on a lampstand, so that anyone who comes in can see its light.

17'There is nothing hidden which will not be brought out into the open, and there is nothing secret which will not be known and come out into the open.

18'Be careful how you listen, for to the man who already has, more will be given; but even what he thinks he has will be taken away from the man who has not.'

19Jesus' mother and brothers arrived, but they were unable to get to him because of the crowd. 20A message was brought to him: 'Your mother and your brothers are waiting outside, and they want to see you.' 21'My mother and my brothers,' he answered, 'are those who listen to God's word and obey it.'

22One day Jesus embarked on a boat with his disciples. 'Let us cross over to the other side of the lake,' he said to them. 23So they set sail. While they were sailing, Jesus fell asleep. A violent squall of wind swept down on the lake, and they were in serious danger of being swamped. 24They came and woke Jesus. 'Master, Master,' they said, 'we're drowning.' Jesus awoke and reprimanded the wind and the boiling surf. They ceased their raging and there was a calm. 25'Where is your faith?' he said to them. They were awestruck and astonished. 'Who can this be?' they said to each other. 'For he gives his orders to the winds and the water, and they obey him.'

26They put in at the Gergesene district, which is opposite Galilee. 27When Jesus stepped out of the boat on to the land, a man from the town who had a demon in him met him. For a long time he had gone naked, and had stayed, not in a house, but among the tombs. 28When he saw Jesus, he shrieked, and flung himself down at his feet. 'What business have you with me, Jesus, Son of the Most High God?' he shouted at the top of his voice. 'Please don't torture me.' 29Jesus had ordered the unclean spirit to come out of the man. Many a time the unclean spirit had seized him, and, although he had been bound with chains and fetters, and had been kept under guard, he had often snapped the bonds apart, and had been driven by the demon into the desert. 30'What is your name?' Jesus asked him. 'A regiment,' he said, for many demons had got into him. 31The demons pleaded with Jesus not to order them into the Abyss.

32A herd of pigs was grazing there on the hillside. They pleaded with him to allow them to go into them. He allowed them to do as they asked. 33The demons came out of the man and went into the pigs, and the whole herd stampeded down the cliff into the lake and were drowned. 34When the herdsmen saw what had happened, they fled and told the whole story both in the town and all over the countryside. 35The people came out to see what had actually happened. They came to Jesus, and found the man out of whom the demons had gone sitting at Jesus' feet, fully clothed and in his senses, and they were terrified. 36Those who had seen what had happened told them the story of how the demon-possessed man had been cured. 37The whole population of the surrounding district of the Gergesenes asked Jesus to go away, for they were gripped with a great fear. Jesus got on board the boat and returned to the other side. 38The man out of whom the demons had gone pleaded to be allowed to stay with him, but Jesus sent him away. 39'Go back home,' he said, 'and tell the story of all that God has done for you.' So he went away and all over the town he proclaimed all that Jesus had done for him.

40When Jesus returned, the crowd welcomed him, for they were all waiting eagerly for him.

41A man called Jairus, who was president of the synagogue, came and threw himself at Jesus' feet. He pleaded with Jesus to come to his house, 42because he had an only daughter of about twelve years of age, and she was dying. When they were on the way, the crowds were crushing in on Jesus.

43There was a woman who had a haemorrhage for twelve years.* Her illness was such that she had never been able to find anyone who could cure her. 44She came up behind Jesus and touched the tassel of his cloak, and on the spot the flow of blood was stopped. 45'Who touched me?' Jesus said. Everyone denied that they had done so. 'Master,' Peter said, 'the crowd are all around you, jostling in on you.' 46'Someone did touch me,' Jesus said, 'for I know that power has gone out of me.' 47When the woman saw that there was no hope of concealment, she came and flung herself trembling at Jesus' feet, and in front of everyone told him the reason why she had touched him and how then and there she had been cured. 48'Daughter,' Jesus said to her, 'your faith has cured you. Go, and God bless you.'

49While he was still speaking, a man arrived from the president's house. 'Your daughter is dead,' he said. 'Don't trouble the teacher any more.' 50When Jesus heard this, he said: 'Don't be afraid! Only trust, and she will be cured!' 51When he came to the house, he did not allow anyone to go in with him except Peter and John and James, and the child's father and mother. 52They were all weeping and wailing for her. 'Stop this crying!' Jesus said. 'She is not dead. She is sleeping.' 53They laughed at him, for they knew that she had died. 54Jesus gripped her hand. 'Child,' he said, 'get up!' 55Her breath came back and then and there she stood up. Jesus ordered that she should be given something to eat. 56Her parents were astonished, but Jesus ordered them not to tell anyone what had happened.

Chapter 9

JESUS called together the Twelve, and gave them power and authority over all demons, and to cure diseases. 2He sent them out to proclaim the Kingdom of God, and to heal.

3'Take nothing for the road,' he said to them. 'Don't take a staff or a beggar's knapsack. Don't take any bread or money. Don't have two shirts. 4Stay in whatever house you first go into until you leave the place. 5If there are any who refuse to welcome you, as you leave

*See Notes on pp. 575-6

that town, shake the last speck of its dust from your feet, as if you were leaving a heathen town, to make them see the seriousness of what they have done.'

6So they went out and made a tour of the villages, everywhere spreading the Good News and carrying on their healing work.

7When Herod the tetrarch heard about what was going on, he did not know what to make of it, because such varying verdicts on Jesus were circulating. By some it was said that John had come back to life. 8Others held that Elijah had appeared, others that one of the ancient prophets had come back to life. 9'I beheaded John,' Herod said. 'Who can this be about whom such reports are circulating?' So he made efforts to meet Jesus.

10When the disciples returned, they told Jesus the story of all that they had done. He withdrew to a town called Bethsaida to be alone, and he took them with him. 11The crowds discovered this and followed him. He welcomed them, and spoke to them about the Kingdom of God, and cured those who needed healing.

12When the day was drawing to a close, the Twelve came to him. 'Send the crowd away,' they said. 'Tell them to go to the surrounding villages and farms to find lodgings and food, for this is a desert place that we are in.' 13'You must give them something to eat,' he said. They said: 'All we have is five loaves and two fishes, unless—and you can't mean that—we are to go and buy food for all these people.' 14For there were about five thousand men there. 'Make them sit down in groups of fifty,' he said to his disciples. 15They did so, and made them all sit down. 16Jesus took the five loaves and the two fishes; he looked up to heaven and said the blessing. Then he broke them into pieces, and gave them to the disciples to serve to the crowd. 17They all ate until they could eat no more; and when what was left over was collected, it amounted to twelve basketfuls of broken pieces.

18When Jesus was alone in prayer, and when his disciples were with him, he put a question to them. 'Who am I popularly supposed to be?' he said. 19'John the Baptizer,' they answered. 'But some say that you are Elijah, others that you are one of the ancient prophets come back to life.' 20He said to them: 'And you—who do you say that I am?' Peter answered: 'God's Messiah.' 21He gave them strict orders to tell this to no one. 22'The Son of Man,' he said, 'must undergo many sufferings. He must be rejected by the elders and chief priests and experts in the Law. He must be killed, and raised to life again on the third day.'

23He said to them all: 'If anyone wishes to walk in my steps, he must once and for all say No to himself, and he must decide to take up his cross daily, and he must keep on following me. 24Anyone who wishes to keep his life safe will lose it; but any man who is prepared to lose his life for my sake will save it. 25What good will it do a man to gain the whole world, if he destroys himself and has to forfeit his life? 26If a man is ashamed of me and of my words, the Son of Man will be ashamed of him, when he comes with the glory of his Father and of the holy angels. 27I tell you truly, there are some of those who are standing here who will not experience death until they see the Kingdom of God.'

28About a week after this conversation Jesus took with him Peter and James and John, and climbed the mountain to pray. 29While he was praying, the appearance of his face changed, and his clothes became as white as a lightning flash. 30Two men came and talked with him. They were Moses and Elijah. 31They appeared in a vision of glory, and they talked with Jesus about the way in which his life was destined to end in Jerusalem. 32Peter and his companions were overcome with sleep, but, when they were fully awake, they saw the glory of Jesus, and the two men standing with him. 33As the two men were leaving Jesus, Peter said to him: 'Master, it is a wonderful thing for us to be here. Let us make three shelters, one for you, and one for Moses, and one for Elijah.' He did not really know what he was saying. 34While he was speaking, a cloud enveloped them. They were awestruck as they entered the cloud. 35Out of the cloud a voice said: 'This is my Son, the Chosen One! Listen to him!' 36After the voice had spoken, they saw that there was no one with Jesus. At that time they said nothing about this, and did not tell anyone about what they had seen.

37Next day, when they had come down from the mountain, a great crowd came to meet Jesus. 38'Teacher,' a man in the crowd shouted, 'please look at my son. He is my only son, 39and a spirit seizes him, and all of a sudden the spirit shrieks and convulses him, and he foams at the mouth. The spirit hardly ever leaves him, and it is breaking the boy up. 40I asked your disciples to eject the spirit from him, but they were quite unable to do so.' 41'This modern generation has so little faith!' Jesus answered. 'There is a fatal perversity about it! How long must I be with you and endure you? Bring your son here!' 42When the boy was coming to Jesus, the spirit tore him and convulsed him. Jesus spoke to the unclean spirit with stern authority, and cured the boy, and gave him back to his father. 43They were all astonished at the greatness of God's power.

While they were still lost in wonder at what he was doing, Jesus said to his disciples: 44'I want what I am going to say to you really to sink into your minds. The Son of Man is going to be handed over into the power of men.' 45They could not understand what he meant when he spoke like this. His meaning was hidden from them to keep them from seeing it, and they were afraid to ask him what he meant by saying this.

46A debate started among the disciples about which of them was greatest. 47Jesus was well aware of what was going on in their minds. He picked up a little child, and made him stand beside him. 48He said to them: 'To welcome this little child in my name is to welcome me; and to welcome me is to welcome him who sent me. It is the man who thinks himself least of all who is truly great.'

49'Master,' John said, 'we saw a man ejecting demons by the use of your name. So we tried to stop him, because he is not a follower of yours like us.' 50'Don't try to stop him,' Jesus said. 'The man who is not your opponent is your supporter.'

51When the time for him to be taken back to heaven was approaching, Jesus resolutely set out on the journey to Jerusalem. 52He sent messengers on ahead. They set out and went into a Samaritan village with the intention of preparing for Jesus' arrival. 53But the villagers refused to give him any hospitality, because he was clearly on his way to Jerusalem. 54When his disciples James and John saw this, they said: 'Master, would you like us to call down fire from heaven and wipe them out?' 55Jesus turned and sternly reprimanded them.* 56So they continued their journey to another village.

57As they were going along the road, a man said to Jesus: 'I will follow you wherever you go.' 58Jesus said to him: 'The foxes have lairs, and the birds of the sky have nests, but the Son of Man has

*See Notes on pp. 575-6

nowhere to lay his head.' 59Jesus said to another man: 'Follow me!' He said: 'Let me go and bury my father first.' 60Jesus said: 'Let the dead bury their dead. You must go and spread the news of the Kingdom of God.' 61Another man said: 'Sir, I will follow you, but let me say good-bye to my family first.' 62Jesus said to him: 'No one who tries to plough looking backwards is of any use to the Kingdom of God.'

Chapter 10

THE next thing Jesus did was to appoint seventy others, and to send them out ahead in twos, into every town and place into which he himself planned to go. 2'The harvest is great,' he said to them, 'but there are few workers. You must pray to the Lord of the harvest to send out workers to gather in his harvest.

3'On your way! I am sending you out like lambs among wolves. 4Don't take a purse, or a beggar's knapsack, or sandals. Don't stop to greet anyone on the road. 5As soon as you go into a house say to it: "God bless this household." 6If a man whom God has blessed lives there, then your blessing will rest on it; but if not, your blessing will return to you. 7Stay in the same house, sharing the food and the drink of the family, for the workman deserves his wage. Don't keep moving your lodging from one house to another. 8In any town you enter, and in any home which gives you hospitality, eat what is put before you. 9Heal the sick in it, and tell them: "God's Kingdom is almost here." 10If you go into any town, and they refuse to welcome you, go out into its streets and say: 11"We wipe off even the dust of your town that sticks to our feet, as if this was a heathen town, as a protest against you. All the same, we want you to realize that God's Kingdom is almost here." 12On the great day, I tell you, Sodom and Gomorrah will get off more lightly than that town.'

13'Tragic will be your fate, Chorazin! Tragic will be your fate, Bethsaida! If the miracles which have been done in you had been done in Tyre and Sidon, they would long ago have sat in penitence in sackcloth and ashes. 14But Tyre and Sidon will get off more lightly at the judgment than you. 15As for you, Capernaum—do you think that you are going to be exalted as high as heaven? You will go down to the depths of hell.'

16'To listen to you is to listen to me; to reject you is to reject me; to reject me is to reject him who sent me.'

17The seventy returned rejoicing. 'Lord,' they said, 'even the demons obey us at your name.' 18He said to them: 'I saw Satan fall like a lightning flash from heaven. 19I have given you power to trample on snakes and scorpions and to tread down all the power of the Enemy, and nothing will harm you. 20All the same, do not rejoice because the spirits obey you; rejoice because your names are written in heaven.'

21At that time the Holy Spirit made Jesus' heart thrill with joy. 'I thank you, Father, Lord of heaven and earth,' he said, 'that you have hidden these things from the wise and the clever and that you have revealed them to those who are as simple as little children. Yes, indeed, Father, I thank you that this is what you chose to do. 22All things have been entrusted to me by my Father, and no one but the Father knows who the Son is; and no one knows who the Father is except the Son, and those to whom the Son chooses to make him known.'

23When they were alone, Jesus turned to his disciples. 'Happy are the eyes which have seen what you are seeing,' he said. 24'For I tell you that many a prophet and many a king wished to see the events that you are seeing, and did not see them, and wished to hear the words that you are hearing, and did not hear them.'

25A legal expert rose to put a test question to Jesus. 'Teacher,' he said, 'what must I do to possess the eternal life that God has promised?' 26'What does the Law prescribe?' Jesus said to him. 'What do you read there?' 27He answered: 'You must love the Lord your God with your whole heart and your whole soul and your whole strength and your whole mind, and, you must love your neighbour as yourself.' 28'That is the right answer,' Jesus said to him. 'You will have life, if you do this.'

29The legal expert wished to show just how expert he was. 'Yes,' he said to Jesus, 'but who is my neighbour?' 30Jesus took up his question. 'There was a man,' he said, 'who was on his way down from Jerusalem to Jericho, when he fell into the hands of brigands. They stripped him naked, and beat him up, and went away and left him more dead than alive. 31It so happened that a priest was coming down the road. When the priest saw him, he passed by on the opposite side of the road. 32In the same way, a Levite arrived at the spot. He went and looked at the man, and then passed by on the opposite side of the road. 33A Samaritan, who was on the road, came to where the man was lying. He was heart-sorry when he saw the state he was in. 34He went up to him, and poured oil and wine on his wounds, and bandaged them. Then he put the man on his beast, and took him to an inn, and looked after him. 35Next morning he took out two silver coins and gave them to the inn-keeper. "Look after him," he said, "and, if you incur any additional expense, I'll square it up with you on my way back." 36Which of these three would you say was a neighbour to the man who fell into the hands of the brigands?' 37'The man who took pity on him,' he said. Jesus said to him: 'You too must go and do the same.'

38In the course of their journey Jesus went into a village. A woman called Martha welcomed him into her house. 39She had a sister called Mary, and Mary sat at the Lord's feet and listened to his talk. 40Martha was so worried about getting a meal ready for them that she was quite distracted. 'Master,' she came up and said, 'don't you care that my sister has left me to attend to everything alone? Tell her to give me a hand.' 41'Martha, Martha,' the Lord answered, 'you are worried and harassed about putting on a meal with a whole lot of courses. 42One will do perfectly well. Mary has chosen the best dish, and it is not going to be taken away from her.'

Chapter 11

JESUS was praying in a certain place, and, when he had finished, one of his disciples said to him: 'Master, teach us a prayer, as John taught his disciples.' 2He said to them: 'When you pray, you must say:

"Father,
     May your name be held in reverence.
     May your Kingdom come.
     3Give us each day bread for the coming day.
     4And forgive us our sins, as we too forgive
          everyone who fails in his duty to us.
     And do not submit us to any ordeal of testing."

5'Suppose one of you has a friend,' he said to them, 'and suppose the friend comes to him in the middle of the night, and says: "Friend, lend me three loaves, 6because a friend of mine on a journey has arrived at my house, and I haven't a scrap of food in the house to give him." 7And suppose the man in the house answers: "Don't bother me! The door is locked for the night, and my children are in bed with me. I can't get up and give you anything." 8I tell you, if he will not get up and give him what he needs for friendship's sake, he will get up and give him all he needs because of his bare-faced persistence.

9I tell you:

> Keep on asking,
>   and you will get;
> keep on seeking,
>   and you will find;
> keep on knocking,
>   and the door will be opened for you.
> 10For everyone who keeps on asking
>   gets what he asks for;
> he who keeps on seeking
>   finds;
> if a man keeps on knocking
>   the door will be opened.
> 11If any of you is a father,
> and his son asks for a fish,
>   is he likely to give him a snake?
> 12Or, if he asks for an egg,
>   is he likely to give him a scorpion?
> 13If, then, although you are naturally evil and ungenerous,
>   you know how to give good gifts to your children,
> how much more will the heavenly Father
>   give the Holy Spirit to those who ask him?'

14Jesus was ejecting a demon which made a man dumb. When the demon came out of him, the dumb man spoke, and the crowds were amazed. 15Some of them said: 'It is with the help of Beelzebul, the prince of demons, that he ejects the demons.' 16Others, with the idea of testing him, demanded that he should produce some visible divine action from heaven. 17He knew what was going on in their minds. So he said to them: 'Any kingdom which is split against itself is on the way to being laid waste, and the houses in it collapse on top of each other. 18If Satan is split against himself, how can his kingdom survive?

And that is the situation, if you say that I eject demons with the help of Beelzebul. 19If I eject demons with the help of Beelzebul, by whose help do your sons eject them? Ask them what they think of this argument of yours. 20But, if it is with the finger of God that I eject demons, then the Kingdom of God has ‑eached you here and now.

21'When a strong man guards his homestead fully armed, his property remains secure and undisturbed. 2But, when a still stronger man attacks and overcomes him, the stronger man takes away the armour on which he relied, and shares out the spoils

23'If a man is not my ally, he is my enemy, and, if a man is not helping my work, he is undoing it.'

24'When an unclean spirit goes out of a man, it roams through waterless places looking for rest, and when it finds none, it says: "I will go back to the house which used to be mine, and which I left." 25So it comes, and finds it swept and in perfect order. 26Then it goes and brings back along with it seven other spirits worse than itself, and they go and make their home there. So the last state of that man becomes worse than the first.'

27While he was saying this, a woman shouted to him from the crowd: 'Happy is the womb which bore you, and the breasts you sucked.' 28But Jesus said: 'True, but rather, happy are those who listen to the word of God and obey it.'

29When the crowds were coming thronging to him, Jesus said: 'This is an evil generation. The people of today want to see some visible action of God. The only action of God which will be given to them is the action of God which was seen in the case of Jonah. 30For, as Jonah was an act of God to the people of Nineveh, so the Son of Man will be an act of God to this generation.

31'When the day of judgment comes, the Queen of the South will rise from the dead at the same time as the people of this generation, and she will condemn them, for she came from the ends of the earth to listen to the wisdom of Solomon, and there is a greater event than Solomon here. 32When the day of judgment comes, the people of Nineveh will rise again at the same time as the people of this generation, and they will condemn them, because Nineveh repented at the preaching of Jonah, and a greater event than Jonah is here.'

33'No one lights a lamp, and puts it into a cellar or under a bowl;

he puts it on the lampstand, so that those who come into the house may see the light.

34'Your eye is the body's lamp. When your eye is sound and generous, the whole body is full of light. When it is diseased and grudging, the whole body is full of darkness. 35Since that is so, you must be on the watch in case the light in you turns to darkness. 36If then your whole body is filled with light, without a particle of darkness, it will be all light, as when a lamp gives you light with its rays.'

37While he was speaking a Pharisee asked him to a meal with him. Jesus went into the house, and took his place at table. 38The Pharisee was very surprised to see that Jesus did not go through the prescribed ritual ceremonial washings before the meal. 39The Lord said to him: 'The fact is that you Pharisees carefully clean the outside of the cup and plate, but your inner life is full of greed and wickedness. 40This is an utterly senseless proceeding. Surely the same person made the outside and the inside too? 41In point of fact, if you give the food that is inside the dishes as a gift to the poor, then everything will be really clean as far as you are concerned.

42'Tragic will be the fate of you Pharisees! You meticulously set aside for God the tenth part of mint and rue and of every vegetable in your kitchen-garden, while you neglect justice and the love of God. You ought to have kept the second without neglecting the first.

43'Tragic will be the fate of you Pharisees! You love the front seats in the synagogue, and you like to be deferentially greeted as you move through the market-places.

44'Tragic will be your fate! You are like hidden graves which men walk over without realizing what they are walking on.'

45'Teacher,' one of the legal experts said, 'statements like these are an arrogant insult to us.' 46Jesus said: 'Tragic will be the fate of you legal experts too! You lay on men's backs intolerable burdens, and you yourselves do not lift a finger to help them with their burdens.

47'Tragic will be your fate! You erect memorials to the prophets whom your ancestors killed. 48Obviously you agree with the verdicts and approve of the actions of your ancestors, for they did the killing and you do the building of the memorials. 49That is why God in his wisdom said: "I will send prophets and apostles to them, and they will kill some, and they will persecute others." 50God did this in order that this generation might become responsible for the murder of all the prophets since the world was created, 51from the murder of Abel to the murder of Zacharias, who was killed between the altar and the house of God. Yes, indeed, I tell you, this generation will be held responsible for all this.

52'Tragic will be your fate, you legal experts! You have removed the key which unlocks the door of knowledge. You have not gone in yourselves, and you have debarred those who are trying to get in.'

53When he left there, the Pharisees began a bitter campaign against him in which they made repeated attempts to provoke him into giving them answers on many subjects, 54by setting verbal traps for him, with the idea of catching him out in any statement he might make.

Chapter 12

MEANWHILE, when the crowds had gathered in their tens of thousands, and when there were so many people that they were trampling on each other, Jesus said certain things which were meant in the first instance for his disciples. 'Be on your guard,' he said, 'against the evil influence of the Pharisees, which is profession without practice. 2What is veiled must be unveiled, and what is hidden must be made known. 3What you have spoken in the dark will be heard in the full light of day. What you have whispered in the ear in your inner rooms will be broadcast from the housetops.'

4'I tell you, my friends, do not fear those who can kill the body, but who are powerless to do anything further. 5I will warn you whom to fear. Fear the One who has the power first to kill you and then to throw you into hell. Yes, indeed, I tell you, fear him!'

6'Five sparrows are sold for two farthings, aren't they? Yet not one of them is forgotten by God. 7So far from being forgotten, the hairs of your head have all been counted. Don't be afraid. You are more valuable than a whole collection of sparrows.'

8'If anyone publicly acknowledges his loyalty to me in front of his fellow men, I tell you, the Son of Man will do the same for him in front of the angels of God. 9But anyone who disowns me in front of men will be disowned in front of the angels of God.

10'If anyone speaks a word against the Son of Man, he will be forgiven for it, but if anyone insults the Holy Spirit, he will not be forgiven.'

11'When you are put on trial before the synagogues and the governors and the civil authorities, do not worry about how to defend yourselves, or about what to say. 12The Holy Spirit will at the time teach you what you must say.'

13A man in the crowd said to Jesus: 'Teacher, tell my brother to give me my share of the estate which has been left to us.' 14'Man,' said Jesus to him, 'who appointed me a judge or an arbitrator between you and your brother?' 15He said to them: 'Watch carefully not to let any kind of greed get a grip of you. It does not follow that, because a man has a superabundance of possessions, his life is one of the things which belong to him.'

16He used a parable to explain his meaning. 'The ground of a rich man,' he said, 'produced an excellent harvest. 17He began to ask himself: "What am I to do? I have no room to store my crops." 18So he said: "I know what I'll do. I will pull down my barns and I will build bigger ones. I will store up all my corn and my possessions in them. 19And I will tell myself: 'You have enough goods stored up to last for many a year. Sit back and relax! Eat and drink and enjoy yourself!' " 20But God said to him: "Fool! This very night you must hand back your life to God! And then who will get all that you have saved up for the future?" 21This is what happens to the man who amasses worldly wealth, but who in God's sight has no riches at all.'

22'That,' said Jesus, 'is why I tell you,
　Stop worrying about what you are going to eat
　　to keep you alive.
　Stop worrying about the clothes
　　you are going to put on your body.
　23There is more to life than food,
　　and more to the body than clothes.
　24Look at the ravens,
　　and learn from them.
　They do not sow or reap.
　　They have no storehouse or barn.
　Yet God gives them their food.
　　How much more valuable you are than the birds!

25‘Can any of you add half a yard to his height
by worrying about it?
26If you can't do a little thing like that
why worry about the rest of life?
27Look at the wild lilies and learn from them.
They do not spin or weave.
Yet, I tell you, that not even Solomon in all his splendour
was robed like one of these.
28You have so little faith!
If God clothes the wild flowers,
which have one brief day,
and which tomorrow are used
to make a fire to heat an oven,
how much more can you depend on him to clothe you?

29‘Don't spend your life
thinking about nothing
but what you are going to eat and drink.
Don't get into a panic about things like that.
30The people in the world who don't know God
spend their lives thinking about things like that.
Your Father knows that you need these things.
31So far from being like that,
you must make his Kingdom
the object of all your endeavour,
and you will get these other things as well.
32You are only a little flock,
but don't be afraid.
It is your Father's decision
to give you the Kingdom.

33‘Sell your possessions,
and give them away in charity.
Get yourselves purses
which will never wear out,
and a treasure in heaven
which will never be exhausted,
for there no thief can get at it,
and no moth can destroy it.
34Your heart is bound to be
where your treasure is.'

35'Always be ready, stripped for action, with your lamps lit. 36Be like men who are expectantly waiting for their master's return from a wedding banquet, and whose aim it is to open the door to him the instant he arrives and knocks. 37Happy are the servants whom their master will find awake, when he comes. I tell you he will roll up his sleeves for action, and will make them sit down like guests, and will come and serve them himself. 38Happy are they, if he finds them like that, even if he comes just before midnight or in the early hours of the morning.

39'It is obvious that if the householder had known at what hour the thief was going to come, he would not have left his house to be broken into. 40You too must be ready, because the Son of Man is going to come at an hour when you do not expect him.'

41'Master,' Peter said to him, 'is this parable meant for us, or for everyone?' 42The Lord said: 'Suppose there is a dependable and sensible steward, whom his master puts in charge of his staff, with instructions to issue them their rations at the right time. 43That servant is a happy man, if his master, when he comes, finds him engaged on that very task. 44He will certainly put him in charge of all his property. 45But, if the servant says to himself: "It will be a long time before my master comes back," and if he begins to beat the manservants and the maidservants, and to eat and to drink until he is drunk, 46that servant's master will come on a day when he is not expecting him. He does not know at what time the master will arrive. And the master will punish him severely, and will assign to him the fate of the unbelievers.

47'If a servant knows what his master wants him to do, and if he makes no preparations and takes no action to do it, he will be beaten with many strokes of the lash. 48But, if he did not know it, even if he has been guilty of actions which deserve a beating, he will be given few strokes of the lash. Great privilege brings great responsibility. When much is entrusted to a man, still more will be demanded from him.'

49'I have come to set the world ablaze. What is it that I want? Would that it were already kindled!

50'I must be plunged into a flood-tide of suffering, and there can be no relief for me, until I have gone through it to the end.

51'Do you think that the result of my coming will be peace in the world? Far from it. I tell you, the result of my coming will be to bring division. ₅₂From now on in one house there will be five people in a state of division, three against two and two against three. ₅₃They will be divided father against son and son against father, mother against daughter and daughter against mother, mother-in-law against daughter-in-law and daughter-in-law against mother-in-law.'

₅₄He said to the crowds: 'When you see a cloud rising in the west, you immediately say: "Rain is on the way," and the rain comes. ₅₅When you feel the south wind blowing, you say: "It will be as hot as an oven," and it is. ₅₆You play at being religious. You know how to read the weather signs from the appearance of the earth and of the sky. Why can you not read the signs of the present crisis?'

₅₇'Why can you not decide yourselves what justice demands? ₅₈When you are on the way to the magistrate with your opponent, do your best to come to terms with him when you are on the road. If you don't, he may well drag you to the judge. Then the judge may well hand you over to the court officer. The court officer may well throw you into prison. ₅₉I tell you, if that happens, you will not be released until you have paid the last farthing in full.'

Chapter 13

IT was at that time that some of the people who were there told Jesus the story of the Galilaeans whom Pilate had murdered at the very moment when they were offering their sacrifices. ₂Jesus said to them: 'Do you think that these Galilaeans were worse sinners than the rest of the Galilaeans, because this happened to them? ₃Far from it, I tell you. But, if you do not repent, you will all suffer the same fate. ₄Or, do you think that the eighteen men who were killed when the tower of Siloam collapsed on them were worse sinners than the rest of the inhabitants of Jerusalem? ₅Far from it, I tell you. But, if you do not repent, you will all suffer the same fate.'

₆He told them this parable. 'There was a man,' he said, 'who had a fig tree planted in his vineyard. He went to look for fruit on it, and found none. ₇"For the last three years," he said to the vine-dresser, "I have been coming and looking for fruit on it, and I have never found any. Cut it down! Why should it exhaust the fertility of the soil?" ₈"Sir," he answered, "leave it for this one more year, and let me dig round it and put in manure. ₉If it bears fruit next year, well and good. If it doesn't, you can cut it down." '

₁₀Jesus was teaching in one of the synagogues on the Sabbath. ₁₁There was a woman there who for eighteen years had in her an evil spirit which caused a weakness in her body. She was bent double, and she was quite unable to straighten herself. ₁₂When Jesus saw her he called her forward. 'You are released from your weakness,' he said to her. ₁₃He laid his hands on her, and then and there her body was straightened, and she praised God.

₁₄The president of the synagogue was indignant because Jesus had healed on the Sabbath. 'There are six days on which work ought to be done,' he said to the crowd. 'Come and be healed on them, not on the Sabbath.' ₁₅The Lord answered: 'Your religion is no more than a façade of conventional piety! Is there any of you who does not untether his ox or his ass from its stall on the Sabbath, and take it out to give it water? ₁₆This woman is a daughter of Abraham. For eighteen years Satan has fettered her. Is it not right that she should be liberated from her fetters, Sabbath though it is?' ₁₇His opponents were all shamed by what he said. But the crowd all rejoiced at all the glorious things that were done by Jesus.

₁₈'What is the Kingdom of God like,' Jesus said, 'and with what will I compare it? ₁₉It is like a grain of mustard seed, which a man took and planted in his kitchen-garden. It grew till it was as big as a tree, and the birds of the sky nested in its branches.'

₂₀Again he said: 'With what will I compare the Kingdom of God? ₂₁It is like leaven which a woman took and inserted into three pecks of flour, with the result that it was all leavened.'

₂₂Jesus continued his tour of the towns and villages, teaching and making his way to Jerusalem. ₂₃'Sir,' a man said to him, 'is salvation something which will come only to a few?' Jesus said to him: ₂₄'Try your hardest to enter through the narrow door, because many, I tell you, will try to get in, and will not be able to. ₂₅Once the householder has got up and locked the door, you will be left standing outside, knocking at the door. "Sir," you will say, "open the door for us." "I don't know where you come from," he will answer. ₂₆Then you will say: "You shared our meals and you taught in our streets." ₂₇"I don't know where you come from," he will say to you. "Your actions were the actions of bad men. Get out of my sight.' " 28There will be tears and agony there, when you will see Abraham and Isaac and Jacob and all the prophets in the Kingdom of God while you are banished from it. 29They will come from the east and from the west and from the north and from the south, and will take their places as guests in the Kingdom of God. 30And some who are now last will be first, and some who are now first will be last.'

31At that time a group of Pharisees came to Jesus. 'Get away from here,' they said, 'because Herod is out to kill you.' 32'Go and tell that fox,' Jesus said, 'that today and tomorrow I am going to eject demons and continue my work of healing. It will take me three days to complete my work. 33But today and tomorrow and the next day I must keep moving on, because it is unthinkable that a prophet should die anywhere else than in Jerusalem.

34'O Jerusalem, Jerusalem! Killer of the prophets! Stoner of those who were sent to you by God! How often I have wanted to gather your children together as a bird gathers her brood under the shelter of her wings—and you refused! 35God no longer has his home among you! I tell you, you will not see me, until the day comes when you will say: "God bless him who comes in the name of the Lord." '

Chapter 14

ONCE on a Sabbath day Jesus went for a meal to the house of one of the leading Pharisees. They were watching him all the time. 2There was a man with dropsy there right in front of him. 3Jesus said to the legal experts and to the Pharisees: 'Is it permitted to heal on the Sabbath, or not?' 4They chose to remain silent. Jesus took the man and cured him and sent him away. 5Then he said to them: 'If any of you has a donkey or an ox, and it falls into a well, will he not pull it out at once, even although it is the Sabbath day?' 6They could find no answer to this argument.

7Jesus told a parable to the guests, when he saw how they tried to choose the top seats. 8'When you are invited by someone to a wedding banquet,' he said, 'don't take the top place, in case someone of higher standing than you may very well have been invited by your host. 9If that happens, the host who invited both you and the other man is sure to come and say: "Give this man your seat." Then you will be humiliated in front of everyone, and you will have to move to the very foot of the table. 10Instead of that, when you are invited as a guest, go and sit at the very foot of the table. Then when the host arrives, he will say to you: "Friend, move up to a higher place." If that happens, you will be honoured in front of all your fellow-guests. 11For everyone who exalts himself will be humbled, and the man who humbles himself will be exalted.'

12'When you give a lunch or a dinner,' Jesus said to the host, 'don't invite your friends or your brothers or your relations or your wealthy neighbours, for they are entirely likely to give you a return invitation, and you will then receive a return payment for your invitation. 13Instead of that, when you give a reception, invite the poor, the maimed, the lame, the blind. 14That is the way to happiness, for they cannot repay you. You will get your repayment at the resurrection of all good men.'

15When one of the guests heard this, he said: 'Happy is the man who is a guest at the feast in the Kingdom of God.' 16Jesus said to him: 'There was a man who planned to give a big dinner to which he invited a large number of guests. 17When the dinner was due to begin, he sent his servants to tell those who had received invitations: "Come! Everything is now ready." 18They all unanimously began to make excuses. The first said: "I have bought a farm, and I must go and see it. Please consider me excused." 19Another said: "I have bought five pairs of oxen, and I am going to try them out. Please consider me excused." 20Another said: "I have married a wife, and so I cannot possibly come." 21The servant came back and reported this to his master. The master of the house was furious. He said to the servant "Hurry out to the streets and the lanes of the town, and bring in the poor and the maimed and the blind and the lame." 22The servant said: "Your orders have been carried out, and there is still room for more." 23"Go out into the roads and the hedgerows," the master said to the servant, "and bring them in, even if you have to compel them to come. I want my house full. 24I tell you none of the invited guests will so much as taste my dinner." '

25The people flocked in their crowds to Jesus. He turned to them and said: 26'No one who comes to me can be my disciple, unless he hates his father and mother and wife and children and brothers and sisters, yes, and himself too. 27No one can be my disciple unless he carries his cross and follows in my footsteps.

28'If any one of you plans to build a tower, does he not begin by sitting down, and calculating the cost, to see if he has enough money to finish it, 29in case, when he has laid the foundations, and then cannot complete it, everyone who sees the half-finished building makes a fool of him. 30"This man," they will say, "began to build and couldn't finish the job." 31Or, if a king is contemplating going to war with another king, does he not begin by sitting down, and considering whether with ten thousand men he can face an opponent who is launching an attack on him with twenty thousand men? 32If he decides that it cannot be done, long before the other gets to close quarters, he sends an embassy to ask for terms of peace. 33Just so, any of you who does not renounce all his possessions cannot be my disciple.'

34'Salt is good, but if the salt has lost its taste, can anything ever give it its saltness back? 35It is useless either for spreading on the land or for throwing on the manure-heap. All you can do with it is to throw it out. Let him who has ears to hear, hear.'

Chapter 15

ALL the tax-collectors and the people with whom no respectable Jew would have had anything to do kept coming to Jesus to listen to his message. 2But the Pharisees and the experts in the Law complained: 'This man welcomes people with whom no respectable Jew would have anything to do, and actually shares their meals with them.'

3Jesus told them this parable. 4'If any of you,' he said, 'has a hundred sheep, and loses one of them, is he not sure to leave the ninety-nine in the desert, and go and search for the lost one, until he finds it? 5And when he has found it, he lifts it joyfully on to his shoulders, 6and goes home and invites his friends and neighbours to come and share his joy. "Rejoice with me," he says, "I have found my lost sheep." 7I tell you that in the same way there will be more joy in heaven over one sinner who repents than over ninety-nine respectable people who do not need to repent.'

8'Or, if any woman has ten silver coins and loses one, is she not sure to light a lamp and to sweep the house and search carefully until she finds it? 9And, when she has found it, she invites her friends and neighbours to share her joy. "Rejoice with me," she says, "I have found the coin I lost." 10I tell you that in the same way the angels of God rejoice over one sinner who repents.'

11'There was a man,' Jesus said to them, 'who had two sons. 12The younger of them said to his father: "Father, give me the share of your estate which is coming to me anyway." So he divided his whole estate between them. 13Soon after, the younger son realized the whole lot into money, and went off to a distant country. There he squandered his whole fortune in a career of debauchery. 14When he had run through everything he had, a severe famine fell on that land, and he was very nearly destitute. 15So he went and took service with a citizen of that country who sent him out to his farm to herd pigs. 16He longed to satisfy the pangs of his hunger with the carob pods which the pigs were eating, and no one gave him anything.

17'When he came to his senses, he said to himself: "How many of my father's hired servants have more food than they can eat, and here am I, ready to die of starvation! 18I will start out, and go to my father, and I will say to him: 'Father, I have sinned against God and against you. 19I am no longer fit to be regarded as your son. Take me back as one of your hired servants.' " 20So he set out, and went to his father. His father saw him coming a long way away, and he was heart-sorry for him. He came running, and threw his arms round his neck, and kissed him. 21The son said to him: "Father, I have sinned against God and against you. I am no longer fit to be regarded as your son." 22But his father said to the servants: "Quick! Bring out the best robe and dress him in it. Give him a ring to wear on his finger, and shoes for his feet. 23Bring the specially fattened calf and kill it. Let us eat and celebrate, 24for this son of mine was dead and has come to life again; he was lost and has been found." So they began to celebrate.

25'His elder son was out on the farm. When he came near the house on his way home, he heard the sound of music and dancing. 26He called one of the servants, and asked what was going on. 27The servant said: "Your brother has arrived, and your father has had the specially fattened calf killed, because he got him back again safe and sound." 28He was furious and refused to go in. His father came and pleaded with him to come in. 29"I have worked like a slave for you for so many years," he said to his father, "and I never disobeyed any order you gave me, and to me you never gave so much as a kid to celebrate with my friends. ₃₀But when this son of yours, who squandered your fortune with prostitutes, arrives, you have the specially fattened calf killed for him." ₃₁"Son," his father said to him, "you are always with me. All that is mine is yours. ₃₂ But we had to celebrate and rejoice, because your brother was dead and has come to life again; he was lost and has been found." '

Chapter 16

'THERE was a wealthy man,' Jesus said to his disciples, 'who employed a manager to take charge of his whole estate. Allegations were made to him that this man was mismanaging his property. So he sent for him. ₂"What's this story I'm hearing about you?" he said. "I want to see your books at once, for you're finished as my manager." ₃The manager said to himself: "What am I going to do now that my employer is going to dismiss me from my job? I haven't the strength to dig, and I haven't the nerve to beg. ₄I know what I'll do to make sure that, when I leave my present job, I'll never lack for a welcome in other people's houses." ₅So one by one he invited those who were in debt to his employer to come and see him. "How much do you owe my employer?" he asked the first one. ₆"A thousand gallons of olive oil," he said. "Here's your bill," the manager said. "Sit down at once, and alter the figure to five hundred." ₇"How much do you owe?" he went on to say to another. "A thousand bushels of wheat," he said. "Here's your bill," he said. "Alter the figure to eight hundred." ₈His employer praised the dishonest manager, because he had acted shrewdly, for, when it comes to practical business with their contemporaries, worldly men are shrewder than unworldly men. ₉My advice to you is, use your money, however dishonestly it may have been acquired, to get yourselves friends, so that, when money is no more, you may find a good home in eternity.

₁₀'The man who is reliable when very little is involved is just as reliable when a great deal is involved; and when a man is dishonest when very little is involved, he will be just as dishonest when a great deal is involved.

₁₁'If you have not shown yourself reliable in this world's ill-gotten wealth, who will trust you with the real wealth? ₁₂And, if you have not shown yourself reliable in dealing with someone else's wealth, who will give you what is your own?'

13'No servant can be a slave to two owners, for he will either hate the one and love the other, or he will be devoted to one and despise the other. You cannot be the servant of the God of heaven and of the god of this world's wealth.'

14The Pharisees were fond of money, and, when they heard all this, they smiled superciliously. 15'You are the kind of people,' Jesus said to them, 'who do your best to acquire a human reputation for goodness, but God knows what you are really like, for there is nothing more loathsome to God than human pride.'

16'The Law and the Prophets were the supreme revelation up to the time of John. Then the Good News of the Kingdom of God began to be proclaimed, and everyone tries to storm his way into it.'

17'Heaven and earth will cease to be before the smallest part of one letter of the Law will lose its authority.'

18'If any man divorces his wife and marries another woman, he commits adultery; and, if anyone marries a woman who has been divorced from her husband, he commits adultery.'

19'There was a wealthy man who dressed in the most expensive clothes made of the finest linen dyed with costly purple dye, and whose everyday meals were lavish banquets. 20And there was a poor man called Lazarus who was left lying at the gate of the rich man's house. Lazarus was a mass of ulcerous sores, 21and he longed to satisfy his hunger with the scraps which were thrown away from the rich man's table. He was so helpless that the dogs came and licked his sores.

22'The poor man died, and the angels carried him away to the arms of Abraham. The rich man also died and was buried. 23He was in Hades and he was in torment. He looked up, and away in the distance he saw Abraham with Lazarus in his arms. 24"Father Abraham," he shouted, "take pity on me, and send Lazarus to dip the tip of his finger in water to cool my tongue, for I am in anguish in this flame." 25"Son," Abraham said, "you must remember that you received your full share of good things during your lifetime, just as Lazarus did of hardships in his. Now the tables are turned, and he is in comfort here and you are in anguish. 26Besides all this, a great gulf has been fixed between us and you, so that those who wish to cross from here to you cannot do so, nor can anyone pass from there to us." ₂₇"Well, then, father," he said, "I have five brothers. ₂₈Please send him to my father's house to warn them of the truth, and to make sure that they do not come to this place of torture as I have done." ₂₉"They have Moses and the prophets," Abraham answered. "Let them listen to them." ₃₀"No, father Abraham," he said, "they will not do that, but, if someone comes to them from the dead, they will repent." ₃₁"If they refuse to listen to Moses and the prophets," Abraham said, "they will not be convinced, even if someone should rise from the dead." '

Chapter 17

JESUS said to his disciples: 'It is inevitable that things which make men sin should come, but tragic is the fate of the man who is responsible for their coming. ₂It would be better for him to have a millstone hung round his neck, and to be hurled into the sea than to be responsible for anything which causes one of these little ones to sin.'

₃'Watch what you are doing! If your fellow man wrongs you, reprimand him, and, if he shows that he is sorry, forgive him. ₄If he wrongs you seven times in one day, and if seven times he turns to you and says that he is sorry for what he did, you must forgive him.'

₅The apostles said to the Lord: 'Give us more faith.' ₆The Lord said to them: 'If you have faith as big as a mustard seed, you would say to this sycamore tree: "Be torn up by the roots and be planted in the sea," and it would obey you.'

₇'If any of you has a servant who is a ploughman or a shepherd, is he likely to say to him when he comes in from the fields: "Come along at once, and sit down at table"? ₈Not likely! What he will say is: "Get ready my dinner. Hitch up your robe, and attend to me while I eat and drink. You can eat and drink when I have finished." ₉Surely he does not thank his servant for doing what he is told to do? ₁₀It is just so with you. When you have done everything you have been told to do, you must still say: "We're nothing special in the way of servants. We have done no more than our duty." '

₁₁When Jesus was on his way to Jerusalem, he was going through the borderland between Samaria and Galilee. 12As he was entering a village, ten lepers met him. They kept their distance 13and shouted: 'Jesus, Master, take pity on us!' 14When he saw them, he said to them: 'Go, and show yourselves to the priests.' While they were on the way, they were cleansed. 15One of them, when he saw that he was cured, turned back praising God at the top of his voice. 16He threw himself down at Jesus' feet in gratitude. And he was a Samaritan. 17Jesus said: 'Were the whole ten not cleansed? Where are the nine?' 18Didn't anyone come back to give praise to God except this foreigner?' 19'Rise and go,' he said to him. 'Your faith has cured you.'

20When Jesus was asked by the Pharisees when the Kingdom of God would come, he answered: 'You cannot see the Kingdom of God coming by watching for visible signs, 21nor will it be possible to say: "Look, here it is!" or, "Look, there it is!" For the Kingdom of God is within you.'

22Jesus said to his disciples: 'The time will come when you will long to see one of the days of the Son of Man, and you will not see it. 23They will tell you: "Look, here he is! Look, there he is!" Don't go and run after them. 24The coming of the Son of Man in his time will be like the lightning flash that lights up the earth from one horizon to another. 25But before that he must undergo many sufferings, and he must be rejected by this present generation. 26What happened in the time of Noah will happen all over again at the time when the Son of Man comes. 27They were eating, they were drinking, they were marrying, they were being married, right up to the day when Noah went into the ark, and the Flood came and wiped them all out. 28In the same way, what happened in the time of Lot will happen all over again. They were eating, they were drinking, they were buying, they were selling, they were planting, they were building. 29And on the day Lot left Sodom fire and brimstone rained down from heaven and wiped them all out. 30It will be exactly the same on the day when the Son of Man appears on the stage of history. 31If on that day a man is on the housetop, and his goods are in the house, he must not go down to take them out; and, equally so, if a man is working in the field, he must not turn back. 32Remember what happened to Lot's wife. 33If a man tries to keep his life safe, he will lose it, and, if a man is willing to lose it, he will preserve it alive. 34On that night, I tell you, there will be two people in one bed; one will be taken and the other will be left. 35There will be two women grinding corn together; one will be taken and the other will be left.* 37'Master,' they asked him, 'where will this happen?' 'Where the body is,' he said, 'the vultures will gather.'

Chapter 18

JESUS told them a parable to illustrate the truth that they must always keep on praying, and never lose heart. 2'In a town,' he said, 'there was a judge, who had no reverence for God and no respect for man. 3There was a widow in that town who kept coming to him and demanding justice against her opponent. 4For a long time the judge refused to act. But in the end he said to himself: "Even if I have no reverence for God and no respect for man, 5I will give this woman justice, because she keeps pestering me, and I don't want her coming until she completely wears me out." ' 6So the Lord said: 'Listen to what the unjust judge says! 7And will not God see justice done for his own chosen ones, who appeal to him night and day? Is he slow to act for them? 8I tell you, it will not be long before he sees justice done for them. But when the Son of Man does come, will he find that men on earth have still not lost their faith?'

9Jesus told the following parable, which was meant for some people who were so confident of their own goodness that they looked with contempt on everyone else. 10'Two men went up to the Temple to pray. One was a Pharisee, the other a tax-collector. 11The Pharisee stood there and this was his prayer, and it was addressed quite as much to himself as it was to God: "O God, I thank you that I am not like other people—rapacious, dishonest, adulterers—or even like this tax-collector here. 12I fast twice a week. I meticulously set aside for you a tenth of my income." 13The tax-collector respectfully kept his distance, and would not even look up to heaven. So far from that, he beat his breast and said: "God! Have mercy on me, the sinner!" 14I tell you, he went home far closer to God than the other, for everyone who exalts himself will be humbled, but, if a man humbles himself, he will be exalted.'

15They tried to bring even the babies to Jesus for him to touch

*See Notes on pp. 575-6

them. When the disciples saw this, they warned them off. 16But Jesus called them to him. 'Let the little children come to me,' he said, 'and don't try to stop them, for it is to such as they are that the Kingdom of God belongs. 17I tell you truly, if a man does not receive the Kingdom of God like a little child, he will certainly not get into it.'

18A leading Jew put a question to Jesus. 'Good Master,' he said, 'what am I to do to get this eternal life that God promised?' 19Jesus said to him: 'Why call me good? No one is good except God. 20You know the commandments—Do not commit adultery, Do not kill, Do not steal, Do not tell lies about anyone, Honour your father and your mother.' 21'I have obeyed these since I was a child,' he said. 22When Jesus heard this, he said to him: 'You still lack one thing. Sell everything you have; share the proceeds among the poor; and you will have treasure in heaven. And come! Follow me!' 23When he heard this, it made him very sad, for he was very rich.

24When Jesus saw how he had reacted, he said: 'With what difficulty will the wealthy get into the Kingdom of God! 25It is easier for a camel to go through the eye of a needle than for a rich man to get into the Kingdom of God.' 26Those who heard this said: 'Then who can be saved?' 27Jesus said: 'The things which are impossible to men are possible to God.'

28Peter said: 'We have left our homes and families to become your followers.' 29'This is the truth I tell you,' Jesus said to them, 'there is no man who has left a house, or a wife, or brothers, or parents, or children for the sake of the Kingdom of God, 30who will not receive them back many times over in this present world, and in the world which is to come, eternal life.'

31Jesus took the Twelve aside, and said to them: 'We are going up to Jerusalem, and everything predicted in the writings of the prophets will happen to the Son of Man. 32He will be handed over to the Romans, and he will be mocked, and treated with wanton insolence, and spat on. 33They will first flog him and then kill him, and on the third day he will rise again.' 34They completely failed to grasp all this. The significance of this statement was hidden from them, and they had no idea of the meaning of what he was saying.

35As Jesus was approaching Jericho, a blind man was sitting at the roadside begging. 36When he heard a crowd passing, he asked what was happening. 37They told him that Jesus of Nazareth was passing along the road. 38He shouted: 'Jesus, Son of David! Take pity on me!' 39The people in front sharply told him to be quiet, but he shouted louder than ever: 'Son of David! Take pity on me!' 40Jesus stopped. He ordered the man to be brought to him. When the man had come to him he asked him: 41'What do you want me to do for you?' The man said: 'Master, the only thing I want is to see again!' 42'See again!' Jesus said to him. 'Your faith has cured you!' 43Immediately his sight returned, and he followed Jesus praising God, and, when the people saw it, they all gave praise to God.

Chapter 19

JESUS entered Jericho, and was on his way through it. 2There was a man called Zacchaeus there. He was the chief tax-collector for the district, and a wealthy man. 3He was trying to see Jesus, but he could not because of the crowd, for he was a little man. 4So he ran on ahead and climbed up into a sycamore tree to see him, for he was to pass that way. 5When Jesus came to the spot, he looked up and said: 'Zacchaeus, hurry up and come down, because I must stay at your house today.' 6Zacchaeus hurried down and gladly welcomed Jesus. 7When they saw this, they began to complain that Jesus had gone to be the guest of a man with whom no respectable Jew would have had anything to do. 8But Zacchaeus stood there and said to the Lord: 'Sir I am going to give half of my belongings to the poor, and, if I have swindled anyone out of anything, I am going to give him back four times as much.' 9Jesus said to him: 'Today salvation has come to this house, for this man too is a son of Abraham. 10The Son of Man came to search for and to rescue the lost.'

11While they were listening to this, Jesus went on to tell them a parable, which was particularly appropriate, because he was nearing Jerusalem, and they thought that the Kingdom of God was going to appear there and then.

12'There was a nobleman,' he said to them, 'who went away to a distant land, there to receive a kingdom for himself, and then to return. 13He sent for ten of his servants, and gave each of them a sum of five pounds. "Trade with this," he said to them, "until I come back." 14But his citizens hated him, and sent an embassy on his heels, to say that they refused to have him as their king. 15He received the kingdom and returned. Then he ordered the servants to whom he had given the money to be summoned to his presence, to find out what profit each had made in his trading.

₁₆'The first came. "Sir," he said, "your five pounds have produced another fifty." "Well done!" he said. "You are a good servant! Because you have shown yourself trustworthy in a very small matter, you are hereby put in charge of ten towns." ₁₈The second came. "Sir," he said, "your five pounds have made other twenty-five pounds." ₁₉The master said to him also: "You too are put in charge of five towns." ₂₀Another came. "Sir," he said, "here is your five pounds. I kept them stored away, wrapped in a cloth, ₂₁because I was afraid of you, because you are a hard man, and you have a habit of appropriating the rewards of a business into which you did not put any money, and of letting someone else do the work, and then taking the profits." ₂₂His master said to him: "You are a thoroughly bad servant! You have pronounced your own condemnation. Were you not well aware that I am a hard man, and that it is my habit to appropriate the rewards of a business into which I did not put any money, and to let someone else do the work, and then to take the profit? ₂₃Why then did you not give my money to the bankers? If you had done that, I would have got it back with interest when I came home." ₂₄So he said to the attendants: "Take the five pounds from him, and give them to the man who has fifty pounds." ₂₅"Sir," they said, "he already has fifty pounds." ₂₆"I tell you," the master said, "if a man has much, he will be given more. If a man has nothing, he will lose even what he has. ₂₇As for these enemies of mine who refused to have me as their king, bring them here and execute them in my presence." '

₂₈After Jesus had said this, he went on ahead on his way to Jerusalem. ₂₉When he was near Bethphage and Bethany, at the hill called Olivet, he sent on two of his disciples. ₃₀'Go into the village opposite,' he said, 'and, as you enter it, you will find a tethered colt, which no one has ever ridden. Untie it, and bring it to me. ₃₁And if anyone asks you: "Why are you untying it?" this is what you will say: "The Master needs it." ' ₃₂Those who had been sent on went away and found everything just as Jesus had told them. ₃₃As they were untying the colt, its owners said to them: 'Why are you untying the colt?' ₃₄They said: 'Because the Master needs it.'

₃₅So they brought it to Jesus. They threw their cloaks on the colt, and mounted Jesus on it. ₃₆As he rode, they spread their cloaks on the road. 37By this time he was nearing the descent from the Hill of Olives. The whole crowd of the disciples began joyfully to shout their praises to God for all the miracles they had seen:

> 38'God bless the king who comes in the name of the Lord!
> Peace in heaven, and glory in the heights of heaven!'

39Some of the Pharisees in the crowd said to him: 'Teacher, reprimand your disciples.' 40'I tell you,' Jesus answered, 'if they remain silent, the stones will break into a shout.'

41When he came in sight of the city, he wept over it. 42'If only,' he said, 'you would realize on this day, which should be your greatest day, the things which would bring you real prosperity—but the tragedy is that you are incapable of seeing them. 43The time will come when your enemies will build a mound from which to attack you, and will encircle you and hem you in on every side. 44They will level the city to the ground, and you and your children in it. They will not leave one stone standing on another in you, because you did not recognize the time when God came to visit you.'

45Jesus went into the Temple precincts and proceeded to drive out those who were selling. 46'Scripture says,' he said to them, ' "My house shall be a house of prayer," but you have made it a brigands' den.'

47He continued to teach in the Temple daily, and the chief priests and the experts in the Law and the leaders of the people tried to find some way to kill him, 48but they could discover no way of doing so, for the people all hung upon his words.

Chapter 20

ONE day, when Jesus was teaching the people in the Temple precincts, and when he was telling them the Good News, the chief priests and the experts in the Law came up to him along with the elders. 2'Tell us,' they said, 'what right have you to act as you do, and who is it who gave you the right to do so?' 3'I too will ask you a question,' Jesus answered. 'Tell me, 4was the source of the baptism which John administered divine or human?' 5They discussed it with each other. 'If,' they said, 'we say, "Divine," he will say: "Why did you not believe in him?" 6But, if we say, "Human," the people will all stone us, for they are convinced that John was a prophet.' ₇So they answered that they did not know the source of John's baptism. ₈So Jesus said: 'No more am I going to tell you what right I have to act as I do.'

₉Jesus told the people this parable. 'A man planted a vineyard,' he said, 'and let it out to tenants, and went abroad for some considerable time. ₁₀At the appropriate time of year he sent a servant to the tenants so that they might give him his due share of the crop. But the tenants beat him up and sent him away empty-handed. ₁₁He went on to send another servant, but they beat him up too, and shamefully maltreated him, and sent him away empty-handed. ₁₂He went on to send a third servant, but they wounded him and threw him out. ₁₃"What am I to do?" the owner of the vineyard said. "I will send my beloved and only son. It may be that they will treat him with respect." ₁₄But, when the tenants saw the son, they discussed the situation with each other. "This is the heir," they said. "Let us kill him, and then the estate will pass into our hands." ₁₅So they threw him out of the vineyard and killed him. What then will the owner of the vineyard do to them? ₁₆He will come and wipe out these tenants, and will give the vineyard to others.' 'God forbid!' they said, when they heard this. ₁₇Jesus looked at them. 'What, then,' he said, 'is the meaning of this passage of scripture:

> "The stone which the builders rejected, ❦
> this has become the headstone of the corner"?

₁₈Anyone who falls against this stone will be shattered to pieces, and it will crush anyone it falls on.'

₁₉At that time the experts in the Law and the chief priests tried to find some way to seize Jesus, but they were afraid of the people, for they were well aware that it was against them that he had directed this parable.

₂₀They kept Jesus under close observation. They sent spies who pretended to be genuinely concerned about the right thing to do. The idea was to seize on what he said, and so to find a reason for handing him over to the power and authority of the governor. ₂₁So they put a question to him. 'Teacher,' they said, 'we know that you speak and teach rightly and that man-made prestige means nothing to you, but that you really do teach the life that God wishes us to live. ₂₂Is it right for us to pay tax to Caesar, or not?' ₂₃Jesus understood their villainy. 24'Show me a shilling,' he said. 'Whose portrait and whose inscription is on it?' 'Caesar's,' they said. 25'If that is so,' he said, 'pay to Caesar what belongs to Caesar, and to God what belongs to God.' 26They were powerless publicly to seize on what he said. They were so astonished at his answer that they were reduced to silence.

27Some of the Sadducees, who deny that there is any resurrection, approached Jesus. They put a question to him. 28'Teacher,' they said, 'Moses prescribed a regulation for us, that, if a man's married brother dies, and dies childless, his brother should marry his wife, and should raise a family for his brother. 29Well then, there were seven brothers. The first married and died childless. 30So did the second, 31and the third married her too. In the same way the whole seven died, and left no children. 32The woman afterwards died too. 33Now, of which of these will the woman be the wife at the resurrection, for the seven had her as wife?' 34'In this world,' Jesus said to them, 'people marry and are married, 35but those who are judged fit to enter the other world and to share in the resurrection of the dead neither marry nor are married. 36Nor can they die any more, for they are like angels, and they are real sons of God, because they are resurrection sons. 37That the dead are in fact raised Moses himself has shown in the passage about the bush, when he speaks of the Lord as the God of Abraham and the God of Isaac and the God of Jacob. 38God is not the God of the dead but of the living. For him they are all alive.' 39Some of the experts in the Law answered: 'Teacher, that was an excellent answer,' 40for they no longer dared to ask him any more questions.

41Jesus said to them: 'How can it be said that the Messiah is David's son? 42David himself says in the Book of Psalms:

> "The Lord said to my Lord,
>   Sit on my right hand,
>   43until I give you the victory over your enemies."

44So then David calls him Lord, and how can he be his son?'

45While all the people were listening, Jesus said to his disciples: 46'Beware of the experts in the Law, for they like to walk about in long flowing robes, and they love to be deferentially greeted, as they move through the market-places. They like the front seats in the synagogue, and the top places at banquets. 47They greedily extract the last penny from credulous widows, and with their long prayers they try to give an impression of exceptional piety. They will receive all the heavier a sentence.'

Chapter 21

JESUS looked up and saw the wealthy people putting their gifts into the Temple treasury. 2He saw a poor widow putting in two little copper coins which were together worth half a farthing. 3'I tell you truly,' he said, 'this poor widow has put in more than all the others put together. 4They all have more than they need, and it is out of their surplus that they have put in their gifts, but she has not enough for her needs, and out of her want she has put in everything she has to live on.'

5When some of them were talking about the Temple, and how it was adorned with lovely stones and gifts, Jesus said: 6'These sights you are gazing at—the time will come when not one stone will be left standing on another, and when every building here will be utterly demolished.' 7'Teacher,' they said, 'when will these events take place, and what will be the sign when they are going to happen?'

8Jesus said: 'Be careful that you are not misled, for many will come claiming that they are my representatives. They will say: "I am he." They will say: "The crucial moment is near." Do not follow them.

9'When you hear of wars and revolutions, don't get into a panic, for these events must happen first, but the end will not come immediately.' 10Then Jesus went on to say: 'Nation will attack nation, and kingdom will attack kingdom. 11There will be great earthquakes, and here and there there will be outbreaks of famine and pestilence; there will be terrifying things and great portents in the sky.

12'Before all this happens, they will attack you and persecute you. They will hand you over to the synagogues, and put you in prison. You will be brought before kings and governors because of your connection with me. 13This will be an opportunity for you to show the world what you believe. 14Make up your minds not to worry beforehand what you are going to say in your defence. 15For I will give you an ability to speak, and a wisdom which none of your opponents will be able to resist or to refute.

16'You will be betrayed by parents and brothers and relations and friends. Some of you will be killed. 17You will be universally hated because of your connection with me. 18But not a hair of your head will be ultimately lost. 19If you see things through to the end, you will win your souls.

20'When you see Jerusalem encircled by armies, then you must realize that the time of her desolation is near. 21At that time those who are in Judaea must flee to the hills; those who are in the city must get out; and those in the country districts must not go into it. 22For these are the days in which the vengeance of God will come, so that everything the scriptures say will come true.

23'It will be a tragic time for those who are carrying children in the womb, or feeding them at the breast, for all over the land there will be terrible suffering, and God's wrath will descend on the people. 24They will fall by the edge of the sword; they will be carried away captive to all countries; and Jerusalem will be trampled upon by the Gentiles; and this will last until the time allotted to the Gentiles runs its course.

25'There will be portents in the sun and in the moon and in the stars, and on earth the nations will not know where to turn, bewildered by the roar of the sea and the waves, 26while men will be fainting from fear, and for the thought of what is going to happen to the world, for the heavenly bodies will be shaken. 27Then they will see the Son of Man coming on a cloud with great power and glory. 28When these things begin to happen, lift up your heads, for your deliverance is near.'

29Jesus used an illustration. 'Look at the fig tree,' he said, 'or indeed at any tree. 30Whenever you see the trees putting on their leaves, you do not need anyone to tell you that summer is near. 31So, whenever you see these events happening, you must realize that the Kingdom of God is near. 32I tell you truly that these things will certainly happen within the life-time of this generation. 33Heaven and earth will cease to be, but my words will never cease to be.

34'Be careful not to let your minds be dulled by dissipation and drunkenness and the worries of making a living, in case that day suddenly closes on you like a trap, 35for it will come on everyone all over the world. 36Watch sleeplessly, and never stop praying that you may be strong enough to come through all that is going to happen, and to stand erect in the presence of the Son of Man.'

37During the day Jesus continued to preach in the Temple, and at night he left the city, and slept in the open air on the hill called Olivet; 38and early in the morning all the people came to listen to him in the Temple.

Chapter 22

THE Festival of Unleavened Bread, which is called the Passover, was just about to begin, 2and the chief priests and the experts in the Law were trying to find some way to kill Jesus. But it was not easy to find one, for they were afraid of the people.

3Satan entered into Judas, who is called Iscariot, who was one of the Twelve, 4and Judas went and discussed with the chief priests and the officers of the Temple police how he could deliver Jesus into their hands. 5They were delighted with his proposal, and they agreed to pay him for his services. 6So he came to an agreement with them, and he began to look for a good opportunity to deliver him into their hands, when the crowd was not there.

7The first day of the Festival of Unleavened Bread came, the day on which the Passover lamb had to be killed and sacrificed. 8Jesus sent off Peter and John. 'Go,' he said, 'and make all the necessary preparations for us to eat the Passover.' 9'Where do you wish us to make the preparations?' they asked. 10'When you have gone into the city,' he said, 'you will meet a man carrying an earthenware water-jug. Follow him to the house he goes into. 11You must say to the house-holder: "The Teacher says to you, Where is the guest room, where I am to eat the Passover with my disciples?" 12He will show you a big upstairs room, with the couches spread with rugs. There make all the necessary preparation.' 13They went off, and found everything exactly as Jesus had told them, and they made all the necessary pre-parations for the Passover.

14When the time came, Jesus took his place at the table with the apostles. 15'I have longed with all my heart,' he said to them, 'to eat this Passover meal with you, before I suffer, 16for I tell you that I will not eat it again, until it finds its fulfilment in the banquet of the Kingdom of God.'

17A cup was handed to him, and he gave thanks to God for it. 'Take this,' he said, 'and share it among yourselves. 18I tell you that from now on I will not drink of the fruit of the vine, until the Kingdom comes.'

19He took a loaf, and, when he had thanked God for it, he broke it into pieces, and gave it to them. 'This means my body,' he said, 'which is given for your sake.* Do this so that you will remember me.' 20In the same way, after the meal he took the cup and said: 'This cup stands for the new relationship between man and God made possible at the cost of my life-blood, which is being shed for your sake.

21'But the traitor's hand is with me at this very table, 22for the Son of Man takes the road he is destined to take, but tragic is the fate of that man by whom the Son of Man is being betrayed.' 23They began to ask each other which of them it could be who was going to do this.

24They began to quarrel about which of them should be regarded as the most important. 25'The kings of the Gentiles,' Jesus said to them, 'lord it over their subjects. It is those who are in a position of authority who receive the title of benefactor. 26But things must be very different with you. With you the man who is greatest must behave like the youngest, and the leader must be like a servant. 27Who would you say is greater? The guest or the servant? Obviously, the guest. But it is as a servant that I am with you.

28'You are the men who have stood by me, when I was under attack. 29My Father assigned the royal power to me, and I assign to you 30the privilege of eating and drinking at my table in my Kingdom, and you will be enthroned as the judges of the twelve tribes of Israel.

31'Simon, Simon, Satan has claimed the right to put the loyalty of all of you through the mill; 32but for you yourself I have prayed that yours may not fail. And, when you have found the way back, you must help your brothers to stand fast.' 33'Master,' Peter said to him, 'I am prepared to go to prison and to death with you.' 34'I tell you,

*See Notes on pp. 575-6

Peter,' Jesus said, 'before the cock crows today you will three times disown me.'

35Jesus said to them: 'When I sent you out with no purse, and with no knapsack, and with no sandals, did you lack for anything?' 'For nothing,' they said. 36'Things have changed now,' he said to them. 'If you have a purse, you must bring it, and a knapsack too; if you have no sword, you must sell your coat and buy one. 37For, I tell you, the passage of scripture which says: "He was reckoned among the criminals" must come true in what is going to happen to me. Yes, what was foretold of me is working itself out to its appointed end.' 38'Master,' they said, 'here are two swords.' 'It is enough,' he said.

39Jesus went out to the Hill of Olives, as he was in the habit of doing, and his disciples accompanied him. 40When he reached the place, he said to them: 'You must pray not to have to face the ordeal of temptation.' 41He himself withdrew a stone's throw from them. He knelt and prayed. 42'Father,' he said, 'if it be your will, save me from having to go through this bitter ordeal. But, not my will but yours be done.' 43An angel from heaven appeared to him, giving him strength. 44He was in an agony of mind, and prayed more intensely. As his sweat dripped on the ground, it was like drops of blood.* 45He rose from prayer, and came to his disciples. He found them sleeping, exhausted by sorrow. 46'Why are you sleeping?' he said to them. 'Up and pray that you may not have to face the ordeal of temptation!'

47Just as he was saying this, a crowd arrived on the scene, with the man called Judas, one of the Twelve, at the head of them. He went up to Jesus to kiss him. 48'Judas,' Jesus said to him, 'are you going to betray the Son of Man with a kiss?' 49When Jesus' comrades saw what was going to happen, they said: 'Master, shall we use our swords?' 50And one of them struck the High Priest's servant, and cut off his right ear. 51'Let them have their way,' Jesus said. And he touched the ear and healed him.

52Jesus said to the chief priests and the officers of the Temple police and to the elders who had come to arrest him: 'Have you come out with swords and cudgels, as if you were out to arrest a brigand? 53I was with you daily in the Temple precincts, and you made no

*See Notes on pp. 575-6

attempt to lay a hand on me. But this is your hour, and the power of darkness is in control.'

54They arrested him and took him away. They brought him into the High Priest's house, and Peter was following at a distance. 55They kindled a fire in the middle of the courtyard, and were sitting round it. Peter was sitting in the middle of them. 56One of the maidservants saw him sitting in the light of the fire. She stared intently at him. 'This man too was with him,' she said. 57Peter denied it. 'Woman,' he said, 'I do not know him.' 58Shortly afterwards another man saw him. 'You too,' he said, 'are one of them.' 'Man,' said Peter, 'I am not.' 59About an hour had passed when another man insisted: 'Quite certainly this fellow was with him. Indeed he was, for he is a Galilaean.' 60'Man,' said Peter, 'I don't know what you're talking about.' At that very moment, while he was still speaking, the cock crew. 61And the Lord turned and looked straight at Peter, and Peter remembered what the Lord had said to him, and how he had said: 'Before the cock crows today you will three times disown me.' 62He went out and wept bitterly.

63The guards who had Jesus in custody flogged him and made him the victim of their horseplay. 64They blindfolded him, and kept asking him: 'Prophesy! Who is it who hit you?' 65And they heaped many another insult on him.

66When day came, the council of the elders assembled with the chief priests and the experts in the Law, and they took him away to their Sanhedrin. 67'Tell us,' they said to him, 'are you the Messiah?' He said to them: 'You will not believe any statement I make, 68and you will not answer any question I ask. 69But from now on the Son of Man will be seated at the right hand of Almighty God.' 70'Are you then the Son of God?' they all said. 'It is you who say so,' he said to them. 71'What further evidence do we need?' they said. 'We have all the evidence we need from his own lips.'

Chapter 23

THEY rose in a body and took Jesus to Pilate. ₂They began to make their accusations against him. 'We found this man,' they said, 'attempting to stir up political trouble in our nation, and trying to stop people paying their taxes to the Emperor, and claiming that he is the Messiah, a king.' ₃Pilate asked Jesus: 'Are you the King of the Jews?' 'If you like to put it so,' Jesus answered. ₄Pilate said to the chief priests and to the crowds: 'As far as I can see, there is no crime with which this man can be charged.' ₅But they insisted: 'He is a trouble-maker. He has been spreading his propaganda all over Judaea. He started in Galilee and now he has reached here.' ₆When Pilate heard this, he asked: 'Is this man a Galilaean?' ₇When he found out that Jesus was under the jurisdiction of Herod, he referred his case to him, for he too was in Jerusalem at that time.

₈Herod was greatly delighted to see Jesus, for he had long wished to see him because of the reports he had heard about him, and he hoped to see some visible demonstration of divine power performed by him. ₉He cross-examined Jesus at some length, but Jesus did not answer him. ₁₀The chief priests and the experts in the Law were present, and continued strenuously to make their allegations against Jesus. ₁₁Herod and his troops treated Jesus with contempt, and made a mockery of him. They arrayed him in a brilliantly-coloured robe, and sent him back to Pilate. ₁₂On that day Herod and Pilate became friends with each other again, for previously they had been estranged from each other.

₁₃Pilate sent for the chief priests and the members of the Sanhedrin and the people. ₁₄'You brought this man to me,' he said, 'on the charge of inciting the people to revolution. I have examined him in your presence, and, so far as I can see, he is not guilty of the charges you are bringing against him. ₁₅And further, Herod did not regard him as guilty either, for he referred his case back to me. He is re-sponsible for no action which merits the death penalty. ₁₆I therefore propose to flog him and release him.'* ₁₈But the whole mob kept shrieking in unison: 'Away with this man! Release us Barabbas!' ₁₉Bar-abbas was a man who had been imprisoned on the charge of being

*See Notes on pp. 575-6

implicated in a rebellion which had arisen in the city, and of murder. 20Pilate again addressed them, for he wished to release Jesus. 21But they shouted back at him: 'Crucify, crucify him!' 22For the third time Pilate said to them: 'Why? What crime has he committed? So far as I can see, he has done nothing to deserve the death penalty. I therefore propose to flog him and to release him.' 23But they insistently shouted their demand that Jesus should be crucified, and their shouts got them their way. 24Pilate gave his decision that they should get what they wanted. 25So he released the man they asked for, the man who had been imprisoned for sedition and murder, and he handed over Jesus to them to do what they liked with him.

26As they were taking Jesus away, they seized a Cyrenian called Simon, who was coming in from the country, and they compelled him to walk behind Jesus, carrying the cross. 27A huge crowd of people followed him, with many women among them, who in their sorrow beat their breasts and wailed their laments. 28Jesus turned to them. 'Daughters of Jerusalem,' he said, 'do not weep for me. Weep for yourselves and for your children, 29for the time is coming when they will say: "Happy are those who could never have a child, and the wombs that never bore a child, and the breasts at which no child ever fed." 30When that time comes, they will say to the mountains: "Fall on us!" and to the hills: "Hide us!" 31For if they do these things in the spring-time, what will they do when winter comes?' 32Two other men who were criminals, were led out to be put to death with him.

33When they came to the place called the Skull, they crucified him there with the criminals, one on his right, and the other on his left. 34Jesus said: 'Father, forgive them, for they do not know what they are doing.' They shared his clothes between them by drawing lots for them.

35The people stood looking on, and the Jewish leaders sneered at him. 'He saved others,' they said, 'let him save himself, if he really is God's Messiah, the Chosen One!' 36The soldiers too made a mockery of him by coming to him and offering him their bitter wine. 37'If you really are the King of the Jews,' they said to him, 'save yourself!' 38Above his head there was a placard: 'This is the King of the Jews.'

39One of the criminals who had been crucified kept hurling insults at Jesus. 'Are you not the Messiah?' he said. 'Save yourself and us!' 40The other sternly reprimanded him. 'Have you no reverence for

God?' he said. 'You have been sentenced to the same punishment as he has been, 41and we with justice, for we are getting what we deserve for our misdeeds, but he has committed no crime. 42Jesus,' he said, 'remember me when you come into your Kingdom.' 43Jesus said to him: 'Very certainly you will be with me in Paradise today.'

44By this time it was about twelve o'clock midday, and darkness came over the whole land until three o'clock in the afternoon, 45for the sun was in eclipse. The curtain of the Temple which veiled the Holy of Holies was ripped down the middle. 46Jesus shouted at the top of his voice. Then he said: 'Father, into your hands I entrust my spirit.' When he had said this, he died.

47When the company commander saw what had happened, he praised God. 'This was an innocent man indeed,' he said. 48When the crowds who had come to watch the spectacle saw what had happened, they all went away beating their breasts. 49All Jesus' friends were standing at a distance, and the women who came with him from Galilee were looking on.

50There was a man called Joseph, who was a member of the Sanhedrin, a kindly man and a strict observer of the Law. 51He had not been in agreement with the policy and action of the Sanhedrin. He came from Arimathaea, a Judaean town, and he was eagerly waiting for the Kingdom of God. 52He went to Pilate and asked for Jesus' body. 53He took it down from the cross, and wrapped it in linen, and laid him in a tomb hewn out of the rock, in which no one had ever yet been laid.

54It was Friday evening, the preparation for the Sabbath, and the Sabbath lamps were just beginning to be lit. 55The women who had come with Jesus from Galilee followed Joseph, and saw the tomb, and watched how his body had been laid in it. 56They went home and prepared spices and perfumes for Jesus' body. They rested during the Sabbath as the commandment ordered.

Chapter 24

VERY early on Sunday morning they went to the tomb with the spices which they had prepared. 2They found the stone rolled away from the tomb. 3They went into it, but they could not find the Lord Jesus' body. 4While they were quite at a loss what to make of this, suddenly two men appeared to them in dazzling clothes. 5They were so terrified that they could not even look up. 'Why are you searching among the dead for him who is alive?' the men said to them. 6'He is not here! He has risen! Remember how, when he was still with you in Galilee, he told you 7that the Son of Man had to be delivered into the power of sinful men, and how he had to be crucified, and how he had to rise again on the third day.' 8They remembered what Jesus had said. 9They returned from the tomb, and told the eleven and all the others all that had happened. 10Mary from Magdala and Joanna and Mary, the mother of James, were there, and, along with the other women who were with them, they tried to tell the apostles all about this. 11To them the story sounded like sheer nonsense, and they refused to believe them. 12Peter went running to the tomb. He stooped down and looked in, and there was nothing there to be seen but the linen grave-clothes. He went back home, astonished at what had happened.

13On that same day two of them were on their way to a village called Emmaus, about eight miles from Jerusalem. 14They were talking to each other about all that had happened. 15While they were talking about it and discussing it, Jesus himself came up to them, and began to walk along the road with them. 16But although they saw him, they were prevented from recognizing him. 17'What are you spending your walk arguing about?' he said to them. They halted and their faces showed the bitterness of their hearts. 18One of them, called Cleopas, answered: 'Are you the only visitor to Jerusalem who has not heard of the recent events there?' 19'What events?' he said. 'What happened,' they said, 'to Jesus of Nazareth who was a prophet and it was obvious to all, God knows, with what power he could speak and act, 20and how our chief priests and leaders handed him over to be condemned to death, and how they crucified him. 21It was our hope that it was he who would liberate Israel. But it did not work out that way, and, to add to it all, it is now three days since all this happened. 22It is true that some women who belong to our circle brought us the most astonishing news. They had gone to the tomb early in the morning, 23and they were unable to find his body, and they came back with a story that they had seen a vision of angels, who told them that he was alive. 24Some of our friends did go to the tomb, and found it empty, as the women had said, but they did not see Jesus.' 25'You are so wilfully blind to the truth!' he said to them. 'You are so slow to believe all that the prophets have said! ₂₆Surely the Messiah had to go through all these sufferings before entering into his glory?' ₂₇And he began from Moses and went down through all the prophets explaining to them all the references in the scriptures to himself.

₂₈They were nearly at the village to which they were going. He made as though he was going farther on. ₂₉But they pressed him. 'Stay with us,' they said. 'It is evening now, and by this time it is late in the day.' So he went in to stay with them. ₃₀As he sat at table with them, he took the loaf, and said the blessing, and broke it in pieces, and gave it to them. ₃₁Suddenly they saw! And they recognized him, and he vanished from their sight.

₃₂They said to each other: 'Were our hearts not strangely warmed as he was talking with us on the road, when he was explaining the meaning of scripture to us?' ₃₃And there and then they started out and went back to Jerusalem, and found the eleven and their friends all gathered together, ₃₄and talking about how the Lord had really risen, and how he had appeared to Simon. ₃₅They told them the story of all that had happened on the road, and how they had recognized him, when he broke the loaf.

₃₆While they were still telling this story, Jesus stood among them. 'God's blessing be on you,' he said to them. ₃₇They were startled and terrified, for they thought that it was a ghost that they were seeing. ₃₈'Why are you in such a state of alarm?' he said to them. 'Why do you let doubts invade your minds? ₃₉Look at my hands and feet! See! It is I! Handle me, and see for yourselves, for a ghost does not have flesh and blood, and you see that I have.' ₄₀After he had said this, he showed them his hands and his feet. ₄₁While they still thought that it was too good to be true, and while they were still in a state of bewildered astonishment, he said to them: 'Have you any food here?' ₄₂They gave him a piece of cooked fish, ₄₃and he took it and ate it while they watched him.

₄₄He said to them: 'While I was with you my message to you was that everything written about me in the Law of Moses and in the Prophets and in the Psalms must come true.' ₄₅He explained everything to them, so that they were able to understand the scriptures. ₄₆'This is what scripture says,' he said, 'that the Messiah must suffer and must rise from the dead on the third day, ₄₇and that repentance which leads to the forgiveness of sins must be proclaimed to all nations in his name. 'And,' he said, 'you must begin from Jerusalem. 48It is you who must tell the world about all this. 49I am going to send you the gift my Father promised you, and you must wait in this city until you are clothed with power from on high.'

50He led them out as far as Bethany, and he lifted up his hands and blessed them. 51While he was blessing them, he parted from them, and was taken up to heaven, 52as they knelt in worship. They went joyfully back to Jerusalem, 53and they spent all their time in the Temple, praising God.

Introduction to John

TRADITION is unanimous that John's Gospel was the last Gospel to be written. Its date is about A.D. 100. Since it is so much later than the other Gospels, it is different in character. By the time it was written three things were happening. First, Christians were studying the records of the life of Jesus closely and with scholarly care. Second, Christianity had gone out far beyond Judaism into the wider world. Third, heresies had begun to arise, and the meaning of the Christian faith had to be stated and restated. John's Gospel has three aims corresponding to these three factors in the situation.

i. John's Gospel was written partly with an historical aim. It was written to supply certain gaps in the narrative of the other three. For instance, John's Gospel tells us of a ministry of Jesus in Jerusalem before his main ministry in Galilee, and his return to Jerusalem for the last days.

ii. John's Gospel was written partly with an apologetic aim. All the other Gospels had arisen within Judaism and necessarily used Jewish categories of thought. But John's Gospel was most likely written in Ephesus, and was written for Greeks. Must then, as one scholar has put it, these Greeks be routed, or even detoured, into Christianity via Judaism? To meet this situation John finds the idea of Jesus as The Word. The Greek word is *Logos*. *Logos* has two meanings, which no one English word can express. *Logos* means *word*, and *Logos* means *mind*. A word is the expression of a thought. Therefore, Jesus is the expression of the thought of God. Or, to take the other meaning, in Jesus we see the mind of God. John says to us: 'If you want to see what God is thinking, if you want to see how God feels to men, and how God thinks of men, look at Jesus. In Jesus the mind of God became a person.'

iii. John's Gospel was written partly with a theological aim. There is a very old tradition about how John's Gospel came to be written. It was, so the story runs, suggested to John that before he died, he should write what he remembered of Jesus, for he must by that time have been a very old man. So it was decided that John should write and that all the others should review it. For seventy years these men had lived under the guidance of the Holy Spirit. So we may think of them sitting down and saying: 'Do you remember how Jesus said?'

'Yes,' another would say, 'and now we know what he meant.' And there would be written down the word and the Spirit-guided interpretation of it. One famous ancient verdict called John's Gospel *the spiritual Gospel*. It is interested not only in the events of Jesus' life, but even more in the meaning of them. It is interested not only in what Jesus said, but also in the meaning and interpretation of what he said. A famous scholar described John's Gospel as 'what Jesus becomes to a man who has known him long.' In it Jesus is still speaking, and the promise that the Spirit would take of Jesus' things and declare them to those who love him (16.14) has come true.

The Story of the Good News
JOHN'S VERSION

Chapter 1

WHEN the world began, the Word was already there. The Word was with God, and the nature of the Word was the same as the nature of God. 2The Word was there in the beginning with God. 3It was through the agency of the Word that everything else came into being. Without the Word not one single thing came into being. 4As for the whole creation, the Word was the life principle in it, and that life was the light of men. 5The light continues to shine in the darkness, and the darkness has never extinguished it.

6On to the stage of history there came a man sent from God. His name was John. 7The purpose of his coming was to declare the truth, and the truth he declared was about the light. The aim of his declaration was to persuade all men to believe. 8He himself was not the light. His only function was to tell men about the light. 9The real light, the light which enlightens every man, was just about to come into the world. 10He was in the world, and, although it was through him that the world came into being, the world failed to recognize him. 11It was to his own home that he came, but his own people refused to receive him. 12But to all who did receive him he gave the privilege of becoming God's children. That privilege was given to those who do believe that he really is what he is. 13They were born, not by the common processes of physical birth, not as the consequence of some moment of sexual passion, not as a result of any man's desire. Their birth came from God. 14The Word became a human person, and lived awhile among us. With our own eyes we saw his glory. It was the glory which an only son receives from his father, and he was full of grace and truth. 15John told all men who he was. His prophetic proclamation was: 'This is he of whom I said, "He follows me in time, but he ranks ahead of me, for he existed before I was born." '

16This was his message, because out of the Word's complete perfection we have all received, and to us there has come wave upon wave of grace. 17For it was through Moses that the Law was given, but it is through Jesus Christ that grace and truth have come. 18No one has ever seen God as he is. It is the Unique One, the Divine One, he who is nearest the heart of the Father, who has disclosed to us the mystery of God.

19This is how John declared the truth. When the Jews of Jerusalem sent priests and Levites to ask him who he was, 20his answer was definite and positive. 'I am not the Messiah,' he openly declared. 21So they asked him: 'What are you then? Are you Elijah?' 'I am not,' he said. 'Are you the promised prophet?' 'No,' he said. 22'Who are you?' they said. 'We want to take back an answer to those who sent us. What have you to say about yourself?' 23He said:

'I am the voice of one shouting in the wilderness,
    "Straighten the road by which the Lord will come,"

as the prophet Isaiah said.' 24Some of the deputation were Pharisees. 25'Why, then,' they asked him, 'are you baptizing, if you are neither the Messiah, nor Elijah, nor the promised prophet?' 26'It is with water I baptize,' John answered. 'Although you are not aware of it, there stands among you 27the One who is to come after me. I am not fit to untie the strap of his sandal.' 28This incident happened in Bethany on the far side of the Jordan, where John was baptizing.

29Next day John saw Jesus coming towards him. 'Look!' he said. 'The Lamb of God, the One who takes away the sin of the world! 30It was of him I said, "A man is coming after me who ranks before me, for he existed before I was born." 31I myself did not know him, but the very reason why I have come baptizing with water is that he might be made plain for all Israel to see. 32I saw the Spirit,' John declared, 'coming down like a dove from heaven and settling on him. 33I myself did not know him. But it was he who sent me to baptize with water who said to me: "He on whom you shall see the Spirit coming down and settling is he who is to baptize with the Holy Spirit." 34I have seen it myself, and I now declare that this is the Son of God.'

35Next day, when John was again standing with two of his disciples, 36he saw Jesus walking past. 'Look!' he said. 'The Lamb of God!' 37When the two disciples heard him say this, they followed Jesus. 38Jesus turned and saw them following him. 'What are you looking for?' he said. 'Rabbi,' they said to him—the translation of the word Rabbi is Teacher—'where are you staying?' ₃₉'Come and see,' he said to them. They came and they saw where he was staying, and they stayed with him for the rest of that day. It was about four o'clock in the afternoon when they met him.

₄₀Andrew, Simon Peter's brother, was one of the two disciples who had heard what John said, and who had followed Jesus. ₄₁The first thing he did was to find his brother Simon. 'We have found the Messiah,' he said to him. (The translation of the word Messiah is Christ.) ₄₂He brought him to Jesus. Jesus looked at him. 'You are Simon, John's son,' he said. 'You will be called Cephas.' (Peter is the translation of Cephas.)

₄₃Next day Jesus intended to leave for Galilee. He met Philip and said to him: 'Follow me!' ₄₄Philip came from Bethsaida, the town from which Andrew and Peter came. ₄₅Philip met Nathanael. 'We have found the person about whom Moses wrote in the Law and whom the prophets foretold,' he said. 'He is Jesus, the son of Joseph, from Nazareth.' ₄₆'Can anything good come from Nazareth?' Nathanael said. 'Come and see,' said Philip. ₄₇When Jesus saw Nathanael approaching, he said: 'Here is a real Israelite! A man who is genuine all through!' ₄₈'How do you know me?' Nathanael said. 'I saw you,' Jesus said, 'at your quiet time under the fig-tree, before Philip spoke to you.' ₄₉'Rabbi,' answered Nathanael, 'you are the Són of God! You are the King of Israel!' ₅₀'Do you believe in me because I said that I saw you under the fig-tree?' Jesus answered. 'You will see greater things than that. ₅₁This is the truth I tell you—you will see heaven standing wide open, and the angels of God ascending and descending on the Son of Man.'

Chapter 2

Two days after this there was a wedding at Cana in Galilee. Jesus' mother was there, ₂and Jesus too was invited to the wedding with his disciples. ₃When the wine ran short, Jesus' mother said to him: 'They have no wine.' ₄'You must not try to tell me what to do,' Jesus said. 'My time has not yet come.' ₅'Do whatever he tells you to do,' his mother said to the servants. ₆Six stone water-jars were standing there, as the Jewish ceremonial customs of purification required, each of them with a capacity of twenty or thirty gallons of water. ₇'Fill the jars with water,' Jesus said to them. They filled them up to the brim. ₈'Now,' said Jesus to them, 'draw some out and take it to the master of ceremonies.' They did so. ₉The master of ceremonies tasted the water which had become wine. He did not know where it had come from, although the servants who had drawn the water knew. He called the bridegroom. ₁₀'Everyone,' he said to him, 'lays on the good wine first, and then, when the guests have had quite a lot to drink, the not so good wine. You have kept the good wine until now.'

₁₁Jesus gave this first demonstration of the power of God in action at Cana in Galilee, and so displayed his glory, and his disciples believed in him.

₁₂After this Jesus went down to Capernaum with his mother and his brothers and his disciples, and they stayed there for a few days.

₁₃The Jewish Passover Festival was shortly to be observed. So Jesus went up to Jerusalem. ₁₄In the Temple precincts he found the sellers of oxen and sheep and pigeons, and the money-changers sitting at their tables. ₁₅He made a whip out of pieces of cord, and he drove them all out of the Temple precincts, and the sheep and the oxen along with them. He scattered the coins of the money-changers and upset their tables. ₁₆He said to the pigeon sellers: 'Take these out of here! Stop turning my Father's house into a shop!' ₁₇His disciples remembered that scripture says: 'Zeal for your house will consume me.' ₁₈'What proof can you give us of your right to act like this?' the Jews said to him. ₁₉'Destroy this Temple,' Jesus answered, 'and in three days I will raise it from the ruins.' ₂₀'It took forty-six years to build this Temple,' the Jews said, 'and are you going to raise it from the ruins in three days?' ₂₁But Jesus was speaking of the temple of his body. ₂₂So when he was raised from the dead, his disciples remembered that he had said this, and they believed the scripture, and realized that what he had said was true.

₂₃When Jesus was in Jerusalem at the Festival of the Passover, many believed in him, for they saw that his actions were visible demonstrations of the power of God. ₂₄But he did not entrust himself to them, ₂₅for he knew all men. He did not need anyone to tell him about human nature, because he was well aware what it is like.

Chapter 3

THERE was a man called Nicodemus, who belonged to the school of the Pharisees, and who was a member of the Sanhedrin. 2This man came to Jesus at night. 'Rabbi,' he said to him, 'we know that you are a teacher who has come from God, for no one could do things which are so obviously demonstrations of divine power, unless God was with him.' 3'I tell you,' said Jesus, 'and it is true, that unless a man is born again from above, he can have no experience of the Kingdom of God.' 4'How can a man be born when he is old? It is obviously impossible for a man to enter his mother's womb a second time, and to be born all over again,' Nicodemus said to him. 5'I tell you,' Jesus answered, 'and it is true, unless a man is born of water and the Spirit, he cannot become a member of the Kingdom of God. 6Physical birth can only beget a physical creature; but spiritual birth begets a spiritual creature. 7You must not be surprised that I said to you that you must all be born again from above. 8The wind blows where it wills, and you hear the sound of it, but you do not know where it comes from and where it is going. And there is the same invisible and unpredictable power in everyone who undergoes this spiritual rebirth.' 9'How can this happen?' Nicodemus answered. 10'Are you the famous teacher of the famous Israel,' Jesus said to him, 'and yet you do not understand this? 11I tell you, and it is true, we speak of that of which we have knowledge; we declare the truth of what we have seen; and you refuse to accept our word for it. 12If you do not believe when I have spoken to you about the familiar things of earth, how will you believe if I tell you about the strange things of heaven? 13There is only one person who has gone up to heaven, and he is the person who came down from heaven, I mean, the Son of Man who comes from heaven.'

14Just as Moses lifted high the serpent in the wilderness, so the Son of Man must be lifted high, 15so that everyone who believes in him may have eternal life. 16For God loved the world so much that he gave his only Son, so that everyone who believes in him should have not destruction but eternal life. 17God did not send his Son into the world to judge the world; he sent him so that through him the world should be saved. 18There is no judgment for the man who believes in him; but if anyone does not believe in him, he already stands condemned, because he has refused to believe in God's only

Son. 19The fact which really judges men is that the light came into the world, and they loved the darkness rather than the light, because their deeds were evil. 20If a man's conduct is bad he hates the light, and refuses to come into the light, for he does not want his actions to be openly convicted. 21But if a man's conduct is dictated by the truth, he willingly comes into the light, for by so doing he will make it clear to everyone that his conduct has its inspiration in God.

22After this Jesus went into the territory of Judaea with his disciples, and there he spent some time with them baptizing. 23John too was baptizing at Aenon near Salim, because there was plenty of water there. A continuous stream of people flocked out to him to be baptized, 24for John had not yet been put into prison. 25A discussion about ceremonial purification arose between John's disciples and a Jew. 26They came to John and said to him: 'Rabbi, the man in whose greatness you publicly declared your belief, when you met him on the far side of the Jordan, is here baptizing, and the people are all going to him.' 27'A man can only receive what God gives him,' John answered. 28'You yourselves can witness to the fact that I said that I am not the Messiah. You can bear witness to the fact that what I did say was that I have been sent on ahead of him. 29It is the bridegroom who has the bride. The bridegroom's friend, who is there to support him and to carry out his orders, is very glad when he hears the voice of the bridegroom. That is what joy means to me, and I have it in full. 30He must go on from strength to strength; I must fade out of the picture.'

31He who comes from above is above all others. If a man has his origin in this world, he belongs to this world, and what he has to say has no other authority than that of this world. He who comes from heaven is above all others. 32He declares what he has actually seen and heard, and yet no one accepts what he declares. 33If a man accepts his declaration, he sets his seal on his conviction that God is absolutely to be relied upon, 34for the messenger of God brings the message of God, for God gives him no meagre share of his Spirit. 35The Father loves the Son, and has put everything under his control. 36To believe in the Son is to enjoy the experience of eternal life; to refuse to believe in the Son is to deprive oneself of the experience of life. More, it is to become the object of the wrath of God.

Chapter 4

When Jesus learned that the Pharisees had heard a report that he was making more disciples and baptizing more converts than John—2although Jesus himself was not in the habit of baptizing at all· it was his disciples who did so—3he left Judaea and went back again to Galilee. 4It was necessary for him to take the road that led through Samaria.

5He came to a town in Samaria called Sychar, near the piece of land which Jacob had given to his son Joseph. 6Jacob's spring was there. Jesus, tired out by his journey, was sitting just as he was beside the spring. It was about twelve o'clock midday.

7A woman from Samaria came to draw water. Jesus said to her: 'Give me a drink of water.' 8His disciples had gone away into the town to buy food. 9The Samaritan woman said to him: 'How can you, a Jew, ask a drink of water from me, a Samaritan woman?' (No Jew would drink out of a cup that a Samaritan had used.) 10Jesus answered: 'If you knew what God's free gift is, and if you realized who it is who is asking you for a drink of water, it is you who would have asked him, and he would have given you living water.' 11'Sir,' the woman said to him, 'you have nothing to draw water with and the well is deep. Where are you going to get this living water from? 12Surely you are not greater than our ancestor Jacob, who gave us this well, and who himself drank from it with his sons and his cattle.' 13'If anyone drinks from this water he will be thirsty again,' Jesus answered, 14'but once a man has drunk the water which I will give him, he will never be thirsty again. The water which I will give him will become a spring of water inside him, always welling up to give him eternal life.' 15'Sir,' the woman said to him, 'give me this water so that I will not be thirsty, and so that I will not need to come all this way to draw water.'

16'Go,' Jesus said to her, 'and tell your husband to come, and come back here.' 17'I haven't got a husband,' the woman said. Jesus said to her: 'You are perfectly right to say that you have no husband. 18You have had five husbands and the man you are now living with is not your husband. You told the truth this time.' 19'Sir,' the woman said to him, 'I see that you are a prophet. 20Our ancestors worshipped on this hill, but you say that Jerusalem is the place where everyone ought to worship.' 21'Believe me,' Jesus said to her, 'a day is coming when you will worship the Father neither on this hill nor in Jerusalem. 22You are worshipping in ignorance; we are worshipping in knowledge; for salvation comes from the Jews. 23But a day is coming —it is here—when the true worshippers will offer the Father a truly spiritual worship, for such are the worshippers whom the Father is looking for. 24God is a spiritual being, and his worshippers must offer him a truly spiritual worship.' 25The woman said to him: 'I know that the Messiah (who is called Christ) is coming. When he comes he will tell us everything.' 26Jesus said to her: 'I am the Messiah, I who am speaking to you.'

27At this Jesus' disciples came up. They were astonished to find Jesus in conversation with a woman, but none of them asked him what he wanted with her or why he was talking to her. 28As for the woman, she left her water-jar and went off into the town. 29'Come,' she said to the people there, 'and see a man who has told me everything I ever did. Can this be the Messiah?' 30They went out of the town and started out to see Jesus.

31Meanwhile his disciples were urging him: 'Rabbi, eat something.' 32'I have food of which you know nothing,' he said to them. 33'Surely someone hasn't brought him something to eat?' the disciples said to each other. 34Jesus said to them: 'My food is to do the will of him who sent me, and to finish what he gave me to do. 35Do you not say: "There are still four months before the harvest comes"? Open your eyes and look at the fields, I tell you, and you will see that they are white for the harvesting. 36Already the harvester is receiving his wages; already he is gathering a crop destined for eternal life, so that the sower and the harvester may rejoice together. 37Here is a situation in which the saying is true—one sows and another harvests. 38I sent you to reap a crop for which you did not toil. Others have toiled, and you have entered into the result of their toil.'

39Many of the Samaritans from that town believed in Jesus, because the woman affirmed that he had told her everything she had done. 40So the Samaritans came and asked him to stay with them, and he did stay there for two days. 41Far more believed when they heard him for themselves. 42'We no longer believe because of your story', they said to the woman. 'We have heard him for ourselves and we know that this really is the Saviour of the world.'

43After staying there for two days Jesus left for Galilee, 44for Jesus himself declared that no prophet is honoured in his own native place. ₄₅When he arrived in Galilee, the Galilaeans welcomed him, for they had seen all that he had done in Jerusalem at the time of the festival, for they too had gone to the festival.

₄₆Jesus went back again to Cana in Galilee, the place where he had turned the water into wine. There was in Capernaum an official of the imperial government whose son was ill. ₄₇When this man heard that Jesus had arrived in Galilee from Judaea he left home and went to Jesus, and asked him to come down and cure his son, for the son was at the point of death. ₄₈'Unless you see visible and astonishing displays of the power of God in action,' Jesus said to him, 'you will never believe.' ₄₉'Sir,' the official said to him, 'come down before my boy dies.' ₅₀'Get on your way,' Jesus said to him. 'Your son will live.' The man believed what Jesus said to him, and set off. ₅₁While he was still on the way down his servants met him with the news that his son was alive. ₅₂He asked them what time it was when he had shown signs of betterment. 'Yesterday,' they told him, 'at one o'clock in the afternoon, the fever left him.' ₅₃Then the father realized that that was the very time at which Jesus had said to him that his son would live. And he and his whole household believed.

₅₄This was Jesus' second demonstration of the power of God in action, after he had come back to Galilee from Judaea.

Chapter 5

AFTER this Jesus went up to Jerusalem to observe one of the Jewish festivals. ₂There is in Jerusalem, beside the Sheep Gate, a bath which in Hebrew is called Bethzatha. It has five porches ₃in which there used to lie a crowd of ailing people, people who were blind and lame and whose limbs were paralysed.* ₅There was a man there who had been ill continuously for thirty-eight years. ₆Jesus saw him lying there. He knew that he had been ill for a long time now. 'Do you want to be cured?' he said to him. ₇'Sir,' the sick man answered,

*See Notes on pp. 575-6

'I have no one to put me into the bath when the water has been disturbed. While I am on my way to the water, someone else always gets down before me.' 8Jesus said to him: 'Get up! Lift your mat! And walk!' 9There and then the man was cured. He lifted his mat and began to walk.

That day was the Sabbath. 10The Jews said to the man who had been cured: 'It is the Sabbath, and you have no right to be carrying your mat.' 11He answered: 'It was the man who cured me who told me to lift my mat and walk.' 12'Who is this man who told you to lift your mat and walk?' they asked him. 13The man who had been cured did not know who Jesus was, for the place was crowded, and Jesus had slipped away.

14Afterwards Jesus met him in the Temple precincts. 'You have been cured,' he said to him. 'From now on stop sinning in case something worse happens to you.' 15The man went away and told the Jews that it was Jesus who had cured him. 16It was because Jesus habitually acted like this on the Sabbath that the Jews tried to prosecute him. 17Jesus answered: 'My Father goes on with his work until now, and I go on with mine.' 18It was because Jesus not only habitually broke the Sabbath, but because he also kept speaking of God as his own father, thus putting himself on an equality with God, that the Jews tried all the harder to kill him.

19Jesus said to them: 'I tell you, and it is true, the Son cannot do anything on his own initiative; he can only do what he sees the Father doing, for whatever the Father does, the Son does too. 20For the Father loves the Son, and shows him all that he himself is doing; and he will show him even greater deeds than these, to fill you with wonder. 21As the Father raises the dead and gives them life, so the Son gives life to those to whom he wishes. 22The Father does not pass judgment on anyone, but he has given all judgment to the Son, 23so that the Son may be universally honoured in the same way as the Father is honoured. Not to honour the Son is not to honour the Father who sent him. 24I tell you, and it is true, if a man listens to my message and believes in him who sent me, he already has eternal life. He is no longer on the way to judgment; he has already crossed the boundary between death and life.

25'I tell you, and it is true, that a time is coming—it has come—when the dead will hear the voice of God's Son, and, if they listen, they will live. 26As the Father himself is the source of life, so he has given the Son power to be the source of life. 27He has given him authority to execute judgment, because he is the Son of Man. 28Do not be surprised at this, for a time is coming when all who are buried in the tombs will hear his voice, 29and they will come out. For those who have lived well, their resurrection will mean life, and for those who have lived badly, their resurrection will mean judgment. 30I can do nothing on my own initiative. As I hear from God, so I judge, and my judgment is just, because my only aim is not to do my own will but to do the will of him who sent me. 31If I make claims on my own behalf, my claims need not be valid. 32But it is another who affirms my claims, and I know that what he says about me is true. 33You sent to John, and John was a witness to the truth. 34I do not need any human being to give evidence in support of my claims. The message I bring you has as its aim your salvation. 35John was a burning and a shining lamp, and for a time you were willing to rejoice in his light. 36But I can produce greater evidence in support of my claims than the evidence of John. The deeds which my Father gave me power to do, these very deeds which I am now doing, these are my evidence that the Father has sent me. 37The Father who sent me has himself given evidence on my behalf. You have never heard his voice, nor have you ever seen his form. 38You do not possess his word dwelling in you, because you refuse to accept him whom he sent. 39You carefully study the scriptures, because you think that in them you have eternal life, and it is these very scriptures which provide you with evidence about me, 40and yet you refuse to come to me to find life.

41'I am not interested in human glory. 42I know that you have not the love of God in your lives. 43I have come as the representative of my Father, and you refuse to receive me. But if someone else comes as the representative of no one but himself, you will receive him. 44How can you believe, when all you are interested in is the human glory you get from each other, and when you are quite indifferent to the glory which comes from the only God? 45Do not think that it is I who will be your accuser to my Father. Moses is your accuser, Moses in whom you place your trust! 46If you believed in Moses, you would believe in me, for it was about me that he wrote. 47 If you do not believe what he wrote, there is no possibility that you will believe what I say.'

Chapter 6

AFTER this Jesus went away across the Lake of Galilee (or Tiberias). ₂Everywhere he went a great crowd went with him, because they recognized the power of God in action in what he did for the sick. ₃Jesus went into the hill country and he was sitting there with his disciples. ₄It was very near the date of the Passover, the famous Jewish festival. ₅Jesus looked up and saw a large crowd of people arriving. 'Where are we going to buy bread for these people to eat?' he said to Philip. ₆He said this as a test of Philip, for he himself knew what he was going to do. ₇Philip answered: 'A year's wages would not buy enough bread for each of them to get a little.' ₈One of his disciples, Andrew, Simon Peter's brother, said to him: ₉'There's a small boy here who has five barley loaves and two little fishes. But what use is that for a crowd like this?' ₁₀Jesus said: 'Get the people to sit down.' There was plenty of grass in the place. So the men sat down, about five thousand of them. ₁₁Jesus took the loaves. He thanked God for them, and shared them out to the people as they lay on the grass. He did the same with the fishes, and they all got as much as they wanted. ₁₂When the people had eaten their fill, he said to the disciples: 'Collect the pieces that are left over. We mustn't waste anything.' ₁₃So they collected them, and filled twelve baskets with the pieces of the five barley loaves which were left over after the people had eaten.

₁₄When the people saw this demonstration of divine power that Jesus had given, they said: 'This must be the Prophet who is to come into the world!' ₁₅Jesus knew that they were just on the point of coming and trying forcibly to make him king. So he withdrew again alone into the hill country.

₁₆When evening came, his disciples went down to the lake, ₁₇and embarked on a boat, and started out across the lake to Capernaum. By this time it was already dark and Jesus had not yet arrived. ₁₈The sea was rising because a gale was blowing. ₁₉When they had rowed three or four miles, they saw Jesus walking on the lake, and approaching the boat, and fear gripped them. ₂₀'It is I,' he said. 'Don't be afraid!' ₂₁They wanted to take him on board the boat, but immediately the boat was at the land for which they were making.

₂₂On the next day, the crowd who had remained on the far side of the lake realized that there had only been one boat there, and that

Jesus had not got into the boat with his disciples, but that his disciples had gone off alone. 23Other little boats from Tiberias approached the place where they had eaten the bread, when the Lord had given thanks. 24So when the crowd saw that neither Jesus nor his disciples were there, they boarded the little boats and went to Capernaum to look for Jesus. 25When they found him on the other side of the lake, they said to him: 'Rabbi, when did you get here?'

26'I tell you,' said Jesus, 'and it is true, you are not looking for me because you recognized the power of God in action, but because you ate your fill of the loaves. 27Do not work for the food which does not last; work for the food which lasts for ever and which gives eternal life, the food which the Son of Man will give to you, for it is he whom the Father, God, has marked out as his own.' 28'What are we to do,' they said to him, 'to do what God requires?' 29'What God requires,' Jesus answered, 'is that you should believe in him whom he has sent.' 30'What visible proof are you going to give to us,' they said to him, 'that we may see it and believe in you? What are you going to do? 31Our fathers ate manna in the desert. As it stands written: "He gave them bread from heaven to eat." ' 32'I tell you,' Jesus said to them, 'and it is true, it was not Moses who gave you the bread from heaven; it is my Father who is giving you the real bread from heaven. 33For God's bread is he who comes down from heaven and gives life to the world.' 34'Sir,' they said to him, 'give us now and always this bread.' 35'I am the bread of life,' Jesus said to them. 'If anyone comes to me, he will never be hungry, and, if anyone believes in me, he will never be thirsty. 36But, I have told you, though you have seen me, you do not believe. 37All that the Father gives to me will come to me; and I will not reject anyone who comes to me, 38because I have come down from heaven, not to do my will, but to do the will of him who sent me.

39'It is the will of him who sent me that of all that he has given me I should not lose a single one; it is his will that I should raise up every one of them on the last day. 40It is the will of the Father that anyone who sees the Son and believes in him should have eternal life, and I will raise him up on the last day.'

41A buzz of critical comment rose from the Jews because Jesus said: 'I am the bread of life which came down from heaven.' 42'Isn't this Jesus, Joseph's son?' they said. 'Don't we know his father and mother? How can he say, as he said just now, that he has come down from heaven?' 43Jesus said: 'Stop your whispering campaign of complaint.

44It is impossible for any man to come to me, unless the Father, who sent me, draws him. But, if he does come, I will raise him up on the last day.

45'It stands written in the prophets: "All will be taught by God." If a man listens to the Father and learns from him, he will come to me. 46Not that anyone has seen the Father. The only one to have seen the Father is he who has come from the presence of God; he has seen the Father. 47I tell you, and it is true, to believe is to have eternal life. 48I am the bread of life. 49Your ancestors ate the manna in the desert—but they died. 50This is the bread which comes down from heaven, and it has come, so that if anyone eats it, he will not die. 51I am the living bread which came down from heaven. To eat this bread is to live for ever. The bread which I will give you is my flesh, given for the life of the world.'

52The Jews began to argue violently with each other. 'How is it possible for this man to give us his flesh to eat?' they said. 53'I tell you,' Jesus said to them, 'and it is true, unless you eat the flesh of the Son of Man and drink his blood, you have no life in you. 54But if anyone eats my flesh and drinks my blood, he possesses eternal life, and I will raise him up at the last day. 55My flesh is the real food, and my blood is the real drink. 56If anyone eats my flesh and drinks my blood, he remains in me and I in him. 57It is the living Father who sent me, and it is through the Father I live; and he who eats me will live through me. 58This is the bread which came down from heaven. It is not like the bread which your ancestors ate, for, although they all ate it, they died. To eat this bread is to live for ever.'

59This is the substance of the teaching Jesus gave in the synagogue at Capernaum. 60Many of his disciples who had been listening said: 'This is a very difficult message. Who can listen to this?' 61Jesus was well aware of the buzz of puzzled conversation that was going on among his disciples. 'Does this shock you?' he said to them. 62'What if you were to see the Son of Man ascending to where he formerly was? 63It is the spirit which gives life; the flesh is of no help. The words I have spoken to you are spirit and life. 64But there are some of you who do not believe.' Jesus said this for he knew from the beginning who did not believe, and he knew who it was who was going to betray him. 65'It is for this reason,' he said, 'that I told you that it is impossible for anyone to come to me, unless it was given to him to do so by the Father.'

⁶⁶From that time on many of his disciples turned back and no longer remained with him. ⁶⁷'Do you too want to go away?' Jesus said to the Twelve. ⁶⁸'Master,' Simon Peter answered, 'who could we go to? You have the words of eternal life, ⁶⁹and we are convinced and sure that you are God's Holy One.' ⁷⁰Jesus answered: 'Did I not choose you, the twelve of you, and one of you is a devil?' ⁷¹He meant Judas, Simon Iscariot's son, for he—one of the Twelve—was going to betray him.

Chapter 7

AFTER that, Jesus moved about in Galilee. He was unwilling to do so in Judaea, because the Jews were trying to find a way to kill him.

²The Jewish Festival of Tabernacles was due soon to be celebrated. ³So Jesus' brothers said to him: 'Leave here and go to Judaea, to give your disciples too a chance to see you in action. ⁴No one acts secretively, if he wishes to focus public attention on himself. If you do these things, make up your mind to show yourself to the world.' ⁵His brothers took this line, because not even they believed in him. ⁶'My time has not yet arrived,' Jesus said to them. 'Your time is any time. ⁷It is impossible for the world to hate you, but it does hate me, because I am a witness to the evil of its deeds. ⁸Go up to the festival yourselves. I am not yet going up to this festival because my time has not yet fully come.' ⁹He said this to them, and stayed on in Galilee.

¹⁰When his brothers had gone up to the festival, then he too went up, not publicly, but secretly. ¹¹The Jews were looking for him at the festival. 'Where is this man everyone is talking about?' they kept saying. ¹²The crowds were buzzing with talk about him. Some of them said: 'He is a good man.' Others said: 'No! On the contrary! He is leading the crowd astray.' ¹³But no one spoke about him openly for fear of the Jews.

¹⁴When the festival was already half finished, Jesus went into the Temple, and began to teach. ¹⁵'Where,' said the Jews in astonishment, 'does this man get this knowledge, when he has never been a college student?' ¹⁶'My teaching,' Jesus said, 'is not my own; it comes from him who sent me. ¹⁷Anyone who is willing to do his will, will know whether this teaching comes from God, or whether I am speaking only on my own authority. ¹⁸The man who speaks with no authority

beyond himself is seeking his own personal glory. It is the man who seeks the glory of him who sent him who speaks the truth. There is no wickedness in him. 19Didn't Moses give you the Law? Yet none of you perfectly obeys the Law. Why are you trying to kill me?' 20'You're demon-possessed,' the crowd answered. 'Who is trying to kill you?' 21'I performed one miracle on the Sabbath,' Jesus said, 'and you are all shocked. 22Now Moses gave you circumcision—not that circumcision started with Moses; it started with the patriarchs—and you circumcise a man on the Sabbath. 23If a man can be circumcised on the Sabbath without breaking the Law of Moses, how can you be angry with me, because I gave a whole man his health on the Sabbath day? 24Don't judge by externals; let your judgment be really just.'

25Some of the people of Jerusalem said: 'Isn't this the man they are trying to kill? 26And here he is speaking boldly and openly and nobody says anything to stop him. Is it possible that the government has actual knowledge that this is the Messiah? 27But he can't be, because we know where this man comes from, but when the Messiah comes, no one is to know where he comes from.' 28As he was teaching in the Temple precincts, Jesus said in a voice that all could hear: 'You know me, and you know where I came from. I did not come on my own initiative. It is the one who is the source of truth who sent me—and you do not know him. 29I know him, because I come from him, and it was he who sent me.' 30They would have liked to seize him, but no one laid a hand upon him, because his hour had not yet come.

31Many of the crowd believed in him. 'When the Messiah comes,' they said, 'surely he will not provide greater demonstrations of the power of God in action than this man has done?' 32The Pharisees heard the crowd buzzing with talk like this about Jesus. So the chief priests and Pharisees sent officers to arrest him. 33'I am to be with you a little longer,' Jesus said, 'before I go back to him who sent me. 34You will search for me, you will not find me, and you cannot come where I am to be.' 35The Jews said to each other: 'Where is he going to go that we will not be able to find him? Can he be going to the Jews who are scattered throughout the Greek world, to teach the Greeks? 36What can he mean when he says that we will search for him and not be able to find him, and that it will be impossible for us to come where he is to be?'

37On the last day of the festival, the great day, Jesus took his stand, and said for all to hear: 'If anyone is thirsty, let him come to me, and let him drink. 38If a man believes in me—as the scripture says—rivers of living water shall flow from within him.' 39In saying this, he was speaking about the Spirit, whom those who believed in him were going to receive, for as yet there was no such thing as the Spirit, for Jesus had not yet been glorified.

40When they heard these words, some of the crowd said: 'This really is the promised Prophet.' 41'This is the Messiah,' others said. 'But surely,' others said, 'the Messiah does not come from Galilee? 42Does the scripture not say that the Messiah is to be a descendant of David, and is to come from Bethlehem where David was?' 43The crowd were split in their attitude to him. 44Some of them wished to arrest him, but no one laid a hand on him.

45So the officers went back to the chief priests and Pharisees, who said to them: 'Why haven't you brought him?' 46'No one ever spoke as this man speaks,' the servants answered. 47'Have you too been led astray?' the Pharisees answered. 48'Has any member of the Sanhedrin believed in him, or any of the Pharisees? 49As for the mob who neither know nor want to know the Law, they are bound for hell anyway.' 50Nicodemus, who had come to Jesus before, and who was one of them, said to them: 51'Does our Law condemn any man without giving him a hearing, and without investigating his actions?' 52'Are you too from Galilee?' they answered. 'Examine the scriptures and you will see that no prophet emerges from Galilee.'

53They all went home.

Chapter 8

BUT Jesus went to the Hill of Olives. 2Early in the morning he went back to the Temple precincts, and the people all flocked to him. He sat down and began to teach them. 3The experts in the Law and the Pharisees brought to him a woman arrested for adultery. They placed her in the centre of the crowd. 4'Teacher,' they said to him, 'this woman was arrested in the very act of adultery. 5Moses laid it down in the Law for us that the penalty in such cases is stoning. What do you say?' 6They intended this as a test question, for they wished to have grounds on which to formulate a charge against him. Jesus stooped down and wrote with his finger on the ground. 7When they continued to question him, he straightened himself. 'If there is anyone here who is sinless,' he said, 'let him start the stoning!' 8And he again stooped down and wrote on the ground. 9When they heard this, beginning from the oldest, they began to leave one by one, and Jesus was left alone with the woman standing there. 10Jesus straightened himself. 'Where are they?' he said. 'Has no one condemned you?' 11'No one, sir,' she said. 'I don't condemn you either,' Jesus said. 'Go and from now on stop sinning.'*

12Jesus again spoke to them. 'I am the light of the world.' he said. 'To follow me is to walk, not in the dark, but to be in possession of the light of life.' 13'You make claims about yourself,' the Pharisees said to him, 'and your claims are not true.' 14'Even if I do make claims about myself,' Jesus answered, 'my claims are true, because I know where I came from and where I am going to. You do not know where I came from or where I am going to. 15You pass judgment on purely human standards. I do not pass judgment on anyone. 16But, if I do pass judgment, my verdict is true, because I am not alone, but I and the Father who sent me combine to judge. 17It is written in your Law that the evidence of two men is true. 18It is I who make claims for myself, and the Father who sent me makes the same claims for me.' 19'Where is your father?' they said to him. 'You do not know either me or my Father,' Jesus answered. 'To know me is to know my Father too.'

20He said this in the Treasury, when he was teaching in the Temple precincts; and no one arrested him for his hour had not yet come.

21Jesus went on to say to them: 'I am going away, and you will try to find me, and you will die in your sin. It is impossible for you to go where I am going.' 22'Is he going to kill himself?' the Jews said. 'Is this what he means when he says that it is impossible for us to go where he is going?' 23'You belong to the world below,' he said to them. 'I belong to the world above. You belong to this world; I do not belong to this world. 24I told you that you will die in your sins, for, if you do not believe that I am who I am, you will die in your sins.' 25'Who are you?' they said to him. 'What I have told you from the beginning,'

*See Notes on pp. 575-6

Jesus said to them. 26'I have many things to say about you, and many judgments to pass on you; but he who sent me speaks nothing but the truth, and I tell the world what he told me.' 27They did not realize that he was speaking to them about the Father. 28'When you lift high the Son of Man,' Jesus said to them, 'then you will realize that I am who I am, and that nothing I do has its source in myself, but I say what the Father taught me to say. 29He who sent me is with me. He has not left me alone, because I always do what pleases him.' 30While he was saying this many believed in him.

31Jesus said to the Jews who had believed in him: 'If you make my message the fixed centre of your life, you really are my disciples, 32and you will know the truth, and the truth will liberate you.' 33'We are Abraham's descendants,' they answered, 'and we have never been slaves to anyone. How can you say that we will be liberated?' 34'I tell you,' Jesus answered, 'and it is true, if a man's actions are sinful, he is the slave of sin. 35The slave has no permanent home in the house; the son has a permanent home in the house. 36If the Son gives you freedom, it will be real freedom. 37I am well aware that you are Abraham's descendants. For all that, you are trying to kill me, because you are incapable of receiving my message. 38It is what I have seen in my Father's presence that I tell you about. You ought to obey the message that has come to you from the Father.' 39'Abraham is our father,' they answered. 'If you are Abraham's children,' Jesus said to them, 'you ought to act like Abraham. 40As it is, you are doing your best to kill me, a man who has told you the truth, the truth that God told me. That is not the way in which Abraham acted. 41You must act as your father acted.' They said to him: 'We were not born as the result of any adulterous union. We have one Father—God.' 42'If God was your father, you would have loved me,' Jesus said to them. 'It is from God I am, and it is from God I come. It is not on my own initiative that I have come, I came because he sent me. 43Why can't you understand what I say? It is because you are incapable of hearing my message.

44'The devil is your father, and you wish to identify your actions with the Desires of your father. He was a murderer from the beginning. He did not take his stand on the truth, because the truth is not in him. It is characteristic of him to tell lies, because he is a liar and the father of falsehood. 45The very fact that I speak the truth keeps you from believing in me. 46Which of you can prove me guilty of sin? If I speak the truth, why do you not believe me? 47If a man's life has its source in God, he will listen to God's words. It is because the source of your life is not in God that you do not listen to me.'

48The Jews answered: 'Are we not perfectly right to say that you are a Samaritan and that you are devil-possessed?' 49'I have no devil,' Jesus answered. 'I honour my Father, and you dishonour me. 50I do not seek my own glory. There is One who does seek it—and he is judge. 51I tell you, and it is true, anyone who obeys my message will never experience death.' 52'Now we know that you are devil-possessed,' the Jews said to him. 'Abraham died, and so did the prophets, but you say, that anyone who obeys your message will never experience death. 53Are you greater than our father Abraham? He died, and the prophets died. Who do you think you are?' 54'If I glorify myself,' Jesus answered, 'my glory means nothing. The Father is the One who glorifies me, that God who, you claim, is your God. 55You do not know him—but I know him. If I say to you that I do not know him, I will be a liar like you; but I do know him, and I do obey his word. 56Abraham your father rejoiced to see my day, and he was glad when he saw it.' 57'You are not yet fifty,' the Jews said to him. 'How can you have seen Abraham?' 58'I tell you,' said Jesus, 'and it is true, before Abraham came into being, I am.' 59They picked up stones to throw at him, but Jesus hid himself, and went out of the Temple precincts.

Chapter 9

As Jesus was walking along the street, he saw a man who had been born blind. 2'Rabbi,' his disciples asked him, 'was it this man's own sin, or was it the sin of his parents, which was responsible for the fact that he was born blind?' 3Jesus answered: 'The reason for this man's blindness is neither any sin of his own nor of his parents; the reason is to allow the activity of God to be displayed in him. 4We must carry on the work of him who sent me so long as it is day; the night is coming when it is impossible for any man to work. 5So long as I remain in the world, I am the light of the world.'

6After saying this, Jesus spat on the ground and made clay with the spittle, and smeared the man's eyes with the clay. 7'Go,' he said to him, 'and wash in the Pool of Siloam.' (The word Siloam means sent.) So he went and washed and came back able to see.

8The neighbours, and those who recognized him as the beggar they used to see, said: 'Isn't this the man who used to sit and beg?' ₉Some said: 'It is him.' Others said: 'No! It's someone very like him.' He himself said: 'I am the man.' ₁₀'How were you made able to see?' they asked him. ₁₁The man answered: 'The man called Jesus made clay and smeared it on my eyes, and told me to go to Siloam and wash. So I went and washed—and saw!' ₁₂'Where is this man?' they said to him. 'I don't know,' he said.

₁₃They took him to the Pharisees, this man who had once been blind. ₁₄Now the day on which Jesus had made the clay and had cured his blindness was the Sabbath. ₁₅The Pharisees too asked him again how he had come to see. He said to them: 'He put clay on my eyes, and I washed, and I can see.' ₁₆'This man does not come from God,' some of the Pharisees said, 'because he does not observe the Sabbath.' But others said: 'Is it possible for a man who is a bad man to perform actions like this, for such actions are visible signs of the power of God at work?' And they differed violently about Jesus.

₁₇They said to the blind man again: 'What have you to say about him? Do you really claim that he cured your blindness?' 'He is a prophet,' he said. ₁₈The Jews did not believe that the man had been blind and that he had been made able to see, until they had called the parents of the man who had been made able to see, ₁₉and asked them: 'Is this your son, and do you say that he was born blind? How can he now see?' ₂₀'We know that this is our son,' his parents answered, 'and we know that he was born blind, ₂₁but how he now sees we do not know, nor do we know the man who made him able to see. Ask him! He is no child! He is quite old enough to speak for himself!' ₂₂His parents took this line because they were frightened of the Jews. For the Jews had already agreed that anyone who expressed the belief that Jesus was the Messiah should be excommunicated. ₂₃That is why his parents said: 'He is not a child! Ask him!'

₂₄They summoned a second time the man who had been born blind. 'Give God the glory,' they said to him. 'We know that this man is a bad man.' ₂₅He answered: 'I do not know whether or not he is a bad man. I do know one thing—I was blind and now I can see.' ₂₆'What did he do to you?' they said to him. 'How did he make you able to see?' ₂₇'I have already told you,' he said, 'and you didn't listen. Why do you want to hear the story all over again? Would you too like to become his disciples?' ₂₈They hurled abuse at him. 'It is you who are his disciple,' they said. 'We are Moses' disciples. ₂₉We know that God spoke to Moses, but we have no idea where this man has come from.'

30'Here indeed is an astonishing state of affairs,' the man answered. 'You don't know where he comes from, and he has made me able to see. 31We know that God does not listen to bad men, but he does listen to anyone who reverences him and obeys him. 32Since the world began, it is an unheard-of thing for anyone to make a man born blind able to see. 33If this man did not come from God, he could not do anything.' 34'You were born in nothing but sin,' they said to him, 'and do you have the nerve to try to teach us?' And they threw him out.

35When Jesus heard that they had thrown him out, he sought him out and said to him: 'Do you believe in the Son of Man?' 36'But who is he, sir?' the man answered. 'I would like to believe in him.' 37Jesus said to him: 'You have not only seen him. It is he who is speaking to you now.' 38'Lord,' he said, 'I believe.' And he knelt in front of him. 39Jesus said: 'It is for judgment that I came into this world, so that those who do not see may see, and that those who see may become blind.' 40When some of the Pharisees who were there heard this, they said: 'Are we included among the blind?' 41'If you were blind,' Jesus said to them, 'you would not be guilty of any sin; as it is, you claim to be able to see, and so your sin remains.'

Chapter 10

'I TELL you,' Jesus said, 'and it is true, if anyone does not enter the sheepfold by the door, but climbs in by some other way, he is a thief and a brigand. 2If a man is a shepherd of the sheep, he enters through the door. 3The doorkeeper opens the door to him, and the sheep recognize his voice, and he calls each of his sheep by its own name, and leads them out. 4When he brings all his sheep out, he walks in front of them, and the sheep follow him, because they recognize his voice. 5They will not follow a stranger; they will run away from him, because they do not recognize the voice of strangers.' 6Jesus addressed this parable to them, but they did not realize what he was saying to them.

7So Jesus spoke again to them. 'I tell you,' he said, 'and it is true, I am the door of the sheep. 8All who came before me are thieves and brigands, but the sheep did not listen to them. 9I am the door. If anyone enters through me, he will go in and out in safety, and will find pasture. 10The thief comes only to kill and destroy. I have come that they may have life and overflowing life. 11I am the good shepherd. The good shepherd is ready to die for the sheep. 12The man who is working only for pay, the man who is not really a shepherd, and who is not the real owner of the sheep, leaves the sheep and runs away when he sees a wolf coming—and the wolf savages the sheep and scatters them—13because he cares for nothing but his pay, and does not really care what happens to the sheep.

14'I am the good shepherd, and I know my sheep, and they know me, 15just as the Father knows me, and I know the Father, and I am ready to die for the sheep. 16I have other sheep which do not belong to this fold. These too I must bring in. They will hear my voice, and there will be one flock, one shepherd. 17The reason why the Father loves me is that I lay down my life so that I may receive it back again. 18So far from anyone forcibly taking it from me, I am laying it down of my own free will. I have the power to lay it down, and I have the power to take it back again. This is the command I have received from my Father.'

19These words caused a further cleavage of opinion among the Jews. 20Many of them said: 'A demon has made him insane. Why do you listen to him?' 21Others said: 'These are not the words of a demon-possessed madman. Can a demon enable the blind to see?'

22It was the Feast of the Dedication. 23It was winter. Jesus was walking in the Temple precincts in Solomon's Porch. 24The Jews surrounded him. 'How long are you going to keep us in suspense?' they demanded. 'Tell us definitely whether or not you are the Messiah.' 25'I have told you,' Jesus answered, 'and you do not believe me. My actions as the representative of my Father are my evidence for my claims. 26But you do not believe, because you are no sheep of mine. 27My sheep recognize my voice, and I know them. They follow me, 28and I give them eternal life. So long as the world lasts, they will never perish, and no one will ever snatch them out of my keeping. 29It is my Father's power which gave them to me, and that power is greater than all else. No one can snatch them out of the Father's keeping. 30I and the Father are one.'

31The Jews picked up stones to stone him. 32Jesus answered: 'You have seen me do many lovely things, things which had their source in the Father. Which of them are you stoning me for?' 33The Jews answered: 'It is not for any lovely action that we are stoning you.

We are stoning you for your blasphemous claims, for you, a man, are making yourself God.' ₃₄Jesus answered: 'Does it not stand written in your Law: "I said, you are gods"? ₃₅Scripture then says that those to whom the message of God came were gods, and scripture cannot be annulled. ₃₆Can you then accuse me, me whom the Father consecrated and sent into the world, of blasphemy, because I said that I am the Son of God? ₃₇If my actions are not the actions of my Father, then don't believe in me. ₃₈But, if they are, even if you don't believe in me, believe in what I do. Then you will know and realize that the Father is in me, and that I am in the Father.'

₃₉Again they tried to seize him, but he slipped through their hands. ₄₀Jesus went away again to Transjordan, to the place where John had first baptized, and remained there. ₄₁Many came to him. 'John himself,' they said, 'did nothing in which the action of God was visibly displayed, but everything John said about this man was true.' ₄₂And many believed in him there.

Chapter 11

A MAN called Lazarus was ill. He belonged to Bethany, the village where Mary and her sister Martha lived. ₂It was Mary who anointed the Lord with perfume, and who wiped his feet with her hair, whose brother Lazarus was ill. ₃The sisters sent a message to Jesus. 'Master,' they said, 'the man you love is ill.' ₄'This illness will not prove fatal,' Jesus said, when he received the news. 'It is designed for the glory of God, and it is meant to be the means of bringing glory to the Son of God.' ₅Martha and her sister and Lazarus were very dear to Jesus.

₆Jesus remained for two days in the place where he was, after he had heard the news that Lazarus was ill. ₇He then said to his disciples: 'We must go to Judaea again.' ₈'Rabbi,' his disciples said to him, 'how can you propose to go back there again, when the Jews so short a time ago tried to stone you?' ₉'Aren't there twelve hours in the day?' Jesus answered. 'If a man walks in the day-time, he does not stumble, because he sees this world's light. ₁₀But if a man walks in the night-time, he does stumble, because there is no light in him.'

₁₁After saying this he went on to say to them: 'Our dear friend Lazarus is asleep, but I am going to him to waken him.' ₁₂'Master,' his disciples said to him, 'if he is asleep, he will get better.' ₁₃It was about the death of Lazarus that Jesus had spoken, but they thought that he was speaking about the slumber of natural sleep. 14Jesus then said to them plainly: 'Lazarus is dead, 15and for your sakes I am glad that I wasn't there, because this has all happened to strengthen your faith. But we must go to him.' 16Thomas, who was called the Twin, said to his fellow-disciples: 'We've got to go too, to die with him.'

17So Jesus went, and found that by this time Lazarus had been in his tomb for four days. 18Bethany was near Jerusalem, about two miles away. 19Many of the Jews had come to Martha and Mary, to comfort them in their grief for their brother's death. 20When Martha heard that Jesus was coming, she went and met him, but Mary remained sitting in the house. 21'Master,' Martha said to Jesus, 'if you had been here, my brother would not have died. 22But, even as things are, I know that God will give you anything you ask him for.' 23'Your brother will rise again,' Jesus said to her. 24Martha said to him: 'I know that he will rise at the resurrection of the dead on the last day.' 25'I am the resurrection and the life,' Jesus said to her. 'In death to believe in me is to live again. In life, for any man, to believe in me is never to die. Do you believe this?' 27'Master,' she said to him, 'I do. I am sure that you are the Messiah, the Son of God, the One who is to come into the world.'

28When she had said this, she went and called her sister Mary. She said to her, without letting anyone else know: 'The Teacher is here, and wants you to come.' 29When Mary heard this, she rose quickly and went to Jesus. 30Jesus had not yet entered the village. He was still in the place where Martha had met him. 31When the Jews, who were with her in the house, and who were trying to comfort her, saw that Mary had risen quickly and had gone out, they followed her, thinking that she was going to the tomb to weep there. 32Mary came to the place where Jesus was. When she saw him, she threw herself down at his feet. 'Master,' she said, 'if you had been here, my brother would not have died.' 33When Jesus saw her, and the Jews who had come with her, weeping, he was deeply and visibly moved, and distressed in spirit. 34'Where have you buried him?' he said. 'Sir,' they said to him, 'come and see.' 35Jesus burst into tears. 36'Look how he loved him!' the Jews said. 37Some of them said: 'Is it not possible that this man, who made the blind man see, could have stopped Lazarus dying too?' 38Jesus was visibly moved again. He came to the tomb. It was a cave, and a stone had been placed at the mouth of it. 39'Take the stone away!' Jesus said. Martha, the dead man's sister, said to him: 'His body

has the stench of death, for it has been in the tomb for four days.'
40Jesus said to her: 'Didn't I tell you that, if you have faith, you will
see the glory of God?' 41They removed the stone. Jesus looked up and
said: 'Father, I thank you that you have heard me. 42I know that you
always hear me. But it is for the sake of this crowd here I spoke. I
want them to believe that you have sent me.' 43When he had said
this, Jesus shouted: 'Lazarus, come out!' 44The dead man came out,
wrapped around hand and foot in the grave-clothes, and with a towel
wrapped round his face. 'Free him from the wrappings,' Jesus said,
'and let him go.' 45Many of the Jews, who had come to visit Mary, and
who had seen what Jesus did, there and then believed in him. 46But
some of them went off to the Pharisees, and told them what Jesus had
done.

47The chief priests and Pharisees assembled the Sanhedrin. 'What
are we to do?' they said. 'This man's actions frequently have all the
marks of divine action. 48If we leave him alone to go on like this,
everyone will believe in him, and the Romans will come and destroy
our Temple, and it will be the end of religious and political freedom.'
49One of them, Caiaphas, the High Priest for that year, said to them:
'You haven't grasped the seriousness of the situation. 50You do not
see that the only reasonable conclusion is that it is better for our
interests for one man to die for the people than for the whole nation
to be wiped out.' 51He did not really think this out for himself. He
said it because he was the High Priest for that year, and so unwittingly
prophesied that Jesus was to die for the nation, 52and not for the
nation only, but in order that the children of God, who were scattered all over the world, should be gathered into one.

53From then on they planned to kill Jesus. 54So Jesus no longer
moved publicly amongst the Jews. He left them and went away to a
district near the desert, to a town called Ephraim, and stayed there
with his disciples.

55The Jewish Passover Festival was near, and people came up in
large numbers from the countryside to Jerusalem before the Passover
to make themselves ceremonially clean. 56As they stood about in the
Temple precincts talking to each other, they kept looking for Jesus.
'What do you think?' they said. 'Surely he is not likely to come to the
festival?' 57For the chief priests and Pharisees had issued instructions
that, if anyone knew where Jesus was, he should give information
which might lead to his arrest.

Chapter 12

Six days before the Passover Jesus went to Bethany. Lazarus, whom he had raised from the dead, stayed there. 2They gave him a dinner there, at which Martha served the guests, and Lazarus was one of those who sat at table with him. 3Mary took a pound of pure and very expensive nard perfume, and anointed Jesus' feet with it, and wiped his feet with her hair. The house was filled with the scent of the perfume.

4Judas Iscariot, one of Jesus' disciples, the man who was going to betray him, said: 'Perfume like this would cost a year's wages for a working man. 5Why wasn't it sold, and the proceeds given to the poor?' 6It was not because the poor meant anything to him that he said this, but because he was a thief, for he had charge of the money-box, and he pilfered from what was deposited in it. 7'Let her alone,' Jesus said. 'Let her observe the last rites now in anticipation of the day when my body will be buried. 8You have the poor with you always, but you do not have me always.'

9The Jews knew that he was there, and they came in their crowds. They came, not only because of Jesus, but also to see Lazarus, whom Jesus had raised from the dead. 10The chief priests decided to kill Lazarus, 11for because of him many of the Jews were abandoning Judaism and beginning to believe in Jesus.

12The next day, when the thronging crowds who had come to the festival heard that Jesus was coming to Jerusalem, 13they took palm branches and went out to meet him. They kept shouting:

'Send your salvation!
Blessings on him who comes in the name of the Lord,
on him who is the King of Israel!'

14Jesus found a young donkey and mounted it, just as it stands written:

15'Have no fear, daughter of Sion!
Your King is coming,
mounted on an ass's colt.'

16His disciples did not at the time understand the meaning of these events, but, when Jesus was glorified, then they remembered that these things had been written about him and had been done to him. 17The crowd, who were with Jesus when he had called Lazarus from the tomb and raised him from the dead, told the story of what he had done. 18It was because they had heard that he had given this visible demonstration of divine power in action that the crowd came to meet him. 19The Pharisees said to each other: 'It is plain to see that nothing is any good. All the world has felt his fatal attraction.'

20There were some Greeks amongst those who came up to worship at the festival. 21They approached Philip, who came from Bethsaida in Galilee, with a request. 'Sir,' they said to him, 'we wish to see Jesus.' 22Philip went and told Andrew, and Andrew and Philip came and told Jesus.

23Jesus said: 'The time has come for the Son of Man to be glorified. 24I tell you, and it is true, if a grain of corn does not fall into the ground and die, it remains alone. But if it dies, it produces a large crop. 25To love your life is to lose it; to hate your life in this world is to keep it, and the end will be eternal life. 26If anyone wishes to serve me, he must follow me, and where I am, my servant will be too. The Father will honour anyone who becomes my servant.

27'I am in distress of soul just now. What am I to say? Am I to say: "Father, save me from this hour"? But no! It is for this purpose that I have come to this hour. 28Father, glorify your name.' A voice came from heaven: 'I have glorified it already, and I will glorify it again.' 29When the crowd who were standing by heard this, they said that it was the noise of thunder. 'An angel spoke to him,' others said. 30Jesus answered: 'It was not for my sake that this voice came, but for yours. 31The time for the judging of this world has come. The prince of this world will now be banished. 32As for me, when I am lifted up from the earth, I will draw all men to me.' 33He said this as an indication of the kind of death he was going to die. 34The crowd answered: 'Our information from the Law is that the Messiah is to remain as long as time lasts. How can you say that the Son of Man must be lifted up? Who is this Son of Man?'

35Jesus said to them: 'It is only for a little while longer that the light is to be with you. Get on your way while you have the light so that darkness may not come down upon you. When a man walks in the dark, he cannot see where he is going. 36While you have the light, believe in the light, that you may become sons of light.' After he had said this, Jesus went away and hid himself from them.

37Although the actions of Jesus had been so visibly filled with divine power, they did not believe in him. 38Their unbelief was the fulfilment of the word which the prophet Isaiah spoke:

'Lord, who has believed our report?
And to whom has the arm of the Lord been revealed?'

39It was impossible for them to believe for the reason given by Isaiah in another passage:

40'He has blinded their eyes;
He has made them impervious to all appeal,
In case they should see with their eyes,
and understand with their heart, and turn,
and I should heal them.'

41It was because he saw Jesus' glory that Isaiah said this. It was about him he spoke. 42In spite of this, many of the national leaders did take the decision to believe in him, but because of the Pharisees, they did not openly affirm their faith, for they did not wish to find themselves barred from the synagogue. 43They were more concerned with their popular reputation than with the honour which only God can give.

44Jesus said for all to hear: 'To believe in me is to believe, not in me, but in him who sent me; 45and to see me is to see him who sent me. 46I have come as light into the world, and therefore to believe in me is no longer to remain in darkness. 47If anyone listens to my words and does not obey them, it is not I who am his judge. It was not to judge the world that I came, but to save it. 48If anyone regards me as of no account, and if anyone does not accept my message, he has his judge. The word I have spoken will be his judge on the last day. 49For I did not speak out of my own authority; it was the Father who sent me who gave me a command what to speak and what to say. 50And I know that his command is eternal life. When I speak, I repeat what the Father has said to me.'

Chapter 13

Before the Passover, Jesus knew that the time had come for him to leave this world and to go to the Father. He had always loved his own in this world, and now he gave them a proof of his love, beyond which love could not go.

₂The evening meal was in progress. The Devil had already put the decision to betray Jesus into the heart of Judas Iscariot, Simon's son. ₃Jesus knew that God had handed all things over to him, and that he had come from God, and was returning to God. ₄He therefore rose from the meal, and stripped off his clothes, and took a towel and fastened it round his waist. ₅He then put water into a ewer, and began to wash his disciples' feet, and to wipe them with the towel which he had round his waist.

₆He came to Simon Peter. 'Master,' Simon Peter said to him, 'are you going to wash my feet?' ₇'At the moment you do not understand what I am doing,' Jesus answered, 'but, when you look back, you will realize the meaning of it.' ₈'You will never wash my feet,' Peter said to him. 'If I do not wash you,' Jesus answered, 'you can never be my partner.' ₉'Don't stop at my feet,' Simon Peter said to him. 'Wash my hands and my head too!' ₁₀Jesus said: 'If a man has been bathed, when he comes in off the street, all that he needs washed is his feet. The whole of him is clean. And you are clean—but not everyone of you.' ₁₁He knew who was betraying him. That is why he said that not all of them were clean. ₁₂When he had washed their feet, he put on his clothes again, and returned to his place at table. 'Do you understand what I have done to you?' he said to them. ₁₃'You address me as Teacher and Master, and you are right to do so, for so I am. ₁₄If I the Master and the Teacher have washed your feet, then you too ought to wash each other's feet, ₁₅for I have given you an example to teach you to treat others as I have treated you. ₁₆I tell you, and it is true, the servant is not superior to his master, nor is the messenger superior to the person who sent him. ₁₇If you know that this is true, you are happy if you act as if it was true.

₁₈'I am not speaking about you all. I know the men whom I have chosen. The passage of scripture must come true: "He who eats my bread has lashed out at me with his heel." ₁₉I am telling you of this before it happens, so that when it does happen, you may believe that

I am who I am. 20I tell you, and it is true, to receive anyone whom I send is to receive me, and to receive me is to receive him who sent me.'

21When Jesus had said this, he was in deep distress in spirit. 'I tell you, and it is true,' he solemnly said, 'that one of you will betray me.' 22His disciples looked at each other, for they had no idea whom he meant. 23One of his disciples, the disciple who was specially dear to Jesus, was reclining on Jesus' right, so that his head was leaning against Jesus' shoulder. 24Simon Peter signed to him. 'Ask him who he is talking about,' he said. 25So then, leaning close to Jesus as he was, he said to him: 'Master, who is it?' 26Jesus answered: 'It is the one for whom I will dip the bread in the dish and give it to him.' So he dipped the bread in the dish, and gave it to Judas, Simon Iscariot's son. 27It was after he had received the bread that Satan entered into him. Jesus said to him: 'Do what you are going to do, and do it quickly.' 28None of those who were present at the table knew why Jesus said this to him. 29Since Judas had charge of the common purse, some of them thought that Jesus was telling him to buy the things they needed for the festival, or to see to the customary Passover gift for the poor. 30Immediately after Judas had received the bread, he went out. It was night.

31After Judas had gone out, Jesus said: 'Now the Son of Man has been glorified, and God has been glorified in him; 32and God will glorify himself in him, and will glorify him here and now. 33Dear children, I will not be with you much longer now. You will look for me, and, as I said to the Jews I now say to you too, you cannot come where I am going. 34I give you a new commandment—to love each other. As I have loved you, you too must love each other. 35It is by your love for each other that all will recognize that you are my disciples.'

36'Master,' Simon Peter said to him, 'where are you going?' 'It is not possible for you now to follow me where I am going,' Jesus answered, 'but afterwards you will follow.' 37'Master,' Peter said to him, 'why can't I follow you now? I will die for you.' 38'So you will die for me?' Jesus answered. 'I tell you, and it is true, before the cock crows, you will disown me three times.'

Chapter 14

'DON'T let your heart be distressed. Keep on believing in God, and keep on believing in me. ₂There are many rooms in my Father's house. If there weren't, would I have told you that I am going to get ready a place for you? ₃If I go and get ready a place for you, I will come back again, and I will take you with me, so that you too may be where I am. ₄You know the way to where I am going.' ₅'Master,' Thomas said to him, 'when we don't know where you're going, how can we possibly know the way?' ₆Jesus said to him: 'I am the true and living way. The only way for anyone to come to the Father is through me. ₇To know me is to know the Father. From now on you do know him and you have seen him.' ₈'Master,' Philip said to him, 'show us the Father, and we will be content.' ₉'Have I been with you all this time, Philip,' Jesus said to him, 'and have you still not realized who I am? To have seen me is to have seen the Father. How can you say: "Show us the Father"? ₁₀Do you not believe that I am in the Father, and that the Father is in me? I myself am not the source and origin of what I say to you. The Father lives in me and acts through me. ₁₁You must believe me when I say that I am in the Father and that the Father is in me. If you do not believe me because of what I say, you must believe me because of what I do. ₁₂I tell you, and it is true, if anyone believes in me he will not only do what I am doing, he will do even greater things, because I am going to the Father. ₁₃I will do whatever you ask in my name, so that the Father may be glorified in the Son. ₁₄I will do anything you ask me in my name.

₁₅'If you love me, you will obey my commands. ₁₆I will ask the Father, and he will give you another Helper to be with you for ever, ₁₇I mean the Spirit of truth. It is impossible for the world to receive him, because it neither sees nor knows him. You know him because he stays with you, and is in you. ₁₈I will not leave you to face life all alone. I am coming to you. ₁₉Very soon the world will no longer see me, but you will see me. Because I live, you too will live. ₂₀When that time comes, you will know that I am in my Father, and that you are in me and that I am in you.

₂₁'To know my commands and to obey them is really to love me. If anyone loves me, he will be loved by my Father, and I too will love him, and I will show myself clearly to him.' ₂₂Judas—not Iscariot—

said to him: 'Master, why is it that you are going to show yourself to us, but not to the world?' 23Jesus answered: 'Anyone who loves me will obey what I say; and my Father will love him, and we will come and make our home with him. 24If a man does not love me, he does not obey what I say. The message I have brought to you is not mine; it comes from the Father who sent me.

25'I have told you this while I am still with you. 26But the Helper, the Holy Spirit, whom my Father will send in my place, will teach you everything, and will remind you of all that I said to you.

27'My last gift to you is peace. It is my own peace that I give to you. My gift is not a gift the world can ever give. Don't let your heart be distressed, and don't let it lose its courage. 28You have heard me telling you that I am going away and that I am coming back to you. If you really loved me, you would be glad that I am going to my Father, for the Father is greater than I.

29'I have told you this now before it happens, so that, when it does happen, you may not lose your faith. 30I am not going to talk very much more to you. The prince of this world is coming, but he has no hold over me. 31It has all got to happen to make the world realize that I love the Father, and that I do exactly what he has instructed me to do. Up! We must go!'

Chapter 15

'I AM the real vine,' Jesus said, 'and my Father is the vine-dresser. 2Any branch in me which bears no fruit, he removes, and any branch which bears fruit, he purifies, to make it bear more fruit. 3You are already purified through the message which I brought to you. 4It is essential that you should remain in me, and I in you. No branch can bear fruit in isolation by itself; it must remain in the vine. Just so, neither can you, unless you remain in me. 5I am the vine; you are the branches. If anyone remains in me, and I in him, he bears much fruit, because apart from me it is impossible for you to do anything. 6If anyone does not remain in me, he is thrown out like a withered branch. Branches like that are collected and thrown into the fire to be burned. 7If you remain in me, and if my words remain in you, ask anything you wish, and it will be done for you.

8'The only way in which you can bring glory to my Father is to bear much fruit, and to show yourselves to be my disciples. 9My love for you is the same as the Father's love for me. Remain in my love. 10To obey my commands is to remain in my love, just as I have obeyed my Father's commands, and remain in his love. 11I have spoken like this to you so that I may find my joy in you, and so that your joy may be complete.

12'It is my command that your love for each other should be the same as my love for you. 13The greatest love that a man can have is to give his life for his friends. 14To be my friends you must do what I command you. 15I am no longer going to call you servants. A servant does not know what his master is doing. I have called you friends, because I have told you everything which my Father told me.'

16'It was not you who chose me; it was I who chose you. I have appointed you to go and bear fruit, fruit that will be permanent, so that my Father may give you anything you ask in my name. 17My command to you is to love each other. 18When you experience the world's hatred, you must realize that it hated me before it hated you. 19If you had belonged to the world, the world would have loved its own. The very reason that the world hates you is that you do not belong to the world, but that I have picked you out of the world. 20Remember what I said to you. The servant is not superior to his master. If they have persecuted me, they will persecute you too. They will respond to your message in the same way as they responded to mine. 21They will do all these things to you because of your connection with me, because they do not know him who sent me.'

22'If I had not come and spoken to them, they would not be guilty of sin. As it is, they have no excuse for their sin. 23To hate me is to hate my Father too. 24If they had not seen me act in a way in which no one else ever acted, they would not be guilty of sin. As it is, they have seen and hated both me and the Father. 25But all this happened that the saying written in their Law might come true: "They have hated me without a cause." '

26'When the Helper, whom I will send to you from the Father, comes, I mean the Spirit of truth, who comes from the Father, he will be a witness for me. 27And you too must be witnesses for me, because you have been with me from the beginning.'

Chapter 16

'I HAVE told you all these things so that, when they happen, your faith will not collapse. 2They will banish you from the synagogues. More—the time is coming when to kill you will be regarded as an act of sacred service to God. 3They will treat you like this because they did not know either the Father or me. 4I have told you these things so that, when the time comes for them to happen, you may remember that I had already told you about them. I did not talk like this to you at first, because I was still with you, 5but now I am going back to him who sent me, and none of you asks me where I am going.

6'But because I have talked like this to you, your heart is filled with distress. 7But I am telling you the truth—it is to your advantage that I should go away, for I must go away before the Helper will come to you. If I do go away, I will send him to you. 8When he comes, he will convict the world of its own sin, and he will convince the world of my righteousness and of the certainty of judgment. 9He will compel the world to see that not to believe in me is sin. 10He will compel them to see that the fact that I am going to the Father and passing beyond your sight is the proof of my righteousness. 11He will compel the world to see that judgment has come, because the prince of this world stands condemned.

12'There is still much that I have to say to you, but at present it would be too much for you to bear. 13When he has come, I mean the Spirit of truth, he will guide you into all the truth. It will not be out of his own knowledge that he will speak; he will speak all that he will hear from God, and he will tell you about the things which are going to happen. 14He will glorify me, for everything he will tell you will have its source in what is mine. 15Everything that belongs to the Father belongs to me. That is why I said that everything he will tell you has its source in what is mine.

16'Very soon you will not see me any more, and then again very soon you will see me.' 17Some of the disciples said to each other: 'What does he mean when he says to us that very soon we will not see him any more, and that then again very soon we will see him? What does he mean when he says that he is going away to the Father? 18What does he mean,' they said, 'when he speaks about "very soon"? We have no idea what he is talking about.'

19Jesus knew that they wanted to ask him what he meant. So he said to them: 'Are you asking each other what I meant, because I said that very soon you will not see me, and that then again very soon you will see me? 20I tell you, and it is true, you will weep and you will lament like mourners at a funeral, but the world will be glad. You will be in distress, but your distress will turn to joy. 21When a woman is having a baby, she is in distress because her time has come. But, as soon as the baby is born, she does not remember the pain any more in her joy that a man child has been born into the world. 22Just so, you for the present are in distress. But I will see you again, and your heart will rejoice, and no one is going to take your joy from you. 23When that time comes, you will not ask me for anything. I tell you, and it is true, the Father will give you anything you ask for in my name. 24Up to now you have asked nothing in my name. Keep on asking and you will keep on receiving, and so your joy will be complete.

25I have talked to you so far in pictures and in figures of speech. The time is coming when I will no longer talk to you in pictures and in figures of speech, but when I will tell you about the Father absolutely clearly. 26When that time comes you will take your own requests to the Father in my name. I tell you that I will not ask the Father to give you an answer. 27I will not need to, because, the Father himself loves you, because you have loved me, and because you have believed that I have come from God. 28It was from the Father I came, when I came into the world. It is to the Father I go, now that I am leaving the world again.'

29'This is plain speaking now,' the disciples said to him. 'This is not just a picture and a figure of speech 30We know now that you know everything, and that there is no necessity for anyone to ask you questions. This makes us quite sure that you have come from God.' 31'Do you believe now?' Jesus answered. 32'The time is coming—it has come—when you will all be scattered to your own homes, and when you will leave me all alone. But I am not alone, because the Father is with me. 33I have told you these things that in me you may have all that makes for true happiness. In the world you are going to have trouble. But courage! I have conquered the world.'

Chapter 17

WHEN he had said this, Jesus looked up to heaven and said: 'Father, the time has come. Glorify your Son that the Son may glorify you, ₂for you have placed all mankind under his authority, so that he may give eternal life to everyone you have given to him. ₃It is eternal life to know you, the only real God, and Jesus Christ whom you sent. ₄I have glorified you on earth by completing the task you gave me to do. ₅And now, Father, give me in your own presence the glory which I had with you, before the world came into existence.

₆'I have shown the men whom you took out of the world and gave to me what you are really like. They belonged to you, and you gave them to me, and they have obeyed the message which you sent to them. ₇They now know that all the gifts you have given to me do come from you, ₈for I have told them what you told me, and they accepted my message, and they know for certain that I came from you, and they have accepted it as true that you sent me.

₉'It is for them that I pray. I do not pray for the world; I pray for those whom you have given me, because they belong to you. ₁₀All that I have is yours, and all that you have is mine, and in them I am glorified. ₁₁I am no longer in the world, but they are in the world. I am coming to you. Holy Father, protect them with your personal protection, as you did me, that they may be one just as we are one. ₁₂When I was with them, I protected them with your personal protection, as you did me, and so well did I guard them that the only one of them who is lost is the man who had to be lost, so that what scripture foretold might come true.

₁₃'Now I am coming to you, and I am telling them all this while I am still in the world that they may have within them that fulness of joy which only I can give. ₁₄I brought them your message, and the world hated them, because they do not belong to the world, just as I do not belong to the world. ₁₅I do not ask you to remove them from the world. What I do ask you to do is to protect them from the evil one. ₁₆They do not belong to the world just as I do not belong to the world. ₁₇Consecrate them to yourself by the truth. Your word is truth. ₁₈I sent them out into the world, just as you sent me into the world. ₁₉I consecrate myself to you for their sakes, that they too may be consecrated by the truth.

20'I do not pray only for my disciples here. I pray too for those who are to believe in me through their preaching. 21I pray that all of them may be one. I pray that just as you, Father, are in me and I am in you, so they too may be in us, for it is this that will make the world believe that you have sent me. 22I have given them the glory which you gave me, so that they may be one as we are one, 23I in them and you in me, that they may be perfectly one, for it is this that will make the world realize that you sent me, and that you loved them as you loved me.

24'Father, it is my wish for all whom you have given me, that they should be with me where I am, so that they may see my glory which you have given me, because you loved me before the creation of the world. 25Righteous Father, although the world does not know you, I know you, and these know that you sent me. 26I have told them what you are like, and I will continue to tell them, so that the love with which you loved me may be in them, and so that I may be in them.'

Chapter 18

WHEN he had said this, Jesus went out with his disciples, across the gulley where the Kedron flows. There was a garden there, and Jesus went into it with his disciples. 2Judas, who was arranging his betrayal, knew the place well, for Jesus and his disciples often met there. 3So Judas obtained a detachment of Roman soldiers, together with a party of the Temple police, who were supplied to him by the chief priests and Pharisees, and went there with lanterns and torches and weapons. 4Jesus was well aware of all that was going to happen to him. He stepped forward and said to them: 'Who are you looking for?' 5'Jesus the Nazarene,' they answered. 'I am he,' he said to them. Judas the traitor was standing there with them. 6When Jesus said to them: 'I am he,' they stepped back and fell to the ground. 7Jesus asked them again: 'Who are you looking for?' 'Jesus the Nazarene,' they said. 8'I told you that I am he,' Jesus answered. 'If it is me you are looking for, let these men go.' 9He said this so that his own statement that he had not lost a single one of those whom God had given him might come true.

10Simon Peter had a sword. He drew it, and struck the High Priest's servant, and cut off his right ear. The servant's name was Malchus.

11'Put your sword into its scabbard,' Jesus said to Peter. 'Shall I not willingly accept whatever the Father sends me, however bitter it may be?'

12The company of soldiers and their commander and the Jewish Temple police seized Jesus, and bound him. 13They began by taking him to Annas. Annas was the father-in-law of Caiaphas who in that year was High Priest. 14It was Caiaphas who had advised the Jews that the sensible thing was that one man should die for the people.

15Simon Peter followed Jesus along with another disciple. That disciple was personally known to the High Priest. So he went into the courtyard of the High Priest's house with Jesus, 16while Peter remained standing outside at the gate. The other disciple who was personally known to the High Priest went out and spoke to the maidservant who was in charge of the door, and brought Peter in. 17The maidservant who was in charge of the door said to Peter: 'You too are one of this man's disciples, aren't you?' 'I am not,' he said. 18The servants and the Temple police had made a fire, and were standing beside it warming themselves, because it was cold. Peter was standing warming himself with them.

19The High Priest questioned Jesus about his disciples and about his teaching. 20Jesus answered: 'I spoke to the world perfectly openly. I have always taught in the synagogue and in the Temple precincts, where all the Jews meet. I have said nothing in secret. 21Why do you question me? Ask those who heard me what I said to them. They know what I said.' 22When Jesus said this, one of the Temple police who was standing by gave him a slap across the face. 'How dare you answer the High Priest like that?' he said. 23'If there is anything wrong with what I have said,' Jesus answered, 'you must produce your evidence to prove that it was wrong. If there is nothing wrong with what I said, why strike me?' 24So Annas sent him bound to Caiaphas the High Priest.

25Peter was standing warming himself. They said to him: 'You too are one of his disciples, aren't you?' He denied it. 'I am not,' he said. 26One of the High Priest's servants, who was a relation of the man whose ear Peter had cut off, said to him: 'Didn't I see you in the garden with him?' 27Peter denied it again. Just then the cock crew.

28Jesus was then taken from Caiaphas' house to the governor's headquarters. It was early in the morning. The Jews did not themselves enter the governor's headquarters. They did not want to risk being ceremonially defiled. They wanted to be able to eat the Passover meal. 29So Pilate came out to them. 'What is the charge you are bringing against this man?' he said. 30'If he had not been a criminal,' they answered, 'we would not have handed him over to you.' 31'Take him yourselves,' Pilate said, 'and try him by your own law.' 'We are not permitted to put anyone to death,' the Jews said to him. 32By saying this they made it certain that Jesus' statement foretelling how he would die would come true. 33Pilate went into his headquarters again. He summoned Jesus. 'Are you the King of the Jews?' he said to him. 34Jesus answered: 'Are you saying this because you have discovered it yourself, or because other people told you that I am?' 35'Am I a Jew?' Pilate answered. 'It is your own nation and the chief priests who have handed you over to me. What have you done?' 36'My kingdom does not belong to this world,' Jesus answered. 'If my kingdom belonged to this world my supporters would have been putting up a struggle to stop me being handed over to the Jews. The plain fact is that my kingdom does not belong to this realm of things.' 37'So you are a king?' Pilate said to him. Jesus said: 'It is you who are calling me a king. The reason why I was born, and the reason why I came into the world, is to declare the truth. If a man is a child of the truth, he listens to what I have to say.' 38'What is truth?' Pilate said to him. After he had said this, he again went out to the Jews. 'There is nothing of which I can find this man guilty,' he said to them. 39'You have a custom that at the Passover time I should release one prisoner as a favour to you. Do you wish me to release the King of the Jews?' 40They shrieked: 'Not this man, but Barabbas!' Barabbas was a brigand.

Chapter 19

PILATE then took Jesus and had him flogged. 2The soldiers twisted some thorny twigs into a crown and put it on his head. They dressed him in a purple robe. 3They kept coming up to him and saying: 'Hail! King of the Jews!' Repeatedly they slapped him across the face. 4Pilate came out again. 'Look!' he said to them. 'I am bringing him out to you, because I want you to know that there is nothing of which I can find him guilty.' 5So Jesus came out wearing the crown of thorns and the purple robe. Pilate said to them: 'Here is the man!' 6When the chief priests and the Temple police saw him, they shrieked:

'Crucify him! Crucify him!' 'Take him and crucify him yourselves,' Pilate said to them, 'for there is nothing of which I can find him guilty.' 7'We have a law,' the Jews answered, 'and by the law he ought to be put to death, because he claimed to be the Son of God.' 8When Pilate heard this he was still more alarmed. 9He went into his headquarters again and said to Jesus: 'Where do you come from?' Jesus refused to answer him. 10'You will not speak to me?' Pilate said. 'Are you not aware that it is in my power to release you, and in my power to have you crucified?' 11'You would have no power over me at all,' Jesus answered, 'if it had not been given to you from above. For that reason the man who betrayed me is guilty of a greater sin than you are.'

12From then on Pilate tried everything to release Jesus. But the Jews kept shrieking: 'If you release this man, you are no friend of Caesar. Anyone who sets himself up as a king is in opposition to Caesar.' 13When Pilate heard this, he brought Jesus out. He took his place upon his official judgment seat, on the place called the Pavement—in Hebrew it is called Gabbatha. 14It was the day before the Passover, and it was about twelve o'clock midday. 'Here is your king!' he said to the Jews. 15They shrieked: 'Away with him! Away with him! Crucify him!' 'Am I to crucify your king?' Pilate said to them. 'Caesar is the only king we have!' the chief priests answered. 16Then Pilate handed Jesus over to them to be crucified.

17So they took Jesus, and he went away carrying his cross for himself, to the place called the Place of a Skull, the Hebrew name of which is Golgotha. 18They crucified him there, and along with him they crucified two others, one on each side and Jesus between them. 19Pilate had an inscription written and fixed to the cross. The writing ran: 'Jesus the Nazarene, the King of the Jews.' 20Many of the Jews read this inscription, because the place where Jesus was crucified was near the city, and it was written in Hebrew and in Latin and in Greek. 21The Jewish chief priests said to Pilate: 'Don't write, "The King of the Jews." "Write, He claimed to be the King of the Jews." ' 22Pilate answered: 'What I have written, I have written.'

23When the soldiers had crucified Jesus, they took his clothes, and divided them into four parts, one part for each soldier. They kept his tunic separate. The tunic was seamless, woven from top to bottom in one piece. 24'We mustn't tear it,' they said. 'It will be better to draw lots to decide who is to get it.' This they did, so that the passage of scripture might come true:

> 'They divided my clothes amongst them,
> and they cast lots for my raiment.'

This is what the soldiers did.

25Jesus' mother, his mother's sister, Mary the wife of Cleopas, and Mary from Magdala were standing beside the cross. 26When Jesus saw his mother with the disciple who was specially dear to him standing beside her, he said to his mother: 'Look! Your son!' 27Then he said to the disciple: 'Look! Your mother!' From then on the disciple took her into his own home.

28After that, since he knew that everything was now completed and done, Jesus said: 'I am thirsty,' so that the words of scripture might come true. 29A jar of bitter wine was standing there. So they put a sponge soaked in bitter wine on a spear and lifted it to his mouth. 30When he had received the bitter wine, Jesus said: 'Finished!' He bowed his head and surrendered his life to God.

31Since it was the day before the Passover, the Jews asked Pilate to have the legs of the crucified men broken, and their bodies removed, to prevent their bodies remaining on their crosses during the Sabbath, for that Sabbath was a specially great day. 32So the soldiers came and broke the legs of the first man, and of the other man who had been crucified with Jesus. 33But, when they came to Jesus, they saw that he was already dead. So they did not break his legs. 34But one of the soldiers pierced his side with a spear, and water and blood immediately issued from it.

35The man who actually saw this happen is a witness to it and his evidence is true (God knows that he is telling the truth), for his aim is that you too may believe. 36This happened that the passage of scripture should come true: 'Not one of his bones shall be broken.' 37And again, another passage of scripture says: 'They shall look on him whom they have pierced.'

38After this, Joseph of Arimathaea asked Pilate for permission to remove Jesus' body. He was a disciple of Jesus, but in secret, because he was afraid of the Jews. Pilate gave him permission. So he came and took Jesus' body away. 39Nicodemus, who had first come to Jesus at night, came too. He brought with him about a hundred pounds of a mixture of myrrh and aloes. 40They took Jesus' body, and wrapped it in strips of linen cloth with the spices, for this is the customary Jewish method of burial.

41There was a garden at the place where Jesus was crucified, and in the garden there was a new tomb, in which no one had ever been laid. 42So, because it was for the Jews the evening of the preparation for the Sabbath, and because the tomb was close at hand, they laid Jesus there.

Chapter 20

ON Sunday Mary from Magdala went to the tomb so early in the morning that it was still dark. When she saw that the stone had been removed from the tomb, 2she went running to Simon Peter and to the other disciple, the disciple who was specially dear to Jesus. 'They have taken away the Master from the tomb,' she said, 'and we don't know where they have put him.' 3Peter and the other disciple set out on the way to the tomb. 4They both began to run. The other disciple ran on ahead, faster than Peter, and reached the tomb first. 5He stooped down and looked in, and saw the linen grave-clothes lying there, but he did not go in. 6Simon Peter arrived after him, and went into the tomb. He saw the linen grave-clothes lying there, 7and he saw the towel, which had been round Jesus' head, lying not with the other grave-clothes, but still in its folds, separately in a place all by itself. 8Then the other disciple, who had arrived at the tomb first, went in, and when he saw the inside of the tomb he was convinced. 9As yet they did not understand that scripture said that Jesus had to rise from the dead. 10So the disciples went back home.

11But Mary stood beside the tomb, outside it, crying. In the midst of her tears she stooped down, and looked into the tomb. 12She saw two angels dressed in white, sitting one at the head, and one at the feet of the place where the body of Jesus had lain. 13'Why are you crying?' they said to her. 'They have taken away my Master,' she said, 'and I don't know where they have put him.' 14When she had said this, she turned round, and saw Jesus standing there, but she did not know it was Jesus. 15'Why are you crying?' Jesus said to her. 'Who are you looking for?' She thought that he was the gardener. 'Sir,' she said, 'if you have removed him, tell me where you have put him, and I will take him away.' 16Jesus said to her: 'Mary!' She turned and said to him in Hebrew: 'Rabbouni!' which means, 'Teacher!' 17'You must not cling to me,' Jesus said to her, 'for I have not yet gone up to the Father. Go to my brothers and tell them that I am going to my Father and your Father, to my God and your God.' 18Mary from Magdala went with the news to the disciples. 'I have seen the Lord!' she said, and she told them what he had said to her.

19On the evening of the same day, the Sunday, when the doors of the room, where the disciples were, were locked because of their fear of the Jews, Jesus came and stood among them. 'God's blessing be on you!' he said to them. 20When he had said this, he showed them his hands and his side. When the disciples saw the Lord, they were glad. 21Jesus said to them again: 'God's blessing be on you! I am sending you as the Father sent me.' 22When he had said this, he breathed on them. 'Receive the Holy Spirit,' he said. 23'If you forgive anyone's sins, they are forgiven. If you retain anyone's sins, they stand retained.'

24Thomas, one of the Twelve, who was called the Twin, was not with them when Jesus came. 25The other disciples said to him: 'We have seen the Lord!' 'Unless I see the mark of the nails in his hands,' he said, 'unless I put my finger in the mark of the nails, and unless I put my hand into his side, I refuse to believe it.' 26A week later the disciples were indoors together again, and Thomas was with them. When the doors were locked, Jesus came and stood among them. 'God's blessing be on you!' he said. 27Then he said to Thomas: 'Look at my hands! Put your finger here! Take your hand, and put it into my side! Stop being unbelieving, and believe!' 28Thomas answered: 'My Lord and my God!' 29Jesus said to him: 'Do you believe, because you have seen me? Blessed are those who have believed, although they have never seen me!'

30Jesus did many other things in the presence of his disciples in which the power of God was demonstrated in action, but they are not written in this book. 31This book was written to make you believe that Jesus is the Messiah, the Son of God, and that your belief may bring you life through his name.

Chapter 21

AFTER this Jesus again showed himself to the disciples on the shore of the Lake of Tiberias. This is the story of how he did so.

2Simon Peter, and Thomas, who is called the Twin, and Nathanael from Cana in Galilee, and Zebedee's sons, and other two of his disciples were together. 3'I am going to the fishing,' Simon Peter said to them. 'We are coming with you too,' they said. They went away and embarked on the boat, and that night they caught nothing. 4Just as the day was breaking, Jesus stood on the beach, but the disciples did not know that it was Jesus. 5'Lads,' Jesus said to them, 'have you caught any fish?' 'No,' they answered. 6'Cast your net on the right-hand side of the boat,' he said to them, 'and you will find some.' So they cast the net, and now they could not haul it in, because there were so many fish in it. 7The disciple who was specially dear to Jesus said to Peter: 'It is the Lord!' When Simon Peter heard him say that it was the Lord, he threw on his tunic, for he was stripped for work, and jumped into the sea. 8The others followed in the boat— they were no great distance from land, only about a hundred yards away—dragging the net filled with fish. 9When they disembarked on the land, they saw a charcoal fire laid, with fish cooking on it, and a loaf. 10'Bring some of the fish you have just caught,' Jesus said to them. 11Simon Peter got on board, and dragged the net to land, full of big fish, one hundred and fifty-three of them; and, although there were so many of them, the net was not broken.

12'Come and have breakfast,' Jesus said to them. None of the disciples dared to ask him who he was, for they knew that it was the Lord. 13Jesus went and took the loaf, and gave it to them, and the fish too. 14This was the third time that Jesus appeared to his disciples, after he had been raised from the dead.

15When they had breakfasted, Jesus said to Simon Peter: 'Simon, son of John, do you love me more than these others do?' 'Yes, indeed, Lord,' Peter said to him, 'you know that I love you.' 'Feed my lambs,' Jesus said to him. 16Jesus said to him a second time: 'Simon, son of John, do you love me?' 'Yes, indeed, Lord,' Peter said to him, 'you know that I love you.' 'Be a shepherd to my sheep,' Jesus said to him. 17Jesus said to him a third time: 'Simon, son of John, do you love me?'

Peter was vexed that Jesus said to him a third time: 'Do you love me?' 'Lord,' he said to Jesus, 'you know everything. You do know that I love you.' 'Feed my sheep,' Jesus said to him.*

18'I tell you, and it is true,' Jesus went on to say to Peter, 'when you were young, you tucked up your robe for action, and went where you chose. But when you are old, you will stretch wide your arms, and someone else will bind you, and carry you to a place not of your own choosing.' 19Jesus said this to indicate the kind of death by which Peter would glorify God. When he had said this, he said to him: 'Follow me!'

20Peter turned and saw following them the disciple who was specially dear to Jesus, the disciple who had been sitting next to Jesus at the evening meal with his head on Jesus' shoulder, and who had asked: 'Lord, who is it who is going to betray you?' 21When Peter saw him, he said to Jesus: 'Lord, what is going to happen to this man?' 22'If it should be my will that he should survive until I come,' Jesus said to him, 'what has that got to do with you? All that concerns you is to follow me.' 23The Christian community got to know about this saying, and they took it to mean that that man would not die. But Jesus did not say to him that he would not die. What he said was: 'If it should be my will that he should survive until I come, what has that got to do with you?'

24It is this disciple who guarantees the truth of these facts, and who has written the story of them, and we know that his evidence is true. 25Jesus did many other things, so many that, if a detailed account of them were written down, I do not think that the world itself would be able to hold the books that would have to be written.

*See Notes on pp. 575-6

Introduction to Acts

THE Book of Acts might be called the second volume of Luke's Gospel. Both books were written by the same man and both books were written to the same man, to Theophilus.

Acts is one of the supremely important books of the New Testament, because without it we would know almost nothing about the history of the early days of the Church. Apart from what we can piece together and deduce from the New Testament letters, Acts is our only source of information about the first age of the Church.

It is misleading to call Acts *The Acts of the Apostles*. Apart from Paul, the only apostles who appear in it are Peter, James and John, and of these three only Peter does any speaking. It would be better to call it *Acts of Apostolic Men*, and not to regard it as a consecutive history, but rather as the opening of a series of windows, through which we catch meaningful and significant glimpses into the life of the early Church.

An historian's sources are all-important. In the early part of Acts Luke had a Jerusalem source (1-5; 15.1-16.5); a Caesarean source (8.26-40; 9.31-10.48); an Antiochene source (11.19-30; 12.25-14.28). But in the later parts of Acts a very interesting fact meets us. In the narrative there are stretches in which it is, 'They did this,' and, 'They did that.' But there are certain sections where it is, 'We did this,' and, 'We did that' (16.9-18; 20.4-16; 21.1-18; 27.1-28.6). On these occasions Luke must have been present. Very likely he kept a travel diary, and these are extracts from it. In these places we have the best of all evidence—an eye-witness account.

In Acts Luke has certain objects.

i. He gives us the story of the expansion of Christianity. The disciples are told that they are to be witnesses in Jerusalem, Judaea, Samaria and to the ends of the earth (1.8). The story of Acts tells how Christianity went out in ever-widening circles, until it reached Rome, the capital of the world.

ii. He wishes to commend Christianity to the Roman government in days when persecution was threatening. So he goes out of his way to tell how fair and just the Roman magistrates always were to the Christians, and how again and again they stated that they saw no harm in Christianity (16.35-40; 18.14; 19.37; 23.29; 25.25). Acts is a defence of Christianity to the Roman government.

iii. He wishes to tell us of the unity of the Church, and of how Jew and Gentile learned to live together in a common fellowship with Christ. So in chapter 15 he shows us the decision of the Church that there should be no difference between Jew and Gentile.

iv. He wishes to tell us that the prime mover in this miraculous expansion was the Holy Spirit (2). He begins with the coming of the Spirit at Pentecost. He goes on to show us Stephen as a man of the Spirit (6.3). It is the Spirit who moves Peter to accept Cornelius (11.12); who makes Philip approach the Ethiopian eunuch (8.29); who instructs the Church at Antioch to send Paul and Barnabas out on their journeyings for Christ (13.2). In Acts every great man and every great movement in the Church is inspired and upheld by the Holy Spirit.

Acts tells us of the miracle of the expansion of the Church, and shows us that it was the Spirit who made that miracle possible.

ACTS OF
APOSTOLIC MEN

Chapter 1

MY DEAR Theophilus, I have already written you a full account of the life and teaching of Jesus 2up to the time when he was taken up into heaven, after he had given his instructions through the Holy Spirit to the apostles whom he had chosen.

3After all that he had gone through, he proved to them on many occasions that he was still alive, for, during a period of forty days, he made himself visible to them, and talked to them about the Kingdom of God. 4While he was still sharing their daily life with them, he gave them orders not to leave Jerusalem, but to wait for the Father's promised gift, of which he had already spoken to them. 5'John,' he said, 'baptized you with water, but very soon you will be baptized with the Holy Spirit.'

6Once when they were all together, they asked him: 'Are you going to restore the royal power to Israel at this present time?' 7'You are not permitted,' he said, 'to know how long things will last or the date when they will happen. These things are solely in the Father's control. 8Apart altogether from that, when the Holy Spirit has come upon you, you will receive power, and you will tell the story of me in Jerusalem, and all over Judaea, and in Samaria, and all over the world.' 9After he had said this, he was taken up before their very eyes, and a cloud received him, and he passed from their sight.

10While they were still gazing up into the sky, as he went away, two men dressed in white appeared to them. 11'Men of Galilee,' they said, 'why are you standing here looking up into the sky? This Jesus, who has been taken away from you up into heaven like this, will come again in the same way as you have seen him going into heaven.'

12They then returned to Jerusalem from the hill called Olivet, which is near Jerusalem, as far away as the Law allows a man to walk on the Sabbath. 13When they came in, they went up to the upper room, which was their headquarters. Peter and John and James and Andrew, Philip and Thomas, Bartholomew and Matthew, James, Alphaeus' son, and Simon the Nationalist, and Judas, James's son, were there. 14These all spent all their time together in prayer with the women, and with Mary, Jesus' mother, and with his brothers.

15At that time Peter rose when all the Christian brothers were there—the assembled company numbered about one hundred and twenty persons. 16'Brothers,' he said, 'the passage of scripture, in which the Holy Spirit long ago foretold through the mouth of David how Judas would offer himself as guide to those who arrested Jesus, had to be fulfilled, 17for he was reckoned as one of our number, and he received his allotted share in our work. 18He bought a piece of ground with the pay his villainy had earned for him, but he fell violently on his face, and his body burst open, so that all his entrails poured out. 19This became public knowledge to all who lived in Jerusalem, and that is why they called that piece of ground Akeldama in their own language, a word which means the Bloody Field. 20Well, then, in the Psalms it stands written:

> "Let his habitation become desolate,
>   and let there be no one to stay in it,"

and,

> "Let another take his office."

21So, then, of the men who accompanied us, during all the time that the Lord Jesus came in and went out among us, 22from the beginning of his ministry, when he was baptized by John, right up to the day when he was taken up and left us—one of these men must be appointed as a witness of his resurrection along with us.'

23So they put forward two, Joseph who was called Barsabbas and whose surname was Justus, and Matthias. 24So they prayed. 'Lord,' they said, 'you know the hearts of all men. Show us which of these two you have chosen 25to take his place in this service, and to become one of our apostolic company, which Judas left to go the way which he had chosen for himself.' 26So they cast lots for them, and the lot fell on Matthias, and he was elected to office with the eleven apostles.

Chapter 2

THE disciples were all passing the day of Pentecost together. ₂All of a sudden a sound came from the sky like a blast of violent wind, and it filled the whole house where they were sitting. ₃There appeared to them what looked like tongues of fire, which divided themselves up, and settled on each one of them. ₄They were all filled with the Holy Spirit, and began to speak in other languages, as the Spirit enabled them to speak.

₅There were Jews staying in Jerusalem, devout men who had come from every nation under the sun. ₆When they heard the sound of this, they came in their crowds. They were bewildered, because each of them was hearing the disciples speaking in his own language. ₇They were astonished and amazed. 'Aren't all these men who are speaking Galilaeans?' they said. ₈'How then is it that each one of us hears them speaking in the language we have spoken since we were born? ₉Parthians and Medes and Elamites, those whose homes are in Mesopotamia, Judaea and Cappadocia, Pontus and Asia, ₁₀Phrygia and Pamphylia, Egypt and the Cyrenian parts of Libya, visitors from Rome, ₁₁Jews and converts to Judaism, Cretans and Arabians, we are hearing them telling of God's great deeds in our own languages.' ₁₂They were all astonished, and completely at a loss what to make of it. 'What is the meaning of this?' they said to each other. ₁₃Others treated the whole affair as a jest. 'They are full of new wine,' they said.

₁₄Peter stood up with the eleven and addressed them in a voice that all could hear. 'Men of Judaea,' he said, 'and all you whose homes are in Jerusalem, understand this and listen to what I have to say. ₁₅These men are not, as you suggest, drunk, for it is only nine o'clock in the morning. ₁₆So far from that, this is what the prophet Joel spoke of:

₁₇"In the last days, God says,
I will pour out a share of my Spirit on all mankind.
Your sons and your daughters will become prophets,
your young men will see visions,
and your old men will dream dreams:

18In those days I will pour out a share of my Spirit
on my slave men and my slave girls,
and they will become prophets.
19I will show wonders in the sky above,
and visible demonstrations of my divine power on the earth below,
blood and fire and a mist of smoke.
20The sun will be turned into darkness,
and the moon into blood,
before the great day of the Lord comes in all its splendour.
21And it shall be that everyone who calls on the name of the Lord
will be saved."

22'Men of Israel, listen to what I have to say. Jesus of Nazareth was
a man attested to you by God by miracles and deeds which were
amazing demonstrations of divine power in action. God was acting
through him, and you saw it, and this is a fact of which you yourselves are well aware. 23In the prearranged plan and knowledge of
God this man was handed over to you, and you killed him, by having
him crucified by heathen men, who had no knowledge of the Law of
God. 24But God loosed the pangs of death, and brought him back to
life again, for it was impossible that he should remain under death's
control. 25For David says of him:

"I saw the Lord always before me,
for he is at my right hand, and therefore I cannot be shaken.
26Therefore my heart was glad, and my tongue rejoiced,
and my life was passed in hope,
27because you will not abandon my soul to the land of the dead,
nor will you allow your Holy One to experience death's decay.
28You have made known to me the paths that lead to life.
You will fill me with gladness, and you will give me your presence."

29'Brothers, as far as the patriarch David is concerned, I can say to
you with no fear of contradiction that he both died and was buried.
His tomb is here to this day. 30Because he was a prophet, and because
he knew that God had given his sworn promise that one of his descendants should sit on his throne, 31he foresaw the resurrection of
the Messiah, and it was about him that he spoke, because in point of
fact the Messiah was not abandoned to the land of the dead, nor did
his flesh experience death's decay. 32That God resurrected this Jesus
is a fact of which we have personal knowledge. 33Now that he has

been exalted to the right hand of God, and now that he has received from the Father the Holy Spirit, whom he had promised, he has given this demonstration of the Spirit, which you are now both seeing and hearing.

34'David did not ascend into the heavens, but he says:

"The Lord said to my Lord, Sit at my right hand
35until I make your enemies a footstool for your feet."

36So then the whole house of Israel must realize for sure that God has made this Jesus whom you crucified both Lord and Messiah.'

37When they heard this, it pierced their very hearts. 'Brothers,' they said to Peter and to the rest of the apostles, 'what are we to do?' 38'You must repent here and now,' Peter said to them, 'and you must, each one of you, be baptized in the name of Jesus Christ. Then your sins will be forgiven, and you will receive the free gift of the Holy Spirit. 39For the promise is to you and to your children, and to all who are a long way away. It is to anyone whom the Lord our God invites.'

40Peter laid the facts about Jesus before them at length. 'Save yourselves from the perverse age in which you live,' he urgently appealed to them. 41So those who accepted his message were baptized, and on that day their numbers received an addition of about three thousand people.

42They spent all their time in listening to the apostles as they taught, and in fellowship, and in breaking bread, and in prayers. 43A sense of awe was in the hearts of all, and many wonderful demonstrations of God's power in action were given through the apostles. 44All those who had come to believe remained together, and had everything in common. 45It was their custom to sell their goods and possessions, and to share out the proceeds among them, as any might need. 46Day by day they spent their time in worshipping in the Temple together, and in breaking bread in each other's houses, and they ate their share of the food with glad and generous hearts. 47They were always praising God, and everyone liked them. The Lord added to their number those who were daily being saved.

Chapter 3

PETER and John were on their way up to the Temple at the hour of prayer, at three o'clock in the afternoon. 2A man who had been born lame was being carried in. He was laid every day at the gate of the Temple called the Beautiful Gate, to beg for alms from the people who were going into the Temple. 3When he saw Peter and John about to enter the Temple, he asked to be given alms. 4Peter looked intently at him, and so did John. 'Look at us,' Peter said. 5He gave them all his attention, in the expectation of getting something from them. 6'I haven't got any silver or gold,' Peter said, 'but I give you what I have. In the name of Jesus of Nazareth—walk!' 7He gripped him by the right hand and lifted him up. His feet and ankles were immediately strengthened. 8He jumped up and stood and walked about, and went into the Temple with them, walking and jumping and praising God. 9Everyone saw him walking and praising God, 10and they recognized him as the man who sat begging at the Beautiful Gate of the Temple. They were amazed and astonished at what had happened to him. 11The man was holding on to Peter and John. All the people came running to them in astonishment, to the portico called Solomon's Portico.

12When Peter saw this, he said to the people: 'Men of Israel, what is there in this to surprise you so much? Why are you staring at us, as if it was by our own power or piety that we had made him walk? 13The God of Abraham and of Isaac and of Jacob, the God of our ancestors, has in this event glorified his servant Jesus, whom you handed over to Pilate, and whom you repudiated, when Pilate's judgment was that he should be released. 14You repudiated the Holy and Just One, and asked as a favour for the release of a man who was a murderer. 15You killed the man who blazed the way that leads to life, but God brought him back to life, a fact which we can personally guarantee. 16It is the name of Jesus and faith in that name which have given strength to this man whom you see and know. It is the faith which this name awakens that has given him perfect health as all of you can see. 17And now, brothers, I know that it was in ignorance that you acted, as did your rulers. 18But this was God's way of fulfilling everything which he foretold through the prophets that the

Messiah should suffer. 19So then repent and turn to God, if you want the record of your sins to be blotted out, 20if you want to enjoy times of refreshing sent by the Lord, and if you want him to send the Messiah, whom he has already appointed—I mean Jesus. 21Heaven must receive him until the time of that restoration of all things of which God spoke long ago through his dedicated prophets. 22Moses said: "The Lord your God will send into the world for you a prophet from your own people, as he sent me. You must listen to everything that he says to you. 23Every living creature who refuses to listen to that prophet will be exterminated from the people of God." 24The whole succession of the prophets, who spoke from Samuel onwards, have proclaimed the coming of this present time. 25You are the descendants of the prophets and the children of the covenant, which God made with your ancestors, when he said to Abraham: "Blessing will come to all the families on earth through your descendants." 26When God sent his servant into the world, he sent him to you first, to bring you this blessing by making each one of you abandon his wicked ways.'

Chapter 4

WHILE Peter and John were speaking to the people, the priests and the chief of the Temple police and the Sadducees came up. 2They were annoyed because the disciples were setting themselves up as teachers of the people, and because they were proclaiming that the resurrection of the dead had happened in Jesus. 3So they seized them and placed them under arrest, for by that time it was evening, intending to deal with them the next day. 4Many of those who had heard Peter's sermon became believers, to the number of about five thousand men.

5On the next day there was a meeting in Jerusalem of their leaders and of the elders and the experts in the Law. 6Annas the High Priest, and Caiaphas and John and Alexander, and the whole high-priestly clan were there. 7They called the disciples forward and asked them: 'By what power, or by the use of what name, did you do this?' 8Then Peter, filled with the Holy Spirit, said to them: 'Leaders of the people and elders, 9if we today are under examination in regard to the help that was given to a sick man, if the point at issue is by whose agency this man has been restored to health and strength, 10we are bound to inform you and the whole people of Israel that this was done by the name of Jesus Christ of Nazareth. You crucified him: God brought him back to life, and it is through him that this man stands before you completely cured. 11This Jesus is

"the stone which was contemptuously rejected by you builders,
   the stone which has become the stone which holds
      the whole building together."

12In no one else is there salvation. His is the only name in all the world, given to mankind, by which you must be saved.'

13When they saw the fearlessness of Peter and John, and when they realized that they were men who had no education and no expert knowledge, they were astonished, and they recognized them as having been among the supporters of Jesus. 14When they saw the man standing with them completely cured, they had no answer.

15They told them to leave the Sanhedrin and to wait outside. They then discussed the problem in private. 16'What are we to do with these men?' they said. 'It is quite clear to everyone who lives in Jerusalem that they have been the means of a very remarkable demonstration of the power of God in action. This is a fact which it is not possible for us to deny. 17To prevent this affair influencing more and more of the people, the best thing that we can do is to warn them that the consequences for them will be very serious, if they do not agree never again to speak to anyone in the name of this person Jesus.' 18So they called them in, and they forbade them absolutely to speak or teach in the name of Jesus. 19Peter and John answered them: 'You must judge for yourselves whether it is right in God's sight to pay more attention to your instructions than to God's, 20 for it is not possible for us to stop speaking about what we have seen and heard.' 21When they had warned them further of the consequences of disobedience, they let them go, for they could find no way to punish them because of the people. They were all praising God for what had happened, 22for the man to whom the divine demonstration of healing had happened was more than forty years old.

23When they were released, they went to their own people, and told them all that the chief priests and the elders had said. 24When they heard the story, they joined in united prayer to God. 'Lord,' they said, 'you who made heaven and earth and the sea and everything in them, 25you who said through the Holy Spirit in the words of our ancestor David your servant:

> "Why did the nations rage,
> and the peoples form their futile plans?
> 26The monarchs of earth rose up,
> and the leaders banded themselves together
> against the Lord and against his Anointed One."

27It is true that in this very city Herod and Pontius Pilate united with the Gentiles and the peoples of Israel against your holy servant Jesus, whom you anointed as Messiah, 28to do to him all that your power and purpose had already decided should be done. 29And now, O Lord, in this present situation, look at their threats, and grant to your servants fearlessly and freely to speak your word, 30and act yourself to heal and to cause wonderful demonstrations of your power to happen through the name of your holy servant Jesus.'

31When they had prayed, the place in which they were assembled was shaken, and they were all filled with the Holy Spirit, and they freely and fearlessly spoke God's word.

32The whole body of those who had placed their faith in Jesus was united in heart and soul. None of them claimed that anything he possessed was his own; they had everything in common. 33The apostles powerfully asserted their personal knowledge of the fact of the resurrection of the Lord Jesus. They were greatly respected by everyone. 34In their fellowship no one was in need. All who possessed estates and houses sold them, and brought the proceeds of the sales, 35and handed them over to the apostles, and it was shared out to each of them as anyone might require.

36Joseph, who had been given the name Barnabas by the apostles (the name means son of comfort), who was a Levite and a Cypriot by race, 37had a piece of ground. He sold it, and brought the money, and handed it over to the apostles.

Chapter 5

A MAN called Ananias with his wife Sapphira sold a piece of property. ₂He took part of the proceeds and handed it to the apostles, ₂but, with his wife's connivance, he retained a certain amount of the purchase price. ₃'Ananias,' Peter said, 'why have you allowed Satan to persuade you to lie to the Holy Spirit by retaining a part of the price of your piece of land? ₄While it remained unsold, did it not remain your own? And, when it was sold, were you not absolutely free to do what you liked with the proceeds? What put it into your head to do this? It is not to men that you have told a lie, but to God.' ₅While Ananias was listening to what Peter was saying, he collapsed and died. Everyone who was listening was terrified. ₆The young men rose and wrapped up his body and carried him out and buried him.

₇About three hours afterwards his wife came in, quite unaware of what had happened. ₈'Tell me,' Peter said to her, 'was it for so much that you sold the piece of land?' 'Yes,' she said, 'for so much.' ₉Peter said to her: 'Why did the two of you come to an agreement to see what the Spirit of the Lord would let you away with? Look, you can hear at the door the footsteps of those who buried your husband, and they will carry you out too.' ₁₀There and then she collapsed at his feet and died. When the young men came in, they found her dead, and carried her out, and buried her beside her husband. ₁₁The whole Church and all who heard about this were terrified.

₁₂Wonderful demonstrations of the power of God in action were publicly performed by the disciples. Their common meeting place was in Solomon's portico. ₁₃None of the others had the courage to attach themselves to them, but the people regarded them with the greatest respect. ₁₄Believers in the Lord were increasingly added to their number, both men and women in crowds. ₁₅So much was this the case that they carried the sick on to the streets, and laid them on beds and stretchers, so that even Peter's shadow, as he passed along, might fall on some of them. ₁₆The crowd came from the towns around Jerusalem as well, bringing the sick and those who were troubled by unclean spirits, and they were all cured.

₁₇The High Priest and his supporters, that is, the party of the

Sadducees, were consumed with envy, 18and they proceeded to arrest the apostles. They committed them to the public prison. 19But during the night an angel of the Lord opened the prison doors and brought them out. 20'Go and take your stand in the Temple,' he said to them, 'and tell the people all about this new life.' 21When they had heard this, they went into the Temple soon after dawn and proceeded to teach. When the High Priest and his supporters arrived, they summoned a meeting of the Sanhedrin, that is, of the whole Jewish senate. They sent orders to the prison for them to be brought. 22The Temple police arrived and found that they were not in the prison. They returned and told their story. 23'We found the prison perfectly securely locked, and the guards standing at the doors,' they said, 'but, when we opened the doors, we found no one inside.' 24When the chief of the Temple police and the chief priests heard this report, they were at a loss to know what had happened to them. 25Someone arrived with the news: 'The men you put in prison are standing in the Temple teaching the people.' 26Then the chief of the Temple police went with his officers and brought them. They used no force, for they were afraid that if they did so they would be stoned by the people.

27So they brought them in and placed them before the Sanhedrin. 28'Did we not strictly order you,' the High Priest demanded, 'not to teach in this name? And you have filled Jerusalem with your teaching, and you are out to fasten the responsibility for this man's death on us.' 29Peter and the apostles answered: 'We must obey God rather than men. 30You murdered Jesus by hanging him on a cross, but the God of our fathers brought him back to life. 31God has exalted him to a place on his right hand as Leader and Saviour, and through him he offers repentance to Israel and forgiveness for their sins. 32We can personally guarantee the truth of these statements, and so can the Holy Spirit, whom God has given to those who obey him.'

33When they heard this, they were infuriated and wanted to kill them. 34But one of the Pharisees, called Gamaliel, a universally honoured teacher of the Law, rose in the Sanhedrin. He gave orders for the men to be removed from the Sanhedrin for a little. 35'Men of Israel,' he said to them, 'think carefully what you are going to do in the case of these men. 36Before this, Theudas appeared on the scene with a claim to be someone, and about four hundred men attached themselves to him. He was killed, and all who accepted his claims were dispersed, and the whole affair came to nothing. ₃₇After him Judas the Galilaean appeared on the scene at the time of the census, and persuaded some of the people to revolt to him. He too was wiped out, and all who accepted his claims were scattered. ₃₈In the present situation my advice to you is, drop the case against these men and let them go, because, if what they are planning and doing is of no more than human origin, it will come to nothing. ₃₉But, if its origin is from God, nothing you can do will destroy them. You must be very careful not to turn out to be the opponents of God.' ₄₀They accepted his advice. They called in the apostles and had them flogged, and ordered them not to speak in the name of Jesus, and let them go.

₄₁They left the Sanhedrin rejoicing that they had been reckoned worthy to be ill-treated for the Name. ₄₂All day in the Temple and from house to house they never stopped teaching, and telling the good news that Jesus was the Messiah.

Chapter 6

AT that time, when the number of the disciples was continually growing, there arose a complaint on the part of the Greek-speaking Jews from overseas against the Hebrew-speaking Jews of Palestine. They alleged that their widows were being passed over in the daily distribution of food. ₂The Twelve summoned the body of the disciples. 'It is not right,' they said, 'that we should abandon the preaching of God's word to spend our time serving food at tables. ₃You, brothers, must select from your number seven men of good reputation, spiritually-minded men with practical ability as well, and we will put them in charge of this duty. ₄This will leave us free to concentrate on prayer and on the task of preaching.' ₅This suggestion commended itself to the general body of the congregation. They selected Stephen, a man full of faith and of the Holy Spirit, and Philip, and Prochorus, and Nicanor, and Timon, and Parmenas, and Nicolaus, a convert to Judaism who came from Antioch. ₆They brought them to the apostles, who prayed and laid their hands on them.

₇The word of God was spreading widely, and the number of the disciples in Jerusalem continued to be greatly increased; and a great many of the priests were accepting the faith.

8Stephen, full of grace and power, publicly gave wonderful demonstrations of the power of God in action. 9Some members of the Synagogue of the Freedmen, as it is called, and of the Cyrenians and Alexandrians, and of those from Cilicia and Asia proceeded to enter into debate with Stephen. 10They were quite unable to put up any defence against the inspired wisdom with which he spoke.

11They then in an underhand way put forward men to say: 'We heard him making blasphemous statements against Moses and against God.' 12They incited the people and the elders and the experts in the Law to action, and they attacked and seized him, and brought him into the Sanhedrin. 13They produced lying witnesses to say: 'This fellow never stops making statements calculated to decry the Holy Place and the Law. 14For we heard him say that this Jesus of Nazareth will destroy this place and will radically alter the customs which Moses handed down to us.' 15All those who were sitting in the Sanhedrin looked intently at Stephen, and his face looked to them like the face of an angel.

Chapter 7

THE high priest said to him: 'Is this so?' 2'Brothers and fathers,' Stephen said, 'give me a hearing. The God of glory appeared to our father Abraham while he was in Mesopotamia, before he came to live in Charran. 3He said to him: "Leave your country and your kindred, and go into the country which I will show you." 4At that time he left the country of the Chaldaeans and settled in Charran. After the death of his father, God removed him from there into the country in which you now live. 5But at that stage he did not give him possession of even one foot of it, but he did promise to give him and his descendants after him possession of it, although at the time he had no child.

6'What God said to him was this. He told him that his descendants would be aliens in a land which belonged to others, and that for four hundred years they would be enslaved and ill-treated there. 7"But," God said, "my judgment will come upon that nation to whom they will be enslaved, and they will afterwards leave that country, and will worship me in this place." 8And God gave Abraham the covenant, of which circumcision is the mark. Thus when Abraham had a son Isaac he circumcised him when he was eight days old, and Isaac became the father of Jacob, and Jacob became the father of the twelve patriarchs.

9'The patriarchs were jealous of Joseph, and sold him into Egypt. But God was with him 10and rescued him from all his troubles. God enabled him by his wisdom to win the approval of Pharaoh, king of Egypt. Pharaoh appointed him governor over the whole of Egypt, and over all his affairs. 11There was a famine over the whole of Egypt and Canaan. There was great distress, and our fathers could find no food. 12When Jacob heard that there was grain to be had in Egypt, he sent our fathers on a first expedition there. 13On their second visit Joseph told his brothers who he was, and Joseph's family became known to Pharaoh. 14Joseph sent and invited Jacob his father and the whole clan—about seventy-five persons—to leave their homes and to come to Egypt. 15So Jacob came down to Egypt, and he died there and so did our fathers. 16Their bodies were taken back to Shechem, and laid in the tomb which Abraham had bought for a sum of silver from the family of Emmor in Shechem.

17'When the time was approaching for the fulfilment of the promise which God had made to Abraham, the number of the people had grown and increased in Egypt. 18This went on until there came to the throne another Egyptian king who had never heard of Joseph. 19This king began a subtle persecution of our nation. He compelled our fathers to expose their children, so that the children would never live to grow up. 20It was at that time that Moses was born. He was a child of quite exceptional beauty. For three months he was brought up in his father's house. 21Then, when he had to be exposed, Pharaoh's daughter adopted him, and brought him up as her own son. 22Moses was educated in all the wisdom of the Egyptians, and he was able both in speech and in action.

23'When he was forty years old, the idea came to him to visit his fellow-countrymen, the sons of Israel. 24He went to the help of one of them, whom he saw being unjustly treated. He stood up for the rights of the ill-used man, and struck the Egyptian. 25He thought that his fellow-countrymen would understand that God was going to rescue them through him. But they did not understand. 26The next day he came upon two of them fighting with each other, and tried to stop them quarrelling. "Men," he said to them, "you are fellow-countrymen. What's the point of injuring each other?" ²⁷But the man who was injuring his neighbour pushed him away. "Who," he said, "appointed you as a ruler or judge over us? ²⁸Do you want to murder me in the way you murdered the Egyptian yesterday?" ²⁹When he heard this, Moses fled. He went into exile in the country of Midian, and there he became the father of two sons.

³⁰'When forty years had passed, when he was in the desert of Mount Sinai, an angel appeared to him in a flame of fire in a bush. ³¹When Moses saw this, he was amazed at the sight. When he went up to look at it, God's voice came to him: ³²"I am the God of your fathers, the God of Abraham, of Isaac, and of Jacob." Moses, shaking with fear, did not dare to look. ³³"Remove your sandals from your feet," the Lord said to him, "for the place on which you are standing is holy ground. ³⁴I have seen the ill-treatment which my people are receiving in Egypt, and I have heard their groans, and I have come down to rescue them. Come now! I am going to send you to Egypt." ³⁵It was this very Moses whom they had rejected. It was to him they said: "Who appointed you a ruler or a judge?" It was this man whom God sent to be their leader and liberator, through the angel who appeared to him in the bush. ³⁶It was he who led them out, after providing wonderful demonstrations of the power of God in action in the country of Egypt and at the Red Sea and in the desert for forty years. ³⁷It was this Moses who said to the Israelites: "God will raise up a prophet from your own fellow-countrymen, as he raised me up." ³⁸He it was who, on the day on which the people assembled in the desert, acted as intermediary between the angel who talked with him on Mount Sinai and our fathers. He received living words to give to us, ³⁹but your fathers refused to obey him. Instead of that they rejected him, and their hearts turned back to Egypt. ⁴⁰They said to Aaron: "Make us gods who will lead us on our journeyings, for, as for this Moses who brought us out of the country of Egypt, we do not know what has happened to him."

⁴¹At that time they made a calf, and offered sacrifice to that idol, and held high revelry to celebrate what their hands had made. ⁴²So God turned from them, and abandoned them to the worship of the host of the sky, as it stands written in the book of the prophets:

"Did you bring sacrifice and offerings to me
    in the wilderness for forty years, O house of Israel?

₄₃Was it not the moving shrine of Moloch you took with you,
and the star of the god Rephan,
the images that you manufactured to worship?
Therefore, I will send you into exile beyond Babylon."

₄₄'It was the Tent of Witness that our fathers had with them in the desert. It was constructed as he who spoke to Moses ordered, following the pattern which Moses had seen. ₄₅It was this Tent of Witness which our fathers brought in with Joshua, when they took possession of the territories of the nations whom God drove out before our fathers, and which they handed down from generation to generation right down to the time of David. ₄₆David was dear to God, and he asked to be allowed to provide a dwelling-place for the God of Jacob. ₄₇But it was Solomon who built a house for him. ₄₈But the Most High does not live in man-made houses. As the prophet says:

₄₉"Heaven is my throne,
and earth is a footstool for my feet.
What kind of house will you build for me? says the Lord,
or what is the place where I am to rest?
₅₀Is it not my hand which has made everything?" '

₅₁'Stubborn men that you are, with hearts and ears no better than the uncircumcised heathen, you are always resisting the Holy Spirit. As your fathers did so, so do you. ₅₂Was there a prophet whom your fathers did not persecute? They killed those who told in advance about the coming of the Just One. And now you have betrayed and murdered him, ₅₃and you are the people who received the Law, transmitted to you by angels—and you have not obeyed it!'

₅₄Stephen's speech so infuriated them that they gnashed their teeth at him. ₅₅But he, filled with the Holy Spirit, gazed up into heaven, and saw the glory of God, and Jesus standing at God's right hand. ₅₆'I see the heavens standing open,' he said, 'and the Son of Man standing at God's right hand.'

₅₇At this they shrieked and shut their ears and rushed at him in a body. ₅₈They threw him out of the city, and stoned him. The witnesses left their clothes in charge of a young man called Saul. ₅₉So they stoned Stephen, and, as they did so, he prayed: 'Lord Jesus, receive my spirit!' ₆₀Then he knelt down, and said in a voice that all could hear: 'Lord, do not hold this sin against them.' When he had said this, he fell asleep in death.

Chapter 8

S AUL thoroughly approved of Stephen's murder.

At that time a savage outbreak of persecution against the Jerusalem church began. With the exception of the apostles, they were all dispersed all over Judaea and Samaria. ₂Devout men took away Stephen's body and buried it, and paid it the last tribute of mourning. ₃Saul began a merciless attack upon the church. He went from house to house, seizing both men and women, and committing them to prison.

₄Those who were dispersed went all over the country, bringing the message of the Good News. ₅Philip went down to a town in Samaria and proclaimed the Messiah to them. ₆The crowds as one man listened eagerly to what Philip was saying, when they heard his words, and saw the demonstrations of divine power in action which he was performing. ₇Unclean spirits came out of many who were possessed by them, shrieking as they came out, and many who were paralysed and lame were cured. ₈There was great joy in that city.

₉There was in that town a man called Simon, who, before Philip arrived, had astonished the people of Samaria with his displays of magic. He claimed to be someone great. ₁₀Everyone of every age and class listened eagerly to him. 'This man,' they said, 'is the power of God which is called "The Great".' ₁₁They listened eagerly to him, because for some considerable time he had been astonishing them with his magic. ₁₂Both men and women were baptized, when they took the decision to believe the Good News which Philip was bringing them about the Kingdom of God, and about Jesus Christ.

₁₃Simon himself took the decision to believe, and, after he had been baptized, he was constantly in Philip's company. He was astonished as he watched things happening which were great demonstrations of the power of God in action.

₁₄When the apostles in Jerusalem heard that Samaria had welcomed the message of God, they despatched Peter and John to them. ₁₅They came down, and prayed for them to receive the Holy Spirit. ₁₆As yet the Holy Spirit had not descended on any of them. They had so far been baptized only in the name of the Lord Jesus. ₁₇Then they laid their hands on them, and they received the Holy Spirit.

₁₈When Simon saw that the Holy Spirit was given through the lay-

257

ing on of the apostles' hands, he offered them money. 19'Give me too this gift,' he said, 'so that anyone on whom I lay my hands may receive the Holy Spirit.' 20Peter said to him: 'May both you and your money perish together, because you thought you could buy for money the gift God gives freely. 21This is a matter in which you have no share or part, for your heart is not right in God's sight. 22Repent of this wickedness of yours. Pray to God to forgive you, if it is possible, that such an idea ever entered your mind. 23It is plain to me that you are no better than the slave of wickedness, on the way to tasting the bitterness like gall which godless worship brings.' 24'It is you who must pray to the Lord for me,' Simon answered, 'so that none of the things you have spoken of may happen to me.'

25So when they had spoken the message of the Lord, and when they had demonstrated its truth by powerful arguments, they started out back to Jerusalem, and on the way they brought the Good News to many Samaritan villages.

26An angel of the Lord spoke to Philip. 'Up,' he said, 'and go south on the road which goes down from Jerusalem to Gaza.' (This is the desert road.) 27So he set out. There was an Ethiopian, a eunuch, a minister of state of Candace, the Ethiopian queen, her chancellor of the exchequer, who had come to worship at Jerusalem, 28and who was now on his way home. He was sitting in his carriage, reading the prophet Isaiah. 29The Spirit said to Philip: 'Go and join the carriage.' 30So Philip ran up, and heard him reading the prophet Isaiah aloud. 'Do you understand what you are reading?' he said. 31'How can I understand,' he said, 'without someone to be my guide?' He invited Philip to get in and sit with him. 32This was the passage of scripture which he was reading:

'He was led like a sheep to be slaughtered,
    and, like a lamb, voiceless when its fleece is being cut,
    he did not open his mouth.
33He was humiliated and he received no justice.
Who shall describe the family from which he came,
    for his life is taken away from the earth?'

34The eunuch said to Philip: 'Tell me, please, who is the prophet speaking about? Is it about himself or about someone else?' 35Then Philip began to speak. Starting from this passage of scripture, he told him the Good News about Jesus. 36As they were going along the road, they came to some water. 'Here is water,' the eunuch said· 'Is there any reason why I should not be baptized?'* ₃₈He ordered the carriage to halt. Philip and the eunuch both went down into the water, and Philip baptized him.

₃₉When they came up out of the water, the Spirit of the Lord seized Philip, and he was gone from the eunuch's sight. The eunuch continued his journey rejoicing. ₄₀Philip arrived in Azotus. He made a tour of all the towns, spreading the Good News, until he reached Caesarea.

Chapter 9

SAUL, still in a frenzy of murderous threats against the disciples of the Lord, went to the High Priest, ₂and asked for an official authorization to go to Damascus to the synagogues there. His purpose was to bring as prisoners to Jerusalem any adherents of the Way whom he might find there, men and women alike.

₃On his journey he had reached the outskirts of Damascus, when all of a sudden a blaze of light from the sky flashed around him. ₄He threw himself to the ground. He heard a voice saying to him: 'Saul, Saul, why are you persecuting me?' ₅'Who are you, Lord?' he said. The speaker answered: 'I am Jesus, and it is I whom you are persecuting. ₆But get up, and go into the town, and you will be told what you must do.' ₇His fellow-travellers stood speechless, for they heard the voice, but saw no one. ₈Saul got up from the ground, but, when he opened his eyes, he was unable to see anything. So they took his hand, and led him into Damascus. ₉For three days he was unable to see, and he ate and drank nothing.

₁₀In Damascus there was a disciple named Ananias. 'Ananias,' the Lord said to him in a vision. 'Here I am, Lord,' he said. ₁₁'Get up,' the Lord said to him, 'and go to the street called Straight, and ask at Judas' house for a man from Tarsus, called Saul. He is praying, ₁₂and in a vision he has seen a man called Ananias coming and laying his hands on him, to give him back his sight.' ₁₃'Lord,' said Ananias, 'the harm this man has done to God's people in Jerusalem is common talk. ₁₄And I have heard too that he has arrived here authorized by

*See Notes on pp. 575-6

the chief priests to arrest all who call on your name.' 15'Go,' the Lord said to him, 'because I have specially chosen this man to be my instrument to tell heathen nations and kings and the sons of Israel about me, 16for I will show him all that he must suffer for my sake.'

17Ananias went off, and went into that house, and laid his hands upon him. 'Brother Saul,' he said, 'the Lord—Jesus who appeared to you on the road as you were on your way here has sent me—to enable you to recover your sight, and so that you may be filled with the Holy Spirit.' 18Thereupon a substance like scales fell from Saul's eyes, and he recovered his sight, and got up, and was baptized. 19When he had taken some food, his strength returned.

Saul remained with the disciples at Damascus for some time. 20He immediately preached Jesus in the synagogues. 'This,' his message was, 'is the Son of God.' 21His hearers listened with astonishment. 'Isn't this the man,' they said, 'who in Jerusalem carried on a merciless campaign against those who call on this name? And wasn't the very purpose for which he came here to bring them as prisoners to the chief priests?' 22But Saul preached with increasing power and bewildered the Jews who lived in Damascus by proving that Jesus is the Messiah.

23After some considerable time, the Jews formed a plot to murder him. 24But Saul got to know about their plot. They were watching the town gates night and day in order to murder him. 25But his disciples took him during the night and lowered him in a basket down over the wall.

26When he arrived in Jerusalem, he tried to attach himself to the disciples. But they were afraid of him, because they did not really believe that he was a disciple. 27Barnabas took him, and brought him to the apostles, and told them the whole story of how Saul had seen the Lord on the road, and of how the Lord had spoken to him, and of how in Damascus he had freely and fearlessly preached in the name of Jesus. 28So he became an accepted member of the community at Jerusalem, 29and he preached freely and fearlessly in the name of the Lord. He talked to the Greek-speaking Jews, and debated with them. They tried to murder him. 30But his fellow-Christians got news of the plot, and brought him down to Caesarea, and sent him off to Tarsus.

31So the church enjoyed peace all over Judaea and Galilee and

Samaria, and continued to be built up, and to live in the fear of the Lord. Through the encouragement of the Holy Spirit the church continued to grow.

32During his travels amongst them all, Peter came down to God's people who lived at Lydda. 33There he came upon a man called Aeneas who had been bed-ridden for eight years. He was paralysed. 34'Aeneas,' Peter said to him, 'Jesus Christ is curing you. Get up, and make your own bed.' There and then he got up. 35Everyone who lived at Lydda and Sharon saw him, and they turned to the Lord.

36At Joppa there was a disciple called Tabitha, a name which means Dorcas, that is, Gazelle. She was constantly engaged in doing good works and in acts of charity. 37It so happened that at that time she fell ill and died. They washed her body, and laid it in an upper room. 38Since Lydda was near Joppa, the disciples had heard that Peter was there. So they sent two men with an invitation to come to them. 'Please include us in your travels,' they said, 'and don't delay.' 39Peter started out and went with them. When he arrived, they took him up into the upper room. All the widows stood there beside him weeping, and showing him the tunics and cloaks Dorcas used to make when she was with them. 40Peter put them all outside. He knelt and prayed. Then he turned to the dead woman and said: 'Tabitha, get up!' She opened her eyes, and saw Peter, and sat up. 41He gave her his hand and helped her to stand. Then he called in God's people and the widows, and presented her to them alive. 42What had happened became known all over Joppa, and many believed in the Lord. 43Peter stayed in Joppa for some considerable time with Simon, a tanner.

Chapter 10

IN Caesarea there was a man called Cornelius, who was a company commander in the Roman army in what was called the Italian battalion. 2He was a devout man and reverenced God, and so did all his household. He was generous in public acts of charity, and constant in private prayer to God.

3In a vision, about three o'clock in the afternoon, he clearly saw an angel of God coming down to him, and saying: 'Cornelius!' 4He gazed at the angel in awe. 'What is it, sir?' he said. The angel said to him: 'Your prayers and your acts of charity have gone up to God, and they have made God think very specially about you. ₅And now you must send men to Joppa, and you must bring here a man Simon, who is called Peter. ₆He is staying as a guest with a man Simon, a tanner, whose house is on the sea-shore.' ₇When the angel who spoke to him had gone away, Cornelius called two of his servants and a devout soldier, who was one of his personal attendants. ₈He told them the whole story, and sent them off to Joppa.

₉On the next day, while they were on their way, and when they were nearing the town, Peter went up on to the flat roof of the house to pray. It was about twelve o'clock midday. ₁₀He became hungry and wanted something to eat. While food was being prepared for him, he fell into a trance, ₁₁in which he saw heaven standing open, and an object like a large sheet coming down. It was let down by the four corners, until it rested on the ground. ₁₂On it there were all the four-footed animals, all the reptiles that creep on the ground and all the birds which fly in the sky. ₁₃He heard a voice. 'Up, Peter!' it said, 'Kill and eat!' ₁₄'Certainly not!' Peter said. 'I have never eaten anything which is defiled and unclean.' ₁₅A second time he heard a voice. 'You must not regard as defiled what God has cleansed,' it said to him. ₁₆This happened three times, and immediately afterwards the sheet was taken back up into heaven.

₁₇While Peter was quite at a loss to understand what the vision he had seen could mean, the men who had been sent by Cornelius had enquired their way to Simon's house, and stood at the gate. ₁₈They called out to ask if Simon called Peter was staying as a guest there. ₁₉While Peter was thinking about the vision, the Spirit said to him: 'Three men are here asking for you. ₂₀Go down, and don't hesitate to go with them, because it is I who have sent them.'

₂₁Peter came down. 'I am the man you are looking for,' he said to the men. 'What brought you here?' ₂₂They said: 'Cornelius, a company commander, a good man and a man who reverences God, and who is held in high reputation by the whole Jewish nation, was instructed by a holy angel to send for you to come to his house, and to listen to what you have to say.' ₂₃Peter invited them in as his guests. The next day he left with them, and some of the members of the congregation at Joppa accompanied him.

₂₄On the following day they entered Caesarea. Cornelius was expecting them, and had invited his relations and his closest friends to join him. ₂₅When Peter was about to go into his house, Cornelius came to meet him and knelt at his feet, and worshipped him. ²⁶Peter lifted him up. 'Get up!' he said. 'I too am a man.' ²⁷So Peter went into the house in conversation with him, and found a large gathering of people there.

²⁸'You are well aware,' Peter said, 'that it is against the Law for a Jew to have any contact with a foreigner, or to visit him in his house. But God has shown me that I must not regard any human being as defiled or unclean. ²⁹That is why I came without any objection when you sent for me. Tell me, then, what was your reason for sending for me?' ³⁰'Four days ago, exactly to this very hour,' said Cornelius, 'I was praying in my house at three o'clock in the afternoon, when a man in shining clothes stood in front of me. ³¹"Cornelius," he said, "your prayer has been heard, and your acts of charity have not gone unnoticed by God. ³²Send, then, to Joppa, and invite Simon, called Peter, to come to you. He is a guest in the house of Simon a tanner, who lives in a house on the sea-shore." ³³So without delay I sent for you, and I am very grateful to you for coming. So now we are all here in God's presence to listen to everything that you have been instructed by the Lord to say.' ³⁴Peter began to speak. 'I am truly convinced,' he said, 'that there is no favouritism with God, ³⁵but that he is ready to receive any man in any nation who reverences him and who does what is right. ³⁶You know the message that God sent to the people of Israel, when he sent the Good News of peace with himself through Jesus Christ—and Jesus is Lord of all. ³⁷You know what happened all over Judaea. You know how it all began in Galilee, after the baptism which John proclaimed. ³⁸You know about Jesus of Nazareth, and how God anointed him with the Holy Spirit and with power, and how he went about helping everyone, and curing all those who were under the tyranny of the devil, because God was with him. ³⁹We are eye-witnesses of all that he did in Judaea and in Jerusalem. You know how they killed him by hanging him on a cross. ⁴⁰On the third day God brought him back to life again, in such a way that he was plainly and unmistakably seen, ⁴¹not by the whole people, but by witnesses who had been already chosen by God, seen, I mean, by us. We actually shared meals with him after he had come back to life again. ⁴²He gave us orders to preach to the people, and to convince them that it is he who has been destined to be the judge of the living and of the dead. ⁴³All the prophets are witnesses to him, and to the fact that everyone who believes in him receives forgiveness of sins through him.'

⁴⁴While Peter was still speaking, the Holy Spirit descended on all

who had been listening to what he was saying. 45The Jewish believers who had come with Peter were all amazed, because the gift of the Spirit had been given so freely and generously to people who were not Jews, 46for they heard them speaking with tongues and praising God. Then Peter said: 47'Can anyone forbid water to be brought, and can anyone try to stop these people being baptized? They have received the Holy Spirit, just as we have done.' 48He gave orders for them to be baptized in the name of Jesus Christ. Then they asked him to wait with them for some days.

Chapter 11

THE apostles and the members of the Christian community in Judaea heard that people who were not Jews had received the message of God. 2When Peter came up to Jerusalem, the Jewish Christians questioned his action. 3'You went into the homes of men who are uncircumcised heathens,' they said, 'and shared meals with them.'

4Peter began at the beginning, and told them the whole story step by step. 5'I was praying in the town of Joppa,' he said, 'when in a trance I saw a vision. I saw an object like a large sheet coming down. It was being let down by the four corners, and it came right down to me. 6I looked at it closely and tried to make out what it was. I saw on it the four-footed animals that walk on the ground, the wild beasts and the reptiles and the birds of the sky. 7I heard a voice. "Up, Peter!" it said. "Kill and eat!" 8"Certainly not, sir," I said, "because no defiled or unclean food has ever entered my mouth." 9The voice spoke a second time from heaven. "You must not regard as defiled," it said, "what God has cleansed." 10This happened three times, and then everything was drawn up again into heaven.

11'At that very moment three men arrived at the house where we were. They had been sent from Caesarea to me. 12The Spirit told me not to hesitate to go with them. These six members of the congregation came with me, and we went into the man's house. 13He told us the story of how he had seen the angel standing in his house, and how the angel had said to him: "Send to Joppa, and bring here Simon called Peter. 14He will tell you how you and the members of your household will be saved." 15No sooner had I begun to speak than the Holy Spirit descended upon them, as he did on us too at the beginning. 16I remembered how the Lord had said: "John baptized with water, but you will be baptized with the Holy Spirit." 17If then God gave them, when they believed in the Lord Jesus Christ, the same gift as he gave to us, when we first believed, who was I to try to hinder God? Could I thwart him?'

18When they heard this story, they at once abandoned their opposition and praised God. 'We can only believe,' they said, 'that God has given to the Gentiles too the repentance which is the way to life.'

19Those who had been dispersed because of the trouble which resulted from the case of Stephen penetrated as far as Phoenicia and Cyprus and Antioch, but they preached the word to no one except to Jews. 20But there were some of them, men who came from Cyprus and Cyrene, who arrived in Antioch and who preached there to the Greeks as well, telling them the Good News of the Lord Jesus. 21The Lord was their ally, and a large number believed and turned to the Lord.

22News of what they were doing reached the ears of the congregation in Jerusalem. So they despatched Barnabas to Antioch. 23When he arrived and saw God's grace in action, he was glad, and he urged them all to remain resolutely loyal to the Lord, 24for he was a good man, full of the Holy Spirit and of faith. The Lord's followers were increased in crowds. 25Barnabas went to Tarsus to look for Saul. 26When he had found him, he brought him to Antioch. For a whole year they were the guests of the church there, and they gave instruction to crowds of people. It was in Antioch that the disciples were first called Christians.

27During that time prophets came down from Jerusalem to Antioch. 28One of them, called Agabus, rose and foretold through the Spirit that there was going to be a severe famine all over the inhabited world. This happened in the time of Claudius. 29The disciples resolved to send help to the Christian community in Jerusalem, each making the contribution he could afford. 30This they did, and they sent their contributions to the elders through Barnabas and Saul.

Chapter 12

AT that time Herod launched a violent attack on certain members of the church. ₂He beheaded James, John's brother. ₃When he saw that this was a policy which delighted the Jews, he went on to arrest Peter. (It was during the Festival of Unleavened Bread.) ₄He seized Peter and put him into prison. He handed him over to four squads of soldiers, each with four men in it, to guard him, for it was his intention to put him on public trial after the Passover Festival.

₅So Peter was closely guarded in prison, but all the time the church was earnestly praying to God for him. ₆On the night before Herod was going to bring him into court, Peter, fettered with two chains, was sleeping between two soldiers, and the guards, stationed in front of the door, were keeping watch over the prison. ₇An angel of the Lord appeared, and a light shone in the building. The angel touched Peter's side, and wakened him. 'Quick!' he said. 'Up!' His fetters fell from his hands. ₈'Fasten your belt,' the angel said, 'and put on your sandals.' Peter did so. 'Put on your coat,' the angel said, 'and follow me.'

₉So he went out and followed him. He did not realize that what was being done by the angel was really happening; he thought that he was seeing a vision. ₁₀They passed through the first and second guards, and came to the iron gate which led into the city. All by itself it opened for them. They went out, and they went one street farther, and then suddenly the angel left him.

₁₁When Peter came to his senses, he said: 'Now I know for certain that the Lord sent his angel and rescued me from what Herod was going to do to me, and from what the Jewish people hoped would happen.' ₁₂When he realized what had happened, he made his way to the house of Mary, the mother of John, who was called Mark. Many had gathered there, and were praying. ₁₃Peter knocked at the door of the gateway, and a maidservant called Rhoda came to answer his knock. ₁₄She recognized Peter's voice, and she was so overcome with joy that, instead of opening the gate, she ran in with the news that Peter was standing at the gate. ₁₅'You're raving,' they said to her. She insisted that he was there. 'It is his angel,' they said. ₁₆Peter went on knocking. When they opened the door, they were astonished to see him. ₁₇He signed to them with his hand to be quiet, and he told them the story of how the Lord had brought him out of prison. 'Take the news to James and to the members of the church,' he said to them. And he went out, and went to another place.

18When day came there was consternation among the soldiers. They could not think what had happened to Peter. 19When Herod had ordered a search to be made for Peter, and had failed to find him, he examined the guards, and ordered them to be executed. Herod then left Judaea, and went down to Caesarea, and stayed some time there.

20Herod was angry with the people of Tyre and Sidon. They came to him in a body, and, when they had gained the support of Blastus, the king's chamberlain, they sued for peace, for their country depended for its food supplies on the king's country. 21A day was fixed, and on it Herod put on his royal robes, and took his seat on the bench in his court, and made an oration to them. 22'It is the voice of a god, and not of a man,' the people kept shouting. 23There and then an angel of the Lord struck him, because he did not give the glory to God; and he was eaten by worms and died.

24The word of the Lord flourished increasingly. 25Barnabas and Saul completed their mission and then returned from Jerusalem. They brought with them John, who was called Mark.

Chapter 13

IN the congregation at Antioch there was a group of prophets and teachers. There were Barnabas and Simeon, who was called Niger, and Lucius who came from Cyrene, and Manaen, who as a boy had been brought up with Herod the tetrarch, and Saul. 2When they were worshipping the Lord and fasting, the Holy Spirit said: 'Come! I want you to assign Barnabas and Saul to the special task to which I have summoned them.' 3When they had fasted and prayed, they laid their hands on them and sent them.

4After they had been given their marching orders by the Holy Spirit, they went down to Seleucia, and from there they sailed to Cyprus. 5When they arrived in Salamis, they proclaimed the message of God in the Jewish synagogues. They had John with them as their helper. 6They made a tour of the whole island as far as Paphos. There they met a Jew who was a religious impostor and a practising sorcerer. His name was Bar-Jesus. 7He enjoyed the patronage of Sergius Paulus, the proconsul, an intelligent man. Sergius Paulus invited Barnabas and Saul to visit him, for he was eager to hear the message of God. 8Elymas the sorcerer—this is the translation of his name—did everything possible to obstruct them, and did his best to sidetrack the proconsul's interest in the faith. 9But Saul, whose other name is Paul, was filled with the Holy Spirit, and looked steadily at him. 10'You utter fraud!' he said. 'You complete villain! You son of the devil! You enemy of all goodness! Will you not stop trying to make men lose the way to God? 11Now the Lord has struck! For a time you will be blind, and you will not be able to see the light of the sun.' There and then a mist and a darkness fell upon him, and he went about looking for people to lead him by the hand. 12When the proconsul saw what had happened, he decided to accept the Christian faith, for he was astonished at the teaching of the Lord.

13Paul and his friends set sail from Paphos, and arrived at Perga in Pamphylia. John left them, and went back to Jerusalem. 14They went across country from Perga and reached Pisidian Antioch. On the Sabbath day they went into the synagogue, and took their seats. 15After the reading of the Law and the Prophets the synagogue officials sent them an invitation. 'Brothers,' they said, 'if you have any message of exhortation for the people, please give it.'

16So Paul rose, and with a gesture of his hand he said: 'Men of Israel, and you who, although you are not Jews, reverence God, give me a hearing. 17The God of this people Israel chose our fathers. During their stay as aliens in Egypt he raised the people to greatness. He demonstrated his power by leading them out of Egypt, 18and for some forty years he supported them in the desert. 19He destroyed seven nations in the country of Canaan, and then gave them possession of that country for a period of four hundred and fifty years. 20Following that, he gave them judges down to the time of the prophet Samuel. 21They then asked for a king, and God gave them Saul, Kish's son. He belonged to the tribe of Benjamin, and he reigned for forty years. 22Then God deposed him, and made David their king. He showed his opinion of David's character when he said: "I have found David the son of Jesse to be a man after my own heart, a man who will do all that I want him to do."

23It is one of this man's descendants whom God, as he promised, has made saviour for Israel—I mean Jesus. 24Before he came, John called upon the whole people of Israel to be baptized as a sign of their penitence. 25When John was nearing the end of his career, he said: "What do you suppose me to be? I am not he. But after me there is someone coming whose shoe laces I am not fit to untie." 26Brothers —I speak both to those of you who are directly descended from Abraham and to those of you who, although you are not Jews, share our worship of God—it is to us that this message of salvation has been sent.

27The citizens of Jerusalem and their leaders failed to recognize him, and they failed to understand what the prophets said, although the books of the prophets are read to them every Sabbath; but by condemning him to death they fulfilled these very prophecies. 28Though they could find no charge to justify his death, they asked Pilate to have him killed. 29When they had finished doing everything to him that scripture said had to be done, they took him down from the cross, and laid his body in a tomb. 30But God brought him back to life again. 31Over a period of some considerable time he appeared to those who came up from Galilee to Jerusalem with him, and they can supply first-hand evidence to the people that this is so. 32We bring to you the Good News that God has made the promise that he gave to our ancestors 33come true for our children, by bringing Jesus back to life, as it stands written in the second psalm:

> 1"You are my son,
>   today I have begotten you."

34As for the fact that he did bring him back to life again, never again to return to death's decay, this is what he says:

> "I will give you the blessings of David holy and certain."

35That is why in another passage he says:

> "You will not allow your holy one to experience death's decay."

36David served the will of God in his own day and generation, and slept the sleep of death, and went to join his ancestors. He thus did actually experience death's decay. 37But he whom God brought back to life again never experienced death's decay. 38Brothers, we want you to know that forgiveness of sins is offered to you through this man, 39and that everyone who believes in him is acquitted from everything for which the Law of Moses could never gain acquittal. 40You must be very careful to see to it that what the prophet spoke about does not happen to you:

41"Look, you scoffers, wonder and perish!
For in your days I will do something,
Something you will never believe,
    even if someone tells you of it." '

42As they were leaving the synagogue, the congregation urged them to come and talk about these things to them again on the next Sabbath. 43When the congregation was dispersed, many of the Jews and many of the Gentiles, who had been converted to Judaism and who worshipped with them, accompanied Paul and Barnabas, who continued to talk to them and to try to persuade them to commit themselves to the grace of God.

44On the next Sabbath almost the whole population of the town gathered to listen to the message of the Lord. 45The Jews were consumed with jealousy when they saw the crowds. They contradicted everything that Paul said, but it was invective rather than argument that they used. 46Paul and Barnabas did not mince their words. 'We were bound to give you the first opportunity to hear God's message,' they said. 'But, since you rejected it, and since by so doing you stand self-condemned as not fit to receive eternal life, we turn to the Gentiles. 47This is what God has instructed us to do:

"I have made you a light for the Gentiles,
    So that through you salvation may be brought
        to the ends of the earth." '

48When the Gentiles heard this, they were glad, and they praised the Lord for the message he had sent; and all who were destined for eternal life became believers. 49The message of the Lord spread all over the countryside.

50But the Jews exerted their influence on pious and aristocratic women and on the leading men of the town, and thus instigated persecution against Paul and Barnabas, and they ejected them from their district. 51They shook the last speck of dust from their shoes, to show them that they regarded them as godless heathens, and went to Iconium; 52and the disciples were filled with the joy of the Holy Spirit.

Chapter 14

IN Iconium they went in the same way into the Jewish synagogue, and they spoke with such effect that a large number of both the Jews and the Greeks believed. 2The Jews who refused to believe incited the Gentiles, and deliberately poisoned their minds against the members of the Christian community. 3They spent some considerable time there, speaking fearlessly with complete confidence in the Lord, who confirmed the message of his grace by enabling them to perform wonderful demonstrations of the divine power in action.

4The population of the town was split in two. Some sided with the Jews and some with the apostles. 5But, when they became aware that there was a move afoot both of the Jews and of the Gentiles and their leaders savagely to attack and to stone them, 6they made their escape to the Lycaonian towns of Lystra and Derbe and the surrounding country. 7There they continued to tell the story of the Good News.

8In Lystra there was a man whose feet were helpless. He had been a cripple since he was born and had never walked. 9He listened to Paul speaking. Paul looked intently at him, and saw that he had faith to be cured. 10He said to him in a commanding voice: 'Get up, and stand erect on your feet!' The man jumped up and began to walk.

11When the crowds saw what Paul had done, they shouted in the Lycaonian language: 'The gods have taken human form, and have come down to us.' 12They called Barnabas Zeus, and Paul Hermes, because he was the chief speaker. 13The priest of Zeus, whose temple was just outside the town gates, brought bulls and garlands to the gates, for he and the people wanted to offer sacrifice. 14When the apostles Barnabas and Paul heard what was going on, they ripped their clothes in distress, and rushed into the crowd. 15'Men,' they shouted, 'why are you doing this? We too are men with feelings exactly the same as yours, and we are bringing you the Good News which invites you to turn from these futile things to a God who is alive, the God who made the sky and the earth and the sea, and everything in them. 16In past ages he allowed all the nations to go their own way. 17And yet he did not leave himself with nothing to point men to himself. He showed his kindness to you by giving you rains from the sky, and the seasons, each with its crops, and by satisfying your hearts with food and joy.' 18Even though they said this, they could hardly stop the crowds sacrificing to them.

19A group of Jews arrived from Antioch and Iconium, and they so worked on the crowds that they stoned Paul, and dragged him out of the town, thinking that he was dead. 20But, when the disciples were standing in a circle round him, he got up and went into the town. The next day he left for Derbe with Barnabas.

21After they had told the Good News to that town, and had made many disciples, they returned to Lystra and to Iconium and to Antioch. 22In each place they fortified the souls of the disciples, and urged them to stand fast in the faith. 'Through many trials,' they said, 'we must find our way into the Kingdom of God.' 23When they had appointed elders for them in each congregation, and when they had prayed and fasted, they committed them to the Lord in whom they had believed. 24So they went through Pisidia, and came to Pamphylia. 25When they had preached their message in Perga, they reached the coast at Attaleia. 26From there they sailed to Antioch, where they had been commended to the grace of God for the task which they had now completed. 27When they arrived there, they called a meeting of the congregation, and told them the story of all that God had done along with them, and how he had opened the door of faith to the Gentiles. 28They spent a long time with the disciples.

Chapter 15

A GROUP of men came down from Judaea, and tried to teach the members of the Christian community that, if they were not circumcised, as the Mosaic practice demanded, it was not possible for them to be saved. 2Paul and Barnabas strongly differed from them and hotly debated with them. It was decided that Paul and Barnabas and some others of them should go up to meet the apostles and elders in Jerusalem to discuss the whole question with them. 3When they had been sent on their way by the congregation, they went through Phoenicia and Samaria, telling the story of the conversion of the Gentiles as they went, and all the members of the Christian communities were delighted to hear it.

4When they arrived in Jerusalem, they were welcomed by the

congregation and the apostles and the elders, and they told them the news of all that God had done in company with them.

₅Some men who had accepted the faith, and who belonged to the party of the Pharisees, rose and said that the Gentiles must be circumcised, and that they must enjoin them to observe the Law of Moses. ₆The apostles and the elders held a meeting to examine the whole matter. ₇After a long debate Peter rose. 'Brothers,' he said to them, 'you are aware that in the very early days of our faith it was God's choice that I should be the means whereby the Gentiles heard the message of the Gospel, and accepted it. ₈And God, who knows the hearts of all, signified his approval by giving them the Holy Spirit, exactly as he gave him to us too. ₉He made no distinction between them and us, for it was by faith that he purified their hearts. ₁₀Why, then, are you trying to make God change his mind, by insisting that the disciples should submit to a yoke which neither we nor our fathers were able to bear? ₁₁Surely the fact is that we believe that it is through the grace of the Lord Jesus Christ that we were saved, just as they have been.'

₁₂At this the whole assembly fell silent. They proceeded to listen to Barnabas and Paul recounting the story of all the wonderful demonstrations of divine power that God had shown among the Gentiles through them.

₁₃When they had finished speaking, James said: 'Brothers, give me a hearing. ₁₄Simeon has related to you the story of the first occasion when God demonstrated his care for the Gentiles, and his intention to take from them a people for himself. ₁₅And this is precisely what the prophets said would happen. You remember the passage:

₁₆"After this I will return,
   and I will rebuild the fallen dwelling of David.
I will rebuild the ruins,
   and I will set it up again,
₁₇in order that the rest of mankind may seek the Lord,
   and all the Gentiles who are called by my name,
₁₈says the Lord who has made these things known long since." '

₁₉'It is therefore my considered judgment that we should not lay unnecessary burdens on the Gentiles who turn to God, ₂₀but that we should instruct them to have nothing to do with anything which has been polluted by contact with idols, and to have nothing to do with unchastity, and not to use as food the flesh of animals which have been killed by strangling, and from which the blood has not been properly drained away.* 21If anyone still personally wants to observe the Law he can do so, for from ancient times there have been those in every town who proclaimed the Law of Moses, and it is still read in the synagogues every Sabbath.'

22Then the apostles and the elders, together with the whole congregation, decided to choose men to represent them, and to send them to Antioch with Paul and Barnabas. It was Judas, called Barsabbas, and Silas, leading men in the Christian community, whom they chose. 23They gave them this written message to take with them: 'As brothers to brothers, we the apostles and elders send our greetings to those in Antioch and Syria and Cilicia who have come into the church from the Gentiles. 24Since we heard that some people from us have disturbed you and have unsettled your minds with their statements, although they were not acting under instructions from us, 25after we had held a meeting, we decided to choose men and to send them to you, with our beloved Barnabas and Paul, 26who are men who have risked their lives for the sake of our Lord Jesus Christ. 27So we have sent Judas and Silas, and they will tell you by word of mouth the same things as are in this letter.

28'The Holy Spirit and we have decided to lay no further burden on you other than these necessary things—29that you must have nothing to do with meat which has formed part of a sacrifice to an idol, that you must not use as food the flesh of animals from which the blood has not been properly drained away, and which have been killed by being strangled, and that you must have nothing to do with unchastity. If you carefully guard against these things, you will do well. Farewell!'

30When they had been sent on their way, they went down to Antioch. There they called a meeting of the congregation, and delivered the letter to them. 31When they had read the letter, they rejoiced in the encouragement it gave them. 32Judas and Silas, for they themselves were prophets, said much to encourage the Christian community, and to settle them more firmly in the faith. 33When they had stayed for some time, the community sent them back to those who had sent them, with every good wish for their welfare.

*See Notes on pp. 575-6

₃₅But Paul and Barnabas stayed on in Antioch, teaching and telling along with many others the Good News of the message of the Lord.

₃₆Some time later, Paul said to Barnabas: 'Let us go back and visit the Christian communities in every town in which we proclaimed the message of the Lord, and let us see how things are going with them.' ₃₇Barnabas wished to take John, called Mark, with them as well. ₃₈But Paul did not think it wise to take with them the man who had been a deserter in Pamphylia, and who had not gone with them to the work. ₃₉There was such a sharp difference of opinion between them that they parted company, and Barnabas took Mark and sailed to Cyprus, ₄₀while Paul chose Silas and went off, after he had been committed to the Lord's grace by the Christian community. ₄₁He made a tour of Syria and Cilicia, strengthening the congregations as he went.

Chapter 16

Paul reached Derbe and Lystra. There was a disciple called Timothy there. He was the son of a Jewess who was a Christian, but his father was a Greek. ₂He was well spoken of by the members of the Christian community in Lystra and Iconium. ₃Paul wanted him to come away with him. So he took him and circumcised him, so as not to prejudice his work among the Jews of those parts, for they all knew that his father had been a Greek.

₄On their way through the towns, they passed on to them the decisions which had been reached by the apostles and elders in Jerusalem, and told them to observe them. ₅So day by day the congregations were strengthened in the faith, and increased in number more and more.

₆They made a tour of the Phrygian and Galatian district, because they had been prevented by the Holy Spirit from telling the message in Asia. ₇When they reached the borders of Mysia, they tried to make their way into Bithynia, but the Spirit of Jesus did not allow them to do so. ₈So they skirted Mysia, and came down to the seacoast at Troas.

₉During the night a vision appeared to Paul. The vision was of a man from Macedonia, standing there pleading with him. 'Come over into

Macedonia and help us,' the man said. 10When Paul had seen the vision, we immediately looked for some means of getting to Macedonia, for we concluded that God had called us to tell them the Good News. 11So we set sail from Troas, and had a straight run to Samothrace. On the next day we reached Neapolis. 12From there we went on to Philippi, the leading town of that district of Macedonia, and a Roman colony. We spent some days in this town.

13On the Sabbath we went out through the town gate along the river bank, where we expected to find a place where the Jews met for prayer. When we reached it, we sat down and began to talk to the women who had come to the meeting. 14There was a woman called Lydia there. She was a dealer in purple dye, and she came from the town of Thyatira. Although she was a Gentile, she was a worshipper of God. She listened, because the Lord had opened her heart, and awakened her interest in what Paul had to say. 15When she and all her household had been baptized, she urged them: 'If you are really convinced that I am a loyal follower of the Lord, come to my house and stay with me.' And she would take no refusal.

16As we were on our way to the place of prayer, a little slave-girl, who was regarded as being inspired by the spirit of Apollo, met us. Her owners made a handsome profit out of her fortune-telling. 17She kept following Paul and us and shouting: 'These men are the servants of the Most High God, and they are proclaiming to us the way of salvation.' 18She kept on doing this for many days. Paul could stand it no longer. He turned and said to the spirit: 'In the name of the Lord Jesus Christ I order you to come out of her.' There and then it came out of her.

19When her owners saw that their hope of profit was gone, they seized Paul and Silas, and forcibly led them to the city square to the town officials. 20They brought them to the magistrates. 'These men,' they said, 'who are Jews, are disturbing our town. 21They are trying to propagate ways of life which it is quite wrong for us who are Romans to accept or to practise.' 22The mob joined in attacking them. The magistrates forcibly stripped them, and ordered them to be flogged. 23When they had given them a severe beating, they threw them into prison, with strict orders to the gaoler to keep them securely. 24Since he had received such an order, he flung them into the inner prison, and fastened their feet in the stocks.

25About midnight Paul and Silas were praying and singing hymns to God. The prisoners were listening to them. 26Suddenly there was so violent an earthquake that the foundations of the prison were shaken. Immediately all the doors burst open, and the fetters of all the prisoners were loosened from the wall.

27When the gaoler awoke, and saw the doors standing open, he drew his sword and was about to commit suicide, for he thought that his prisoners had escaped. 28'Don't injure yourself,' Paul shouted to him. 'We are all here.' 29The gaoler called for lights and rushed in, shaking in every limb. He threw himself down at the feet of Paul and Silas. 30He brought them out and said: 'Sirs, what must I do to be saved?' 31They said: 'Commit yourself to the Lord Jesus Christ, and you and your family will be saved.' 32They told the message of the Lord to him and to his whole household.

33There and then, although it was in the middle of the night, he took them in and bathed the weals the flogging had left on them. He and all his family were at once baptized, 34and he took them into his house and provided them with a meal. He rejoiced, and so did all his family, that he had become a believer in God.

35When day came, the magistrates sent their attendants to say: 'Let these men go!' 36The gaoler reported this message to Paul. 'The magistrates,' he said, 'have sent orders for your release. So now, come out, and go on your way, and all good things go with you!' 37But Paul said to him: 'They publicly flogged us without a trial, and they flung us into prison—and we are Roman citizens! And now are they going to put us out and hush the business up? They are not going to get away with that! Tell them to come themselves and take us out!' 38The attendants reported to the magistrates what Paul had said. The magistrates were terrified when they heard that they were Roman citizens. 39So they came and apologized to them, and took them out, and requested them to leave the town. 40When they had left the prison, they went to Lydia's house, and, when they had seen the members of the Christian community, and had spoken encouragingly to them, they left.

Chapter 17

When they had taken the road through Amphipolis and Apollonia, they arrived in Thessalonica, where there was a Jewish synagogue. 2As he always did, Paul went into the synagogue, and for three Sabbaths he argued with them on the basis of scripture, 3expounding the scriptures and citing passages as evidence that the Messiah had to suffer and come back to life again after he had died. 'This Jesus of whom I am telling you is the Messiah,' he said. 4Some of them were convinced and attached themselves to Paul and Silas, including many of the Greeks, who, without becoming Jews, attended the synagogue to worship God, and the wives of many of the leading men in the community.

5The Jews bitterly resented the success of Paul and Silas. They got hold of some rascally street-corner idlers, and organized them into a mob, and attempted to set the city in an uproar. They attacked Jason's house. They were looking for Paul and Silas, to bring them before the public assembly of the people. 6When they were unable to find them, they dragged Jason and some of the members of the Christian community to the magistrates. 'The men,' they shouted, 'who are reducing the whole civilized order of things to chaos, have arrived here too, 7and Jason has received them as his guests. Their conduct is in flat contradiction of the decrees of Caesar, for they are declaring that someone else called Jesus is king.' 8The crowd and the magistrates were disturbed when they heard this, 9and they bound over Jason and the others to keep the peace, and let them go.

10The members of the Christian community immediately sent Paul and Silas away to Beroea under cover of night. When they arrived there, they made their way to the Jewish synagogue. 11The Jews there were more generous in their sympathies than those in Thessalonica. They listened eagerly to the Christian message, and they examined the scriptures every day, to find out if what Paul was saying was really true. 12Many of the Jews took the decision to believe, and so did a considerable number of wealthy Greek women, and men too. 13When the Thessalonian Jews learned that the message of God had been proclaimed by Paul in Beroea too, they came there also, and proceeded to incite the crowds to riot and disorder. 14The Christian community immediately sent Paul off on the road to the sea-coast. Silas and Timothy remained there in Beroea. 15Paul's escort convoyed him as far as Athens. They left him after he had given them instructions to Silas and Timothy to join him as soon as possible.

16While Paul was waiting for them in Athens, the sight of the city in the grip of idol-worship angered him. 17In the synagogue he carried on an argument with the Jews and with the Gentiles, who, without becoming Jews, attended the synagogue to worship God. And every day he talked in the city square with those whom he happened to meet.

18Some of the Epicurean and Stoic philosophers encountered him. Some of them said: 'What can this fellow with his ill-digested scraps of knowledge mean?' Others said: 'He seems to be a preacher of foreign divinities.' This was because Paul was telling the good news of Jesus and the resurrection. 19They took him and brought him to the Court of the Areopagus. 'May we know,' they said, 'what this new and strange teaching of yours is all about? 20Some of the things you are trying to introduce sound very strange to us. We would like to know what they mean.' 21The Athenians and the foreigners who live in Athens spend all their time in nothing other than in talking about and listening to whatever is the latest novelty.

22Paul took his stand in the middle of the Court of the Areopagus. 'Men of Athens,' he said, 'I cannot help seeing that generally speaking you tend to be a very religious people. 23As I was walking through the city, and as I was looking at the objects of your worship, in addition to all the other things, I came on an altar inscribed: "To an Unknown God." I have come to tell you about that which you worship without knowing what you are worshipping.

24'The God who made the world and everything that is in it is the Lord of heaven and earth. He does not have his home in man-made temples, 25nor can he be served by human hands, as if he stood in need of anything that men could give him. It is he who gives to all men life and breath and all things. 26He created every nation of mankind of one common stock, and gave them their homes all over the world. He fixed the appointed periods of every nation's rise and fall, and settled the boundaries within which they were to live. 27He created them to seek God, with the hope that they might grope after him in the shadows of their ignorance, and find him—and indeed he is close to each one of us. 28"In him we live and move and are," as even some of your own poets have said, "We are his children." 29Since we are the children of God, we ought not to think that the Deity is like an image of gold or silver or stone, fashioned by human art and design. 30God shut his eyes to the folly of those times when men knew no better. But now he is issuing his orders to all men everywhere to repent, 31because he has fixed a day on which his righteous judgment will come upon the world, through a man whom he has destined for that task. He has provided proof to all men that this is so by bringing this man Jesus back to life when he was dead.'

32When they heard of the resurrection of dead men, some laughed the whole matter out of court. But some said: 'We would like you to talk to us again about this.' 33With the discussion at this stage Paul left the court.

34There were some who attached themselves to him, and who decided to become believers. Among them were Dionysius, a member of the Court of the Areopagus, and a woman called Damaris, and others along with them.

Chapter 18

AFTER that Paul left Athens and went to Corinth. 2There he made the acquaintance of a Jew called Aquila. Aquila's family belonged to Pontus, but he had newly arrived from Italy with Priscilla, his wife. They had had to leave Italy, because Claudius had issued an order that all Jews must remove themselves from Rome. Paul went to visit them. 3Because he was of the same trade as they were, he stayed with them, and worked with them, for they were leather-workers by trade.

4He argued the case for Christianity every Sabbath in the synagogue, and tried to convince both Jews and Greeks. 5When Silas and Timothy came down from Macedonia, Paul began to devote himself entirely to preaching, insisting to the Jews that the Messiah was Jesus. 6When they opposed him with invective rather than with reason, he shook out his clothes at them, as a Jew might shake the polluted dust from his clothes, when he left a heathen town. 'The responsibility for your fate is your own,' he said to them. 'No blame attaches to me. From now on I will go to the Gentiles.' 7So he changed his lodging, and went to stay in the house of a man called Titius Justus, a worshipper of God, though not a Jew. This man's house was next door to the synagogue.

8Crispus, the president of the synagogue, became a believer in the Lord with his whole household. Many of the Corinthians who listened to Paul became believers and were baptized. 9During the night the Lord said to Paul in a vision: 'Don't be afraid! Go on speaking, and don't stop! 10For I am with you, and no one will try to harm you, because there are many people in this city who belong to me.' 11Paul settled among them for a year and six months, engaged in the work of instructing them in the message of God.

12When Gallio was proconsul of Achaia, the Jews made a concerted attack on Paul, and brought him to Gallio's court of justice. 13'This man,' they said, 'is trying to persuade people to worship God in a way that is illegal.' 14When Paul was going to speak, Gallio said to the Jews: 'If, you Jews, this was a matter of crime or of fraud, it would be reasonable for me to agree to give you a hearing. 15But, if this is a matter of debates about words, and about names, and about your own law, you must deal with it yourselves. I have no desire to give judgment on such things.' 16He forcibly ejected them from his court. 17They all took Sosthenes, the president of the synagogue, and beat him up in full view of Gallio's judgment seat. But Gallio was not concerned with things like that.

18Paul stayed on for some considerable time longer. Then he said goodbye to the members of the Christian community, and sailed away to Syria, accompanied by Priscilla and Aquila. At Cenchreae he had his hair cut off, because he had taken the Nazirite vow. 19When they reached Ephesus, he left them and went by himself into the synagogue, and debated with the Jews. 20When they asked him to stay longer, he refused, 21but, when he had said goodbye to them, he said: 'God willing, I will come back again to you.' So he sailed away from Ephesus. 22He arrived in Caesarea, and from there went up to Jerusalem, and greeted the congregation there. Then he went down to Antioch. 23After spending some time there, he went on a tour of the various places in the Galatian territory and in Phrygia, strengthening all the disciples as he went.

24A Jew, called Apollos, who was a native of Alexandria, arrived in Ephesus. He was a man of culture, and able to make very effective use of the scriptures. 25He had received instruction in the Way of the Lord. He was filled with enthusiasm, and in his speaking and teaching he gave an accurate account of the story of Jesus. But the only baptism he knew was John's. 26He began to speak freely and fearlessly in the synagogue. When Aquila and Priscilla had heard him speaking, they took him and gave him a more accurate account of the Way of God. 27When he wished to cross over to Achaea, the Christian community encouraged him to do so, and wrote to the disciples there to give him a welcome. When he arrived, he was of great assistance to those who through the grace of God had become believers, 28for he strenuously out-argued the Jews in public debate, by proving through the use of the scriptures that the Messiah is Jesus.

Chapter 19

WHILE Apollos was in Corinth, Paul went to Ephesus by way of the inland route. There he met a group of disciples. 2He asked them if they had received the Holy Spirit, when they became believers. 'No,' they said. 'We have not even heard that there is a Holy Spirit.' 3'What kind of baptism did you receive?' he said. 'John's baptism,' they said. 4Paul said: 'John's baptism was a baptism which was a sign of repentance. It was in the One who was coming after him that he told the people to believe, that is, in Jesus.' 5When they heard this, they were baptized in the name of the Lord Jesus. 6When Paul laid his hands on them, the Holy Spirit came upon them, and they began to speak with tongues and to prophesy. 7In all there were about twelve of these men.

8Paul went into the synagogue, and for three months he freely and fearlessly debated about the Kingdom of God, and tried to persuade men to accept it. 9When some in their obstinate refusal to believe resorted to slanderous statements about the Way in the presence of the whole congregation, Paul left them, and withdrew the disciples with him, and carried on the debate daily in the lecture hall of Tyrannus. 10This went on for two years, with the result that everyone who lived in the province of Asia, both Jews and Greeks, heard the message of the Lord. 11Through the hands of Paul, God performed extraordinary miracles, 12so that sweat-bands or towels which had been in contact with Paul's skin were taken away to those who were ill, and their illnesses left them, and the evil spirits went out of them.

13Some of the itinerant Jewish exorcists ventured to pronounce the name of the Lord Jesus over those who had evil spirits. 'I charge you by the Jesus whom Paul preaches,' was their formula. 14There were seven sons of a Jewish high priest called Scaeva who were doing this. 15But the evil spirit answered them: 'I know who Jesus is, and I understand who Paul is—but who are you?' 16The man in whom the evil spirit was jumped on them, and mastered and overpowered them all. The result was that they fled from that house naked and wounded.

17When this became known to all the Jews and Greeks who lived in Ephesus, they were terrified, and the name of the Lord Jesus came to be regarded as something quite extraordinary. 18Many of them accepted the Christian faith and came and confessed the error of their ways, and revealed the secrets of their spells. 19Many of those who practised sorcery brought their books and publicly burned them. When they reckoned up the value of them, they found it came to more than two thousand pounds.

20So the word of the Lord was powerfully increased and was mightily effective.

21After all this had happened, Paul under the guidance of the Spirit formed a plan to make a tour of Macedonia and Achaea, and then to go on to Jerusalem. 'After I have been there,' he said, 'I must see Rome too.' 22He sent two of his helpers, Timothy and Erastus, to Macedonia, while he himself stayed on in Asia for some time.

23At that time the Way was involved in a violent commotion. 24There was a man called Demetrius, a silversmith, who made silver models of the temple of Artemis, and who thereby provided very considerable profit for the craftsmen. 25He called a meeting of the craftsmen and of all who were similarly employed. 'Men,' he said to them, 'you well know that our financial prosperity depends on this business. 26You have the evidence of your eyes and ears that, not only in Ephesus, but practically all over Asia, this fellow Paul has persuaded a great many people to change their ideas altogether, for he says that the gods which are manufactured by hand are not gods at all. 27Not only is there a risk that our business is going to fall into disrepute, but there is also a danger that the temple of the great goddess Artemis may come to be regarded as of no importance, and that she whom Asia and the whole civilized world worships will be despoiled of her majesty.' 28When they heard this they were furiously angry. 'Great is Artemis of the Ephesians!' they kept shouting.

29Confusion spread all over the city. They seized Gaius and Aristarchus, fellow-travellers of Paul from Macedonia, and dragged them along with them, as they rushed like one man to the city theatre. ₃₀Paul wished to go into the crowd, but the disciples would not allow him. ₃₁Some of the Asiarchs, who were friendly with him, sent and urged him not to risk going into the theatre. ₃₂Some kept shouting one thing, and others another, for the meeting was in complete confusion, and the majority of them did not know why they had met.

₃₃Some of the crowd conjectured that Alexander must be the ringleader of the trouble, for the Jews were pushing him forward. Alexander wanted to speak to the people in his own defence, so he gestured to the crowd to be silent. ₃₄When they realized that he was a Jew, the crowd roared like one man, and for about two hours they shouted continuously: 'Great is Artemis of the Ephesians!'

₃₅When the city secretary had succeeded in quietening the mob, he said: 'Men of Ephesus, who is not well aware that the city of Ephesus is warden of the temple of the great Artemis, and of the sacred image which fell from heaven? ₃₆No one can deny that this is so. You must therefore keep calm and do nothing reckless. ₃₇You have brought these men here, although they are guilty neither of sacrilege nor of blasphemy against our goddess. ₃₈If Demetrius and his fellow-craftsmen have a complaint against anyone, assizes are held, and there are proconsuls. Let the parties to the dispute bring charges against each other. ₃₉If you have any further claim to make, the matter must be settled in a legally constituted assembly of the people. ₄₀In point of fact we run the very real danger of being charged with rioting because of today's proceedings, for there is no legitimate reason that we can offer for this uproar.' ₄₁With these words he dismissed the assembly.

Chapter 20

WHEN the uproar had subsided, Paul sent for the disciples, and, after he had spoken encouragingly to them, he said goodbye to them, and left to go to Macedonia. ₂He made a tour of those parts, and gave the people there many an encouraging talk. Then he went to Greece. ₃When he had been there for three months, the Jews hatched a plot against him, just when he was on the point of sailing for Syria. He, therefore, decided to return through Macedonia. ₄Sopater of Beroea the son of Pyrrhus, accompanied him, and so did Aristarchus and Secundus of Thessalonica, Gaius of Derbe, and

Timothy, and Tychicus and Trophimus of Asia. ₅They went on ahead, and waited at Troas for us. ₆We sailed from Philippi, after the Passover week was finished, and five days later we caught up with them at Troas, where we spent a week.

₇On the Saturday evening we met for our common meal. Paul, who was due to leave the next day, began to talk to them, and prolonged his talk till midnight. ₈There were many lamps in the upper room in which we were meeting. ₉A young man, Eutychus, was sitting in the window-seat. As Paul went on talking, he grew sleepier and sleepier. Completely overcome by sleep, he fell from the third storey to the ground below, and was picked up dead. ₁₀Paul went down and took him in his arms, and lay on top of him. 'Stop this uproar,' he said. 'His life is still in him.' ₁₁Paul went back upstairs, and shared in the common meal with them. He talked long with them until the dawn came, and then he left. ₁₂They took the boy away alive, and they were greatly relieved.

₁₃We went on ahead to the ship, and set sail for Assos. We were to take Paul on board there. That was the arrangement he had made, for he intended to travel on foot. ₁₄When he met us at Assos, we took him on board, and proceeded to Mitylene. ₁₅Next day we sailed from there and arrived off Chios. The following day we crossed to Samos, and on the day after that we reached Miletus, ₁₆for Paul had decided not to put in at Ephesus. He did not wish to be delayed in Asia, for he was hurrying to reach Jerusalem, if possible, in time for the day of Pentecost.

₁₇From Miletus Paul sent to Ephesus, and asked the elders of the congregation there to come to see him. ₁₈When they arrived, he said to them: 'You yourselves well know the kind of life I lived all the time I lived amongst you from the day I first set foot in Asia. ₁₉You know how I served the Lord with all humility and with tears, amidst all the trials I had to endure because of the plots of the Jews. ₂₀You know that I did not shrink from telling you all that was for your good, and from teaching you publicly and in your own homes. ₂₁You know that to Jews and Greeks I continually insisted on the necessity of the repentance which turns to God and on faith in our Lord Jesus. ₂₂Now I am going to Jerusalem, because the Spirit will not let me do anything else. What will happen to me there, I do not know. ₂₃I only know that, as I go from town to town, the Holy Spirit leaves me in no doubt that imprisonment and troubles are waiting for me there.

24But I do not reckon my life of any importance, nor do I regard it as precious to myself, so long as I can finish my course, and complete the task which the Lord Jesus gave me to do for him, the task of bearing my personal witness that the Good News of the grace of God is true.

25'And now I know that none of you, amongst whom I went about preaching the Kingdom, will ever see me again. 26I want to go on record as saying to you today that I am responsible for the death of no man's soul, 27for I never shrank from telling you the whole purpose of God. 28Be careful about your own spiritual life, and care for the flock in which the Holy Spirit has appointed you as guardians. Make it your aim to be the shepherds of the church of God, which he has bought for himself at the price of the blood of his own One.

29'I know that after I am gone fierce wolves will get in among you, and will not spare the flock. 30I know that from your own members men will emerge who will preach a perverted version of the truth in an attempt to seduce the disciples from their loyalty, and to persuade them to follow them. 31That is why you must be sleeplessly on the watch. That is why you must remember that night and day for three years I never stopped giving each one of you with tears the advice which kept you right.

32'Now I commit you to God and to the message of his grace, that message which is able to build you up, and to give you a share in the blessedness of all who have been consecrated to him. 33I had no desire to possess any man's money or finery. 34You yourselves know that these hands of mine worked for my own needs, and the needs of my companions. 35I have always shown you that we must work like this to help those who are weak. We must always remember the words of the Lord Jesus and never forget that it was he who said: "It is a happier thing to give than to get." '

36After Paul had said all this, he knelt down with them all and prayed. 37They all wept bitterly, and flung their arms round him, and kissed him lovingly again and again. 38What grieved them most of all was that he had told them that they would never see him again. They escorted him to the ship.

Chapter 21

WHEN we had torn ourselves away from them and set sail, we made a straight run to Cos. The next day we reached Rhodes, and from there we sailed to Patara. ₂There we found a ship about to make the crossing to Phoenicia. We went on board and set sail. ₃We sighted Cyprus, and left it on our port beam. We sailed on to Syria, and put in at Tyre, for there the ship was to discharge her cargo. ₄We sought out the local disciples, and stayed there for a week. They told Paul through the Holy Spirit not to proceed with his journey to Jerusalem. ₅When we had come to the end of our time there, we left to continue our journey. All of them, with their wives and children, escorted us outside the town. We knelt down on the beach, and prayed, and said goodbye to each other. ₆Then we went on board the ship, and they returned to their homes. ₇When we had completed our voyage from Tyre, and had reached Ptolemais, we greeted the Christian community there, and stayed with them for one day. ₈We left on the next day, and arrived at Caesarea. We went into Philip the Evangelist's house—he was one of the Seven—and stayed with him. ₉He had four unmarried daughters, who were prophetesses.

₁₀While we were staying there for several days, a prophet called Agabus came down from Judaea. ₁₁He came to us and took Paul's belt, and tied up his own hands and feet with it. 'The message of the Holy Spirit,' he said, 'is that this is the way in which the Jews in Jerusalem will bind the man to whom this belt belongs, and will hand him over to the Gentiles.' ₁₂When we heard this, both we and the local people pleaded with Paul not to go up to Jerusalem. ₁₃Paul answered: 'What do you mean by going on like this, weeping and trying to crush the courage out of my heart? I am ready, not only to be imprisoned, but even to die in Jerusalem for the sake of the Lord Jesus.' ₁₄When he would not be persuaded, there was nothing left for us to say but: 'The Lord's will be done.'

₁₅At the end of our time in Caesarea, after we had made all the necessary preparations for the journey, we set out on the road up to Jerusalem. ₁₆Some of the disciples from Caesarea came with us, and they took us to Mnason, a native of Cyprus, and one of the very

first disciples, in whose house hospitality was to be provided for us.
17When we arrived in Jerusalem, the Christian community gladly
welcomed us. 18On the next day Paul took us with him to pay a visit
to James. All the elders were also present. 19When he had greeted
them, Paul gave them a detailed account of all that God had done
among the Gentiles through his ministry. 20They praised God, when
they had heard the story. 'Brother,' they said to Paul, 'you see how
many thousands of Jews have accepted the Christian faith, and all of
them remain devoted adherents of the Law. 21Rumours have reached
them that you teach all the Jews who live in Gentile communities to
desert their loyalty to Moses, and that you tell them not to circumcise
their children, and not to follow their ancestral customs. 22What are
we to do about this? They will, of course, all hear that you have
arrived in Jerusalem. 23We have a suggestion to make which you
would do well to act on.

'We have four men here who have put themselves under a voluntary vow. 24Take these men. Join them in their ritual purifications.
Accept financial responsibility for their expenses. Then they will be
able to embark on their vow by having their heads shaved. Then
everyone will realize that the rumours they have heard about you
have no foundation in fact, but that, so far from that, you yourself
keep the Law, and guide your conduct by it. 25As for the Gentiles who
have become believers, we have already issued our decision that they
must have nothing to do with meat that has formed part of the
sacrifice to an idol, that they must have nothing to do with meat
from which the blood has not been properly drained away, that they
must have nothing to do with meat from animals which have been
killed by strangling, and that they must have nothing to do with unchastity.'

26Paul took the men, and on the next day, after he had undergone
ritual purification with them, he went into the Temple to give notice
of the date when the period of purification would be completed,
and when the necessary sacrifice could be offered for each of them.
27When the week's period, which purification required, was almost
completed, the Asian Jews saw Paul in the Temple precincts. They
incited the mob to riot and seized Paul. 28'Men of Israel,' they shouted,
'help! This is the man whose teaching is everywhere directed against
God's people and against the Law and against this place. And, what is
more, he has brought Greeks into the sacred precincts, and has
defiled this holy place.' 29They made this charge because they had

previously seen Trophimus, the Ephesian, in Paul's company in the city, and they thought that Paul had brought him into the sacred precincts.

30The whole city was seething with excitement. There was a concerted rush of the people, and they seized Paul and dragged him out of the Temple precincts. Immediately the gates were shut. 31While they were trying to murder Paul, a report reached the officer commanding the company of soldiers on garrison duty that the whole of Jerusalem was in an uproar.

32He immediately took soldiers and centurions, and rushed down to them. When the mob saw the officer and the soldiers, they stopped beating Paul. 33The commander came up and seized him, and ordered him to be bound with two chains. 'Who is he?' he asked. 'And what has he done?' 34Some of the mob shouted one thing and some another. When he could not discover what the facts were because of the disturbance, he ordered Paul to be taken into the barracks. 35When Paul reached the steps, he had actually to be carried by the soldiers because of the violence of the mob, 36for the mass of the people followed, screaming: 'Kill him!'

37Just as Paul was going to be taken into the barracks, he said to the commander: 'Will you allow me to say something to you?' 'Do you know Greek?' the commander said. 38'Are you not the Egyptian who some time ago started a revolt and led the four thousand Assassins out into the desert?' 39'I am a Jew,' Paul said, 'a native of Tarsus in Cilicia, a citizen of a most illustrious city. Will you please permit me to speak to the people?'

40When the commander had given his permission, Paul took his stand on the steps, and made a gesture to the people with his hand. They were hushed to silence and Paul addressed them in the Hebrew language.

Chapter 22

'BROTHERS and fathers,' he said to them, 'give me a hearing, and give me a chance to defend myself to you.' 2When they heard him addressing them in the Hebrew language, they were still quieter. 3'I am a Jew,' Paul went on, 'born in Tarsus in Cilicia, but brought up in this city. I was trained in the school of Gamaliel with all the strictness which our ancestral Law demands. I am as whole-heartedly

289

devoted to God as any of you here today. 4I was such a persecutor of the Way that I wished to put its followers to death. I chained and imprisoned both men and women, 5and that is a fact to which the High Priest and all the council of the elders can provide evidence. I received letters of introduction from them to our brother Jews in Damascus, and I set out there to bring those of the Way who were there to Jerusalem to be punished.

6When I was approaching Damascus on my journey, suddenly about midday a great light from the sky flashed around me. 7I fell to the ground. I heard a voice. "Saul, Saul," it said to me, "why are you persecuting me?" 8"Who are you, Lord?" I answered. "I am Jesus the Nazarene," the voice said to me, "and it is I whom you are persecuting." 9My travelling companions saw the light, but they did not hear the voice of the speaker. 10"What am I to do, Lord?" I said. "Get up," the Lord said to me, "and go into Damascus, and there you will be told about all you are destined to do." 11I had been blinded by the brilliance of that light. So, led by the hand by my companions, I went into Damascus.

12A certain Ananias, a man who devoutly kept the Law, and who was highly esteemed by all the Jews who resided in Damascus, 13came to me. He stood beside me. "Brother Saul," he said, "receive your sight again!" There and then I recovered my sight, and looked up at him. 14"The God of our fathers," he said to me, "has appointed you to know his will, and to see the Just One, and to hear him actually speaking, 15because you are to be a witness for him to all men of what you have seen and heard. 16And now, why delay? Up! Call on his name, be baptized, and wash away your sins!"

17When I had returned to Jerusalem, and while I was praying in the Temple precincts, I fell into a trance. 18I saw Jesus and heard him saying to me: "Hurry! Get out of Jerusalem as fast as you can, for they will not accept what you affirm about me." 19"Lord," I said, "they themselves know that I used to go from synagogue to synagogue imprisoning and flogging those who believe in you. 20They know that when Stephen, your martyr, was murdered, I was standing there, and that I fully agreed with his death, and that I was guarding the clothes of those who killed him." 21"Go!" he said to me, "for I will send you far away to the Gentiles." '

22Until he said this, they were willing to give him a hearing, but at these words they shouted: 'Away with him! A creature like this is not fit to live.' 23They were shrieking, and waving their cloaks, and throwing dust into the air. 24The commander ordered that Paul should be taken into the barracks. He gave orders for him to be cross-examined under the lash, for he wanted to find out why they shouted at him like that.

25When they were strapping him down, preparatory to flogging him, Paul said to the centurion who was standing by: 'Have you any right to flog a man who is a Roman citizen—and to flog him without a trial?' 26When the centurion heard this, he went and reported it to the commander. 'What are you going to do?' he said. 'This man is a Roman citizen.' 27The commander came up. 'Tell me,' he said to Paul, 'are you a Roman citizen?' 'Yes,' said Paul. 28'I had to pay heavily to obtain this citizenship,' the commander answered. 'I am a citizen by birth,' said Paul. 29Those who had been about to cross-examine him stood back at once. The commander was alarmed when he realized that Paul was a Roman citizen, and that he had put him in chains.

30On the next day the commander wished to ascertain the real reason why Paul was accused by the Jews. So he released him from prison, and ordered the chief priests and the whole Sanhedrin to assemble. He brought Paul down and confronted him with them.

Chapter 23

Paul looked steadily at the Sanhedrin. 'Brothers,' he said, 'all my life I have had a completely clear conscience before God, and I still have.' 2Ananias the High Priest ordered those who were standing beside Paul to hit him on the mouth. 3'God is going to strike you,' Paul said, 'you white-washed wall! Are you going to sit there in legal judgment on me, and at the same time quite illegally order me to be struck?' 4'Are you insulting God's High Priest?' those who were standing by said to Paul. 5'Brothers,' said Paul, 'I did not know that he was High Priest, or I would not have spoken like that, for scripture says: "You must not abuse the ruler of the people." '

6Paul knew that one half of the Sanhedrin were Sadducees and that the other half were Pharisees. So he shouted for all the Sanhedrin to hear: 'Brothers, I am a Pharisee, and I come from a line of Pharisees. What I am on trial for is the hope of the resurrection of the dead.' 7When he said this, there was a violent division between the Pharisees and the Sadducees, and the meeting was split in two, because the Sadducees say that there is no resurrection, and that there are neither angels nor spirits, while the Pharisees believe in all three. 9The meeting developed into a shouting match. Some of the experts in the Law, who belonged to the party of the Pharisees, rose to speak. 'We can find nothing wrong with this man,' they insisted. 'What if a spirit or an angel has spoken to him?' 10The dispute grew so violent that the commander was afraid that they would tear Paul apart. So he ordered his troops to come down and forcibly to remove Paul from the meeting, and to take him into the barracks.

11The next night the Lord came and stood beside Paul. 'Courage!' he said. 'You have declared my story in Jerusalem, and you must speak for me in Rome too.'

12When day came, the Jews formed a plot. They took a solemn oath that they would neither eat nor drink, until they had killed Paul. 13More than forty of them were involved in this conspiracy. 14They went to the chief priests and elders. 'We have taken a solemn oath,' they said, 'to abstain from all food, until we have killed Paul. 15So what we want you and the Sanhedrin to do is to inform the commander that you propose to make a fuller investigation into his case. That will make it necessary for him to bring Paul down to you. We are prepared to see to it that he will not reach the court alive.'

16Paul's nephew heard of the proposed ambush. He went into the barracks and told Paul about it. 17Paul called one of the centurions. 'Take this young man to the commander,' he said. 'He has something to report to him.' 18So the centurion took him to the commander. 'The prisoner Paul,' he said, 'called me and requested me to bring this young man to you, because he has something to tell you.' 19The commander took his arm and drew him aside. When they were alone, he asked him: 'What is it that you have to report to me?' 20'The Jews,' he said, 'have made an agreement to ask you to bring Paul down to the Sanhedrin tomorrow, on the grounds that the Sanhedrin is going to carry out a fuller enquiry into his case. 21You must not allow them to persuade you to do so, for more than forty of them have taken a solemn vow neither to eat nor drink, until they have murdered him, and they are waiting in ambush for him. They are ready now, and they are only waiting for you to promise to do as they will request.' 22The commander dismissed the young man with strict orders not to tell anyone that he had given him this information.

23He called two of his centurions, and said to them: 'Get ready an infantry force of two hundred men to go to Caesarea, together with seventy cavalrymen and two hundred spearsmen. Have them standing by from nine o'clock in the evening onwards.' 24He also instructed them to provide horses to mount Paul, and to bring him safely to Felix the governor. 25He then wrote a letter in the following terms: 26'Claudius Lysias to his Excellency, the governor Felix, greetings. 27This man was seized by the Jews and was about to be killed by them. I intervened with my troops and rescued him, for I learned that he is a Roman citizen. 28Since I wished to know the reason why they accused him, I brought him down to their Sanhedrin. 29I discovered that the accusation related to questions of their own Law, and that he was accused of nothing which merited death or imprisonment. 30I was informed that they intended an attempt on this man's life. I therefore send him to you. I have instructed his accusers to state before you what they have against him.'

31The soldiers took Paul, as they had been instructed, and brought him by night to Antipatris. 32On the next day they left the cavalry to go with him, while they returned to barracks. 33When they reached Caesarea, they delivered the letter to the governor, and handed Paul over to him. 34When he had read the letter, he asked Paul what province he came from. When he learned that he came from Cilicia, 35he said: 'I will deal with your case, whenever your accusers arrive.' He gave orders that Paul was to be kept under guard in Herod's headquarters.

Chapter 24

FIVE days later the High Priest Ananias came down, with a group of elders and with an advocate called Tertullus. They laid information against Paul before the governor. 2When Paul had been summoned, Tertullus began the case for the prosecution. 'Your Excellency Felix,' he said, 'to you we owe the prolonged peace which we enjoy, and you in your foresight have initiated a series of reforms for this nation 3of every kind and in every place, and we welcome all this with all gratitude. 4I do not want to detain you for any length of time, so I ask you in your clemency to give us a brief hearing. 5We have found this man to be a troublesome pest. He is a disruptive influence among all the Jews all over the world. He is the ring-leader of the Nazarene party. 6He even tried to desecrate the Temple precincts. We arrested him,* 8and by examining him yourself you can discover from himself the facts about all the crimes of which we accuse him.' 9The Jews joined in the attack, and alleged that these charges were true.

10The governor signed to Paul to speak. 'Since I know,' Paul answered, 'that you have been the judicial head of this nation for many years, I confidently embark upon my defence. 11You can easily check the fact that it is no more than twelve days ago that I went up to worship in Jerusalem. 12They did not find me arguing with anyone in the Temple precincts, or collecting a crowd, either in the synagogues or in the city. 13They cannot produce any evidence to support the charges which they are now bringing against me. 14This I do admit to you—I do worship the God of our fathers as the Way—they call it a sect—teaches; but at the same time I accept everything that is laid down in the Law and written in the prophets, 15and I have the same hope in God as they themselves accept, I mean that there will be a resurrection of both good and bad. 16That is why I too always discipline myself to have a clear conscience before God and men.

17'It is some years since I have been in Jerusalem. I arrived there to bring gifts to my people, and to offer sacrifices to God. 18It was when I was engaged in this that they came upon me in the Temple precincts. I had gone through all the necessary purifications. I was not the centre of a crowd, and there was no disturbance. The whole trouble has been caused by some Jews from Asia, 19who ought to be here in your court to make whatever accusations they have to bring against me. 20Failing that, these men here ought to state of what crime they found me guilty when I appeared before the Sanhedrin, 21other than this one statement which I publicly made, when I was standing in their meeting: "What I am on trial for in your court today is the resurrection of the dead."'

22Felix reserved his judgment, for he was very well informed of the facts about the Way. 'When Lysias the commander comes down,' he said to them, 'I will investigate your case.' 23He then gave orders to the centurion that Paul was to be kept in custody and that he was to be given a certain amount of liberty, and that no one was to stop his friends from rendering him any service.

*See Notes on pp. 575-6

24Some days afterwards Felix came with his wife Drusilla, who was a Jewess. He sent for Paul, and listened to him talking about faith in Christ Jesus. 25When Paul was discoursing about goodness and self-control and the coming judgment, Felix became alarmed. 'Leave me for the present,' he said. 'When I have time to spare, I will send for you.' 26He had at the same time hopes that Paul would give him a bribe. So he sent for him very frequently, and had many conversations with him. 27At the end of two years Felix was succeeded by Porcius Festus. Felix left Paul in prison, because he wished to curry favour with the Jews.

Chapter 25

THREE days after he entered his province Festus went up from Caesarea to Jerusalem. 2The chief priests and the leading Jews laid information against Paul, and they pleaded with Festus as 3a special favour to have Paul sent up to Jerusalem. Their intention was to ambush him and to murder him on the road. 4Festus' answer was that Paul was being held at Caesarea, and that he himself intended soon to leave for there. 5'The best thing your authorities can do,' he said, 'is to come down with me, and to make their accusations against the man, if he has committed any crime.'

6He spent no more than eight or ten days with them, and then went down to Caesarea. On the next day he took his place in his court, and ordered Paul to be brought in. 7When Paul came in, the Jews who had come down from Jerusalem surrounded him, and brought against him many serious charges, which they were quite unable to substantiate. 8It was Paul's defence that he was guilty of no crime against the Jewish Law, or against the Temple, or against Caesar. 9Festus wished to curry favour with the Jews. He therefore said to Paul: 'Are you willing to go to Jerusalem, and to be tried before me there on these charges?' 10'It is Caesar's court of justice in which I am standing,' said Paul, 'and it is precisely there that my case must be tried. I am entirely innocent of any crime against the Jews, as you very well know. 11If I am a criminal, and if I have done anything that merits the death penalty, I have no objections to dying, but, if there is no substance in these accusations which are being made against me, then no one can make a free gift of me to the Jews. I appeal to

Caesar.' 12Festus conferred with his council. 'You have appealed to Caesar,' he said. 'You will go to Caesar.'

13Some days after this, King Agrippa and Berenice arrived in Caesarea to pay their respects to Festus. 14As they were staying for some time, Festus consulted the king about Paul's case. 'There is a prisoner here,' he said, 'who was left behind by Felix. 15When I was in Jerusalem, the Jewish chief priests and elders laid information against him, and demanded his condemnation. 16I replied that it is not the Roman custom to hand over any accused man, before he has an opportunity to confront his accusers face to face, and to defend himself against the charge made against him. 17When they came here, I did not delay the matter. On the next day I took my place in my court, and ordered the man to be brought in. 18When his accusers rose to speak, they charged him with none of the crimes that I had expected. 19The questions at issue with him were about their own religion, and about one Jesus who had died, but whom Paul asserted to be alive. 20I was at a loss to know how to hold an enquiry into matters like that. I therefore asked him if he was willing to go to Jerusalem, and to be tried on these charges there. 21But Paul appealed that he should be kept in custody until the Emperor should decide his case. I therefore ordered him to be so kept until I could remit his case to Caesar.' 22'I should like to have a personal talk with this man,' Agrippa said to Festus. 'You shall have a talk with him tomorrow,' said Festus.

23On the next day Agrippa and Berenice arrived in full state, and went into the audience hall with the top-ranking army officers and the most prominent citizens of the town. At the order of Festus, Paul was brought in. 24Festus said to King Agrippa and to the whole audience: 'You are looking at the man about whom the whole body of the Jews petitioned me in Jerusalem and here. They vociferously insisted that he must not be allowed to live any longer. 25As far as I could see, he has done nothing to merit the death penalty, but when he himself appealed to the Emperor, I decided to send him to him. 26I have no definite facts to report in writing about him to my imperial master. I have therefore brought him before you all, and especially before you, King Agrippa, so that a preliminary enquiry may be held, and so that I may thus have some definite information to include in my report, 27for it seems unreasonable to me to remit a person to the Emperor without making it clear what he is charged with.'

Chapter 26

Y ou have our permission to tell your story,' Agrippa said to Paul. Paul stretched out his hand, and began his defence. 2'I count myself fortunate, King Agrippa,' Paul said, 'that it is before you that I am today about to defend myself against all the accusations brought against me by the Jews. 3I count myself specially fortunate, because you are an expert in all Jewish customs and questions. I therefore ask you to give me a patient hearing.

4'All the Jews well know the kind of life I lived from the days of my youth, for it was lived amongst my own people and in Jerusalem. 5Their knowledge of me goes back a long way. If they were willing to do so, they could give evidence that my life was the life of a Pharisee, lived in obedience to the principles of the strictest sect of our religion. 6And now it is because my hope is that God will keep the promise which he made to our fathers that I stand here on trial today. 7It is that very hope which the twelve tribes strive to attain, by worshipping God with strenuous devotion night and day. It is for cherishing this hope, your Majesty, that I am accused—and my accusers are Jews! 8Why should you regard it as incredible that God raises the dead?

9'I was myself convinced that it was my duty to do all that I could to oppose Jesus the Nazarene. 10This I did in Jerusalem. I shut up many of God's people in prison, after I had received authority from the chief priests to do so. When they were being put to death, I cast my vote against them. 11I went from synagogue to synagogue punishing them, and trying to force them to curse the name of Jesus. In my insane rage I engaged in a campaign of persecution even in cities outside Palestine.

12'As part of all this, I was on my way to Damascus with the authority and the commission of the chief priests. 13On the road at midday, your Majesty, I saw a light from the sky, brighter than the sun, shining around me and my fellow-travellers. 14We all fell to the ground. I heard a voice. "Saul, Saul," the voice said to me in the Hebrew language, "Why are you persecuting me? You only hurt yourself by kicking against the goads." 15"Who are you, Lord?" I said. The Lord said: "I am Jesus, and it is I whom you are persecuting. 16Up! Stand on your feet! I have appeared to you, because I have chosen you to be my servant, and to tell people the story of the vision of me you have seen, and of the visions of me you will see. 17I will rescue you from the people and from the Gentiles. It is to the Gentiles that I am going to send you. 18I want you to open their eyes, so that you will make them turn from darkness to light, and from the power of Satan to God, for I want them to receive forgiveness of their sins, and a share in the blessedness of those who through faith in me have become God's consecrated people."

19Therefore, King Agrippa, I did not disobey the heavenly vision, 20but first to those in Damascus, then in Jerusalem, then all over the country of Judaea, then to the Gentiles, I brought the message to repent, and to turn to God, and to make their conduct match their repentance. 21That is why the Jews seized me in the Temple precincts and tried to murder me. 22God gave me his support. Today I stand declaring my faith to people from the top to the bottom of society. I am saying nothing beyond what the prophets and Moses said would happen—23that the Messiah must suffer, and that, because he was the first to rise from the dead, he would bring the message of light to the Jewish people and to the Gentiles.'

24When Paul came to this stage in his defence, Festus shouted: 'You're raving, Paul. All this study is driving you mad.' 25'Festus, your Excellency,' Paul said, 'I am not raving. So far from that, I am speaking words of truth and sanity. 26King Agrippa knows about these things, and I do not need to mince my words to him. I do not believe that any of the things I have been speaking of have escaped his notice. This thing was not done in a corner. 27King Agrippa, do you accept the message of the prophets? I know you do.' 28Agrippa said to Paul: 'You think that it won't take you long to make a Christian out of me.' 29'I could pray to God,' said Paul, 'that, whether it takes a long time or a short time, not only you but all who are listening to me today should be made such as I—apart from these chains.'

30The king rose, and so did the governor and Berenice and those who had been seated with them. 31When they had withdrawn, they discussed the case with each other. 'There is nothing in this man's conduct,' they said, 'which merits death or imprisonment.' 32'This man,' Agrippa said to Festus, 'could well have been released, if he had not appealed to Caesar.'

Chapter 27

WHEN the verdict that we should sail for Italy was reached, Paul and a group of other prisoners were handed over to a centurion of the Imperial regiment, called Julius. ₂We embarked on a ship whose home port was Adramyttium, which was about to make the voyage to the ports on the Asian coast, and set sail. Aristarchus, a Macedonian from Thessalonica, accompanied us. ₃Next day we put in at Sidon. Julius treated Paul kindly, and allowed him to visit the friends and to enjoy their hospitality. ₄We put to sea from there, and sailed under the lee of Cyprus, because of head-winds. ₅We then sailed across the open sea off the coast of Cilicia and Pamphylia, and arrived at Myra in Lycia. ₆There the centurion found an Alexandrian ship which was bound for Italy, and put us on board it.

₇For many days our passage was slow, and it was with difficulty that we arrived off Cnidus. Since we could make no progress because of the head-wind, we sailed under the lee of Crete, off Salmone. ₈We coasted along with difficulty until we came to a place called Fair Havens, which was near the town of Lasea.

₉A great deal of time had been lost, and by this time sailing was dangerous, because it was late September and the fast of the Day of Atonement was already over. So Paul warned them. ₁₀'Men,' he said, 'I see that this voyage is going to involve damage and serious loss, not only to the cargo and the ship, but also to our lives.' ₁₁The centurion was influenced more by the captain and the ship-owner than by what Paul said.

₁₂That place was not suitable for wintering in. So the majority favoured a plan to sail on from there, in the hope that it might be possible for them to make Phoenix, and to winter there. Phoenix is a harbour in Crete open to the south-west and north-west winds. ₁₃When a light southerly breeze sprang up, they thought that they had as good as achieved their purpose. So they weighed anchor, and coasted along Crete, keeping inshore. ₁₄Soon after a hurricane-like wind—the wind called the north-easter—rushed down on them, blowing from off the island. ₁₅The ship was caught in the wind. It was impossible to keep her head to it. So we yielded to the wind, and ran before it.

₁₆When we had run under the lee of a little island called Cauda, we succeeded with difficulty in getting control of the dinghy. 17When they had hauled it on board, they used their tackle to undergird the ship. They were afraid they would run on to the Syrtis quicksands, so they lowered the top-gear and allowed the ship to run.

18We were violently battered by the storm, and on the next day they began to jettison the cargo. 19On the third day they manhandled the ship's spare gear overboard. 20For many days the sun and the stars were invisible, and the storm continued to rage. In the end we began to abandon all hope that we would ever come through it alive.

21When they had gone without food for a long time, Paul gathered them round. 'Men,' he said, 'you should have listened to me, and you should not have sailed from Crete. Then your only profit from the voyage would not have been this damage and loss. 22But, even as things are, take my advice, and keep your hearts up. Not one of you will lose his life. The only thing that will be lost is the ship. 23For tonight there stood by me an angel of the God to whom I belong and whom I worship. 24"Don't be afraid, Paul," he said. "You must stand before Caesar, and God has given you the lives of all your companions on this voyage." 25Keep your hearts up, men! For I trust in God that everything will turn out exactly as I have been told. 26But we have to be cast ashore on an island.'

27It was the fourteenth night, and we were drifting helplessly across the Sea of Adria. It was about midnight when the sailors suspected that land was approaching. 28They took soundings, and found a depth of twenty fathoms. A little farther on they took soundings again, and found a depth of fifteen fathoms. 29They were afraid of piling up on a rocky coast. So they let go four anchors from the stern, and prayed for daylight.

30The sailors were attempting to get out from the ship. They had actually begun to let the dinghy down into the sea, on the excuse that they were going to lay out anchors from the bow. 31'Unless these men stay in the ship,' Paul said to the centurion, 'you cannot hope to survive.' 32The soldiers then cut the ropes of the dinghy, and let it fall away.

33Just before daybreak Paul urged them all to take some food. 'For fourteen days,' he said, 'you have been in constant suspense without food, and have eaten nothing. 34I strongly advise you to take some food. This is essential, if you are going to survive. For I assure you that not a hair of anyone's head will be lost.' 35When he had said this, he took a loaf, and gave thanks to God in front of them all, and broke it in pieces, and began to eat. ₃₆This put fresh heart into them, and they took some food. ₃₇All together there were two hundred and seventy-six of us on board the ship. ₃₈When they had eaten all they wanted, they lightened the ship by jettisoning the cargo of grain into the sea.

₃₉When day broke, they did not recognize the land. They noticed a bay with a sandy beach, and they planned, if possible, to run the ship ashore there. ₄₀They slipped the anchors, and let them fall into the sea. At the same time they unleashed the lashings of the steering-paddles. They hoisted the foresail to the wind, and made for the beach. ₄₁They struck a spit of land, and beached the ship. The bow stuck fast and remained immovable. The stern began to break up under the pounding of the waves. ₄₂It was the soldiers' plan to kill the prisoners, in case any of them should swim away and make their escape. ₄₃But the centurion put a stop to that, because he wished to save Paul's life. He ordered those who could swim to jump overboard and to make for the land. ₄₄The rest he ordered to make for the shore, some on planks, and some on parts of the ship. And thus it was that they all reached the land in safety.

Chapter 28

WHEN we had safely reached the land, we learned that the island was called Malta. ₂The natives showed us quite extraordinary kindness. It had begun to rain and it was cold; so they lit a bonfire and brought us to it.

₃Paul had twisted together a bundle of sticks and laid it on the fire. Because of the heat a viper came out, and fastened on his hand. When the natives saw the beast hanging from his hand, they said to each other: 'This man must be a murderer. He escaped from the sea, but justice has not let him live.' ₅Paul shook the beast off into the fire, and was none the worse of it. ₆They were expecting him to proceed to swell up, or suddenly to drop dead. They watched him for a long time. When they saw that nothing out of the way was happening to him, they changed their minds, and began to say that he was a god.

₇In the nearby countryside there were estates which belonged to the chief magistrate of the island. His name was Publius. He welcomed us, and entertained us hospitably for three days. ₈It so happened that Publius' father was lying ill with recurrent attacks of fever and with dysentery. Paul went to visit him. He prayed and laid his hands on him and cured him. 9When this happened, the other people in the island who were ill came too, and were cured. 10The result was that they heaped honours upon us, and, when we sailed, they put on board everything we could need.

11After three months we set sail in a ship which had wintered in the island. She was an Alexandrian ship, and she had the Heavenly Twins as her figurehead. 12We put in at Syracuse, and stayed there for three days. 13From there we sailed round and reached Rhegium. The day after, a south wind blew, and two days' sailing took us to Puteoli. 14There we met some members of the Christian community, and at their urgent invitation we stayed with them for a week. And so we came to Rome.

15The members of the Christian community had heard about us, and they came to meet us as far as the Forum of Appius and the Three Taverns. When Paul saw them, he thanked God, and was greatly encouraged. 16When we got to Rome, Paul was allowed to live by himself, with a soldier to guard him.

17Three days after this Paul invited the leaders of the local Jews to come to see him. When they were all there, he said to them: 'Brothers, although I had done nothing hostile to the Jewish nation and nothing to contravene our ancestral customs, I was handed over to the Romans in Jerusalem. 18When the Romans had examined me, they wished to release me, because there were no grounds in my life and conduct for a charge involving the death penalty. 19When the Jews objected to my release, I could not do anything else but appeal to Caesar—not that I had any accusation to make against my nation. 20It is because I stand for the hope which all Israel shares that I am wearing this chain, and that is why I have requested to see you and to talk to you.' 21'We,' they said to him, 'have received no letters from Judaea about you, and no member of the Jewish community who arrived here has brought any report or rumour that you have been involved in anything criminal. 22We think it only right to hear from yourself what your views are. The only thing we do know about this sect is that there is universal opposition to it.'

23They fixed a day with him, and they came to him in his lodging in still greater numbers. From morning to night he expounded the Kingdom of God to them, supporting his statements with vigorous arguments, and trying to persuade them to accept Jesus by citing passages from the Law of Moses and from the prophets. 24Some of them were convinced by what he said; others refused to accept it. 25They were far from being in agreement with each other. Before they left, Paul said one thing more. 'The Holy Spirit,' he said, 'well said to your fathers through the prophet Isaiah:

> 26"Go to this people and say:
>   you will certainly hear,
>   but you will certainly not understand
>   the meaning of what you hear;
>   you will certainly see,
>   but you will certainly not perceive
>   the meaning of what you see.
> 27The mind of this people has become lazily shut,
>   and their ears have become hard of hearing,
>   and they have deliberately obscured their own sight,
> lest at any time they should see with their eyes,
>   and hear with their ears,
>   and understand with their minds,
>   and turn and find their cure in me."

28I want you to know that the saving power of God has been sent to the Gentiles. They will listen.'*

30Paul stayed there for two whole years at his own expense. He welcomed everyone who came to see him. 31All the time he continued to proclaim the Kingdom of God, and to teach the facts about the Lord Jesus Christ, completely freely and fearlessly, and there was no attempt to stop him.

*See Notes on pp. 575-6

General Introduction to the Letters of Paul

IT is unfortunate that the Letters of Paul were ever called epistles, for the word epistle tends to remove them out of the ordinary run of things into a special theological and literary category. They are in the real sense of the term letters.

Greek letters were written to a pattern and a formula, and Paul's letters exactly observe the pattern which every Greek letter followed. Here is a letter written by a newly-enlisted soldier called Apion to his father Epimachus. Its date is some time in the second century A.D.

'Apion to Epimachus his father and lord heartiest greetings. First of all I pray that you are in good health and continually prosper and fare well with my sister and her daughter and my brother. I thank the Lord Serapis [his god] that, when I was in danger at sea, he saved me. As soon as I entered Misenum I received my travelling money from Caesar, three gold pieces. And I am well. I beg you therefore, my dear father, write me a few lines, first regarding your health, secondly regarding that of my brother and sister, thirdly that I may kiss your hand, because you have brought me up well, and on this account I hope to be quickly promoted, if the gods will. Give many greetings to Capito, and to my brother, and sister, and to Serenilla, and my friends. I send you a little portrait of myself at the hands of Euctemon. My military name is Antonius Maximus. I pray for your good health.'

The pattern of the letter is first, the address, second, a prayer and a thanksgiving, third, the general contents, fourth, the closing greetings. This is exactly the pattern of Paul's letters. Paul's letters are real letters.

Further, Paul's letters are not treatises. He did not sit down at a desk in undisturbed study and contemplation. They are all written in the dust and heat of the day. They are all written to meet some situation which was threatening the churches he loved so well. They are not timeless theological essays; they are written to meet some particular occasion. This is what sometimes makes them very difficult. Reading them can be like listening to one side of a telephone conversation. We have often to deduce what the situation was from the letters themselves. Paul wrote for the day to day needs of the church. True, he brought the eternal truths to these situations, but he would have been astonished, if he had known that his letters would still be being read and studied far down the twentieth century.

Still further, Paul did not hand-write his letters, apart sometimes from some very few sentences and the authenticating signature at the end. He dictated them. We even know the name of one of his secretaries, for Tertius slipped in his own name and greetings in the Letter to the Romans (Romans 16.22). We must not therefore think of Paul sitting at his desk carefully polishing each sentence, until the style was faultless and the grammar perfect. We must think of him striding up and down his room, seeing in his mind's eye the people to whom he was writing, and pouring out a flood of often impassioned and excited words to the secretary who strove to take it all down. The letters of Paul are not literary products; they come from the arena of life. They have not the cool detachment of the theologian in his study; they throb with the passionate concern of the pastor for his people.

Introduction to the Letter to the Romans

THE Letter to the Romans was written from Corinth in A.D.57. It tells us itself of its occasion. One of the schemes which lay closest to Paul's heart was the collection given by the younger churches for the mother church at Jerusalem (1 Corinthians 16.1-4; 2 Corinthians 8 and 9). Here was a way really to mark the unity of the church, and really to demonstrate the concern for each other of each of its parts. When Paul wrote Romans the collection had been made. He was on the point of conveying it to Jerusalem, and he was conscious of the dangers that awaited him there, dangers which were in fact to lead to his arrest and his imprisonment. But Paul was thinking ahead. After he had been to Jerusalem, he planned to go to Spain. He had never been in Rome, and he had neither founded nor visited the church there. But his purpose was to visit the Roman church on his way to Spain (Romans 15.24-33). So, to prepare them for the visit which he hoped to pay, he wrote this letter.

Of all Paul's letters the Letter to the Romans comes nearest to being a treatise. It has been described by the adjective 'testamentary'. This is Paul's testament, the essence of his faith.

He begins by demonstrating that neither the Jewish nor the Gentile world had been able to get into a right relationship with God (chapters 1 and 2). The failure is total and universal (3.10-18).

True, the Jews possessed the law, but even the law was powerless to help. It in fact fomented sin, for it often happens that to forbid a thing is the surest way to awaken the desire for it (chapter 7).

What then is the way to a right relationship with God? It is the way of faith. That is the way that Abraham took. Circumcision and the law had nothing to do with it, because God blessed Abraham, and Abraham became the friend of God, before he was circumcised and long before the law ever came into the world.

The essence of the right relationship with God is not the hopeless task of keeping the law; it is justification by faith. In this great phrase Paul is using the word justification in a special sense. To justify a person ordinarily means to find reasons why a person was right to act as he did. But God justifies the ungodly (4.5), and it cannot mean that God finds reasons to prove that the sinner is right to be a sinner. In Greek the word for to *justify* is *dikaioun*. Greek verbs which end in *-oun* do not mean to make a person something. They mean to treat, reckon, account a person as something. And when Paul speaks about God justifying the sinner, he means that God treats the sinner as if he had been a good man. God treats the rebel as if he had been a loving son. And it is justification *by faith*, because it is only when we have absolute faith in what Jesus tells us about God that we can think about God like that at all.

Man as man is a sinner, for Paul holds to the fact of original sin (chapter 5). By that Paul does not mean a taint or a tendency to sin. He means that, because of the oneness, the solidarity, of the human race all men literally sinned in Adam. In chapter 5 he sets out his logical argument for this in five steps.

i. Adam sinned by breaking a definite commandment of God.

ii. The consequence was that death entered the world, for death is the consequence of sin.

iii. Between Adam and Moses there was no law, for the law was not yet given. There could therefore be no transgression of a law which did not exist.

iv. In spite of that men continued to die.

v. Why? Because, such is the solidarity of the human race, that all men had literally sinned in Adam, and therefore died (5.12).

The only thing that can reverse this process is the coming of Jesus Christ into the world, for, by becoming one with him, as we were once one with Adam, we can become alive (5.17-19).

But the question arises, if God treats the bad man as if he had been good, does this give us a licence to sin? Far from it! In baptism we become one with Jesus Christ, and then the old life of sin is left behind, and a new life is begun. Baptism is like dying to sin and rising to righteousness with Jesus Christ (chapter 6). And this new life is for ever supported by the Spirit helping us (chapter 8).

In chapters 9-11 Paul deals with the problem of the Jews. Why did they, God's chosen people, reject God's Son, when he came? That too, Paul finds, is all part of the purpose of God. The Jews rejected Christ in order that the gospel might go out to the Gentiles. But the day will come when the Gentiles will bring the Jews back in again, and Jew and Gentile will both be gathered in.

With Paul theology and ethics always go hand in hand, and chapters 12-15 are chapters of ethical guidance and advice. The letter ends with a note of introduction for Phoebe, and a list of greetings to Paul's friends.

Here in this letter we are faced with Paul's greatest principle—salvation by faith alone. As it has been put: 'All is of grace, and grace is for all.'

The Letter to the
ROMANS

Chapter 1

THIS is a letter from Paul 7to all those in Rome whom God loves, and who have been called by him to be his people. Grace to you and every blessing from God our Father and from the Lord Jesus Christ.

1I write to you, because I have been called by God to be an apostle, and because I have been specially commissioned to bring men the good news of God. 2It was this good news that God promised long ago through his prophets in the sacred scriptures. 3The good news is about his Son, who in his human lineage was a direct descendant of David, 4and who, because of the supreme holiness of his character, was by the resurrection designated beyond all question the Son of God. It is Jesus Christ our Lord I mean, 5and it is through him that I have received the privilege of an apostleship, the task of which it is for his sake to lead all men of all nations into that submission to him which is the product of faith. 6You too are included among those to whom my apostleship extends, for to you too the invitation of Jesus Christ has come.

8I want to begin by saying that I thank my God through Jesus Christ for you all, because the report of your loyalty to Christ is being broadcast all over the world. 9God himself can tell you, the God whom I serve with every fibre of my being in my work for the good news of his Son, that I unceasingly remember you in my prayers. 10I constantly pray that at long last it may be God's will that a way should open up for me to visit you. 11For I long to see you, because I want to share with you some of the gifts the Spirit gives, so that the foundations of your faith may be strengthened, 12or rather, that you and I may both be cheered and encouraged, when we meet, I by your faith and you by mine. 13I want you to know, brothers, that I have often had it in my mind to come to visit you, although up to now something has always happened to stop me, because I have harvested men for God all over the Gentile world, and I would like to do so among you too. 14I owe a duty to Greeks and to non-Greeks, to the intellectuals and to the simple folk. 15That is why I am so eager to tell the good news to you in Rome too.

16I am quite sure that the good news will never let me down, for it is the saving power of God to everyone who accepts it, first to the Jews, then to the Greeks. 17In it God's way of setting men right with himself is revealed as beginning and ending in faith, just as it stands written: 'It is the man who is right with God through faith who will find life.'

18No one can fail to see that the wrath of God from heaven is directed against all the impious wickedness of men who are wickedly obstructing the progress of the truth. 19What man can know about God is clear for them to see, for God made it clear to them. 20Ever since the world was created, the invisible nature of God, his eternal power and deity, are clear for the mind to see through the things which God has made. Men are therefore left without defence, 21because, although it was open to them to know God, they gave him neither praise nor gratitude. They allowed themselves to become involved in futile speculations which did nothing but darken their foolish minds. 22Their alleged wisdom was in fact folly. 23They substituted images, made in the shapes of mortal men, and of birds and beasts and reptiles, for the glory of the immortal God.

24God therefore allowed them to go their own way, until, driven by the desires of their hearts, they ended up in a moral degeneration in which they were partners in dishonouring their own bodies. 25This they did because they were men who substituted their untruth for God's truth. They have given their reverence and their worship to that which is created instead of to the Creator—praise be to him for ever and ever! Amen. 26God therefore allowed them to go their own way, until they ended up as victims of their own dishonourable passions. Their women substituted unnatural intercourse with each other for natural intercourse with men. 27In the same way, men abandoned natural intercourse with women, and were inflamed with passion for each other. Men perpetrated shameless things with men, and brought on themselves the inevitable consequences which such misguided conduct was bound to bring. 28They deliberately refused to recognize God. God allowed them to go their own way, until they reached a stage when they were mentally and morally vitiated, and did things which no man ought to do. 29They are filled with every kind of wickedness and evil, with the desire for that which no man has any right to desire, with viciousness. Their lives are permeated with envy, murder, quarrelling, underhand plotting, malignity. 30They became whispering scandal-mongers, slanderers, God-forsaken and God-defying, arrogant, braggarts, ingenious in the discovery of novelties in vice, disobedient to parents. 31They are without conscience, without honour, without family affection, without pity. 32Although they were well aware that in the judgment of God those who are guilty of such conduct deserve to die, they not only practise it themselves, but they also applaud others who practise it.

Up to this point Paul has been addressing the Gentile world. Now he turns to address the Jews.

Chapter 2

So then, my friend, if you, whoever you are, presume to pass judgment on other people, you have left yourself with no defence, for in the very act of judging some one else, you condemn yourself, for you yourself do exactly the same things as you condemn in others. 2You say that you are well aware that God's judgment rightly falls on people who do the kind of things that I have just been talking about. 3So then, you, my friend, condemn people who do things like that, and yet you yourself are in the habit of doing exactly the same things. Is it your idea that you yourself will escape God's judgment? 4Or, are you contemptuously trading on the wealth of God's kindness and forbearance and patience? Are you not aware that the kindness of God is meant to lead you to repentance?

5In the stubbornness and impenitence of your hearts you are storing up wrath for yourself on the day of wrath, the day when God's just judgment will burst upon the world. 6For God will settle accounts with every man on the basis of what each man has done. 7To those who in inflexible devotion to goodness seek for glory and honour and immortality, he will give eternal life. 8For those who in selfish ambition are disobedient to the right and obedient to the wrong, there will be anger and wrath. 9There will be trouble and anguish for the soul of every man whose conduct is evil, for the Jew first and for the Greek too. 10There will be praise and honour and every blessing for everyone whose conduct is good, for the Jew first and for the Greek too. 11For God has no favourites.

12If a man does not know the law, and sins, he will perish, although it will not be on the basis of the law that he is judged. If a man does know the law, and yet sins, it is on the basis of the law that he will be judged. 13If a man does no more than hear what the law says, that does not make him innocent in God's sight; but if a man does what the law commands, he will be innocent. 14When the heathen who do not possess any law do by natural instinct what the law demands, although they possess no law, they are their own law. 15, 16They show that the requirements of the law are written on their hearts. On the day when God judges the secrets of men through Jesus Christ, as my gospel says he will, their conscience will agree with the verdict, and their own inmost thoughts will accuse them, or even sometimes excuse them.

17You bear the name of 'Jew'; you have a law on which to lean; you pride yourself on your relation to God; 18you know his will; your instruction in the law gives you the ability to distinguish between competing moral choices; 19you are confident that you are qualified to be a leader of the blind, a light to those who are in darkness. 20You claim to be able to provide discipline for the foolish and instruction for the child. You believe that in the law you possess the embodiment of knowledge and truth. 21Well then, in view of all this, if you claim the right to teach others, what about teaching yourself?

You preach against stealing—do you yourself steal? 22You forbid adultery—do you yourself commit adultery? You abhor idols—do you yourself rob temples? 23You pride yourself that you have a law—do you yourself dishonour God by breaking the law? 24As scripture says: 'The name of God is insulted in heathen society because of your conduct.'

25Circumcision is only of value, when your whole conduct is based on the law; but, if you habitually break the law, your circumcision might as well be uncircumcision. 26If a man who is not circumcised obeys the just requirements of the law, surely he can be regarded as being as good as circumcised? 27The man who is physically uncircumcised, but who perfectly keeps the law, will judge you, if you habitually break the law, in spite of your written code of laws and your circumcision.

28The real Jew is not the man who is a Jew in visible externals, nor is external bodily circumcision the real circumcision. 29The real Jew is the man who is a Jew in his inner being, and the real circumcision is a thing of the heart. It is a spiritual thing, not conformity to any set of rules and regulations. When a man is really like that, he will receive the praise, not of men, but of God.

Chapter 3

WHAT then has a Jew got that no one else has got? Or, what is the use of circumcision? ₂Much in every way! First and foremost, there is the fact that the Jews were entrusted with the sacred words of God. ₃What then if some of them were unfaithful? Is their infidelity going to destroy God's fidelity? ₄God forbid! Even if every man was proved to be a liar, God must still be true. As scripture says of him: 'You must be proved right when you speak; you must triumph when you are on trial.'

₅You might plead that in point of fact our wickedness provides an opportunity for the proof of God's justice. What are we to deduce from that? Are you going to go on to argue that it was therefore unjust of God to launch the divine wrath upon us? This is the way in which the human mind might argue. ₆God forbid! On that argument, how could God judge the world at all? ₇Your argument is: 'If the effect of my falsehood is to enable God's truth to bring him more and more glory, why then am I still condemned as a sinner? Why should we not do evil in order that it may issue in good?' ₈This is in fact the very argument that some people slanderously allege that I use. An argument like that bears its condemnation on its face.

₉What then? Do we Jews enjoy any advantages? By no means! We have already charged all men, Jews and Gentiles alike, with being under the domination of sin. ₁₀It stands written:

'There is none who is righteous, not even one,
  ₁₁there is none who understands,
     there is none who seeks for God.
  ₁₂All have swerved aside, and all have gone bad;
     there is no one who practises goodness,
     not one single one.
  ₁₃Their throat is an open tomb,
     they use their tongues for treachery,
     the venom of asps is on their lips.
   ₁₄Their mouth is full of cursing and bitterness;
   ₁₅their feet are swift to shed blood.
  ₁₆The way they have chosen can bring them nothing
     but ruin and wretchedness.
  ₁₇They know nothing of the way which brings blessedness,
   ₁₈they never think of reverence for God.'

19We know that everything the law says, it says to those who are within the sphere of the law. This is designed to produce a situation in which no man is left with any defence, and in which the whole world has become subject to God's judgment. 20And this is brought about by the fact that no one can ever get into a right relationship with God through doing the things which any legal system prescribes. All that any legal system can do is to make men aware of what sin is.

21But a new situation has arisen. The world has been shown a way of being put into a right relationship with God apart from any kind of law. It is nevertheless a way which is already attested by the law and the prophets. 22It is a way of being put into a right relationship with himself which God has provided. That right relationship is reached through faith in Jesus Christ, and it is offered to all who have faith. There is no distinction. 23All have sinned; all have lost the divine glory which they were meant to have. 24And all can enter into a right relationship with God as a free gift, by means of his grace, through the act of deliverance which happened in Jesus Christ. 25It was God's purpose that Jesus Christ should be the one through whose sacrificial death sin can be forgiven through faith. Such a sacrifice was necessary to demonstrate God's justice, because in his forbearance he had not exacted from the men of past generations the penalty which their sins deserved. 26And it was necessary in order to demonstrate his justice at this present time, by showing that, although he is just, he nevertheless puts the man who has faith in Jesus into a right relationship with him.

27What then becomes of pride in our achievements? It is excluded. On what principle is it excluded? Is it on the principle that our achievement in keeping the law brings merit? No, it is excluded because the only thing that matters is faith. 28It is our argument that a man is put into a right relationship with God by faith, and that the performance of the things which any law demands has nothing to do with it. 29Is God the God of the Jews only? Is he not the God of the Gentiles too? Indeed, he is the God of the Gentiles too. 30He must be, if it is true that God is one. And since he is one, he will bring those who are circumcised into a right relationship with himself by means of faith, and he will bring those who are not circumcised into the same relationship through faith. 31Does this then mean that we are using faith to abolish the law? God forbid! We are placing the law on a firmer foundation.

Chapter 4

From the point of view of physical descent Abraham is our fore-father. What are we to say that his special discovery was? ₂We can say that, if Abraham was put into a right relationship with God through his own achievement, he has legitimate grounds for pride. But in point of fact, in regard to his relationship with God he has nothing on which to pride himself. ₃What does scripture say? 'Abraham took God at his word, and that act of faith was accepted as putting him into a right relationship with God.' ₄If a man produces some piece of work, his pay is credited to him, not as a gift given to him, but as a debt owed to him. ₅But, if a man does not claim to have produced anything, but simply puts his faith in the God who brings godless men into a right relationship with himself, then his faith is accepted as putting him into a right relationship with God. ₆You get exactly this situation in David's saying about the congratulation of the man whom God accepts apart altogether from anything that he has done:

₇'O the bliss of those who have broken the law
    and have been forgiven,
      whose sin has been put out of sight.
₈ O the bliss of the man whose sin is not debited against him
    by the Lord.'

₉Does this description of bliss apply only to those who are circum-cised, or also to those who are uncircumcised? Let me repeat what I said: 'Abraham's act of faith was accepted as putting him into a right relationship with God.' ₁₀How was it so accepted? Was it while he was circumcised, or while he was uncircumcised? It was in fact not while he was circumcised, but while he was uncircumcised. ₁₁He received the badge of circumcision as the hall-mark of that right relationship with God, which was the result of his faith, before he was circum-cised. This happened in order that he might be the father of all who have faith while they are uncircumcised, so that this faith may be credited to them as righteousness. ₁₂And it happened in order that he might also be the father of those who are not only circumcised, but who also take that same way of faith as our father Abraham did, while he was still uncircumcised.

₁₃The promise to Abraham and to his descendants was that Abraham should enter into possession of the world. It was not through any kind of law that this promise came to him; it came through that right relationship with God, which is the result of faith. 14For, if it was through any kind of law that they entered into this possession, then faith is emptied of all its meaning, and the promise is cancelled. 15Law and wrath are bound to go hand in hand. But where no law exists, there can be no such thing as a breach of the law. 16This is why the whole matter is based on faith. It was so based that it might all move in the realm of grace. This had to be so, in order to confirm the promise that was made to every one of Abraham's descendants. This promise was not made only to those who base their life on the Jewish law; it was also made to those who base their life on that same faith as Abraham had. For Abraham is the father of all of us. 17As scripture says of him: 'I have appointed you as father of many nations.' This promise was made in the presence of God, the God in whom Abraham had put his faith, the God who makes the dead live, the God whose summons goes out to things which do not yet exist, as if they already did exist. 18When there were no grounds for hope, Abraham took his stand on hope, and by an act of faith he did believe that he would become the father of many nations, as God had said—'So many will your descendants be.' 19His faith did not waver, although he was well aware that his body was as good as dead—for he was about a hundred years old—and that the life was gone from Sarah's womb. 20He never allowed lack of faith to make him question God's promise. So far from that, his faith was so strengthened that he praised God 21in the unshakable conviction that God is able, not only to make promises, but also to make his promises come true. 22That is why it was credited to him as righteousness. 23The fact that it was so credited is recorded, not only for Abraham's sake, 24but for our sake also, because it is also going to be credited to those who believe in him who raised from the dead our Lord Jesus, 25who was delivered to death that our sins might be forgiven, and raised to life that we might enter into a right relationship with God.

Chapter 5

IT is through faith that we have been put into a right relationship with God. We therefore are at peace with him because of what our Lord Jesus Christ has done for us. 2Through him we possess the entrance into that grace in which we stand, and our pride is in the glorious hope that God has given us. 3More than that—we take a pride in our troubles, for we know that trouble produces fortitude, 4and fortitude produces a character which has stood the test, and character produces hope, 5and this hope never lets us down, for God's love has been poured into our hearts through the Holy Spirit who has been given to us. 6For, while we were still in all our weakness, in God's good time Christ died for godless men. 7It is very unlikely that anyone would be willing to die for a just man; it is just barely possible that some one might even dare to die for a good man. 8But God proves how much he loves us by the fact that Christ died for us while we were still sinners. 9Already, here and now, we have been put into a right relationship with God through the death of Jesus. Since that is so, we can be even more confident that through him we will be saved from the wrath to come. 10It was the death of his Son which restored us to friendship with God, even when we were hostile to him. And, if that is so, now that we are God's friends, how much surer we can be that we will be saved by his continuing life! 11And this is not merely a future hope. Here and now we can take a legitimate and joyful pride in our relationship with God, made possible through the work of our Lord Jesus Christ, for by him we have been made friends with God.

12It was through one man that sin gained an entry into the world, and through sin came death. And so death spread to all men, because all had sinned. 13Before there was law in the world, there was sin, but so long as there is no law, sin is not debited to anyone's account. 14Now, although that is so, from the time of Adam until the time of Moses death exercised its sway over even those who had not actually sinned in the way in which Adam broke the command he had received.

In Adam the one who was to come was foreshadowed. 15But there is no comparison between Adam's sin and God's free gift. By one man's sin the whole of mankind was involved in death. But the grace of God and the free gift, which came through the grace of the one man Jesus Christ, came in a far greater flood-tide of power to all mankind. 16There is no comparison between the effect of God's free gift and the effect of that one man's sin. The verdict which followed the one sin was a verdict of condemnation; but the gift of grace which followed so many sins leads to a verdict of acquittal. 17It is true that because of one man's sin death held sway because of that one man; but it is still truer that those who receive the far more effective power of grace with the free gift of a right relationship with God will reign in life because of what the one man Jesus Christ has done. 18So then, the conclusion is that just as one man's act of sin resulted in condemnation for all men, so one man's act of righteousness resulted in life-giving acquittal for all men. 19For, just as by one man's sin the rest of mankind were constituted sinners, so by one man's obedience the rest of mankind can be constituted righteous. 20Into this situation there entered the whole legal system, with the inevitable result that breaches of the law increased. But the increase in sin was more than counter-balanced by the far greater increase in grace, 21so that, to counteract sin's deadly reign, grace might hold sway in that right relationship with God, which leads to eternal life, and which was made possible through the work of Jesus Christ our Lord.

Chapter 6

WHAT inference are we to draw from all this? Are we—the suggestion is yours—to keep on sinning so that there may be more and more grace? 2God forbid! We are men who have died to sin. How can we go on living in it? 3You must be well aware that all of us who have been baptized into union with Christ have by that baptism been united with him in his death. 4Through this baptism, which united us with him in his death, we were buried with him, so that, just as Christ was raised from the dead by the glory of the Father, we too should live a completely new kind of life. 5If we have been so united with him that we died a death like his, we shall also be so united with him that we shall experience a resurrection life like his. 6For we are well aware that the person we were in our pre-Christian days has been crucified with him, so that our sin-dominated personalities might be destroyed and we might be released from our slavery to sin. 7Once a man is dead he cannot be prosecuted for his sin. 8If we shared Christ's death, we believe that we shall share his risen life too. 9We know that the resurrected Christ is never again to die; he is removed for ever from the sway of death. 10For in the death he died he died once and for all to sin; in the life he lives he lives continuously to God. 11So you must regard yourselves too as dead to sin, and in your Christian life you must regard yourselves as living continuously to God.

12So then, there must be an end to the reign of sin in your mortal body. Sin must no longer command your obedience to the body's desires. 13You must no longer place the various parts of your body at the service of sin, to be used as weapons in the hand of wickedness. You must take your decision to place yourselves at the service of God, as those who were dead and are alive, and you must offer every part of your body to God, to be used as weapons in the hand of all that is right. 14For sin will no longer hold sway over your life, for you are no longer under law; you are under grace.

15What then? Are we to use the fact that we are not under law but under grace as a reason for sinning? God forbid! 16It must be obvious to you that, if you place yourselves at anyone's service as his obedient slaves, you are the slaves of the person to whom you give your obedience. So you may choose to be the slaves of sin, and thereby end in death, or, you may choose to dedicate yourselves to obedience, and thereby end in a right relationship with God. 17You were once slaves of sin, but, thank God, you chose to give whole-hearted obedience to the pattern of teaching to which you have been committed. 18You have been emancipated from sin, and you have become slaves of goodness. 19I am using human language, because it is all that weak human nature can grasp. For just as you yielded your bodies and all their parts to the servitude of impurity and to a lawlessness which issued in ever more lawlessness, so you must now yield them to goodness and walk the way to holiness. 20When you were the slaves of sin, goodness exercised no control over you. 21What good did it do you then? It left you nothing but a legacy of shame. For these things cannot end in anything but death. 22But now there is a new situation. You are emancipated from sin and enslaved to God. And the result is that you are on the way to holiness, and the end of that road is eternal life. 23For death is the wage that sin pays, but God's free gift is eternal life, lived in union with Christ Jesus our Lord.

Chapter 7

YOU must be well aware, brothers, for I am speaking to those who are familiar with a legal system, that the law has authority over a man only during his life-time. 2A married woman is legally bound to her husband during his life-time. But, on the death of her husband, so far as she is concerned, the marriage law ceases to exist. 3So then, if during the life-time of her husband she lives with another man, she is branded as an adulteress. But, on the death of her husband, she is no longer bound by the marriage law, and consequently she is not an adulteress if she marries another man. 4Just so, my brothers, as far as the law is concerned you too are dead, because you have become part of the crucified body of Christ. This was to end your marriage to the law, and to allow you to be married to someone else, I mean to him who was raised from the dead. This was meant to make our lives fruitful for God. ₅So long as we were dominated by our lower nature, our sinful passions were active in our bodies, because the law incited them to work, thereby making our lives fruitful for death. ₆But a new situation has arisen. Our relationship to the law is completely obliterated. The law once held us in its grip, but now, as far as the law is concerned, we are dead. And the result is that we serve God in the new life of the Spirit, and not in the old life of the letter of the law.

₇What conclusion are we to draw from all this? Are we to conclude that the law and sin are one and the same thing? God forbid! All the same, this is true—I would not have known what sin is unless through the action of the law. What I mean is, I would not have known what it is to covet unless the law had said: 'You must not covet.' ₈It was through the commandment that sin found a bridgehead in me, and thus wakened in me all kinds of wrong desires. For where there is no law, the life goes out of sin. ₉I once enjoyed life in a state in which I knew nothing about the law. Then the commandment came into my life and sin sprang to life, ₁₀and life became death for me. So far as I was concerned that very commandment which was meant to bring life brought death. ₁₁For it was through the commandment that sin gained a bridgehead in me, and seduced me, and through it for me turned life into death. ₁₂So the law in itself is holy, and the commandment in itself is holy, just and good.

₁₃Did then that which was good turn life into death for me? God forbid! It was sin that turned life into death for me, and it did so by using to produce death that which in itself is good. This happened that the true characteristic of sin should be exposed, and that through its perverted use of the commandment sin should be shown to be superlatively sinful. ₁₄We know that the law is spiritual, but I am made of flesh and blood. I have been sold into sin's slavery. ₁₅My own actions are a mystery to me. What I do is not what I want to do but what I hate doing. ₁₆The fact that I do not want to do what I do proves that I agree that the law is good. ₁₇The fact is that it is not I who do it; it is the sin which has its home in me. ₁₈I am well aware that, as far as my lower nature goes, nothing good has its home in me. For the ability to wish to do the fine thing I possess; the power to do it I do not possess. ₁₉It is not the good that I want to do that I actually do; it is the evil that I do not want to do that I keep on doing. ₂₀If I do what I do not want to do, it is no longer I who do it. It is the sin which has its home in me which does it. ₂₁I find it to be a principle of life that, even when I want to do the right thing, the one thing that I can do is the wrong thing. 22In my inner self I delight in the law of God, 23but I am aware of a different law, operating in the physical parts of my body, and waging a constant campaign against the law which my reason accepts, and reducing me to captivity to that sinful principle which operates in my physical body. 24I am a wretched creature. Who will rescue me from this body which turns life into death? 25God alone can through Jesus Christ our Lord! Thanks be to him! So then, I am in a situation in which with the spiritual part of my nature I serve God's law, and with the lower part of my nature I serve sin's law.

Chapter 8

WE can therefore say that there is now no condemnation for those whose life is one with the life of Christ. 2For, when through union with Christ Jesus I came under the law of the life-giving Spirit, I was emancipated from the law of death-bringing sin. 3For what the law was unable to do—that is to say, to effect this emancipation from sin—because human nature rendered it impotent and ineffective, God did. He did it by sending his own Son with a human nature like our sinful nature. He sent him to deal with sin, and to deal with it as a human person. 4He thus left sin without a case, and, because he won the victory over sin, the legitimate demand of the law is satisfied in us too, in us whose lives too are no longer directed by our lower nature, but by the Spirit. 5Those who have allowed their lower nature to become the rule of their lives have an attitude to life which is dominated by their lower nature; those who have taken the Spirit as the rule of their lives have an attitude to life which is dominated by the Spirit. 6To have a mind dominated by our lower human nature is to turn life into death; to have a mind dominated by the Spirit is to have real life and every blessing. 7For the mind that is dominated by our lower human nature is hostile to God, for it neither does, nor ever can, submit to God's law. 8It is impossible for those who are ruled by their lower human nature to please God. 9But you are not ruled by your lower human nature; you are ruled by the Spirit, if it is true that the Spirit of God has really made his home in you. No one who does not possess the Spirit belongs to Christ. 10But, if Christ is in you, the physical part of you may be doomed to death because of sin, but the spiritual part of you is destined for life because of the right relationship with God into which you have entered. 11If the Spirit of God, who raised Jesus from the dead, has his home in you, God, who raised Christ from the dead, will give life even to your bodies, subject to death though they are, through the power of his Spirit, who comes and makes his home within you.

12So then, brothers, our duty is not to the lower part of our human nature, nor are we bound to live as it dictates. 13For, if you live as the lower part of your human nature dictates, you are on the way to death. But, if by the help of the Spirit you put to death the life your animal instincts make you want to live, you will really live. 14Only those who are led by God's Spirit are God's sons. 15This Spirit you have received does not leave you in the old relationship to God of terrified slavery. No! This Spirit you have received makes you a son in the family of God, and through this Spirit we can cry to God: 'Father, dear Father!' 16This same Spirit joins with our spirit in the assurance that we really are children of God. 17If we are children of God, then we are heirs to all the promises of God. Yes, fellow-heirs with Christ, if our aim in life is to share his glory by sharing his suffering.

18In my reckoning, whatever we are called upon to suffer in this present time cannot compare with the glory which is going to burst upon us. 19For the whole created universe eagerly and expectantly awaits the day when God will show the world who his sons are. 20For the whole created universe was involved in a process of meaningless frustration, not of its own choice, but by the decree of God who did so subject it. But the situation was never hopeless, 21because even the created universe itself will be liberated from its servitude to death's decay, and will come to enjoy the glorious liberty of the children of God. 22For we know that up to now the whole created universe groans in all its parts, like a woman in the birthpangs. 23This is not only true of the created universe. We too, even although we have received in the Spirit a foretaste of what the new life will be like, groan inwardly, as we wait longingly for God to complete his adoption of us, so that we will be emancipated from sin, both body and soul. 24It is for this hope that we have been saved. But, if what we hope for is already there to be seen, it is not hope at all. For why should anyone go on hoping and waiting for what is already there for him to see? 25But, if we keep on hoping for what we cannot see, then eager hope and patient waiting are combined.

26Even so, the Spirit helps us in our weakness. We do not know what to pray for, if we are to pray as we ought, but the Spirit himself intercedes for us, when the only prayers that we can offer are inarticulate cries. 27He who penetrates into the inmost depths of the human heart knows what the Spirit means, for it is by God's will that the Spirit pleads for God's people. 28We know that through the work of the Spirit all the different events of life are being made to work for good, for those who keep on loving God, those whom his purpose has called. 29For long ago, before they ever came into being, God both knew them and marked them out to become like the pattern of his Son, for it is his purpose that his Son should be the first and eldest of a great family. 30Not only did God mark out his own; he also called them. This call was an invitation to enter into a right relationship with himself, and for them this right relationship is the way to glory.

31What then are we to conclude in view of all this? If God is for us, who is against us? 32If God did not spare his only Son, but gave him up for the sake of us all, can we not be sure that with him there is nothing that he will not freely give us? 33Who can bring any charge against God's chosen ones? Not God, for it is God who acquits us. 34Who can condemn? We have as our intercessor Christ who died. Rather, I ought to say, Christ who was raised from the dead, and who is now at God's right hand. 35Who can part us from Christ's love for us? Shall trouble or distress or persecution or famine, nakedness or danger or the sword? 36As scripture says:

> 'All the day long we face death for your sake;
> we are regarded as sheep to be slaughtered.'

37But he who loved us has enabled us, not only to overcome these things, but to emerge triumphant over them. 38I am quite sure that nothing in death or in life, no angel and no superhuman being, nothing in the world as it is and nothing in the world as it will be, 39no power of the heights and no power of the depths, nor anything else in all the created universe will be able to part us from the love which God has shown us in Christ Jesus our Lord.

Chapter 9

WHEN I say that there is a great grief and an unceasing anguish in my heart, I am speaking the truth as a Christian. This is no lie, and my conscience under the direction of the Holy Spirit supports me in everything I say. 3I could pray that a curse to banish me from the presence of Christ might fall upon me, if such a fate would save my brothers, my natural kith and kin. ₄For they are Israelites. God made them members of his own family. The glory, the covenants, the law, the worship of the Temple, his promises—he gave them all to them. ₅Theirs are the fathers, and in human descent it is from them that the Messiah comes. God who is over all be blessed for ever and ever! Amen.

₆And yet it is not as though the word of God had completely failed, for it is not all who are descended from Israel who are really Israel. ₇Not all are Abraham's real children because they happen to be his physical descendants. In point of fact scripture says: 'It is through Isaac that the line of your descendants will be traced.' ₈This means that it is not those who are simply physically Abraham's children who are the children of God. It is the children born as a result of God's promise who are reckoned as Abraham's real descendants. ₉The statement of the promise in fact is: 'At this time next year I will come, and Sarah will have a son.' ₁₀There is further proof to be added to this. Rebecca had two children, and our ancestor Isaac was the father of both. ₁₁Before they were even born, and before they had done anything good or bad, she was told: 'The older will be the servant of the younger.' ₁₂This was to ensure that the choice between them, involved in the purpose of God, might be permanently based, not on any human achievement, but simply on God's call. ₁₃This is exactly what scripture says: 'I loved Jacob, but I hated Esau.'

₁₄What then are we to conclude? Are we to say that this is injustice on the part of God? God forbid! ₁₅He says to Moses: 'I will have mercy on whom I choose to have mercy, and I will have pity on whom I choose to have pity.' ₁₆So then everything depends, not on man's will, or effort, but on God's pity. ₁₇Scripture says to Pharaoh: 'I have brought you on to the stage of history for the sole purpose of making you the object of the demonstration of my power, and so that the story of what I have done may be told all over the world.' ₁₈So then, if God wills to show mercy on anyone, he does so; and if God wills to make anyone more stubborn than ever, he does so.

₁₉If that is so, you may well argue, why does he blame me? Obviously no one can resist what God wills. ₂₀I might well ask you, my friend, who are you to answer God back? Surely you would not give the created the right to say to the creator: 'Why did you make me like this?' ₂₁Has the potter not the right to do what he likes with the clay? Has he not a perfect right to make out of the same lump one article which is designed for the drawing-room, and one which is designed for the kitchen? 22God must have wished to demonstrate his wrath and to display his power. In spite of that he bore very patiently with the men and women he had created, men and women who deserved nothing but his wrath and who were fit for nothing but destruction. 23What if it was for the sake of the men and women whom he had created to be the objects of his pity, the men and women he had prepared for glory before they ever came into the world, that he held his hand, because he wanted to show them the wealth of that glory of his, which he had always intended for them? 24Such are we, and it is we whom he has called, not only from among the Jews, but from among the Gentiles too. 25As he says in Hosea:

'To those who were not a people
    I will give the title of "my people";
and to her who was not loved,
    I will give the title of "the beloved";
26and in that very place where they were told:
    "You are not my people,"
they will be given the title
    "sons of the living God".'

27Isaiah's prophetic proclamation about Israel is: 'The sons of Israel may be as many in number as the sand of the sea, but it is only the remnant who will be saved. 28Finally and summarily, the Lord will do on earth what he said he would do.' 29As Isaiah said in a previous passage:

'If the Lord of hosts had not left us children,
    we would have become like Sodom,
    and we would have been like Gomorrah.'

30What then are we to conclude? We must conclude that the Gentiles who were not trying to find a right relationship with God received such a relationship, and it was a relationship which was the result of faith, 31while Israel which was looking for some kind of law through which it might enter into a right relationship with God found no such law. 32And why? Because they looked for it, not as the product of faith, but, as they believed, the product of their own performance. They stumbled over the stumbling-stone. 33As scripture says:

'I will place a stumbling-stone in Sion,
    a rock to make men trip,
but he who puts his faith in him will not be disappointed.'

Chapter 10

BROTHERS, with all my heart I long and pray to God for their salvation. 2This I will say for them—they have a zeal for God, but it is superficial and ill-informed. 3They have failed to realize that it is God who brings men into a right relationship with himself, and they have tried to establish such a relationship by their own unaided efforts, and have refused to submit to God's method of bringing it about. 4It is Christ who completes what it was the goal of the law to do, and who thereby opens a right relationship with God to everyone who has faith.

5About the right relationship with God which is based on trying to keep the law, Moses writes that, if a man did obey the law, he would find life in the right relationship that such obedience would bring—an impossible task! 6But this is how the message of the right relationship which comes through faith speaks: 'Do not say to yourself: "Who will go up to heaven?" (that is, to bring Christ down), 7or, "Who will go down to the abyss?" (that is, to bring Christ up from the dead).' 8No! What does it say?

> 'The word is near you,
> on your lips and in your heart.'

The word it is speaking about is the message of faith which we are proclaiming to you. 9For if you publicly assert with your lips your belief that Jesus is Lord, and if you believe with all your heart that God raised him from the dead, you will be saved. 10For it is the heart's faith which brings a man into a right relationship with God, and it is the open assertion of that faith with the lips which brings a man to salvation. 11For scripture says: 'No one who has faith in him will have his hope disappointed.' 12For there is no difference between Jew and Greek. The same Lord is Lord of all, and his wealth is enough for all who call upon him. 13For, 'Everyone who appeals to the name of the Lord will be saved.'

14How then can men appeal to someone in whom they have not put their faith? And how can they put their faith in someone of whom they have never heard? And how can they hear without someone to bring them the message of him? 15And how can they bring the message of him unless they have been sent by God to do so? As scripture says: 'How welcome is the coming of the messengers who bring good news!' 16But not all have accepted the good news. For Isaiah says: 'Who has believed the message we brought?' 17So then, faith must be the consequence of hearing the message, and the message comes through the word which tells of Christ and which was sent by him. 18But, I ask, have they not in fact heard? Indeed they have, for

> 'Their voice has gone out to the whole earth,
>   and their words to the limits of the inhabited world.'

19But, I ask, if that is so, did Israel not realize the meaning of the message? First, a quotation from Moses:

> 'I will treat a nation that is no nation
>   in such a way as to make Israel jealous,
> I will treat a foolish people
>   in such a way as to make Israel angry.'

20Then Isaiah, greatly daring, says:

> 'I was found
>   by those who were not looking for me,
> I made myself seen
>   by those who were not asking about me.'

21But to Israel he says: 'All the day long I have held out my hands in appeal to a disobedient and hostile people.'

Chapter 11

I ASK then, did God reject his people? God forbid! How could I agree to that, I who am an Israelite, a descendant of Abraham, a member of the tribe of Benjamin? 2God did not reject his people whom before time began he chose to be his own. No! Do you not know what scripture says in the story of Elijah? Do you not remember how Elijah pleads with God against Israel? 3'Lord,' he said, 'they have killed your prophets. They have demolished your altars. I alone am left, and they are out for my life.' 4But what is God's answer to him? 'I have left for myself seven thousand men who have never knelt to Baal in worship.' 5So at this present time there is a remnant, and the choice of it is due to grace. 6And, if their choice is due to grace, then that choice is no longer a consequence of their own performance, for, if that were so, grace would no longer be grace. 7What then? Israel as a whole failed to obtain what it sought; the chosen few did obtain it. The hearts of the rest were made impervious to the appeal of God. 8As scripture says:

> 'God gave them a spirit benumbed into insensibility,
>   eyes designed not to see, ears designed not to hear,
>   a state which has lasted right down to this present day.'

9David too says:

> 'Let their well-spread table become a trap and a snare;
>   let it become the very thing which causes their ruin
>   and trips them up, and brings them retribution.
> 10Let their eyes be blinded to take away the ability to see,
>   let their backs be bent for ever beneath their burden.'

11So then I ask, did their error involve them in irretrievable disaster? God forbid! So far from that, it was through their sin that salvation went out to the Gentiles, and the intention was that the inclusion of the Gentiles should awaken Israel to envy. 12If their sin enriched the world, and if their failure enriched the Gentiles, how much more will it mean when no longer the remnant but the whole nation becomes the people of God?

13It is to you Gentiles that I speak. I am an apostle to the Gentiles, and I magnify my office, 14for my one aim is somehow to provoke the people of my own flesh and blood to envy the Gentiles their privilege, and so to succeed in saving some of them. 15If the rejection of the Jews results in the reconciliation of the world to God, to what can you compare their reception, except to life from the dead? 16If the first handful of dough is consecrated, then the whole lump must be consecrated, and if the root is consecrated, the branches must be consecrated too.

17If some of the original branches of the olive-tree have been lopped off, and if you, like a wild olive, have been grafted in in their place, and if you thereby become sharers in the rich root of the olive-tree, 18you must not pride yourselves on being superior to the original branches. If you do feel moved to such a pride, remember that it is not you who support the root, but the root which supports you. 19So then, you will say: 'The branches were lopped off to allow me to be grafted in.' 20Very well! It was their refusal to take the way of faith that caused them to be lopped off; it was your acceptance of the way of faith that put you where you are. Your feelings should not be feelings of pride, but of awe. 21For, if God did not spare the original branches, he will not spare you either. 22So then, remember both the kindness and the severity of God. Remember his severity to those who fell into sin; remember his kindness to you. In that kindness you must continue to trust, and not in your own achievement. Otherwise you too will be cut away. 23As for them, if they cease to persist in their refusal to take the way of faith, they will be grafted in again. For God is able to graft them in again. 24For, if you were cut out from what is naturally a wild olive-tree, and if against all nature you were grafted into a cultivated olive-tree, how much more will they who are the original olive-branches be grafted back into the stock which is their own?

25Brothers, I want you to grasp this divine secret which God has revealed to his own, because I do not want you to get the impression of your own cleverness. The insensitiveness of the hearts of the Jewish nation is not a total insensitiveness, and it will only last until the full number of the Gentiles has come in. 26After that has happened, all Israel will be saved. As scripture says:

'The Rescuer will come from Sion,
  he will drive all godlessness from Jacob.
27This is the covenant I will make with them,
  when I take away their sins.'

28Looked at from the point of view of the gospel, they have incurred God's hatred, and it is all for your sake. Looked at from the point of view of God's eternal choice, they are still loved by God for the sake of the fathers. 29For God cannot go back on his gifts or his call. 30You once disobeyed God, but now through their disobedience you have found God's mercy. 31Just so, in the present situation they have been disobedient, but God's purpose is that they should find mercy through the mercy which you have found. 32For God made all men prisoners to disobedience, for it was his purpose to show mercy to all.

33How deep is the wealth of the wisdom and knowledge of God! His decisions are beyond man's mind to understand! His ways of working are beyond man's power to trace!

34'Who has understood the mind of the Lord?
    Or, who has been his counsellor?
35 What man ever gave anything to God
    that put God in his debt?'

36For everything had its beginning from him, and owes its continued existence to him, and will find its end in him. Glory be to him for ever! Amen.

Chapter 12

So then, brothers, I urge you by the mercies of God to offer your bodies to God as a living, consecrated sacrifice, which will delight God's heart, for that is the only worship which a rational being can offer to God. 2Stop always trying to adjust your life to the world's ways. You must get a new attitude to life; your whole mental outlook must be radically altered, so that you will be able to decide what God's will is, and to know what is good and pleasing to him, and perfect.

3I say to everyone among you—and it is the special place which God's grace gave me which gives me the right to say it—you must not have a more exalted idea of your own importance than you have any right to have. You must use your mind to arrive at a sober estimate of yourself, an estimate based, not on your own performance, but on the measure of faith that God has given to each of you. 4In a single body there are many parts, and each part has its own function. 5In the same way, although we are many, our union with Christ makes us one body, and we are individually living parts of one another. 6The grace of God has given us each special gifts, which are all different, and each man must use his gift. If a man has the gift of prophecy, he must use it in proportion to his faith. 7If he has the gift of administration, he must use it in administration. If he is a teacher, he must use it in teaching. If by his words he can lift up men's hearts, he must use them to do so. 8If a man can contribute to someone else's need, he must do so generously. If he has the gift of leadership, he must exercise it with enthusiasm. If he is helping those in distress, he must do so gladly.

9Your love must not be a superficial pretence. You must hate evil, and you must give your unshakable loyalty to what is good. 10Your brotherly love must make you one loving family. You must lead the way in honouring each other. 11Your zeal must never flag. You must keep your enthusiasm at boiling-point. You must always be serving the Lord. 12You must be filled with optimistic joy. You must meet trouble with the power to pass the breaking-point and not to break. You must persevere in prayer. 13You must share what you have with God's people who are in need. You must be eager to practise hospitality. 14You must bless your persecutors; you must bless them and not curse them. 15You must be joyous with the joyful, and you must be sad with the sorrowful. 16You must live in harmony with one another. You must not be haughtily contemptuous; you must be happy to seek the society of people who in the world's eyes are quite unimportant. You must avoid conceit. 17You must not live on the principle that one bad turn deserves another. You must aim only at the things which all men regard as lovely. 18If it is possible, so far as it depends on you, your personal relationships with everyone must be good. 19My dear friends, never be out for vengeance. Leave room for the wrath of God, for scripture says: 'Retribution belongs to me,' the Lord says. 'I will repay.' 20So far from that, if your enemy is hungry, give him something to eat. If he is thirsty, give him something to drink. For, if you do that, you will make him feel the pangs of burning shame. 21Never let yourself be defeated by evil, but always defeat evil with good.

Chapter 13

EVERYONE must submit to the governing authorities. All authority owes its existence to the act of God, and the existing authorities were instituted by God. 2Since this is so, to rebel against authority is to resist what God has ordered. Those who do resist will have no one to blame but themselves for any punishment they will incur. 3It is not good conduct but bad conduct which has any reason to fear the magistrates. Do you want to be in a position in which you need have no fear of those in authority? If your conduct is good, you will receive nothing but approval from them. 4The man in authority is the servant of God, and he exists for the sake of what is good. If you are guilty of misconduct, then you must necessarily be afraid. It is not for nothing that a man in authority has the power of life and death. He is the servant of God, and his function is to exercise punishment and to demonstrate the divine wrath on evil-doers. 5It is therefore necessary to submit to authority, not simply because you are afraid of God's wrath, but also because you respect your own conscience. 6For the same reason you must pay your taxes, for the magistrates are God's officers, intent on carrying on this very duty of maintaining good order. 7Pay all men what is due to them. If you are due tribute to anyone, pay it. If you are due taxes to anyone, pay them. Give respect to whom respect is due, and honour to whom honour is due.

Be in debt to no one—apart from the debt of love which you

always owe to one another, for to love your neighbour is to fulfil the whole law. ₉The commandments, 'You must not commit adultery; you must not murder; you must not steal; you must not covet'—and any other commandment there may be—are all summed up in this one sentence: 'You must love your neighbour as yourself.' ₁₀Love never wrongs its neighbour. Therefore love is the law's complete fulfilment.

₁₁Further, you are well aware what moment in history we have reached. You know that it is high time to wake from sleep, for our salvation is closer to us than when we first took the decision to believe. ₁₂The night is almost over. Day is almost here. We must therefore strip ourselves of the conduct which belongs to the dark, and we must clothe ourselves in the armour of soldiers of the light. ₁₃We must behave ourselves with propriety, as those who live in the full light of day. We must have nothing to do with revelry and drunkenness, with debauchery and shameless immorality, with quarrelling and jealousy. ₁₄You must clothe yourselves with the Lord Jesus Christ, and you must stop planning how to satisfy the desires of yourselves at your worst.

Chapter 14

WELCOME the man who is weak in the faith, but do not begin by introducing him to discussions about debatable matters. ₂One man has faith enough to believe that he may eat all kinds of food. Another, who is weaker in the faith, feels compelled to be a vegetarian. ₃The man who believes that food laws are quite irrelevant must not look down with contempt on the man who carefully observes them; and the man who carefully observes them must not think that he has the right to judge the man who thinks them unnecessary, for God has welcomed him. ₄Who are you to pass judgment on another man's servant? It is by the judgment of his own master that a man stands or falls. And, what is more, he will stand, for the Lord can make him stand. ₅One man regards one day as more holy than another day; another man regards all days as alike. Each man must make up his own mind, and reach his own conviction, on such a matter. ₆If a man feels like that about a certain day, he does so with the honour of God in his mind. If a man eats meat, he eats with the honour of God in his mind, because he says his grace for what he eats. If a man does not eat meat, he abstains from eating with the honour of God in his mind, for he too says his grace to God. ₇No man's life concerns only himself, and no man's death concerns only himself. In life we live for the Lord; in death we die for the Lord. In life and in death we belong to the Lord. 9The very reason why Christ died and came to life again was to make him Lord of the dead and of the living. 10As for you, why do you pass judgment on your brother? Or, why do you regard your brother with contempt? We shall all stand at God's judgment seat. 11For scripture says:

> 'As I live, says the Lord,
>   every knee shall bow to me,
>   and every tongue shall acknowledge me
>   as God.'

12So then, each of us will have to answer for himself to God.

13So then, let us resolve to stop passing judgment on each other. Instead of that, let us resolve never to place an obstacle in any Christian's way, and never to do anything which would make it easier for him to go wrong. 14My Christian faith gives me the knowledge and the conviction that there is nothing which in itself is impure. Only if a man thinks that something is impure does it become impure to him. 15But, if your fellow-Christian is distressed because of the food you eat, your conduct is no longer based on love. You must not let what you eat become the ruin of a man for whom Christ died. 16You must not do the right thing in such a way that it gets you a bad reputation. 17For the Kingdom of God does not consist in eating or not eating, and drinking or not drinking. It consists in justice and peace and joy—and all in the atmosphere of the Holy Spirit. 18To serve Christ in this way is to please God and to win the approval of men. 19We must then concentrate all our efforts on the things which produce right relationships between one another and which build us into a real fellowship. 20Do not for the sake of food undo all that God has done. It is quite true that all things are pure, but it is quite wrong for any man to make the Christian way more difficult for others by what he eats. 21The really fine thing is to abstain from eating meat, and to abstain from drinking wine, and to abstain from anything which makes the way more difficult for your fellow-Christian. 22By all means retain your faith, but retain it as a personal matter between you and God. He is a fortunate man who has no self-questionings when he comes to a decision that a thing is right. 23And, if a man eats, and is still not sure whether he is doing the right thing or not, he stands condemned for eating, because his action does not spring from faith, and what is not based on faith is sin.

Chapter 15

IF our faith is strong, it is our duty to accept the scruples of those whose faith is not so strong as ours as part of the burden which we must carry. It is not our duty to consider only ourselves. ₂It is our neighbour that each of us must consider, and our aim must be his good and the upbuilding of his faith. ₃For Christ certainly did not consider only himself. Far from it, for scripture says:

> 'The reproaches of those who reproached you
> fell upon me.'

₄Everything that was written long ago was written for our instruction. Its aim was to enable us, through the fortitude and the encouragement which the scriptures give, to maintain our hope. ₅I pray that God, from whom fortitude and encouragement come, may grant to you to live in Christlike harmony with each other, ₆so that your hearts and voices may be united in a chorus of praise to the God and Father of our Lord Jesus Christ.

₇Welcome each other, therefore, as Christ welcomed you—and all for the glory of God. ₈I mean that Christ became the servant of the Jewish people to confirm God's promises to the fathers, and thus to demonstrate that God is true to his word, ₉and also to give the Gentiles reason to praise God for his mercy. As scripture says:

> 'Therefore I will praise you among the Gentiles,
> and I will sing to your name.'

₁₀And again it says:

> 'Gentiles, rejoice with his people!'

₁₁And again:

> 'Praise the Lord, all Gentiles, and let all the peoples add
> their praise to him.'

₁₂And again, Isaiah says:

> 'The root of Jesse shall come,
> he who will be raised up to rule the Gentiles,
> and on him shall the Gentiles set their hope.'

₁₃May the God who gives you hope make your faith an experience which is filled with joy and peace, so that by the power of the Holy Spirit your hearts may be brimming over with hope.

14I personally, my brothers, have no doubt at all that you are full of goodness, filled with all kinds of knowledge, and well able to give advice to each other. 15All the same, in parts of this letter I have written to you with some considerable boldness, to remind you of what you already know. 16My warrant for so doing is the special privilege given to me by God. 17This privilege made me the servant of Christ Jesus to the Gentiles, and gave me the telling of the good news as my priestly task. It gave me as my aim the task of making the Gentiles an offering, consecrated by the Holy Spirit, and thus acceptable to God. 18I will venture to speak only of the things in which I was the agent of Christ to lead the Gentiles into obedience to him by my words and by my actions, 19and by the compulsion of miraculous demonstrations of the power of God in action, and by the power which the Holy Spirit gave me. And so from Jerusalem right round to Illyricum I have completed the proclamation of the good news of Christ. 20My ambition has always been to tell the good news of Christ not in places where the name of Christ is already known, for I do not want to build on a foundation which some one else has laid. 21My ambition is expressed in the words of scripture:

'Those to whom the story of him has never been told
    shall see him,
    and those who have never heard of him
    shall understand.'

22That is why I was repeatedly prevented from coming to visit you. 23As things now are, I have no longer any scope for work in these parts. I have been longing to visit you for many years, and I hope to do so now, 24whenever I go to Spain. For I hope to see you on the way through, and to have your help on my way there, after I have had the pleasure of spending some time with you. 25At the moment I am off to Jerusalem with help for God's people there. 26For Macedonia and Achaia decided to make a contribution to the poor members of God's people in Jerusalem. 27This they decided to do, and indeed they are in their debt. For, if the Gentiles have shared in the spiritual blessings of the Jews, they are bound to regard it as nothing less than a duty to give them help in material things. 28So then, when I have completed this business, and when I have delivered the proceeds of the collection intact, I shall leave for Spain, and I shall visit you on the way. 29I know that when I come to you, I will come with a full blessing from Christ.

30I appeal to you by our Lord Jesus Christ, and by the love which the Spirit inspires, to join with me in straining every nerve in prayer to God for me, 31that I may escape the clutches of the unbelievers in Judaea, and that God's people in Jerusalem may welcome the help I bring to them, 32because through God's will I want to come joyfully to you and so to be rested and refreshed in your company. 33God, the giver of peace, be with you all. Amen.

Chapter 16

THIS is to introduce to you our fellow-Christian Phoebe, who is active in the service of the congregation at Cenchreae, 2and to ask you to give her a Christian welcome, worthy of God's people. Please assist her in any matter in which she may need your help, for she has given help to many, myself included.

3Give my good wishes to Prisca and Aquila, who have so often shared with me in Christian work, 4for they have risked their lives for my life. Not only I, but all the Gentile congregations too, are grateful to them. 5Give my good wishes to the congregation which meets in their house. Give my good wishes to my dear Epaenetus, who was the first convert to Christ in Asia. 6Give my good wishes to Mary, who has worked so hard among you. 7Give my good wishes to Andronicus and Junias, my fellow-countrymen and my fellow-prisoners, for they are distinguished members of the apostolic company, and they were Christians before I was. 8Give my good wishes to Ampliatus, my dear Christian friend. 9Give my good wishes to Urbanus, who shares with me in the work and in the fellowship of Christ, and to my dear Stachys. 10Give my good wishes to Apelles, that sterling Christian. Give my good wishes to the Christian members of the household of Aristobulus. 11Give my good wishes to my fellow-countryman Herodion. Give my good wishes to the members of the household of Narcissus who are Christians. 12Give my good wishes to Tryphaena and Tryphosa, who are such strenuous workers in the Lord's service. Give my good wishes to my dear Persis, who has toiled so hard in the Lord's service. 13Give my good wishes to Rufus, that choice Christian, and to his mother, who was a mother to me too. 14Give my good wishes to Asyncritus, to Phlegon, to Hermes, to Patrobas, to Hermas, and to all the members of their Christian community 15Give my good wishes to Philologus and to Julia, to Nereus and to his sister, and to Olympas, and to all God's people who are members of their Christian community. 16Greet each other with the kiss of peace. All the congregations of Christ send their good wishes.

17I urge you, brothers, to keep your eye on those who are trouble-makers and who make it easier for others to go wrong, in defiance of the teaching you have received. Have nothing to do with them. 18For men like that are the servants, not of our Lord Jesus Christ, but of their own appetites, and with their smooth and flattering talk they seduce the hearts of innocent people. 19The story of your Christian obedience is known to everyone. You make me very happy, but I want you to be experts in goodness and innocent of evil. 20It will not be long until the God of peace so crushes Satan that you will trample on him. The grace of our Lord Jesus be with you.

21Timothy, my colleague, sends you his good wishes, and so do Lucius and Jason and Sosipater, my fellow-countrymen. 22I Tertius, who took down this letter from Paul's dictation, send you Christian greetings. 23Gaius who has given me hospitality, and whose hospitality embraces the whole congregation, sends you his good wishes. Erastus, the city treasurer sends you good wishes and so does our Christian brother Quartus.

25To him who is able to make you stand four-square,
  as the good news I preach and the message Jesus Christ pro-
    claimed promised that he can,
  that good news and that proclamation which came in the rev-
    elation of the secret purpose of God,
  that purpose which was for long ages veiled in silence,
26but has now been full disclosed and through the writings
  of the prophets and the command of God made known to
  all the Gentiles, to lead them to the obedience
  which is born of faith—
27to the God who alone is wise be glory for ever
  through Jesus Christ. Amen.

Introduction to the First and Second Letters
to the Corinthians

THE story of Paul's work in Corinth is told in Acts 18.1-17. Corinth was one of the places where Paul stayed longest, for we are told that he worked in Corinth for eighteen months. There are no letters which give us so vivid a picture of life in the early church, for, as it has been said, these letters take the roof off the church, and let us see what was going on inside.

It will help to have in our minds a scheme of the course of Paul's correspondence with Corinth.

i. It began with a letter which is prior to our first Corinthian letter. This letter is referred to in 1.5.9. It was a letter which told the Corinthians to have nothing to do with the immorality of the heathen world. It was not until A.D.90 that Paul's letters were collected, and by that time it may well have been that the editors did not quite know how to arrange them. It may be that this previous letter became embedded in 2 Corinthians, and it is perhaps contained in 2 Corinthians 6.14-7.1. The sense suits, and, if that section is removed, it makes good sense to pass from 6.13 to 7.2.

ii. Certain information came to Paul from Corinth, and in the meantime he had sent Timothy to Corinth to mend matters (1.4.17). The information came from members of Chloe's household, who had come to Ephesus from which Paul wrote (1.1.14); from a letter which the Corinthians had sent Paul, and which is answered in 1.7.1-1.15.58; and from Stephanas, Fortunatus and Achaicus, the bearers of the Corinthians' letter (1.16.7).

iii. Paul answered this in our first letter.

iv. The letter was ineffective and Paul paid a quick visit to Corinth. The evidence of this visit is in 2.12.14, and 2.13.1,2, where he speaks of a third visit, and, if there was to be a third, there must have been a second. This visit was also a failure and a heartbreak to Paul (2.1.23; 2.2.1).

v. Since the visit was ineffective, he wrote again, this time a very stern letter, which he came near to regretting having sent (2.2.4; 2.2.9; 2.7.8). It may be that this painful letter is in 2 Corinthians 10-13, which is one of the most heartbroken letters that Paul ever wrote. It is likely that it ought to come before 2 Corinthians 1-9, and that it was misplaced when the letters were edited. He also sent Titus to Corinth to try to settle things.

vi. Paul then left Ephesus to journey to Corinth by way of Macedonia. He was desperately worried, but in Macedonia he met Titus, who brought news that the trouble was over. And then Paul wrote the letter we have in 2 Corinthians 1-9, in which there is the calm after the storm.

As we have seen, in the first letter Paul dealt with the news which Chloe's people had brought him, and with the letter which the Corinthians had sent him. The problems were as follows.

i. First, there are the problems of which Chloe's people informed Paul.

a) The Corinthian church is torn and divided by sects and parties (1.1.10-1.4.21).

b) There has been a shocking case of immorality involving a son and his stepmother.

c) Members of the congregation do not hesitate to go to law with each other, for the Greeks were always a litigious people (1.6.1-11).

d) There is flagrant and blatant sexual immorality even among so-called Christian people (1.6.12-20).

ii. The subjects on which the Corinthians asked Paul's advice were many and varied.

a) There were questions about marriage (1.7.1-40). Paul's answers to these questions, answers in which he clearly prefers the unmarried state, are governed by the fact that he expected the Second Coming at any moment, and therefore wished people to have no earthly ties at all. He believed himself and all men to be living in a very temporary situation.

b) There were questions about meat which had been offered to idols (1.8.1-1.11.1). In those days nearly all social occasions were held in heathen temples. Only a token part of the sacrifice was burned on the altar, and part of the rest was given to the worshipper, who made a feast of it and invited his friends. If a Christian refused to attend such parties, he cut himself off from nearly all social occasions.

c) There were questions about worship in church.

1. There was the question about women who tried to worship with their heads uncovered (1.11.2-16). In those days for a woman to go bare-headed was the sign that she was a loose woman, and was an invitation to immorality.

2. There were questions about the Lord's Supper. In those days the Lord's Supper included the Love Feast, but what should have been a

noble expression of Christian fellowship had become an occasion for the stressing of social distinctions and the formation of cliques (1.11.17-34).

3. There was the problem of spiritual gifts. The phenomenon of speaking with tongues, and the way in which people coveted it, were bidding fair to reduce the church services to chaos (1.12-1.14).

iii. Finally, there were questions about the resurrection of the body. By the resurrection of the body Paul meant rather the survival of a man's total personality as an individual than the resurrection of the physical body (1.15.1-58).

In the second letter, as we have seen, we should very likely read chapters 10 to 13 first. In them Paul is forced to meet the accusations of his opponents, and, much against his will, to state his own claims. Finally, chapters 1 to 9 show us the relief after the anxiety.

The Corinthians letters show us another thing which to Paul was very important. The Jerusalem church was the mother church, but it was a very poor church. Paul had therefore organized a collection for the Jerusalem church from the younger churches. He speaks of it in both letters (1.16.1-11; 2.8.1-9.15). To Paul this collection was a way of marking the unity of the church, by showing that each church felt a Christian responsibility for the others. To give is to demonstrate oneness.

In the Corinthian correspondence we see better than anywhere else in the New Testament the practical problems of the early church.

The First Letter to the
CORINTHIANS

Chapter 1

THIS is a letter from Paul, called by God's will to be an apostle of
Jesus Christ, and from Sosthenes, our colleague, 2to God's congregation at Corinth, those whose union with Christ has consecrated
their lives to God, those whom God has called to be his own, and to
everyone everywhere who calls on the name of our Lord Jesus Christ,
their Lord and ours. 3Grace to you and every blessing from God our
Father and from the Lord Jesus Christ.

4I always thank my God for you. I thank him for his grace which
was given to you in Christ Jesus. 5For through your union with him
your lives have been enriched in everything, with the result that you
are equipped with every kind of knowledge and with complete
ability to communicate it. 6You are in fact the proof that what Christ
promised has happened. 7The result is that there is no spiritual gift
which you do not possess, while you eagerly await the time when our
Lord Jesus Christ will again burst upon the stage of history. 8It is he
who will so strengthen you to the very end that on the day when our
Lord Jesus comes no one will be able to level any charge against you.
9You can rely on God by whom you were called to share the life of
his Son, Jesus Christ, our Lord.

10I urge you, brothers, by the name of our Lord Jesus Christ, to live
in harmony with one another, and not to allow divisions to exist
between you. You must be united and unanimous in your general
attitude to life and in each particular decision. 11I say this because,
brothers, a report has reached me through Chloe's people. They tell
me that there are quarrels in your society. 12I refer to the fact that
each one of you has his slogan: 'I belong to Paul'; 'I belong to Apollos';
'I belong to Cephas'; 'I belong to Christ.' 13Has Christ been torn into
pieces? Was it Paul who was crucified for you? Was it in Paul's name
that you were baptized? 14I am thankful that the only people among
you I did baptize were Crispus and Gaius. 15That at least stops any of

you claiming that you were baptized in my name. 16I did baptize Stephanas' family too. Beyond that, I cannot think of anyone whom I baptized. 17For Christ did not send me to baptize, but to bring the good news, nor did I use the artifices of rhetoric, for I did not want the simple fact of the cross of Christ to be emptied of its power by human cleverness.

18The story of the cross makes nonsense to those who are on the way to ruin, but to us who are on the way to salvation it is the power of God. 19For scripture says:

> 'I will destroy the wisdom of the wise,
> I will bring to nothing the cleverness of the clever.'

20Where is the sage? Where is the expert in the law? Where is the clever debater whose questions never looked beyond the horizons of this world? Has God not turned this world's wisdom into folly? 21In God's wisdom the world through its wisdom never succeeded in getting to know God. God therefore decided to save those who believe by the folly of the message we preach. 22And folly they believe it to be, for the Jews ask for miraculous demonstrations of the power of God in action, and the Greeks look for wisdom, 23but we preach Christ, and Christ on his cross, a message which to the Jews is actually a barrier to belief, and which to the Gentiles is nonsense. 24But to those whom God has called, both Jews and Greeks, he is Christ the power of God and the wisdom of God. 25For the folly of God is wiser than the wisdom of men, and the weakness of God is stronger than the strength of men.

26Brothers, you see God's way of calling you. There are few among you who are wise as the world counts wisdom; there are few who are influential; there are few of aristocratic birth. 27But God has chosen the things the world counts foolish to shame the wise; God has chosen the things the world counts weak to shame the strong. 28God has chosen the things which the world counts quite undistinguished in birth, and which it despises, things which the world regards as mere nothings, to destroy things as they are. 29And he did this to ensure that no human being should have any cause for pride in the presence of God. 30It is his doing that you have entered into fellowship with Jesus Christ. God has made him our wisdom, our goodness, our way to holiness, our liberation. 31And he did this to ensure that what scripture says might come true: 'If any man is proud, he must be proud of what the Lord has done for him.'

Chapter 2

When I came to see you, brothers, I did not come proclaiming God's secret with any special kind of rhetorical or philosophical brilliance. ₂I had in fact made up my mind that in my preaching to you I would forget everything except Jesus Christ, and him upon his cross. ₃I was very conscious of my own inadequacy; I was apprehensive and very nervous, when I came to you. ₄My message and my preaching were not delivered in professionally persuasive language. But they were characterized by the undeniable presence of the Spirit and of power. ₅This was my deliberately chosen method, because I wanted your faith to depend, not on man's cleverness, but on God's power.

₆There is a wisdom which we do teach to mature Christians, but it is not this world's wisdom, nor is it the wisdom of this world's rulers, for they are already passing from the scene. ₇What we do teach is the secret wisdom of God, which only God's own people can understand, a wisdom which until now has remained concealed, but which long ago before time began God framed and destined for our glory. ₈None of this world's rulers knew it. If they had known it, they would not have crucified the Lord of glory. ₉No! It is the wisdom of which scripture says:

> 'God has prepared for those who love him
> what no eye has ever seen, and no ear has ever heard,
> and what no human mind has ever even thought of.'

₁₀It is through the Spirit that God has given us the revelation of his truth, for the Spirit searches out everything, even the deep things of God. ₁₁What human being knows a man's mind, except the man's own inmost spirit? Just so, no one knows God's mind except God's Spirit. ₁₂It is not the spirit of the world that we have received, but the Spirit whose source and origin is God, to enable us to understand the gifts which God in his grace has given to us. ₁₃When we interpret spiritual truths to people who have the Spirit, we speak about these gifts in language which was not taught us by human wisdom, but which was taught us by the Spirit. ₁₄A man who does not possess the Spirit refuses to accept the truths which the Spirit of God gives him. Such a man regards them as nonsense. He cannot understand them because a man needs the Spirit rightly to evaluate them. ₁₅The man who has the Spirit can rightly evaluate everything, and he himself is subject to no man's judgment. 16To quote scripture:

'Can anyone know the mind of the Lord?
Can anyone instruct him?'

And we do have the mind of Christ.

Chapter 3

BROTHERS, it was quite impossible for me to speak to you as I would speak to people who have the Spirit; I had to speak to you as to people whose horizons were limited to this world, as to those who had never got beyond the stage of infancy in their Christian faith. 2In my teaching I gave you milk to drink. I could not give you solid food; you were not able to digest it, and you are not able to do so even yet, 3for you are still worldly people. While envy and quarrelling flourish among you, you cannot but admit that you are still worldly people, and that your conduct is based on purely human motives. 4When one of you says: 'I belong to Paul', and another: 'I belong to Apollos', are you not behaving like men untouched by Christ? 5What after all is Apollos? What is Paul? We are both servants of God through whom you entered the Christian faith; and each of us carried out the task God gave him to do. 6I planted the seed; Apollos watered it; but it was God who made the plant grow. 7It is not the man who plants the seed, or the man who waters it, who is really important; the really important person is God who makes it grow. 8There is no difference between the man who plants the seed and the man who waters it. Each of them will receive his own reward for his own work. 9We work together and we work for God. You are God's garden; you are God's building.

10In the privilege and the task which God gave me, like a wise master-builder, I laid the foundation. Someone else is erecting the building upon it. Each man must be careful how he erects his building. 11No one can lay any other foundation than the one which has been laid, for that foundation is Jesus Christ. 12Whatever superstructure a man raises on that foundation—be it of gold, or silver, or precious stones, or wood, or hay, or stubble—13each man's work will be shown up in its true character. The day of judgment will clearly show what it is, for that day will break upon the world's sight with fire, and the fire will test the character of each man's work. 14If the work which a man has built on that foundation survives the test, he will receive a reward. 15But if a man's work perishes in the flames, he will lose it, but he himself will be saved, but like a man rescued from a fire. 16Are you not aware that you are God's temple, and that the Holy Spirit has his home in you? 17If anyone destroys God's temple, God will destroy him, for the temple of God is holy—and you are that temple.

18Do not allow anyone to mislead you. If any of you thinks he is wise, as this world reckons wisdom, he must become a fool in order to become really wise. 19For this world's wisdom is nonsense as God sees it. For scripture says:

> 'He traps the wise in their own cleverness.

20And again:

> 'The Lord knows that the arguments of the sages are futile.

21You talk about 'belonging' to people. You must never make your connection with any man a cause for pride. 22It is not a case of you belonging to some human person. For everything belongs to you— Paul and Apollos and Cephas, the world and life and death, the present and the future—23and you belong to Christ, and Christ belongs to God.

Chapter 4

YOU must think of us as Christ's servants and as stewards of the secrets of God. 2Now the first quality that anyone looks for in a steward is reliability. 3To be called upon to undergo your judgment, or the judgment of any human court, matters very little to me. For that matter, I do not even judge myself. 4My conscience is clear, but that does not necessarily mean that I am acquitted. My judge is the Lord. 5You must therefore stop this habit of passing premature judgments. You must wait until the Lord's coming, for he will light up the things which are hidden in darkness, and will lay bare the motives of the heart. And then each man will receive from God such praise as he deserves.

6Brothers, although these things do not really apply to us at all, I have for your sakes applied them to myself and Apollos by way of example, because I want you by taking us as an example to learn the principle that to go beyond what scripture says is forbidden, and so to stop your self-important practice of singing the praises of one leader and blackguarding another. 7Who sees anything specially outstanding in you? What do you possess that you did not receive? If you received it as a gift, why pride yourself as if it had not been a gift but an achievement? 8No doubt you have arrived at a stage when you have not an unsatisfied longing left! No doubt you have arrived at a stage when you are spiritual millionaires! No doubt you have entered into your kingdom and left us far behind! I wish that you had entered into your kingdom, and that we could share it with you! 9For I think that God has brought us apostles on to the scene like the little company of captives who bring up the rear of a victorious general's pageant of triumph and who are doomed to die in the arena. We have become a public spectacle to the world, both to angels and to men. 10We are fools for Christ's sake; you are wise with Christian wisdom. We are weak; you are strong. Yours is the glory; ours, the disgrace. 11To this hour we live in hunger and in thirst; we are ill-clad; we are beaten up; we are homeless vagrants. 12We sweat it out, working with our hands. We meet insult with blessing; persecution, with endurance; slander, with appeal. 13To this day we are regarded as no better than the scum of the earth and the off-scourings of humanity.

14I am not writing like this to shame you. I am doing it to warn you, for I regard you as my dear children. 15You may have thousands of guardians in your Christian life; you have only one father. For it was I who through the gospel became your father in the Christian faith. 16I therefore appeal to you to take me as your pattern and example. 17It is for this very reason that I am sending Timothy to you. He is my dear child and faithful in the Lord's service. He will remind you of the way I live as a Christian, and which I everywhere teach in every congregation. 18There are some who are inflated with defiant self-conceit, not really believing that I intend to come to visit you. 19But I will come, and, if the Lord wills, I will come soon, and then I will discover, not how these inflated characters can talk, but what they can do. 20For the Kingdom of God does not consist of talk but of power. 21Make your own choice! Do you want me to come to you with a rod of discipline, or lovingly and in the spirit of gentleness?

Chapter 5

I HAVE actually received a report that there is a case of sexual immorality among you, and a case so shocking that it is not practised even by pagans, for a man is living with his step-mother, as man and wife. ₂In face of this are you still inflated with self-conceit? Should this not rather have been a matter for tears of sorrowful shame? A man who perpetrated a deed like that should have been totally expelled from your fellowship. ₃Although I am absent from you in body, I am present in spirit, and, as if I were present, in the name of the Lord Jesus I have already come to a decision about the man who has done this terrible thing. ₄When you have met, and when I am present with you in spirit, acting in the power of our Lord Jesus ₅you must banish such a man from the fellowship of God's people, and consign him to Satan. This you must do so that this salutary and painful discipline may mortify this man's fleshly desires, so that on the day of the Lord his spirit may be saved. ₆Your proud pretensions have an ugly look about them. Are you not well aware that an evil influence can from the smallest beginnings spread like an infection through a whole community? ₇Get rid of the last remnants of the tainted life that once you lived, so that not a suggestion of evil infection may be left. That is the way you ought to be in any event, for the last evil taint ought to have been eradicated from your life, just as before the Passover sacrifice the last particle of leaven is removed from every house. For Christ is for us the Passover lamb, sacrificed for our deliverance. ₈Let us then live life as if it was a continual festival, with not a taint of evil or wickedness left, but in the purity of sincerity and truth.

₉I wrote to you in my letter not to associate with immoral people. ₁₀I obviously did not mean the people out in the world who are immoral or sinfully greedy, and thieves or idolaters. If you had to avoid them, you would have to retire from the world altogether. ₁₁What I did write was that you must refuse to associate with anyone who claims the name of fellow-Christian, if he is living an immoral life, if he is sinfully greedy, if he is an idolater, if he uses abusive language, if he is a drunkard or a thief. With such a man you must not even share a meal. ₁₂What business of mine is it to exercise judgment on the man outside the church? But it is obviously your business to exercise judgment on people inside it. ₁₃God will exercise judgment on people outside the church. Remove the evil man from your fellowship.

Chapter 6

IF any of you has a dispute with another member of the church, can he really bring himself to take his case to the pagan law-courts, and not to God's people? 2Is it possible that you are not aware that it is God's people who are going to judge the world? And, if the world is to be judged by you, are you really incompetent to exercise judgment in the most trivial matters? 3Are you not aware that we are to judge angels? How much more then mundane matters of everyday life? 4If you do embark upon law-suits about such mundane matters, how can you submit them for decision to men who have no kind of respect within the Christian community? 5Shame on you! Are you asking me to believe that in your own society there is not a single wise man, able to give a decision between one Christian and another? 6Must Christian go to law with Christian, and that before people who are not Christians? 7In point of fact, to have such law-suits with each other at all is to fail to maintain the standard of the Christian life. Why do you not rather submit to be injured? Why do you not rather submit to being swindled? 8So far from that, it is you who do the injuring and the swindling—and it is your fellow-Christians who are your victims. 9Bad men will never enter the promised possession of the Kingdom of God. Make no mistake! Fornicators, idolaters, adulterers, homosexuals, perverts, 10thieves, those whose desires are never satisfied, drunkards, those who use abusive language, robbers, will never enter into the promised possession of the Kingdom of God—and you know it! 11And that is what some of you were like, but you have been washed clean in baptism; you have started out on the road to holiness; through the name of the Lord Jesus Christ, and through the Spirit of our God you have entered into a new relationship with God.

12'There is nothing which I may not do,' you say. I quite agree, but it is not everything whose results make it worth doing. 'There is nothing which I may not do,' you say. I quite agree, but there is nothing by which I will allow myself to be dominated. 13'Food is for the stomach,' you say, 'and the stomach for food.' True, but the day will come when God will destroy both the stomach and the food. The body was never meant for fornication; it was meant for the Lord, and the Lord for the body. 14God raised the Lord from the dead, and he will raise us also by his power. 15Are you not aware that your bodies are parts of Christ? And am I then going to take the limbs which rightly belong to Christ and make them the limbs which belong to a prostitute? God forbid! 16You must be well aware that, if a man joins himself to a prostitute, he becomes physically one with her. For as scripture says: 'These two shall become one person.' 17But, if a man joins himself to the Lord, he becomes spiritually one with him. 18Have nothing to do with fornication. Every other sin which a man may commit is outside his body, but the fornicator sins against his own body. 19Are you not aware that your body is the temple of the Holy Spirit, who dwells within us, and whom we have received from God, and that you therefore do not belong to yourselves? 20He bought you for himself—and it did not cost him nothing. Therefore honour God with your body.

Chapter 7

WITH reference to the contents of your letter, and in particular in regard to the point you make that it is an excellent thing for a man to have nothing to do with women, my verdict is this. 2In order to avoid illicit sexual relationships, each man must have his own wife, and each woman her own husband. 3A husband must discharge to his wife the sexual duty which he owes her, and so must a wife to her husband. 4The wife is not in sole control of her own body; the husband has his rights. Equally, the husband is not in sole control of his own body; the wife has her rights. 5You must not wrongly withhold from each other that to which each of you has a right, unless it is by mutual consent, for a limited period, and for the purpose of concentrating upon prayer. Thereafter you must resume your normal relationship with each other again. This is necessary to prevent Satan from tempting you, because self-control is very difficult for you. 6I am stating this as a concession, not laying it down as a command. 7My own personal wish is that all men should be like myself. But each man has his own special gift from God, one of one kind, and another of another.

8My advice to those who are not married and to widows is that it is an excellent thing, if they remain as I myself have remained. 9But, if they find self-control impossible, then they must marry, for it is better to marry than to live a life continually inflamed with unsatisfied sexual desire. 10To those who are married my orders are—and they are not mine but the Lord's—that the wife must not separate from her husband. 11If she does so separate, she must remain unmarried or be reconciled to her husband. And a husband must not divorce his wife. 12To the rest there is no definite word of the Lord that I can quote, but my own advice is this. If a Christian has a pagan wife, and if she is willing to live with him, he must not divorce her; 13and if a Christian wife has a pagan husband, and if he is willing to live with her, she must not divorce her husband. 14The pagan husband is brought into the circle of God's people through his wife, and the pagan wife is brought into the circle of God's people through her Christian husband. If that principle were not so your children would be pagan, but in point of fact they are within the circle of God's people. 15If the pagan partner wishes to separate, he or she must do so. The Christian brother or sister is at liberty to take his or her own decision in such matters. God meant marriage to be a perfect human relationship between two people. 16Remember that as a wife, for all you know, you may very well be the means of saving your husband. Remember that as a husband, for all you know, you may very well be the means of saving your wife.

17The one thing to remember is that each man must go on living the life God gave him to live, and living in the circumstances in which he was when God called him. These are in fact the principles that I lay down in all the congregations. 18Was any man called already circumcised? Then he must not try to obliterate the mark of circumcision. Has any man been called uncircumcised? Then he must not have himself circumcised. 19Both circumcision and uncircumcision are quite irrelevant. What matters is obedience to God's commands 20Each man must remain in the same circumstances in which his call to be a Christian came to him. 21Were you a slave when you were called? Don't let that worry you. All the same, if you can obtain your freedom, you are better to make use of the opportunity than to refuse it. 22The man who was called to be a Christian as a slave is the Lord's free man; and equally, the man who was called to be a Christian as a free man is Christ's slave. 23You have been bought at a price. Do not become the slaves of men. 24Brothers, it is the duty of each man in the sight of God to remain in the condition in which he was when God's call came to him.

25In regard to those who have accepted a voluntary virginity, I cannot cite any definite commandment of the Lord; but I give my own opinion, and I give it as one who is to be trusted, because I have received God's mercy. 26In view of the present threatening situation in my opinion this is an excellent thing, I mean that it is an excellent thing that a man should stay as he is. 27Are you bound to a wife? Then do not seek any loosening of the marriage bond. Has your marriage been dissolved? Then do not seek a wife. 28But, if you do marry, you have committed no sin; and, if a virgin marries, she has committed no sin. But people who do so will encounter all the everyday problems that such a physical relationship brings. And I would want to spare you that. 29But this, brothers, I do say—there is not much time left now, and, since that is so, from now on those who have a wife must live as if they had no such ties. 30Both those who mourn and those who rejoice must live from now on as if mourning and rejoicing were quite irrelevant. If people buy, they must do so on the understanding that they have no secure possession of anything. 31Those who are involved in the world's business must live as if they were not immersed in it, for this world in its present changing form will not last much longer. 32I want you to be free from distracting worries. An unmarried man's one thought is for the Lord's business. His one aim is to please the Lord. 33But, once a man has married, his one thought is for this world's business. His one aim is to please his wife. 34The result is that he lives a divided life. The one thought of an unmarried woman and of a virgin is for the Lord's business. Her one aim is to be dedicated to God in body and in spirit. But, once a woman has married, her one thought is for this world's business. Her one aim is to please her husband. 35It is for your good I am telling you this. I have no desire to put a leash on your liberty. All I am urging on you is that you should live a lovely life in undistracted concentration on the Lord.

The situation referred to in verses 36-38 is uncertain. In general, the advice of these verses is given to a man in regard to 'his virgin,' and the propriety of marriage for her. There are three possibilities.

(a) The advice may be to a father, who is uncertain whether it is his Christian duty to keep his unmarried daughter in a state of perpetual virginity, or to allow her to marry.

(b) The advice may be to a man in regard to the girl to whom he is engaged to be married, and who is uncertain whether his Christian faith makes marriage undesirable and perpetual virginity the truly Christian state.

(c) It is just possible that the reference is to a practice which certainly existed in the church later. Whether it existed in the time of Paul is not certain. In this practice a man and a woman decided to live together, but to have no sexual relationships at all. This was obviously a relationship which put a severe strain on both. And the question may be whether, when such a relationship is in danger of becoming intolerable, marriage is allowed.

In view of the three possible references there are three possible translations, and we give all three translations of verse 36.

(a) *Advice to a father*

36If a father thinks that he is acting unfairly towards his unmarried daughter, if she has passed the years of youth and has arrived at maturity, then he ought to let matters take their course. Let her do as she likes. There is no sin in that. Let them (i.e. the girl and her lover) marry.

(b) *Advice to someone engaged to be married*

36If a man thinks that he is acting unfairly to the girl to whom he is engaged to be married in deciding not to marry, if passions are strong, then he ought to let matters take their course. Let him (or her) do as he (or she) wishes. There is no sin in that. Let them marry.

(c) *Advice to those who have undertaken to live together with no sexual relationships*

36If a man thinks that he is acting unfairly towards the girl with whom he has decided to live but not to have any sexual relationships, if passions are strong, then he ought to let matters take their course. There is no sin in that. Let them marry.

37But, if a man's mind is firmly made up, from choice and not from compulsion, and if he is in full control of his own will, and has come to a final decision and has made up his mind that the girl must remain a virgin, he will do well. **38**This is to say that, if a man gives his virgin daughter in marriage (or, marries his fiancée, or, marries the girl he had decided to live with and to remain unmarried), he does well; but if he does not, he will do still better.

39For a woman, her marriage cannot be dissolved during the lifetime of her husband. But, if her husband dies, she is at liberty to be married to anyone she wishes, only it must be a Christian marriage. **40**But in my opinion she is happier if she remains as she is—and I think that I too have God's Spirit.

Chapter 8

This chapter deals with the problem of eating meat which had formed part of a sacrifice to a heathen idol, a subject to which Paul returns in 10.25-32. In this matter the Christian was faced with three problems which in the first century were very real.

(a) A sacrifice was seldom burned entire. A token part was burned, and then part of the meat became the perquisite of the priest, and part was given to the worshipper. The worshipper usually gave a meal with his share of the meat to his friends in the precincts of the heathen temple. Most social occasions were so held. An invitation to dine usually read like this: 'I invite you to dine with me at the table of the Lord Serapis,' or of some other god. The question was whether or not a Christian could attend such a meal. The verdict is that he could not attend, because he could not sit at the table of Christ and the table of demons, with whom the heathen gods were identified. This meant that the Christian was to a large extent cut off from social life.

(b) The priests received far more meat than they could use. They sold it to the shops, whence it was sold to the public. Paul's verdict is that the Christian can buy in the shops and ask no questions.

(c) Sometimes the worshipper took the meat home with him and used it for a meal in his own house. In this case Paul's verdict is that the Christian may eat what is put before him, and ask no questions. But, if someone with a sensitive conscience warns him that the meat was meat offered to an idol, then he must not eat, more for the protection of the other person's conscience than for his own sake.

However remote the whole question is from modern life, it clearly presented a social problem of the first importance for the Christians of New Testament times.

And now with regard to the points you raise about meat that has formed part of a sacrifice to an idol, we are well aware that, as you say, 'We all have knowledge.' Your kind of 'knowledge' inflates a man with self-conceit; love builds him up in character. ₂If a man fancies that he has attained to some degree of knowledge, he has not yet reached the stage when he has any knowledge at all in the real sense of the term. ₃But if anyone loves God, he is recognized by God as his.

₄Well then, with regard to the matter of eating meat which has formed part of a sacrifice offered to an idol, we know very well, that, as you say, 'An idol stands for something which has no real existence in the order of the universe,' and that, 'There is only one God.' ₅For, even if there are so-called gods in heaven or on earth—and indeed there are plenty of 'gods' and plenty of 'lords'—₆as far as we are concerned

> There is one God, the Father,
>   from whom everything comes,
>   and to whom we go;
> and one Lord Jesus Christ,
>   through whom all things came into being,
>   and through whom we live.

₇But it is not everyone who possesses this knowledge. There are some people who up to now have been accustomed to idol-worship, and, when they eat a piece of meat which was part of a sacrifice made to an idol, they still cannot escape the feeling that this meat is the property of a false god. Their conscience is over-sensitive, and, since they cannot help feeling they are doing the wrong thing, their conscience is violated. 8Food will not affect our standing with God. We are not minus something, if we do not eat; and we are not plus something, if we do eat. 9But you must be careful that this liberty of yours does not turn out to be the very thing which becomes a barrier in the way of those who are weak in the faith. 10It is in the heathen temples that people hold their social occasions, and the meat for the meal is their share of the meat that was offered to the idol. Well then, if someone whose conscience is weak and over-sensitive sees you with your superior knowledge sitting as a guest at a party in the shrine of a heathen idol, will he not be encouraged by your action to eat meat which has formed part of a sacrifice offered to an idol? 11The result will then be that the man with the sensitive conscience is encouraged to violate his conscience, and so your superior knowledge becomes his ruin—and he is your fellow Christian for whom Christ died. 12By thus sinning against your fellow-Christians, and by thus striking a blow at their conscience in all its sensitiveness, you are sinning against Christ. 13That is why if anything I eat makes it easier for my brother to go wrong, I will never eat meat again, for I refuse to do anything which will make it easier for my brother to go wrong.

Chapter 9

Do I not possess the liberty of a Christian? Have I not the rights of an apostle? Have I not seen Jesus the Lord? Did the Lord not give me you as my handiwork? 2I may not be an apostle in the eyes of others; in yours at least I certainly must be. The fact that you are Christians is the seal which guarantees that I genuinely am an apostle.

3To those who want to put me on trial this is my defence. 4Have we no right to food and drink at the expense of the Christian community? 5Have we no right to take a Christian wife with us on our travels, as the other apostles do, including the Lord's brothers and Cephas? 6Or, are Barnabas and I the only apostles who are not exempt from having to work for a living? 7Who ever serves as a soldier at his own expense? Who ever plants a vineyard without eating the grapes? Who ever tends a flock without getting any of its milk? 8It is not only human authority that I have for speaking like this. Does the law not say the same? 9For there is a regulation in Moses' law: 'You must not muzzle the ox, when it is threshing the grain.' (That is, the ox must be free to eat what it is threshing.) Is it about oxen that God is concerned? 10Or, is it not quite clearly with us in mind that he says this? Quite certainly it was written with us in mind, for the ploughman is bound to plough and the thresher to thresh in the expectation of receiving a share of the produce. 11We sowed the seeds which brought you a harvest of spiritual blessings. Is it too much for us to expect in return to reap some material help from you? 12If others have the right to make this claim on you, surely we have still more?

But we have never made use of this right. So far from that, we put up with anything, rather than risk doing anything that would hamper the progress of the gospel. 13Are you not aware that those who perform the sacred ritual of the Temple use the Temple offerings as food, and that those who serve at the altar share with the altar in the sacrifices which are placed on it? 14In the same way, the Lord gave instructions that those who preach the gospel should get their living from the gospel. 15As for myself, I have never claimed any of these rights, nor am I writing now to see that I get them. I would rather die first! No one is going to turn the one claim in which I take a pride into an empty boast! 16If I preach the gospel, I have nothing to be proud of. I can't help myself. For me it would be heartbreak not to preach the gospel. 17If I do this because I choose to do it, I would expect to get paid for it. But if I do it because I can do no other, it is a task from God with which I have been entrusted. 18What pay do I get then? I get the satisfaction of telling the good news without it costing anyone a penny, and of thus refusing to exercise the rights the gospel gives me.

19I am a free man, and no man's slave; yet I have made myself every man's slave in order to win more men for Christ. 20When I was working among the Jews, I lived like a Jew, in order to win the Jews. When I was working among those who accept the law, I lived like a man who accepts the law—although I myself do not accept it—in order to win those who accept the law. 21When I was working among Gentiles, to whom the Jewish law means nothing, I lived like a man who has no use for the law—although I am far from disregarding the law of God, and very much subject to the law of Christ—in order to win those who do not accept the law. 22To those who are weak in the faith and over-sensitive in conscience, I have made myself like them, in order to win them. I made myself all things to all men, in order to save some of them by every possible means. 23Everything I do is done for the sake of the gospel, so that I may be a partner in its blessings.

24You are well aware that on the race-track all the runners run the race, but only one receives the prize. Just so, you must run to win. 25No athlete ever relaxes his self-discipline. They discipline themselves to win a crown that must fade; we do so to win a crown that cannot fade. 26I do not run without a goal clear before me. I do not box like a man engaged in shadow-boxing. 27I batter my body; I make it realize that I am the master, for I do not want to preach to others, and then to find that I myself have failed to stand the test.

Chapter 10

BROTHERS, you must never forget that our ancestors all journeyed under the pillar of cloud, and all passed safely through the Red Sea. 2In the cloud and in the sea they were all baptized as followers of Moses. 3They all ate the same supernatural food, 4and they all drank the same supernatural drink, for they drank from the supernatural rock which accompanied them on their journey—and that rock was Christ. 5Nevertheless most of them incurred the displeasure of God, and the desert was strewn with their dead bodies. 6These events are intended as symbolic warnings to us not to set our hearts on evil things, as they did. 7Nor must you become idolaters, as some of them did. As scripture says: 'The people sat down to eat and drink and rose up to indulge in their heathen sport.' 8Nor must we commit fornication as some of them did, in consequence of which twenty-three thousand died in a day. 9Nor must we try to see how far we can go with God and get away with it, as they did, and in consequence were destroyed by serpents. 10Nor must you grumble against God, as some of them did, and in consequence were killed by the Angel of Death. 11What happened to them is intended as a symbolic warning to us. These events were recorded as advice to us, for we are living in the age to which all the ages have been leading up. 12One warning emerges from all this—anyone who thinks that he is standing securely must be careful in case he collapses. 13You have been involved in no trials except those which are part of the human situation. You can rely on God not to allow you to be tested beyond what you are able to cope with. No! When trial comes he will send you along with it the way out of it, to enable you to bear it.

14Therefore, my dear friends, have nothing to do with idolatry. 15I assume that I am speaking to sensible people. Decide for yourselves whether what I say is reasonable or not. 16You would agree that the cup of blessing for which we give thanks is a means of sharing in the blood of Christ. You would agree that the bread which we break is a means of sharing in the body of Christ. 17Because there is one loaf and because we all receive a share of the one loaf, although we are many, we are one body. 18Look at actual Jewish practice and belief. The worshippers receive their share of the meat of the sacrifice and eat it; the altar receives its share. Does that not make altar and worshippers partners? 19What is my argument? That a thing offered to an idol has any real existence? Or that an idol itself has any real existence? 20No, but I am arguing that the sacrifices of the pagans are offered to demons and not to God, and I do not want you to become partners with the demons. 21You cannot drink the cup of the Lord and the cup of demons. You cannot share the Lord's table and the demons' table. 22Or, do we want to make God jealous? Are we stronger than he is?

23I quite agree with you that we are free to do anything—but that is not to say that everything is to our good. It is perfectly true that we are free to do anything—but it is not everything that strengthens life and character for ourselves and for others. 24No one must concentrate solely on his own good; he must be equally interested in the other man's good. 25Eat anything that is sold in the meat-market, and never mind asking questions to satisfy your conscience, 26for the earth and everything in it belongs to the Lord. 27If a non-Christian invites you to a meal and you decide to go, eat everything that is put before you, and never mind asking questions to satisfy your conscience. 28But, if anyone present says to you in warning: 'This meat was part of a sacrifice offered to an idol,' then don't eat it. Don't eat it for the sake of the man who warned you and for the sake of his conscience. 29I am not talking about your conscience. (Your conscience is clear.) It is the other man's conscience I am talking about. (His conscience is oversensitive.) 'But,' you say, 'why should my liberty have to submit to the judgment of another man's conscience? 30If I partake and thank God, why am I bitterly attacked for eating food for which I said grace?' 31Your eating, your drinking, your every action must be to the glory of God. 32You must live in such a way that you give no offence either to Jews or to Greeks or to the church of God. 33I try not to get up against anyone in anything, for it is not my own good that I am out for, but the good of all. The one thing I want is for them to be saved. 11.1And you must try to copy me, as I try to copy Christ.

Chapter 11

The practical background of verses 2-16 of this chapter is the fact that in the Middle East in the time of Paul a woman who went about unveiled in public would be regarded as a loose woman. On the other hand a woman's veil was her protection and her authority. Without her veil she was open to any man's approach; with her veil she was unmolested. The trouble was that in Corinth women in their new Christian emancipation were liable to act in a way which would shock the public and bring discredit on the Christian community.

You say that I am never out of your memory, and that you never lose your grip on the instruction I handed on to you. This is greatly to your credit. 3I want you to understand that Christ is the head of every man, that man is the head of woman, and that God is the head of Christ. 4If in public worship any man prays or preaches with his head covered, he dishonours his head. 5But if any woman prays or preaches with her head uncovered, she dishonours her head. It is exactly the same as if her head was shaved. 6For if a woman is going to abandon wearing a veil, she might as well go the whole way and have her hair cut short. If it is disgraceful for a woman to have her hair cut short or to shave her head, then she ought to continue to wear a veil. 7A man ought not to cover his head, for he is the image and glory of God, but woman is the glory of man. 8For man was not made from woman, but woman from man. 9And further, man was not created for the sake of woman, but woman for the sake of man. 10So then, for the sake of the angels a woman ought to wear on her head the veil which gives her her own authority. 11But it must be remembered that from the Christian point of view man is essential to woman, and woman is essential to man. 12Originally woman was made from man; and now man comes into being through woman. And everything comes into existence from God. 13Exercise your own judgment. Can you honestly say that it is fitting for a woman to engage in public prayer to God unveiled? 14Does not nature itself teach us that for a man long hair is a disgrace, 15but for a woman long hair is her glory? This is so because she has been given her hair as a covering. 16If anyone thinks that he would like to go on arguing about this, let it suffice to say that we have no such custom as the participation of unveiled women in public worship, nor have the congregations of God.

In the first days of the church the Sacrament of the Lord's Supper was closely connected with a congregational meal known as the *Agapē*, or Love Feast. This was a real meal, and should have been a valuable way of expressing the fellowship of all classes and conditions of men within the unity of the church. But in Corinth the congregation at the *Agapē* had broken up into cliques and sections and groups, and that which was meant to symbolise unity had become the cause of disunity.

17One piece of instruction I must give you about a matter which is not to your credit. The fact is that your meetings as a congregation do more harm than good. 18In the first place, I am informed that, when you meet as a congregation, you are split into mutually exclusive groups, and I am prepared to believe that to some extent this is so. 19I suppose that there are bound to be differences in your society, if for no other reason than to make it clear which of you are of sterling faith. 20When you meet together it is impossible for you to eat the Lord's Supper, 21for each of you is in far too big a hurry to eat his own meal, and the result is that some go hungry while others are drunk. 22Have you no homes of your own where you can eat and drink? Or, do you think so little of the church of God that you think nothing of publicly humiliating members who are poor? What am I to say to you? Am I to commend you for conduct like this? I certainly do not!

23The tradition which I have handed on to you goes right back to the Lord. That tradition tells that on the night on which he was being delivered into the hands of his enemies, the Lord Jesus took a loaf, 24and, when he had thanked God, he broke it into pieces and said: 'This means my body which is for you. You must continue to do this to make you remember me.' 25In the same way, after the meal, he took the cup too, and said: 'This cup stands for the new relationship with God made possible at the cost of my death. You must continue to do this, as often as you drink it, to make you remember me.' 26For every time you eat this loaf and drink the cup you are publicly proclaiming the Lord's death, until he comes again.

27The consequence is that anyone who eats the bread or drinks the cup of the Lord in a way that contradicts all that the Lord meant it to be will be guilty of a crime against the body and blood of the Lord. 28A man must examine himself before he eats his share of the bread and drinks his share of the cup, 29for a man's eating and drinking become a judgment on himself, if in eating and drinking he does not realize that the church is the body of Christ, and therefore a unity with no divisions. 30This is the reason why many of you are ill and weak, and why a considerable number of you have died. 31If we would examine ourselves, we would not be undergoing the judgment of God. 32But, when we do undergo judgment, we are being disciplined by the Lord to save us from being involved in the final condemnation of the world. 33So then, brothers, when you meet for a common meal wait for one another. 34If anyone is hungry, he must eat at home. This will prevent your meeting together from becoming the means whereby you incur judgment. I will settle the other matters when I come.

Chapter 12

WITH regard to the points you raise about the gifts which the Spirit gives, I want you to realize what the position really is. 2You know that when you were pagans you were ever and again swept away to the worship of dumb idols, under the influence now of one leader and now of another. 3I therefore want you to understand that no one speaking under the influence of the Spirit of God can say: 'A curse on Jesus!' And no one except under the influence of the Holy Spirit can say: 'Jesus is Lord.'

4There are different kinds of spiritual gifts, but they are the gifts of the same Spirit. 5There are different spheres of service, but the service is of the same Lord. 6There are different kinds of effects, but it is the same God who produces them in every case and in every person. 7The visible effect which the Spirit produces in each of us is designed for the common good. 8To one man there is given through the Spirit power to express intellectual wisdom in words; to another by the same Spirit there is given power to communicate knowledge in words. 9By one and the same Spirit faith is given to one man, and the gift of healing to another; 10the power to work miracles to another; the gift of prophecy to another; the ability to discern whether or not spirits are from God to another; the gifts of different kinds of ecstatic speech to another; the ability to interpret such speech to another. 11It is one and the same Spirit who produces all these different effects, and who, as he wishes, distributes them to each individual person.

12The body is a single unity, although it has many parts, and all the parts of the body, many as they are, are one united body. It is exactly so with Christ. 13Whether we are Jews or Greeks, whether we are slaves or free men, through the action of the one Spirit our baptism has united us into one body. We are all saturated with the one Spirit. 14The body does not consist of one part, but of many. 15If the foot should say: 'Because I am not a hand, I am not part of the body,' that does not make it any the less part of the body. 16If the ear should say: 'Because I am not an eye, I am not part of the body,' that does not make it any the less part of the body. 17If the whole body was an eye, what would happen to the sense of hearing? 18If the whole body was an ear, what would happen to the sense of smell? But in point of fact God has appointed each part in the body as he wished. 19If all the parts of the body were one part, where would the body be? 20But in point of fact there are many parts, but there is one body. 21The eye cannot say to the hand: 'I don't need you.' Nor, to take another example, can the hand say to the feet: 'I don't need you.' 22So far from that, the parts of the body which seem to be weaker are in fact more essential. 23We attach greater honour to those parts of the body which we regard as dishonourable. The unlovely parts of our body are surrounded with a greater modesty, 24of which the lovely parts have no need. But God has blended the body together, and has given more honour to the parts which lack honour. 25His design was that there might be no division in the body, but that the parts of the body should be equally concerned for each other's welfare. 26So, if one part of the body suffers, all the parts suffer in sympathy with it; and, if one part is honoured, all the parts share its joy.

27You are the body of Christ, and each of you is a part of it. 28In the church God has appointed, first, apostles; second, prophets; third, teachers; then, those who have the power to work miracles; then, those who possess gifts of healing or of helping others; those who have the ability to administer the affairs of the church, and those who have the gift of various kinds of ecstatic speech. 29Obviously everyone is not an apostle. Obviously everyone is not a prophet or a teacher. Obviously everyone does not have the power of working miracles 30or special gifts of healing. Obviously everyone cannot speak in ecstatic speech or interpret such speech. 31Set your hearts on possessing the greater gifts. And now I am going to show you the way which is by far the best.

Chapter 13

Even if I could speak the languages of men and of angels,
  if I am without love,
I am no better than a clanging gong
    or a clashing cymbal.
2Even if I have the gift of prophecy,
  even if I understand all the secrets
    which only the initiates know;
  even if I am wise with all knowledge;
  even if I have faith so complete
    that it can move mountains,
    if I am without love,
  there is no value in my life.
3Even if I dole out everything I possess,
  even if I welcome a martyr's death in the flames,
    if I am without love,
  it is all no good to me.

4Love is patient with people; love is kind.
There is no envy in love;
    there are no proud claims;
    there is no conceit.
5Love never does the graceless thing;
    never insists on its rights,
    never irritably loses its temper;
    never nurses its wrath to keep it warm.
6Love finds nothing to be glad about
    when someone goes wrong,
    but is glad when truth is glad.
7Love can stand any kind of treatment;
    love's first instinct is to believe in people;
    love never regards anyone or anything as hopeless;
    nothing can happen that can break love's spirit.
8Love lasts for ever.
    Whatever prophecies there may be,
      they will some day be ended;
    whatever utterances of ecstasy there may be,
      they will some day be silenced;

whatever knowledge there may be,
 it will some day pass away.
₉We have but fragments of knowledge
 and glimpses of prophetic insight;
₁₀but when the complete will come,
 the fragmentary will be ended.
₁₁When I was a child,
 I had a child's speech;
 I had a child's mind;
 I had a child's thoughts.
But, when I became a man,
 I put away childish things.
₁₂Now we see bewildering shadows in a mirror,
 but then we shall see face to face;
now I know a fragment of the truth,
 but then I will know as completely as I am known
₁₃The truth is that these three things last for ever—
 faith, hope, love—
 and the greatest of them is love.

Chapter 14

Throughout this chapter there runs a contrast between speaking with tongues, or speaking in a tongue, and prophesying. Speaking in a tongue does not mean speaking in a foreign language. There was, and still is, a phenomenon in which a man poured out a torrent of sounds in an ecstasy and in no known language without any conscious effort on his part, and as if some spiritual power was speaking in him and through him. And there were also those who had the gift of interpreting this ecstatic and otherwise unintelligible flow of sounds. This gift was greatly admired and much coveted in the church at Corinth. On the other hand, there was prophecy. Prophecy does not here mean foretelling the future; it means powerfully proclaiming the message of God. Unlike the ecstatic speaking in tongues prophecy was completely intelligible, and in this chapter is very nearly the equivalent of preaching.

SPARE no effort to possess love, and set your heart on the gifts the Spirit gives, and especially on the ability to proclaim the message of God with prophetic power. ₂When a man is speaking in ecstatic language, he is speaking not to man but to God, for no one understands what he is talking about. He is no doubt under the influence of the Spirit, but he speaks in a way that no ordinary person can understand. ₃But when a man proclaims the message of God, he speaks in such a way that his words build up the spiritual life of his hearers, and bring them courage and comfort. ₄When a man is speaking in ecstatic language, he is no doubt building up his own spiritual life; but the man who proclaims God's message builds up the spiritual life of the whole congregation. ₅I would be happy if you all spoke in ecstatic language; but I would be still happier if you all proclaimed God's message. The man who clearly proclaims the message of God is greater than the man who speaks in ecstatic language, unless such a speaker explains what it all means, for only then will the spiritual life of the whole congregation be built up.

₆If, brothers, I do come to you and speak to you in ecstatic language, what good will I do you, unless by my words I unveil the truth to you, or bring you new knowledge, or proclaim the message of God to you, or give you instruction? ₇Even in the case of inanimate musical instruments, for example a flute or a harp, unless they preserve the correct interval between the notes, how can anyone recognize the tune that is being played on the flute or the harp? ₈If no one can tell what call the bugle is sounding, how can anyone prepare for battle? ₉Just so, if you in your ecstatic language do not produce any intelligible and meaningful speech, how can anyone understand what you are saying? Your words will go whistling down the wind. ₁₀I do not know how many different languages there are in the world. No race is without its language. ₁₁But, if I do not understand the meaning of the language, I will be speaking gibberish to the speaker, and he will be speaking gibberish to me. ₁₂It is exactly the same with you. In your eagerness for spiritual gifts, you must set your heart on excelling in building up the spiritual life of the congregation. ₁₃That is why a man who speaks in ecstatic language must pray to be able to interpret what he says. ₁₄If I pray in ecstatic language, it is my spirit which prays. My mind is producing nothing at all. ₁₅What about it then? My prayers must be inspired, but my prayers must be the product of my own mind as well; my hymns must be inspired, but my hymns must be the product of my own mind as well. ₁₆If you pour out your ecstatic praises to God, how can the ordinary man who is there say Amen to your thanksgiving, since he has no idea what you are talking about? ₁₇No doubt your thanksgiving is a thing of beauty, but the spiritual life of the other man is not built up by it. ₁₈I thank God that I have the gift of ecstatic language more than any of you has. ₁₉But, for all that, in the congregation I would rather speak five intelligible words, to instruct others as well as myself, than ten thousand words in ecstatic language which no one can understand.

20Brothers, don't be childish. True, in evil you must be as innocent as babes, but you must be adult in your thinking. 21It stands written in the law:

> 'By men of strange tongues,
>   and by the lips of strangers,
> I will speak to this people,
>   and even then they will not listen to me,
>   says the Lord.'

22'Strange tongues' are, therefore, designed to convince, not those who believe, but those who do not believe. The clear proclamation of the truth is designed to help, not the unbeliever, but the believer. 23If there is a meeting of the whole congregation, at which everyone speaks in ecstatic language, if ordinary people or non-Christians come in, they are bound to think that you are crazy. 24But if everyone is clearly proclaiming God's message, and a non-Christian or an ordinary person comes in, the whole service challenges and convicts his conscience. 25The secrets of his heart are laid bare, and the result will be that he will fling himself down and worship God. 'Truly,' he will say, 'God is among you.'

26How then, brothers, are we to sum all this up? When you meet together, each of you has something which he wishes to contribute to the gathering, a hymn, a piece of instruction, something that has been specially revealed to him, an ecstatic utterance, an interpretation of such an utterance. Everything must be done with the intention of building up the spiritual life of the congregation. 27If there is to be any speaking in ecstatic language, no more than two, or at the most three, must speak. They must speak in turn, and one person must interpret. 28If there is no interpreter available, then the man who wishes to speak in ecstatic language must not address the congregation at all. He must speak to himself and to God. 29Two or three may deliver their message from God with prophetic power. The others must exercise their judgment on what is said. 30If another person sitting in the congregation receives a special message from God, the first speaker must stop speaking. 31You can all give your message from God one at a time, and then everyone will be instructed and everyone will be encouraged. 32Those who want to deliver a prophetic message can, and must, control their inspiration, 33for God is not the God of disorder but of peace.

Following the custom of all the congregations of God's people, 34the women must remain silent at the meetings of the congregation.

They are not permitted to speak. They must remain in the subordinate position which the Jewish law assigns to them. ₃₅If they wish to find out about anything, they must put their questions to their own husbands at home, for it is quite improper for a woman to speak at a meeting of the congregation. ₃₆Did the word of God originate from you? Or, are you the only people to whom it came?

₃₇If anyone claims prophetic or special inspiration, he must realize that what I write is a commandment of the Lord. ₃₈If he refuses to recognize this, he is himself not to be recognized. ₃₉So, my brothers, set your heart on being able to proclaim God's message clearly. Do not try to stop those who speak in ecstatic language. ₄₀But everything must be done properly and in order.

Chapter 15

BROTHERS, I want to remind you of the gospel which I preached to you, and which you received, the gospel on which you have taken your stand, ₂and by which you are being saved, if you keep a tight grip of it, in the form in which I preached it to you, unless your decision to believe was all for nothing. ₃As a first essential, I handed on to you the account of the facts that I myself had received. That account told that Christ died for our sins, as the scriptures said he must; ₄that he was buried, that he was raised to life again on the third day, as the scriptures said he would be; ₅that he appeared to Cephas and then to the Twelve; ₆that he then appeared to more than five hundred Christian brothers at one and the same time, of whom the majority survive to the present day, though some of them have died. ₇Next, he appeared to James, then to all the apostles. ₈Last of all, he appeared to me too, and my birth into the family of Christ was as violent and unexpected as an abortion. ₉For I am the least of the apostles. I am not fit to be called an apostle at all, because I persecuted God's church. ₁₀It is by the grace of God that I am what I am. Nor did that grace come to me to no effect. So far from that, I have toiled harder than all the rest of them put together, although it was not I who did the work but the grace of God which is my constant companion. ₁₁So then, whether I or they were the preachers, this is the substance of our preaching, and this is the faith which you accepted.

₁₂If then the substance of the Christian message is that Christ has been raised from the dead, how can some of you say that there is no resurrection of the dead? 13If there is no resurrection of the dead, then neither has Christ been raised. 14But, if Christ has not been raised, both the Christian message we preached to you and your faith are emptied of all meaning. 15If this is so, a further consequence is that we have clearly been making false statements about God, because we affirmed about God that he raised Christ, when in fact, if it is true that the dead are not raised, he did not do so. 16For, if the dead are not raised, neither has Christ been raised. 17And, if Christ has not been raised, then your faith is all a delusion; you are still at the mercy of your sins. 18Then further, we are bound to conclude, those who have died holding the Christian faith are dead and gone for ever. 19If our Christian hope does not reach beyond this life, then of all men we are most to be pitied.

20But in point of fact Christ has been raised from the dead. Just as the first-fruits are the guarantee that all the rest of the harvest will follow, so his resurrection guarantees that those who have died will rise again. 21For since it was through a man that death came into the world, it is also through a man that resurrection of the dead came. 22In Adam all die, and, just so, in Christ all will be brought to life. 23But each in his own order. First of the whole harvest is Christ; then at his coming those who belong to Christ. 24Then the end will come, and, after Christ has destroyed every rule and authority and power in the spirit-world, he will hand over the Kingdom to God the Father. 25He must reign until God has reduced all his enemies to complete subjection. 26Death will be the last enemy to be destroyed. 27Scripture says: 'God has completely subjected all things to him.' But, when scripture says that 'all' things have been subjected to him, it is quite clear that that does not include God himself, who subjected all things to him. 28When all things have been subjected to him, then the Son too will himself be subjected to him who subjected all things to him, for the final purpose is that God should be all in all.

29Again, what will happen to those who get themselves baptized on behalf of the dead? If the dead are not raised to life at all, what is the point of their being baptized for them? 30And as for us—why are we in hourly peril of our life? 31Brothers, by the pride I have in our joint fellowship in Jesus Christ our Lord, I swear I take my life in my hands every day. 32If I had to fight with men like wild beasts at Ephesus, what was the point of it for me?

> 'Let us eat and drink,
>   for tomorrow we shall die'

is a sound policy, if the dead are not raised. 33Make no mistake—'bad companions corrupt good morals.' 34Return to your sober senses, and stop your sinning. There are some of you who are utterly ignorant of God. I say it to shame you.

35But someone will ask: 'How are the dead to be raised to life? What kind of body will they have?' 36Only a fool would ask a question like that! When you sow a seed, it does not come to life unless it dies. 37And, when you sow a seed, what you sow is not the body which it is going to become, but a naked seed, maybe of corn or of some other grain. 38God gives it the body he has chosen for it, and to each seed he gives its own body. 39All flesh is not the same flesh. Men have one kind of flesh, and animals another, and birds another, and fishes another. 40There are heavenly bodies and there are earthly bodies. The heavenly bodies have one kind of splendour and the earthly bodies another. 41The sun has one kind of splendour, the moon another kind of splendour, the stars another kind of splendour. One star differs from another in splendour.

42It is so with the resurrection of the dead. What is buried in the earth, like a seed, in decay is raised imperishable. 43What is buried in dishonour is raised in glory. What is buried in weakness is raised in power. 44It is a physical body that is buried in the ground like the seed; it is a spiritual body that is raised. If there is a physical body, there is bound also to be a spiritual body. 45Thus scripture says: 'The first man Adam became a life-having person.' The last Adam became a life-giving spirit. 46But it was not the spiritual which came first; it was first the physical, then the spiritual. 47The first man was made of the dust of the earth; the second Man is from heaven. 48What the man made of dust was, all men made of dust are. What the Man from heaven is, all the heavenly are. 49We have worn the likeness of the man of dust; so we shall wear the likeness of the heavenly Man.

50Brothers, what I mean is this. Flesh and blood can never possess the Kingdom of God, nor can that which is subject to decay possess immortality. 51Look! I will tell you the secret that God has revealed. We shall not all die, but we shall all be changed, 52in a split second, in the time it takes to blink an eye, when the last trumpet sounds. For the trumpet shall sound, the dead shall be raised never to die again, and we shall be changed. 53This nature, which is subject to decay, must be clothed with the life that can never decay. This nature, which is subject to death, must be clothed with the life that can never die. 54When this nature which is subject to decay is clothed with the life which can never decay, and when this nature which is subject to death is clothed with the life which can never die, then the saying of scripture will come true:

> 55'Death is swallowed up, and victory is complete!
> Where, O death, is your victory?
> Where, O death, is your sting?'

56It is sin which gives death its sting, and it is the law which gives sin its power. 57But thanks be to God who gives us the victory through our Lord Jesus Christ. 58Therefore my dear brothers, stand firm and immovable. Work always for the Lord to the limit and beyond it in the certain knowledge that the Lord will never allow all your toil to go for nothing.

Chapter 16

ABOUT the collection for God's people—you must follow the same instructions as I gave to the congregations in Galatia. 2On the first day of the week, each of you must personally lay aside and save up a sum in proportion to his earnings. And then, when I come, you will not have to start organizing collections. 3When I arrive, I will give letters of introduction to those whom you approve for the task, and I will send them to Jerusalem to be the bearers of your gift. 4If it should seem worthwhile for me to go myself, they will make the journey with me.

5I will come to you after I have completed my journey through Macedonia—for I am on my way through Macedonia just now—6and it is possible that I may stay with you, or even spend the winter with you, so that you may help me on my way, wherever I may be going. 7I do not want to pay you a visit just now in the passing, for I hope to stay with you for some time, if the Lord permits it. 8It is my intention to stay on in Ephesus until the Day of Pentecost, 9for ample opportunity for effective work lies before me here, although there is strong opposition.

10If Timothy comes, see that you make him feel at home among you, for he is doing the Lord's work as I am. 11No one must look down on him. Send him on his way to join me with good-will, for I and the brothers are expecting him.

12As for our brother Apollos, I strongly urged him to visit you with the other brothers, but at the moment he was quite determined not to come, although he will come, when an opportunity arises.

13Always be on the alert. Stand firm in the faith. Play the man. Be strong. 14Your every action must be dictated by love.

15You know, brothers, that the household of Stephanas were the first converts in Achaea, and you know that they have organized themselves for the service of God's people. 16Well then, I urge you to accept the leadership of such men and of all who work and toil with them. 17I am glad that Stephanas and Fortunatus and Achaicus have arrived, because their presence has compensated for your absence. 18For they have set my mind at rest—and yours too. Such men deserve to have their services recognized.

19The congregations of Asia send you their good wishes. Aquila and Priscilla, with the congregation which meets in their house, send you warmest Christian greetings. 20All the brothers send you their good wishes. Greet one another with the kiss of peace.

21I Paul write this greeting in my own handwriting.

22If anyone does not love the Lord, a curse be on him! Marana tha. Our Lord, come!

23The grace of the Lord Jesus be with you. 24My love to you all in Christ Jesus.

The Second Letter to the
CORINTHIANS

Chapter 1

THIS is a letter from Paul, an apostle of Christ Jesus because God willed it so, and from Timothy our colleague, to God's congregation at Corinth, together with all God's people all over Achaea. ₂Grace to you and every blessing from God our Father and from the Lord Jesus Christ.

₃Let us give thanks to the God and Father of our Lord Jesus Christ. He is the merciful Father, the God from whom all courage and comfort come. ₄It is he who encourages us in all our troubles, and he does so to give us the power to encourage others who are in every kind of trouble with that same encouragement which we ourselves have received from him. ₅We have been involved in an overflowing tide of the sufferings of Christ; but equally through Christ the overflowing tide of his encouragement has been our support. ₆If we are in trouble, it is meant for your encouragement and your salvation. If we are given courage and comfort, it is for your encouragement, encouragement which becomes more real and effective when you bear with gallantry the same sufferings as we too have experienced. ₇And our hope for you is well founded, because we know that, if you have to share in the sufferings, you will share in the encouragement too.

₈We want you to know, brothers, about the trouble in which we were involved in Asia. It fell upon us with such excessive and intolerable weight that we despaired even of survival. ₉So serious was the situation that in our heart of hearts we believed that we had been sentenced to death. But it all happened to make us put our trust, not in ourselves, but in the God who raises the dead. ₁₀It was he who rescued us from such threats of death, and it is he who will rescue us. In him we have set our hope, and he will go on rescuing us. ₁₁All the time you too must be helping us by praying for us; and then the thanksgivings of many will rise to God for us, as they thank God for the gracious gift he gave us, as a result of many prayers.

12There is one thing in which we do take pride—the witness of our conscience that out in the world, and especially in our relationships with you, we have behaved with that simplicity and sincerity which are the gifts of God. It was not worldly wisdom but divine grace that always shaped our conduct. 13There is nothing in the letters we write to you but what you can read and understand—no hidden meanings. 14So far you do understand, but only partly. It is my hope that your understanding will become complete. Then you will come to recognize that on the day of the Lord Jesus your pride is in us, and ours in you.

15It was because I was so confident that you and I understand each other that I first planned to visit you. My plan was to give you a double favour. 16My plan was to travel to Macedonia by way of you, and to visit you again on my way back from Macedonia, and to be despatched by you on my way to Judaea. 17This was my original plan. Can you really believe that I light-heartedly and irresponsibly failed to keep it? Do you really believe that when I make plans I make them like a man with no moral standards at all, so that I can vacillate between yes and no to suit my own convenience? 18As surely as God keeps his word, I did not speak to you in terms of a vacillating and ambiguous yes and no. 19Jesus Christ the Son of God, who was preached among you through us—I mean through Silvanus and Timothy and myself—did not sway between yes and no. So far from that, with him the divine Yes happened. 20In him all God's promises find their yes. That is why when to the glory of God we say 'Amen' we say it through him—'through Jesus Christ our Lord.' 21It is God who assures us of the fact that we along with you belong to Christ; it is God who set us apart for our task; 22it is God who marked us as his own; it is God who gave us the Holy Spirit in our hearts as the foretaste and guarantee of all that is to come.

23I call upon God to witness to the truth of what I am going to say. I stake my life on it. It was because I did not want to hurt you that I did not come again to Corinth. 24It is not that we want to domineer over you in regard to what you are to believe, for you stand firm in the faith. But we are partners with you in your quest for joy.

Chapter 2

ABOUT this I made up my mind—I was determined not to pay you another distressing visit. ₂For, if I distress you, who is there left to cheer me, except the very persons I distressed? ₃This is the very reason why I wrote to you. I wrote because I did not want to come and be distressed by the very people who should have made me happy, for I was quite sure that, if I was happy, you would all be happy too. ₄I wrote that letter to you with a deeply troubled mind and a very sore heart. I wrote it in tears, and my object in writing to you was, not to distress you, but to tell you of my overflowing love for you.

₅If a certain person has been the cause of distress, it was not I whom he has distressed. He has at least—I don't want to overstress the matter—to some extent distressed all of you. ₆This punishment inflicted by the majority of the congregation is sufficient for a man like that. ₇You should therefore rather forgive him and encourage him. You do not want the man to be utterly overwhelmed by excess of grief. ₈I urge you therefore to affirm your love for him. ₉The reason why I wrote that letter was to test you, to see if you were prepared to give me your unquestioning obedience. ₁₀If you forgive a man for anything he has done, so do I. What I have forgiven—if there was anything for me to forgive—I have forgiven for your sake in the presence of Christ. ₁₁For we must not allow Satan to get the better of us. We know his schemes all too well.

₁₂When I went to Troas to tell the good news of Christ, I found that the Lord had provided ample opportunity for me to do so. ₁₃I was worried because my colleague Titus was nowhere to be found. So, instead of waiting there, I said good-bye to them, and left for Macedonia.

₁₄Thanks be to God, for he always gives us a place as sharers in the victory procession of Christ, and, just as at such an earthly triumph, the perfume of incense fills the streets, so God through us has displayed in every place the fragrance of the knowledge of himself. ₁₅You might call us in our work for God the means whereby the fragrance of Christ comes to those who are on the way to salvation and to those who are on the road to ruin. ₁₆For those who are on the way to ruin it is a deadly and poisonous stench; for those who are on their way to salvation it is a living and life-giving perfume. And who is fit for this task? ₁₇We are not like so many who make a commercial racket of preaching God's word. No! When we preach God's message, we do so in transparent sincerity, as sent by God and in the presence of God, and as servants of Christ.

Chapter 3

ARE we beginning to flourish our credentials all over again? Is it possible that we, like some people, need letters of introduction to you or from you? ₂You are our letter, written on our hearts, open to everyone to know and to read. ₃Clearly, you are a letter, written by Christ, and delivered by us. This letter is written, not in ink, but with the Spirit of the living God, written not on stone tablets but on human hearts.

₄We can make such a claim because of our confidence in God through Christ. ₅Not that we are in our own resources adequate for our task, nor would we claim that in ourselves we have achieved anything. Far from it! Any adequacy we have has its source in God, ₆for it is he who has made us capable of being servants of a new kind of relationship with himself, a relationship which is not dependent on any written code of laws, but on the Spirit. For the written law brings death, but the Spirit gives life.

₇If the dispensation of the law, which brings death, and which was carved in letters of stone, came into existence in a blaze of splendour, such splendour that the people of Israel could not look for any length of time at Moses' face because of its brightness, although it was a brightness which was only a transient and fading splendour, ₈how much greater must be the splendour of the dispensation of the Spirit? ₉If the dispensation which ends in man's condemnation by God had its splendour, how much more overflowing must be the splendour which puts a man into a right relationship with God? ₁₀Indeed, what was at one time clothed in splendour is now divested of its splendour, because of the new and surpassing splendour which has emerged. ₁₁For, if that which was transient and fading had its splendour, how much greater must be the splendour of that which lasts for ever?

₁₂With a hope like this, we have always spoken frankly and freely. ₁₃We have not been like Moses, who put a veil over his face to keep the people of Israel from watching the fading splendour, until it finally disappeared. ₁₄Their minds became impenetrably insensitive. To this very day their eyes are covered by the same veil, when they hear the lesson from the old covenant being read in the synagogue. That veil is still not taken away, because it is only when a man becomes a Christian that the veil is destroyed. 15But to this very day, when the writings of Moses are read in the synagogue, the veil still covers their hearts. 16But scripture tells us of Moses that, whenever he went in to speak with the Lord, he took off the veil, and so, whenever a man turns to the Lord, the veil is taken away. 17By the Lord he means the Spirit, and where the Spirit of the Lord is there is liberty, 18and, because there is no veil on our faces, the faces of us all reflect the glory of the Lord. We are thus being transformed into his very likeness, always moving on to greater and greater glory—and this is the work of the Lord, who is the Spirit.

Chapter 4

SINCE, in God's mercy to us, we have been given this piece of service to do, we never get discouraged. 2So far from that, we have renounced those practices which are so shameful that they have to be kept hidden; we do not live like clever rogues, nor have we the trick of twisting the word of God to suit ourselves. No! Our way of trying to commend ourselves to every man's conscience in the sight of God is to bring the truth into the full light of day, 3and, if the good news is being hidden, it is hidden only to those who are on the way to ruin. 4In their case the god of this world has blinded the minds of those who refuse to believe, with the result that they cannot see the light that has dawned on them, the light of the good news of the glory of Christ, who is exactly like God. 5It is not ourselves that we preach. We preach Jesus Christ as Lord, and ourselves as your servants for Jesus' sake. 6It is the God who said: 'Light will shine out of darkness,' who has made his light shine in our hearts to illumine them with the knowledge of the glory of God, seen in the face of Jesus Christ.

7We have this treasure, but we ourselves in whom the treasure is contained are no better than pots of clay. It has to be so, to make it clear that the supreme power belongs to God, and does not have its source in us. 8We are under pressure on every side, but never without a way out. We are at our wit's end, but never at our hope's end. 9We are pursued by men, but never abandoned by God. We are knocked down, but never knocked out. 10We always carry about in our bodies the death that Jesus died, so that in our mortal bodies his life too may be displayed. 11For us life means the continual danger of death for

Jesus' sake, for thus men will be enabled to see the life that Jesus gives in our body, subject though it is to death. 12So death is at work in us, but life is at work in you. 13Scripture says: 'I believed, and therefore I spoke.' We have the same spirit of faith and we too believe, and therefore we too speak. 14For we know that the God who raised the Lord Jesus will raise us too with Jesus, and will bring us into his presence along with you. 15Everything is for your sakes, and the purpose of it all is that grace, as it reaches more and more people, should beget an ever-increasing flood-tide of gratitude to the glory of God.

16That is why we never lose heart. So far from that, even if the physical part of us inevitably deteriorates, spiritually we are renewed every day. 17We have our troubles, but they are transitory and unimportant, and all the time they are producing for us a superlative and eternal glory, which will far outweigh all the troubles. 18And, all through it, it is not the things which are seen but the things which are unseen on which our gaze is fixed, for the things which are seen last only for their brief moment, but the things which are unseen last for ever.

Chapter 5

OUR present earthly body is like a tent in which a man lives temporarily when he is on a journey from one place to another. But we know that, if this temporary home is demolished, we have a house which God will give us, a house not built by any human hands, made to last in heaven for ever. 2In this present body we do indeed sigh deeply for what we have not got, for we long with all our hearts to have the house of our heavenly frame put on us over the top of this one, 3for, if we are so clothed, we will not be found naked. 4We who are in the temporary tent of this body sigh deeply, indeed we do. We feel oppressed, not because we want to strip ourselves of it, but because we want our new frame put on over the top of it, because then our mortality will be engulfed in the ocean of life. 5It is God who has fashioned us for this very purpose, and who has given us the Spirit as the pledge and the first instalment of the life into which we shall one day enter.

6So then we are always in good heart. We know that, so long as this body is our home, we are exiles from the Lord. 7It is by faith that we have to live, not by what we can actually see. 8We are in good heart. We would much prefer to leave our home in this body, and to make our home with the Lord. 9It is therefore our one ambition to please him whether we have to stay in this world or whether we have to leave it. 10For all of us must appear before the judgment seat of Christ, and then each of us will receive what is due to him for his actions in this body, whether his conduct was good or bad.

11We know what the fear of God is, and it is in light of that knowledge that we try to persuade men. Our own life lies completely open to God, and, I hope, lies equally open to the verdict of your own conscience. 12We are not trying to give ourselves a testimonial all over again, but we are trying to give you a chance to show your pride in us, because we want you to have an answer to those whose pride is in outward prestige and not in inner character. 13If we seem to have taken leave of our senses, it is for God's sake. If we are sane and sensible, it is for your sake. 14For us there is no escape from the love of Christ, for we have reached the certainty that one died for all men. And, if one died for all, we cannot escape the conclusion that all were dead. 15So he died for us, and therefore all through life men must no longer live for themselves, but must live for him who for them died and was raised to life again.

16The consequence of all this is that from now on we evaluate no man on purely human standards. There was a time when we evaluated Christ by human standards; we no longer do so. 17When a man becomes a Christian, a new act of creation happens to him. His old life is gone for ever; a new life has come into being. 18And the whole process is due to the action of God, who through Christ turned our enmity to himself into friendship, and who gave us the task of helping others to accept that friendship. 19The fact is that God was acting in Christ to turn the world's enmity to himself into friendship, that he was not holding men's sins against them, and that he placed upon us the privilege of taking to men who are hostile to him this offer of his friendship. 20We are therefore Christ's ambassadors. It is as if God was making his appeal to you through us. As the representatives of Christ we appeal to you to accept the offer of friendship that God is making to you. 21For our sakes God identified Christ, who was entirely innocent of sin, with human sin, in order that we through him might be identified with the goodness of God.

Chapter 6

WE are God's collaborators. You have received the grace of God. We therefore urge you not to let it all go for nothing. ₂God says:

> 'In the hour of my favour I heard you,
> and in the day of deliverance I came to your help.'

Now the hour of God's favour has come; now the day of deliverance is here. ₃We put no obstacle in any man's way, for we do not want our ministry to be open to criticism and blame. ₄So far from that, we try to commend ourselves in every circumstance of life as the servants of God. We have met troubles, hardships, desperate situations with unfailing fortitude. ₅We have endured the lash, imprisonment, the violence of the mob. We have toiled so hard that we have gone without sleep and food. ₆Our life has been marked by purity, by wisdom, by patience, by kindness, by the possession of the Holy Spirit, by love which is utterly sincere. ₇Our message has been characterized by the truth and the power of God. Goodness has been our armour both to commend and to defend the faith. ₈We have known honour, and we have known disgrace. We have been slandered, and we have been praised. We have been called impostors, and we have spoken the truth. ₉No one knows us, and everyone knows us. We have been dying for a long time, and we are still, as you can see, very much alive. We have been through the training-school of suffering, and still survive. ₁₀We have known our sorrows, yet joy is ever with us. To look at us, you would think we are destitute, but we have brought God's wealth to many. On the face of it we have nothing, yet we possess everything.

₁₁I have been very frank with you, my Corinthian friends. My heart is wide open to you. ₁₂On our side there is no restraint at all. If there is restraint, it is in your hearts. ₁₃I use a child's phrase—Let's have a fair exchange! Open your heart the same as I have opened mine.

₁₄Stop trying to run in double harness with unbelievers. Can there be any partnership between right and wrong? Can there be any fellowship between light and darkness? ₁₅What agreement can there be between Christ and Beliar? How can a believer share with an unbeliever? ₁₆How can God's temple ever come to any possible agreement with idols? And we are the temple of the living God. As God has said:

'I will make my home amongst them,
   and I will move about amongst them,
   and I will be their God,
   and they will be my people.'

17So then he goes on to say:

'You must come out and leave them.
   You must separate yourselves from them, the Lord says.
You must have nothing to do with what is unclean,
   and then I will accept you.
   18And I will be a father to you,
   and you will be sons and daughters to me,
   says the Lord, the Almighty.'

Chapter 7

SINCE, then, my dear friends, we are in possession of promises like these, let us purify ourselves from anything that would defile us in body or in spirit, and let us aim at a completely consecrated life lived in the fear of God.

2Make room for us in your hearts. We have wronged no one; we have corrupted no one; we have taken advantage of no one. 3I am not saying this with any thought of condemning you. I have told you already that you are so dear to us that we wish nothing better than to face death and to share life with you. 4I am very frank with you; I am very proud of you. We may be involved in all kinds of trouble, but in spite of that my courage and comfort are complete, and my cup of joy is overflowing.

5Even after we arrived in Macedonia life was as exhausting as ever. We were surrounded by troubles. Outwardly, we were involved in battles; inwardly, we were the prey of fears. 6But God, who brings comfort and courage to the discouraged, cheered us by the arrival of Titus. 7It was not only his arrival which cheered us; it was also the encouraging treatment he received when he was with you, for he told us how much you long to see us, how sorry you are for the past, and how enthusiastically you support me. And all this made me happier yet. 8If I did distress you with that letter, I am not sorry. Even if at the time I was sorry about it—for I see that the letter did distress you, even if it was only for a time—9I am glad now, not glad that you were distressed, but glad that your distress led to a change of mind in you. Your distress was all part of the purpose of God, and was meant to ensure that you should not be the losers by anything we did. 10For distress, accepted as God means it to be accepted, produces a change of mind which leads to salvation, and which brings no regret to follow. But distress, regarded from the world's point of view, brings death. 11Just look at what this distress, sent in God's purpose and accepted in God's way, did for you! Look how eager it made you to show that you are innocent! Look how vexed you were with the whole situation! Look what fear it awoke, what longing to see me, what enthusiasm to defend me, what eagerness that justice should be done! You have proved yourselves to be completely guiltless in the whole affair. 12So then, if I did write that letter to you, it was not for the sake of the wrong-doer, nor was it for the sake of the person wronged. It was to demonstrate to you yourselves in the sight of God your own devotion to me. 13That is why we have been so comforted and encouraged.

But we have more to be thankful for than our personal encouragement. We were more than delighted to hear how happy you all made Titus by the way in which you made it possible for him to rest and relax in your company. 14I am specially gratified by this, because I did sing your praises to him, and I was not disappointed. Everything we have said to you is true, and just so the proud claims we made about you to Titus have been proved true too. 15And he thinks of you all the more affectionately, when he remembers how willing you all were to accept his instructions, and how you welcomed him with fear and trembling. 16It makes me happy to feel with what complete confidence I can depend on you.

Chapter 8

BROTHERS, we want you to know how the grace of God has been given to the congregations in Macedonia. 2Even when they were in the middle of an ordeal of severe trouble, their overflowing joy and their desperate poverty somehow combined to result in an equally overflowing wealth of generosity. 3They gave what they were able to give, I assure you, yes, and more than they were able to give. Absolutely spontaneously, they insistently pled with us for the privilege of sharing in the effort to help God's people in Jerusalem. 5Their generosity far exceeded our hopes. First, they gave themselves to the Lord, and then, because it was God's will, they gave themselves to us.

6It was Titus who was in charge of the first moves in the organisation of this gift. So we have invited him to visit you, and to see that it is brought to its conclusion. 7You are outstanding in every sphere, in faith, in speech, in knowledge, in all kinds of enthusiasm, in your love for us. I want you to be equally outstanding in the giving of this gift.

8When I speak like this, I am not issuing orders. I am using the story of the eagerness of others to test the genuineness of your love. 9You know the gracious generosity of our Lord Jesus Christ. You know that, although he was rich, he chose to become poor for your sakes, to make you rich through his poverty. 10I offer you my own personal opinion about this matter. You were not only the first to do this. As far back as last year, you were the first to want to do it. 11And now, in my opinion, the time has come, when the best thing that you can do for your own sakes is to finish the job, so that your eagerness to plan it may be equalled by your determination to complete it as generously as your resources allow. 12If the will to give is there, God will accept whatever gift a man's resources make it possible for him to give; he does not demand a gift which is beyond a man's resources to give. 13I am not asking you to give in such a way as to bring relief to others and distress to yourselves. What I am asking is that you should share and share alike. 14At the present moment your more than enough should be used to help their less than enough, so that some day their more than enough may be used to help your less than enough. In that way it will be a case of share and share alike. 15As scripture said about the manna:

'The man who gathered much
        did not have too much,
    and the man who gathered little
        did not have too little.'

16Thank God that he made Titus as enthusiastically eager to help on your behalf as I am myself. 17He welcomed our request to go to you. In fact, he went so eagerly that there was no need to ask him to go. 18We are sending with him that Christian brother whose praise all the congregations sing because of his services to the gospel. 19Not only is he universally praised; on this occasion he has also been elected by the congregations to accompany us on our journey with this gift which we are organizing for the Lord's glory and to show our eagerness to help. 20We are taking every precaution to ensure that no one can find anything to censure in our administration of this generous gift. 21It is our aim to act in such a way that both God and men will recognize that our actions are honourable. 22So with them we are sending our Christian brother. We have had varied and frequent opportunities to test his enthusiasm to be of service, and on this present occasion he is all the more eager to help because of the great confidence he has in you. 23As for Titus, he is my partner and my collaborator in helping you. As for the other brothers, they are envoys of the congregations and a credit to Christ. 24Give them proof of your love, and proof that the proud claims I made about you are true. Such proof will through them reach the congregations.

Chapter 9

IT is superfluous for me to write to you about your aid for God's people in Jerusalem. 2I know how eager you are to help. In fact, I am always boasting about it to the Macedonians. 'Achaia,' I told them, 'has had everything ready since last year.' The story of your enthusiasm has stimulated and challenged most of them. 3I am sending the brothers to you because I do not want the proud claims we made for you in this matter to turn out to be quite unjustified, and I want to make sure that you are ready, as I said you were, 4for I do not want the Macedonians to arrive with me and to find you quite unprepared. It would be acutely embarrassing for us—not to mention you—for us to be so sure of you and for that to happen. 5I therefore thought it necessary to urge these brothers to go on ahead to you, and to get ready in advance the gift you promised to give. I want everything to be ready in good time, so that it will really look like a gift you wanted to give and not like an extortion that has been forced out of you.

6Remember this—meagre sowing means meagre reaping; generous sowing means generous reaping. 7Each person must make up his own mind what he is going to give. He must not give as if giving hurt him, or as if the money was being forced out of him. God loves a man who enjoys giving. 8God can give you more than enough of every good gift, enough for you to have plenty for yourselves always and in any circumstances, and to have enough left over to contribute to every good cause. 9As scripture says:

> 'He gave generously to the poor;
> his kindness lasts for ever.'

10God, who gives seed to sow and bread to eat, will give you an abundant supply of seed, and he will make it grow into a plentiful harvest, which will be the result of your charity to others. 11He will always make you rich enough to be generous to every claim on you, and your generosity will make many people thank God when we have distributed it to those who need it; 12for this piece of Christian service, which you have accepted as your duty, not only supplies the needs of God's people, it also overflows in a tide of thanksgiving to God. 13This service, which you are rendering, will be proof to those who receive it that you really are pledged to obedience when you publicly declare your faith in the gospel of Christ. They will also see how generously you share what you have with them and with all. And, when they see this, they will praise God for it. 14Because God gave you a superabundance of his grace, their warmest affection will go out to you, and they will be praying for you. 15Thank God for his gift, which has no price, and which is beyond words to tell of.

Chapter 10

I PAUL am making a personal appeal to you, and I make it by the gentleness and the kindness of Christ. You say that when I am actually with you, I have nothing to say for myself, but that, when I am away from you, I can put on a brave show. 2Please do not make it necessary for me to come and act with that same bravery, for I am perfectly certain that I can count on myself to act with boldness against some who declare that, as they see it, our conduct is governed by worldly rather than by Christian motives. 3True, we live in the world, but the battles we fight are not worldly battles. 4The weapons we use in our campaign are not the weapons the world uses. They are filled with divine power to demolish strongholds. We demolish false arguments, 5and every towering obstacle, erected to prevent men from knowing God. We capture every thought, and compel it to become obedient to Christ. 6Once you have rendered complete obedience to us, we are ready to punish any act of disobedience.

7Look at the obvious facts of the situation. If anyone is sure that he belongs to Christ, he had better take another look at himself, because we belong to Christ just as much as he does. 8The Lord gave me my authority to enable me to build up your spiritual life, not to demolish it. And suppose I have been making apparently excessive claims for it, my claims will in fact be completely vindicated. 9I do not want you to get the idea that I am the kind of person who would try to scare you by means of my letters. 10Some of you, I know, do allege: 'His letters are weighty and powerful, but he has no kind of presence when you meet him, and as a speaker he is beneath contempt.' 11Anyone who talks like that would do well to take into his calculations the fact that what we are in word in our letters in our absence we are in action in our presence.

12Of course, we would not venture to include ourselves among those who have such a high opinion of themselves, or to compare ourselves with them. They measure themselves by themselves; they are a mutual admiration society—a senseless proceeding. 13But we do not make claims that go beyond all proper limits. Our claims are limited to the sphere which God allotted to us—and that sphere includes you. 14For we are not exceeding our permitted boundary, as we would be if our limit did not extend to you, for indeed we were the first to reach you with the good news of Christ. 15We make no claims at all in regard to the work that others have done in spheres which are beyond our limits. Our hope is that, as your faith increases, we may have a still greater and greater place among you, but always a place within our limits. 16Then we will be able to bring the good news to regions beyond you, without making any claims about work done in some one else's sphere. 17As scripture says: 'If a man is going to take pride in anything, let him take pride in what God has done.' 18It is not the man who recommends himself who is approved; it is the man whom God recommends.

Chapter 11

I WISH that you would bear with me in a little folly. Please do! 2I am jealous for you with God's jealousy, for it was I who arranged your engagement to Christ as a chaste virgin bride to her one husband. 3But I am afraid that your minds may be corrupted, and that you may be seduced from your single-hearted devotion to Christ, just as the serpent with his clever lies seduced Eve. 4For, if someone comes and preaches another Jesus to you, different from the Jesus we have preached, or if you receive a different Spirit from the Spirit you received, or a different gospel from the gospel you were given, you have no difficulty in tolerating it. 5I do not believe that I am in any way inferior to these super-apostles. 6I may be inexpert in speech, but I am not in knowledge; and this is something that always and in all circumstances we have made perfectly clear.

7I accepted a low place to enable you to have a high one, for I preached the good news to you, and I did not take one penny piece for doing so. Was this where I went wrong? 8I robbed other congregations by taking pay from them to enable me to serve you. 9When I was staying with you, and when I was hard up, I bothered none of you for help. The brothers who came from Macedonia supplied me with all I needed. It was my principle, and it always will be, never to be a burden to you. 10As surely as the truth of Christ is in me, I will allow nothing anywhere in Achaea to despoil me of my pride in being able to make this claim. 11Why? Because I do not love you? God knows I do love you!

12I will go on doing as I am doing, because I want to deny every opportunity to those who are looking for an opportunity to make it seem that the work on which they pride themselves is the same as ours. 13Such men are not real apostles; they are not honest workmen; they disguise themselves as apostles of Christ. 14And no wonder, for Satan himself can disguise himself as an angel of light. 15It is therefore easy enough for his servants to disguise themselves as servants of goodness. But in the end they will get what their conduct deserves.

16I repeat, I do not want anyone to think me a fool. But even if you do think I am, accept me as a fool. Give me a chance to do just a little talking about the claims I am proud of. 17This isn't a Christian way to talk. All right! In this business of talking about the things I am proud of, I am talking like a fool. 18There is a lot of talking about human prestige going on; I am going to do some talking too. 19You are wise men; you find no difficulty in suffering fools gladly. 20You are quite prepared to put up with it, if someone treats you like slaves, if some one makes a meal of you, if someone preys on you, if some one gives himself airs, if someone slaps you across the face. 21If it comes to behaviour like that—to my shame!—you can charge me with being too much of a weakling to act like that. But, if anyone dares to make proud claims—this is fools' talk—I can be just as daring. 22Are they Hebrews? So am I. Are they Israelites? So am I. Are they descendants of Abraham? So am I. 23Are they servants of Christ? This is madman's talk—I am a better servant than they are. I have worked far harder. I have been in prison far oftener. I have been scourged far more severely. I have often been in peril of my life. 24Five times I received the forty less one lashes from the Jews. 25I have been beaten with rods three times. I have been stoned once. I have been ship-wrecked three times. I have been twenty-four hours in the water. 26I have been frequently on the road. I have been in dangers from rivers, in dangers from brigands, in dangers from my fellow countnymen, in dangers from the Gentiles, in dangers in cities, in dangers in the lonely places, in dangers at sea, in dangers from Christians who were no Christians. 27I have worked and I have toiled. I have often gone without sleep. I have been hungry and thirsty. I have often had to go without food. I have known cold and exposure. 28Apart altogether from the things I pass over, there is the daily pressure on me which my concern for all the congregations brings. 29Who is weak without me sharing his weakness? Who is led astray without my burning concern?

30If I must make my claims, I will base them on the things which show my weakness. 31The God and Father of our Lord Jesus, he who is blessed for ever, knows that I am telling the truth. 32In Damascus the governor under King Aretas ringed the city of the Damascenes with guards to ensure my arrest, 33but I was lowered in a basket through an opening in the wall, and thus escaped his clutches.

Chapter 12

I MUST keep on talking about myself and about my claims—not that it does any good. I come now to visions and revelations given by the Lord. 2I knew a man who was a Christian, and fourteen years ago—I have no idea whether it was a physical experience or a vision, God knows—he was snatched up to the third heaven. 3I know that this man—I have no idea whether it was a physical experience or a vision, God knows—4was snatched up into paradise, and that there he heard things which cannot be reduced to speech, and which no human being has any right to utter. 5For a man like that I will make claims; for myself I will make no claims, except about the things which show my weakness. 6If I do wish to make claims, they will not be the claims of a fool, for what I say will be the truth. But I spare you this, because I do not want anyone to have a higher opinion of me than he can form on the basis of what he sees me do and hears me say. 7To prevent me therefore from being too uplifted by the superlative nature of the visions I experienced, I was given a physical condition which brought me pain like a stake twisting in my body. It was Satan's messenger, sent to batter me, to keep me from being too uplifted. 8Three times I pled with God about this, and asked him to take it away. 9'My grace is all you need,' he said to me. 'It is in weakness that my power becomes most powerful.' I shall therefore find my highest joy and my greatest pride in my weakness, for then the power of Christ will settle on me. 10So then, I have no objection to weaknesses, to insults, to hardships, to persecutions, to desperate situations for Christ's sake, for it is when I am weak that I am strong.

11I am behaving like a fool—it is you who forced me to. It ought to have been you who were vouching for my claims. I am in no way inferior to your super-apostles, even if I am a mere nobody. 12The things which are the characteristic hall-marks of any apostle happened among you. You saw me live a life in which again and again I passed the breaking-point and did not break, a life marked by demonstrations of the power of God in action, by wonders and by miracles. 13In what way were you made to feel inferior to the rest of the congregations, apart from the fact that I myself never bothered you for help? Forgive me for wronging you like that! 14I am ready to come to visit you for the third time. I will not be a nuisance to you. It is not your money I want; it is you. Children should not be saving up to help their parents; it is parents who should be saving up to help their children. 15As for you, I will most gladly spend all I have, and be myself completely spent for you. If I love you too much, will that make you love me less? 16We can take it as agreed that I was not a burden to you. But there is another charge—constitutionally I am supposed to be an unscrupulous rascal, and I am supposed to have trapped you by trickery. 17Did I take advantage of you through any of the people I sent to you? 18I asked Titus to visit you, and I sent our colleague along with him. Are you going to say that Titus took advantage of you? Did he and I not act under the guidance of the same Spirit? Did we not follow exactly the same course of action?

19Are you under the impression all along that it is to you we have been making our defence? It is before God, and as Christians, that we speak. My dear friends, everything we have said, we have said for the upbuilding of your spiritual life. 20I am afraid that, when I come, I may find you different from what I would like you to be, and that you may find me different from what you would like me to be. I am afraid that I may find in your society quarrelling and jealousy, explosive tempers and unbridled personal ambitions, slanderous talk and malicious gossip, swelling pride and general disorder. 21I am afraid that, if I come again, God may humiliate me in front of you, and that I may have to shed tears over many who sinned in the past, and who have not repented of their impurity, their sexual immorality, and the blatant licentiousness of their lives.

Chapter 13

I AM coming to visit you for the third time. Scripture says: 'Every fact must be established by the evidence of two or three witnesses.' ₂I have a warning to give to all those who sinned in the past, and to everyone else. I warned you before, on my second visit to you, and now in my absence I warn you again, if I come to you again, I will show no mercy. ₃You are looking for proof that Christ speaks through me—and you will get it. In his dealings with you he is no weakling; so far from that, he demonstrates his power among you. ₄True, it was in weakness that he died on the cross; but it is the power of God which gives him continuing life. True, we are one with him, and therefore we share his weakness, but, when we have to deal with you, the source of our life, as it is with his life, is the power of God.

₅It is yourselves you must examine, to see if you really are living in the Christian faith. It is yourselves you must test. You must be well aware that Christ Jesus is within you—unless you have failed the test altogether. ₆I hope that you will realize that we have been tested and have not failed the test. ₇It is our prayer to God that we may have to do nothing to hurt you. It is not that we want it demonstrated that we can meet the test. The one thing we want is that you should do the right thing, even if it should look as if we had failed the test. ₈For we cannot act against the truth; we can only act for it. ₉We are quite happy to be weak, provided you are strong. Our one prayer is for the complete correction of your lives. ₁₀My one reason for writing this letter to you before I come to visit you is to make sure that, when I do arrive, I will not have to deal with you severely with the authority which the Lord gave me, an authority to be used always to build up and never to pull down.

₁₁And now, brothers, good-bye! Try to correct your lives. Don't reject my appeals to you. Agree with one another. Live at peace with one another, and the God of love and peace will be with you. ₁₂Greet one another with the kiss of peace. All God's people send you their good wishes.

₁₃The grace of the Lord Jesus Christ, the love of God, the fellowship the Holy Spirit gives be with you all.

Introduction to the Letter to the Galatians

THE Letter to the Galatians is a short letter, but there is no letter which has more of the very essence of Paul in it, and it may well have been the first letter that Paul wrote to his people.

From the beginning to the end of his life Paul had his enemies, and in the Letter to the Galatians he is defending himself from them. So this letter has been said to be like 'a sword flashing in a great swordsman's hand'. In this letter two things are under attack.

i. Paul's apostleship was under attack. Paul was not one of the original Twelve; he had begun life as a savage persecutor, out to obliterate Jesus and his church, and therefore Paul was vulnerable to attack. Further, the qualification for apostleship was that a man must have been a member of the original followers of Jesus and must have been a witness of the resurrection (Acts 1.21,22), and once again Paul was open to attack.

Paul never denied his past (1.13,14), but what he did claim was that his apostleship was nothing less than a special appointment from Jesus Christ and from God the Father (1.1;1.11,12).

ii. This gave him a gospel which was particularly and peculiarly his. But it was not a gospel which was different from that of the church. It was known to and fully approved by the leaders of the church (2.2). But Paul's gospel had one characteristic. It was intended by God, and accepted by the church, as being specially for the Gentiles (1.16; 2.7-9). It was this gospel which was under attack.

It was under attack by a certain kind of Jewish Christian. There were Jews who genuinely believed that, since the Jews were the chosen people, and since Jesus was God's greatest gift to men, a man must become a Jew before he could become a Christian, and that therefore he must first become circumcised, and then he must obey the Jewish law, with all its regulations about food, and about Sabbath observance, and about separation from the Gentiles (3.1-6).

To Paul the trouble about this was that the implication was that a man could, so to speak, earn the favour of God by doing certain things to his body, and obeying certain rules and regulations. To Paul the only way to get right with God was faith, which meant throwing oneself unconditionally on the free mercy of God, as Abraham had done so many centuries before (3.10-22). As Paul saw it, all that a man could do was to take what God offered, in faith in the love of Jesus

Christ. So there was always this clash between faith and works, and this is what Galatians is all about.

iii. But what about the law? Was it not holy, given on Mount Sinai, the law of God? The law still had its uses, as Paul saw it. It defines sin, and thereby makes a man conscious of sin—but it cannot cure sin. It is like the slave who took the schoolboy to the door of the school, but had to leave him there. The law showed a man his sin, and by so doing, drove a man to the mercy of God in faith, because no one can keep the law. The law showed a man that any attempt to save himself must end in defeat. He must in faith accept the offer of God that Jesus brought to men (3.19-29).

iv. The Christian therefore has complete freedom from the law. Does this mean that the Christian can do what he likes? No, because this Christian freedom is conditioned by the Christian's sense of responsibility to others and his love for Jesus. He is free—but he is never free to injure his brother, or to grieve God. He is free to live the life the Spirit gives him, and to be released from his own lower nature (5.1-26).

v. So the letter comes to its close with practical injunctions and a final appeal from Paul.

This is the letter which tells all men that the only way to be right with God is to take what God offers in penitence and in love. Then into life will come the liberty which is, not licence, but true freedom to serve men and to love God.

The Letter to the
GALATIANS

Chapter 1

THIS is a letter from Paul, and from all the brothers who are with
him, to the congregations in Galatia. I write to you as an apostle,
and my apostleship comes from no human source and was conferred
on me by no human agent. It was conferred on me through the direct
action of Jesus Christ and of God the Father, who raised him from the
dead. 3Grace to you and every blessing from God our Father and from
the Lord Jesus Christ, 4who gave himself for our sins. His purpose was
to rescue us from this present evil world, for this was the will of our
God and Father. 5Glory be to him for ever and ever. Amen.

6I am surprised that you are so quickly deserting the God who
called you by the grace of Christ and transferring your loyalty to a
different gospel—7not that it is another gospel, for there is no such
thing. It is nothing other than an attempt by certain people to upset
you and to pervert the gospel of Christ. 8But even if we or an angel
from heaven should preach a gospel to you which is at variance with
the gospel we have already preached to you, let God's curse be on
him. 9As I have already said, and as I repeat now, if anyone is preaching to you a gospel which is at variance with the gospel you have
already received, let God's curse be on him.

10When I talk as bluntly as I am talking now, is it men's approval I
am out to win, or is it God's? Do I sound as if I was trying to ingratiate
myself with men? If I were still trying to ingratiate myself with men,
I would not be the servant of Christ.

11I tell you, brothers, the gospel which I preach is no human affair.
12I owe my knowledge to no man's instruction and to no man's
teaching. No! It came to me by direct revelation from Jesus Christ.

13You have heard of my former career when the religion of the
Jews was my religion. You are well aware that there were no bounds
to my persecution of God's church, and that I tried to blast it out of
existence. 14In my fanatical enthusiasm for my ancestral traditions, I

outstripped most of my contemporaries and my compatriots in my progress in the Jewish way of life and belief. 15But God had a purpose for me even before I was born. He called me by his grace, 16and he chose to reveal his Son to me, and through me to others. His purpose was that I might tell the good news about him to the Gentile world. When he called me, I did not seek the advice of any human being, 17nor did I go up to Jerusalem to visit those who were apostles before I was. No! The first thing I did was to go off to Arabia. Then I came back again to Damascus.

18Then three years later I went up to Jerusalem to make the acquaintance of Cephas, and I stayed with him for a fortnight. 19The only other apostle I saw was James the Lord's brother. 20Before God what I am writing to you is absolutely true. 21Then I went to the districts of Syria and Cilicia. 22To the Christian congregations in Judaea I was personally unknown. 23All that they had heard was a report that their former persecutor was now preaching the faith which he had once tried to blast out of existence. 24And what had happened to me provided them with a reason for praising God.

Chapter 2

FOURTEEN years elapsed before my next visit to Jerusalem. On that occasion I went up with Barnabas, and I took Titus too along with me. 2This visit was the result of direct divine guidance. I had a private meeting with the most respected leaders of the church, at which I referred to them the gospel which I am in the habit of preaching among the Gentiles. I took this step because I wanted to be sure that my efforts in the past and in the present had not been, and would not be, all to no purpose. 3Not even Titus, who was with me, Greek though he is, was compelled to be circumcised. 4The question of his circumcision was indeed raised by certain spurious Christians who had been insinuated into the discussion in an underhand way. They had wormed their way in, with the purpose of spying out a way to launch an attack on the Christian freedom which we possess, for it was their intention to reduce us to spiritual slavery. 5Not for a moment did we yield to their attempts to subject us to the law. My one aim was to preserve the integrity of the gospel for you. 6The leading figures in the church—what they were makes not the slightest difference to me; status symbols mean nothing to God—the leading lights, I say, had no new suggestions to put forward. 7On the contrary, they recognized that I had been entrusted with the gospel for the uncircumcised Gentiles, just as Peter had been entrusted with the gospel for the circumcised Jews. 8For he whose power was operative in and for Peter to make him an apostle to the circumcised Jews was equally operative in and for me to make me an apostle to the Gentiles. 9So then, James and Cephas and John, whom all regard as pillars of the church, recognized the special grace which had been given to me. They pledged themselves to accept me and Barnabas as partners in a partnership in which our sphere should be the Gentiles and theirs the Jews. 10The only thing they did ask us to do was to remember the poor, which was the very thing that I had already every intention of doing.

11When Cephas came to Antioch, I opposed him to his face, for he stood self-condemned. 12He had been in the habit of sharing meals with the Gentiles until a group of men from James arrived. When they arrived, he began to withdraw, and finally tried completely to separate himself from fellowship with the Gentiles, because he was scared of the party who insisted on the observance of the Jewish law. 13The rest of the Jewish Christians became involved in this two-faced conduct, to such an extent that even Barnabas was swept away in this situation in which the conduct of these people was a complete denial of their alleged Christian beliefs. 14When I saw that they were leaving the straight road of the true gospel, I said to Cephas in front of them all: 'You were born and bred a Jew, and you are prepared to mix with the Gentiles and to abandon the Jewish way of life. How then can you try to compel the Gentiles to live by the Jewish law?'

15We are Jews by birth; we are not Gentile sinners—as a Jew would call them. 16But we very well know that no man can get into a right relationship with God by means of doing the things that any law prescribes. The only way to get into a right relationship with God is through faith in Christ Jesus. So we took the decision to become believers in Christ Jesus, in order to get into a right relationship with God through faith in Christ, and not through doing what any law prescribes, because no one can get into a right relationship with God by trying to do what any law prescribes.

17If in our aim to get into a right relationship with God through Christ it becomes obvious that we too are sinners, does this mean that Christ is the promoter of sin? God forbid! 18The way in which I would really prove myself a sinner would be by rebuilding that whole edifice of legalism which I have already pulled down. 19My very attempt to obey the law compelled me in the end to live a life in which the law has for me become a dead letter. Only thus could I live to God. I have been crucified with Christ. 20My own life is dead; it is Christ who lives in me. True, my physical life goes on, but its mainspring is faith in the Son of God who loved me and gave himself for me. 21I am not going to treat the grace of God as if it did not exist. For, if it is possible to get into a right relationship with God by means of any law, then Christ might as well not have died.

Chapter 3

M¥ Galatian friends, the trouble with you is that you will not use your common-sense! Who has put a spell on you? The story of Jesus on his cross was told to you so vividly that it seemed to be happening before your very eyes. 2Will you answer me one question? Did you receive the Spirit as a consequence of observing the law, or simply because you heard the offer and accepted the way of faith? 3How can you be so senseless? You began in the Spirit. Are you going to end up by trying to win salvation by doing something to your body? 4Are you simply going to write off all the great facts of your Christian experience? Surely it cannot all go for nothing! 5Does he who gives you the Spirit so generously, and who works miracles among you, do so because you observe the law, or because you heard the offer and accepted the way of faith? 6You have exactly the same experience as Abraham. Abraham took God at his word, and that act of faith was accepted as putting him into a right relationship with God.

7So then, you are bound to see that it is the people who rely entirely on faith who are the sons of Abraham. 8Scripture foresaw that it would be by faith that God would bring the Gentiles into a right relationship with himself, and recounts how the good news was announced to Abraham long ago: 'All nations shall be blessed in you.' 9So then, all who rely on faith are blessed along with Abraham the man of faith. 10All those who rely on obedience to the prescriptions of the law are under a curse, for scripture says: 'Anyone who does not consistently do everything that is written in the book of the law is accursed.' 11It is clear that no one can get into a right relationship with God by obedience to any kind of legal system, because, 'It is the man who is right with God through faith who will find life.' 12It is not by faith that the law operates. What the law actually says is that those who keep its prescriptions shall find life by means of them. 13But

Christ ransomed us from the curse of the law by taking the curse upon himself for our sakes, for scripture says: 'Everyone who is hanged from a tree is accursed.' 14This happened that the blessing which was given to Abraham might go out to the Gentiles in Christ Jesus, so that through faith we might receive the Spirit as he promised.

15Brothers, I take an analogy from ordinary everyday life. Even in the case of an ordinary business contract, no one cancels it and no one adds clauses to it once it has been finally ratified. 16Now the promises were made to Abraham and to his *issue*. When God made the promise, he did not say, 'and to your *issues*,' as if he was speaking about many. He said 'and to your *issue*,' in the singular, as if he was speaking about one definite person, and that one person is Christ. 17What I mean is this—the law, which came into existence four hundred and thirty years later, cannot cancel an agreement already made by God, and so render the promise inoperative. 18For, if the right to inherit the promise depends on any kind of law, then it no longer depends on a promise; but in point of fact it was through a promise that that right was graciously given to Abraham by God. 19What then is the function of the law? The law was introduced into the situation to define what wrong-doing is. But it was only intended to last until Abraham's 'issue,' to whom the promise had been made should come. The law was transmitted through angels and in the person of a mediator. 20This is to say that the validity of the law depends on two parties, one to give it and one to keep it, and on a mediator to bring it from the one to the other. But a promise depends on only one person, the person who makes it, and when there is only one person involved there is no necessity for a mediator. And in this case God is the one person, and on him alone the promise depends.

21Is this then to say that the law and the promises are in opposition to each other? God forbid! If there was any such thing as a law which is able to give men life, then it really would have been possible to get into a right relationship with God by relying on such a law. 22But, as scripture says, no one ever kept any such law, and therefore the whole universe is imprisoned in the power of sin. The situation was designed so that the promise which depends on faith in Jesus Christ might come true for those who have such faith.

23Before the coming of the era of faith we were the law's prisoners, locked up in its power until the coming of the way of faith which was destined to be revealed. 24The law was therefore the servant who brought us to the door of the school of Christ, so that in Christ's school we might be made right with God through faith. ₂₅Once faith had come, we did not need any such servant any more.

₂₆This is true because you are all sons of God through faith because of your connection with Christ Jesus. ₂₇For all those who have be-come one with Christ through baptism are, as it were, clothed with the life of Christ. ₂₈Because your connection with Christ makes you one with each other, in your society there can be no Jew or Greek, no slave or free man, no male and female. ₂₉If you are Christ's, then you are descendants of Abraham, with the right to possess all that God promised him.

Chapter 4

WHAT I mean is this—so long as the heir is a minor, he is to all intents and purposes no different from a slave, although he is the owner of the whole estate. ₂Even although he is the owner he is under the control of guardians of his person and trustees of his property, until the date his father fixed arrives. ₃It is the same with us. When we were spiritually minors we were no different from slaves, under the control of that elementary knowledge of God which was all the world could attain. ₄But when the necessary period had been completed, God sent his Son, born as any child is born, brought up under the Jewish law, ₅to ransom those whom the law held in its power, for it was his purpose that the time of slavery should end and the time of sonship begin. ₆That you are sons is proved by the fact that God sent the Spirit of his Son into our hearts, crying: 'Father! Dear Father!' ₇The result is that you are no longer in the position of a slave; you are in the position of a son. And, if you are in the position of a son, God has made you an heir.

₈There was a very different time, when you did not know God, and when you had consented to become slaves to gods who are not really gods at all. ₉But as things now are you have come to know God—or, to put it more correctly, you are known by God. How then can you turn back to the weak and poverty-stricken rudiments of religion that once were all you knew? How can you want to relapse into that servitude all over again? ₁₀You scrupulously observe days and months and special occasions and years. ₁₁You worry me, for I cannot help being afraid that all the toil I spent on you has gone for nothing.

₁₂I appeal to you, brothers, to put yourselves in my place, as indeed

I put myself in yours. I have no complaints against you. 13You know
that the first of my two visits to you was due to the fact that I was ill,
and it was that illness which gave me the chance to bring the good
news to you. 14That physical illness might well have been a temptation to you to despise me, and to recoil in disgust from me. But, so
far from that, you received me as if I were an angel of God, and as
you would have received Christ Jesus himself. 15You were so happy
to have me! What has happened? I declare that, if it had been possible,
you would have plucked out your eyes and given them to me. 16Do
you regard me as your enemy because I tell you the truth? 17These
people pay a great deal of attention to you, but not with any honourable motive. What they really want is to separate you from me, and
to make you pay a great deal of attention to them. 18It is an excellent
thing to have people taking an interest in you, so long as their motives
are honourable, and I would gladly see you enjoying that interest and
attention always and not only when I am actually with you. 19You
are already my dear children, but now I have to endure the birth-
pangs all over again, until the nature of Christ is brought to birth
within you. 20I wish I was with you just now. I wish I did not need to
talk to you like this. But I must, because I am at my wit's end to know
what to do about you.

21You want to submit yourselves to the law. Tell me, then, will you
not listen to what the law says? 22Scripture tells us that Abraham had
two sons. One was the slave-girl's son, and the other was the free
woman's son. 23The slave-girl's son was born by natural human
processes; the free woman's son was born as a result of the promise of
God. 24These things form an allegory. These two women stand for
two covenants. The one, that is, Hagar, represents the covenant
which had its beginning on Mount Sinai, and which bears children
destined for slavery. 25Hagar stands for Mount Sinai in Arabia, and
she corresponds to the present Jerusalem, for she and her children are
slaves. 26But the heavenly Jerusalem is the free woman, and it is she
who is our mother, 27for scripture says:

'Rejoice, you barren one, who bore no child,
    break out into a shout of joy,
        you who have never known the pangs of childbirth.
For the children of the woman who was left all alone
    shall be more than those of the woman who has a husband.'

28You, brothers, are children of God's promise, as Isaac was. 29In the
old days long ago the child born in the purely human way perse-

cuted the child born as a result of the action of the Spirit—and the same still happens today. ₃₀But what does scripture say? 'Drive out the slave-girl and her son, for the slave-girl's son will not be allowed to share the inheritance with the free woman's son.' ₃₁You can see from all this, brothers, that we are not the children of any slave-girl; we are the children of the free woman.

Chapter 5

CHRIST set us free, and means us to stay free. Take your stand on that, and never again submit to any yoke of slavery.

₂I, Paul, tell you that, if you get yourselves circumcised, Christ will be no good to you. ₃Once again I solemnly state to every man who gets himself circumcised that he is under obligation to carry out every item of the law. ₄If you try to get into a right relationship with God through any legal system, you have by that very act severed your connection with Christ. You have removed yourselves from the sphere of grace. ₅It is by the help of the Spirit that we eagerly await the hoped-for right relationship with God which comes from faith. ₆Once a man becomes a Christian, whether or not he is circumcised is meaningless. What matters is faith working in love.

₇You were making excellent progress. Who stopped you obeying the truth? ₈Whatever arguments were used to persuade you certainly did not come from the God who calls you. ₉Once even the slightest infection gets into a society, it spreads until the whole society becomes infected. ₁₀The fact that you and I are united in the Lord makes me completely confident that you will agree with me. But the person who is upsetting you will have to pay the penalty—and it does not matter who he is. ₁₁As for me, brothers, if I still proclaim the necessity of circumcision, why am I still being persecuted? If indeed I was still proclaiming circumcision as a necessity, then those who believe in circumcision would no longer find the cross offensive. ₁₂I wish the people who are disturbing you would castrate themselves, let alone circumcise themselves!

₁₃Brothers, you were called to be free. But one thing you must guard against. You must not use your freedom as an opportunity to give full play to the demands of your lower nature. No! You must use it lovingly to serve one another. ₁₄For the whole law is summed up in one sentence: 'You must love your neighbour as yourself.' ₁₅But, if you go on biting and savaging one another like wild animals, you must be careful that you do not end up by destroying one another.

16What I mean is this—make the Spirit the rule of your life, and then you will never be out to satisfy the desires of your lower nature. 17For the desires of our lower nature run counter to the desires of the Spirit, and the desires of the Spirit run counter to the desires of our lower nature. These two are permanently opposed to one another, and the result is that the very things you want to do are the very things you cannot do. 18But, if you are led by the Spirit, you are not under the domination of law. 19Anyone can see the kind of things for which the lower part of our nature is responsible, things like fornication, impurity, blatant immorality; 20idolatry and sorcery; enmity, strife and jealousy; outbursts of explosive temper, selfish ambition, divisions, the party spirit, 21envy; drunkenness, revelling, and the like. 21I told you before, and I tell you again, people who practise things like these will never enter into possession of the Kingdom of God. 22But the harvest which the Spirit produces is love, joy, peace; patience, kindness, goodness; fidelity, 23the strength of gentleness, self-control. No law forbids things like that. 24Those who belong to Christ Jesus have once and for all crucified their lower nature with its passions and desires. 25If the Spirit is the ruling principle of our lives, we must march in step with the Spirit. 26We must have no desire for empty prestige, no provoking of one another, no jealousy of one another.

Chapter 6

Brothers, if anyone is detected in some wrong act, you who are spiritual must correct him. You must do so gently, and you must, each of you, look to yourself, in case you too are tempted. 2Help each other to carry your burdens, for, if you do, you will fulfil Christ's law. 3If anyone has a good opinion of himself, when in fact he has nothing to be pleased about, he is deluding himself. 4It is his own work that a man must test, and then any sense of achievement that he has will be the result of judging himself by himself, and not of comparing himself with someone else. 5For everyone has to shoulder his own personal pack. 6If anyone is under instruction in the Christian message, he should share with his teacher all the good things he has. 7Make no mistake—you can't make a fool of God! A man will reap whatever he sows. 8If a man sows in the field of his own lower nature, from that lower nature he will reap a life that is doomed to decay. But if he sows in the field of the Spirit, the harvest will be eternal life. ₉We must never get tired of doing the fine thing, for, when the right time comes, we will reap the harvest of it, if we never relax our efforts. ₁₀So then, whenever we get the chance, we must do good to everyone, and especially to those who are members of the family of the faith.

₁₁See in what big letters I am writing to you in my own handwriting! ₁₂It is these people who wish to make an impressive outward display of their religion who are trying to compel you to get yourselves circumcised. In point of fact, they really want to escape persecution for the cross of Christ. ₁₃These advocates of circumcision don't themselves make any great success of their law-keeping. They want you to be circumcised to enable them to boast that they have persuaded you to accept as essential an outward mark on your body. ₁₄God forbid that I should boast about anything except about the cross of our Lord Jesus Christ, that cross by which the world has been crucified to me and I to the world! ₁₅Whether a man is circumcised or not circumcised is of no importance. What matters is the creating of the man all over again. ₁₆Mercy and every blessing on all those who will make this the rule of their life and conduct, and on God's Israel.

₁₇In future let no man go on making things difficult for me, for the scars I bear on my body brand me as the slave of Christ.

₁₈Brothers, the grace of our Lord Jesus Christ be with your spirit. Amen.

Introduction to the Letter to the Ephesians

THE Letter to the Ephesians has been called 'The Queen of the Epistles'. But it presents us with certain problems.

Some of the oldest and the best manuscripts of the Greek New Testament do not have the words *in Ephesus* in the first verse of the letter. In them the letter, as the Revised Standard Version has it, is written: 'To the saints who are also faithful in Christ Jesus.' We further note that, unlike the usual letters, it has no personal greetings at the end. The simplest explanation of these facts is that the letter we know as the Letter to the Ephesians was in fact a circular letter, which was sent out to the churches of Asia Minor, and Ephesus among them. If it is a circular letter, it is all the more important, for it was meant, not for one congregation, but for a group of congregations.

There are some who do not think that it is one of Paul's letters at all. They feel that the style and the thought are so different from Paul's usual style and thought that he cannot have written it. But it must be remembered that this letter comes from very near the end of Paul's life, and that it was written when he was in prison, and therefore had far more time to write it than he had to write the other letters which he had to dash off on the spur of the moment to meet some threatening situation in one of his churches.

The Letter to the Ephesians was written about A.D.62, and it is one of a group of letters—Colossians, Philemon and Philippians are the others—which were written when Paul was in prison in Rome. Certain that he would receive no justice from the Jews, Paul had exercised the right of a Roman citizen, and had appealed direct to the Emperor (Acts 25.10,11). We know that he was in prison for at least two years before his case came up (Acts 28.30), and during this period he wrote these letters. In the Letter to the Ephesians he more than once mentions the fact that he was in prison when he was writing (3.1; 6.1; 6.20).

The theme of the letter is simple, but very great. We may state it in four propositions.

i. This is a world of disunity. Man himself is a disunity, torn by his passions and desires. And this disunity obviously separates a man from God (2.1-10). Further, men are separated from each other. There is the dividing wall which separates the Gentile from the Jew (2.1-22).

ii. It is God's aim to bring unity into this literally distracted world. This is the purpose of God.

iii. That unity of man with himself, of man with man, and of man with God is to be brought about in and through Jesus Christ (1.9; 4.13). That is to say, God's instrument of reconciliation is Jesus Christ.

iv. But Jesus Christ has ascended to heaven, and he too needs an instrument, and his instrument, the body through which he works, is the church (1.23; 5.23).

So then the thought of the Letter to the Ephesians revolves round two closely connected propositions—God's instrument of reconciliation is Jesus Christ, and Jesus Christ's instrument of reconciliation is the church.

As a missionary, it is Paul's great privilege to bring this message to the Gentiles; and as a pastor, it is his task to lay before the church the life the Christian must live.

The Letter to the
EPHESIANS

Chapter 1

This is a letter from Paul, who became an apostle of Jesus Christ because God willed it so, to God's consecrated people in Ephesus, the loyal Christians there. 2Grace to you and every blessing from God our Father and from the Lord Jesus Christ.

3Praise to the God and Father of our Lord Jesus Christ, for he in the heavenly places has blessed us with every spiritual blessing, because our life is bound up with the life of Christ. 4It was through this connection with Christ that before the creation of the world God chose us to be his own consecrated people, and to live lives faultless in his sight. In his love 5he had already destined us for adoption into his own family through the work of Jesus Christ, for this was the purpose of his will. 6All this he did that men might praise that glorious grace of his which he gave to us in his Beloved and through no merits of our own. 7It is in and through Christ and the sacrifice of his life that we have been liberated, a liberation which means the forgiveness of sins. It all happened because of the wealth of his grace. 8This grace he gave us in superabundance to equip us with all wisdom and with all insight. 9He revealed to us the secret of his will, and of the purpose which long ago he had in Christ. 10This purpose is finally to bring to their conclusion all the events in history, and to make of all things, things in heaven and things on earth, one perfect whole in Christ. 11And we too have received a share in him, for this was our destiny in the intention of that God who works out everything as the purpose of his will directs. 12The purpose of all this was that we Jews, who were the first to set our hopes on Christ, should cause his glory to be praised, 13and it is through him that you Gentiles too have heard the message of the truth, the good news of your salvation. It is in him that you took your decision to believe, and received the promised Holy Spirit, who marks you out as his, 14that Holy Spirit who is the first instalment and the pledge of all that one day you will possess.

The final end of all this is the liberation of God's own people, so that his glory may be praised.

15This is why, since I heard of your faith in the Lord Jesus and your love to all God's consecrated people, 16I never stop thanking God for you, and remembering you in my prayers. 17For it is my prayer that the God of our Lord Jesus Christ, the glorious Father, may give you the Spirit to make you wise in heavenly things, and to reveal to you full knowledge of himself. 18I pray that your inner vision may be flooded with light, to enable you to see what hope the fact that he has called you gives you, to see the glorious wealth of the life that he has promised you as members of his dedicated people, 19to see how surpassingly great is his power to us who believe, that power demonstrated in the action of the mighty strength 20which was operative in the case of Christ, when he brought him back to life again, and seated him at his right hand in the heavenly places. 21There he gave him a place far above all spiritual powers, above every ruler and authority and power and lord, above every possible title of honour, not only in this world but also in the next. 22He subjected everything to him, and he gave him as the supreme head to the church; 23and the church is his body, the complement of him who completes all things everywhere.

Chapter 2

You Gentiles were spiritually dead in your trespasses and sins. 2It was in them that you lived an earthbound life, under the domination of the controller of those evil powers who haunt the air, of that spirit who is now active in those who are disobedient to God. 3We Jews were no different, for we too at one time lived a life dominated by the desires of our lower nature, doing what the human body wanted and what the human mind planned. We were just as much in danger of the divine wrath as anyone else. 4But God is rich in mercy, and, because of his great love for us, 5he raised us to life with Christ, even though we were spiritually dead in sins. It is to grace that you owe your salvation. 6Because of our union with Christ Jesus he raised us from spiritual death, and gave us a seat with him in the heavenly places. 7He did this to demonstrate to all future ages the surpassing wealth of his grace in his kindness in Christ Jesus to us. 8For it is to grace that you owe your salvation through faith. The whole process comes from nothing that we have done or could do;

it is God's gift. 9Any achievement of ours is ruled out to make it impossible for anyone to boast. 10It is he who made us what we are, for through Jesus Christ we have been created for that life of goodness which God already prepared for us to live.

11You will therefore do well to remember that you were once Gentiles from the physical point of view. You Gentiles were once called 'the uncircumcised' by the Jews who call themselves 'the circumcised.' The circumcision of which they speak is a physical and man-made thing. 12You will do well to remember that at that time you knew nothing of a Messiah. You were aliens with no share in the divine nation of Israel. You were complete strangers to the covenants which contain the promise of God. You lived in a world without hope and without God. 13But because of your relationship with Christ Jesus the situation has changed. You who were far away have been brought near through the death of Christ.

14It is he who has solved the problem of our relationships with God and man. He has destroyed the fence's dividing wall and made both Jew and Gentile into one. By his incarnation he destroyed the old enmity, 15for he abolished the law with its commandments and its decrees. This he did in order that their common relationship to himself might make the two into one new man, and thus their new relationship to him gave them a new relationship to each other. 16It was his purpose to make Jew and Gentile into one united body through the cross, and thus by it to kill the ancient enmity, and to bring both back to God. 17So he came and brought the good news of this new divine and human relationship both to you Gentiles, who were far away, and to the Jews, who were near, 18for through him we both possess the right of access through the one Spirit to the Father. 19So then, it follows that you are no longer foreigners and aliens; you are fellow-citizens with God's consecrated people, and members of the household of God. 20The prophets and the apostles are the foundations of the structure into which you have been built, and Christ Jesus himself is the corner-stone. 21It is he who holds the whole building together and who makes it grow into a holy temple in the Lord. 22In your union with him you too are being built in as a part with all his other people, to make you through the Spirit a dwelling-place for God.

Chapter 3

BECAUSE of this I, Paul, Christ's prisoner for you Gentiles as I am, am praying for you. ₂I am sure that I can assume that you have heard of my divinely allotted ministry, a ministry given to me to bring to you Gentiles that grace of God which I myself have already experienced. ₃It was by direct revelation that God told me of his secret plan, about which I have briefly written to you in the earlier part of this letter, ₄and by reading it you can judge for yourselves if I have really grasped the secret of the real meaning of Christ. ₅In former times that secret was not told to men in the way in which it has now been disclosed by the Spirit to God's consecrated apostles and prophets. ₆That secret is that the Gentiles through the gospel are partners with the people of God, fellow-members of the one body, sharers in the promise in virtue of their connection with Christ Jesus. ₇Of that gospel I was made a servant, as a result of the free gift of the grace of God which I experienced, an experience which came to me through the action of his power. ₈I am the least of all God's consecrated people, and yet God in his grace gave me the privilege of bringing the good news of the wealth of Christ to the Gentiles, a wealth the limit of which no man can ever find. ₉It was my God-given task to shed a flood of light on the working out of that secret, up to now hidden from all eternity in the mind of God, the creator of all things. ₁₀The purpose of all this was through the church to make known the many-coloured wisdom of God to the demonic rulers and powers in the heavenly places, ₁₁for this was the eternal purpose that God had planned to work out in Christ Jesus our Lord. ₁₂And because of Christ Jesus and our faith in him we can enter God's royal presence with no fear and in perfect trust. ₁₃So then, it is my prayer that you will not be discouraged by the troubles that I am going through for you, for in my troubles is your glory.

₁₄For this cause I kneel in prayer to the Father, ₁₅that Father who is the origin and ideal of all fatherhood in heaven and on earth, ₁₆praying to him that in the wealth of his glory he may grant to you to be strengthened in power through his Spirit in your inner being, ₁₇praying that your faith may be such that Christ may make your hearts his home, praying that love may be that in which your life is rooted and on which it is founded. ₁₈I pray that in fellowship with all God's consecrated people you may have strength to grasp how broad and long and high and deep Christ's love is, 19to know that love of his which is greater than we can ever understand, for then your life will be filled with all God's fullness.

20Now to him who can do for us far more than our lips can ask or our minds conceive through that power of his which is at work in us, 21to God be glory in the church and in Christ Jesus from age to age, for ever and ever. Amen.

Chapter 4

PRISONER though I am, my life is still lived in the presence and power of the Lord. You have been called by God to be his own. So then, I urge you to live a life which befits such a call. 2I urge you to live a life of complete humility and gentleness, a life of patience, a life in which you always lovingly bear with one another. 3I urge you to be eager to preserve that unity which the Spirit can give, a unity in which you are bound together in a perfect relationship to one another. 4There is one body and there is one Spirit, just as the fact that God has called you has set before you one hope. 5There is one Lord; there is one faith; there is one baptism. 6There is one God and Father of all, who reigns over all, and works through all, and is in all.

7Each of you has received his own share of grace, in proportion as the free gift of Christ has given it to you. 8That is why it is said:

> 'He ascended on high,
>   after he had taken his prisoners captive,
>   and gave gifts to men.'

9What can 'he ascended' mean other than that he first descended into the lower parts of the earth? 10The one who descended is the same as the one who ascended far above all heavens, so that he might fill all things with his presence and himself. 11And these were the gifts he gave—some to be apostles, some to be prophets, some to be preachers of the good news, some to be pastors and teachers. 12Their function is to equip God's consecrated people for the service they must give; it is their function to build up the body of Christ. 13Then we shall go on to be one united band of brothers, one in our faith and in our knowledge of the Son of God. Then we shall grow into mature manhood, until we reach the stature of Christ in all his completeness. 14Then we shall no longer be infants, tossed and blown about by every chance blast of teaching, at the mercy of the slick cleverness of men, craftily calculated to lead us astray. 15We must rather speak the truth with the accent of love, and then in everything we shall become more and more closely united with him who is the head, I mean Christ. 16For it is through its connection with him that the whole body, formed into one harmonious whole through each ligament with which it is equipped, as each part of it performs its own function, develops its own growth, and so builds itself up in love.

17This I say—and in the Lord's name I solemnly call on you to listen to it—you must no longer live the kind of life the heathen live, a life of utter futility. 18For their minds are darkened and they are alienated from the life of God, because of the deliberate ignorance of their minds and the sheer imperviousness of their hearts. 19They have lost all decent feelings, and have abandoned themselves to shameless immorality, which ends in all kinds of filthy practices, in their greed for the things which no man has any right even to desire. 20This is not the way that you have learned about Christ. 21I have no doubt that you have been told about him, and that you have received Christian instruction in the truth as it is embodied in Jesus. 22You must therefore, as you have been taught, divest yourselves of that old personality, which was characteristic of the way in which you used to live, and which was rotting away, seduced by its own desires. 23You must have a completely new attitude of mind. 24You must put on that new personality, which was divinely created, and which shows itself in that justice and holiness, which are the products of the truth.

25So then, banish all falsehood from your lives. You must speak the truth to your fellowmen, because we are as closely bound up with each other as the parts of the body are. 26Sometimes it is a duty to be angry, but your anger must never be sinful anger. Never come to the end of any day still angry with anyone. 27Give the Devil no place or opportunity in your life. 28The man who stole must steal no longer. He must rather work his hardest, doing an honest day's work with his own hands. His aim must be to have enough to share it with the man who has less than enough. 29You must never use foul language. So far from that, any word of yours must be good for meeting the need of the occasion. Then it will be a means of grace to those who hear it. 30Do not bring sorrow to God's Holy Spirit, that Spirit by whom God's sign of ownership has been set upon you, to mark you out for the day of deliverance. 31All bitterness and bad temper and anger, the loud voice and the slanderous tongue must be removed from your lives, and so must all maliciousness. 32You must be kind to one another; you must be compassionate; you must forgive one another, as God in Christ forgave you.

Chapter 5

So then you must try to be like God, for you are his children and he loves you. 2Your life must be lived in love, and must have as its pattern the life of Christ, who loved us and gave himself for us, as a sacrifice and offering acceptable to God. 3Fornication and any kind of indecency or conscienceless greed should not even be so much as mentioned in your society, for it is not fitting for God's consecrated people even to talk about things like that. 4You must have nothing to do with obscene language and with stupid or frivolous talk. These things are not becoming for you. No! Gratitude to God should be the accent of your talk. 5For you are well aware that no one who is guilty of sexual excess, no one who is morally impure, no one who is characterized by that greed, which has made gain its god, has any part in the Kingdom which is Christ's and God's.

6You must not allow anyone to mislead you with empty words. It is things like that which bring God's wrath on those who disobey him. 7You must never have anything to do with people like that. 8You were once all darkness, but now your connection with the Lord has made you light. You must behave as those who are at home in the light. 9For light brings as its harvest everything that is good and right and true. 10You must submit everything to the test of the approval of the Lord. 11You must have no share in the sterile deeds of darkness; you must rather expose them. 12It is shameful even to talk about the things they do and try to keep hidden. 13Everything that is exposed by the light is lit up; and anything that is lit up itself becomes all light. 14As the hymn has it:

> 'Sleeper, awake,
> and rise from the dead,
> and Christ will shine on you!'

15Pay careful attention to the kind of life you live. Behave as sensible and not as senseless men. 16Seize each opportunity as it comes, for we are living in evil times. 17Don't behave like fools. You must always try to understand what the Lord wants you to do. 18Don't get drunk with wine—that way debauchery lies. No! Fill yourselves with the Holy Spirit. 19Speak to each other in psalms and hymns and songs inspired by the Spirit. Sing and make music to the Lord with all your heart. 20Never stop thanking God the Father for everything in the name of our Lord Jesus Christ. 21Your reverence for Christ must banish all feeling of superiority to others.

22Wives must be subject to their husbands, for that is their Christian duty. 23For a husband is head of his wife as Christ is head of the church, for he is the Saviour of the church, which is his body. 24As the church is subject to Christ, so too wives must be in everything subject to their husbands. 25Husbands, you must love your wives, as Christ too loved the church and gave himself for it. 26It was his purpose to cleanse and consecrate it by the washing of baptism and the preaching of the word, 27for he wished to present the church to himself in all its splendour, without stain or wrinkle or any such thing, for he wished it to be dedicated and faultless. 28It is thus that husbands too ought to love their own wives, as they love their own bodies. To love one's body is to love oneself. 29No one ever hated his own body. So far from that, he nourishes it and cherishes it, as Christ too nourishes and cherishes the church, 30because we are parts of his body. 31For this cause a man will leave father and mother, and will be inseparably joined to his wife, and they two will become so completely one that they will no longer be two persons, but one. 32There is here a very great symbol. As I see it, that saying is a symbol of the relationship of Christ and the church. 33I say no more, except that each one of you husbands must love his wife as he loves himself, and that every wife must respect her husband.

Chapter 6

CHILDREN, you must obey your parents. This is your Christian duty, and it is right that you should do so. 2Honour your father and mother—this is the first commandment with a promise attached to it. 3If you do, you will have a prosperous and a long life in the land. 4You fathers also have your duties. You must not make your children resentful by your treatment of them. You must bring them up in Christian discipline and training.

5As for you slaves, you must obey your human masters, with proper respect and fear, in honest loyalty, as you would obey Christ. 6You must not work only when someone is watching you, as if the only thing that matters is human approval. You must work as Christ's slaves, genuinely trying to do what God wants you to do.

7You must give your service with good-will, as if it was the Lord you were working for, and not a human master, 8for you well know that each man, whether he is a slave or a free man, will receive from the Lord the equivalent of anything good that he has done. 9As for you masters, you must act towards your slaves in the same way.You must stop using threats, for you well know that both they and you have a Master in heaven, and there is no favouritism with him.

10Finally, your union with the Lord and with his mighty power must give you a dynamic strength. 11Put on the complete armour which God can give you, and then you will be able to resist the stratagems of the Devil. 12For our struggle is not against any human foe; it is against demonic rulers and authorities, against the cosmic powers of this dark world, against spiritual forces of evil in the heavens. 13So then, take the complete armour which God can give you, and then, when the evil day comes, you will be able to see things through to the end, and to remain erect. 14So then take your stand. Buckle the belt of truth round your waist. Put on righteousness for a breastplate. 15Put preparedness to preach the gospel of peace on your feet, like shoes. 16Through thick and thin take faith as your shield. With it you will be able to extinguish all the flaming arrows of the Evil One. 17Take salvation as your helmet. Take the sword the Spirit gives. That sword is the word of God. 18Keep on praying fervently, and asking God for what you need, and on every occasion let the Spirit be the atmosphere in which you pray. To that end sleeplessly and always persevere in your requests to God for all God's consecrated people. 19Pray for me too, and ask God to give me a message when I have to speak. Pray that I may be able fearlessly to tell men the secret of the good news, 20for which I am an ambassador, though now in chains. I need your prayers to enable me to speak it with the fearlessness with which I ought to speak.

21Tychicus, our dear brother and a loyal Christian servant, will tell you everything and will let you know how things are with me, and what I am doing. 22I am sending him to you for this very purpose, to let you know what is happening to me, and to encourage your hearts.

23Every blessing to the brothers, and love and faith combined from God the Father and the Lord Jesus Christ. 24Grace be with all those who love our Lord Jesus Christ with a love which will never die.

Introduction to the Letter to the Philippians

THE Letter to the Philippians is another of the letters written by Paul when he was in prison in Rome, and its date is about A.D.62. When he wrote it, he had already faced one part of his trial (1.7). He is not yet in despair about his freedom (1.25,26), and yet, in spite of his hopes, he writes as if death was not very far away (1.20-23; 2.17).

There was no church to which Paul was closer than the church at Philippi. He loved the Philippians and the Philippians loved him (1.3-11). The measure of his closeness to them is seen in the fact that from his other churches Paul was too proud to accept any help. He would rather work his fingers to the bone than take charity (1 Thessalonians 2.9), but from the Philippians he was happy to take and to take more than once (4.10-18).

There were troubles in Philippi, but they were minor troubles. There is nothing in this letter of the dangers and heresies which threatened the very life of the church.

There were those who were rather his competitors than his comrades in preaching (1.15-18). There were those who tried to persuade the Christians to accept circumcision (3.1-4). There were, as might happen in any congregation, two women who had quarrelled and who would not make it up again (4.2,3). And Paul's cure for everything is to have the same attitude of humble service as Jesus Christ had in his life (2.1-18).

Through this letter the warmth of Paul's affection shines and throbs and glows, and in this letter there is the nobility of that courage of his which was ready to face death or life.

The Letter to the
PHILIPPIANS

Chapter 1

THIS is a letter from Paul and Timothy, servants of Christ Jesus, to all God's consecrated Christian people who are in Philippi, and to those who are in charge of the congregation there and those who are engaged in its service. 2Grace to you and every blessing from God our Father and from the Lord Jesus Christ.

3In all my memories of you I have cause for nothing but thanksgiving. 4In my every prayer for you all it is always with joy that I pray. 5I thank God for the way in which you have been my partners in the work of the gospel from the first day it arrived among you right up to the present. 6And I am quite sure of this—that God who began a good work in you will continue it until it is completed on the day when Jesus Christ comes. 7It is right for me to feel like this about you all, because of the place you have in my heart, for you are my partners in the work that God's grace gave me the privilege of doing, both in my imprisonment, and when I have to stand my trial to defend and to establish the truth of the gospel. 8God knows that I am telling the truth when I tell you how I yearn for you with the same affection as Christ Jesus himself does. 9It is my prayer that your love may overflow with deeper and deeper knowledge, and with a greater and greater sensitive awareness of every kind, 10for then you will be able to decide between the different courses of action which present themselves to you, for I want you to be pure and blameless to meet Christ on the day when he comes. 11I want you to be filled with that harvest of goodness which Jesus Christ alone can give, and which moves men to glorify and praise God.

12I want you to know, brothers, that, contrary to all that might have been expected, what has happened to me has resulted in the progress of the gospel. 13The result has been that the whole praetorian guard and all the others could not fail to see that it is as a Christian that I have been imprisoned. 14The very fact that I am in prison has given more and more of our fellow-Christians an ever-increasing confidence in the Lord to dare more and more fearlessly to preach the Christian message.

15It is quite true that there are some who preach Christ from motives of jealousy and controversy; but there are others who preach him in good will. 16It is love which makes some preach Christ, because they know well that it is for the defence of the gospel that I am lying in prison. 17Others proclaim Christ in a spirit of competitive rivalry with very mixed motives. Their idea is to make my imprisonment still harder to bear. 18What does it matter? Whatever else is true, it is true that in every way, whether the preaching is only an excuse for other things, or whether it is done in all sincerity, Christ is being proclaimed—and therefore I am quite happy about it. 19Yes, and I will continue to be happy, for I know that all this will end in my release, because you are praying for me and because the Spirit of Jesus Christ is generously helping me. 20It is my dearest wish and hope that I will never let myself down, but that, as always so now, I may have the courage to speak so freely that men may honour Christ because of my conduct, whether I live or die. 21For to me life is Christ, and death leads to still greater life. 22If I am to go on living life in this world, then I will have the chance to go on doing useful work. But it is not mine to know what choice I will have to make. 23I find it very difficult to decide between the two alternatives. I long to leave this world and to be with Christ—for that is far better. 24But for your sakes it is more necessary for me to go on living in this world, 25and, because I am convinced of this, I know that I am going to remain with you all, and that I am going to continue to stand by you all, to help you to make still further progress, and to have still more joy in the faith. 26I want to visit you again and so to give you the opportunity to have still more Christian pride in me.

27One thing I do want to say to you—in your day to day conduct in the ordinary life of society you must live in a way that befits the gospel of Christ. I want you to live in such a way, that whether I come and see you, or whether I am absent, I will hear that you are standing fast, one in spirit and one in heart, one in your united contest for the faith of the gospel, 28facing your opponents without a trace of nervous fear. Then your courage will be the clear proof to them that they are doomed and that you will be saved—a proof supplied by God himself. 29For you have received the privilege of serving Christ, not only by believing in him, but also by suffering for him. ₃₀You have to fight the same battle as you once saw me fight, and which, as you hear, I am still fighting.

Chapter 2

IF there is such a thing as Christian encouragement, if there is such a thing as love's comforting power, if you and I are really sharing in the partnership which only the Holy Spirit can make possible, if you really wish to show me a heartfelt sympathy which is like the mercy of God, ₂make my joy complete by being in perfect harmony of mind, by joining in a common love for God and for each other, by sharing in a common life, by taking every decision in unity of mind, ₃by never acting from motives of competitive rivalry or in the conceited desire for empty prestige. If you want to make my joy complete, instead of that each of you must humbly think the other better than himself; ₄each of you must concentrate, not on his own interest, but on the interests of others also. ₅Try always to have the same attitude to life as Jesus had.

> ₆He shared the very being of God,
>   but he did not regard his equality to God
>   as a thing to be clutched to himself.
>   ₇So far from that, he emptied himself,
>   and really and truly became a servant,
>   and was made for a time exactly like men.
>   In a human form that all could see,
>   ₈he accepted such a depth of humiliation
>   that he was prepared to die,
>   and to die on a cross.
>   ₉That is why God has given him the highest place,
>   and has conferred on him
>   the name that is greater than any name,
>   ₁₀so that at the name of Jesus every creature
>   in heaven, and on earth, and beneath the earth
>   should kneel in reverence and submission,
>   ₁₁and so that everything which has a voice
>   should openly declare
>   that Jesus Christ is Lord,
>   and thus bring glory to God the Father.

12You have always been obedient. So then, my dear friends, not only as you did when I was with you, but now much more when I am not with you, keep on toiling in fear and trembling to complete your salvation. 13For it is God who is at work in you, to put into you the will to desire and the power to achieve what his purpose has planned for you. 14Do everything without grumbling and without arguing, 15and then no one will be able to question your morals or your sincerity, and you will be faultless children of God, although you live in an age in which life is twisted and perverted. Even in an age like that you must shine like stars in the world. 16You must go on offering them the word of life, for, if you do, on the day when Christ comes I will be able proudly to claim that I did not run a loser's race, and that all my toil has not gone for nothing. 17When men make their sacrifices to the gods, they pour out upon them a sacrificial cup of wine. Your faith and your service are a sacrifice to God, and it may be that my life, like that cup of wine, must be poured out to crown and complete your sacrifice. 18If it must be so, I am glad and I share my joy with you; and in the same way you must be glad and share your joy with me.

19I hope, if the Lord Jesus wills it, to send Timothy to you soon, to cheer my heart with news of how things are going with you. 20I have no one whose heart and mind are so much in tune with mine. He is the one man who will take a genuine interest in your affairs. 21For they are all self-centred instead of being Jesus Christ-centred. 22You well know his sterling worth, and you are well aware how he has served with me, like a son with a father, for the advancement of the gospel. 23I hope then to send him as soon as I see how things are going to go with me. 24I am confident that, if the Lord wills it, I myself will soon come to you.

25I thought it necessary to send back to you Epaphroditus, our fellow-Christian, who has done Christ's work and fought Christ's battles with me. He is the messenger you sent to serve me in my need, but now I send him home to you, 26because he was homesick to see you all, and because he was worried, because he knew that you had heard that he had been ill. 27And indeed he was so ill that he nearly died. But God took pity on him, and not only on him but on me too, to save me from having one grief after another. 28I am all the more eager to send him, to give you the joy of seeing him again and to relieve my own anxiety. 29Welcome him home gladly with a Christian welcome. Honour him and such as him, 30because for the sake of Christ's work he narrowly escaped death, for he risked his life to give to me for you the service which you yourselves could not give.

Chapter 3

Nothing remains, brothers, but for me to wish you the joy that comes from being united with the Lord. To me it is no trouble to repeat what I have already written, and to do so will help to keep you safe.

2Beware of these dogs! Beware of these manufacturers of wickedness! Beware of those whose circumcision is no better than mutilation! 3It is we who are really circumcised, for we offer God a worship directed by his Spirit. Our pride is in Christ Jesus. We place no reliance on human externals, 4although I might well base my claims on such things. If anyone thinks that he can rely on physical marks and human achievements, I have an even stronger claim. 5I was circumcised on the eighth day after I was born. I am a pure-blooded Israelite. I belong to the tribe of Benjamin. I am a Hebrew and the son of Hebrew parents. In my attitude to the Jewish law I was a Pharisee. 6So enthusiastic was my devotion to the law that I was a persecutor of the church. As far as the goodness which the law prescribes and demands is concerned, I was beyond criticism. 7But whatever achievements in my life and career I would once have reckoned among the profits of life, I have written off as a dead loss for the sake of Christ. 8Yes, and more than that—I am prepared to write off everything as a dead loss for the sake of getting to know Christ Jesus my Lord, for that knowledge is something which surpasses everything in the world. For his sake I have abandoned everything, and I regard all else as of no more value than filth for the garbage heap. For me the only thing of value in the world is to gain Christ, 9and to make my life one with his. I am not right with God through any legalistic achievement of my own. All I want is the relationship with God which only God himself can give me, all founded on faith in Christ. 10My one aim is to know Christ, and to experience the power of his resurrection, and to share with him in his sufferings. My aim is to die the death he died, 11so that, if it may be, I may reach the resurrection from the dead.

12I do not claim that I have already attained this, or that I have already reached perfection. I press on to try to grasp that for which Christ Jesus has already grasped me. 13Brothers, I do not regard myself as having already grasped the prize. But I have one aim in life—to forget what lies behind, and to strain every nerve to reach what lies ahead. 14And so I press on to the goal to win the prize to which God in Christ Jesus calls me upward and onward. 15This must be how all of us who are mature Christians feel about life. If there is any point on which you feel differently, God will make it clear to you too. 16This one thing I say, let us never fall below the standard of conduct we have already reached.

17Brothers, make a united effort to follow the example I have given you, and keep watching those who model their conduct on the pattern they have seen in us. 18For there are many of whom I have often spoken to you, and of whom I now speak even with tears, whose conduct makes them the enemies of the cross of Christ. 19They are doomed to destruction. They worship their own appetites. They glory in their shame. They have never a thought beyond the horizons of this world. 20We are citizens of heaven, and we eagerly wait for the Lord Jesus Christ to come from heaven as our Saviour. 21He will change the form of the body which we now possess, with all its earthly limitations and humiliations, and will make it exactly like his own glorious body; and he will do so by the exercise of that power of his, which enables him to bring that and everything else under his sway.

Chapter 4

My brothers, I love you and I long for you. You are my joy and you will be my crown. And in view of all that I have said to you, this, my dear friends, is how you must demonstrate your unswerving loyalty to the Lord.

2I urge Euodia and I urge Syntyche to settle their differences in Christian unity. 3And I make a special appeal to you, my dear partner, to do all you can to help these women, for they have shared with me in the strenuous work of the gospel, along with Clement too, and with the rest of my fellow-workers whose names are in the book of life. 4Never lose your Christian joy. Let me say it again! Never lose it! 5You must make it common knowledge that you never insist on the letter of the law. It will not be long now until the Lord comes. 6Don't worry about anything. In every circumstance of life tell God about the things you want to ask him for in your prayers and your requests to him, and bring him your thanks too. 7And God's peace, which is beyond both our understanding and our contriving, will stand guard over your hearts and minds, because your life is linked for ever with the life of Christ Jesus.

8It only remains to say, brothers, that your thoughts must continually dwell on everything that is true, on everything that is nobly serious, on everything that is right, on everything that is pure, on everything that is lovely, on everything that is honourable, on all that men call excellence, and on all that wins men's praise. 9You must keep putting into practice the lessons you have learned from me, the instruction you have received from me, and the example I have given you in speech and in action. And then the God of peace will be with you.

10It is my great and truly Christian joy to know that, after so long an interval, your care for me has flowered again. I know that your care has always been there, but you never had the opportunity to show it. 11Don't think that I am saying this because I am thinking of all the things I have to do without. I have learned how to be content in any circumstances. 12I know how to live with less than enough, and I know how to live with more than enough. I have learned the secret of how to live in any situation and in all circumstances, of how to eat well and of how to go hungry, of how to have more than enough and how to have less than enough. 13He who fills me with his dynamic power has made me able to cope with any situation. 14All the same, I am very grateful to you for sharing with me when I am in trouble.

15You yourselves well know, my Philippian friends, that in the earliest days of the gospel, when I had left Macedonia, you were the only church by whom in partnership I was offered, and from whom I accepted, any financial help. 16Even when I was in Thessalonica you more than once sent help for my needs. 17It is not the gift that I am concerned about. What I am concerned about is the heavenly profit which accumulates to your account! 18You owe me nothing! You have more than paid your debt! I have all that I could possibly want now that I have received from Epaphroditus the gifts you sent. These gifts of yours were like a sweet-smelling offering to God, a sacrifice which he is glad to accept, and in which he delights. 19My God will supply everything you need out of the splendour of his wealth given you in Christ Jesus. 20Glory be to our God and Father for ever and ever! Amen.

21Give my good wishes to every one of God's dedicated people. Our fellow-Christians who are here with me send their good wishes to you. 22All God's people send you their good wishes, especially those on the imperial staff. 23The grace of the Lord Jesus Christ be with your spirit.

Introduction to the Letter to the Colossians

THE Letter to the Colossians was written about A.D.62, when Paul was in prison in Rome awaiting trial (4.3,18). It has a close resemblance to the Letter to the Ephesians and was written at the same time.

Paul himself had neither founded nor visited the church at Colosse (2.1). Its founder was probably Epaphras (1.7), and it was most likely founded in the missionary activity which took place when Paul was in Ephesus (Acts 19.10).

The congregation in Colosse was in good heart (1.3-8), and the letter was written rather to meet a situation which was threatening than a situation which had actually emerged. What was that situation?

At the back of the Letter to the Colossians there was a heresy which is at the back of much of the New Testament. Its name was Gnosticism, which means wisdom, and, in order to understand this letter, we have to understand this heresy.

The Gnostic began with the basic assumption that in the world there are two realities, spirit and matter, and that both are eternal; they have both been there since before the beginning of time. Out of this matter the world was made in the beginning; but the characteristic of this matter is that it is flawed; it is bad stuff. Therefore everything made out of it is bad. The inevitable consequence is that the body is bad. If the body is essentially and incurably bad, we may do one of two things with it. We may either practise a rigid asceticism in which we starve and neglect the body, or, since the body is bad anyway, and since it does not matter what happens to it, we may give it its way, and sate and glut its passions. In regard to the body, Gnosticism issues either in asceticism or in antinomianism.

But this belief has the most important consequences for the doctrine of creation. Spirit is altogether good, and God is spirit; matter is essentially flawed and evil. It follows that God cannot touch matter, and it therefore also follows that God cannot be the creator of the world. How then was the world created? God sent out an emanation and this emanation sent out another emanation and so on and on in an endless chain, until we come to a very distant emanation, who is so far from God that he can touch and handle matter. This distant emanation is the creator of the world. Further, as the emanations grow further and further from God, they become, first, more and more ignorant of God, and, finally, more and more hostile to God, so that the emanation who created the world is both totally ignorant of, and hostile to, the true God. The world is made of bad stuff by a lesser and ignorant god, who knows nothing of the true God, and who is hostile to him.

To get from this world to God, the soul has to pass up through the endless chain of emanations. To do this it needs to know their names and the pass-words. Gnosticism is therefore only for the clever intellectuals, and simple folk cannot know true religion at all. This is the heresy which the Letter to the Colossians combats. Let us trace the combat.

i. The Gnostics did not believe in the uniqueness of Jesus. Jesus was only one in the chain of the emanations between man and God. He might stand very high in the chain, maybe highest of all, but he is no more than one link in the chain. To meet this Paul insists that Jesus is nothing less than the image of God (1.15), that in him all knowledge and wisdom dwell (2.3), that he is indeed the fullness of God (1.19; 2.9). The Gnostic would of course deny the incarnation. The body is bad; Jesus could not have a body. But to Paul Jesus is all of God in bodily form (2.9).

ii. The Gnostic said that creation was carried out by an ignorant and hostile god. Paul insists that Jesus Christ the Son of God was God's agent in creation (1.16). The true love and power which are operative in redemption are also operative in creation.

iii. The Gnostic declared that he was offering a philosophy (2.8) possible only for the intellectual élite, the chosen few. Paul insists that Christianity is for every man and that every man can become perfect before God (1.28).

iv. The Gnostic sometimes practised asceticism. He passed food laws and regulations; he prescribed days and seasons and fasts; his motto was, 'Touch not, taste not, handle not.' This is all completely unchristian and against Christian freedom (2.16-23).

v. On the other hand, the Gnostic might let the body, bad anyway, have its way, and so become guilty of gross immorality. This, says Paul, a Christian must never do (3.5).

Paul closes the letter with his usual ethical section and his greetings.

We see how in this letter Paul takes the Gnostic heretical claims one by one, and meets them with Christ. This letter defends the church against a heresy which would have wrecked Christianity.

The Letter to the
COLOSSIANS

Chapter 1

THIS is a letter from Paul, who became an apostle of Christ Jesus because God willed it so, and from our colleague Timothy, ₂to the consecrated and loyal members of the Christian fellowship in Colosse. Grace be to you and every blessing from God our Father.

₃We always thank God, the Father of our Lord Jesus Christ, for you in our prayers, ₄because of the reports which have reached us of your Christian loyalty and of the way in which you show your love for all God's dedicated people. ₅You have this loyalty and love, because of the hope which is waiting ready for you in heaven, the hope of which you have already heard, ₆when the gospel arrived among you and its truth was preached to you. That gospel is spreading and producing lovely lives all over the world, just as it is among you from the day you first heard of God's grace and realized what it truly is. ₇You were taught it by Epaphras, our dear fellow-servant, who is Christ's loyal worker and our representative to you. ₈It was he who told us of that love of yours which the Spirit has inspired.

₉That is why, from the day on which news of you reached us, we never stop praying for you, and asking that you may be given spiritual wisdom and understanding, for then you will have complete insight into what God wants you to do. ₁₀We pray that your life and conduct will be worthy of the Lord and such as will be altogether pleasing to him. We pray that your life will be productive of all kinds of good action, and that you will continue to come to know God better and better. ₁₁We pray that in God's glorious strength you will receive power to cope with anything, a power which will enable you gladly to meet life with fortitude and patience. ₁₂We pray that you will be ever grateful to the Father who has made you fit to receive a share in the possession which he promised to his dedicated people in the realm of light. ₁₃It was he who rescued us from the grip of the power of darkness, and transferred us to the Kingdom of his dear Son. ₁₄It is through this Son that we have received the liberation which comes when sins are forgiven. 15He is the perfect likeness of the invisible God; his is the supremacy over all creation. 16For he is the agent by whom all things were created, in heaven and upon earth, visible and invisible, spiritual powers and beings, whether they be thrones or lordships or authorities or powers. He is the agent and the goal of all creation. 17He exists before everything else, and everything else holds together in him. 18The church is his body, and he is its head. He is its beginning, for he was the first to return from the dead, which means that there is no part of the universe in which the topmost place is not his, 19for by God's own decision God in all his completeness made his home in him. 20More, it was God's decision to effect through him an act of universal reconciliation to himself of everything in heaven and on earth, and it was through his death on the cross that God did bring the whole universe into a right relationship with himself.

21Once you were estranged from God; your minds were hostile; your conduct was evil. 22But now the situation has changed. God has changed your enmity into friendship to himself by the incarnation and death of his Son, and has thus brought you into his own presence, dedicated, innocent and blameless, 23provided that you remain firmly founded in your faith, immovable in the hope of the gospel which you have heard, the gospel which was proclaimed to the whole created world under heaven, the gospel of which I Paul have been made a servant.

24I am now happy to suffer for your sake. It is my privilege to fulfil the uncompleted sufferings which the work of Christ still entails, human being though I am, for the sake of his body, which is the church. 25Of that church I was made a servant because of the part in his work that God gave me to do for your sake. My particular office is to tell to men the whole message which God has sent, 26to tell the secret which only a disciple can know, the secret which has been hidden throughout the ages and the generations, and which has now been revealed to God's dedicated people. 27It was God's will to make the glorious wealth of his secret known to them, and to make it known to all nations. The secret is that Christ is in you, and therefore yours is the hope of future glory. 28It is he of whom we tell. And in so doing it is every man whom we warn; it is every man whom we instruct in all wisdom; for it is our aim to present every man as a mature Christian. 29It is for this that I toil, and it is his power working mightily in me which nerves me for the struggle.

Chapter 2

I WANT you to know the intensity of my efforts for you and for the people in Laodicea and for all those who have never personally met me. ₂I want their hearts to be encouraged. I want them to be welded together in love. I want them to experience all the wealth of conviction that insight brings, for then they will come to know and understand God's secret which only a disciple can know—and that secret is Christ. ₃In him all the treasures of wisdom and knowledge are hidden. ₄I am telling you this to prevent anyone leading you astray with speciously persuasive talk. ₅For, even if I am physically absent from you, I am with you in spirit, and it makes me very happy when I see the disciplined order and the staunch front which your Christian faith displays.

₆The tradition you have received is that of Jesus as Messiah and Lord. Your whole life and conduct therefore must be that of men who are indissolubly linked to him. ₇You must live as men who have their roots in him and whose life is founded on him and who are continually being reinforced by the faith which you were taught, and all the time you must be overflowing with gratitude. ₈You must be careful not to become the victims of an arid and misleading intellectualism, which is based on merely human tradition and on that elementary knowledge, which is all the world can supply, and not on Christ. ₉For it is in Christ that godhead in all its completeness dwells in bodily form. ₁₀It is in your union with him that your own life reaches perfected completeness. He is supreme over every demonic power and authority. ₁₁In your union with him too you were circumcised with a circumcision which was not a physical operation, but which consisted in stripping off your lower sensual nature, for that is the circumcision which Christ effects on you. ₁₂For in baptism you were buried with him, and in baptism you were also raised with him from the dead through your faith in the power of God, which was operative in raising him from the dead. ₁₃You were dead in sins; you were uncircumcised strangers to God, but God made you alive with Christ, for he forgave us for all our sins. ₁₄He cancelled the bond by which we were self-committed to the decrees of the law, and by which we stood condemned. He completely removed it and nailed it to the cross. ₁₅On the cross he stripped the demonic powers and authorities of their power, and made a public spectacle of them, as if they had been captives in a victor's triumphal procession.

16You must not therefore let anyone criticize you in matters of what it is right or wrong to eat or drink, or with regard to the alleged correct observance of festivals, new moons and sabbaths. 17These things are no more than the shadow of the things to come; the reality belongs to Christ. 18There are self-appointed umpires around who delight in asceticism and in angel worship, and who are always trying to penetrate further into their own world of fantasies. Their minds, dominated by a false idea of the importance of external things, inflate them with a senseless conceit. You must not let them disqualify you. 19They lose their grip on him who is the head, and it is only through its connection with him that the whole body, equipped and welded together by the joints and ligaments, grows as God meant it to grow.

20Your death with Christ means that the world's rudimentary teaching has nothing more to do with you. Why then go on living as if your life was dominated by the world? 21Why pay any more attention to those whose slogans are: 'Don't handle this! Don't taste that! Don't touch the next thing!'? 22All these regulations refer to things which are bound to perish in the course of being used. They move in the sphere of human regulations and human teaching. 23These things may bring a reputation for wisdom with their rigoristic piety, their deliberate self-abasement, their ascetic treatment of the body, but they are of no real value in the struggle against sensual indulgence.

Chapter 3

IF then you have been raised to life with Christ, your heart must be set on the great realities of that heavenly sphere, where Christ is seated at the right hand of God. 2Your constant concern must be with the heavenly realities, not with worldly trivialities. 3For you died to this world, and now you have entered with Christ into the secret life of God. 4When Christ, who is your life, comes again for all the world to see, then all the world will see that you too share his glory.

5Once, finally and for all you must put an end to the use of any part of your body for worldly and immoral purposes. Your new state must mean the death, as far as you are concerned, of fornication, impurity, unbridled passion, desire for the forbidden things, the spirit which makes a god of gain—for that is a kind of idolatry. ₆These are the things which incur the wrath of God. ₇There was a time when your life and conduct too were characterized by these things, a time when they were an integral part of your life. ₈But now you too must remove them all from your life—the long-nourished anger, the blaze of temper, maliciousness, abusiveness, foul language. These must no longer stain your lips. ₉There must be no more dishonesty to each other, for you have stripped off the old nature and all its works and ways, ₁₀and you have clothed yourselves with the new nature, which is progressively renewed, until it reaches fuller and fuller knowledge of God, and comes nearer and nearer to being in the image of its creator· ₁₁And so we have arrived at a state of things in which there is no distinction between Jew and Greek, circumcised and uncircumcised, barbarian, Scythian, slave and free man. Christ is all that matters, and there is neither person nor thing in which Christ is not.

₁₂You are God's chosen people, dedicated and dear to him. You must therefore clothe yourselves in compassion, in kindness, in humility, in gentleness, in patience. ₁₃You must bear with each other, and, if anyone has something to complain about in someone else, you must forgive each other. You must forgive each other as the Lord forgave you. ₁₄And, to crown all, you must clothe yourselves in love, which holds all the other qualities together and completes them. ₁₅Only Christ can enable men to live in a right relationship with each other. It is this unifying power of his which must dictate your every decision, for you were meant to be one united body. You must be thankful. ₁₆You must open your hearts to the message of Christ so that in all its riches it may find its home there. You must with all wisdom continually teach and advise each other. With heartfelt gratitude to him you must sing to God in psalms·and hymns and songs inspired by the Spirit. ₁₇Whatever you do and whatever you say, you must do and say it all as the representatives of the Lord Jesus, and all the time you must be giving thanks to God the Father through him.

₁₈You wives must accept the authority of your husbands, for this is fitting in a Christian household. ₁₉You husbands must love your wives, and must not be harsh to them.

₂₀You children must always obey your parents, for this is pleasing to God and proper for a Christian. ₂₁You fathers must not make life intolerable for your children, in case you take all the heart out of them.

₂₂You slaves must obey the orders of your human masters in every detail. You must not be the kind of workman who works only when he is watched, as if the only person you have to satisfy is some human being. You must be an honest workman, and the one person whose verdict you must respect is the Lord. 23Put the whole of yourselves into whatever you are doing, and do it, not as if you were doing it for men, but as if you were doing it for the Lord, 24for you well know that it is from the Lord you will receive the reward into which he has promised that you will enter. The master of whom you are the slaves is Christ. 25Wrong-doing will bring its own reward—and there is no favouritism with God.

Chapter 4

You masters must treat your slaves justly and fairly, for you well know that you too have a Master in heaven.

2You must never grow discouraged in prayer, and, when you pray, you must be unwearied in thanksgiving. 3Pray for us too. Pray to God to give us the opportunity to preach, to tell the secret of Christ, which only the disciple can know, that secret for the sake of which I am in prison. 4Pray to him to enable me to speak in such a way that I will open that secret to all, for that is what it is my duty to do. 5You must behave wisely to those outside the church. You must eagerly seize every opportunity that comes to you. 6Your conversation must always have charm and wit. You must study the art of giving the right answer to everyone you talk to.

7Tychicus, our dear Christian brother, our trusty helper, and our fellow-servant in the Lord's service, will give you all the news about how things are with me. 8The reason why I am sending him is to give you all the news about us and to cheer you up. 9I am sending with him Onesimus, our dear and trusty brother, who is one of yourselves. They will tell you all the news from here.

10Aristarchus, my fellow-prisoner, sends you every good wish, and so does Mark, Barnabas' cousin. You have already received instructions about him, to give him a welcome, if he comes to visit you. 11Jesus called Justus sends his good wishes too. These are the only Jewish Christians who are working with me for the Kingdom of God, and they have been a comfort to me. 12Epaphras, who is one of yourselves and Christ's servant, sends you his good wishes. He never stops praying strenuously for you, asking that you should stand fast, mature in your faith, firm in your convictions, always engaged in doing the will of God. 13I can testify how hard he works for you and for the people in Laodicea and in Hierapolis. 14Our dear friend Luke the doctor sends his good wishes, and so does Demas. 15I send all my good wishes to our fellow-Christians in Laodicea, and to Nympha and the congregation which meets in her house. 16When this letter has been publicly read in your group, make arrangements for it to be read in the congregation in Laodicea too. And you too must have the letter which is on the way to you from Laodicea read to your congregation. 17Say to Archippus: 'See that you fully discharge that duty which was entrusted to you in the Lord's service.'

18In my own handwriting—every good wish from Paul. Remember my chains. Grace be with you.

Introduction to the First and Second Letters to the Thessalonians

THE background to the Letters to the Thessalonian church is to be found in the story of Paul's work at Thessalonica in Acts 17.1-9.

Behind that story there is a situation of the first importance for the early Christian missionaries. As we learn from the story in Acts, Paul's stay in Thessalonica extended over no more than three weeks, and it ended in a situation in which he had to be smuggled out by night. As we learn from the letters themselves, the whole situation had left the new converts a legacy of serious trouble, in which life had become very dangerous (1.1.6; 1.2.9-16; 2.1.5).

The question which faced Paul was this. Was it possible in three weeks' work to lay the foundations of a Christian community, which would stand fast when things were difficult? If so, the evangelization of Europe in a life-time was a practical proposition. Or, was missionary work to be a long, slow process, in which the missionaries had to settle in a place for months or even years before a church could really be said to be founded? Thessalonica presented a test case.

It is no wonder that Paul was worried. In his worry he sent Timothy to find out how things were going (1.2.17-19; 1.3.1-6). It was when Timothy and Silas caught up with him again in Corinth (Acts 18.5) that Paul wrote his letters. In the letters three things appear.

i. Paul had no need to worry. The Thessalonians were standing fast (1.1.3-10; 1.3.6-10). It was clear that even a short campaign, even if it ended in the flight of the missionary, could be permanently effective.

ii. But there were other things. Paul had to meet criticism of himself. He was criticized as being concerned with what he could get out of his converts in power and in money. So he hotly denies that he had used flattery, that he had sought prestige, that he had been dictatorial (1.2.1-8). Above all, he hotly denies that he had ever made anything out of his converts, and points out that he had toiled night and day at his trade, so as not to be a burden to anyone (1.2.9-12; 2.3.7).

iii. A serious theological problem had arisen, and this problem is at the very heart of the Thessalonian correspondence.

An essential part of the Christian message was the return of Jesus Christ, the Second Coming. At that time the church, including Paul, expected the Second Coming at any moment. They expected it today, tomorrow, certainly within their own lifetime. In Thessalonica this produced two problems.

a) The Thessalonians were disturbed about what was to happen to those who died before the Second Coming arrived. Would they miss the glory? Paul assures them that those who died in Christ would lose nothing (1.4.13-18).

b) An even more serious problem came from the fact that many of the Thessalonians had stopped work, and were doing nothing but stand about talking in excited groups, waiting for the Second Coming. Ordinary everyday life had collapsed in this hysterical expectation. Paul tells them that there will be signs before the Second Coming emerges, and above all a last conflict with the forces of evil (2.1.3—2.2.16). He urges them not to stand idle and gossiping, but to get on with the day's work and to live life as it comes (2.3.6-13). His attitude is that, when Jesus Christ comes, a man cannot be found doing anything better than an honest day's work.

The Thessalonian letters show the practical problems of the early missionary and the theological problems which a not fully grasped faith must bring.

The First Letter to the
THESSALONIANS

Chapter 1

THIS is a letter from Paul and Silvanus and Timothy to the congregation of the Thessalonians who belong to God the Father and to the Lord Jesus Christ. Grace to you and every blessing.

2We always thank God for you all, when we mention you in our prayers. 3We continually remember in the presence of our God and Father the activity of your faith, and the toil of your love, and the constancy of your hope in our Lord Jesus Christ. 4You are brothers to us and dear to God. We know that God has chosen you, because our gospel came to you not simply as a message in words; it came with the dynamic power of the Holy Spirit, and carrying complete conviction. 5Equally, you know what we were like when we were with you, and that it was for your sake that we were what we were. 6As for you, you took us and the Lord as your example, for the coming of the Christian message brought you at one and the same time serious trouble and the joy which the Holy Spirit gives. 7The result was that you became an example to all in Macedonia and Achaea who accept the Christian faith. 8It is not only in Macedonia and Achaea that the message of the Lord has sounded out from you. The story of your loyalty to God has so spread all over that there is no need for us to say anything about it. 9Everywhere people are talking about you, and telling the story of the welcome you gave us, and of how you turned to God, and left your idols to become the servants of the real and living God, 10and to await the coming of his Son from heaven, that Son whom God brought back to life when he had died, Jesus who rescues us from the wrath which is coming on the world.

Chapter 2

You yourselves know, brothers, that our visit to you was not wasted time. ₂As you know, we came to you after experiencing insult and injury at Philippi. But God made us able freely and fearlessly to tell you the good news of God—and not without a struggle. ₃Our appeal to you is not the result of some delusion; there is no element of sensuality in it; it is not designed to deceive. ₄No! God tested us and thought us fit to be entrusted with the good news. That is the way in which we speak, not as if we were trying to win human approval. God tests men's hearts, and it is at his approval that we aim. ₅We did not come with flattering talk, as you are well aware, nor, God is our witness, did we ever use our message as a disguise for exploiting you. ₆We never tried to acquire a human reputation either in your eyes or in the eyes of anyone else. ₇We could quite well have made heavy demands as the envoys of Christ. So far from that, when we were living among you, we were as gentle as a nurse cherishing her children. ₈We cared for you so much that it was our desire to share with you, not only the good news of God, but even our very lives, because you were so dear to us. ₉You remember, brothers, how, when we proclaimed the good news of God to you, we laboured and toiled, how we worked night and day, to avoid being a burden to any of you. ₁₀You can give evidence, and so can God, how devoutly and justly and blamelessly we behaved to you who are believers. ₁₁As you know, we treated you as a father treats his children. ₁₂To each one of you individually we made our appeal and our plea, calling on you out of our own experience of Christ, to live lives worthy of the God who is calling you into his glorious Kingdom.

₁₃There is another reason why we continually thank God. We thank him because, when you received the message of God, which you heard from us, you accepted it not as a human message, but, as indeed it is, as a message from God—and that message is at work in you who believe. ₁₄You followed the example, brothers, of the Christian congregations in Judaea, because you too underwent the same suffering at the hands of your fellow-countrymen as they did at the hands of the Jews. ₁₅For the Jews killed both the Lord Jesus and the prophets, and persecuted us. They defy God; they are the enemies of the human race; ₁₆for they try to stop us bringing to the Gentiles that message by which the Gentiles can be saved. By this they put the finishing touch to their record of sin. But God's wrath has finally caught up with them.

17When, brothers, you and I were lost to each other for a short time, you were for us out of sight, but not out of mind. And so we longed all the more eagerly to see you face to face. 18We therefore wished to come to you—more than once I, Paul, planned this—but Satan blocked our road. 19What hope or joy or achievement can we lay claim to when we stand before our Lord Jesus when he comes— what except you? 20For it is you who are our glory and our joy.

Chapter 3

So then, when we could not stand it any longer, we decided that there was nothing for it but for us to be left behind in Athens alone, 2while we sent Timothy, our colleague and God's fellow-worker in spreading the good news of Christ, to encourage you to stand fast for your faith, 3and to urge that no one should be shaken by these troubles. You yourselves well know that, when we become Christians, we are bound to be involved in trouble. 4When we were with you, we warned you that we would be in trouble, and, as you know, it has turned out to be so. 5That is why, when I could stand it no longer, I sent to find out how your faith was surviving, for I was worried in case the tempter had tempted you, and all our hard work had gone for nothing.

6Timothy has just come back from you to us, and has brought us good news about your faith and love. He tells us that you always think kindly of us, and that you are longing to see us, just as much as we are longing to see you. 7So then, in all our distress and trouble the story of your faith has set our mind at rest about you. 8It makes life worth living for us, if you remain unshakably true to your Lord. 9How can we adequately thank God for you, and for all the joy you have brought us before our God? 10Night and day we keep pouring out our prayers to be allowed to see you again and to repair any deficiencies in your faith.

11It is our prayer that our God and Father himself and our Lord Jesus may open up the way for us to visit you. 12It is our prayer that the Lord may make your love for each other and for all men to grow until it overflows, just as ours does for you. 13It is our prayer that he may strengthen your hearts, until you can stand in blameless holiness before our God and Father, when our Lord Jesus comes with all those who are dedicated to him.

Chapter 4

IT remains to say, brothers, that there is something which I want to ask you to do and to urge upon you as a Christian fellowship. You have received instructions from us on how you must behave to please God, and indeed you do so behave. I want you to intensify your efforts more and more. ₂You know what orders the Lord Jesus gave us to give to you. ₃It is God's will that you should walk the road to holiness and that you should have nothing to do with fornication. ₄It is his will that each of you should know how to be master of his own body, to keep it in the road to holiness and to use it honourably. ₅You must not allow your body to be at the mercy of the passions and desires, as the heathen who are ignorant of God do. ₆No one must try to over-reach his fellowman in business, or try to exploit him, because, as we have already very definitely told you, the Lord exacts the penalty for all such actions.* ₇For God did not call us to live a life soiled with impurity; he called us to walk the road to holiness. ₈Therefore, to disregard these instructions is to disregard not man but God, who gives his Holy Spirit to us.

₉About the love which should be characteristic of the Christian fellowship, there is no necessity that I should write to you, for you yourselves have been taught by God to love one another. ₁₀And indeed you do keep this rule of love to all your fellow-Christians all over Macedonia. But, brothers, we urge you to intensify your efforts. ₁₁We urge you to have no other ambition than to live quietly, and to mind your own business, and to do an honest day's work, as we instructed you to do. ₁₂Then the people outside the church will admire your life and conduct, and you will be able to live in independence.

₁₃I do not want you, brothers, to get wrong ideas about those who sleep death's sleep, because I do not want you to grieve like those who are not Christians and who have nothing to hope for. ₁₄We believe that Jesus died and rose again. We therefore also believe that in the

*See Notes on pp. 575–6

same way God will bring with Jesus those who died in the Christian faith.

15What we are going to say to you, you must regard as a message from the Lord. We who are still alive, and who will survive until the Lord comes, will not take precedence over those who have already fallen asleep in death. 16The Lord himself will come down from heaven, with a shout of command, with the archangel's voice, when God's trumpet-call sounds. Then Christians who died believing in Christ will rise first. 17Then, after that, we who are still left alive will be caught up with them into the clouds, to meet the Lord in the air. And so we shall be always with the Lord. 18So then, this is the message with which you can comfort and encourage each other.

Chapter 5

THERE is no necessity, brothers, for me to write to you about the periods and dates of these events, 2for you yourselves well know that the day of the Lord is to come as a thief comes during the night. 3When people are talking of how peaceful and secure life is, then destruction will be on them, as suddenly as the labour pains come to a pregnant woman—and there will be no escape for them. 4But you, brothers, are not in the dark. The great day cannot catch up on you like a thief, 5for you are all sons of the light and sons of the day. We do not belong to the night or to the dark. 6So then, we must not sleep as the rest of the world does. We must be sleeplessly and soberly on the watch. 7Sleepers sleep at night; those who get drunk are drunk at night. 8But we who belong to the day must be sober. We must put on faith and love as a breastplate, and the hope of salvation as a helmet, 9for God has not destined us to be the victims of the divine wrath; he has destined us to win salvation through our Lord Jesus Christ, 10who died for us. He died for us so that, awake or asleep, we should live in his presence and his company. 11So then we must encourage each other, and we must always make life stronger and better for each other—as indeed you do.

12We ask you, brothers, to give full recognition to those who work so hard in your society, for they are your leaders in the Christian fellowship, and they are there to give you good advice. 13Hold them in the highest respect and affection because of the work they do. Nothing must ever be allowed to interrupt your personal relationships with each other. 14We appeal to you, brothers, to warn those who will not accept discipline, to encourage the nervous and timid, to help the weak, to have patience with everyone. 15You must see to it that no one tries to repay injury with injury. You must always aim at doing nothing but kindness to each other and to all.

16You must be happy all the time. 17You must never stop praying. 18You must find something to be grateful to God for in everything, for this is the way in which God wishes you who are Christians to live. 19You must not try to put a stop to the activity of the Spirit. 20You must not contemptuously dismiss the work and words of the prophets. 21You must test everything and retain what is good. 22You must have nothing to do with any kind of evil.

23It is my prayer that the God of peace may completely consecrate you. I pray that you may be kept sound in spirit, soul and body, for then you will be blameless, when our Lord Jesus Christ comes. 24You can rely on him who called you to do this for you.

25Brothers, pray for us too. 26Greet all the brothers with the kiss of peace. 27In the name of the Lord I charge you to have this letter read to the whole congregation.

28The grace of our Lord Jesus Christ be with you.

The Second Letter to the
THESSALONIANS

Chapter 1

THIS is a letter from Paul and Silvanus and Timothy to the congregation of the Thessalonians, who belong to God our Father and to the Lord Jesus Christ. ₂Grace to you and every blessing from God the Father and from the Lord Jesus Christ.

₃For us, brothers, it is nothing less than a duty always to thank God for you. That we should do so is fitting, because your faith goes from strength to strength, and your love for each other, of each for all and all for each, grows ever greater. ₄So much so is this the case that we cannot help telling God's other congregations how proud we are of you because of your fortitude and your unswerving loyalty amidst all the persecutions and the troubles you are going through. ₅It all goes to prove the justice of God's judgment, for it is designed to enable you to show that you deserve to be citizens of the Kingdom of God for which you are suffering. ₆For God in his justice is bound to square the account by sending trouble to those who trouble you, ₇and by sending relief to you who are now going through troubles, and to us too, when the Lord Jesus bursts from heaven on to the stage of history with his mighty angels ₈and in flaming fire, to execute divine vengeance on those who refuse to recognize God, and on those who refuse to obey the gospel of our Lord Jesus. ₉Men like that will pay the penalty of eternal destruction and banishment from the presence of God and his mighty glory. ₁₀This is what will happen on that great day when he comes to be welcomed with glory by his own dedicated people, and with awe and wonder by all who put their faith in him, and by you too, for you accepted the truth which out of our own experience we declared to you. ₁₁Our constant prayer for you is that our God will find you worthy of the invitation he sent to you, and that he may turn all your good intentions into actions, and powerfully help you to live the life that faith demands. ₁₂Then the name of the Lord Jesus will be glorified because of you, and you because of him, in the grace of our God and of the Lord Jesus Christ.

Chapter 2

WE want to speak to you, brothers, about the coming of our Lord Jesus Christ and about the way in which we are to be gathered to him. 2We want to ask you not to be suddenly thrown off your balance, and not to get into a state of panic because of some message which claims to be inspired, or some statement or some letter purporting to come from us, and alleging that the day of the Lord has already come. 3You must allow no one to deceive you in any way. That day cannot come until the Great Rebellion has taken place, until there appears upon the scene the man who is the incarnation of lawlessness, the man with God's doom on him, 4the universal enemy, the one who in his pride exalts himself against every divinity acknowledged by men and every object of man's worship, the one who in the end invades God's temple and takes his seat there, with the claim that he is God. 5You cannot have forgotten that I told you all this when I was still with you. 6You know about the restraining power which at present holds things in check, so that the Wicked One will not burst upon the world until his own proper time. 7For the power of lawlessness is secretly at work even now, but it will remain secret only until the restraining power is removed from the scene. 8Then the Lawless One will openly emerge, and the Lord Jesus will blast him out of existence with the breath of his mouth and with the blinding brilliance of his coming. 9It is the power of Satan which will be operative in the coming of the Lawless One. He will come equipped with all kinds of power and will produce miracles and wonders calculated to deceive. 10With all sin's power to mislead, he will come to those who are doomed to perish because they shut their minds to the love of truth which could have saved them. 11So God sends them a power which deludes them into believing what is a lie, 12and the end will be the judgment of all who refused to believe the truth and who deliberately chose sin.

13Brothers, you are dear to God, and we can do no other than always thank God for you, because God chose you as the first to be saved by the Spirit's consecrating power and by your acceptance of the truth. 14It was for that that he called you through the good news which we brought to you, because he wanted you to have as your own the glory of our Lord Jesus Christ. 15So then, brothers, stand fast, and keep a tight grip of the traditions you were taught by us, whether by word of mouth or by our letter. 16It is my prayer that our Lord Jesus Christ himself and God our Father, who loved us and gave us through his grace encouragement for time and eternity and a good hope, 17may give comfort and courage to your hearts, and make them strong always to do and to speak all that is good.

Chapter 3

IT only remains, brothers, to ask you to pray for us. Pray that the word of the Lord may make the same splendid progress as it did with you. 2Pray that we may be rescued from perverse and wicked men, for it is not all who have faith. 3You can rely on the Lord to strengthen you and protect you from the Evil One. 4The Lord gives us confidence in you, and we are sure that you are keeping, and will keep, our instructions. 5It is our prayer that the Lord may direct your hearts to remember the way in which God has loved you and all that Christ triumphantly went through for you.

6It is our order to you, brothers, in the name of the Lord Jesus Christ, to withdraw yourselves from any brother who is living a work-shy and indisciplined life and whose conduct does not agree with the tradition you received from us. 7You yourselves are well aware how you ought to take us as your pattern and example. For we did not live in an indisciplined idleness when we were with you. 8We never accepted our maintenance from anyone for nothing. So far from that, we sweated and toiled, we worked night and day, to avoid being a burden to any of you. 9It was not that we did not have the right to maintenance; it was to provide you with ourselves as a pattern and example to copy. 10For even when we were staying with you we used to insist to you that no man who was not willing to work should be allowed to eat. 11News has reached us that in your society there are some who are living workshy and indisciplined lives, idle in their own affairs, and interfering in everyone else's. 12Our instructions and our plea to such in the name of the Lord Jesus Christ are that they should go on quietly with their own business, and so earn their own living. 13As for you, brothers, never get tired of living the good life. 14If anyone pays no attention to what we have said in this letter, mark him well. Refuse to associate with him in the hope that that will make him ashamed of himself. 15I do not say that you must treat him as an enemy; you must warn him as a brother.

16I pray that the Lord of peace himself may give you every blessing at all times and in every way. The Lord be with you all.

17In my own handwriting—every good wish from Paul. This is the sign which authenticates every letter. This is my autograph. 18The grace of our Lord Jesus Christ be with you all.

Spirit and Matter
A Note on the Background of Thought in New Testament Times

THERE is a certain line of thought which was very common in the pagan world in New Testament times, and which invaded the thought of the church. We shall meet it in the Pastoral Epistles, that is, in First and Second Timothy and Titus, in Second Peter and in Jude, which are closely connected, and in First and Second John. Instead of explaining it each time we meet it in these various letters, it will be better if we outline it in the one place, so that the one account of it can be referred to in the introduction to all of these letters.

Greek thought was always suspicious of the body. So many of man's sins and troubles could be traced to the fact that he had a physical body, with all the weakness and all the tendency to sin, which are, so to speak, inherent in the body. So Plato could say that the body is 'the prison-house of the soul'. Epictetus could refer to himself as 'a poor soul shackled to a corpse'. Seneca could speak of 'the detestable habitation of the body'. This line of thought regarded the body, not as something to be saved, but as something to be destroyed, whereas from the very beginning Christian thought regarded man as body, soul and spirit, all of which had their place in God's plan, and all of which could be saved. Christian thought never regarded salvation as being the end of one half of man, the physical half; it regarded salvation as being the saving of the total man.

This line of Greek thought is the basis of Gnosticism, of which we have already spoken in the introduction to the Letter to the Colossians. A Gnostic was a man who, as they claimed, had *gnōsis*, which is wisdom, and Gnosticism is the way of wisdom.

Gnosticism is based on a complete dualism. That is to say, it is based on a complete opposition between spirit and matter. It held that from the beginning spirit, that is God, and matter had existed. Creation was, therefore, not creation out of nothing, but creation out of already existing matter. The trouble was, as they saw it, that this matter was essentially flawed and evil; it was bad stuff; and it was out of this bad stuff that the world was created.

Since God is pure spirit and altogether good, he cannot himself touch this evil matter at all. He therefore put out a series of emanations or aeons, as they called them. There were many of these aeons. Each one in the series was a little further from God. Each one in the series was a little more ignorant of God. Finally, at the end of the series you come to aeons who are not only ignorant of God, and distant from God, but also hostile to God. It was by such an aeon, the Demiurge, the world-maker they called him, that this world was created. The world then was not created by the true God, but by an ignorant and hostile god. All this had certain consequences.

If matter is bad, then the body is bad as such. It cannot be reformed, or cured, or amended; it is bad as such. Such a belief will issue in one of two things.

a) It can issue in asceticism, in which the body is to be neglected and starved and held down, and in which all the things of the world are to be despised and used as little as possible. This line can become tied up with the Jewish Law, which with its food laws and regulations can be taken to be at least part of the rigid asceticism which is demanded.

b) It can equally issue in antinomianism, the complete neglect of all laws of morality. For, if the body is already evil, it does not matter what you do with it. Since it is in any event bad, its passions and desires may be sated and glutted, and it will make no difference.

It must be noted that this antinomian line of thought can pervert the doctrine of grace into its ally. In Romans 6 Paul deals with those who advocate sinning to give grace more and more chances to abound. The argument is that the grace of God is the greatest thing in the world; it can forgive every sin; therefore the more you sin, the more you give this wonderful grace the chance to operate. Sin then is a good thing, for it simply brings more and more grace.

So then, there was a line of thought which argued, either that sin did not matter, or that sin was a good thing in that it produced more and more grace.

All this line of thought has obvious repercussions about what will be believed about Jesus. If matter is evil, and if Jesus is the Son of God, then it follows that Jesus cannot have had a human body, so they argued. This produced the belief called Docetism. *Dokein* means *to seem*; Docetism is *Seemism*. They believed that Jesus only *seemed* to be a man. He had no real body; he was a phantom in human shape. So they said that he left no footsteps on the ground, when he walked. When you touched him there was nothing there to touch. There was no such thing as the incarnation, because it was impossible for the

Son of God to take an essentially evil body. The manhood and the humanity of Jesus were destroyed.

It also, of course, impinges on the doctrine of the resurrection. If Jesus had nothing but a phantom body, he did not ever really suffer; and if the body is essentially evil, then clearly there was no bodily resurrection. It becomes easy to see how very dangerous this teaching was.

But this Gnosticism produced something else. It also disturbed human relationships. If matter is evil, then the supreme aim is for the spirit of man to escape from the evil of the body and to rise to God. But, as we have seen, between this world with its evil matter and the God who is pure spirit there stretch a whole series and ladder of aeons. Each of these aeons was equipped with a name and with a genealogy. Long and complicated histories and stories were attached to each of them. Further, to get past them, a whole series of pass-words was required. To learn these myths and genealogies, to acquire these pass-words, needed high intellectual power. It was not possible for simple people. And so full salvation, full escape from matter to spirit, from the world to God, was only possible for an intellectual élite. And so Gnosticism, instead of enabling Christians to love one another, produced a situation in which Christians learned to despise one another, and the fellowship of the church was broken and interrupted.

Continuous glimpses of this line of thought will be seen behind the New Testament books, and especially behind the Pastoral Epistles, Second Peter and Jude, and First and Second John. The reader should watch for these signs as he reads.

Introduction to the First and Second Letters to Timothy and the Letter to Titus

THESE three letters are always called the Pastoral Epistles, a title which was given to them by Paul Anton in 1726. Prior to that they had been called the Ecclesiastical Epistles because they had so much instruction to give about the church. They are called the Pastoral Epistles, because they have so much to say about the character and the duty of those who are the pastors of the church. It has been said that their message can be summed up in the words of 1 Timothy 3.15: 'How to behave in the household of God'.

As we read them, one thing must always be remembered. They come from a time when the church was like a little island in a surrounding sea of paganism. It was so short a time since the converts had come into the church from paganism; the influences of paganism were so strong. The danger of relapse was insistent and constant. That is why it has been said that these letters are the most relevant of all New Testament letters in the mission field to this day. It is then only to be expected that they will have much to say about the Christian duty.

There is a duty to those outside the church. The Christian office-bearer must be well spoken of by people outside (1 Timothy 3.7). Religion must be no conventional thing which has no dynamic in it (2 Timothy 3.-19). A profession which practice denies is not to be tolerated (Titus 1.16).

The Christian has a duty to the state. He must pray for those who rule, and he must himself be a good citizen (1 Timothy 2.1,2; Titus 3.1).

The duties and the necessary characteristics of the various people within the church are laid down. The elders and the bishops are described (1 Timothy 3.1-8; 5.17-22; Titus 1.5-9). The deacons are described (1 Timothy 3.8-13). By this time the church had in it an order of widows (1 Timothy 5.3-16). The place of women is laid down, and they are forbidden to teach, a necessary restriction in Greek society, in which a forward woman would have automatically been regarded as an immoral woman (1 Timothy 2.11-15).

The duties of slaves are laid down, for the Christian slave must be a good slave (1 Timothy 6.1,2; Titus 2.9,10). The danger of riches is stressed (1 Timothy 6.6-10, 17-19).

There is much stress on keeping the faith, that is, on maintaining strict orthodoxy (2 Timothy 1.13,14; 3.14; Titus 1.9; 2.1).

This is all the more necessary, because at the back of these letters there is a heresy and a mistaken teaching to which continuous reference is made. It has myths; it has endless genealogies; it has speculations. It is given to argument and to discussion; it has a morbid craving for controversy; it has no true knowledge. It forbids people to marry, and tries to lay down ascetic food laws and is connected with Judaism. It declares that the resurrection is already past (1 Timothy 1.3-11; 4.1-5; 4.7; 6.4,5; 2 Timothy 2.14-16; 2.18; 4.2; Titus 1.10; 1.14; 3.9). It is easy to see that this is just the kind of situation that Gnostic speculations produced.

There are a great many scholars who do not think that these letters come from the hand of Paul as they stand. The style is different, much more matter of fact. The church with its elders and bishops and deacons and widows seems a much more highly developed institution than ever it was in the missionary days of Paul. Faith tends to be orthodoxy rather than personal relationship with Jesus Christ. In Paul's life as we know it there is no room for a ministry to Crete (Titus 1.5), unless Paul was released after his arrest and was free to work for some time before he was finally martyred. This is possible, but, if it was so, we have no information.

And yet in these letters there are a number of passages which are very personal to Paul and his life (1 Timothy 1.1-20; 2 Timothy 1.11,12; 1.15-18; 3.10,11; 4.6-21; Titus 3.12,13). It is just possible that what happened was that, after Paul's death, a devoted friend and follower of his took certain personal letters he had from Paul and added a message for the church of his day, and sent it out in the name of his great missionary master.

The First Letter to
TIMOTHY

Chapter 1

THIS is a letter from Paul, who is an apostle of Christ Jesus by the command of God our Saviour and of Christ Jesus our hope, ₂to Timothy his own true son in the faith. Grace, mercy and every blessing to you from God the Father and from Christ Jesus our Lord.

₃When I set out for Macedonia, at my urgent request you stayed on in Ephesus. What I wanted you to do was to give my orders to certain individuals to stop teaching doctrines which are a contradiction of the Christian faith, ₄and to give up spending their time and energy in the study of myths and genealogies to which there is no end, and which only provide recondite and abstruse speculations instead of helping to further God's scheme of salvation, the central principle of which is faith. ₅This order of mine has no other object than to promote the love which issues from a clean heart, a good conscience, and a sincere and genuine faith. ₆There are some people who have aimed at all the wrong things. They have lost the right way, and have ended up in a welter of arid and futile speculative discussions. ₇They would like to be instructors in the Christian ethic, but in fact they do not know what they are talking about, and they have no proper understanding of the things on which they lay so much stress.

₈We know that the law is a splendid thing, when it is used as it ought to be used. ₉We know very well that the law is not directed against the good man; it is directed against the lawless and the law-defying, against the impious and the sinner, against the irreligious and the irreverent, against patricides and matricides, against murderers, ₁₀fornicators, homosexuals, kidnappers, liars, perjurers, against anyone or anything which is hostile to sound teaching, ₁₁the teaching which agrees with the glorious good news sent by the blessed God to mankind, the teaching with which I have been entrusted.

₁₂It was Christ Jesus our Lord who gave me the strength for the responsibility of this task. My gratitude goes out to him because he believed that he could trust me, and appointed me to do this service for him, 13in spite of the fact that I formerly abused and persecuted and wantonly insulted him. But he treated me with mercy, because I acted in ignorance in the days before I came to believe. 14My sin was great, but the grace of our Lord was still greater, and with it there came the faith and love which are to be found in Christ Jesus. 15Christ Jesus came into the world to save sinners—this is a saying which you can believe and accept absolutely—and I am the worst of them. 16But I received mercy, and it was for this reason. Christ Jesus wanted me to be the first in whom he might display all his patience for everyone to see, because he wanted me to be an example of those who were going to believe in him, and so find eternal life. 17To the eternal King, immortal, invisible, the only God, be honour and glory for ever and ever. Amen.

18Such are the instructions which I entrust to you, son Timothy, and I do so with confidence, because I remember how what the prophets said about you first directed me to you. I want you to remember what they said, and to wage a good campaign, 19armed with faith and a clear conscience. It is because they defied conscience that there are some who have made shipwreck of their faith. 20Among these are Hymenaeus and Alexander. I have consigned them to Satan. They must be taught by discipline not to insult God.

Chapter 2

First of all, I urge you to offer petitions, prayers, intercessions, thanksgivings for all men. 2Pray for kings and for all who hold high office. Thus we will be able to live a quiet and peaceful life, in all reverence to God and in all dignity to man. 3Such prayer is a lovely thing. It is the kind of prayer that God our Saviour wants to hear, 4for he wants all men to be saved and to arrive at a knowledge of the truth. 5There is one God, and one Mediator between God and man, Christ Jesus in his humanity, 6for he sacrificed himself as the price of freedom for all men. And that sacrifice of his is the proof and guarantee, given in his good time, that God's desire is indeed the salvation of all mankind. 7Of this truth I was appointed a herald and apostle—it is the truth I am telling you and no lie—to teach the Gentiles the true faith.

8I would therefore wish that wherever you meet for public worship prayers should be offered by the men of the congregation. The hands they lift to God in appeal must be pure. Angry arguments must have no place in your meeting. 9In the same way, women must dress neatly, modestly and soberly. They must not use elaborate hair-styles; they must not wear jewellery of gold and pearls; they must not dress in extravagantly expensive clothes. 10They must be clothed in good conduct, as befits women who profess to be worshippers of God. 11It is a woman's duty to learn quietly and to live submissively. 12I do not allow a woman to teach or to have authority over men. A woman must keep quiet, 13for Adam was made first, then Eve. It was not Adam who was led astray. 14It was the woman who was led astray, and who became the victim of sin. 15But women will be saved by motherhood, if they continue to live faithfully and lovingly, modestly walking the way to holiness.

Chapter 3

IT has been said, and said truly, that to be ambitious to be the leader and guardian of the community is to set one's heart on a noble task. 2The superintendent of the community must therefore be a man whom no one can criticize. He must be the faithful husband of one wife. He must be abstemious, wise in the art of living, with an ordered beauty in his life. He must be hospitably inclined and he must be skilled in teaching. 3He must not be too fond of wine. He must be gentle and not pugnacious. He must be peaceable and money must have no attraction for him. 4He must preside well over his own family, with children who give him complete obedience and perfect respect. 5If a man does not know how to preside over his own household, how can he look after one of God's congregations? 6He must not be a new convert, in case he should become inflated with a sense of his own importance, and so incur the same judgment that was passed on the Devil for his pride. 7He must have a good reputation among those who are not members of the church, for he must never incur the risk of making himself a target for abuse, and he must never provide ammunition for the slanderer.

8In the same way, the deacons must be serious men. They must not be the kind of men who say one thing to one person and another to another. They must not be too fond of wine, nor must they be prepared to make money by disreputable methods. 9They must combine a disciple's knowledge of the Christian faith with a clear conscience. 10They must first undergo a period of probation. If they emerge from it with a clear record, they must then enter upon the work of a deacon. 11Their wives too must be serious women. They must not be given to malicious scandal-mongering. They must be abstemious and completely trustworthy. 12Deacons must be the faithful husbands of one wife. They must control their children, and preside well over their own households. 13Deacons who successfully carry out their office win for themselves a high standing in the church, and they receive the right to speak very freely in matters of the Christian faith.

14I am writing this letter to you, although I hope to come to see you fairly soon. 15I am sending it to you, because, if I am delayed, I want you to know how to behave in God's household, and God's household is the church of the living God, a pillar and buttress of the truth. 16No one can deny the greatness of the truth of our religion, the truth which only a disciple can understand:

> He appeared in a human body;
> was vindicated in the spirit;
>   was seen by angels;
> was preached among the nations;
>   was believed in all over the world;
>   was taken up in glory.

Chapter 4

THE Spirit expressly says that in later times there will be some who will become deserters from the faith, and who will listen to spirits, who will lure them from the right way, and to the teaching of demons. 2The demons will operate through men whose teaching is a mixture of insincerity and lies, men whose own conscience bears the brand-mark of the Devil burned into it. 3Such teachers try to stop people marrying. They try to teach them to abstain from certain foods, foods which God created to be received with gratitude by those who are believers and who know the truth. 4For everything that God created is good. Nothing is to be rejected. Everything is to be received with thanksgiving, 5for it is consecrated by God's word and by prayer.

6If you remind the Christian fellowship of these basic truths, you will be a good servant of Christ Jesus, and all the time you will continually nourish your soul on the words of faith, and on that fine teaching of which you have become a follower. 7You must have nothing to do with myths, which are quite profitless for religion, and which are no better than old wives' tales. Train yourself for the life whose goal is God. 8Physical training has a limited usefulness, but to live the life whose goal is God has an unlimited usefulness, for it promises life now and life to come. 9This is a saying which you can believe and accept absolutely. 10It is for that reason that we accept both the strict discipline of training and the stern struggle of the contest, because we have set our hope on the living God, who is the Saviour of all men, and above all the Saviour of those who believe.

11Hand on these instructions and this teaching. 12It would be wrong for anyone to look down on you because you are young. It is rather your duty to provide an example of what a believer should be, in your speech, in your conduct, in love, in reliability, in purity. 13While you are waiting for me to come, give your attention to the public reading of scripture, to the exhortation of the congregation, and to teaching. 14Do not neglect the special gift the Spirit gave you. It was given to you through the words of the prophets, when the elders as a body laid their hands on you. 15Give your continuous attention to these things. They must be your whole life, and then no one will be able to fail to see your all-round progress. 16Pay attention to yourself and to your teaching. If you do, you will save both yourself and your hearers.

Chapter 5

IF you have occasion to find some fault with an older man, do not do so harshly. Appeal to him, as you would to a father. Treat younger men as your brothers, 2older women as your mothers, younger women as your sisters. Then your relationship with them will be completely pure.

3You must honour widows, who are genuinely widows. 4If a widow has children or grandchildren, her own younger relatives must first learn to discharge what is a religious duty to their own family, and to repay the debt which they owe to their parents and grandparents, for this is what God approves. 5But a genuine widow, who is left all alone in the world, has no other hope than God, and night and day she spends all her time telling him her needs and praying to him. 6As for a widow who lives a life of extravagant luxury, although she may be physically alive, she is spiritually dead. 7Pass on these instructions, for the widows must be beyond criticism. 8To make no provision for one's own people, and especially for one's own family, is to deny our

Christian faith, and to be worse than an unbeliever. ₉To be enrolled, a widow must be at least sixty years old. She must have been the faithful wife of one husband. ₁₀She must have a reputation for good works. She can only be enrolled, if she has brought up children, if she has practised hospitality, if she has been prepared to render the most menial service to God's people, if she has been in the habit of helping people in trouble, if good works of every kind have been the aim and object of her life. ₁₁Do not place younger widows on the roll. For, when passion makes them grow restive under the discipline of Christ, they want to marry, ₁₂and so stand condemned, because they have broken their pledge to him. ₁₃At the same time they learn to be idle, and to spend their time on a continual round of social visits. They learn not only to be idle; they learn to gossip, and to poke their noses into everyone's business, chattering about things that should not be talked about at all. ₁₄I would like the younger widows to marry, to have children, to preside over a house and home, and to give none of those who are hostile to us an opportunity to spread their slanders about us. ₁₅Some of them have already lost the way, and gone to the Devil. ₁₆Any Christian man or woman who has widows within the family circle must personally support them. The congregation must not be asked to carry a burden of responsibility for people like that; it must be left free to support those who are genuinely widows.

₁₇Elders who exercise an efficient leadership should be reckoned as worthy of double pay, especially those strenuously engaged in preaching and teaching. ₁₈For scripture says: 'You must not muzzle the ox when it is treading the corn,' and, 'The workman deserves his pay.' ₁₉Do not accept any charge against an elder, unless it is supported by the evidence of two or three witnesses. ₂₀Consistent sinners must be publicly convicted to make the others healthily afraid. ₂₁Before God and Christ Jesus and the holy angels I charge you to keep these rules, and never to prejudge an issue or to act other than impartially. ₂₂Do not be in too big a hurry to ordain anyone to the eldership. Do not get yourself involved in the sins of others. Keep yourself clean. ₂₃Don't go on drinking nothing but water. Use a little wine for the sake of your stomach and your frequent attacks of sickness.

₂₄Some men's sins are so notorious that the court knows all about them long before they come up for trial. The sins of others have not caught up with them yet. ₂₅In the same way good deeds are evident for all to see, and, even if they are not, they cannot in the end be hidden.

Chapter 6

ALL those who are under the yoke of slavery must recognize that their masters have a right to all respect. If they fail to see this, the name of God and the Christian teaching will get a bad reputation. 2If their masters happen to be believers, they must not treat them with any the less respect because they are brothers within the Christian community. So far from that, they must try to be all the better slaves, because those who are receiving their service are their brothers in faith and love.

This is what you must teach, and this is what you must urge upon your hearers. 3If anyone's teaching is at variance with this, and if he does not take his stand on sound instruction—and by that I mean the instruction which our Lord Jesus Christ gave—and on truly religious teaching, 4he is inflated with conceit. Instead of having a real grasp of the truth, he has an unhealthy passion for speculations and for hair-splitting arguments, which are bound to issue in jealousy and in controversy, insults, and in an atmosphere poisoned with suspicion 5and in continuous friction, which are all characteristic of men who have become mentally depraved and deprived of the truth. They are characteristic of men who regard their religion as a profit-making concern. 6And indeed there is great profit in religion for the man who has learned the secret of needing nothing outside himself. 7For we brought nothing into the world, for the very good reason that, when we come to leave it, we can take nothing out of it. 8Given food to eat and clothes to wear, we have quite enough to be going on with. 9Those who want to be wealthy run the risk of encountering many a temptation, and falling into many a trap, and of developing a great many senseless, and even hurtful, ambitions, which are liable to plunge men into wreck and ruin. 10For the love of money is the root from which all evils grow. It is this uncontrolled craving for money which has made some people lose the way, and caused them to experience the sting of many a bitter pang.

11You are a man of God, and therefore you must have nothing to do with these things. Justice, godliness, fidelity, love, fortitude, gentleness—these you must make the object of all your endeavour. 12Strain every nerve, as the noble athlete of faith, to win the prize of eternal life. It was to this you were called, when you nobly and publicly confessed your faith in the presence of many witnesses. 13I charge you in the presence of God, the universal giver of life, and of Christ Jesus, who before Pilate nobly witnessed to his faith, 14never to blot your copy-book, never to lay yourself open to criticism, but to obey your orders, until the Lord Jesus Christ appears. 15And that appearance will be displayed in his own good time by the blessed and only Sovereign, the King of kings, the Lord of lords, 16the One who alone possesses immortality, whose home is in the light that no man can approach, whom no man has ever seen or can see. To him be honour and might that knows no end! Amen.

17Tell those who are wealthy in this world's goods not to be arrogant, and not to place their hopes on money with all its uncertainty, but on God who richly provides us with everything to enjoy. 18Tell them to be kind, to find their wealth in lovely deeds, to be quick to give and ready to share. 19Then they will provide themselves with a treasure on which they can build well for the future. Thus they will grasp the life which is real life.

20My dear Timothy, keep what has been entrusted to you safe. Turn your back on godless and meaningless chatter, and on the contradictory statements of that knowledge, which it is a lie to call knowledge. 21There are some who profess to have knowledge, but, as far as the faith is concerned, they have missed the mark.

Grace be with you all.

The Second Letter to
TIMOTHY

Chapter 1

This is a letter from Paul, who is an apostle of Christ Jesus, to his dear son Timothy. I am an apostle because God willed that I should be, and my work is to bring to men the promised life which Christ Jesus can give them. ₂Grace, mercy and every blessing to you from God the Father and from Christ Jesus our Lord.

₃I serve God with a good conscience as my forefathers did before me, and I thank him, when night and day I continually remember you in my prayers. ₄I remember the tears you shed when we parted, and I am longing to see you again. Nothing could make me happier than that. ₅I am reminded of the sincerity of your faith. It was a faith like that, which long before this had its home in the heart of your grandmother Lois and your mother Eunice—and I am quite sure that it is in your heart too. ₆That is why I want to remind you to kindle to a flame God's gift, which came to you, when I laid my hands upon you at your ordination. ₇For God did not give us the spirit of cowardly fear; he gave us the spirit of power, of love, and of self-discipline. ₈Don't be ashamed publicly to declare your loyalty to our Lord. Don't be embarrassed that I am in gaol for his sake. Join the company of sufferers for the gospel, and God will give you strength. ₉It is that same God who saved us and called us to a life dedicated to himself. He did not call us because we had done anything to deserve it. He called us because it was his purpose to do so. He called us in the grace which has been given to us in Christ Jesus. That grace existed in God's purpose before time began, ₁₀and has now been fully displayed for all to see through the coming to earth of our Saviour Christ Jesus, who destroyed death and brought life and immortality to light through the good news. ₁₁For the service of the good news I was appointed a herald, an apostle and a teacher. ₁₂That is the reason why I am in the situation in which I now am. But I am not ashamed of it. I know the person to whom I have entrusted my life, and I am absolutely sure that he can protect what I have placed in his safe-keeping, until the great day comes. 13Take as the standard by which you live the sound instruction which you received from me. Live in that loyalty and love which come into life when Christ Jesus becomes the very atmosphere in which you exist. 14By the help of the Holy Spirit, who has his home within you, keep safe the noble gift which has been entrusted to you.

15You already know that everyone in the province of Asia has deserted me, including Phygelus and Hermogenes. 16I pray for God's mercy for the family of Onesiphorus. His visits have always been like a breath of fresh air to me. He was not ashamed to visit me in gaol. 17So far from that, when he arrived in Rome, he made every effort to search for me until he found me. 18The Lord grant him to find mercy from the Lord on the great day! And you know even better than I do all the service he rendered to the church in Ephesus.

Chapter 2

Fortify your life with the dynamic influence of that grace which enters life, when Christ Jesus becomes the atmosphere in which we live. 2Take the instruction I gave you in the presence of many witnesses, and hand it over to men on whom you can rely, and who are such that they will be competent to communicate to others what they themselves have learned. 3Like a good soldier of Christ Jesus, join the company of those who are prepared to suffer for their faith. 4No soldier on active service gets involved in civilian affairs; he has no other aim than to satisfy his commanding officer. 5No athlete will win the victor's laurel crown, unless he keeps the rules of the game. 6The farmer who has done all the hard work has the first right to share in the crops. 7Think over what I am saying to you. The Lord will make you able to understand all about it.

8Remember Jesus Christ, risen from the dead, descended from David. This is what my gospel teaches. 9It is for the sake of that gospel that I am at present suffering, even to the length of being imprisoned as a criminal. But no one can put the word of God in prison. 10It is for the sake of God's chosen ones that I can pass the breaking-point and not break. I want them too to win that salvation which is ours because of what Christ Jesus has done for us, and with it the glory that is eternal. 11It has been said, and said truly:

If we have died with him,
we shall live with him;
12if we endure,
we shall reign with him;
if we deny him,
he too will deny us;
13if we are faithless,
he remains faithful,
for he cannot deny himself.

14Keep on reminding them of all this. Charge them before God not to engage in pugnacious debates about verbal niceties. Debates like that are an unprofitable occupation, and do nothing but undermine the faith of the hearers. 15Do your best to present yourself to God as a man of sterling worth, a workman who has no need to be ashamed of his work, a sound expositor of the true word. 16Avoid empty and irreverent chatter. Those who indulge in it make fast and excellent progress in irreligion. 17The damaging effects of their teaching will spread like a cancerous ulcer. Hymenaeus and Philetus are men like that. 18Their idea of the truth is well off the mark, for they say that our resurrection has already taken place, a statement which upsets some people's faith. 19The firm foundation God laid still stands, sealed with this inscription: 'The Lord knows those who are his,' and, 'Everyone who takes the name of the Lord on his lips must turn his back on wickedness.' 20In any great house there are utensils not only of gold and silver; there are utensils of wood and earthenware too. Some are put to an honourable use, and some to a menial use. 21Anyone who cleanses himself from the things we have been talking about will be a utensil fit for honourable use, dedicated to God, useful to his master, equipped to render every useful service. 22Leave the hot passions of youth behind. Consistently take as your aim justice, fidelity, love, right relationships with those whose appeal is sincerely to the Lord. 23Refuse to take any part in senseless and illiterate speculations, for you are well aware that they can result in nothing but controversies. 24The Lord's servant must not be quarrelsome; he must be characteristically kindly. He must be a good teacher. He must have a mind above resentment. 25When he has to exercise discipline upon those who oppose him, he must do so in the strength of gentleness, for it may be that God will lead them to repentance and to a knowledge of the truth. 26True, they were captured alive by the Devil, but it may be that they will come to their senses and escape from his trap, and end up by accepting God's will.

Chapter 3

You must realize that in the last days difficult times will come. 2There will be men who love nothing but self and money. They will be boastful, arrogant and abusive. They will have no respect for parents, and no gratitude to any man. They will be without reverence to God 3and without natural affection to men. They will be implacable in their enmities and slanderous in their words. They will be intemperate and savage. They will see nothing to love in goodness. 4They will be treacherous, reckless, inflated with conceit. They will love pleasure more than they love God. 5They will retain the outward conventions of religion, but they will consistently deny its dynamic. Refuse to associate with people like that. 6It is people like that who insinuate themselves into houses and thus get into their clutches silly women, who are burdened by their sins of the past and driven by all kinds of desires, 7women who go from teacher to teacher, and who remain quite incapable of ever arriving at a knowledge of the truth. 8Jannes and Jambres rebelled against Moses, and they too rebel against the truth. They are men with corrupt minds and a counterfeit faith. 9But they will not get very far. Their folly will be publicly exposed as that of Jannes and Jambres was.

10But you have been my comrade in my teaching, my way of life, my purpose, my faith, my patience, my love, my fortitude. 11You have been my partner in my persecutions and my sufferings. You know what happened to me in Antioch, in Iconium, in Lystra. You know what persecutions I had to go through. The Lord rescued me from all of them. 12All who choose to live a godly life as Christians will be persecuted. 13Malicious men and impostors will go from bad to worse, deceiving others and themselves deceived. 14You must refuse to move from the things you have been taught and have accepted as true, and you must never forget from whom you learned them. 15Nor must you forget that from your childhood days you have known the sacred scriptures, which, if you have faith in Christ Jesus, can give you the wisdom that leads to salvation. 16Every divinely inspired scripture is also useful for the teaching of the truth, for the refutation of error, for moral correction, and for training in the good life. 17Its aim is to make the man of God fit for his task, and to equip him for every kind of useful work.

Chapter 4

I CHARGE you before God and Christ Jesus, who will judge the living and the dead, I charge you by his coming appearing and his coming reign, 2proclaim your message. Urge it upon people whether you can take an opportunity or have to make an opportunity. Use argument, rebuke, appeal, with all the patience that good teaching needs. 3The time will come when they will refuse to listen to sound teaching. They will collect a motley assortment of teachers to tickle their ears by telling them the things they want to hear. 4They will deliberately shut their ears to the truth, and will wander down the byways of mythology. 5You must retain your sanity of mind. You must be prepared to suffer. You must act like a man who has good news to tell. You must leave no part of your Christian service incomplete.

6Men pour out a cup of wine as a sacrifice to their gods, and the last drops of my life are being poured out on the altar of sacrifice. The time for me to strike camp has come. 7My wrestling days are over, and I have fought well. For me the race is finished now. And I have kept my pledge. 8Now there awaits me the victorious athlete's laurel crown, which is the prize of life lived well. The Lord, the just Judge, will give it to me on that great day, and not only to me, but to all who lovingly longed for him to appear.

9Do your best to come to see me soon. 10Demas has left me. He fell in love with this world. He has gone to Thessalonica. Crescens has gone to Galatia, and Titus to Dalmatia. 11Only Luke is with me. Get Mark and bring him with you. He can render me useful service. 12I have sent Tychicus to Ephesus. 13When you come, bring me the cloak I left in Carpus' house at Troas. Bring me the books, and specially the parchments. 14Alexander the coppersmith did me a lot of harm. The Lord will give him what he has earned for what he has done. 15You too must watch him, because he bitterly opposed our message.

16At my first appearance in court on trial, no one supported me. Everyone deserted me. I pray that it may not be held against them. 17But the Lord stood by me and gave me strength, and so through me the Christian message in all its fullness was proclaimed, and all the Gentile world heard it, and I was rescued from the lion's mouth. 18The Lord will rescue me from every wicked attack on me. He will keep me safe until his heavenly kingdom comes. Glory be to him for ever and ever! Amen.

19Give my good wishes to Prisca and Aquila, and to Onesiphorus' family. 20Erastus stayed on at Corinth. I left Trophimus ill at Miletus. 21Do your best to come before winter sets in. Eubulus sends you his good wishes, and so do Pudens and Linus and Claudia and all your fellow-Christians. 22The Lord be with your spirit. Grace be with you all.

The Letter to
TITUS

Chapter 1

THIS is a letter from Paul, God's servant and Jesus Christ's apostle. It was to awaken faith in God's chosen people and to bring them the knowledge of the truth, as it is contained in our religion, that I was made both servant and apostle. 2That religion is founded on the hope of eternal life. Long ago God—and he cannot lie—promised this life. 3Now in his own good time God has displayed his message for all to see, through the proclamation of it, with which I was entrusted by the direct command of God our Saviour. 4I am writing to you Titus, for you are my true son in the faith which we both share. Grace to you and every blessing from God our Father and Christ Jesus our Saviour.

5My intention in leaving you behind was that you should tidy up the loose ends of things which I did not manage to finish, and that you should appoint elders in every town. In any such appointments you are to follow my instructions, 6and you are to appoint only men who are above suspicion of moral fault, men who are the faithful husbands of one wife, men whose own children are Christian believers, not open to any charge of loose living or out of control. 7The superintendent of the community is God's servant, and as such he must necessarily be a man who is above suspicion of moral fault. He must not be self-opinionated or violent in temper. He must not be too fond of wine or pugnacious. He must not be prepared to make money by disreputable methods. 8He must keep open house for strangers. He must be ready to welcome goodness wherever he sees it. He must be wise in the art of living, just, devout, master of himself. 9He must never lose his grip of the message which he has been taught and on which he must rely, for thus he will have the ability to appeal to his hearers with sound doctrine, and to refute opponents.

10There are many, especially among the Jewish members of the church, who are a law to themselves. Their talk is wild and futile, and they produce nothing but error and confusion in the mind of their hearers. 11It is essential that they should be silenced, for they are upsetting whole families by teaching things that should not be taught, and by doing so for motives which are shamefully mercenary. 12It was one of themselves, one of their own prophets, who said: 'The Cretans are always liars, vicious beasts, lazy gluttons.' 13This statement is true. You must for that very reason sternly convict them of the error of their ways. Only thus will they return to a sound faith, 14and stop devoting themselves to Jewish myths and to rules and regulations imposed by men who turn their back on the truth. 15To the pure everything is pure; to the corrupt and unbelieving nothing is pure. They are corrupt both in mind and conscience. 16They profess to know God, but by their conduct they deny him. They are detestable, disobedient, disqualified for any good activity.

Chapter 2

As for yourself personally, what you say must be in keeping with sound doctrine. 2You must instruct the older men to be abstemious, serious, wise in the art of living, sound in faith, in love and in fortitude. 3In the same way the older women must live as if every act in life is an act of worship. They must not indulge in scandal-mongering. They must not be so addicted to drink that they cannot do without it. They must be teachers of all that is fine, 4and so train the younger women to love their husbands and their children, 5to be wise in the art of living, to be chaste, to be domesticated, to be kind, to accept the authority of their own husbands. This is the way to ensure that no one can spread bad reports about the message of God. 6In the same way you must urge the younger men to live wisely and well. 7You must yourself provide in everything an example of fine living. In your teaching you must show integrity and dignity. 8Your speech must be wholesome, and such that no one can find fault with it. Then your opponent will be shamed into silence, when he can find nothing discreditable to say about us. 9Slaves must try to give complete obedience and satisfaction to their masters. They must not answer back. 10They must never be guilty of pilfering. They must show themselves to be completely honest and reliable, for to work like that is the way to become ornaments of the teaching we have received from God our Saviour.

11For the grace of God has broken into history for the salvation of all men. 12It is training us to renounce the life in which God is banished from the scene, and in which the world's desires hold sway, and in this age to live a well-ordered, upright and godly life, 13while all the time we are waiting for our blessed hope to be realized, when the splendour of our great God and Saviour Jesus Christ bursts upon the world. 14He gave himself for us, to liberate us from all wickedness, and to make us a people purified to be his own, and eager to live a noble life. 15This is your message. Plead with men and argue with men to accept it, and always with the accent of authority. Don't allow anyone to look down on you.

Chapter 3

MAKE it a regular part of your teaching to remind your people to submit to the government and the authorities, to obey them, and to be ready to undertake any honest work. 2Consistently remind them that they must not use insulting language, or be quarrelsome; that they must always be fair and more than fair to others, and that in their dealings with everyone they must show themselves to be men and women whose strength is always in their gentleness. 3We too were once foolish and disobedient and astray. We too were the slaves of all kinds of passions and pleasures. Malice and envy were the characteristics of our daily life. We were detested by others and we hated each other. 4But, when the kindness and the generous love of God our Saviour appeared upon the scene, 5not in consequence of anything that we had done in any goodness of our own, but solely in his own mercy, he saved us through the water of rebirth and that renewal which the Holy Spirit gives. 6Through Jesus Christ our Saviour he poured out the Spirit richly upon us. 7For it was his purpose to put us, through his grace, into a right relationship with himself, and to enable us to enter into possession of the eternal life which God had promised and for which we hope. 8This has been said, and said truly.

These are the points that I want you to stress, for I want to make sure that those who have come to believe in God will make it their object to engage in honest work. Such work is not only honest; it is also useful to society. 9Avoid senseless speculations and genealogies, dissension and wordy battles about legalistic points. They are a waste of time and get nowhere. 10If a man disregards the beliefs of the community and goes his own way, you must warn him a first time and a second time. After that have nothing to do with him. 11You can be sure that a man like that is a perverted sinner who stands self-condemned.

12When I send Artemas or Tychicus to you, come and join me at Nicopolis as soon as you can. It is there that I have decided to spend the winter. 13Do your best to help Zenas the lawyer and Apollos on their way, and see to it that they have everything they need. 14Our people must be instructed to engage in honest work. They must earn the necessities of life, and they must not contribute nothing to the common good.

15All the people who are with me send their good-wishes. Give my good wishes to all our faithful friends. Grace be with you all.

Introduction to the Letter to Philemon

THE Letter to Philemon is unique among the letters of Paul for it is the only personal letter, written to an individual, that we have from his pen.

It was written about A.D.62, when Paul was in prison in Rome, and it was written to Philemon, a member of the church at Colosse. It was written to help Onesimus. Onesimus was Philemon's slave, and he had run away. He probably was a thief as well as a runaway, for Paul promised to make good any theft Onesimus had been guilty of (verse 18). Just as a modern criminal might run to London or to New York, to lose himself in the vast crowds of the great city, so Onesimus had fled to Rome. Somehow or other he had made contact with Paul there, and he had become a Christian. He had become very dear to Paul, and Paul would have liked to keep him with him, but Paul would do nothing without the good-will of Philemon.

So Onesimus had to be sent back to his master, and all the more so because a Christian must do the right thing. So Paul sent him back. Paul was taking a risk. There were as many as sixty million slaves in the Roman Empire. They clearly had to be rigidly kept down. The fate of the runaway slave was extremely hard, if he was recaptured. He might well be killed, for his master had the right of life and death over him. In the eyes of the law of Rome a slave was not a person but a thing. He might well be branded on the forehead with a red-hot iron with the letter F, standing for *fugitivus*, runaway. At the best, he would certainly expect to be cruelly beaten.

Nevertheless Paul sent Onesimus back. But he makes a request to Philemon. Philemon is to receive him, not only as a returned runaway, but as a Christian brother beloved.

The end of the story we do not know, but surely we can be sure that Philemon responded to the pleading of Paul.

It is to be noted that Paul does not mention emancipation. Any move to try to abolish slavery at this stage would have been to court disaster. A rising of the slaves could only have ended in massacre. But something had happened. If the slave has become a dear brother, then the sting of slavery is drawn, and the principle has been stated which will end sooner or later in emancipation.

So in this letter we find the great apostle concentrating all his efforts for the sake of a runaway slave.

The Letter to
PHILEMON

THIS is a letter from Paul, a prisoner for Christ Jesus' sake, and from our colleague Timothy, to our dear friend and fellow-worker Philemon, and to the congregation which meets in your house, 2and to our sister Apphia, and to our fellow Christian soldier Archippus. 3Grace to you and every blessing from God our Father and from the Lord Jesus Christ.

4I never mention you in my prayers without thanking God for you, 5for I am always hearing of your faith in the Lord Jesus and your love for all God's dedicated people. 6It is my prayer that your fellowship with us in the faith we share may be effective in giving us an ever-deepening understanding of all the blessings which have become part of our life, and so may lead us nearer and nearer to Christ. 7Your love has made me very happy, and has been to me a source of much courage and comfort, because, my brother, you have been the means by which the hearts of God's people have been refreshed.

8So then, although our relationship as Christians entitles me with every confidence to order you to do what is your duty, 9yet because we love one another I appeal rather than command. I take this line though I am such as I am—Paul, the ambassador of Christ, and now in prison for Christ Jesus' sake. 10I appeal to you in regard to Onesimus, who is nothing less than my own child, because in prison I became his father in the faith. 11He is living up to his name now.* For there was a time when he was useless to you, but now he is useful both to you and to me. 12I am sending him to you, and with him I am sending my own heart. 13I am in prison here for the sake of the good news, and I would have liked to keep him with me, to render me the service which you yourself would gladly have given me. 14But I wished to do nothing without your consent, for I wanted your kindness to me to be, not a gift which you were compelled to give me, but a gift which you gave of your own free-will. 15It may be that he was taken away

*See Notes on pp. 575–6

from you for a time so that you might get him back for eternity, 16no longer as a slave, but as something far more than a slave, as a brother, specially dear to me, and how much more dear to you as a man and as a Christian!

17So then, if you regard me as your partner in the faith, welcome him as you would welcome me. 18If he has defrauded you of anything, or, if he owes you anything, charge it to me. 19Here is my written and signed guarantee that I will repay it—(signed) Paul. It is unnecessary for me to remind you that you owe me nothing less than your very self. 20So, brother, do me this favour as a Christian duty, and, like a Christian, put an end to my anxiety.

21I write to you confident that you will agree to my request, sure that you will do even more than I ask. 22At the same time, please get a room ready for me, for I hope that your prayers will be answered, and that God will allow me to visit you.

23Epaphras, my fellow-prisoner for Christ Jesus' sake, sends you his good wishes, 24and so do Mark, Aristarchus, Demas and Luke, my fellow-workers. 25The grace of the Lord Jesus Christ be with your spirit.

Introduction to the Letter to the Hebrews

THE Letter to the Hebrews might well be called the letter of the great unknown. No one knows who wrote it. Away back in the third century Origen had said: 'Who wrote the Letter to the Hebrews God alone knows.' How then did it get attached to the name of Paul? When the New Testament came to be put together as a book, the test of whether or not any single book was to get into it was whether or not the book had been written by an apostle, or at least by an apostolic man, a man who had been in contact with the apostles. No one knew who had written the Letter to the Hebrews, but it was far too great and far too valuable a book to omit and to lose. So it was, as it were, put under the protection of Paul, the great letter-writer, and was included with his letters.

Five hundred years before the writer to the Hebrews wrote his letter, Plato the great Greek had spoken of a doctrine which had left a deep mark on Greek thought. He had spoken of the *forms* or *ideas*. There were, he said, the perfect ideas, the perfect forms, the perfect patterns, the perfect archetypes of all things laid up in heaven. Everything on earth was a pale and imperfect copy of these forms and ideas; and the task of life was to get from the world's imperfections to heaven's perfections, to get from earth's unreality to heaven's reality. As the writer to the Hebrews saw it, in Jesus heaven's perfection had come to earth.

Before Jesus everything had been fragmentary and evanescent (1.1), but Jesus is greater than everything that went before. He is greater than the angels (chapter 1). He is greater than Moses (chapter 3). He is greater than Joshua (chapter 4). Everything that had been foreshadowed and hinted at came to its perfection in Jesus.

But in one respect, in the greatest of all things, this was specially true. The priest had a very special position in ancient religion. The Latin for priest is *pontifex*, which means a bridge-builder. The priest was the person who built a bridge between God and man. In particular the Jewish High Priest had a very special function on the Day of Atonement. No human being ever went into the Holy of Holies in the Temple, except the High Priest, and even he on only one day in the year, the Day of Atonement. The priest on behalf of the people went into the presence of God. To the writer to the Hebrews the ancient priesthood is only the imperfect shadow of the real thing.

Jesus is the real priest, the priest who himself can go into the presence of God, and who can open the way for others to follow.

So the writer to the Hebrews tells how Jesus is the perfect priest. Two things are necessary for any priest—he must have sympathy with men, and he must be divinely appointed (chapter 5). That was supremely true of Jesus.

There are things which show the obvious imperfection of the old priesthood. The old priesthood had to offer sacrifice for its own sins before ever it offered sacrifice for the sins of the people. Jesus does not need to do that, because he has no sin (7.27). The old sacrifices had to be made over and over again, day in and day out throughout the years. But the sacrifice Jesus made is made once and for all and never needs to be made again (10.1-3).

The imperfection of the old sacrifices is obvious. If they were really effective, they would not need to be made over and over again. The blood of animals can never really make atonement. But Jesus is not only the perfect priest, he is the perfect offering too; and the offering he brings is himself, and his perfect obedience (10.5-14).

There is nothing surprising in this, because the new covenant, the new relationship to God had already been foretold (Jeremiah 31.31-34; Hebrews 9.15-18), and the new kind of priesthood, the priesthood after the order of Melchizedek (Genesis 14.17-21; Psalm 110.4; Hebrews 7) had already been foretold too.

So Jesus is both the perfect priest and the perfect offering, and therefore in him the way to God is open wide. So for the writer to the Hebrews two things are to be said to the Christian.

First, *Let us go in*. The access to God is wide open, because of what Jesus the great High Priest has done. Let us then draw near (4.16; 10.19-22).

Second, *Let us go on*. Those to whom he was writing had become a little weary, a little regretful for what they had left, a little discouraged and they were on the verge of turning back. But to them there comes the invitation, to go, not backwards, but forwards, and to go in faith (5.11-6.12; chapter 11).

Let us go in, and, Let us go on, are the twin rallying-calls of the great unknown who wrote the Letter to the Hebrews.

The Letter to the
HEBREWS

Chapter 1

LONG ago God spoke to our ancestors by means of the prophets, but the revelation which was given through them was fragmentary and varied. ₂But now, as time as we know it is coming to an end, he has spoken in one whose relation to himself is that of Son, that Son into whose possession he gave all things, and by whose agency he created the present world and the world to come. ₃This Son is the radiance of his glory, just as the ray is the light of the sun. He is the exact impression of his being, just as the mark is the exact impression of the seal. It is he who sustains all things by the dynamic power of his word. And, after he had effected the cleansing of men from their sins, he took his place at the right hand of the Majesty in the heights of heaven, ₄for he was as much superior to the angels as the title he had been given as his possession by God was greater than theirs.

₅To which of the angels did God ever say:

> 'You are my Son;
> today I have begotten you'?

And again:

> 'I will be his Father,
> and he will be my Son'?

₆Again, when he leads his firstborn Son on to the stage of world history, he says:

> 'Let all God's angels worship him.'

₇Of the angels he says:

> 'God makes his angels winds,
> and his servants a flame of fire.'

8But of the Son he says:

'Your throne, O God, will last for ever and ever;
    the righteous sceptre is the sceptre of your kingdom.
9You have loved justice, and you have hated lawlessness.
    That is why God, your God, has singled you out
        from your fellows,
    and has given you the thrilling joy
        of being anointed for kingship.'

10And again:

'It was you, O Lord, who in the beginning
    laid the foundations of the earth;
and it was your hands
    which made the heavens.
11They will be destroyed, but you remain.
    They will all grow old, as clothes grow old.
12You will fold them up like a cloak,
    and they will be changed, as clothes are changed.
But you are always the same,
    and your years will never come to an end.'

13To which of the angels has he ever said:

'Sit at my right hand,
    until I make your enemies a footstool for your feet'?

14Clearly, the angels are serving spirits, despatched each on his own errand, to help those who are to receive the salvation which God has promised.

Chapter 2

IT is therefore necessary that we should pay all the more attention to what we have been told. Otherwise, we may well be like a ship which drifts past the harbour to shipwreck. 2For, if the message delivered through angels, as the law was, was valid, and, if every transgression of it, and disobedience to it, carried its just penalty, 3how can we escape, if we disregard so much greater a way to salvation? For the way of salvation offered to us had its origin in the Lord's own words, and its validity was guaranteed to us by those who actually heard it from his own lips. 4God too continuously supplied further evidence of its truth in events in which his own power is plainly visible, in all kinds of acts of supernatural power, and in the distribution of the gifts the Holy Spirit gives, as God decides.

5For it was not to angels that God subjected the new order of which we are speaking. 6There is a passage of scripture, in which one of the sacred writers puts it on record:

'What is man that you should remember him,
  or what is the son of man that you should be concerned with him?
7You made him for a little time lower than the angels.
  But afterwards you crowned him with glory and honour,
8and you subjected all things beneath his feet.'

When it says that he subjected all things to him, it means that he left nothing unsubjected to him. But as things are we do not in fact yet see all things in a state of subjection to man. 9What we do see is Jesus. For a short time he was made lower than the angels. But now we see him crowned with glory and honour, because of the death he suffered, for it was the gracious purpose of God that Jesus should experience death for all.

10God will be the end of all things as he was the beginning, and it was fitting for him, in bringing many sons to glory, to make the pioneer of their salvation perfect through his sufferings. 11For the consecrating priest and the consecrated people have one Father That is why he does not hesitate to call them brothers:

12'I will tell of your name to my brothers,
  I will sing your praises in the assembly of God's people.'

12And again he says, as any man might say:

13'I will put my trust in God.'

and again:

'Here am I and the children God gave me.'

14The children share in a flesh and blood human nature, and he too in exactly the same way shared in the same things. The purpose of his doing so was to destroy him who had death in his control, I mean, the Devil, 15and so to liberate those for whom life was a kind of slavery, because of their fear of death. 16For obviously it is not angels that he is out to help; it is, as scripture says, the children of Abraham whom he helps. 17He therefore had to be completely identified with his brothers, for only then could he become in divine things a compassionate high priest on whom men can rely, and so bring forgiveness to the people for their sins. 18For, because he himself went through the ordeal of suffering, he is able to help others who are now going through that same ordeal.

Chapter 3

So then, brothers in consecration, sharers in the calling which comes from heaven and calls to heaven, fix your attention on Jesus. Jesus is the Apostle and High Priest of the faith which we profess, 2and he was faithful to God who appointed him to that office. Moses too was faithful to God in all God's house. 3The founder of a house has always greater honour than the house itself. So then Jesus is deemed to be worthy of greater honour than Moses. 4Every house is founded by someone; it is God who founded all things. 5It was in the capacity of a servant that Moses was faithful in God's house. His function was to point to the things which God was going to say in the future. 6But it was as a son that Christ was faithful over the house of God. And we are God's house, if we retain our courage, and our pride in the hope that is ours.

7So then, as the Holy Spirit says:

'Today I plead with you, listen to his voice.
8Do not be stubborn,
    as you were when you rebelled against him,
    on the day when you sorely tried his patience
        in the desert.
9There your ancestors tried me,
    and put me to the test,
    and saw what I could do 10for forty years.
That was why I was angry with that generation.
I said: "In their hearts they always go astray,
    and they never learned my ways."
11As I swore in my anger,
    they shall never come in to me,
    and share my rest.'

12Brothers, you must be very careful to avoid a situation in which the heart of any of you becomes so wicked in its refusal to believe that he thereby becomes a deserter from the living God. 13So long as it is possible to use the word 'Today' in that appeal of God, you must rather daily urge one another not to allow any of you to be made stubborn against God by sin's seductive influence. 14For we have been made partners with Christ, if only we preserve firm the confidence we had at the beginning. 15When it was said:

> 'Today I plead with you, listen to his voice.
> Do not be stubborn,
>   as you were when you rebelled against him,'

16who was it who heard God's appeal, and who rebelled? Who but all those who came out of Egypt under Moses' leadership? 17With whom was God angry for forty years? Was it not with those who sinned, and who fell dead in the desert? 18To whom did he swear that they would never enter his rest, if it was not to those who disobeyed him? 19So we see that it was their refusal to believe which made it impossible for them to enter.

Chapter 4

So then, so long as the promise of entrance into his rest remains open to us, the one thing we must dread is that any of you should be judged to have missed it. 2We too have heard the good news, just as they did, but the message they heard did them no good, because there was no faith in those who heard it for it to be blended with. 3It is we who have believed who are entering that rest. What he said was:

> 'I swore in my anger
>   that they should never enter into my rest.'

This is said, although God's work has been completed since the creation of the world. 4For somewhere scripture has said about the seventh day: 'God rested from all his work on the seventh day.' 5Let me repeat it. In the passage we have already quoted we find: 'They shall never enter into my rest.' 6Those who in the old days received the good news of that rest never did enter into that rest because of their refusal to believe. It therefore remains for someone to enter this rest. 7God therefore again fixes a day, for in David, so long a time afterwards, he says 'Today,' for in the passage we have already quoted he says:

> 'Today I plead with you, listen to his voice.
> Do not be stubborn.'

8If Joshua had in fact given them rest, God would not afterwards have spoken to them about another day. 9The deduction therefore must be that there still remains a Sabbath rest for the people of God. 10For, if anyone enters into God's rest, he too rests from his work, as God did from his. 11Let us then make every effort to enter into that rest, so that no one may make the mistake of being guilty of the same kind of disobedience.

12For the word of God is effectively alive; it is sharper than any double-edged sword; it penetrates right to the division of soul and spirit, of joints and marrow. It scrutinizes a man's thoughts and intentions. 13There is no created thing or being which is out of sight to him. Everything is stripped and exposed to the eyes of the one to whom we have to render account of ourselves.

14Since then we have a great high priest, who has passed through the heavens, Jesus the Son of God, we must never lose our grip of the faith we have publicly professed. 15It is not a high priest who is unable to sympathize with the weaknesses that we possess; it is a high priest who in every respect has gone through the same ordeal of temptation as we have to go through, and who emerged sinless. 16We must then fearlessly and confidently come to the throne of grace, and then we will find mercy and grace to help us in every situation when we need them.

Chapter 5

EVERY high priest who is selected from his fellowmen is appointed to act for them in matters concerning God. His function is to offer to God gifts and sacrifices for men's sins. 2Because he himself is clothed in weakness, he can deal gently with those who do not know the truth and who lose the way. 3Because of this weakness he is under obligation to offer sacrifices for his own sins, just as he does for the sins of the people. 4No one takes this honour upon himself; he is called to it by God, just as Aaron was.

5So Christ too did not give himself the glory of becoming high priest; that glory was given to him by God, who said to him:

> 'You are my Son;
> today I have begotten you.'

6In the same way he says in another passage:

'You are a priest for ever
in the order of Melchizedek.'

7In the days of his human life, with loud cries and tears, he brought his prayers and requests to God, who was able to save him from death, and his prayers were heard because of his reverence for God. 8Son though he was, for him suffering was the way to learn obedience. 9So he became perfect, and thus became the source of eternal salvation for all who obey him, 10and he was given by God the title of a priest in the order of Melchizedek.

11On Melchizedek I have a great deal to say, and it is not easy for me to put it in a way that you will understand, for you have become dull of hearing. 12By this time you ought to be teaching others. But in point of fact you need someone to teach you all over again the elementary principles of God's message to you. It is milk you have come to need, not solid food. 13If a man is still being fed on milk, he is unable to take in instruction on the good life, for he is still a baby. 14Solid food is for mature men; it is for those whose faculties are disciplined by practice to distinguish between right and wrong.

Chapter 6

So then, we must leave behind elementary Christian instruction, and move on to mature teaching. There is no point in laying the foundations all over again. I mean the basic teaching about repentance from the way of life the end of which is death, and about faith in God, 2teaching about purificatory rites, the laying on of hands, the resurrection of the dead, and eternal judgment. 3And move on we shall, if God allows us. 4For, once people have been enlightened, once they have experienced the heavenly gift and have received a share of the Holy Spirit, 5once they have experienced the goodness of God's word and the dynamic powers of the age to come, 6if they then fall away, it is impossible again to renew their repentance, for they are personally crucifying the Son of God all over again, and are publicly treating him with cynical contempt. 7So long as the ground, which drinks in the rain which often falls upon it, produces a useful crop for those by whom it is cultivated, it continues to receive its share of blessing from God. 8But if it produces a crop of thorns and thistles, it is no use to anyone; it is in danger of being cursed by God; and it will end up by being burned.

9My dear friends, even if we do use language like this, we remain convinced that you are not as bad as this, but that you still possess the necessities of salvation. 10God is not unjust; he will not forget all that you did, and the way in which you showed your love for him in your past and present service of his dedicated people. 11It is our earnest desire that each of you should show the same eagerness in your efforts to reach the full and final realization of your hope. 12You must not become lazy. You must take as your examples those who through faith and perseverance are entering into the possession of the promises of God.

3For, when God made his promise to Abraham, since he had nothing greater by which to swear, he swore by himself. 14'I pledge myself to bless you,' he said, 'and to give you many descendants.' 15And thus Abraham patiently waited, and so received what God had promised. 16Men swear by someone greater than themselves, and an oath is a guarantee which ends all dispute. 17So then, when God wished to give to those who are destined to receive what he promised an even more compelling proof of the unalterable character of his purpose, he introduced an oath, as well as a promise, between himself and them. 18Thus by means of two unalterable things, in which it is impossible that he should lie, God wanted those who have sought safety with himself to have a powerful incentive to hold fast to that hope which is set before us. 19That hope we hold, and it is for us the anchor of the soul. It is both sure and certain. It enters with us into the inner sanctuary behind the curtain. 20There Jesus has already gone, to make it safe for us to follow, for he has become a priest for ever in the order of Melchizedek.

Chapter 7

THIS Melchizedek was King of Salem, and priest of the most high God. He met Abraham, when Abraham was returning from the defeat of the kings, and blessed him. 2Abraham assigned to him as his share a tenth part of everything. In the first place, the translation of his own name, Melchizedek, is King of Righteousness. In the second place, he is King of Salem, and that means King of Peace. 3There is no mention of his father; there is no mention of his mother; no ancestor of his is ever mentioned. His days are never said to have had any beginning, and his life is never said to have had any end. He is like the Son of God; he remains a priest for ever.

4Look how outstanding this man is! Abraham the patriarch gave him a tenth part of the best of the spoils. 5Those of Levi's sons, who receive the priestly office, possess with it an injunction which legally entitles them to exact tithes from the people, that is, from their own fellow-countrymen, although they are descendants of Abraham. 6Melchizedek was not of Levitical descent at all, and yet he exacted tithes from Abraham, and blessed the man who was the possessor of the promises of God. 7There can be no question that it is the inferior who is blessed by the superior. 8Further, in the case of the Levitical priesthood it is mortal men who receive tithes. In the case of Melchizedek the evidence of scripture is that he is alive. 9Further, it would be possible to say that in the person of Abraham Levi too, who has the right to exact tithes, had tithes exacted from him, 10for he could be said to be in the body of his forefather Abraham when Melchizedek met him.

11It was on the basis of the levitical priesthood that the people had received the law. If that priesthood had been perfectly able to do what it was designed to do, there would obviously have been no need for a different kind of priest to emerge, a priest of the order of Melchizedek, and not of the order of Aaron. 12Now, if the priesthood is changed, then of necessity there is a change of the law too, 13for Jesus Christ, of whom we are speaking, belonged to a different tribe, from which no one ever served at the altar, 14for it is clear that our Lord sprang from the tribe of Judah, and Moses said nothing about priests in connection with that tribe. 15This is still clearer, when another priest emerges, a priest like Melchizedek. 16This priest became a priest, not through any regulation based on the rule of physical descent, but through the force of an indestructible life. 17The evidence for this is that it is said of him:

> 'You are a priest for ever
> in the order of Melchizedek.'

18There has been a cancellation of the previous rule, because it was weak and ineffective. 19The law was unable to do what it was designed to do, but a better hope has been brought on to the scene, and through it we can find the way to approach God.

20The levitical priests became priests without any oath being taken. 21He became a priest after an oath had been taken, because God said to him:

> 'The Lord has taken his oath,
> and will never change his mind.'

22And in as far as it was with an oath that Jesus became priest, in so far he has become the surety of a better relationship between God and man. 23Under the levitical system, a great many became priests, because death would not allow them to remain for long in the priesthood. 24But, because he remains for ever, he is a priest who needs no successor. 25That is why he is for all time able to save those who come to God through him, for he is always alive to intercede with God for them.

26This is the kind of priest we need, holy, untainted with evil, stainless, quite different from sinners, exalted above the heavens. 27Unlike the levitical high priests, he has no need first daily to offer sacrifices for his own sins, and then to offer them for the sins of the people. He did this once and for all when he offered himself. 28The law appoints as high priests men who are characteristically weak creatures, but the sworn statement, which came later than the law, appointed a Son, who remains perfect for ever.

Chapter 8

Now the point of what we have just been saying is that it is just such a high priest that we actually have. He has taken his seat at the right hand of the throne of the Majesty in heaven. 2He serves God in the Holy of Holies, I mean, in the real tabernacle, which the Lord, not man, set up. 3Every high priest is appointed to offer gifts and sacrifices. It is therefore necessary for this high priest too to have something to offer. 4If he was on earth, he would not be a priest at all, for there already are priests, who offer the gifts which the Jewish law prescribes. 5The service that such priests render is no more than a shadowy copy of the heavenly reality. That it is a copy is shown by the fact that, when Moses was about to build the tabernacle, God's instructions to him were: 'See that in everything you copy the pattern which was shown to you on the mountain top.' 6But in the new situation our high priest has been given a ministry which is as much superior to that of the levitical priests as the covenant of which he is the mediator is a better covenant, for this covenant was established on the basis of better promises.

7If that first covenant had been beyond criticism, there would have been no necessity to introduce a second into the situation. 8But that it is not beyond criticism is shown by the fact that God says in criticism of those who acknowledge no other:

'The time is coming, the Lord says,
    when I will establish a new and different covenant
    with the house of Israel and the house of Judah.
⁹It will not be like the covenant which I made with their fathers,
  at the time when I took them by the hand
    to bring them out of the country of Egypt.
The new covenant is necessary,
    because they did not abide by the covenant which I made
          with them.
So I let them go their own way, the Lord says.
¹⁰This is the covenant which I will make with the house of Israel,
    when that time comes, the Lord says.
I will put my laws into their minds,
    and I will write them on their hearts.
I will be their God, and they will be my people.
¹¹There will be no necessity for any of them to teach his fellow-
          citizen,
    or for any of them to teach his brother,
    and to say to him: "Know the Lord,"
For from the humblest to the greatest everyone will know me.
¹²I will forgive their iniquities,
    and I will not remember their sins any more.'

¹³When God speaks of a new covenant of a different kind, he makes the first covenant obsolete, and what is obsolescent and aging is not far from extinction.

Chapter 9

THE first covenant had indeed a ritual of worship laid down, and it had a sanctuary, although a this-worldly one. ²For a tabernacle was constructed, in the outer part of which there stood the lamp-stand and the table with the bread of the presence. It was called the Holy Place. ³Beyond the second curtain there was the part of the tabernacle called the Holy of Holies. ⁴It had in it the golden altar of incense and the sacred chest of the covenant, which was completely encased in gold. Inside the sacred chest there was a golden jar containing the manna. There was also Aaron's staff, which once budded. And there were the two stone tablets of the covenant with the ten commandments written on them. ⁵Above it were the cherubim of the glory of God, with their wings over-arching the mercy-seat, as the lid of the chest was called. It is not possible for me at present to enter into a detailed discussion of all this.

6This then is the way in which these things were arranged. Into the outer part of the tabernacle the priests continually enter in the course of carrying out the various acts of the ritual of worship. 7But into the inner part of the tabernacle only the high priest goes, and that only once a year. He never enters without taking blood with him. This he offers to God for himself and for the sins which the people have committed, without even knowing that they had committed them. 8By this the Holy Spirit makes it clear that the way into the inner sanctuary is not disclosed so long as the first tabernacle still exists. 9The first tabernacle symbolically stands for this present age, and the gifts and sacrifices which are offered in it are such that they cannot give the worshipper perfect peace of conscience. 10Founded as they are upon laws about food and drink and different kinds of ritual washings, they are no more than external regulations, remaining in force only until the time when by the action of God religion is totally reformed and reconstructed.

11, 12When Christ appeared on the scene, he came as a priest of the good things which were to come. The tabernacle in which he serves is greater and more perfect. It is not made by human hands. That is to say, it is not part of the created world at all. Once and for all he went right through it into the Holy of Holies. It was not the blood of goats and calves that he took with him as a sacrifice. It was his own blood. And thus he secured eternal deliverance for us. 13For, if sprinkling with the blood of goats and bulls, and with the ashes of a heifer, so physically purifies those who have become ritually unclean that they are rendered fit to enter God's presence in worship, 14how much more will the blood of Christ, who offered himself to God as a victim without blemish in a spiritual and eternal sacrifice, cleanse our conscience from the conduct which leads to death, and fit us for the service of the living God?

The point in the passage which follows depends on a play on words. The Greek word *diathēkē* means two things. It means both *covenant* and *will*. The writer to the Hebrews plays on these two meanings. The switch from one meaning to the other is made in verse 16, and the argument is that the benefits of a *diathēkē, covenant, will,* cannot be received until the testator has died. So for the new *diathēkē, covenant, will,* to become operative and effective the death of Christ had first to happen. A play on words is seldom translatable from one language into another, and this one is not. But it has to be kept in mind that the word for *covenant* is the same as the word for *will*.

15Christ has therefore become the connecting link between God and man, and through him the new covenant has come into being. A death has occurred—the death of Christ—as a result of which men have been rescued from their sins committed under the first covenant. And so those who have been called by God are enabled to receive the gift which God promised from all eternity. 16In the case of a will, it is essential that the death of the testator should be established. 17It is only upon death that a will becomes valid and effective, for a will cannot be operative while the testator is still alive. 18It was for this very reason that even the first covenant was not inaugurated without blood. 19For, after every commandment in the law had been announced to all the people, Moses took the blood of calves and goats, together with water, scarlet wool and hyssop, and sprinkled the book itself and all the people. 20'This,' he said, 'is the blood of the covenant which God enjoined you to keep.' 21In the same way he sprinkled the tabernacle too and everything that was used in worship. 22In fact, it would almost be true to say that in the regulations of the law everything must be cleansed by blood, and that there can be no forgiveness, unless blood has been shed.

23These are only copies of the heavenly things and they have to be cleansed by these rites. The heavenly things themselves need greater sacrifices than these. 24For it was not into a manmade sanctuary that Christ entered, a mere symbol of the real sanctuary; it was into heaven itself, now to appear before God on our behalf. 25Nor is he there to repeat the sacrifice of himself over and over again, as year after year the high priest goes into the sanctuary with blood that is not his own. 26For, if that had been the way of it, he would have had to suffer over and over again, ever since the world was created. In actual fact he appeared once and for all, at the consummation of history, to wipe out sin through the sacrifice of himself. 27For men it is appointed to die once—and after that comes judgment. 28So Christ was once and for all sacrificed to bear the sins of all. And, now that sin has been dealt with, he will appear a second time, this time not to deal with sin, but to bring salvation to those who are eagerly waiting and watching for him.

Chapter 10

THE Jewish law was no more than a shadow of the good things which are to come; you will not find in it the true expression of these realities. By going on making the same sacrifices which are offered year after year for ever the law can never perfect those who are trying to find the way into God's presence. ₂If these sacrifices could have done this, they would obviously have ceased to be offered, because the worshipper would have been once and for all cleansed, and would no longer be haunted by the sense of sin. ₃So far from that, these sacrifices do no more than keep reminding a man of his sins year after year. ₄For it is not in the power of the blood of bulls and goats to take sins away.

₅This is why Christ, as he was coming into the world, said to God:

> 'You had no desire for sacrifice and offering.
>   You prepared a body for me.
> ₆Animal sacrifices burned whole on the altar
>   and offerings for sin
>   brought no pleasure to you.
> ₇Then I said: "Here I am.
>   As scripture says of me in the roll of the book,
>   I have come, O God, to do your will." '

₈First he said: 'You neither wish for, nor find any pleasure in, animal sacrifices and offerings, in sacrifices burned whole on the altar, in offerings for sin'—and these are the offerings which the law prescribes. ₉Then he said: 'Here I am. I have come to do your will.' Thus he cancels the first, that is, animal sacrifice, to establish the second, that is, perfect obedience. ₁₀And it is by that will of God that we have been made fit to enter God's presence through the once and for all sacrifice of the body of Jesus Christ.

₁₁Every Jewish priest stands every day carrying out the ritual of worship, and offering the same sacrifices over and over again, and these sacrifices are such that they never take sins away. ₁₂But Christ offered one sacrifice for sins, a sacrifice which is effective for ever, and then took his seat at the right hand of God, ₁₃where he awaits the complete subjection of his enemies. ₁₄For by one sacrifice, valid for ever, he enabled men to enter into perfect communion with God.

15We have the declaration of the Holy Spirit that this is true. 16For after he had said:

'This is the covenant which I will make with them
    after these days, the Lord says;
I will put my laws into their hearts,
    and I will write them upon their minds,'

17he then goes on to say:

'And their sins and their disobedience
    to my laws I will completely forget.'

18And, when these have been forgiven, there is no longer any need for an offering for sin.

19Through the sacrificial death of Jesus we, brothers, have complete freedom to enter the Holy of Holies by a new and living way, 20which he inaugurated for us. We can pass right through the curtain, for as the curtain was rent, so his body was rent for us. 21We have a great high priest, who presides over the house of God. 22Let us then come to him in complete sincerity of heart and conviction of faith, with our hearts so sprinkled with the blood of his sacrifice that we no longer have a guilty conscience, and with our bodies washed with pure water. 23Let us hold inflexibly to the hope which we tell the world we possess, for we can rely on the word of him who promised it to us. 24We must think how to stimulate each other to love and to lovely living. 25We must not, as some do, abandon meeting together; we must rather encourage each other to do so, and all the more because you see that it will not be long now until the great day comes.

26For, if we go on deliberately sinning after receiving the knowledge of the truth, there is no longer any possible sacrifice for sin left. 27All that is left is to await in terror the judgment, and the fury of fire which will destroy the opponents of God. 28If anyone treats the law of Moses as if it did not exist, the penalty is death without pity on the evidence of two or three witnesses. 29How much more severe, do you think, must be the punishment deserved by the man who has spurned the Son of God, who has regarded as a common thing the covenant blood through which he was made fit to enter God's presence, and who has wantonly insulted the Spirit through whom God's grace has come to us? 30For we know who said: 'The right of just punishment is mine; I will repay.' And again: 'The Lord will judge his people.' 31It is a terrifying thing to fall into the hands of the living God.

32Cast your minds back to your early days. At that time, when you had seen the light, you met with gallantry a hard struggle with sufferings. 33Some of you had abuse and torture heaped upon you, to provide a public spectacle. Some of you deliberately chose to share the experiences of those who were involved in those troubles. 34You voluntarily shared the sufferings of those who were in prison. You gladly accepted the violent confiscation of your possessions, for you knew that you possessed something better and more lasting. 35You must not throw away your confidence, for it will bring you a rich reward. 36What you need is the power to see things through. If you have that, you will obey the will of God, and so receive what he has promised.

> 37'Soon, very soon now,
>   he who is to come will come,
>   and will not delay.
> 38 And by his fidelity the good man who is mine
>   will find life.
>   But, if he is afraid to face things,
>   I have no pleasure in him.'

39We are not afraid to face things; we are not men destined to be lost; we are men of faith destined to save our souls.

Chapter 11

FAITH is the confidence that the things which as yet we only hope for really do exist. It is the conviction of the reality of the things which as yet are out of sight. 2It is because of this faith that the heroes of the past received the approval of God.

3It is by faith that we understand that the universe was constructed by the word of God, for the seen had to take its origin from the unseen.

4It was through faith that Abel offered to God a better sacrifice than Cain did. It was because of his faith that he was approved as a good man, for God showed his approval of the gifts he offered. His faith made him, even after his death, a living and speaking example to us. 5By faith Enoch was removed from this world without experiencing death. He vanished from this world because God removed him. We can rightly attribute this to his faith, because it is recorded in scripture that before his removal his life had pleased God, 6and without faith it is impossible to please God, for anyone who wishes to come to God must believe that God exists, and that he rewards those who search for him. 7It was through faith that Noah received from God a message about events which were still out of sight. He received it reverently, and built an ark to save his household. Through his faith he proved the error of the world's ways, and entered into possession of that goodness in the Lord's sight which comes through faith.

8It was through faith that Abraham obeyed the call of God, and went out to a land which he was to receive, because God had promised it to him. He set out, although he did not know where his journey was going to take him. 9It was through faith that he lived like an alien in a foreign country in the land that had been promised to him. He had his home in tents, and so had Isaac and Jacob who shared possession with him of the promise God had made, 10for he was waiting for the city with its foundations, the city of which God is the architect and builder. 11It was through faith that he received the power to beget a child, even although Sarah was unable to have children, and even although he himself was beyond the age to become a father, for he had made up his mind that, since God had made a promise, he could depend on God to keep it. 12The result was that from one man, and that a man who from the point of view of begetting children was as good as dead, there came descendants as many as the stars in the sky in number, and as countless as the grains of sand on the sea-shore.

13These all died in faith. They never received what God had promised. They only saw and greeted God's promises in the far-off distance. They never denied the fact that they were strangers, and that they had no permanent home anywhere on earth. 14When people speak like that, they make it clear that they are looking for a country of their own. 15If their thoughts had always been turning back to the country they had left, they could easily have found an opportunity to return to it. 16But in point of fact they are reaching out to a better country, I mean a heavenly one. That is why God is not ashamed to be called their God, for he had prepared a city for them.

17, 18It was through faith that Abraham, when he was tested, as good as offered up Isaac as a sacrifice to God. Isaac was his only son, and God had told him that the line of his descendants would descend through Isaac, and yet he was ready to offer him in sacrifice to God.

19He had reasoned it out that God could raise his son to life again even from the dead—and symbolically he did indeed receive him back again. 20It was through faith that Isaac called down future blessings on Jacob and Esau. 21It was through faith that the dying Jacob blessed each of Joseph's sons, and bowed in worship before God, leaning on the top of his staff. 22It was through faith that Joseph, when the end was near, spoke about the time when the Israelites would leave Egypt, and gave instructions as to what was to be done with his bones, when that time came.

23It was through faith that, when Moses was born, he was hidden by his parents for three months, because they saw that he was an exceptionally beautiful child, and so disregarded the king's edict. 24It was through faith that, when Moses grew up, he refused to be called the son of Pharaoh's daughter. 25He preferred to share their ill-treatment with the people of God than to enjoy the short-lived pleasure sin can bring, 26for he regarded the insults and injury, which God's Anointed One must suffer, as greater wealth than the treasures of Egypt, for his eyes were fixed on his reward. 27It was through faith that Moses left Egypt. He was not afraid of the king's anger. He held inflexibly to his chosen course, as one who sees the invisible God. 28It was through faith that he kept the Passover, and carried out the sprinkling of the doors with blood, to keep the Destroying Angel from touching the eldest sons of the Israelite families. 29It was through faith that they crossed the Red Sea, as if it had been dry land. But, when the Egyptians attempted the same crossing, they were drowned. 30It was through faith that the walls of Jericho collapsed, after the Israelites had marched round them each day for seven days. 31It was through faith that the prostitute Rahab did not share in the destruction of those who did not believe in Israel's God, because she had given the spies a kindly welcome.

32What more need I say? There is no time for me to tell of Gideon, Barak, Samson, Jephthah, David, Samuel and the prophets. 33It was through faith that they conquered kingdoms, established justice, found God's promises come true. It was through faith that they muzzled the mouths of lions, 34quenched raging flames, escaped the threat of the sword. It was through faith that their weakness was changed into power, that they became strong in battle, that they routed the serried ranks of foreign armies. 35It was through faith that women received back their dead resurrected to life again. Some were battered to death in torture. They refused to accept release, for they wanted to win a better resurrection. 36Some had to face mockery and the lash, and the even worse fate of chains and imprisonment. 37They were stoned; they were sawn in two; they died murdered by the sword. They went about clad in sheepskins and goatskins. They had not even the bare necessities of life. Life was for them a series of crushing blows; they lived in constant ill-treatment. 38The world did not deserve people like that. They wandered in the lonely places and among the hills; caves and holes in the ground were their homes.

39All these through their faith won the approval of God, but they did not receive what God had promised to his people, 40because God in his providence had a better plan for us. His purpose was that we and they should reach the final blessedness together.

Chapter 12

So then, in the arena of life we are surrounded by a vast crowd of spectators. We must therefore, as an athlete strips for action, strip off every encumbrance and the sin which clings to us, and we must run with gallant determination the race which stretches in front of us. 2And all the time we must concentrate on nothing but Jesus, in whom our faith had its beginning and must have its end, for he, for the joy that lay ahead of him, courageously accepted the cross, with never a thought for the shame, and has now taken his seat at the right hand of God. 3The way to avoid the failure of your nerve and heart is to compare your situation with the situation of him who met the opposition of sinners with such constancy and courage.

4In your struggle with sin you have not yet had to resist to the point of having to die for your faith. 5Have you forgotten that challenging passage of scripture, which speaks to you as sons?

'My son, always remember the value of the discipline
    which comes to you from the Lord,
  and never be depressed and discouraged,
    when he corrects you.
6The Lord disciplines the man he loves,
    and punishes every son
  whom he accepts into his family.'

7You must accept it as discipline. God is treating you as sons. Is there any son whom his father does not discipline? 8If you are left without the discipline in which all sons share, then you are bastards and not real sons. 9Again, we had human fathers who disciplined us, and we respect them for it. Should we not be much more ready to submit to a spiritual Father in order to learn to live? 10They exercised discipline over us for a short time, and as they thought best; but he disciplines us for our good, and his aim is to make us fit to share his holiness. 11No discipline seems pleasant at the moment; it is always painful. But afterwards it repays those who were trained by it with the happy harvest of a good life.

12So then, fill the listless hands with energy; strengthen the trembling knees; 13make straight paths for your feet to walk in, so that the lame limb may not be dislocated, but cured.

14Aim at right relationships with everyone. Set your heart on that consecration without which no one can see the Lord. 15See to it that no one deprives himself of the grace of God. See to it that no poisonous weed grows up to make trouble for you and to contaminate the whole community. 16See to it that no one is guilty of sexual immorality, or lost to all religious feeling, as Esau was, for he sold his birthright for a single meal. 17You know that, when he afterwards wished to claim the blessing he had sold, he was rejected. There was no possibility for him to think again, although he tried with tears to undo what he had done.

18It is not to Mount Sinai that you have come, to a material and blazing fire, to gloom and thick darkness, to a hurricane of wind, 19to the blare of the trumpet, to a voice which spoke such terrible words that those who heard it pled that it should say no more. 20For they were appalled by the order that, if even a beast touched the mountain, it should be stoned to death. 21The sight was so terrible that Moses said that it left him trembling and afraid. 22No! You have come to Mount Sion and to the city of the living God, to the heavenly Jerusalem and to thousands upon thousands of angels. 23You have come to the firstborn sons of God's family registered in heaven, in worshipping assembly. You have come to God who is the judge of all, to the spirits of good men who have reached the goal of life, 24to Jesus the mediator of the new covenant, to the sprinkled sacrificial blood, which has a greater message than the blood of Abel.

25Take care not to refuse to listen to him who speaks. Those who refused to listen to the man Moses, who on earth was the messenger of God's truth, did not escape. Still less will we escape, if we turn our backs on Christ, the one who comes from heaven. 26At that time his voice shook the earth, but now he has promised: 'Once again I will shake, not only the earth, but heaven too.' 27That phrase, 'once— and only once—again', can only mean the complete removal of the things that are shaken—for they are only created things—and then only the things that cannot be shaken will remain. 28Since then we are receiving a kingdom that cannot be shaken, we must be grateful to God, and, to show our gratitude, we must worship him in the way that pleases him, with reverence and fear, 29for our God is a devouring fire.

Chapter 13

CHRISTIANS must never stop loving their fellow-Christians. 2Do not forget the duty of hospitality, for there are those who through it have entertained angels without being aware that they were doing so. 3Remember those who are in prison with a sympathy which shares their chains with them. Do not forget those who are being ill-treated, for you have not yet left this life, and the same fate can happen to you. 4You must regard marriage as an honourable state. Nothing must violate the marriage bond. Fornicators and adulterers have God as their judge. 5Never let the love of money dominate your life. Be content with what you have. God himself has said: 'I will never let go my grip of you; I will never abandon you.' 6If that is so, we can meet life fearlessly, for we can say:

'The Lord is my helper.
I shall not be afraid.
What can any man do to me?'

7Remember those who were once your leaders. It was they who brought God's message to you. Look back on the way in which they left this life, and make their loyalty your example. 8Jesus Christ is the same yesterday, today and for ever. 9Do not allow yourselves to be swept away by all kinds of strange teachings. The best thing to fortify your souls is the grace of God, not regulations about what we may eat and not eat, which have never been of the slightest use to those who use them as rules of life. 10The Jewish priests, who carry out the ritual of the earthly tabernacle, get as the perquisite of their office their share of the sacrificial meat to eat, but we have an altar from whose sacrifices they have no right to eat. 11The high priest brings the blood of the animals into the Holy of Holies as a sin-offering, but the bodies of these animals are burned outside the camp. 12That is why Jesus had to suffer outside the city, in order, through his own blood, to make the people fit to enter the presence of God. 13So then, we must go out to him outside the camp, and we must accept the same abuse as he accepted. 14For here we have no permanent city; we are looking for the city which will come. 15Through him then we must bring a sacrifice of continual praise to God. The sacrifice I mean is given by lips which publicly affirm their faith in him. 16Never forget to live a life of goodness and sharing. It is sacrifices like that which delight God.

17Obey your leaders, and accept their leadership. Their care for you is ceaseless and unsleeping. They look after you as men who will answer for the responsibility placed upon them. Make their task of leadership a happy and not a distressing experience. To make their task an unhappy one would do you no good at all.

18Keep praying for us, for we believe that our conscience is clear, for our only desire is to live a good life. 19I urge you all the more strenuously to pray for us, so that you and I may meet again all the sooner.

20God brought our Lord Jesus back from the dead, and his sacrificial death made him the great shepherd of the sheep and the inaugurator of the eternal covenant. 21And may that God of peace equip you with every good thing you need to enable you to do what he wants you to do, and may he make us and our life such as he would wish us and it to be through Jesus Christ, to whom be glory for ever and ever! Amen.

22I ask you, brothers, please to bear with this message of encouragement and comfort, for indeed it is a short letter that I have sent you. 23I would like you to know that our brother Timothy has been released from prison, and, if he arrives in time, he will be with me when I see you.

24Give my best wishes to all your leaders and to all God's consecrated people. The people from Italy send you their good wishes. 25Grace be with you all.

Introduction to the Letter of James

IT is not by any means certain who the James is who wrote this letter, but he may well have been James the brother of Jesus.

The Letter of James has always suffered from the fact that Luther called it 'a right strawy epistle', and would have banished it from the New Testament altogether. Luther's objection to it was that he thought that it contradicted Paul. Paul had said that no man could ever be justified by works, that every man had to be justified, had to be put right with God, by faith alone. But James seems to say, and to say with vigour, that what matters is works (2.14-26). To Paul Abraham was justified by faith (Romans 4.1-12); to James Abraham was justified by works (2.21). But Paul and James are not really at variance. They are not saying contradictory things; they are saying complementary things. It has been well put this way: 'A man is not saved *by* works, but he is saved *for* works.' No man can earn the love of God, but once a man knows through faith that God loves him, he knows, or he knows nothing of the meaning of Christianity, that he must spend all his life trying to live a life that is worthy of that love. We are not saved by works; but the only proof that we are saved is that we live a life a little more like that of our Saviour and our Lord.

In many ways this is a strange letter. In the Greek it only mentions the name of Jesus twice (1.1; 2.1). It is an intensely practical letter, and is the very essence of practical Christianity.

One of the strange things about it is that it is impossible to make a connected analysis of it. It consists of a series of disconnected paragraphs of advice and admonition. It speaks of the necessity of constancy in trial (1.2-4); of the necessity of doing as well as hearing (1.22-25); of the dangers of partiality and of snobbish respect of persons (2.1-7); of the necessity of adding works to faith (2.14-26); of the terrible dangers of the tongue (3.1-12); of the true wisdom (3.13-18); of the folly of planning without God (4.13-17); of the necessity of steadfastness, because Christ is coming (5.7-11); of the power of prayer (5.13-18); and it has a special sense of the danger of riches (2.6,7; 5.1-6). It is a series of cameo-like utterances, with no logical connection with each other, and simply set down one after another.

This is the fact which may tell us what this letter may well have begun by being. When the Jewish rabbis gave instruction in preaching, their instruction always was that the preacher must never linger long on any one subject. To keep and to maintain the interest of the hearer he must move quickly from subject to subject. The Hebrew word for preaching is in fact *charaz*, which is literally the word for stringing beads or pearls. Preaching was like stringing a series of pearls together.

This is exactly what James is. It is like a series of pearls of wisdom strung together with no connection. So we may well believe that this letter was originally a sermon, either a synagogue or a church sermon, preached by James, and afterwards taken down and made into a general letter of advice.

The Letter of
JAMES

Chapter 1

GREETINGS from James, servant of God and of the Lord Jesus
Christ, to the twelve tribes scattered in exile from their home-
land.

₂My brothers, you must regard it as nothing but joy when you are
involved in all kinds of trials, ₃for you must realize that when faith has
passed through the ordeal of testing the result is the ability to pass
the breaking-point and not to break. ₄This ability must go right on to
the end, and then you will be perfect and complete, without a weak
spot. ₅It is characteristic of God to give generously and ungrudgingly
to all. So then, if anyone is lacking in wisdom, he must ask God for it,
and it will be given to him. ₆But he must ask in faith and with no
doubts, for the man who doubts is like a wave of the sea, blown about
at the mercy of every wind. ₇That kind of man need not think that
he will receive anything from God. ₈A man like that can never make
up his mind, and is quite unable to steer a steady course.

₉The brother who is nobody in the eyes of the world must take
pride in the way that the hard experiences of life, rightly accepted,
raise him to new heights of character. ₁₀The brother who is wealthy
must take pride in the way in which life brings him low, for he will
last no longer than a wild flower blooms. ₁₁For the sun rises, and the
sirocco blows and withers the grass, and the flower wilts, and its
beauty is gone. So the life of the rich man is a journey to decay.

₁₂Happy is the man who meets trial with the unbreakable spirit, for,
after he has come through the ordeal, just as the victorious athlete in
the games receives the laurel crown, so he will receive as his prize the
life which God has promised to those who love him. ₁₃If in his ordeal
a man is tempted to sin, he must not say: 'I am being tempted by God.'
God cannot be tempted by evil, nor does he ever tempt anyone else.
₁₄Each man is tempted when he is seduced and enticed by his own
desire. ₁₅Then the next thing that happens is that this desire conceives

and becomes the mother of sin. And then, when sin is full-grown, it spawns death.

16My dear brothers, don't be misled. 17All God's giving is good, and every perfect gift comes down from above, from the Father of the lights of the heavens. In him there is no change, nor does he turn away from us and leave us in the shadows. 18By an act of his own will, through the word of truth, he brought us into being, for, just as the first-fruits of the harvest are specially dedicated to him, so he intended us to have the first and highest place in all creation.

19My dear brothers, there is something that you must bear in mind Everyone must be quick to listen, slow to speak, and slow to become angry. 20Human anger can never produce the kind of conduct God desires. 21So then, you must strip off everything that would soil life and all that malice that is like an alien growth on life, and in a teachable spirit you must receive implanted in your heart the word which is able to save your souls.

22You must not only listen to the word; you must act on it. Otherwise, you indulge in self-deception. 23To listen to the word and not to act on it is to be like a man who looks in a mirror at the face that nature gave him. 24He looks at himself, and then he goes away, and immediately forgets what he looks like. 25It is the man who looks into the perfect law, which is the source of liberty, and who takes his stand on it, the man who is not simply a forgetful listener, but who is an active doer, who will be blessed by God, because he is a man of action.

26A man may regard himself as religious, but, if he has no control over his tongue, he is deceiving himself, and his religion is futile. 27The religion which in the sight of God the Father is pure and stainless consists in helping orphans and widows in their distress, and in keeping oneself from becoming contaminated by the world.

Chapter 2

MY brothers, you cannot at one and the same time believe in our glorious Lord Jesus Christ and be a snob. 2Suppose a man elegantly dressed and wearing a gold ring on his finger comes into your meeting, and suppose a poor man dressed in soiled and shabby clothing comes in at the same time. 3And suppose you pay special attention to the elegantly dressed man. Suppose you say to him: 'Would you be kind enough to sit there?' while you say to the poor man: 'Stand there!' or, 'Squat on the floor at my feet!' 4Do you not thereby inconsistently introduce class distinction into your fellow-ship, and does this not mean that you arrive at your judgments of people from the wrong motives altogether?

5Listen, my dear brothers! Didn't God choose those who by the world's standards are poor to be rich in faith, and to enter into possession of the kingdom which he has promised to those who love him? 6But you dishonour the poor man. Is it not the case that the rich treat you as tyrants treat their slaves? Is it not true that it is they who drag you to the law-courts? 7Is it not they who hurl their insults at the fair name of Jesus, which was pronounced over you, when you became his in baptism? 8The law of the Kingdom is stated in the passage of scripture: 'You must love your neighbour as yourself,' and perfectly to obey that law is to do well. 9But, if you continue to allow snobbery to dictate your attitude to other people, you are committing a sin, and you stand condemned by the law as law-breakers. 10To keep the rest of the law in its entirety, but to fail to keep it in one particular part, is legally to become guilty of breaking the law as a whole. 11For the same person said both: 'You must not commit adultery' and: 'You must not commit murder.' It may be that you do not commit adultery, but, if you commit murder, you have become a law-breaker. 12You must so speak and you must so act as men who are going to be judged by the law that makes men free. 13Judgment will be merciless for the man who acted mercilessly. But mercy can laugh at judgment.

14My brothers, what good is it for a man to say that he has faith, if he never does anything to prove it? Can faith save him? 15Suppose a fellowman or woman has no clothes to wear and no food for a daily meal, 16and suppose one of you says to a person in such a situation: 'Go and God bless you! May you have a fire to warm yourself and a meal to eat!' And suppose you do not give that person even enough to keep body and soul together, what use is that? 17Faith is like that. If faith does not issue in action, if it is all alone by itself, it is dead.

18But someone will say: 'You get different kinds of people. One man may well claim to be a man of faith, while another man may equally well claim to be a man of action.' I challenge you to prove to me that you have faith in any other way than by actions. For my part, I am perfectly willing to prove my faith to you by my actions. 19You believe that there is one God? Excellent! The demons believe so too—and shudder with terror. 20You poor fool! Do you want proof that faith is useless without action? 21Take the case of our ancestor Abraham. Was it not because of his actions that he was accepted by God as a good man? Was it not in fact by his action in offering Isaac on the altar? 22It must be obvious to you that his faith and his actions combined to act together, and that his faith was completed by his actions. 23So the passage of scripture which says: 'Abraham had faith in God, and that faith made him accepted by God as a good man' came true, and he was called God's friend. 24It must be clear to you that it is in consequence of his actions that God reckons a man to be a good man, and not only in consequence of faith. 25In the same way, was it not as a consequence of her actions that the prostitute Rahab was reckoned to be good? Was it not because she welcomed the Jewish messengers, and helped them to escape by a different route? 26The body is dead when there is no breath in it, and faith is dead when it has no actions to accompany it.

Chapter 3

My brothers, you ought not to try to become teachers in large numbers, for you are well aware that we teachers will be judged by a sterner standard than ordinary people. 2We all make many a slip, but, if a man does not slip up in his words, he is a perfect man, able to control every part of himself. 3We put bits into the mouths of horses to make them obey us, and thus we turn their whole body in any direction we wish. 4Take the case of ships. In spite of their size, and even when they are being driven by fierce winds, by a very small rudder they can be guided to change course, just as the steersman's wish directs. 5Just so, the tongue is a small part of the body, but it makes great claims.

Take the case of a forest fire. A tiny spark can set a whole forest ablaze. 6The tongue is a fire. Among the parts of the body the tongue represents this wicked world. It infects the whole body with the taint of evil. It sets the whole course of our existence on fire with a fire that is fed from the flames of hell. 7Every kind of beast and bird, every kind of reptile and fish, can be, and has been, brought under control by mankind. 8The tongue is the one thing that no man can control. It is an evil which is out of all control, full of deadly poison. 9With it we bless the Lord and Father, and with it we curse men made in the likeness of God. 10Blessing and cursing issue from the one mouth. My brothers, it is all wrong that this should happen. 11Obviously, a spring cannot gush out sweet and bitter water from the same opening. 12Clearly, my brothers, a fig-tree cannot produce olives, or a vine figs. No more can salt water produce fresh water.

13Have you a wise and understanding man in your society? He must demonstrate by the excellence of his life and conduct that all he does is done in that gentleness which is the hall-mark of wisdom. 14If in your heart there is a zeal which is bitter and fanatical, if you are actuated by selfish ambition, you must not treat others with arrogant conceit, and you must not defeat the truth with your falsehoods. 15This is not the wisdom which comes down from above. This is a wisdom which never sees beyond the horizons of this world, which is quite unspiritual, and which is demon-inspired. 16Where there is fanaticism and personal ambition, there is bound to be a chaotic state of affairs, in which every kind of evil flourishes. 17The wisdom which comes from above is in the first place pure. Then it produces harmony between man and man; it never stands on the letter of the law; it is never obstinate; it is characteristically merciful; it produces a rich crop of kindly acts; it is free from doubts and hesitations; it never acts a part. 18Goodness has its own harvest. But the harvest grows only when its seed is sown where harmony holds sway, and it is for those who are the makers of such a harmony.

Chapter 4

WHAT causes feuds and fights in your society? Are they not the outward expression of that inner warfare which results from your instinctive desire for pleasure? 2You want something; you cannot have it; you are ready to commit murder. You passionately desire something; you are unable to get it; you fight and feud. The reason why you do not have what you want is that you do not ask God for it. 3And when you do ask, you do not get what you ask for, because you ask for the wrong reasons. All you want to do with what you get is to spend it on your own pleasure. 4You have broken all your vows! Do you not know that friendship with the world means enmity to God? If a man chooses to be a friend of the world, he thereby makes himself an enemy of God. 5Or, do you think that scripture is meaningless when it says: 'God yearns jealously for the loving devotion of the spirit he implanted in us'?* 6But to meet the greater need he gives the greater grace. That is why scripture says:

'God is hostile to the arrogant,
but favours the humble.'

*See Notes on pp. 575–6

7So then, accept the authority of God. Take a stand against the devil, and he will run away from you. 8Come to meet God, and he will come to meet you. You are sinners; you must therefore cleanse your hands from evil deeds. Your loyalty is divided; you must therefore purify your heart from false loves. 9You will be well to be wretched, to mourn and to weep. Your laughter must change to mourning, and your gladness to gloom. 10Come in self-abasement to the Lord, and he will lift you high.

11Brothers, you must stop your habit of disparaging criticism of each other. To disparage a brother or to criticize him is to disparage Christ's law of love and to criticize it. And, if you criticize the law, then you are not obeying the law; you are critics of it. 12There is one law-giver and judge—the One who is able to save and to destroy. Who then are you to judge your fellowman?

13'Today or tomorrow,' some of you say, 'we will travel to this or that town, and we will spend a year there, trading and making money.' Stop and think a minute! 14You do not know what life will be like for you tomorrow. Your life is like a mist—seen for a moment, then vanishing for ever. 15Instead of speaking as you do, what you ought to say is: 'If it is the Lord's will, we shall live to do this or that.' 16In point of fact, you take a pride in your self-confident assertions— and all such self-confident pride is wrong. 17So then, for a man to know the right thing and not to do it is sin.

Chapter 5

YOU who are rich must stop and think! You must weep and wail for the miseries that are hastening on you! 2Your wealth has rotted; your splendid garments are the food of moths; 3your gold and silver are eaten with rust. That rust is the proof of the real value of these things—and it will eat into your own bodies like fire. You have piled up wealth in a world that is coming to an end. 4The pay that you never paid to the workers who reap your fields cries out against you. The clamorous protests of those who harvested your fields have reached the ears of the Lord of hosts. 5You have lived in this world in the luxury which saps a man's moral fibre and in dedication to wanton pleasure. You fattened yourselves like specially fattened cattle—and the day of slaughter has come. 6You condemned the innocent man; you murdered him; and he does not resist you.

7So then, brothers, you must be patient until the Lord comes. Take the case of the farmer. He waits for the ground's precious crop in patience, until it has received the autumn and the spring rain. ₈You too must be patient, and you must hold inflexibly to your purpose, for it will not be long now until the Lord comes. ₉Brothers, you must not spend your time lugubriously blaming one another for your troubles, if you want to escape God's judgment. The Judge is here—standing at the door. ₁₀Brothers, take the prophets, who spoke as the representatives of the Lord, as an example of patience in suffering. ₁₁We have no doubt of the ultimate bliss of those who met suffering with the power to see things through. You have heard the story of Job, and of how he had this power, and you know how the Lord brought Job's sufferings to a triumphant conclusion. For the Lord is compassionate and merciful.

₁₂Above all, my brothers, when you make a promise you must not use an oath. In such circumstances you must not swear by heaven, or by earth, or by anything else. If you mean Yes you must say Yes, and if you mean No you must say No, if you do not wish to become liable to judgment.

₁₃Is there anyone in your society who is in distress? He must pray. Is there anyone happy? He must sing a hymn. ₁₄Is there anyone in your society who is ill? He must call in the elders of the congregation, and they must pray over him, and anoint him with oil in the name of the Lord. ₁₅Such a prayer, offered in faith, will cure the sick man, and the Lord will put him on his feet again, and whatever sins he has committed will be forgiven. ₁₆Confess your sins to each other, and pray for each other, for that is the way to be cured. The prayer of a good man is powerfully effective. ₁₇Elijah was a man every bit as human as we are. He prayed earnestly that there should be no rain, and for three years and six months no rain fell on the land. ₁₈Then he prayed again, and the rain fell from the sky, and the ground produced its crops again.

₁₉My brothers, if anyone wanders away from the truth, and someone turns him back again, I want you to know that the man who turns a sinner back from his wandering way will save that sinner's soul from death, and will draw a veil over a host of sins of his own.

Introduction to the First Letter of Peter

IT is just possible that the First Letter of Peter is two letters joined together into one. In 4.11 we find a doxology, and the usual place for a doxology to come is at the end. In 3.21 we find a reference to baptism. So some people have thought that from the beginning down to the doxology we have a sermon preached on the occasion of a baptismal service, and that from 4.12 to the end we have a separate address given when trial and persecution were threatening the church. This could well be so, but for the purposes of this introduction we shall treat the letter as one whole.

The First Letter of Peter might well be called the letter of Christian responsibility.

i. It stresses the responsibility of the Christian to God and to Jesus. It is characteristic of this letter that it never mentions a Christian privilege without also mentioning a Christian responsibility. You have received the good news. *Therefore* gird your minds (1.12,13). The good news has been preached to you. *Therefore* put away all malice (1.25–2.1). Christ has suffered. *Therefore* live well (4.1–6). The end is near. *Therefore* live the Christian life (4.7–11). And always this has to be done with the example of Jesus Christ before us (2.21). In First Peter privilege and responsibility go hand in hand.

ii. It stresses the duty of the Christian to the person outside the church. This letter never forgets the propaganda value of a Christian life, and that the best argument for Christianity is a Christian. The Christian is to prove the falsity of the charges against Christianity by the excellence of his life (2.12,15). The Christian wife is to win her pagan husband for the faith without a word being spoken (3.1,2).

iii. It stresses the duty of the Christian to the state. The Christian is to be a good citizen (2.13–17). He is to be a good servant, even when he is treated with injustice, for then he will be like Jesus (2.18–25).

iv. It stresses the Christian's duty to family and to community (2.1–12). Christianity begins at home, and in the community in which a man lives.

v. It stresses the Christian's responsibility to the church, of which he must be a good and willing servant (5.1–5).

The other great line of this letter is its encouragement in the face of coming trial.. The Christian will suffer, but his suffering must never be as an evil-doer, but always as a Christian (4.12-19), and the end is sure (5.6-11).

From beginning to end the First Letter of Peter is the letter of Christian responsibility in every sphere of life.

There are many scholars who doubt whether this letter was written by Peter at all. The only persecution which took place in Peter's lifetime was the persecution set on foot by Nero in Rome about A.D.64, and that persecution did not extend to the provinces, and to the places to which this letter is written (1.1). This did not happen until the time of Domitian about A.D.95 or of Trajan about A.D.111. This is true, but the news of the persecution at Rome instigated by Nero could well have reached Asia Minor and could have sent through the Christians a shudder of terror, when they thought of what had not yet happened, but at any time might happen to them. It is not necessary to abandon Peter's authorship of this letter.

The First Letter of
PETER

Chapter 1

THIS is a letter from Peter, Jesus Christ's apostle. I write to the exiles scattered all over Pontus, Galatia, Cappadocia, Asia and Bithynia, 2to those who have been chosen in the providence of God the Father, who are travelling on the road to holiness in the power of the Spirit, who are destined to obey Jesus Christ and to share in the new relationship with God which God made possible by his sacrificial death. May more and more of God's grace and blessing be with you.

3Praise be to the God and Father of our Lord Jesus Christ, who in his great mercy made our lives begin all over again, and who through the resurrection of Jesus Christ from the dead gave us a living hope, 4and the certainty that one day we will enter into that immortal, undefiled and unfading life which he promised to you, and which he is keeping in heaven for you. 5Your faith has made the power of God the guardian of your lives, until you reach that salvation which will burst upon the world, when time comes to an end. 6You must rejoice in all this, even if at the moment you are involved in a situation in which you are bound to be distressed by all kinds of troubles. 7Even gold which has stood the test of the refiner's fire perishes in the end. But the purpose of all this is that you should emerge with a tried and tested faith, which is more valuable than gold, for such a faith will find praise and glory and honour, when Jesus Christ dawns upon the world again. 8You have never seen him, yet you love him. You do not see him now, yet you believe in him, and your faith makes you rejoice with a joy which is beyond words to tell, and which is tinged with glory. 9And the secret of your joy is that, as the final result of your faith, you are on the way to receiving the salvation of your souls.

10This salvation was the subject of the searching and the investigating of the prophets, who prophesied about the grace which was to come to you. 11They tried to find out to what person and to what time Christ's Spirit within them pointed, when that Spirit declared beforehand the sufferings Christ would have to endure, and the glories which would follow the sufferings. 12It was revealed to them that their search was not for their own sakes, but for yours, for the things they foretold have now been announced to you through those who brought the good news to you through the Holy Spirit sent from heaven. And these are things which even the angels long to see into.

13So then your minds must be stripped for action. You must live soberly. You must set all your hope on the grace which is coming to you when Jesus Christ will appear again. 14You must live like obedient children, and you must not allow your lives to be shaped by the influence of the passions which used to dominate you in the days of your ignorance. 15So far from that, you must show yourselves holy in all your conduct, as he who called you is holy, 16for it stands written: 'You must be holy, because I am holy.'

17The God whom in your prayers you call Father does not arrive at his verdict on any man by favouritism; he judges each man by his actions. You are exiles of eternity, and you must therefore spend your time on this earth in reverent living, 18for you know well what it cost to liberate you from the slavery of that life of futility which you inherited from your fathers. The price did not consist of things which are doomed to decay, of silver and gold. 19The price was the precious life-blood of Christ, who was, as it were, the sacrificial lamb with no flaw or blemish. 20He was destined for this task before the creation of the world, and for your sakes he came for all men to see as time comes to its end. 21It was for the sake of you he came, for you who through him believe in God, who raised him from the dead and gave him glory. So then, your faith and your hope look to God.

22Now that obedience to the truth has purified your souls, and now that you have reached a genuine love for your brother-Christians, you must love each other sincerely and intensely, 23for you have been born all over again through the agency of the living and lasting word of God, and this time your father is not a mortal man but the immortal God. 24For:

> 'Human life is like grass,
>   and all its splendour is like the grass's flower.
> The grass withers; the flower fades;
>   but the word of the Lord remains for ever.'

25And this word is the word of good news which has been preached to you.

Chapter 2

So then, you must strip yourselves of all malicious and twisted conduct, of two-faced and envious behaviour, of all slanderous gossiping. 2As newly-born children want nothing but their mother's milk, so you must set your heart on the pure milk that flows from the word of God, for it is by it that you will grow up in a steady progress towards salvation. 3Surely, in the psalmist's words, you have experienced the kindness of the Lord. 4He is the living stone, rejected as worthless by men, yet chosen and precious to God. So then, you must come to him, 5as if you yourselves were living stones, and you must let yourselves be built into a living temple, in which you will become a holy priesthood, to offer spiritual sacrifices, which God will be glad to accept through Jesus Christ. 6For, as scripture has it:

'See! I am laying in Sion
    a chosen and precious corner-stone,
and whoever believes in him will never
    have his hope disappointed.'

7His preciousness is for you who believe in him. But to those who refuse to believe,

'The very stone which the builders rejected
has become the corner-stone,'

8and he becomes

'A stone over which men will stumble,
and a rock which will trip them up.'

They stumble because they refuse to obey the word—a fate for which they were destined.

9But you are a chosen race, a royal priesthood, a nation different from other nations, a people designed by God to be his own, and it is your task to proclaim the noble deeds of him who called you out of darkness into his wonderful light.

10 'Once you were not a people at all;
  now you are the people of God.
  Once there was no mercy for you;
  now you have received mercy.'

11 My dear friends, I plead with you as exiles of eternity and strangers in this world, to abstain from those passions which are part of sinful human nature, for they wage a continuous campaign against your soul. 12 Live a lovely life among the heathen, and then, when they spread their malicious stories about you as bad men, they will see the lovely way you live, and end up by praising God on the day God comes to judge.

13 Accept the authority of the institutions of human society for the Lord's sake, whether it be that of the emperor, who is the supreme authority, 14 or of governors, on the ground that they are sent by him to punish criminals and to praise good-living citizens. 15 For it is God's will that by your good behaviour you should silence the ignorant accusations of senseless men. 16 You must live like free men, but not like men who use their freedom as a pretext for vice. So far from that, you must use your freedom to become God's slaves. 17 You must honour all men; you must love the members of the Christian community; you must reverence God; you must continue to honour the emperor.

18 You slaves must accept the authority of your masters with all respect, not only in the case of those who are kind and considerate, but also in the case of those who are perversely unfair. 19 For a man indeed deserves praise, if, because of his continual consciousness that he is living in the presence of God, he uncomplainingly bears pain, even when he is suffering undeservedly. 20 What credit is it to you if you get a beating for doing wrong, and bear it uncomplainingly? But to suffer when you have behaved well, and to bear it uncomplainingly, is something which is a credit to you in the sight of God. 21 This is the very situation to which you have been called, for Christ too suffered for you, and in so doing, he left you an example, for he wanted us to follow in his steps.

22 'For he committed no sin,
  and no one ever heard him speak a twisted word.'

23 He did not answer insult with insult. He did not answer ill-treatment with threats of revenge. No! He committed himself and his cause to the Judge whose verdict is just. 24 In his own body he carried

our sins to the cross, for he wanted us to be able to die to sin and to live to goodness. It is by his wounds that you have been healed. 25Once you were straying away like sheep, but now you have turned to the shepherd and guardian of your souls.

Chapter 3

IN the same way, you wives must accept the authority of your husbands. Your aim must be that any of them who refuse to believe will be won over by the conduct of their wives, without a word being spoken, 2when they see how reverent and pure your conduct is. 3Your beauty must not be the superficial beauty which depends on elaborate hair-styles and expensive jewellery and the wearing of fashionable clothes. 4No! Your beauty must be the beauty of your inner character and personality. It must consist of the beauty of a gentle and serene character, a beauty which the years cannot wither, for in God's sight that is what is really precious. 5This was the beauty with which once upon a time consecrated women, whose hopes were set on God, adorned themselves. They accepted the authority of their husbands. 6It was in this way that Sarah obeyed Abraham, calling him master. And you have now become Sarah's daughters, if you continue to live well, and if you refuse to allow anything to reduce you to frightened panic.

7In the same way, you husbands must live understandingly with your wives. You must treat them with special respect, for women are the weaker sex. They too, you must remember, are sharers with you in God's gift of life eternal. For only if you live like that will there be no barrier between your prayers and God.

8Finally, you must be one in your attitude to life, and one in your sympathy with each other. Love must be the hall-mark of your society. You must be deeply concerned for others. There must be no pride in you. 9You must never repay injury with injury, or abuse with abuse. You must ask God to bless people who treat you badly. It is to act like that that you were called and that is the way in which you will receive for yourselves the blessing God has promised you.

10'For, if a man wants a life he can love,
    and if he wants to experience good fortune,
  he must restrain his tongue from evil,
    and his lips from twisted speaking.

11He must turn away from what is wrong, and do what is right.
He must make right relationships with his fellowmen
the object of all his endeavour and his search,
12for God looks with favour on the good,
and is always ready to hear their prayer,
But his face is set against wrong-doers.'

13Who can harm you, if you make what is right the object of all your endeavour? 14Even if you have to suffer because of doing the right thing, you will still have joy. Don't allow their threats to terrify or distress you. Make Christ your Lord, and give him a unique place in your hearts. 15Always have your answer ready, when anyone asks you to give an account of the hope all Christians share, 16but do so with gentleness and with reverence. Keep your conscience clear, for then, when slanderous stories are spread about you, those who abuse your fine Christian life will be ashamed of what they said about you. 17For, if it is God's will, it is better to suffer for doing the right thing than for doing the wrong thing. 18For Christ too died once and for all for our sins. He, the good, died for us, the bad, and he died to open the way to God for you. He underwent physical death, but in his spirit he was brought to life, 19and in his spirit he went and preached to the spirits in prison. 20These were the spirits of men, who long ago refused to obey God, when in the time of Noah God in his patience withheld his hand, while the ark was being built. In the ark a few people, eight souls in all, were brought safely through the water. 21That water was the symbol to which the water of baptism, which now saves you, corresponds. For baptism is not simply the removal of physical dirt from your bodies; it is a confession of faith to God by a good conscience—and it is the resurrection of Jesus Christ that makes this saving process possible. 22And he is at God's right hand, for he went to heaven after angels and demonic authorities and powers had been made subject to him.

Chapter 4

WHEN he was here in the body Christ accepted suffering, and you must arm yourselves with the same resolution, for in this earthly life the way to be done with sin lies through suffering. 2The object of such suffering is to enable a man to live the rest of his earthly life in obedience, not to human passions, but to God's will. ₅In your past life you had ample time to follow the heathen way of life. Your conduct was characterized by shameless immorality, by giving your passions their way, by habitual drunkenness, by carousals and drinking parties, and by idolatries which outrage common decency. ₄Your former associates therefore find it strange when you no longer join them in their headlong rush into the maelstrom of debauchery, and their surprise makes them abusive. ₅But they will have to answer for their conduct to him who is ready to judge the living and the dead. ₆For the object of preaching the good news to the dead was that, although in this human life they had received the judgment of death which all men receive, they might yet in their spiritual existence learn to live as God wants them to live.

₇It will not be long now until the end of the world comes. Keep calm and keep sober—you will pray all the more effectively, if you do. ₈Above all, love each other intensely, for love draws a veil over many a sin. ₉Keep open house for all, and never grudge it. ₁₀Each of you has his own special gift, and all of you must use your gifts in the service of one another. Only thus will you use as you ought the varied grace which God has entrusted to you. ₁₁If any of you speaks to the fellowship, he must speak as a man with a message from God. If anyone is called upon to undertake some service, he must do so in the strength which God supplies. All your actions must be designed to bring glory to God through Jesus Christ, for his is the glory and the power for ever and ever. Amen.

₁₂My dear friends, do not be surprised at the ordeal by fire in which you find yourselves involved, as if something strange was happening to you, for it has been sent to test you. ₁₃So far from that, rejoice in so far as you are sharing in the sufferings of Christ, for, if you do so, when his glory flashes upon the world, you will greet it with a surge of joy. ₁₄If they throw the name of Christ in your teeth as an insult, it is all joy, because then the Spirit of God in all his splendour rests upon you. ₁₅I say this because none of you must ever have to suffer as a murderer, or as a thief, or as a criminal, or as unjustifiably interfering with other people's affairs. ₁₆But if any of you has to suffer for being a Christian, he must not be ashamed to do so. He must make the name of Christian a name which brings honour to God. ₁₇For the time has come for judgment to begin, and to begin from the house of God. And if it begins with us, what will be the end for those who refuse to accept the good news that God has sent?

18'And if it is going to be difficult
for the good man to be saved,
what will happen
to the impious and the sinner?'

19Those for whom suffering is the will of God must continue to live well, and must commit their lives to the Creator on whom they can rely.

Chapter 5

IT is to the elders in your fellowship that I address my appeal. I too am an elder. With my own eyes I saw Christ suffer, and I will share with you in the glory which is destined to flash upon the world. 2Be true pastors of the flock of God which is in your charge. Exercise your oversight over them, not like men who have been conscripted into office, but like willing volunteers, as God would have you to do; not for the mean motive of what you can get out of it, but as men eager for the task; 3not with any desire to domineer over those allotted to your charge, but as examples to the flock. 4And when the chief shepherd appears, you will receive the glorious crown, which will never wither.

5In the same way, you younger men must submit to the authority of your elders. All of you in your service of each other must put on the apron of humility, because:

'God is hostile to the arrogant,
but favours the humble.'

6Submit yourselves with no thought of self-assertion to the strong control of God, and then in his good time he will honour you. 7Bring all your worries to him to carry for you, for he is always concerned about you.

8You must be abstemious. You must be on the alert. Your enemy the Devil prowls around, like a roaring lion, looking for someone to devour. 9You must resist him with a rock-like faith, and you must realize that, so long as they are in the world, all members of that Christian brotherhood of which you are a part must right to the very end experience the same kind of suffering. 10For a short time you will have to suffer, but the God of all grace who through Christ called you into his eternal glory will restore you, establish you, strengthen you, and give you a firm foundation for your life. 11To him be power for ever and ever. Amen.

12I am writing this letter to you with the help of Silvanus, who is in my estimation a brother in whom you can have every confidence. I write to encourage you, and to add my personal testimony that this is the true grace of God. Stand fast in it.

13The Christian church in its modern Babylon—chosen just as you have been chosen—sends its good wishes, and so does my son Mark.

14Greet each other with the kiss of Christian love. Every blessing be on you all who belong to Christ.

Introduction to the Second Letter of Peter

THE writer of this letter is not out to tell his readers anything new; he is out to remind them of what they already know and of what they should never have forgotten (1.12,13).

In particular they should have known that the great promise of Christianity is that through it men can escape from the corruption of this world (1.4). But false teachers have come in, and have brought with them eternal danger, for the whole lesson of history, as exemplified in the cases of Noah and Lot, is that God destroys the sinner and rescues his own from the evil of their age (2.4-10).

The description of these false teachers is vivid. By implication we learn that they dealt in myths (1.16), that they interpreted scripture to suit themselves (1.20,21), and that they twist the meaning of things to their own destruction (3.16). They are utterly licentious and immoral (2.2; 2.13-18). They promise freedom, but they themselves are the slaves of corruption (2.17-19). They escaped the defilement of sin only to plunge into it again. It would have been better for them never to have known the right, than to have known it, and then to have relapsed into gross immorality (2.20-22).

This was only to be expected, for it was prophesied that evil men would arrive on the scene (3.1-3). They think that Christ will not come again; but he is coming. The delay is only God's way of giving men a further chance to amend their lives, and in any case they must remember that in the sight of God a thousand years is as a day (3.1-10). The prospect of Christ's coming and God's judgment demands a life of goodness (3.11-18).

Here, clearly, we have still another case of men who taught that sin did not matter, and who perverted the grace of God into an excuse for sinning as they pleased (pp. 148-150).

'Lilies that fester smell far worse than weeds,' and the corruption of the best always results in the worst. These men were threatening to turn the Christian gospel into an excuse for sin, and the writer of this letter is fighting a battle to keep the Christian faith and life as they ought to be.

It has to be said that a very great many scholars, from John Calvin onwards, have been very doubtful if Peter really is the author of this letter. There are three main reasons for this doubt.

First, the style of this letter is so different from the first letter which bears Peter's name that it is next to impossible that the same man could have written both. This is one of the most florid, rhetorical and flamboyant pieces of style in the New Testament.

Second, in 3.15, 16, the writer writes to his readers as if the letters of Paul were well known to them. This seems to imply that the letters of Paul had been collected and published and were part of the literature of the church. But Paul's letters were private letters, and they were not collected and edited and published for all to read until at least A.D.90. In the early sixties, when Peter died, it would hardly have been possible to write like this.

Third, he talks of the people who said that the Second Coming was not going to happen, because things have been just the same 'since the fathers fell asleep' (3.4). This seems to mark out the readers of this letter as at least second generation Christians, whose fathers, who had first heard the Christian message, are now dead.

It may be that the writer of this letter was someone who knew well what Peter had said in his preaching and his writing, and who knew well what he would say in the present situation, and who wrote in his great teacher's name.

The Second Letter of
PETER

Chapter 1

This is a letter from Simon Peter, Jesus Christ's servant and apostle to those who through the justice of our God and Saviour Jesus Christ have been privileged to receive a faith as precious as our own. 2May God's grace and every blessing be given ever more richly to you, and may you enter ever more and more deeply into the knowledge of God and of Jesus our Lord.

3This I can pray with confidence, for his divine power has gifted us with everything necessary for life and godliness, because we have come to know him who called us to share his own glory and excellence. 4It was through the excellence of his glory that we received the precious and very great gifts he promised to us, and it is through these gifts that you are enabled to escape the world's corruption, which is the fruit of unbridled passion, and so to become sharers in the divine nature. 5And this is the very reason why you must make up your minds to make every effort to equip your faith with virtue, your virtue with knowledge, 6your knowledge with self-mastery, your self-mastery with fortitude; your fortitude with godliness, 7your godliness with Christian friendliness; your friendliness with love. 8For, if you possess these virtues, and if you keep on growing in them, it will keep you from being ineffective and unproductive on your road to an ever deeper knowledge of our Lord Jesus Christ. 9If such virtues are lacking in a man's life, he is blind and short-sighted, and he has forgotten that his life has been cleansed from the sins that once defiled it. 10Brothers, you must be all the more eager to confirm the fact that you really have been called and chosen. If you live like this, you will never collapse on the march, 11for then the way into the everlasting Kingdom of our Lord and Saviour Jesus Christ will open ever more generously to you.

12I therefore propose to keep on constantly reminding you of these things, although you know them already, and although you are well grounded in the truth which you already possess. 13I regard it as my duty, so long as this transient life remains to me, to keep on reminding you of these things, for I want to prevent you from falling into a sleepy lethargy, 14for I am well aware that my earthly pilgrimage has not long to go now, because our Lord Jesus Christ himself has told me so. 15And I will make every effort to see to it that after my death you will be able to call these things to mind, whenever need arises.

16It is not skilfully contrived fictions that we made use of to tell you about the power and the coming of our Lord Jesus Christ. So far from that, we were eye-witnesses of his majesty. 17There was a time when he received honour and glory from the Father, a time when there came to him, sent from the majestic glory, that voice which said: 'This is my Son, the beloved and only one in whom I have found my delight.' 18At that time we too heard that voice sent from heaven, for we were with him on the sacred mountain. 19This makes us even more sure of the message of the prophets. You will be wise to pay attention to it, for it is like a lamp shining in a dark place, until the day dawns, and the morning-star rises in your hearts. 20But it is of the first importance that you should realize that no prophecy in scripture is a matter for one's own individual interpretation, 21for no prophecy came through some man's will. No! Prophecy came because men were moved by God to speak, under the influence of the Holy Spirit.

Chapter 2

FALSE prophets emerged in Israel, and there will be false teachers among you too. They will introduce pernicious heresies by underhand methods, and they will repudiate the Master who bought them for himself. Their conduct will result in their own speedy destruction. 2They will have many followers in their blatant immoralities, and through them the true way will be brought into disrepute. 3They will be out for what they can get, and they will use plausibly constructed stories to exploit you. Long ago sentence was passed on them, and it has never been revoked. Their doom is not asleep.

4We know that God did not spare the angels who sinned. We know that he committed them to hell in pits of darkness to be kept for judgment. 5We know that God did not spare the ancient world, and we know that, when he despatched the flood on the world of impious men, he saved Noah, the preacher of righteousness, along with seven others. 6We know that God reduced the cities of Sodom and Gomorrah to ashes, and sentenced them to complete destruction. We know that in that catastrophe God provided an example of what is going to happen to the impious. 7We know that he rescued Lot, who was a good man, and who was distressed by the blatantly immoral conduct of the wicked. 8For to that good man in his life amongst them the sights he saw and the things he heard made their lawless conduct a daily agony to his law-abiding soul. 9We can therefore be sure that the Lord knows how to rescue God-fearing men from their ordeal, and equally he knows how to keep the wicked under punishment to await the day of judgment, 10especially those whose conduct is dominated by the polluted passions of their lower nature, and characterized by contempt for all authority.

Foolhardy and self-opinionated, they have no compunction in insulting the celestial glorious ones, 11whereas angels, who are their superiors in strength and power, do not attack other celestial beings with insults, even when they are seeking judgment against them in the presence of the Lord. 12They are no better than brute beasts, born by nature to be caught and killed. They heap their insults on anything they do not understand. And like beasts they will certainly be destroyed. 13Injury they inflicted, and injury they will receive in return. To revel in broad day light is their idea of pleasure. They are disfiguring blemishes on your society. Even when they share your meals with you, they are luxuriating in the deceptions which they practise, 14They strip with their eyes every woman they look at. They are insatiable in looking for sin. Those whose moral defences are weak are the victims of their seductions to sin. They are stripped for action in the race to get. God's curse is on them! 15They have left the straight road and have gone wandering. They have taken the same road as Balaam, the son of Bosor, who loved ill-gotten gain. 16But Balaam was forcibly brought face to face with his disobedience to God. A dumb animal spoke to him with a human voice, and halted the prophet in his mad career.

17These men are wells with no water in them. They are mists driven by a squall of wind. The depths of darkness are reserved for them. 18With their bombastic and empty talk they use the seductions of physical passion and blatant immorality to make victims of those who are just beginning to escape from the errors of the society in which they used to live. 19They promise them freedom, while they themselves are enslaved by corruption; for a man is a slave to that by which he has been mastered. 20If through coming to know our Lord and Saviour Jesus Christ they escaped the defilements of the world, and if they again became involved in them, and were again mastered by them, they finish up worse than they began. ₂₁For it would have been better for them never to have known the way of goodness than to have known it and then to have abandoned the sacred commandment which they were taught. ₂₂In their case the proverb has turned out to be true: 'A dog returns to his own vomit,' and: 'The sow that has been washed returns to rolling in the mud.'

Chapter 3

My dear friends, this is the second letter which I have now written to you. In both of them it has been, and is, my aim to stimulate you to do some straight thinking by reminding you of what you already know. ₂My aim is to compel you to remember the words already spoken to you by God's dedicated prophets, and the command of the Lord and Saviour which you received from your apostles. ₃Right at the beginning you must realize that in the last days there will come men who will pour cynical scorn on the faith, and who know no law but their own desires. ₄'What has happened to his promised coming?' they will demand. 'Already a generation has passed to its rest, and the situation remains exactly as it always has been since the world was created.' ₅Such men have chosen to shut their eyes to the fact that long ago the heavens existed, and an earth was formed out of water and through water by the word of God. ₆And it was by these waters that that ancient world was inundated and destroyed. ₇But the present heavens and earth are by that same word reserved for fire. They are being kept for the day of judgment, when godless men will be destroyed.

₈My dear friends, there is one fact you must never forget. One day to the Lord is the same as a thousand years, and a thousand years are the same as one day. ₉It is not dilatoriness—although some people think it is—which keeps the Lord from fulfilling his promise; it is his patience with you. He does not want any to be destroyed; he wants them to find their way to repentance. ₁₀The day of the Lord will come as unexpectedly as a thief. When it comes the heavens will vanish with a sound like roaring fire. The heavenly bodies will disintegrate in flames. The earth, and everything in it that man has made, will be laid bare.* ₁₁In view of this coming dissolution of the universe, ask

*See Notes on pp. 575–6

518

yourselves what kind of people you ought to be! Think in what consecrated godliness of conduct you ought to live! 12Think how you ought to live in constant expectation of the coming of the day of God, and how you ought to do everything possible to hasten its coming! For on it the heavens will be dissolved in fire, and the heavenly bodies will melt in flames. 13But, because God has promised that it shall be so, we await the new heavens and the new earth, in which justice will have its home.

14So then, my dear friends, since this is what you are waiting for, make up your minds to exert every effort to see to it that that day will find you spotless and blameless, at peace with God. 15You must regard our Lord's patience as your opportunity of salvation. This is what our dear colleague Paul too wrote to you in the wisdom God gave him. 16This is what he says in all his letters, when he speaks of this subject in them. In his letters there are some passages which are not too easy to understand, passages which men, whose knowledge of the faith is inadequate and who lack stability, twist to suit themselves, as they do with the rest of the scriptures—to their own ruin. 17So then, my dear friends, you have been warned in advance. You must therefore take every precaution not to become involved in, and swept away by, the error of men who disregard the laws of God, for, if that happens, you will have no firm ground left to stand on. 18You must steadily grow in grace and you must steadily come to know more and more of our Lord and Saviour Jesus Christ. Glory be to him now and for all eternity!

Introduction to the First Letter of John

IT has been well said that a suitable title for this letter would be *The Tests of Life*. In it there is a phrase which occurs again and again—By this we know. In each case there is a test of what the true Christian is, and by inference an indication of the mistakes of the misguided people who are threatening to wreck the Christian community. Let us then look at these tests.

i. The first test is that we can only prove that we really do know God by keeping his commandments (2.3; 2.5; 5.2). This is clearly a rebuke to the Gnostics who said that sin does not matter, and to the Christians who twisted the grace of God into an excuse for sinning. We can only prove that we are Christians by walking as Jesus walked (2.5).

ii. The second test is that we can only prove the reality of our faith by doing right, by believing in Jesus, and by loving our fellow men (3.10,16,19,24). John is quite clear that to hate your brother is to be as bad as a murderer (3.15). Forthrightly he lays it down that to say that we love God, and at the same time to hate our brother, is to be a liar (4.20). The most correct theology and the most faultless morality without love are not Christian. Once again, the Gnostics who despised their fellow men stand condemned.

iii. The third test is that the real Christian must believe that Jesus really did come in the flesh (4.2). The Christian must believe in the real flesh and blood manhood of his Saviour. He must believe in a real and genuine incarnation. Once again, the Gnostics who said that Jesus was no more than a phantom in human form and who denied him a flesh and blood body are condemned.

iv. The fourth test is willingness to listen to the word and the message of God (4.6). The Gnostics claimed to have special and private information, to have, indeed, a gospel of their own. The real Christian never thinks that he knows better than the gospel.

v. The fifth test is the possession of the Holy Spirit (4.13). The true Christian lives in the guidance and in the strength of the Spirit.

To love and to obey God, to believe in Jesus and to be convinced of his true manhood, always to love our fellow men, and to live in the Spirit, these for John are the tests of the truly Christian life.

The First Letter of
JOHN

Chapter 1

OUR theme is the Word which is life. We tell you of what was there from the beginning, of what we heard, and saw with our own eyes, of what we looked at, and touched with our own hands. ₂This life was full displayed for all to see. We saw it, and we speak from personal experience. It is news of this eternal life, which was with the Father, and which was full displayed to us, that we are now bringing to you. ₃We bring you the message of what we saw and heard. We do so because we have fellowship with God and with his Son Jesus Christ, and we want you to share with us in that fellowship. ₄We are writing this to you, because we want our joy to be complete.

₅The message which we have heard from him and which we are transmitting to you is this—God is light and there is no darkness in him. ₆To claim to have fellowship with God, and at the same time to walk in darkness, is to speak and act a lie. ₇To walk in the light, as he is in the light, is to have fellowship with each other. And the blood of Jesus his Son purifies us from all sin. ₈To claim that we have no sin is an act of self-deception, and a proof that we have no idea of the truth. ₉If we confess our sins, we can depend on him, even although he is just, to forgive us our sins, and to purify us from every kind of wickedness. ₁₀To say that we have never committed a sin is as good as to call him a liar, and to prove that we have no idea what his message means.

Chapter 2

MY dear children, I am writing like this to you to keep you from committing any sin. But, if anyone does sin, we have one to plead our cause with the Father, I mean Jesus Christ—and he is good. ₂He himself is the sacrifice, by which the defilement of our sins is removed, and not only the defilement of our sins but also of those of the whole world. ₃The only test by which we can really know that we do know him is this—do we obey his commandments? ₄If anyone claims to know him, and does not obey his commandments, that man is a liar, who does not know what truth is. ₅But in anyone who obeys his message, love for God has reached perfection. Here is the one test which proves that our lives are indissolubly bound to his. ₆Anyone who claims that his life is indissolubly linked to the life of Christ must live the same kind of life as he did.

₇My dear friends, it is not a new commandment that I am writing to you about. It is an old commandment which you have possessed from the beginning of your Christian life. The old commandment is the message which you have heard. ₈But there is a sense in which it is a new commandment that I am writing to you about. What I am writing to you about came true in him and in your own experience. It is new because we are now in a situation in which the darkness is passing away, and in which the real light is already shining. ₉If a man claims to be in the light, and at the same time hates his brother, he is still in the dark. ₁₀To love your brother is to live in the light; it is to live a life in which there is nothing to make a man stumble. ₁₁To hate your brother is to be in the dark, and to walk in the dark. For a man to live like that is to have no idea where he is going, because his eyes are blinded by the dark.

₁₂I write to you, my dear children,
  because your sins have been forgiven for his sake.
₁₃I write to you, fathers,
  because you know him who existed when the world began,
    and who still exists.
 I write to you, young men,
  because you have conquered the Evil One.
₁₄I have written to you, my children,
  because you know the Father.
 I have written to you, fathers,
  because you know him who existed when the world began,
    and who still exists.
 I have written to you, young men,
  because you are strong,
    because God's word has its home in you,
      and because you have conquered the Evil One.

₁₅You must not be in love with the world, and the things of the world. No one can be in love with the world and in love with God at one and the same time. 16Everything that is characteristic of the world, the desires of the passions, the way in which the sight of what we have not got kindles our desires for it, the tawdry glamour of this world's life, has its source, not in the Father, but in the world. 17There is no permanence in the world and the things it sets its heart upon, but to do God's will is to last for ever.

18Children, it is the last hour. You were told that Antichrist is coming, and now many Antichrists have arisen. This is how we know that it is the last hour. 19They left our fellowship, but they never really belonged to it. If they had really belonged to our fellowship, they would have remained with us. They left us to make it clear that none of them belong to us. 20They speak as if they were the only ones anointed by God with his Holy Spirit. But you too have had that experience, and all of you possess knowledge. 21It is not because you do not know the truth that I have written to you; it is because you do know it, and you are well aware that no lie has its source in the truth. 22Surely the supreme lie is to deny that Jesus is the Messiah. The one who denies the Father and the Son is Antichrist. 23To deny the Son is to deny the Father too; to acknowledge the Son is to have the Father too. 24What you heard when you first became Christians must remain immovably in you. If what you heard when you first became Christians remains immovably in you, then you too will remain in indissoluble union with the Son and the Father. 25And the promise that he made to us is eternal life.

26I have written to you about those who are trying to lead you astray. 27As for you, the anointing with the Spirit, which you received from him, remains with you, and you do not need anyone to teach you. So far from that, the fact that you were anointed with the Spirit gives you all knowledge. His teaching is the truth itself and no lie. Therefore, you must remain united with Christ, as he taught you.

28My dear children, your life must be indissolubly united with his even here and now, and then, whenever he appears, we will have nothing to fear, and we will not try to hide in shame from him, when he comes. 29You know that he is good, and therefore you must be well aware that everyone who practises goodness draws his life from him.

Chapter 3

THE fact that we have been called the children of God must compel us to see how great a love the Father has given us. We are not only called his children; we are his children. The world does not recognize us, because it did not recognize him. ₂My dear friends, already here and now we are God's children, but what we shall be has not yet been revealed. What we do know is that, when Christ appears, we shall be like him, because we shall see him as he is. ₃If any man has this hope, the hope that is founded on Christ, he purifies himself as Christ is pure.

₄To commit sin is to break God's law. Sin is in fact the breaking of that law. ₅Christ himself was completely free from sin, and he appeared, as you are well aware, to remove sins altogether. ₆If a man's life is linked with the life of Christ he stops sinning. If a man goes on sinning, this is the proof that he has neither seen nor known Christ. ₇Dear children, you must not allow anyone to lead you astray. The man who does the right thing is a good man, just as Christ is good. ₈The man who goes on sinning is a child of the Devil, for there never was a time when the Devil was not a sinner. The reason why the Son of God appeared was to destroy the Devil's work. ₉No one who has God for his father continues to sin, because God's seed is a permanent part of him. He cannot go on sinning, because God is his father. ₁₀The test which makes it evident who are God's children and who are the Devil's children is that, if a man does not do what is right, and if a man does not love his fellowman, he is not God's child.

₁₁This is so because from the beginning the one thing that you have been taught is to love one another. ₁₂We must never be like Cain, who was a child of the Evil One, and murdered his brother. And why did he murder him? Because his own conduct was bad and his brother's was good. ₁₃Do not be surprised, brothers, if the world hates you. ₁₄It is because we love our fellowmen that we know that we have crossed the boundary between death and life. Not to love is to remain in the realm of death. ₁₅To hate one's fellowman is to be a murderer, and you know well that no murderer possesses eternal life as a permanent part of his being. ₁₆The action of Christ in laying down his life for us has shown us what love is; and we too are bound to lay down our lives for our fellowmen. ₁₇If a man is comfortably equipped with this world's necessities, and if he sees a brother man in need, and shuts his heart against him, how can he claim that God's love is an integral part of his life? 18Dear children, our love must not be a thing of words and of fine talk; it must be a thing of action and of sincerity.

19It is when we have a love like that that we will know that our life has its source in the truth, 20and, if there are times when our conscience condemns us, we will be able to assure ourselves before him by remembering that God is greater than our conscience, and that he knows all about us. 21My dear friends, if our conscience does not condemn us, we can come to God with confidence, 22and receive from him whatever we ask, because we keep his commandments and do what pleases him. 23It is his command that we should accept the claims of his Son Jesus Christ, and that we should love one another, for this is the commandment he gave us. 24If a man keeps God's commandments, God enters into his life, and he enters into God's life. It is through the Spirit, whom he gave us, that we know that he has entered into our life.

Chapter 4

MY dear friends, do not trust every man who claims to be inspired by the Spirit. You must test such claims to inspiration to see if they really do have their origin in God, for many prophets inspired by false spirits have gone out into the world. 2The test by which you can recognize God-given inspiration is this. Everyone who claims to be inspired, and who accepts and states as an article of faith that Jesus Christ came in a human flesh and blood body, does draw his inspiration from God. 3Everyone who claims to be inspired, and who denies this article of faith about Jesus Christ, does not draw his inspiration from God. This is in fact the spirit of Antichrist. You were told that Antichrist was to come; but he is already in this world, here and now. 4But, my dear children, your life has its source in God, and yours is the victory over them, because the Spirit who is in you is greater than the spirit who is in the world. 5Their life has its source in the world. Therefore, their message has its source in the world. That is why the world listens to them. 6Our life has its source in God. If a man knows God, he listens to us; if a man does not belong to God, he does not listen to us. That is how we recognize which spirit is the spirit of truth, and which is the spirit of error.

7My dear friends, we must love one another, for love's source is

God, and to love is to be God's child and to know God. 8Not to love is not to know God, because God is love. 9As far as we are concerned, God's love was displayed in all its splendour by his action in sending his only Son into the world, and so through him giving us life. 10The wonder of love is not that we loved God but that he loved us enough to send his Son to remove the barrier that our sins had erected between us and him. 11My dear friends, if God loved us like that, it is our bounden duty to love each other. 12No one has ever seen God. But, if we love each other, God becomes an integral part of our lives, and his love is perfected in us.

13The proof that our life is joined to God's life, and his to ours, is to be found in the share of the Spirit which he has given to us. 14Further, we declare from personal knowledge, because we were eye-witnesses of the facts, that God sent his Son to be the Saviour of the world. 15If any man accepts, and states as an article of faith, that Jesus is the Son of God, God enters into his life, and he into God's. 16As for us, we have personal knowledge of, and faith in, the love which God has for us.

God is love. So then, if a man lives a life of love, he enters into the life of God, and the life of God enters into him. 17As far as we are concerned, love reaches its peak in that we are certain that on the day of judgment we have nothing to fear, because our relationship to this world is the same as his was. 18In love there is no fear. So far from that, perfect love banishes fear. Fear is connected with punishment. If a man is still afraid, he has not yet experienced love in all its perfection. 19Our love has its source and origin in God's love, for God loved us before we loved him. 20If anyone claims that he loves God, while at the same time he hates his brother, he is a liar. For, if a man does not love his fellowman, whom he has seen, he cannot possibly love God, whom he has not seen. 21And indeed the commandment that he has given us is that the man who loves God must love his fellowman too.

Chapter 5

To believe that Jesus is the Messiah is to be a child of God. To love the father is to love his child. 2We are therefore bound to realize that to love God and to obey his commandments must mean to love his children too. 3To love God is to obey his commandments, and his commandments are not burdensome, 4because to be a child of God is to be victorious over the world, and the victory which conquers the world is our faith. 5Surely the man who is victorious over the world is none other than the man who believes that Jesus is the Son of God.

6This is he who came through the water of his baptism and the blood of his cross—I mean Jesus Christ. It was not only by the water that he came; it was by the water and the blood. It is the Spirit who is the witness to this, because the Spirit is truth. 7That truth is guaranteed because there are three witnesses, 8the Spirit, the water, and the blood, and the three agree. 9We accept human evidence on these terms, and surely the evidence of God has still greater weight, and this evidence is the evidence of God. This is the evidence that he has given in regard to his Son. 10If a man believes in the Son of God, he finds his evidence in his own heart. If a man refuses to believe God, by that very action he as good as calls God a liar, because he has refused to accept the evidence which God gave in regard to his Son. 11The evidence in question is this—that God gave us eternal life, and that his Son is the source of this life. 12To have the Son is to have life; not to have the Son is not to have life.

13My purpose in writing this letter to you is to give you the assurance that you do possess eternal life. I am writing to you who already know who and what the Son of God is, and who have committed yourselves to him. 14The reason why we can approach God with complete confidence is that, if we ask for anything that is in accordance with his will, he listens to us. 15If we know that he listens to us, whenever we ask him for anything, we know that the things for which we have asked him are already ours.

16If anyone sees his fellowman committing a sin which is not a deadly sin, he must pray to God for him, and he will be the means whereby the sinner receives life. This is in the case of those whose sin is not deadly sin. There is such a thing as deadly sin. To pray about that is a different matter. 17All wrong-doing is sin, but there is sin which is not deadly sin.

18We know that no child of God keeps on sinning. We know that the Son of God keeps him safe, and that the Evil One cannot touch him. 19We know that, although the whole world lies in the power of the Evil One, we belong to God. 20We know that the Son of God has come, and has given us understanding to know the One who is real. Our lives are indissolubly bound to the One who is real, because they are indissolubly bound to his Son Jesus Christ. This is the real God, and this is eternal life. 21My dear children, be on your guard against false gods.

Introduction to the Second Letter of John

THIS little letter does no more than reiterate the advice and the warnings of the first letter. The recipients are commanded to love one another, to be obedient to the commandments of God, and never to move from the belief that Jesus came to this world in full flesh and blood manhood. The letter is not so much a rebuke for any past mistakes; it is rather a warning to put its readers on their guard, should any of the false teachers visit them.

The only problem in the letter is who the elect lady is. She may have been a person and an individual, but the tone of the letter makes it much more likely that John is writing to a group and a community, and it is more likely that the phrase the elect lady stands for a church and not a person, and that the elect sister in verse 13 is a sister church.

The Second Letter of
JOHN

THIS is a letter from the Elder to the Lady chosen by God, and to her children, whom I truly love. Nor am I the only person to love you and yours. All who know the truth love you too. ₂It is for the sake of the truth, which has its home among us, and which will always remain with us that I write. ₃Grace, mercy and every blessing to you from God the Father and from Jesus Christ, the Father's Son, in truth and in love.

₄It made me very happy to find that some of your children are making truth the rule of their lives and are thus obeying the commandment we have received from the Father. ₅And now, dear lady, it is not as if I was pressing some new commandment on you. I am reminding you of a commandment we have known since the very beginning of our Christian life. I have only one thing to urge on you—that we should love one another. ₆To love means to live in obedience to God's commandments. This is the commandment which you have been taught from the beginning, and it must be for you the rule of life. ₇I say this because many deceivers have gone out into the world, who do not acknowledge Jesus Christ as coming in flesh and blood manhood. Such a teacher is a deceiver and Antichrist. ₈Be on your guard. You must be careful not to lose all that you worked for. Rather, you must see to it that you receive your reward in full. ₉Every so-called progressive who ceases to take his stand on the teaching of Jesus Christ has lost God. But, if a man continues to take his stand on that teaching, he has both the Father and the Son. ₁₀If anyone visits you, and does not bring this teaching, refuse to have him in your house. Give him no greeting. ₁₁For to give a man like that your good wishes is to become a partner in his evil work.

₁₂There are many things about which I could write to you, but I do not want to communicate with you by paper and ink. I hope to visit you soon, and to talk with you face to face, for then our joy will be complete. ₁₃The children of your sister, chosen by God, send you their good wishes.

Introduction to the Third Letter of John

BEHIND this little letter there is one of the most interesting and important situations in the New Testament.

In the early days of the church there were two kinds of ministry. There was the settled ministry, the ministry of the local congregation, the elders and the deacons. This kind of ministry did its work in one place and within one congregation, much as the ministry functions now. But there was also an itinerant ministry. The prophets and the apostles were not confined to one congregation. They moved throughout the whole church. Their authority was, so to speak, universal and not confined to any one place or any one congregation. *The Teaching of the Twelve Apostles* is the earliest book of Church Order which we possess. It must date back to very early in the second century, to a time very near that at which this little letter was written. This book gives the order for the Eucharist, and then at the end it says: 'But allow the prophets to hold the Eucharist as they will' (*The Teaching of the Twelve Apostles* 10.7). That this itinerant ministry was not without its problems is seen in the passage which immediately follows: 'Concerning the prophets and apostles, act thus according to the ordinance of the gospel. Let every apostle who comes to you be received as the Lord, but let him not stay more than one day, or if need be a second as well; but if he stays three days, he is a false prophet. And when an apostle goes forth let him accept nothing but bread; but, if he asks for money, he is a false prophet' (11.3-6). From this we can see that the itinerant apostles and prophets brought their own problems.

In particular they brought one big problem. They brought the inevitable clash between the itinerant and the settled ministry. The stronger the institution of the settled congregation became, the less it liked the invasions of the nomadic prophets and apostles, especially when these wanderers tried to tell them what to do. And after years of authority the wandering prophets and apostles found it hard to understand that they were no longer welcome.

This is exactly the situation we have in this letter. John is one of the old school. In fact, he was probably the last survivor of the old school. The essence of the situation is in verses 5-10. John pleads for the welcome and the support of those wandering prophets and apostles, who have given up everything to undertake this itinerant ministry.

He pleads that they should be welcomed and supported and helped on their way. But in verses 9 and 10 we read of Diotrephes who wanted nothing to do with these wanderers, who will not receive them, and who would actually debar them from the congregation. Diotrephes is the representative of the settled ministry and he finds the arrival of these wanderers nothing less than a nuisance and a disturbance. Demetrius (verse 12) is presumably still prepared to accept the old order.

So then, in this little letter we see the clash between the itinerant and the settled ministry, with the settled ministry resenting the invasion of these incomers with their claim to special and universal authority. In this letter the aged John throws all his weight on the side of the wandering prophets and apostles. But it was a losing battle and before very long the wandering evangelists had vanished from the scene, and the local ministry became the backbone of the structure of the church.

The Third Letter of
JOHN

THIS is a letter from the Elder to my dear Gaius, whom I truly love.

2My dear friend, it is my prayer that everything is going well with you, and that you are in good health. I know that it goes well with your soul. 3It made me very happy, when some of our fellow-Christians came and told me of your devotion to the truth. I am well aware that you make the truth the rule of your life. 4Nothing gives me greater pleasure than to know that my children are making the truth the rule of their lives.

5My dear friend, you show your loyalty in what you do for your fellow-Christians, strangers though they are to you. 6They have told to the congregation here the story of your Christian love. Please help them on their way in a way that is fitting for servants of God. 7It was for the sake of Christ's name that they set out, and it is their custom to accept nothing from pagans. 8It is our duty to support such men, for by so doing we will become their fellow-workers in the truth.

9I sent a letter about this to the congregation, but Diotrephes cannot stand any interference with what he thinks is his place, and he refuses to recognize our authority. 10So, if I come, I will take occasion to remind the congregation of his conduct. He spreads malicious and untrue stories about us. Not content with that, he refuses to accept our fellow-Christians who wish to visit your congregation. He tries to stop those who would gladly receive them and tries to expel them from the congregation.

11My dear friend, do not imitate a bad example; imitate what is good. The man who does good belongs to God; the man who does evil has never seen God. 12Everyone speaks well of Demetrius, as does the truth itself. We too affirm his worth, and you know that our evidence is true.

₁₃There are many subjects on which I could write to you, but I do not want to communicate with you by pen and ink. ₁₄I hope to see you soon, and we will talk face to face. ₁₅Every blessing to you! The friends here send you their good wishes. Give our good wishes individually to all our friends with you.

Introduction to the Letter of Jude

JUDE, or Judas, was a common name, and we cannot be quite sure who the Jude is who wrote this letter. But there is one very interesting possibility. He describes himself as the brother of James. The only James who was great enough to be called simply James with no further description was the James who was the head of the Jerusalem church. He was the brother of Jesus, and so it may well be that the writer of this letter is Jude, the brother of Jesus (Mark 6.3).

The letter is obviously an emergency production. Jude was going to write a treatise on the faith, but faced with this threatening situation he took up his pen to deal with it (verse 3), and what he has to deal with is the perversion of the truth (verse 4).

Anyone who reads the two letters carefully will see that the contents of this letter are very nearly the same as the second chapter of the Second Letter of Peter. The same danger is threatened; the same licentiousness and ungodly immorality is there; the same prophecy is cited. There is little doubt that the writer of the Second Letter of Peter found this little letter of Jude so cogent and so eloquent and so powerful that he incorporated it into his own.

In the end Jude pleads with his readers to keep themselves in the love of God (21), and to exert every effort to rescue those who had gone so far astray (22,23), and then he comes to the end with the most magnificent doxology in the New Testament (24,25).

Once again we see a Christian teacher wrestling with the perversion of the Christian gospel into an excuse to sin (pp. 148-150).

There is only one other notable thing in this little letter. It does what the New Testament writers very, very seldom do. It quotes books outside the Old Testament and outside scripture altogether. The passage about the argument of Michael with the devil about the body of Moses comes from an apocryphal book called *The Assumption of Moses* (verses 8 and 9), and later on he goes on to quote a passage from the Book of Enoch, which was a book of the same kind (verses 14 and 15). This could mean that Jude comes from a time so early that the canon of Old Testament scripture was not yet finally fixed.

The Letter of
JUDE

THIS is a letter from Jude, Jesus Christ's servant and James'
brother, to those who have been called by God, and whose lives
are lived in the love of God and under the protection of Jesus Christ.
2It is my prayer that you should experience more and more of the
mercy and the love of God, and that you should be blessed ever
increasingly with every good thing.

3My dear friends, while I was devoting all my energies to writing
a treatise for you on the salvation we all share, I felt the necessity to
write to you here and now to urge you strenuously to defend the faith
which was once and for all handed over to God's dedicated people.
4I regard this as necessary because there are some who have insinuated
themselves into your fellowship—they were long ago marked out for
this judgment—godless men they are, who pervert the grace of God
into an excuse for blatant immorality, and who deny our only
Master and Lord, Jesus Christ.

5You have already been given full and final knowledge of the
Christian faith. Nevertheless I want to remind you that the Lord*
who rescued the people of Israel from their slavery in the country of
Egypt later destroyed those who were guilty of unbelief. 6The angels
too who did not observe their own rank, and who left their proper
place, he keeps under guard in eternal chains beneath darkness, to
await the judgment of the great day. 7You have another instance of
this in Sodom and Gomorrah and the neighbouring towns. They
in the same way practised sexual immorality and pursued unnatural vice. They provide an example of what happens to people
who live like that, for they were subjected to the penalty of eternal
fire.

8So too these men today with their so-called visions defile their
bodies, and treat the Lord's authority with contempt, and insult the
glorious celestial ones. 9When Michael the archangel was arguing

*See Notes on pp. 575-6

with the Devil in their dispute about who was to get possession of Moses' body, he did not venture to add insult to condemnation. All he said was: 'The Lord rebuke you.' 10These men attack with their insults everything they do not understand. The things which, like brute beasts, they instinctively do understand are the very things which ruin them. 11Tragic will be their fate, for they have walked in the footsteps of Cain, they have flung themselves into Balaam's error for pay, they rebelled like Korah, and like Korah they are doomed. 12These men are blots on your Love Feasts; they bring no reverence to the sacred meals they share with you. They are supposed to be shepherds of the flock, but the only people they look after are themselves. They are clouds, driven by the wind, yet giving no rain. They are trees, fruitless in autumn, doubly dead, torn up by the roots. 13They are wild sea-waves foaming out their shameless acts. They are wandering stars, and the deepest depths of hell for ever and ever await them.

14It was of these too that Enoch prophesied in the seventh generation after Adam. 'The Lord will come,' he said, 'with tens of thousands of his holy angels 15to execute universal judgment, and to convict the godless of the godless conduct of which they have been guilty, and of the wild words they have spoken against him in their sin and their godlessness.' 16These men are filled with smouldering discontent. They are in a state of chronic resentment against life. Their conduct is determined by nothing but their own desires. Their talk is insolent and arrogant. They give their fulsome admiration to those out of whom they think they can get something.

17As for you, my dear friends, you must remember the statements already made by the apostles of our Lord Jesus Christ. 18During the last time, they said, there will be men to whom religion is a matter for a jest, and who have no principle of action other than their own godless desires. 19They are the kind of men who are a disruptive influence. They know no life beyond the life of this world. They are completely unspiritual. 20As for you, my dear friends, you must continue to build your life on the foundation of your most sacred faith. You must live lives of prayer in the atmosphere of the Holy Spirit. 21You must keep yourselves in the love of God. You must await the mercy of our Lord Jesus Christ, through which you will receive eternal life. 22Some, who cannot make up their minds, you must treat with pity. 23Some you must rescue by snatching them from the fire. With some you must deal with mingled pity and fear. You must hate even clothes stained by contact with a sensual man.

24And to him who is able to keep you from falling, and to bring you blameless into his glorious presence with glad rejoicing, 25to the only God our Saviour, through Jesus Christ our Lord, be glory, majesty, dominion, authority, before time began, and now, and until time ends.

Introduction to the Revelation

To a modern reader the Revelation is the strangest book in the New Testament. In the New Testament it stands alone, and there is nothing like it. But in point of fact it is a specimen of a kind of book which was very common between the Testaments, and of which many other examples exist. It is often called by another name; it is often called the Apocalypse. The Greek word *apokalupsis* means a revealing, an unveiling, a drawing of the curtain aside. And many Apocalypses were written both by Jews and Christians in the years before and after Jesus came. What then were these strange books, and what did they tell of?

The Jews never forgot that they were God's chosen people, and they never lost their faith and hope that some day this would be proved for all to see, and that they would become masters of the world, for they tended to think that they were chosen for power and for glory rather than for service and responsibility.

At first they believed that they would become great when there emerged a king of David's line to lead them to conquest. This was the Messiah whom they expected, and they thought of him in human terms. As time went on they began to think in terms of a supernatural instead of a human leader. But as time passed, and as they were subject in turn to the Babylonians, the Assyrians, the Persians, the Greeks, the Romans, as they realized their own smallness and the world's vastness, they began to see that their greatness could never be achieved by human means at all. After all, Palestine was only one hundred and twenty miles from north to south, and less than fifty miles from east to west. So they began to believe, not in any human leader, but in the direct intervention of God. The day would come when God himself would come striding into history and lead them to greatness and to glory.

So they began to have the belief that all time is divided into two ages. There is this present age, which is wholly bad, wholly under the domination of Satan, and quite beyond cure and reformation. There is the age which is to come, which was the golden age of God and of his people. But how was the one to turn into the other? It would happen on the Day of the Lord, the great day when God himself would enter history. It would be a day of cosmic disintegration, when the sun would be turned into darkness and the moon into blood, and the mountains hurled into the sea, and when all order would become chaos. It would be a day of dreadful judgment; and then the new world would be born, and all would be well.

The Apocalypses were the books in which seers and visionaries set out what they believed would happen on the Day of the Lord. All Apocalypses therefore tend to be unintelligible, because they are trying to describe the indescribable, to express the inexpressible, to put into signs and symbols the terrors and the glories of the end time.

Now this is what our Apocalypse does. Only for it the end is not the Day of the Lord, but the coming again of Jesus Christ in majesty and glory and victory. To paint this picture it takes over much of the imagery and the dramatic apparatus which had attached to the Day of the Lord. Old Testament passages like Isaiah 24, Joel 2, Zephaniah 1 are the basis of the picture. This is a typical Apocalypse, describing the indescribable events which will happen when this world vanishes and the new world is born. We have only to see this to see that it cannot be taken literally. It is a poet's vision far more than it is an historian's story. It is the word of a prophet and a visionary (1.3; 22.9,10), not a literal time-table and description of celestial events.

It begins with the letters to the seven churches, which were the churches in which the seer John's writ ran (1.3). But from chapter 4 onwards it is a series of visions of the end time. The opening of the seven seals (6.1–8.1), the sounding of the seven trumpets (8.2–13.18), the pouring out of the seven bowls (15.1–18.24), the vision of worship and judgment (19.1–20.15), the picture of the new order (20.1–22.5) are all symbolic visions of the end time.

It shows us nothing of the Jesus of the Gospels; it shows us the warrior Christ. It has been said that the Revelation is the most Jewish book in the New Testament. This is true. There is hardly anything in it which cannot be paralleled from the Old Testament. In one thing it is very strange to us, but very Jewish. It calls Jesus the Lamb oftener than any book in the New Testament (eg. 5.8; 6.1; 7.17; 8.1; 14.1). But it is a strange picture, for we hear of the wrath of the Lamb and the victory of the Lamb and the might of the Lamb. This is a Jewish picture. The great Jewish heroes like David and Judas Maccabaeus were depicted as horned lambs. There is no gentleness here at all, only ineluctable power.

And what is at the back of all this? When we read the Revelation, one thing strikes us straight away. Its attitude to the state is quite different from any other book in the New Testament. The other books respect the state and tell Christians to be good citizens (Romans 13.1-7;

1 Timothy 2.2; 1 Peter 2.13-17). But in the Revelation Rome is the great harlot, drunk with the blood of the saints and the martyrs, for in it Babylon stands for Rome (17.1-6). What had gone wrong?

Bit by bit the Roman Emperor had come to be regarded as a god. He embodied the spirit of Rome, and in very gratitude for good rule people had first worshipped the spirit of Rome, and then the Emperor as the incarnation of that spirit. At first the Emperors were embarrassed by this, for they had not sought it. But they began to see how they could use it. Rome stretched from Britain to the Euphrates and from the Danube to North Africa. What could give some kind of unity to this vast polyglot Empire which comprised most of the world? The one thing that could unify it was Caesar worship. So the day came, when once a year every citizen had to burn a pinch of incense to the godhead of Caesar and say: 'Caesar is Lord.' This the Christians would never do. Christ and Christ alone was Lord. And that was why they were persecuted. If they had conformed and had burned the incense and said the sentence, they could have gone off and worshipped anything. But they would not, and so they became what the poet called 'the panting, huddled flock, whose crime was Christ.'

The Revelation comes from that time when men had to choose between Caesar and Christ, when to be true to Christ was to be liable to die. That is why it hates Rome, and that is why it looks so eagerly forward to the end of the present evil age, and the time when Christ's enemies will be vanquished and he will reign for ever and ever.

THE REVELATION TO JOHN

Chapter 1

THIS is the record of the revelation given by Jesus Christ. God gave it to him to show to his servants what must soon happen, and he through his angel sent and made it known to his servant John. ₂John publicly proclaimed the message given to him by God and affirmed by Jesus Christ, telling all that he had seen.

₃God's joy will come to the man who reads
  the words of this prophetic message
    to the assembled people,
  and to those who listen to them,
  and to those who obey what is written in it,
  for it will not be long now until the crucial moment
    of fulfilment comes.

₄This is John's message to the seven churches in the province of Asia.

Grace to you and every blessing,
  from him who is and was and is coming,
  and from the seven spirits before his throne,
  ₅and from Jesus Christ,
    who declared God's truth and whose word can be trusted,
    who was the first to rise from the dead,
    who is the ruler of all earthly kings.
To him who loves us,
  and who liberated us from our sins
    at the cost of his blood,
  ₆and who made us a kingdom
  every member of which is a priest
    to his God and Father,
  to him be glory and dominion for ever and ever. Amen.
  ₇Look! he is coming with the clouds.
    Everyone will see him,
  and so will those who pierced him,
    and all the nations of the earth

will weep in remorse for what they did to him.
Even so! Amen!

₈I am Alpha and Omega, the one who is the beginning and the end, says the Lord, who is and who was and who is coming, the one who holds all things in control. ₉I, John, your fellow-Christian, and your partner in the trouble, in the Kingdom, and in the gallant endurance which being a follower of Jesus involves, was in the island called Patmos, because I had preached God's word and had publicly declared my faith in Jesus. ₁₀On the Lord's Day I fell into a trance, in which I heard behind me a voice like the sound of a trumpet. ₁₁'Write what you are seeing on a scroll,' it said to me, 'and send it to the seven churches, to Ephesus, to Smyrna, to Pergamum, to Thyatira, to Sardis, to Philadelphia, and to Laodicea.'

> ₁₂I turned to see
> whose voice it was that was speaking to me,
> and, when I had turned,
> I saw seven golden lampstands.
> ₁₃And in the middle of them
> there was a figure like a man.
> He was wearing a robe
> that reached down to his feet,
> and he had a golden girdle
> encircling his breast.
> ₁₄The hairs of his head were as white
> as snow-white wool;
> his eyes were like flaming fire;
> ₁₅his feet were like burnished brass,
> refined in a furnace;
> his voice was like the sound
> of torrents of waters
> ₁₆In his right hand
> he had seven stars;
> and out of his mouth
> there came a sharp double-edged sword,
> and his face
> shone like the sun in full blaze.

₁₇When I saw him, I fell at his feet like a dead man. He laid his right hand on me. 'Have no fear,' he said. 'I am the first and the last. ₁₈I am the living one. I was dead, and now I am alive for ever, and the keys of death and Hades are mine. 19Write down what you have seen, what is and what will be hereafter. 20This is the secret meaning of the seven stars, which you saw in my right hand, and of the seven golden lamp-stands. The seven stars are the angels of the seven churches, and the seven lampstands are the seven churches.'

Chapter 2

WRITE this message to the angel of the church at Ephesus.

This is a message to you from the one who holds the seven stars in his right hand, and who walks among the seven golden lamp-stands. 2I know the life that you have lived. I know how hard you have toiled, and how gallantly you have met your troubles. I know how impossible you find it to tolerate evil men. I know that there was a time when you tested those who claim to be apostles, and who have no right to that title, and proved them liars. 3Indeed you have met your troubles with gallantry. Indeed you have suffered for your Christian loyalty, and you have never abandoned the struggle. 4But I do have this criticism of you to make. You have lost the love that once you had, when you first became Christians. 5Think back to the standards that once you had, and repent, and live again the life you lived, when you first became Christians. If you do not, I am coming to you, and, unless you repent, I will remove your lampstand from its place. 6But you do have this in your favour—you hate the practices of the Nicolaitans, and so do I. 7It is the duty of anyone who can hear to listen to what the Spirit is saying to the churches. I will give the victor in the battle of life the right to eat the fruit of the tree of life, which is in the garden of God.

8Write this message to the angel of the church at Smyrna.

This is a message to you from the one who is the first and the last, the one who was dead and who rose to life again. 9I know the troubles you are going through. I know you are destitute of this world's goods. But for all that you are rich in true wealth. I know the slanders of those who call themselves Jews, but who are Satan's synagogue. 10Do not be afraid of what is going to happen to you. The Devil will throw some of you into prison. It will be to test you, and you will have a ten day time of trouble. Prove yourself to be willing to die for your faith, and I will give you life as your victor's crown. 11It is the duty of everyone who can hear to listen to what the Spirit is saying to the churches The second death can never hurt the victor in the battle of life.

12Write this message to the angel of the church at Pergamum.

This is a message from the one who has the sharp, double-edged sword. 13I know where your home is. I know that it is where Satan has his seat of power. And yet I also know that you never lose your grip of me, and that you did not deny your loyalty to me even in the time of Antipas, who was so steadfast in declaring his loyalty to me that he was put to death among you, where Satan has his residence. 14But I do have a few criticisms of you to make. You have among you some who have accepted the teaching of Balaam, who taught Balak to lay a trap for the Israelites, by teaching them to eat meat which has been part of a sacrifice to a heathen idol, and to practise sexual immorality. 15So you too have some who have accepted the very similar teaching of the Nicolaitans. 16You must repent. If you do not, I am coming to you soon, and I will make war on them with the sword of my mouth. 17It is the duty of everyone who can hear to listen to what the Spirit is saying to the churches. To the victor in the battle of life I will give a share of the manna that was hidden away, and I will give him a white stone, and on the stone a new name will be inscribed, a name undisclosed to anyone except to the person who receives it.

18Write this message to the angel of the church at Thyatira.

This is a message from the Son of God, from the one whose eyes are like flaming fire, and whose feet are like burnished brass. 19I know the life you have lived. I know your love, your loyalty, your service, and the gallantry with which you have met your troubles. I know that your conduct was good, when you first began the Christian life, and that it is even better now. 20But I do have this criticism to make of you. You tolerate that Jezebel of a woman who claims to be a prophetess, and whose teaching seduces my servants into committing fornication, and eating meat which has been part of a sacrifice to a heathen idol. 21I gave her time to repent, and she refuses to repent of her fornication. 22I will lay her on a bed of pain, and I will hurl her partners in adultery into terrible trouble, unless they realize how wrong her conduct is, and stop participating in it. 23I will strike her children dead, and all the churches will know that the most secret thoughts of men's minds and the most secret feelings of their hearts are no secrets to me. Each man's conduct will decide what reward or punishment I will assign to him. 24But on all the rest of you in Thy-atira, who have not accepted this teaching, and who have no knowledge of 'the deep secrets of Satan,' as they call them, I make no other demand 25than to order you not to relax your grip on what you have, until I come. 26To the victor in the battle of life, and to the man who to the end lives the kind of life I have commanded him to live, I will give authority over the nations. 27He will shatter them with a rod of iron; they will be smashed like broken pieces of pottery. 28His authority will be like the authority I received from my Father. And I will give him the morning star. 29It is the duty of everyone who can hear to listen to what the Spirit is saying to the churches.

Chapter 3

Write this message to the angel of the church at Sardis. This is a message from the one who has the seven spirits of God and the seven stars. I know the life that you have lived. I know that you have the reputation of being alive, but you are in fact dead. 2Awake from your sleep, and strengthen what is left, for it too is on the way to death, for, as far as I can see, in the sight of God nothing that you should have done has been done. 3So then, keep remembering the faith you have received, and the instruction you were given. Keep on obeying it, and make up your mind to repent. If you do not awake from your sleep, I will come like a thief, and you will not know the moment when I will come upon you. 4In spite of it all, you still have a few people in Sardis who have not stained their clothing, and they will walk with me, dressed all in white, because they deserve to do so. 5The victor in the battle of life will be thus clothed in white robes. I will never erase his name from the book of life. I will acknowledge him as mine before my Father and his angels. 6It is the duty of everyone who can hear to listen to what the Spirit is saying to the churches.

7Write this message to the angel of the church at Philadelphia. This is a message from the one whose nature is holiness and truth, the one who has the key of David. When he opens, no one can shut; when he shuts, no one can open. 8I know the life that you have lived. A door of opportunity, which no man can shut, stands open in front of you, and it is I who have given it to you. I know that you have only a little strength, but you have been obedient to my instructions, and did not disown your loyalty to me. 9I am going to deliver into your hands those who belong to the synagogue of Satan, those who claim to be Jews, but who are liars, and who are not. I will make them come and do homage to you, and I will make it clear to them that you are dear to me. 10You have kept my instructions to face your troubles gallantly. I will therefore keep you safe from the crisis time of ordeal which is going to descend on the whole world to test all the inhabitants of the earth. 11I am coming soon. Never relax your grip on what you have, and then no one will be able to take away your victor's crown. 12I will make the victor in the battle of life a pillar in the temple of my God. Never again will he leave it. I will write on him the name of my God, and the name of the city of my God, the name of the new Jerusalem, which is to come down from heaven from my God. 13It is the duty of everyone who can hear to listen to what the Spirit is saying to the churches.

14Write this message to the angel of the church at Laodicea.

This is a message from the one who is the guarantor of all God's promises, the witness on the truth of whose word you can rely, the moving cause of God's creation. 15I know the life that you have lived. I know that you are neither cold nor hot. If only you were either cold or hot! 16So, because you are tepid, and neither hot nor cold, you make me want to be sick! 17You claim to be rich and wealthy. You claim to have everything you need. You are not aware that in your destitution and blindness and nakedness you are in fact a wretched creature who is to be pitied. 18I therefore strongly advise you to buy from me gold refined in the fire, to make you really rich; and white clothes in which to dress yourself, to keep you from becoming a public spectacle, naked and ashamed; and ointment to put on your eyes, to make you able really to see. 19My way of showing that I love people is to reprove and discipline them. Make up your mind to repent. Make a lasting enthusiasm of your religion. 20I am standing at the door knocking. If anyone hears my voice, and opens the door, I will come in and we will share our meal together, I with him, and he with me. 21To the victor in the battle of life I will give the privilege of sitting with me on my throne, just as I won the victory, and took my seat with my Father on his throne. 22It is the duty of everyone who can hear to listen to what the Spirit is saying to the churches.

Chapter 4

After this I had another vision. There in front of me a door stood open in heaven, and the voice like the sound of a trumpet, which I had heard speaking to me before, spoke to me. Come up here,' it said, 'and I will show you what must happen in the future.' ₂Immediately I fell into a trance. I had a vision of a throne standing in heaven, and of someone sitting on the throne. ₃When I looked at the one sitting on the throne, it was like looking at the sheen of a jasper or carnelian stone, and all around the throne there was a rainbow, gleaming like an emerald. ₄In a circle surrounding the throne I saw twenty-four thrones. And on the thrones I saw twenty-four elders sitting. They were wearing white robes, and they had victors' golden crowns on their heads. ₅Out from the throne there came flashes of lightning and peals of thunder. In front of the throne there were burning seven blazing torches, which are the seven spirits of God. ₆The space in front of the throne looked like a sea of glass, like crystal.

In the middle of the scene, round about the throne, there were four living creatures, covered with eyes, back and front. ₇The first living creature was like a lion; the second living creature was like an ox; the third living creature had a man's face; the fourth living creature was like an eagle in flight. ₈Each of the four living creatures had six wings, and they were covered all over with eyes, inside and out Day and night they never rested from singing:

> 'Holy, holy, holy is the Lord God,
> he who holds all things in control,
> he who was and who is and who is coming.'

₉Whenever the four living creatures give glory and honour and thanksgiving to the one who sits on the throne, and who lives for ever, ₁₀the twenty-four elders throw themselves down in front of the one who sits on the throne, and worship him who lives for ever and ever. They lay their crowns before the throne, and this is their song:

> ₁₁'Our Lord and God, yours is the right
> to receive glory and honour and power,
> for you created all things,
> and it was through your will
> that they came into being, and were created.'

Chapter 5

THEN in the right hand of the one who was sitting on the throne I saw in my vision a scroll, covered on both sides with writing, front and back. It was sealed with seven seals. ₂Then I saw a strong angel and heard him announcing for all to hear: 'Is there anyone here fit to open the scroll and to break its seals?' ₃No one in heaven or on earth or under the earth was able to open the scroll or to see what was in it. ₄I began to cry bitterly, because no one could be found who was fit to open the scroll and to see what was in it. ₅One of the elders said to me: 'Stop crying! The victory of the Lion from the tribe of Judah, the Root of David, has given him the right to open the scroll and to break the seven seals.'

₆Then I saw in my vision a Lamb standing in the middle of the throne, in the centre of the circle of the four living creatures and of the twenty-four elders. The Lamb had all the marks of a victim slain for sacrifice. He had seven horns and seven eyes. The seven eyes are the seven spirits of God, which are sent by him all over the earth. ₇The Lamb went and received the scroll from the right hand of the one who was sitting on the throne. ₈When he had received the scroll, the four living creatures and the twenty-four elders threw themselves down in front of him. Each of the elders had a harp. And they had golden bowls filled with incense, which is the prayers of God's dedicated ones. ₉They sang a new song, and this is what they sang:

> 'You have the right to take the scroll,
>   and to break its seals,
>   because you were slain,
>   and at the cost of your life-blood
>   you bought for God
>   men out of every tribe and language
>   and people and nation,
>   ₁₀and you made them into a kingdom
>   every member of which is a priest to serve God,
>   and they will reign on earth.'

₁₁The vision continued, and I heard the voice of many angels encircling the throne, and of the living creatures and the elders. There were myriads and myriads, and thousands and thousands of them ₁₂And this is what they were saying for all to hear:

'The Lamb who was slain
 has the right to receive
power and wealth and wisdom and strength,
 honour and glory and thanksgiving.'

13And I heard the whole of the created world in heaven and on earth and under the earth and in the sea and everything they contain speaking, and this is what they were saying:

'Blessing and honour and glory and power
 to the one who is sitting on the throne,
 and to the Lamb for ever and ever.'

14The living creatures said Amen, and the elders threw themselves down and worshipped.

Chapter 6

IN my vision I saw the Lamb open the first of the seven seals, and I heard one of the four living creatures say in a voice like thunder: 'Come!' 2In my vision I saw a white horse. Its rider had a bow. He was given a victor's crown, and he rode out conquering and to conquer.

3When the Lamb opened the second seal, I heard the second living creature say: 'Come!' 4Another horse came out, blood-red in colour. Its rider was given the right to take peace from the earth, and to make men slaughter one another. And he was given a great sword.

5When he opened the third seal, I heard the third living creature say: 'Come!' And in my vision I saw a black horse. Its rider was holding a pair of scales in his hand. 6I heard what sounded like a voice speaking from the middle of the four living creatures. 'It will take a whole day's wages to pay for a quart of flour,' the voice said. 'It will take a whole day's wages to pay for three quarts of barley. But you are forbidden to damage the olive and the wine.'

7When he opened the fourth seal, I heard the voice of the fourth living creature say: 'Come!' 8And in my vision I saw a horse blanched and pale. Its rider's name was Death, and with him as his follower came Hades. He was given power over a quarter of the earth. He was allowed to kill by the sword, by famine, by pestilence, and by the wild beasts of the earth.

9When he opened the fifth seal, I saw at the foot of the altar the souls of those who had been slaughtered, because they had preached the word of God, and had publicly declared their belief in it. 10They shouted their appeal to God: 'Sovereign Lord, holy and true, how long is it going to be until you act in judgment, and take vengeance for our murder on the inhabitants of the earth?' 11Each of them was given a white robe. They were told to rest a little while longer, until there should be completed the number of their fellow-servants who were to be killed, as they had been.

12In my vision I saw what happened, when the Lamb opened the sixth seal. There was a violent earthquake. The sun became as black as black sackcloth. The moon looked as if it was all made of blood. 13The stars fell from the sky to the earth, like figs from a fig-tree shaken by a gale of wind. 14The sky vanished like a scroll being rolled up. Every hill and island was removed from its place. 15The kings of the world, and the great ones, and the generals, and the wealthy, and the powerful, all men, slave and free alike, hid themselves in the caves and among the rocks of the hills. 16They said to the hills and the rocks. 'Fall on us, and hide us from the one who is sitting on the throne and from the wrath of the Lamb. 17For the great day of their wrath has arrived, and who can survive it?'

Chapter 7

THE vision continued, and in it I saw four angels standing at the four corners of the earth. They were holding back the four winds of the earth, to stop any wind blowing on the earth or on the sea, or against any tree. 2In my vision I saw another angel coming up from the east. He had the living God's seal. He shouted to the four angels who had been given power to damage the land and the sea. 3'You must not damage the land or the sea or the trees,' he said, 'until we have marked the foreheads of the servants of God with God's seal.' 4I was told the number of those who were marked with the seal. The number was one hundred and forty-four thousand, sealed from all the tribes of the Israelites:

5Of the tribe of Judah, twelve thousand were sealed;
of the tribe of Reuben, twelve thousand;
of the tribe of Gad, twelve thousand;
6of the tribe of Asher, twelve thousand;
of the tribe of Naphtali, twelve thousand;

of the tribe of Manasseh, twelve thousand;
7of the tribe of Simeon, twelve thousand;
of the tribe of Levi, twelve thousand;
of the tribe of Issachar, twelve thousand;
8of the tribe of Zebulun, twelve thousand;
of the tribe of Joseph, twelve thousand;
of the tribe of Benjamin, twelve thousand were sealed.

9The vision continued, and in it I saw a vast crowd of people, too many for anyone to count. They came from every nation and from all tribes and peoples and languages. They were standing in front of the throne, and in front of the Lamb. They were wearing long white robes, and they were holding palm branches in their hands. 10They were shouting:

> 'It is our God who is seated on the throne,
>   and the Lamb,
>   who have brought us in safety
>   through all our troubles.'

11All the angels stood in a circle round the throne and the elders and the four living creatures. They threw themselves down on their faces in front of the throne and worshipped God, 12and this is what they said:

> 'Amen! Blessing and glory and wisdom
>   and thanksgiving and honour and power
>   and strength belong to our God for ever and ever.
>   Amen!'

13One of the elders said to me: 'These men who are wearing the long white robes—who are they and where did they come from?' 14'Sir,' I said, 'you will have to tell me.' 'These,' he said to me, 'are the men who have come through the terrible time of trouble. They have washed their robes, and have made them white through the blood of the Lamb. 15That is why they are there before God's throne.

> Night and day they serve him in worship
>   in his temple,
>   and he who sits on the throne will company with them
>   in all his glory.
> 16Never again will they hunger or thirst;
>   the sun will not beat down on them,
>   nor any scorching heat,

₁₇because the Lamb who is in the centre of the throne
will be their shepherd.
He will be their guide
to the springs of the water of life,
and God will wipe away all tears from their eyes.'

Chapter 8

WHEN the Lamb opened the seventh seal, there was a silence
in heaven for about half an hour. ₂In my vision I saw the
seven angels who stand in the presence of God being given seven
trumpets.

₃Another angel came and stood beside the altar. He was carrying
a golden censer. He was given a large quantity of incense to mingle
with the prayers of all God's dedicated people, as he offered them on
the golden altar in front of the throne. ₄The smoke of the incense
went up before God from the angel's hands with the prayers of God's
dedicated people. ₅Then the angel took the censer and filled it with
fire from the altar and hurled it at the earth, and there were peals of
thunder and flashes of lightning and an earthquake.

₆Then the seven angels with the seven trumpets prepared to sound
them.

₇The first angel sounded a blast on the trumpet, and there came
hail and fire mingled with blood, and it was hurled on the earth. A
third of the land was burned up, and a third of the trees were burned,
and all the green grass was burned.

₈Then the second angel sounded a blast on the trumpet, and what
looked like a great mountain blazing with fire was hurled into the
sea. A third part of the sea turned into blood, ₉and a third of
the living creatures in the sea died, and a third of the ships were
wrecked.

₁₀Then the third angel sounded a blast on the trumpet, and a great
star, flaming like a torch, fell from heaven. It fell on a third of the
rivers and the springs of water. ₁₁The name of the star was Wormwood. A third of the waters turned into wormwood, and the waters
brought death to many men because of their bitterness.

₁₂Then the fourth angel sounded a blast on the trumpet, and a
third of the sun was struck, and a third of the moon, and a third of the
stars, with the result that a third of them were darkened, and the day
lost a third of its light, and so did the night.

13In my vision I saw an eagle in flight in the middle of the sky, and I heard it shout: 'Tragic, tragic, tragic will be the fate of the inhabitants of the world, when the trumpets speak which the rest of the angels are to sound.'

Chapter 9

THEN the fifth angel sounded a blast on the trumpet, and in my vision I saw a star which had fallen from the sky to the earth. To this star was given the key of the shaft of the Abyss. 2The star then opened the shaft of the Abyss. From the shaft there rose smoke, like the smoke of a vast furnace, and the sun and the air were darkened by the smoke rising from the shaft. 3Out of the smoke locusts spread all over the ground. They were given the same power as normal scorpions have. 4They were instructed not to damage the grass of the earth, or any of the green things or of the trees. They were to do no damage to anything except to men who did not have God's seal on their foreheads. 5They were not permitted to kill them, but they were to torture them for five months. The pain they were to inflict was to be like the pain a scorpion inflicts, when it stings a man. 6At that time men will search for death and will not be able to find it; they will long to die, but death will evade them.

7In appearance the locusts were like horses caparisoned for battle. On their heads they had what looked like golden crowns. Their faces were like human faces. 8They had hair like women's hair. Their teeth were like lions' teeth. 9They had breastplates like iron breastplates. The sound of their wings was like the sound of many chariots and horses charging into battle. 10They had tails like scorpions, with stings. It was in their tails that their power to hurt men for the five month period lay. 11They had the angel of the Abyss as their king. In Hebrew he is called Abaddon; in Greek his name is Apollyon, which means the Destroyer.

12The first woe has passed. There are still two more woes coming.

13Then the sixth angel sounded a blast on the trumpet. Then I heard a voice, coming from the horns of the golden altar, which stood in the presence of God. 14'Release the four angels who are held bound at the great river Euphrates,' it said to the sixth angel with the trumpet. 15So the four angels who were there, all ready for that very hour and day and month and year, were released to kill a third of mankind. 16Their squadrons of cavalry numbered two hundred million. I was told the number of them. 17In the vision this was how I saw the horses and their riders. The riders were wearing breast-plates of flame colour, blue and sulphur-yellow. The horses had heads like lions' heads, and flames and smoke and sulphur issued from their mouths. 18A third of mankind were killed by these three plagues, by the flames and the smoke and the sulphur, which issued from their mouths. 19The power of the horses lay in their mouths and in their tails, for their tails were like snakes with heads, and with them they inflicted wounds.

20But the men who were left, and who had not been killed by these plagues, did not repent. They did not abandon their manmade gods. They did not stop worshipping demons and idols of gold and silver and bronze and stone and wood, which cannot see or hear or move. 21They did not repent of their murders, their sorceries, their im-morality, their thefts.

Chapter 10

IN my vision I saw another strong angel coming down from heaven. He was wrapped in a cloud; the rainbow was on his head; his face was shining like the sun; and his legs were like pillars of fire. 2He was holding in his hand a little scroll which was unrolled. He placed his right foot on the sea, and his left on the land. 3Then he shouted with a shout like a lion's roar, and, when he shouted, the seven thunders spoke with their voices. 4When the seven thunders spoke, I was about to write down what they said. But I heard a voice speaking from heaven. 'You must seal with secrecy what the seven thunders said,' I was told, 'and you must not write it down.' 5The angel, whom I saw standing on the sea and on the land, raised his right hand to heaven, 6and swore by him who lives for ever and ever, by him who created heaven and everything in it, and earth and everything in it, and the sea and everything in it, that there would be no more delay, 7but that at the time of the trumpet blast which the seventh angel was to sound, the secret purpose of God would be completed, as he had told his servants the prophets.

8Then the voice I had heard from heaven spoke to me again. 'Go,' it said, 'and take the scroll, which the angel who is standing on the sea and on the land is holding open in his hand.' 9So I went to the angel, and asked him to give me the little scroll. 'Take it,' he said to me, 'and eat it. Your stomach will find it bitter, but your mouth will find it as sweet as honey.' ₁₀So I took the little scroll from the hand of the angel, and ate it. In my mouth it tasted as sweet as honey; but, when I ate it, it turned my stomach sour. ₁₁I was told: 'Once again you must prophesy about many peoples and nations and languages and kings.'

Chapter 11

I WAS given a cane like a measuring-rod. 'Up!' I was told, 'and measure the temple of God, and the altar, and count those who worship in it. ₂Omit the outer court from your calculations, and do not measure it. It has been given to the Gentiles, and they will trample on the holy city for forty-two months. ₃I will give my two witnesses the task of proclaiming my message, dressed in sackcloth, through-out the one thousand two hundred and sixty days.' ₄It is these wit-nesses that the two olive trees and the two lampstands, which stand in the presence of the Lord, represent. ₅If anyone tries to harm them, fire will issue from their mouths, and will devour their enemies. This is the death that anyone who tries to harm them must die. ₆These witnesses possess the power to shut up the sky, and to stop any rain falling during the period they are proclaiming the message of God. They also possess power over the waters, to turn them into blood, and to smite the earth with every kind of plague, as often as they wish. ₇When they have completed their declaration of the truth, the beast who rises from the Abyss will make war on them, and will conquer them, and kill them. ₈Their dead bodies will lie on the street of the great city, which is symbolically called Sodom and Egypt, the city in which their Lord also was crucified. ₉Men of all peoples and tribes and languages and from all nations will see their dead bodies for three and a half days, and they will refuse to allow their bodies to be buried. ₁₀The whole population of the world will be so glad to see them dead that they will celebrate their death, and give presents to each other to mark it, because these two prophets were responsible for the merciless and universal castigation of all men. ₁₁After the three and a half days the breath of life from God went into them. They stood up, and those who saw them were terrified at the sight of them. ₁₂Then they heard a shout from heaven. 'Come up here!' it said to them. And they went up into heaven in a cloud as their enemies watched. ₁₃At the same moment there was a violent earth-quake, and a tenth part of the city collapsed in ruins. Seven thousand people lost their lives in the earthquake. Those who were left were terrified, and praised the God of heaven.

14The second woe is over. The third woe is coming soon.

15The seventh angel sounded a blast on the trumpet, and voices in heaven began to shout:

> 'Our Lord and his Messiah
>   have become the sovereigns of the world,
>   and he will reign for ever and ever.'

16The twenty-four elders, who sit on their thrones in the presence of God, flung themselves down and worshipped God, 17and this is what they said:

> 'We give you thanks, Lord God,
>   you in whose power are all things,
>   you who are and who were,
>   that you have taken your great power
>   and entered upon your royal rule.
> 18The nations raged;
>   your wrath went out,
>   for the time for the dead to be judged has come,
>   the time to give their reward
>   to your servants the prophets,
>   and to your dedicated people,
>   and to those who reverence your name,
>   both great and small,
>   the time to destroy those who are destroying the earth.'

19God's temple in heaven was opened, and within the temple the ark of the covenant could be seen. The lightning flashed and the thunder pealed, and there was an earthquake and a violent storm of hail.

Chapter 12

THEN a sight full of meaning appeared in the sky. It was a woman, clothed with the sun, standing on the moon, and with a crown of twelve stars on her head. 2She was pregnant, and in her labour and her agony she cried aloud for her child to be born. 3Then another sight full of meaning appeared in the sky. It was a huge flame-coloured dragon, with seven heads and seven horns, with a royal crown on each of its heads. ₄Its tail swept from their places a third of the stars in the sky, and hurled them to the earth. The dragon stood waiting in front of the woman, who was waiting for her child to be born, for he intended to devour the child as soon as he was born. ₅So the woman had her baby, a boy, who is destined to rule all nations with an iron rod. Her child was snatched up to God and to his throne. ₆The woman fled to the desert, where there was a place prepared by God, waiting for her. She was to be cared for there for one thousand two hundred and sixty days.

₇War broke out in heaven, in which Michael and his angels fought against the dragon. The dragon with his angels put up a fight, ₈but he was not strong enough to win, and in the end no place was any longer left for them in heaven. ₉So the great dragon, the ancient serpent, who is called the Devil and Satan, and who is responsible for leading the whole world astray, was hurled to the earth, and his angels with him. ₁₀I heard a voice speaking in heaven for all to hear, and this is what it said:

'Now our God has won the victory;
   now God has displayed his power and his sovereignty,
   and the authority of his Messiah,
because the accuser of our brothers,
   who accused them night and day in the presence of God,
   has been hurled out of heaven.
₁₁The blood of the Lamb,
   and their fearless declaration of their faith,
have won for them the victory over him,
   for they did not love their lives
   enough to refuse to die for their faith.
₁₂So then, rejoice, you heavens,
   and you who live in them!
But tragic is your fate, earth and sea,
   for the Devil has come down to you,
and great is his wrath,
   for he knows that his time is short.'

₁₃When he saw that he had been hurled to the earth, the dragon pursued the woman who had had the boy baby. ₁₄But the woman was given two great eagle's wings, to enable her to fly away to her place in the desert, where she was to be cared for for a time, times and half a time, that is, three and a half years, where the serpent could not reach her. ₁₅Out of his mouth the serpent hurled after the woman a stream of water like a river, in an attempt to sweep her away in the torrent. ₁₆But the earth came to the help of the woman. It opened its mouth and drank up the river which the dragon had hurled from his mouth. ₁₇The dragon was infuriated with the woman. He went off to make war on the rest of her children, I mean, on those who obey God's commandments, and who declare their loyalty to Jesus. ₁₈He stood on the sea-shore.

Chapter 13

Iₙ my vision I saw a beast rising from the sea. It had ten horns and seven heads. On each of its ten horns there was a royal crown, and on each of its heads there was a name which was a deliberate insult to God. ₂The beast which I saw in my vision was like a leopard; its feet were like a bear's feet; its mouth was like a lion's mouth. The dragon assigned to the beast his power and far-reaching authority. ₃I saw that one of its heads looked as if it had been fatally injured, but its mortal wound had been healed. The whole earth went after the beast in fascinated wonder. ₄They worshipped the dragon, for he had assigned his authority to the beast, and they worshipped the beast. 'The beast,' they said, 'is unique and irresistible.'

₅The beast was allowed to use grandiloquent language which was a deliberate insult to God. It was given the right to exercise authority for forty-two months. ₆It poured out a torrent of insults against God. It insulted his name, and the place where he lives, and the inhabitants of heaven. ₇It was allowed to make war on God's dedicated people, and to conquer them, and it was given authority over people of every tribe and nation and language and race. ₈The whole population of the world will worship it, except those whose names were inscribed before the world began in the roll of the living, which belongs to the Lamb who was killed.

₉If a man can hear, he must listen to this message.

₁₀'If a man is destined for captivity,
    to captivity he goes;
  if a man is to be slain by the sword,
    by the sword he is to be slain.'

This is where the gallantry and loyalty of God's dedicated people must be displayed.

₁₁Then in my vision I saw another beast rising from the land It had two horns like a lamb, and, when it spoke, it was like a dragon speaking. ₁₂It exercised all the authority of the first beast, while the first beast looked on. It made the earth and all its inhabitants worship the first beast, the beast whose mortal wound had been healed. ₁₃It performed great miracles. It even made fire come down from heaven to earth while people looked on. ₁₄Through the miracles that it was allowed to do in the presence of the beast it led astray the inhabitants of the earth. It told the inhabitants of the earth to make an image in honour of the beast who was wounded by the sword and came to life again. ₁₅It was allowed to give breath to the image of the beast, and thus it made the image of the beast able to speak, and it was allowed to cause all who refused to worship the image of the beast to be put to death. ₁₆It caused everyone, important and unimportant, rich and poor, free men and slaves to be branded with a mark on their right hand or on their forehead. ₁₇Without this mark, the name or the number which stands for the name, no one was allowed to buy or sell. ₁₈To solve this problem needs wisdom. An intelligent man can calculate for himself the number of the beast, for the number represents a man's name, and, if you count the letters of his name, their value as numbers is six hundred and sixty-six.

The point of this obscure passage is that neither Greek nor Hebrew has any signs for the numbers. The letters of the alphabet do duty for the numerals as well, as if A were to equal 1; B,2; C,3, and so on. Since that is so, if the letters in any name are given their numerical value, they can be added up and so give a sum total. In point of fact, 666 is the sum of the Hebrew letters in the Hebrew form of Nero Caesar, who was the first and the most notorious persecutor of the church.

Chapter 14

IN my vision I saw the Lamb standing on Mount Sion. With him there were one hundred and forty-four thousand people with his name and the name of his Father inscribed on their foreheads. ₂I heard a sound from heaven, like the sound of cataracts of water and like a crashing peal of thunder. The sound I heard was like the music of harpers playing on their harps. ₃They were singing a new song before the throne and before the four living creatures and the elders. No one could learn that song except the hundred and forty-four thousand, who had been ransomed from the world. ₄These are men who never soiled their lives with women, for they kept themselves in virgin purity. These are men who follow the Lamb wherever he goes. They were ransomed, and thus separated from the rest of men, as the first-fruits of that harvest which God and the Lamb will gather in. ₅They have never been known to tell a lie; they are faultless in their purity.

₆In my vision I saw another angel, flying in mid-heaven, with an eternal gospel to proclaim to the inhabitants of the earth, to every nation and tribe and language and people. ₇'Reverence God,' he shouted for all to hear, 'and give him the glory, for the hour of his judgment has come! Worship him who made heaven and earth, the sea and the springs of water!'

₈Another angel followed the first angel. 'Fallen, fallen is Babylon the great,' he said, 'Babylon who made all the nations drink the wine of her fornication, the wine doomed to the wrath of God.'

₉Another angel followed the first two. 'Anyone who worships the beast and his image,' he said for all to hear, 'and anyone who accepts the mark of the beast on his forehead or on his hand ₁₀will also drink of the wine of the wrath of God, poured undiluted into the cup of his anger. He will be tormented with sulphurous fire in the presence of the holy angels and in the presence of the Lamb. ₁₁The smoke of their torture rises to all eternity. Those who worship the beast and his image, and anyone who receives the mark of his name, have no rest, day or night!' ₁₂A situation like this demands the gallantry of God's dedicated people, of those who continue to maintain their obedience to the commandments of God and their loyalty to Jesus.

₁₃Then I heard a voice from heaven. 'Write,' it said, 'God's joy will come to the dead who from now on die with their connection with their Lord unbroken.' 'Yes, indeed,' said the Spirit, 'for after their toil they will have their rest, and the record of what they did goes with them.'

₁₄In my vision I saw a white cloud. Sitting on the cloud I saw one like a human figure, wearing a victor's crown of gold on his head, and carrying a sharp sickle in his hand. ₁₅Another angel came out of the temple, and shouted to him who was sitting on the cloud: 'Set to with your sickle and reap. The time to reap has come, for earth's harvest is ripe, and more than ripe.' ₁₆So he who was sitting on the cloud swung his sickle on the earth, and the earth was reaped.

₁₇Then another angel came out of the temple in heaven. He too had a sharp sickle. ₁₈Then still another angel came from the altar. He was the angel who controls fire. He shouted to the angel with the sickle. 'Set to with your sharp sickle,' he said, 'and gather in earth's grape harvest from the vine. Its clusters are ripe.' ₁₉So the angel swung his sickle on the earth, and gathered its grapes, and threw them into the great winepress of God's wrath. ₂₀The juice was squeezed out of the grapes outside the city, and blood flowed from the winepress as high as the horses' bridles for two hundred miles round about.

Chapter 15

THEN I saw another great and astonishing sight in heaven, a sight which was full of meaning. I saw seven angels with seven plagues. These were the last plagues of all, because in them the wrath of God reached its climax and its consummation.

₂Then I saw what looked like a sea of glass, mingled with fire. I saw, standing beside the sea of glass, those who had emerged victorious from their struggle with the beast, and with his image, and with the number of his name. ₃They were singing the song of Moses, the servant of God, and the song of the Lamb, and this is what they were singing:

> 'Lord God, you hold all things in your power,
>   and great and marvellous are your deeds.
> Just and true are your ways, King of the nations.
> ₄Who will not reverence you, Lord,
>   and who will not glorify your name?
>   For you alone are holy.
> All the nations will come,
>   and will worship in your presence.
> because the justice of your decrees
>   has been made plain for all to see.'

₅My vision continued. The sanctuary of the Tent of Witness in heaven was opened. ₆Out of the sanctuary there came the seven angels with the seven plagues. They were robed in linen, clean and shining. They were wearing golden girdles round their breasts. ₇One of the four living creatures gave the seven angels seven golden bowls, full of the wrath of God, who lives for ever and ever. ₈The sanctuary was filled with smoke from the glory of God and from his power. No one could enter the sanctuary, until the seven plagues of the seven angels were completed.

Chapter 16

THEN I heard a voice shouting from the sanctuary to the seven angels. 'Go,' it said, 'and pour out on the earth the seven bowls of the wrath of God.'

₂So the first angel went and poured out his bowl, and ulcerous and malignant sores attacked the men who had the mark of the beast, and who worshipped his image.

₃The second angel poured out his bowl on the sea, and the sea turned into blood, like the blood of a corpse, and every living creature in the sea died.

₄The third angel poured out his bowl on the rivers and the springs of water, and they turned into blood. ₅Then I heard the angel who presided over the waters saying:

'You who are and were, the Holy One,
   it is in your justice
      that you have pronounced this sentence.
₆Because they poured out
      the blood of God's dedicated people
         and of the prophets,
   you have given them blood to drink.
   They have got what they deserved.'

₇Then I heard the altar saying:

'Yes, Lord God,
   you hold all things in your control;
   your judgments are true and just.'

₈Then the fourth angel poured out his bowl on the sun, and the sun was allowed to burn men with its flame. ₉Men were dreadfully burned. They hurled their insults at the name of God, who has the power to unleash such plagues, and they refused to repent and to give him glory.

₁₀Then the fifth angel poured out his bowl on the throne of the beast. His kingdom was enveloped in darkness. They tried to bite out their tongues in their agony. ₁₁They hurled their insults at the God of heaven for their pains and their sores, but they did not repent for what they had done.

₁₂Then the sixth angel poured out his bowl on the great river

Euphrates, and its waters were dried up to prepare the way for the kings from the east. 13In my vision I saw issuing from the mouth of the dragon and the mouth of the beast and the mouth of the false prophet three evil spirits like frogs. 14They were the spirits of demons, and they were able to perform miracles. They went out to the kings of the inhabited world to muster them for the battle which is to be fought on the great Day of God, who holds all things in his control. 15I am coming like a thief. Happy is the man who stays awake, and who keeps his clothes beside him, for then he will not have to walk naked and thus have all men see his shame. 16So they mustered the kings in the place called in Hebrew Armagedon.

17Then the seventh angel poured out his bowl in the air. Then there came a shout out of the sanctuary from the throne: 'It is done!' 18Then there came flashes of lightning and peals of thunder, and an earthquake of such violence that there never was an earthquake like it for violence, since men came into being on the earth. 19Then the great city was split into three parts. The cities of the nations collapsed. Babylon the great did not escape her fate, for God gave her the cup of the wine of his furious wrath. 20Every island vanished, and the mountains disappeared. 21Huge hailstones, weighing as much as a hundredweight, rained down on men from the sky. Men hurled their insults at God for the plague of the hail, because the plague was devastating in the extreme.

Chapter 17

ONE of the seven angels, who had the seven bowls, came and spoke to me. 'Come!' he said. 'I will show you the sentence of condemnation which has been passed on the great prostitute, that city which is built on many waters. 2She has acted the prostitute with the kings of the earth, and the inhabitants of the earth have become drunk with the wine of her fornication.' 3So he carried me away to the desert in a trance. In my vision I saw a woman seated on a scarlet beast. The beast was covered with names which are a deliberate insult to God. It had seven heads and ten horns. 4The woman was robed in purple and scarlet. She was bedecked with gold and jewels and pearls. She had a golden cup in her hand, filled with obscenities and with the filth of her fornication. 5On her forehead there was inscribed a name with a secret meaning—Babylon the great, mother of prostitutes and of earth's obscenities. 6In my vision I saw the woman drunk with the blood of God's dedicated people and with the blood of those who had declared their faith in Jesus.

To me the woman was a most astonishing sight. 7The angel said to me: 'What is so astonishing to you in all this? I will explain to you the secret meaning of the woman and of the beast she is riding, the beast with seven heads and ten horns. 8The beast which you saw was once alive and is not now alive. It will rise from the Abyss, and it is on the way to destruction. Those of the inhabitants of the earth whose names were not written, since the world was created, in the roll of the living will look in wonder at the beast. They will stand astonished at it, because it was once alive, and is not now alive, and will appear. 9The solution of this requires a mind equipped with wisdom. The seven heads are seven hills on which the woman sits enthroned. They are also seven kings. 10Five of them have already fallen; one is the king now in existence; the other has not yet come. And, when he does come, he is destined to remain for only a short time. 11The beast which was once alive, and which is not now alive, is itself also an eighth. At the same time it belongs to the seven, and it is on its way to destruction. 12The ten horns which you see in your vision are ten kings, who have not yet entered upon their reigns. They are to receive authority for one hour and are to exercise it in co-operation with the beast. 13These kings share one common purpose—to hand over their power and their authority to the beast. 14They will go to war with the Lamb, and the Lamb will conquer them, because he is Lord of lords, and King of kings. Sharing the Lamb's battle and victory are those who are called and chosen and loyal.

15'The waters, on which the prostitute sits, which you saw in your vision,' the angel said to me, 'are crowds of peoples and nations of every language. 16The ten horns, which you saw, and the beast will come to hate the prostitute. They will leave her stripped and desolated. They will devour her flesh. They will burn her in flames to ashes. 17For God put it into their minds to carry out his purpose by coming to a common decision to hand over their sovereignty to the beast, until all that God has said should be completed and done. 18The woman you saw is the great city which has sovereignty over the kings of the earth.'

Chapter 18

M^Y vision continued, and in it I saw another angel coming down from heaven. He was an angel of great authority, and the earth was lit up by his splendour. ₂He shouted in a resounding voice:

> 'Fallen, fallen is Babylon the great.
>> She has become the home of demons,
>> the haunt of every unclean spirit,
>> the haunt of every unclean and loathsome bird,
> ₃because she made all the nations
>> drink of the wine of her fornication,
>>> the wine doomed to the wrath of God.
> The world's kings committed fornication with her,
>> and the demands of her wanton luxury
>>> have made the world's merchants rich.'

₄I heard another voice from heaven, and this is what it said:

> 'Come out of her, my people,
>> if you do not wish to be partners in her sins,
> and if you do not wish
>> to share in her plagues.
> ₅For her sins are heaped as high as heaven,
>> and her crimes are not forgotten by God.
> ₆Give her what she gave to others;
>> repay her twice over for all that she has done.
> In the cup that she mixed for others
>> mix her a drink that is twice as strong.
> ₇Give her torment and grief,
>> to match the splendours and the luxury
>>> that once she gave herself.
> She says in her heart:
>> "I am a queen on a throne!
>> I am no widow forlorn!
> Sorrow will never touch me!"
> ₈Because of all this, in one single day
>> her plagues will assail her—
>>> pestilence and sorrow and famine—

565

she will be burned to ashes in flames,
    for mighty is the Lord,
    and he has pronounced her doom.'

9The world's kings were her companions in fornication and in wanton luxury. Now they will weep and lament over her, when they see the smoke of the conflagration in which she will be burned. 10In their terror at her torment they will stand far away and say:

'Tragic, tragic is the fate of the great city,
    of Babylon the mighty city!
    For in one brief hour her doom has come!'

11The world's merchants too will weep and mourn for her, because there will be no one now to buy their cargoes any more, 12cargoes of

gold and silver and jewels and pearls;
    cloths of fine linen and purple and silk and scarlet;
    all kinds of perfumed woods, ornaments made of ivory,
        all kinds of things made of precious wood
            and bronze and iron and marble;
    13cinnamon and spice, incense and myrrh and
            frankincense;
    wine and oil and fine flour and wheat;
    cattle and sheep, horses and chariots;
    slaves and human lives.

14'Gone is the fruit of your heart's desire!
    Perished your brilliance and your splendour!
    And no one will ever see them again.'

15The merchants who dealt in these things, and who grew rich because of their trade with her, will stand far away in their terror at her torture, in tears and in sorrow. 16They will say:

'Tragic, tragic is the fate of the great city,
    she who was robed in fine linen and purple
        and scarlet,
    she who was gilded with gold,
        and bedecked with jewels and pearls,
    17for in one brief hour,
        wealth so great was turned into a desert!'

And every ship's captain, and every sea-faring man, all sailors, and all whose trade is on the sea, stood far away, 18and shouted as they watched the smoke of the conflagration in which she was burning: 'Truly the great city was unique!' 19They flung dust on their heads, and in their tears and sorrow they cried:

'Tragic, tragic is the fate of the great city,
the city by whose wealth,
all who had ships at sea grew wealthy,
for in one brief hour
she has become a desert!'

20'Rejoice over her, O heaven,
rejoice you dedicated people of God,
you apostles and you prophets,
because God has passed on her,
the sentence she passed on you!'

21Then a strong angel took a stone like a huge millstone, and hurled it into the sea, and, as he did so, he said:

'Thus will Babylon the great city
be hurled violently down,
and will disappear from sight for ever.
22Never again will the melody
of harpers and minstrels,
of flute-players and trumpeters,
be heard in you.
Never again will craftsmen of any trade
be found in you.
The sound of the mill
will never again be heard in you.
23The light of a lamp
will never again be seen in you.
The voice of the bridegroom and the bride
will never again be heard in you.
Your merchants were once
the world's commercial aristocrats.
Your sorceries led
all the nations astray.
24She stands exposed as the murderer
of the prophets,
and of God's dedicated people,
and of all the world's slaughtered martyrs.'

Chapter 19

My vision continued, and in it I heard what sounded like the roar of a vast crowd in heaven, and this is what they were saying:

'Alleluia!
Victory, glory and power belong to our God,
    2for his judgments are true and just.
He has sentenced the great prostitute,
    who was the corrupter of the earth with her fornicati on
    and he has taken vengeance on her
        for the murder of his servants.'

3A second time they shouted:

'Alleluia!
The smoke rises from her for ever and ever.'

4The twenty-four elders and the four living creatures threw them selves down, and worshipped God as he sat on his throne. 'Amen they said. 'Alleluia!'
    5Then a voice came from the throne, and this is what it said:

'Praise our God,
    all you servants of his,
    all you who reverence him,
        both great and small!'

6Then I heard what sounded like the sound of a vast crowd, and like the sound of cataracts of water, and like the crash of thunder, and this is what they were saying:

'Alleluia!
For the Lord our God,
    who holds all things in his control,
    has begun his reign.
    7Let us rejoice and thrill with gladness,
        and let us give him glory,
    for the wedding day of the Lamb has come
    8and his Bride has prepared herself for it.
Fine linen, dazzlingly white,
    has been given to her for her dress.'

The fine linen stands for the good deeds of God's dedicated people.

9Then he said to me: 'Write this—God's joy will come to those who have been invited to the Lamb's wedding banquet!' He went on to say to me: 'This is a genuine message from God.' 10I threw myself down at his feet to worship him. 'This is what you must not do,' he said. 'I too am a fellow-servant with you and your brothers, for we both possess the declaration of the truth which Jesus brought to us. It is God alone whom you must worship. For the same Spirit speaks in the declarations of Jesus and in the words of the prophets.'

11Then I saw heaven standing open, and on to the scene there came a white horse. Its rider's name was Faithful and True, for both as a judge and as a warrior he is just. 12His eyes were like flaming fire; on his head he had many royal crowns. Inscribed on him, he had a name known only to himself. 13The robe he was wearing was soaked with blood. The name by which he is called is The Word of God. 14The armies of heaven followed him, mounted on white horses, and dressed in fine linen, white and clean. 15A sharp two-edged sword issued from his mouth. With it he was to smite the nations, for he will rule them with an iron rod. He treads the winepress of the anger of the wrath of God, who holds all things in his control. 16He has a name inscribed on his robe and on his thigh—King of kings and Lord of lords.

17Then I saw an angel standing in the sun. He shouted to all the birds flying in mid-sky. 'Come!' he said. 'Gather for God's great banquet! 18Come and eat the flesh of kings and the flesh of generals, the flesh of strong men, the flesh of horses and their riders, the flesh of all men, free men and slaves, small and great.' 19Then I saw the beast and the world's kings and their armies mustered to join battle with the rider of the horse and his army. 20The beast was captured, and so was the false prophet, who in the presence of the beast had performed miracles, by which he had led astray those who had received the mark of the beast, and those who worship his image. These two were hurled alive into the lake of fire with its sulphurous flames. 21The rest of them were killed by the sword, which issued from the mouth of the rider of the horse, and the birds all gorged themselves with their flesh.

Chapter 20

THEN I saw in my vision an angel coming down from heaven. In his hand he was holding the key of the Abyss and a huge chain. 2He seized the dragon, the ancient serpent, who is the Devil or Satan, and bound him for a thousand years. 3Then he hurled him into the Abyss, and locked him in, and sealed the opening over him, to keep him from leading the nations astray any more, until the thousand year period had been completed. Following on that period, he has to be released again for a short time.

4Then in my vision I saw thrones. Sitting on them were the souls of those who had been executed, because they had declared their faith in Jesus, and for the sake of the word of God. They had not worshipped the beast or his image, and they had not received his mark on their foreheads and on their hands. To them the right of judgment had been given. They came to life again, and they shared Christ's reign for a thousand years. 5The rest of the dead did not come to life again until after the thousand year period had been completed. This is the first resurrection. 6God's joy will come to the man who has a share in the first resurrection! He is one of God's dedicated people. The second death has no power over these. They will be priests of God and of Christ, and they will share his reign for a thousand years.

7Then, when the thousand year period has been completed, Satan will be released from his imprisonment. 8He will go out to lead astray the nations all over the world, in all its four quarters. He will muster Gog and Magog, all God's enemies, for battle. In number they will be like the sand of the sea. 9They covered the whole breadth of the world as they marched up, and they surrounded the camp of God's dedicated people and the city he loves. Then fire came down from heaven and devoured them. 10Then the Devil who led them astray was hurled into the lake of sulphurous fire, into which the beast and the false prophet had already been thrown. Day and night they will be tortured for ever and ever.

11Then I saw a great white throne and someone sitting on it. Earth and heaven fled from his presence, and not a trace of them remained. 12Then in my vision I saw the dead, great and small, standing in front of the throne. The record books were opened. Another book was brought—the register of the living. The dead were judged on the basis of what was written in the books, by the record of what they had done. 13The sea gave back its dead. Death and Hades gave back their dead. And each man was judged by the record of what he had done. 14Death and Hades were hurled into the lake of fire. The lake of fire is the second death. 15Everyone whose name was not found to be recorded in the book of the living was hurled into the lake of fire.

Chapter 21

THEN I saw in my vision a new heaven and a new earth, for the first heaven and the first earth were gone. The sea no longer existed. 2I saw the holy city, new Jerusalem, coming down out of heaven from God, made ready like a bride, dressed in all her finery for her husband. 3Then I heard a voice speaking from the throne for all to hear. 'The home of God in all his glory is with men,' it said, 'and he will live with them. They will be his people and God himself will be with them, and he will be their God. 4He will wipe away every tear from their eyes. Death will cease to exist. There will no longer be any sorrow or crying or pain. The old order of things has gone!'

5Then he who was seated on the throne said: 'See! I am making everything new. Write this down,' he said, 'because you can believe what I am saying, for it is true.' 6Then he said to me: 'It is done! I am Alpha and Omega, the beginning and the end. I will allow the thirsty to drink from the spring of the water of life—and all as a free gift. 7The victor in the battle of life will enter into possession of all this. I will be his God and he will be my son. 8But for the cowards, for those who refuse to believe, for those whose lives are an abomination, for murderers and fornicators, for sorcerers and idolaters and for liars of every kind, their fate is the lake, burning with sulphurous fire, which is the second death.'

9Then one of the angels, who held the seven bowls which were filled with the seven last plagues, came and spoke to me. 'Come here,' he said, 'and I will show you the bride, the Lamb's wife.' 10He took me away in a trance to a great high mountain, and showed me the holy city Jerusalem coming down out of heaven from God, 11with the sheen of God's splendour on it. Its radiance was like the radiance of a very precious stone, like a jasper, clear as crystal. 12It had a huge high wall with twelve gates. At the gates there were twelve angels. Names were inscribed on the gates, and the names were the names of the twelve tribes of Israel. 13There were three gates on the east, three gates on the north, three gates on the south, and three gates on the west. 14The city wall had twelve foundation stones, with the twelve names of the Lamb's twelve apostles on them.

15The angel who was speaking to me had a golden measuring-rod to measure the city and its gates and its wall. 16The city was built in the shape of a square. The length and the breadth were equal. He measured the city with his rod, and the length of the sides was fifteen hundred miles. Its length and breadth and height were all equal. 17He measured the height of the wall, and it came to two hundred and sixteen feet. (This is in human figures, which the angel was using.) 18The wall was constructed of jasper. The city was of pure gold, as clear as glass. 19The foundations of the city wall were adorned with jewels of every kind. The first foundation stone was a jasper; the second, lapis lazuli; the third, chalcedony; the fourth, emerald; 20the fifth, sardonyx; the sixth, carnelian; the seventh, chrysolite; the eighth beryl; the ninth, topaz; the tenth, chrysoprase; the eleventh, turquoise; the twelfth, amethyst. 21The twelve gates consisted of twelve pearls. Each gate was made of a single pearl. The city streets were of pure gold, like translucent glass.

22 saw no temple in the city. Its temple is the Lord God, who holds all things in his control, and the Lamb. 23The city has no need of the sun or the moon to shine in it, for the splendour of God illumines it, and its lamp is the Lamb. 24The nations shall walk by its light. The world's kings will bring their splendour to it. 25Its gates will never be shut in the day-time—and it will never be night there. 26The splendour and wealth of the nations will be brought to it. 27Nothing unclean will ever be allowed into it, nor anyone whose conduct is foul and false. Only those whose names are written in the Lamb's roll of the living will be allowed to enter it.

Chapter 22

THEN he showed me the river of the water of life, sparkling like crystal. It issues from the throne of God and of the Lamb. 2It flows down the middle of the city street. On each side of the river grows the tree of life. The tree produces twelve crops of fruit. It gives a crop for each month in the year. The leaves of the tree are meant to be a cure for the nations. 3No accursed thing shall exist any more. The throne of God and the Lamb will be there, and his servants will worship him. ₄They will see him face to face; his name will be on their foreheads. ₅There will be no night any more. They do not need the light of any lamp or even the light of the sun, because the Lord God will give them light. And they will be kings for ever and ever.

₆Then he said to me: 'You can believe what I am saying to you because it is true. The Lord, the God who inspired the prophets, has sent his angel to show his servants what must soon happen. ₇I am coming soon! God's joy will come to the man who obeys the prophetic message of this book!'

₈It was I John who heard these messages and saw these visions. When I heard and saw them, I threw myself down in worship at the feet of the angel who showed them to me. ₉'That is what you must not do,' he said to me. 'I am your fellow-servant, and the fellow-servant of your brothers the prophets, and of all who obey the words of this book. It is God alone whom you must worship.' ₁₀He went on to say to me: 'Do not seal up as secret the prophetic message of this book, for the crisis time is near. ₁₁The evil man must continue in his evil-doing. The filthy man must continue in his filthiness. The good man must continue to live the good life. The man who is dedicated to God must continue in his dedication.'

₁₂'I am coming soon,' Jesus says, 'and I am bringing my reward with me. I will settle accounts with each man on the basis of the life he has lived. ₁₃I am Alpha and Omega, the first and the last, the beginning and the end.'

₁₄'God's joy will come to those who wash their robes, for then they will have the right to the tree of life, and to entry through the gate into the city. ₁₅Outside there are dogs and sorcerers, fornicators and murderers and idolaters, and everyone who loves and acts a lie.'

₁₆'I Jesus have sent my angel to give you this solemn message from me to bring it to the churches. I am the Root of David and my descent is from him. I am the bright morning star. ₁₇The Spirit and the bride say: "Come!" If any man hears the invitation, he must answer: "Come!" If anyone is thirsty, he must come. Here is the invitation, to everyone who wants the water of life, to come and take it—and all for nothing.'

₁₈I make a solemn declaration to everyone who hears the prophetic message of this book. If anyone makes any addition to it, God will add to him the plagues recorded in this book. ₁₉If anyone removes anything from the words of this book's prophetic message, God will take away his share in the tree of life and in the holy city, described in this book.

20He who has sent this solemn message says: 'Yes indeed! I am coming soon!' So be it! Come, Lord Jesus!

21The grace of the Lord Jesus be with you all.

Notes

MATTHEW

p. 19 Some manuscripts add here *without a cause.*

p. 23 Some manuscripts add here, *For the Kingdom and the power and the glory are yours for ever. Amen.*

p. 50 Some manuscripts here add verse 21, *This kind comes out only by prayer and fasting.*

p. 51 Some manuscripts insert here verse 11, *For the Son of Man came to save the lost.*

p. 53 Some manuscripts add here, *And anyone who marries a divorced woman commits adultery.*

p. 62 Some manuscripts insert here verse 14, *Tragic will be the fate of you experts in the law and you Pharisees with your façade of ostentatious piety! For you greedily extract the last penny from credulous widows, and then with your long prayers try to give an impression of exceptional piety. You will receive all the heavier a sentence.*

p. 76 Other manuscripts add here, *Another took a spear and pierced his side, and water and blood came out.*

MARK

p. 95 Here some manuscripts insert verse 16, *If a man has ears to hear, let him hear.*

p. 101 Verses 44 and 46, which are the same as verse 48, are omitted by the best manuscripts.

p. 106 Some manuscripts here add verse 26, *'But if you refuse to forgive, your Father in heaven will not forgive your sins either.'*

p. 116 Here some manuscripts insert verse 28, *So the passage of scripture which says, 'He was reckoned with the transgressors' came true.*

LUKE

p. 127 Here some manuscripts have, *and on earth his peace and his favour towards men.*

p. 131 Here some manuscripts have, *You are my Son, the Beloved and Only One. Today I have begotten you.*

p. 147 Here some manuscripts add, *She had spent her whole living on doctors.*

p. 150 Here some manuscripts add, *You do not know the kind of men you ought to be. The Son of Man did not come to destroy lives but to save them.*

p. 171 Here some manuscripts insert verse 36, *There will be two men in the field; one will be taken and the other one will be left.*

p. 181 Some manuscripts omit the words from here to the end of verse 20.

p. 182 Some manuscripts omit verses 43 and 44.

p. 184 Here some manuscripts insert verse 17, *At the festival he was obliged to release one prisoner for them.*

JOHN

p. 201 Here some manuscripts insert verse 4, *They were waiting for the famous movement of the water, for from time to time an angel of the Lord would come down, and the water in the bath was disturbed, and whoever was the first to step into the bath after the water had been disturbed was cured of whatever disease he was suffering from.*

p. 210 The best and most ancient manuscripts of the New Testament do not contain this story.

p. 238 Verses 15-17: In the Greek of this passage two different words are used for 'to love'. It is almost certain that there is no difference in meaning between them, but if a difference in meaning is to be expressed the passage may be translated as follows:

15 When they had breakfasted, Jesus said to Simon Peter: 'Simon, son of John, do you love me more than these others do?' 'Yes, indeed, Lord,' Peter said to him, 'you know that you are dear to me.' 'Feed my lambs,' Jesus said to him. 16 Jesus said to him a second time: 'Simon, son of John, do you love me?' 'Yes, indeed, Lord,' Peter said to him, 'you know that you are dear to me.' 'Be a shepherd to my sheep,' Jesus said to him. 17 Jesus said to him a third time: 'Simon, son of John, am I dear to you?' Peter was vexed that Jesus said to him the third time: 'Am I dear to you?' 'Lord,' he said to Jesus, 'you know everything. You do know that you are dear to me.' 'Feed my sheep,' Jesus said to him.

ACTS

p. 259 Here some manuscripts insert verse 37, '*If you believe with your whole heart,*' Philip said, '*it can be done.*' '*I believe,*' he answered, '*that Jesus Christ is the Son of God.*'

p. 274 Both here and at verse 29 there are variations in the text. Some manuscripts omit, *that you must have nothing to do with unchastity.* Some omit, *which have been killed by being strangled.* Some add after *unchastity, and not to do to others anything they would not wish them to do to themselves.*

p. 294 Here certain manuscripts insert verses 6b, 7, 8a. 6b *It was our intention to try him under our own law,* 7 *but Lysias, the commander arrived and used considerable force to remove him from our hands,* 8a *and ordered his accusers to appear before you.*

p. 303 Here some manuscripts insert verse 29, *After he had said this, the Jews went away, hotly debating with each other.*

1 THESSALONIANS

p. 436 An alternative translation of verses 4-6 is: 4 *Each of you must know how to possess a wife in a holy and honourable way,* 5 *not with lustful passion, like the heathen who do not know God.* 6 *In this matter no one must overreach his fellow-man, or invade his rights, for, as we have already very definitely told you, the Lord exacts the penalty for all such actions.*

PHILEMON

p. 467 Paul here makes a word-play on the name *Onesimus*, which means *useful* or *profitable*.

JAMES

p. 499 An alternative translation of this passage is: 'The spirit which God implanted in us is envious in its desires.'

2 PETER

p. 518 The reading is uncertain here. Some manuscripts have *will vanish;* others have *will be burned with fire.*

JUDE

p. 535 Some manuscripts here have *God*; others have *Jesus*, which may be the Greek form of *Joshua*, as in Acts 7.45 and Hebrews 4.8.